UNITED NATIONS CONFERENCE ON TRADE AND DEVELOPMENT
Geneva

THE LEAST DEVELOPED COUNTRIES
REPORT 2006

Prepared by the UNCTAD secretariat

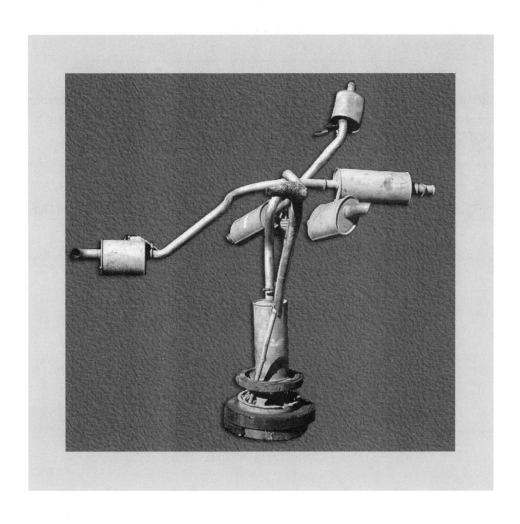

UNITED NATIONS
New York and Geneva, 2006

Note

Symbols of United Nations documents are composed of capital letters with figures. Mention of such a symbol indicates a reference to a United Nations document.

The designations employed and the presentation of the material in this publication do not imply the expression of any opinion whatsoever on the part of the Secretariat of the United Nations concerning the legal status of any country, territory, city or area, or of its authorities, or concerning the delimitation of its frontiers or boundaries.

Material in this publication may be freely quoted or reprinted, but full acknowledgement is requested. A copy of the publication containing the quotation or reprint should be sent to the UNCTAD secretariat at: Palais des Nations, CH-1211 Geneva 10, Switzerland.

The Overview from this Report can also be found on the Internet, in both English and French,
at the following address:
http://www.unctad.org

UNCTAD/LDC/2006

UNITED NATIONS PUBLICATION
Sales No. E.06.II.D.9
ISBN 92-1-112701-7
ISSN 0257-7550

WHAT ARE THE LEAST DEVELOPED COUNTRIES?

Fifty countries are currently designated by the United Nations as "least developed countries" (LDCs): Afghanistan, Angola, Bangladesh, Benin, Bhutan, Burkina Faso, Burundi, Cambodia, Cape Verde, Central African Republic, Chad, Comoros, Democratic Republic of the Congo, Djibouti, Equatorial Guinea, Eritrea, Ethiopia, Gambia, Guinea, Guinea-Bissau, Haiti, Kiribati, Lao People's Democratic Republic, Lesotho, Liberia, Madagascar, Malawi, Maldives, Mali, Mauritania, Mozambique, Myanmar, Nepal, Niger, Rwanda, Samoa, Sao Tome and Principe, Senegal, Sierra Leone, Solomon Islands, Somalia, Sudan, Timor-Leste, Togo, Tuvalu, Uganda, United Republic of Tanzania, Vanuatu, Yemen and Zambia. The list of LDCs is reviewed every three years by the Economic and Social Council (ECOSOC) in the light of recommendations by the Committee for Development Policy (CDP).

The following criteria were used by the CDP in the 2006 review of the list of LDCs:

(a) A "low-income" criterion, based on the *gross national income (GNI) per capita* (a 3-year average, 2002–2004), with thresholds of $750 for cases of addition to the list, and $900 for cases of graduation from LDC status;

(b) A "human assets" criterion, involving a composite index (the *Human Assets Index*) based on indicators of (i) nutrition (percentage of the population undernourished); (ii) health (child mortality rate); (iii) school enrolment (gross secondary school enrolment rate); and (iv) literacy (adult literacy rate); and

(c) An "economic vulnerability" criterion, involving a composite index (the *Economic Vulnerability Index*) based on indicators of (i) natural shocks (index of instability of agricultural production; share of population displaced by natural disasters); (ii) trade shocks (index of instability of exports of goods and services; (iii) exposure to shocks (share of agriculture, forestry and fisheries in GDP; merchandise export concentration index); (iv) economic smallness (population in logarithm); and (v) economic remoteness (index of remoteness).

For all three criteria, different thresholds are used for addition to, and graduation from, the list of LDCs. A country will qualify to be added to the list if it meets the three criteria and does not have a population greater than 75 million. A country will qualify for graduation from LDC status if it has met graduation thresholds under at least two of the three criteria in at least two consecutive reviews of the list. After a recommendation to graduate a country has been made by the CDP and endorsed by ECOSOC and the General Assembly, the graduating country will be granted a three-year grace period before actual graduation takes place. In accordance with General Assembly resolution 59/209, this standard grace period is expected to enable the relevant country and its development partners to agree on a "smooth transition" strategy, so that the loss of LDC-specific concessions at the end of the grace period does not disturb the socioeconomic progress of the country.

Acknowledgements

The Least Developed Countries Report 2006 was prepared by a team consisting of Charles Gore (team leader), Lisa Borgatti, Marquise David, Michael Herrmann, Ivanka Hoppenbrouwer-Rodriguez, Zeljka Kozul-Wright, Madasamyraja Rajalingam and Utumporn Reungsuwan. Penelope Pacheco-López also joined the team from 1 February, 2006, and Veronica Escudero participated in the final stages of preparation of the Report from 1 April, 2006. Specific inputs were also received from Pierre Encontre. The work was carried out under the overall supervision of Habib Ouane, Director, Special Programme for Least Developed, Landlocked and Island Developing Countries within UNCTAD.

Two ad hoc expert group meetings were organized as part of the preparations for the Report. The first, "Mobilizing and Developing Productive Capacity for Poverty Reduction", was held in Geneva on 20 and 21 June 2005. It brought together specialists in three distinct fields — the macroeconomics of development, the development of technological capabilities and the employment–poverty nexus — as well as representatives of some UN agencies which emphasize the importance of production and employment for poverty reduction. The participants in the meeting were as follows: Yves Ekoué Amaizo (UNIDO), Rizwanul Islam (ILO), Massoud Karshenas, Mark Knell, Thandika Mkandawire (UNRISD), Juan Carlos Moreno-Brid, (ECLAC) Banji Oyelaran-Oyeyinka, Eric Reinert, Jaime Ros, Tony Thirlwall, Rolf van der Hoeven (ILO) and Marc Wuyts. The meeting discussed the conceptual and analytical approach to the issue of productive capacities, the initial ideas on which were elaborated by Zeljka Kozul-Wright. The second expert group meeting, "New Productive Development Policies in LDCs", was held in Geneva on 3 and 4 October 2005. It brought together two experts on new industrial policies, Anthony Bartzokas and Mario Cimoli (ECLAC), and an expert on new agricultural policy, Andrew Dorward, to discuss the overlaps between new thinking in these different fields, as well as its relevance for LDCs.

Background papers or specific inputs for the Report were commissioned from Adrian Atkinson, Amit Bhaduri, Ayman Ismael, Kenneth King, Mark Knell, Penelope Pacheco-López, Rajah Rasiah, Jaime Ros, Ignacy Sachs, Roberto Simonetti and Marc Wuyts. Claes Johansson of the UNDP Human Development Report Office in New York also provided inputs for part I of the Report.

Joerg Mayer, of the Macroeconomics and Development Policies Branch of the Division on Globalization and Development Strategies within the UNCTAD secretariat, provided specific advice. The staff of the Central Statistics Branch of the same Division also fully supported the work.

Secretarial support was provided at different times by Cora Alvarez, Mounia Atiki, Sylvie Guy, Paulette Lacroix, Mary McGee, Regina Ogunyinka, Veronica Rivera Cruz, Sivanla Sikounnavong and Stephanie West. Diego Oyarzun-Reyes designed the cover, and the text was edited by Graham Grayston. The overall layout, graphics and desktop publishing were done by Madasamyraja Rajalingam.

The financial support of the Government of Norway is gratefully acknowledged.

Contents

Part One
RECENT ECONOMIC TRENDS AND UNLDC III DEVELOPMENT TARGETS

Part Two
DEVELOPING PRODUCTIVE CAPACITIES

List of Boxes

List of Charts

Annex Chart

Box Charts

List of Tables

Box Tables

Explanatory Notes

The term "dollars" ($) refers to United States dollars unless otherwise stated. The term "billion" signifies 1,000 million.

Annual rates of growth and changes refer to compound rates. Exports are valued f.o.b. (free on board) and imports c.i.f. (cost, insurance, freight) unless otherwise specified.

Use of a dash (–) between dates representing years, e.g. 1981–1990, signifies the full period involved, including the initial and final years. An oblique stroke (/) between two years, e.g. 1991/92, signifies a fiscal or crop year.

The term "least developed country" (LDC) refers, throughout this report, to a country included in the United Nations list of least developed countries.

In the tables:

Two dots (..) indicate that the data are not available, or are not separately reported.
One dot (.) indicates that the data are not applicable.
A hyphen (-) indicates that the amount is nil or negligible.
Details and percentages do not necessarily add up to totals, because of rounding.

Abbreviations

ACP	African, Caribbean and Pacific
AGOA	African Growth and Opportunity Act
AIDS	acquired immune deficiency syndrome
APQLI	augmented physical quality of life index
ATC	Agreement on Textiles and Clothing
CDP	Committee for Development Policy
DAC	Development Assistance Committee
EBA	Everything But Arms
EC	European Community
ECLAC	Economic Commission for Latin America and the Caribbean
ECOSOC	Economic and Social Council
EDI	Economic diversification Index
EPZ	export processing zone
ESAF	Enhanced Structural Adjustment Facility
EVI	Economic Vulnerability Index
FAO	Food and Agriculture Organization of the United Nations
FDI	foreign direct investment
FSAP	financial system assessment programme
GATS	General Agreement on Trade in Services
GATT	General Agreement on Tariffs and Trade
GDP	gross domestic product
GNI	gross national income
GSP	Generalized System of Preferences
GSTP	Generalized System of Trade Preferences
HAI	Human Assets Index
HIPC	heavily indebted poor country
HIV	human immunodeficiency virus
ICTs	Information and communication technologies
IDA	International Development Association
IF	Integrated Framework for Trade-Related Technical Assistance
IFI	international financial institutions
IFPRI	International Food Policy Research Institute
ILO	International Labour Organization
IMF	International Monetary Fund
LDCs	least developed countries
MDGs	Millennium Development Goals
NEPAD	New Partnership for Africa's Development
NGO	non-governmental organization
NTB	non-tariff barrier
ODA	official development assistance
ODCs	other developing countries
OECD	Organisation for Economic Co-operation and Development
POA	Programme of Action for the LDCs for the Decade 2001–2010
PPP	purchasing power parity
PRS	Poverty Reduction Strategy
PRSP	Poverty Reduction Strategy Paper
R&D	research and development
RPED	Research Programme in Enterprise Development

SIDS	Small Island Developing States
SITC	Standard International Trade Classification
SMEs	small and medium-sized enterprises
TNC	transnational corporation
UNAIDS	United Nations Joint Programme on HIV/AIDS
UN COMTRADE	United Nations Commodity Trade Statistics Database
UNCTAD	United Nations Conference on Trade and Development
UNDP	United Nations Development Programme
UNECA	United Nations Economic Commission for Africa
UNESCO	United Nations Educational, Scientific and Cultural Organization
UNIDO	United Nations Industrial Development Organization
UNLDC III	Third United Nations Conference on the Least Developed Countries
UNSD	United Nations Statistical Division
WDI	World Development Indicators
WHO	World Health Organization
WTO	World Trade Organization

Overview

This Report is intended as a resource for policymakers in the least developed countries (LDCs) and for their development partners. Part I focuses on recent economic trends in the LDCs and the progress that those countries are making towards achieving the quantitative development targets of the Programme of Action for the Least Developed Countries for the Decade 2001–2010 (POA), agreed at the Third United Nations Conference on the LDCs (UNLDC III) held in Brussels in 2001. Part II focuses on the issue of developing productive capacities in the LDCs. The Overview summarizes the basic policy argument in a nutshell for the busy reader, and then the basic evidence upon which this argument is founded.

THE POLICY ARGUMENT IN A NUTSHELL

Productive capacities matter

In recent years, many LDCs have achieved higher rates of economic growth than in the past and even higher growth of exports. But there is a widespread sense — which is apparent in the concern to ensure "pro-poor" growth — that this is not translating effectively into poverty reduction and improved human well-being. Moreover, the sustainability of the accelerated growth is fragile as it is highly dependent on commodity prices, including oil prices, trends in external finance, preferences for exports of manufactured goods, and climatic and weather conditions. In the late 1970s and 1980s, many LDCs experienced growth collapses in which gains from earlier growth spurts were reversed, and the vulnerability to this happening again remains.

Developing productive capacities is the key to achieving sustained economic growth in the LDCs. It is through developing their productive capacities that the LDCs will be able to rely increasingly on domestic resource mobilization to finance their economic growth, to reduce aid dependence and to attract private capital inflows of a type that can support their development process. It is also through developing their productive capacities that the LDCs will be able to compete in international markets in goods and services which go beyond primary commodities and which are not dependent on special market access preferences.

Developing productive capacities is also the key to reducing pervasive poverty in the LDCs. Although aid transfers to the LDCs are increasingly being used to alleviate human suffering, substantial and sustained poverty reduction cannot be achieved with such expressions of international solidarity alone. It requires wealth creation in the LDCs and the development of domestic productive capacities in a way in which productive employment opportunities expand.

The development of productive capacities will be particularly important during the next 15 years because the LDCs are at a critical moment of transition in which they face a double challenge. Firstly, more and more people are seeking work outside agriculture and urbanization is accelerating. For the LDCs as a group, the decade 2000–2010 is going to be the first decade in which the growth of the economically active population outside agriculture is predicted to be greater than the growth of the economically active population within agriculture. This transition will affect more than half the LDCs during the decade and even more in the decade 2010–2020. Secondly, the LDCs must manage this transition in an open-economy context. As shown in earlier LDC Reports, very few LDCs have restrictive trade regimes at the present time and most have undertaken rapid and extensive trade liberalization. But their existing production and trade structures offer very limited opportunities in a rapidly globalizing world driven by new knowledge-intensive products with demanding conditions of market entry. At the same time, rapid opening up in more traditional sectors is exposing existing producers to an unprecedented degree of global competition. Benefiting from recent technological advances requires advancing towards and crossing various thresholds in human capital, R&D and management practice, which most LDC economies have lacked the resources to do. The relentless logic of cumulative causation threatens to push LDCs even further behind.

If productive employment opportunities do not expand sufficiently for the growing labour force in the LDCs — in non-agricultural activities as well as within agriculture — there will be increasing pressures for international migration from the LDCs and high levels of extreme poverty will persist. The development of productive capacities is also necessary to secure the fiscal basis for good governance and to ensure effective sovereignty. Without the development of their productive capacities, more and more LDCs will face recurrent, complex humanitarian emergencies.

Productive capacities should be at the heart of development and poverty reduction policies

It is becoming widely accepted that the developing world needs not just lower tariffs or improved market entry, but also enhanced supply capacities in order to benefit from the open, global economy through producing and trading competitive goods and services. New international initiatives under discussion, such as "aid for trade", recognize that without productive capacities there will be little to trade and that these capacities will not emerge automatically from the workings of market forces alone, but from the interplay of entrepreneurship, public policy and international action. To the extent that the "aid for trade" initiative results in increased aid for, inter alia, export supply capacities, this is a move in the right direction.

However, in general, national and international policies do not adequately address the challenge of developing productive capacities in the LDCs. There is a need for a paradigm shift which places the development of productive capacities at the heart of national and international policies to promote development and poverty reduction in the LDCs.

Productive capacities are defined in this Report as *the productive resources, entrepreneurial capabilities and production linkages which together determine the capacity of a country to produce goods and services and enable it to grow and develop.* For tradable goods and services, what matters is the capacity to produce in an internationally competitive manner. Productive capacities develop within a country through three closely interrelated processes: capital accumulation, technological progress and structural change. Capital accumulation is the process of maintaining and increasing stocks of natural, human and physical capital through *investment*. Achieving technological progress is the process of introducing new goods and services, new or improved methods, equipment or skills to produce goods and services, and new and improved forms of organizing production through *innovation*. Structural change is the change in the inter- and intrasectoral composition of production, the pattern of inter- and intrasectoral linkages and the pattern of linkages amongst enterprises. Such change often occurs through investment and innovation, and the emerging production structure in turn influences the potential for further investment and innovation.

To put productive capacities at the heart of development and poverty reduction policies means to focus on promoting capital accumulation, technological progress and structural change in the LDCs. National and international policies should seek to start and to sustain a virtuous circle in which the development of productive capacities and the growth of demand mutually reinforce each other. This should be done in a way in which productive employment opportunities expand in order to ensure poverty reduction.

Developing productive capacities requires new policy orientations

This paradigm shift is not something totally new. But it would be a new policy orientation for the LDCs and their development partners, even though developing productive capacities is part and parcel of the Brussels Programme of Action for the LDCs. It would entail a production- and employment-oriented approach to poverty reduction which would encompass, rather than be narrowly focused on, increasing social sector spending and achieving human development targets. It would also entail a development-driven approach to trade rather than a trade-driven approach to development. An approach to developing productive capacities which is simply trade-centric will not be sufficient for sustained and inclusive growth in the LDCs.

The paradigm shift would also strengthen current efforts to develop productive capacities in the LDCs — such as in policies to improve their investment climate — through:

- Macroeconomic policies oriented to promoting growth, investment and employment;
- A multi-level approach which not only seeks to set the framework institutions and macroeconomic environment, but also includes policies to change meso-level production structures and institutions, as well as micro-level capabilities and incentives;
- An active approach to promoting entrepreneurship;
- A strategic approach to global integration in which the speed and degree of liberalization in different economic spheres take account of the goal of developing productive capacities.

National and international policies to develop productive capacities in the LDCs should prioritize the relaxing of key constraints on capital accumulation, technological progress and structural change. The identification of key constraints needs to be done on a country-by-country basis. However, one consequence of the combination of a deficiency of domestic demand on the one hand, and of weak capabilities, infrastructure and institutions for being internationally competitive on the other hand, is that productive resources and entrepreneurial capabilities are underutilized within the LDCs owing to lack of demand and structural weaknesses. There is surplus labour, latent entrepreneurship, untapped traditional knowledge, a vent-for-surplus through exporting and unsurveyed natural resources. Policy thus needs to be geared to mobilizing these underutilized potentials. As Albert Hirschman has put it, "Development depends not so much on finding optimal combinations for given resources and factors of production as on calling forth and enlisting for development purposes resources and abilities that are hidden, scattered, or badly utilized".

Within the LDCs, increasing productivity and employment for long-run sustainable growth requires a twin strategy of investing in dynamically growing sectors while at the same time building capacity in sectors where the majority of labour is employed. A strategy of investing only in dynamic sectors in attempts to "leapfrog" may not be enough to reduce poverty, mainly because the fastest-growing sectors may often not be where the majority of the poor are employed and may require skills and training that the poor do not possess. The challenge then is to broaden the impact of the dynamically growing sectors of the economy, while deepening their linkages with other sectors in the economy — sectors where the majority of the poor are underemployed. At the same time, it is paramount to ensure that the poor can be provided with skills and training for labour absorption in these growing areas of the economy.

The most effective approach would support and stimulate simultaneous investments in agriculture, industry and services, along the value chain of the promising sectors, as well as promotion of exports including, in particular, upgrading and increased local value-added of abundant natural resources. The focus should be on triggering growth through investment and production linkages and seeking to sustain an interactive economic growth process through the dynamic interrelationship between the primary, secondary and tertiary sectors. Agricultural growth linkages, in which there is a virtuous circle in which demand stimulus from agricultural growth generates investment, entrepreneurship and employment in non-agricultural activities, particularly non-tradables, are likely to be relevant in many LDCs and at the heart of efforts to create a more inclusive process of development which supports sustainable poverty reduction.

Poverty reduction can occur rapidly if policy catalyses and sustains a virtuous circle in which the development of productive capacities and the growth of demand mutually reinforce each other, and there is a transformation of productive structures towards more skilled and technology-intensive production systems consistent with higher value-added activities and strong productivity growth. This will require the building of a virtuous circle of increased savings, investment and exports through a combination of market forces and public action. This implies mobilizing, strengthening and transforming the enterprise sector from SMEs to larger globally competitive enterprises, diversification of their export structures and establishing a dense network of linkages across firms and farms, in and between both the rural and non-rural sectors. Much of the effort will be focused on strengthening the role of domestic enterprises. However, foreign firms (through FDI and other channels) can be a beneficial factor in this process, provided that learning economies and spillover effects prevail — and possible costs can be mitigated.

The process requires a better balance between domestic and international sources of growth. Increased exports and export diversification are an absolutely essential part of the strategy. However, an exclusive emphasis on exports rather than domestic demand, or vice versa, or on developing productive capacities in tradables rather than non-tradables, or vice versa, is likely to be counterproductive. Both matter for growth and poverty reduction. Increased domestic demand also results from increasing incomes and poverty reduction, and this builds a further feedback mechanism supporting the momentum of growth as productive employment opportunities expand.

An economic transformation process can take place only if an enabling policy framework is put in place that would bring about the process of capital accumulation, structural change and technological progress. This will require not only a re-evaluation of the current national and international policies, but also the building up of the necessary institutions, particularly the private enterprise sector (firms), and financial and knowledge systems. In addition to the need for investment and improvement of the physical infrastructure, economic agents themselves (firms) need to be created or strengthened, entrepreneurship needs to be mobilized, underutilized traditional knowledge revived and productive employment created for underutilized labour.

At the national level, there is a need for more development-oriented poverty reduction strategies, as argued in the last two Least Developed Countries Reports. These would focus on developing production capacities in a way which creates productive employment opportunities. But a good national poverty reduction cannot be fully effective in an adverse international enabling environment, and it can also be enhanced by appropriate international support measures. The scaling-up of aid is occurring and there are promises that this will continue. However, as aid inflows increase, it is important that the composition of aid shifts back towards the development of productive capacities. Increased aid for physical infrastructure — transport, telecommunications and energy — is certainly part of this. But it is also necessary to go beyond this, and in particular, to strengthen production sectors and linkages, and also to support enterprise development and the improvement of domestic financial and knowledge systems. New international support measures which can promote the development of productive capacities in the LDCs need to be developed.

RECENT ECONOMIC TRENDS AND PROGRESS TOWARDS ACHIEVEMENT OF UNLDC III DEVELOPMENT TARGETS

Recent economic trends

The average GDP growth rate in the LDCs as a group in 2004 was the highest for two decades. This was underpinned by record levels of merchandise exports and record levels of capital inflows, particularly in the form of grants and FDI. Most of the oil-exporting LDCs did particularly well, benefiting from higher oil prices in 2004 especially. But the good economic performance was not confined to those countries. Real GDP growth was 6 per cent or more in 15 LDCs in 2004, including 11 LDCs which do not export oil.

Within this overall growth performance the trend towards increasing divergence amongst the LDCs, which first emerged in the early 1990s, has continued. Real GDP per capita stagnated or declined in 2004 in 15 out of 46 LDCs for which data are available.

This divergence is partly related to the differential access to external finance. Both FDI inflows and ODA grants, the two major elements driving the surge in capital inflows, were highly concentrated. Ten LDCs absorbed 84 per cent of FDI inflows in 2004. In nominal terms, aid actually doubled between 1999 and 2004. But 30 per cent of this increase was absorbed by Afghanistan and the Democratic Republic of the Congo. For other countries, the nominal increase in aid was much smaller. Indeed, it either stagnated or declined in real terms in almost half of the LDCs during the same period, including 9 out of the 10 island LDCs.

Another issue of concern is the sustainability of the recent economic performance. The ratio of gross domestic savings to GDP, which is already much lower than in other developing countries, actually declined from 13.4 per cent in 2003 to 11 per cent in 2004. During that period, the LDCs' reliance on external finance savings to finance capital formation increased. Many LDCs are also particularly vulnerable because they are net importers of both food and oil. The combination of price increases in these sectors can considerably worsen their persistent trade deficits. The effects of very high recent oil prices are not evident, given the years for which data are available.

The sustainability of the recent growth performance will depend in particular on the extent to which existing and additional ODA and FDI are channelled into productive investment, both private and public, and support increased domestic savings, structural change and an upgrading and diversification of productive capacities. Unfortunately, a large share of the increase in ODA is attributable to debt relief and emergency assistance, which together accounted for 35 per cent of total net ODA disbursed to LDCs in 2003 and 27 per cent disbursed in 2004. FDI inflows remain oriented towards exploiting extractive sectors. The external debt stock of the LDCs continues to increase in spite of major debt relief measures. In 2003, interest payments and profit remittances were equivalent to about 60 per cent of the value of grants received (excluding technical cooperation).

Finally, economic growth will not be sustainable unless it is a type of growth which leads to improvements in human well-being that are socially inclusive. The results of the economic growth which are now occurring are, in this regard, quite mixed (see below).

Progress towards achievement of UNLDC III development targets

The most striking feature of progress towards the achievement of the UNLDC III targets since 2001 is the much stronger engagement of development partners than in the 1990s with respect to aid, debt relief and market access. During the 1990s, many LDCs engaged in significant and far-reaching economic reforms, including extensive trade liberalization, financial liberalization and privatization. But aid fell by 45 per cent in real per capita terms between 1990 and 1998. However, as noted above, this trend has now been reversed, with aid inflows doubling in nominal terms since 1999. Important progress has also been made on debt relief for some LDCs; and these efforts to increase development finance for the LDCs have been complemented with new initiatives to move towards the objective of duty-free and quota-free access for all LDC products. There has also been significant progress in the untying of aid.

These positive trends are encouraging. However, aid inflows have still not reached the levels commensurate with the aid-to-GNI targets in the POA. Moreover, the recent surge in aid has been driven by debt forgiveness grants and emergency assistance grants, and a large proportion of the increase in aid has been concentrated in Afghanistan and the Democratic Republic of the Congo. Up to 2004, the increase in aid also reinforced the trend away economic infrastructure and production sectors towards social sectors. Despite debt relief for some, the overall debt burden of the LDCs continues to increase. Moreover, in spite of the special market access initiatives, the proportion of total developed country imports from LDCs admitted free of duty actually declined from 77 per cent to 72 per cent between 1996 and 2003 if oil and arms imports are excluded.

Economic growth and investment rates are higher than in the 1990s in many LDCs. But only 6 out of the 46 LDCs for which data are available met or exceeded the POA target of growth of 7 per cent per annum between 2001 and 2004. Ten out of 39 LDCs for which data are available met the investment target of 25 per cent of GDP during 2001–2004.

Eighteen out of the 46 LDCs for which data are available were unable to achieve per capita growth rates of more than 1.0 per cent per annum during the period 2001–2004, which is far too low to have a serious effect on the extreme poverty in which about half the population of LDCs live. Moreover, progress towards human development goals is very mixed. More progress is being made in human development dimensions that are directly affected by the quantity and quality of public services (primary education, gender equity education and access to water) than with regard to those that are the outcome of both public services and levels of household income (hunger and child mortality).

In the end, the sustainability of economic and social progress in the LDCs will ultimately depend on building up their productive base so that they can increasingly rely on domestic resource mobilization and private rather than official sources of external finance, and can compete in international markets without special market access preferences. The POA targets wisely have a wider reach than the MDGs, emphasizing the importance of developing productive capacities. However, the increased external resources being provided by development partners will not translate into sustained economic and social progress unless development finance for LDCs continues to be scaled up effectively, to be complemented with more effective trade development measures and to be linked to efforts to develop domestic productive capacities.

DEVELOPING PRODUCTIVE CAPACITIES: KEY FINDINGS AND ANALYSIS

Potential versus actual growth

The least developed countries have the potential to achieve very high rates of economic growth and to reduce poverty rapidly if constraints on the development of their productive capacities are relaxed. The Report demonstrates this with an analytical framework and empirical estimates of how fast the LDCs could grow during the period 2002–2015 if their productive capacities were developed. The analysis indicates that the growth rate target of more than 7 per cent, which is part of the Brussels Programme of Action for the LDCs, is achievable. But it requires a fast catch-up growth scenario in which there is full employment of the labour force and various potential sources of labour productivity growth, which are available to all poor countries, are exploited. In particular, it requires structural change to enable increasing returns to scale and external economies, faster human capital accumulation, and faster acquisition and absorption of technologies already in use in other countries.

This catch-up growth scenario will not be possible without substantially increased investment rates. These must be financed from substantially increased domestic savings, or substantially increased external resource inflows, or some combination of the two. Accelerated export growth will also be necessary in order to pay for the increased imports which will be required for sustaining faster economic growth. There will also need to be an increased technological effort to acquire and utilize modern technologies in use in other countries. The full-employment output growth trajectory will not be achieved unless there are strong demand-side incentives to invest. Realizing the potential growth rates will thus be possible only if key constraints on the development of productive capacities are addressed.

As these constraints are very strong in the LDCs, the actual growth rates achieved by the LDCs have thus been much lower than these potential growth rates. Taking a long view, real GDP per capita grew at only 0.72 per cent per annum for the group of LDCs as a whole during 1980–2003. For 41 LDCs for which data are available, 17 had negative average annual GDP per capita growth rates over this period and in only 9 did the average annual GDP per capita growth rate exceed 2.15 per annum over the period, which was a rate sufficient for their income per capita to be converging with that in high-income OECD countries.

The recent improved growth performance in some LDCs noted above is certainly encouraging. However, closer analysis of the year-to-year changes which have occurred in the LDCs shows that historically many LDCs have experienced short periods of rapid growth, but these have been followed by economic crises in which there are often quite severe output losses and economic recoveries of varying strengths and completeness. Of the 40 LDCs for which data are available, only 7 have experienced steadily sustained growth – Bangladesh, Bhutan, Burkina Faso, Cape Verde, the Lao People's Democratic Republic, Lesotho and Nepal. All the other LDCs have experienced economic contractions of varying duration and severity since achieving political independence.

Of the 33 LDCs which have experienced economic crises with major output losses, there are only 12 whose real GDP per capita is now higher than it was at its peak in the 1970s or early 1980s. These countries include a number of high-performing economies such as Mozambique and Uganda which have grown rapidly after economic collapse. The other 21 LDCs, — just over half of the countries for which data are available — have experienced growth collapses in the sense that their real GDP per capita in 2003 was lower than it had been between 20 and 30 years earlier. Eleven out of those 21 LDCs have simply not recovered at all from the growth collapse. However, amongst the other 10, there are a number of countries, such as Gambia and Rwanda, whose growth record since the mid-1990s has been good but which still have not recovered to achieve earlier levels of real GDP per capita. The recent improvement in growth performance of the LDCs as a group reflects the fact that increasing numbers are recovering.

As the catch-up growth scenario shows, the potential for rapid and sustained growth exists in the LDCs if they can develop their productive capacities. If such development does not happen, even countries which are growing faster now are likely to experience the same kind of growth collapses as characterized past LDC growth experience.

Trends in the development of productive capacities

Capital accumulation

Despite improvements in the 1990s, capital formation was still only 22 per cent of GDP in the LDCs as a group in 1999–2003 and domestic private investment was particularly weak. Capital formation in the LDCs is far below the rate which is estimated to be required for the fast catch-up growth scenario discussed above (35 per cent of GDP) and also below that required for a slow catch-up scenario (28 per cent of GDP), in which technological acquisition occurs more slowly than in the fast catch-up scenario.

A further concern is that actual rates of human capital formation in the LDCs in the 1990s were slower than in other developing countries. The average number of years of schooling of the adult population in the LDCs was three years in 2000, which was less than the level in other developing countries in 1960. The brain drain is also increasing in many LDCs. In 2000, one in five of the stock of "high-skill workers" in the LDCs, defined as those with tertiary education (13 years of schooling or more), was working in an OECD country.

The inadequate rates of physical and human capital formation reflect weaknesses in domestic resource mobilization to finance capital formation, as well as weaknesses in the way in which external capital inflows are supporting domestic processes of capital accumulation. Gross domestic savings rose to 13.6 per cent of GDP in 1999–2003. But with this savings rate it is impossible, without external capital inflows, even to achieve positive rates of GDP per capita growth. Estimates of genuine savings, which take account of capital depreciation and natural resource depletion, also indicate that, without ODA grants, there were negative savings for all years between 1991 and 2003, and that the genuine savings rate, without ODA grants, was also declining. Thus, although the growth performance of the LDCs as a group improved considerably in the 1990s, their domestic productive resource base — as measured by genuine savings without ODA grants — has been shrinking.

Government revenue and expenditure are also low, particularly in countries which do not have access to mineral resource rents. During 2000–2003, government final consumption expenditure in the LDCs was equivalent to $26 per capita compared with $186 per capita in other developing countries.

External capital inflows can play an important catalytic role in kick-starting and supporting a virtuous cycle of domestic resource mobilization in which expanding profitable investment opportunities generate increased savings and increased savings in turn finance increased investment. There is a major opportunity here because since 2000 the sharp decline in ODA to LDCs which occurred during the 1990s has been reversed, and FDI inflows into LDCs, though geographically concentrated, are also increasing. But the limited evidence suggests that FDI inflows are not crowding in domestic private investment. Moreover, there are various features of the current aid regime which imply that ODA is not playing a catalytic role in boosting domestic resource mobilization and expanded domestic capital accumulation.

Particularly important is the fact that the composition of aid is oriented away from physical capital formation and productive sectors. Between 1992–1995 and 2000–2003, ODA commitments to economic infrastructure and production-oriented sectors declined from 45 per cent to 26 per cent of the total commitments of all donors to LDCs. If one focuses simply on aid commitments to production sectors (agriculture, industry, mining, construction, trade and tourism), it will be seen that this constituted only 6.8 per cent of total aid commitments in the period 2000–2003. ODA commitments to banking and financial services were only 1 per cent of total aid commitments in 2000–2003.

Structural change

For the LDCs as a group there has been little structural change since the early 1980s, though there are significant differences between LDCs. The share of agriculture in GDP in the LDCs is declining slowly (from 37 per cent in 1980–1983 to 33 per cent in 2000–2003). Both industrial and service activities are expanding (in rounded numbers, from 23 per cent to 26 per cent of GDP and from 39 per cent to 42 per cent of GDP respectively over the same period). But much of the increase in industrial value-added is concentrated in a few LDCs and the types of industrial activities which are expanding most in the LDCs are mining industries, the exploitation of crude oil and the generation of hydroelectric power rather than manufacturing. Moreover, the types of services which are expanding most are low value-added and survivalist petty trade and commercial services.

Whilst the LDC group as a whole has seen a relatively modest increase in manufacturing value-added, there is considerable unevenness in this process. Between 1990–1993 and 2000–2003, half of the total increase in manufacturing value-added in the LDC group as a whole was attributable to the growth of manufacturing in Bangladesh. Many of the LDCs individually have seen a considerable contraction of manufacturing value-added. Between 1990–1993 and 2000–2003 manufacturing value-added as a share of total value added declined in 19 out of 36 LDCs for which data are available and stagnated in two. Between 1990 and 2000, moreover, a total of 14 out of 25 LDCs saw a decline in their share of medium- and high-technology manufactures in total manufactures.

Labour productivity

The evidence shows that, on average, it required 5 workers in the LDCs to produce what one worker produces in other developing countries, and 94 LDC workers to produce what one worker produces in developed countries in 2002–2003. Worse still, the productivity gap is widening. Labour productivity in the LDCs as a group in 2000–2003 was just 12 per cent higher than in 1980–1983, whilst it increased by 55 per cent on average in other developing countries. Significantly, although agricultural value-added per agricultural worker rose slightly in the LDCs, non-agricultural value-added per non-agricultural worker actually declined by 9 per cent between 1980–1983 and 2000–2003. Non-agricultural labour productivity declined in four fifths of the LDCs for which data are available over this period, a fact which indicates that there is a widespread and major problem in productively absorbing labour outside agriculture.

Trade integration

The goods and services which the LDCs can supply competitively to world markets are ultimately limited by the goods and services which they can produce and how efficient they are in producing them. This is the basic source of the marginalization of the LDCs in world trade. Even if the LDCs exported all their output, their share of world exports of goods and services would be only 2.4 per cent, even though their share of the world population is over 10 per cent.

Moreover, just as the production structure of the LDCs is strongly oriented to exploiting natural resources, so their export structure is also strongly oriented in that way. Primary commodities contributed about two thirds of total merchandise exports in 2000–2003. An important feature of the trends in the merchandise export composition of the LDCs is that manufactures exports have been increasing. In 1980–1983, manufactured exports constituted only 13 per cent of total merchandise exports for the LDCs as a group and now they constitute about one third. However, the shift away from primary commodities into manufactures is occurring much more slowly than in other developing countries and has not gone as far. It is concentrated in low-skill labour-intensive products, particularly garments, which have often developed to take account of special preferences and are now vulnerable with the end of the Agreement on Clothing and Textiles. Export production is not well rooted in domestic systems of production and, at worst, exists as enclaves of dynamism with almost no production linkages with the rest of the economy. Medium- and high-technology manufactured goods exports accounted for less than 3 per cent of the total merchandise trade of LDCs in 2000–2003, whilst they constituted 40 per cent of the total merchandise trade of other developing countries. Moreover, the expansion of manufactured exports has also been concentrated within a few LDCs.

The data also show that there has been a very limited pattern with regard to upgrading *within* primary commodity exports. For the LDCs as a group, the share of processed minerals and metals within total mineral and metal exports fell from 35 per cent to 28 per cent between 1980–1983 and 2000–2003. The share of processed agricultural goods within total agricultural exports increased from 23 per cent in 1980–1983 to 18 per cent in 2000–2003. The main positive sign of upgrading in the composition of commodity exports has been a shift, within unprocessed agricultural products, from static to more dynamic products. If one uses an UNCTAD definition of dynamic products as those with an elasticity of demand greater than one, it is seen that the most important dynamic products are fish and fishery products and spices.

Technological progress and the development of technological capabilities

The overall lack of structural change, the very slow rate of productivity growth and the limited range of goods in which LDCs are internationally competitive are all symptomatic of a lack of technological learning and innovation within LDCs. The patterns of production and trade indicate that the level of accumulation of knowledge-based assets is generally low. But there is also regression rather than accumulation in these assets in many LDCs.

Using traditional indicators of technological effort (such as R&D, patenting, numbers of scientists and researchers and publications), it is apparent that there is a major knowledge divide between the LDCs, other developing countries and developed countries.

- R&D expenditure in both LDCs and other developing countries is very low compared with that in OECD countries. Gross expenditure on R&D in 2003 (or the latest available year) was 0.2 per cent of GDP in the LDCs and 0.3 per cent of GDP in other developing countries, compared with 2.2 per cent of GDP in OECD countries.
- The number of researchers and scientists engaged in R&D activities per million population in the LDCs in 2003 (or the nearest year) is just 27 per cent of the level in other developing countries and 2 per cent of the level in OECD countries.
- During the period 1990–1999, only 0.1 per cent of the scientific and technical journal articles in physics, biology, chemistry, mathematics, clinical medicine, biomedical research, engineering and technology, and earth and space sciences originated in LDCs.
- Between 1991 and 2004, only 20 US patents were granted to citizens of LDCs, compared with 14,824 to citizens of other developing countries and 1.8 million to citizens of OECD countries.

It would be wrong, however, to infer that innovation and problem-solving are not occurring in the LDCs. There are many incremental innovations with significance for domestic needs that are not being captured by these traditional indicators. R&D expenditure is certainly not the only indicator. But firm-level data from Investment Climate Surveys also indicate deficiencies in technological capabilities, particularly in domestic enterprises. Investment in capital equipment is identified as the most important channel of technological acquisition by firms in these surveys. However,

- As a share of GDP, machinery and equipment imports into LDCs in the period 2000–2003 were lower than those into other developing countries (3 per cent versus 4.8 per cent of GDP), and the gap between the two groups of countries has widened since the early 1980s.
- In real per capita terms, machinery and equipment imports into LDCs during 2000–2003 were at almost the same level as in 1980. Real capital goods imports per capita were about $10 per capita (in 1990 dollars), which was seven times lower than real capital goods imports of other developing countries

The basic weakness of human resources within the LDCs, indicated by the general statistics on years of schooling and the brain drain given above, makes the social basis for building technological capabilities very weak. This is also apparent in technically-related education. In 2001, technical and vocational education constituted only 2.6 per cent of total secondary enrolment in the LDCs on average, as against 10.4 per cent in developing countries and 25 per cent in OECD countries. Enrolment in tertiary technical subjects is very low, mainly because enrolment in tertiary education in the LDCs in general is much lower than in other developing countries and OECD countries. In recent years, tertiary enrolment was equivalent to only 6 per cent of the population aged 20–24 in LDCs, compared with 23 per cent in other developing countries and 57 per cent in high-income OECD countries. Within tertiary enrolment, the share of enrolments in science and agriculture in LDCs is at approximately the same levels as in other developing countries and OECD countries. But the share of engineering enrolments within tertiary enrolment is just over half the level in other developing countries. Tertiary-level enrolments, particularly in technical subjects, are important for developing the managerial and technical skills to use modern technologies efficiently and to adapt imported technologies to local conditions. This indicates a major gap in the general competences which provide the basis for technological capabilities.

Differences amongst the LDCs

Given the diversity in the growth performance of the LDCs, the Report identifies trends in the development of productive capacities in three groups of LDCs divided into three groups: converging economies, which are defined as those which achieved an average growth of real GDP per capita of more than 2.15 per annum during the period 1980–2003; weak-growth economies, which are those that did not achieve this level but had positive growth of real

GDP per capita over the period; and regressing economies, in which real GDP per capita was declining over the period.

Analysis of the differences amongst the economies in terms of physical capital formation and its financing shows significant differences. At the start of the 1980s, there was not that much difference in the investment rates in the three groups of countries. But by 1999–2003, the ratio of gross capital formation to GDP had increased by 12 percentage points on average in the converging economies and by 6 percentage points in the weak-growth economies, and had declined in the regressing economies. It is clear that increased investment is associated with higher and more sustained growth rates. In the converging economies, the increased investment was also associated with rising domestic savings. This also occurs in the weak-growth economies. But the rise in investment is particularly related to increases in FDI inflows which occurred after 1993. On average, three-quarters of the increase in the rate of capital formation in the weak-growth economies can be attributed to increased FDI inflows. With regard to grants, it is clear that during the 1980s grants as a share of GDP increased significantly in the converging economies, but subsequently decreased. In contrast, grants are increasing as a share of GDP in both the weak-growth and the regressing economies.

There are also major differences between the three groups of economies in terms of patterns of structural change, productivity growth and trade integration. Again focusing on the difference between the converging economies and regressing economies, it is apparent that the converging economies are characterized by (i) a decline in the share of agriculture in GDP; (ii) an increase in manufacturing value-added; (iii) rising labour productivity in both agriculture and non-agricultural sectors; (iv) an increase in the share of trade in GDP; and (v) an increase in the share of manufactures exports in merchandise exports. In the regressing economies (i) the share of agriculture in GDP is rising; (ii) de-industrialization, in the sense of a declining share of manufactures in GDP, is occurring; (iii) labour productivity is declining in both agriculture and non-agriculture; (iv) trade is declining as a share of GDP; and (v) although manufactures exports are increasing as a share of total merchandise exports, this is occurring much more slowly than in the converging economies.

From these patterns, it is clear that the dynamics of production structures matter for economic growth in the LDCs. Just as within other developing countries, industrialization, and in particular the expansion of manufacturing activities, is characteristic of the LDCs which have experienced the highest and most sustained economic growth. Moreover, de-industrialization, understood here as a decline in the share of manufacturing activities in GDP, and also an increase in the share of agriculture in GDP, are characteristic features of economic regression. The successful LDC experience does not diverge from the classic long-term patterns of structural transformation which have been found when sustained economic growth occurs.

The patterns of structural change, productivity growth and trade integration within the converging economies are indicative of much greater technological progress than in the weak-growth and regressing economies. However, data for trends in machinery and equipment imports do not indicate significant differences between the country groups. This is related to the fact that the level of such imports is associated with FDI inflows. However, it suggests that the development of technological capabilities may be an area of weakness even in converging economies, and that their growth processes remain vulnerable.

The problem of productive absorption of labour

In almost all the LDCs there is an imbalance between the rate of growth of the labour force, which is very rapid owing to population growth, and the rate of capital accumulation and technological progress, which is generally slow. As a result, most workers have to earn their living using their raw labour, with rudimentary tools and equipment, little education and training, and poor infrastructure. Labour productivity is low and there is widespread underemployment. This is the basic cause of persistent mass poverty in the LDCs.

The total labour force of the LDCs is estimated at 312 million people in 2000. Between 1990 and 2000, the labour force increased by 71 million, and between 2000 and 2010 it is expected to grow by a further 89 million to reach 401 million people. A large share of the increment in the total labour force between 2000 and 2010 (22 per cent), will occur in Bangladesh. However, all LDCs are experiencing a large growth in their labour force during the present decade. In 36 out of 50 LDCs for which data are available, the labour force is expected to increase by over 25 per cent.

The most important way in which labour has found productive work within LDCs over the last 25 years has been through agricultural land expansion. But this is becoming more and more circumscribed.

Firstly, as more and more arable land is being brought into cultivation in the LDCs, there is increasing dependence on fragile lands (such as arid regions, steep slopes and fragile soils). This is likely to become a major problem because extreme poverty can make it difficult for many households to use sustainable agricultural practices, and thus there are problems of land degradation and declining soil fertility. There are 31 LDCs in which over 30 per cent of the population live on fragile lands.

Secondly, land under crop cultivation per person engaged in agriculture is generally declining. For the LDCs as a group, the average size of the cultivated holding per economically active agriculturalist has fallen by 29 per cent over the last 40 years. Taking this ratio as a rough proxy of farm size, it is evident that in 32 out of the 50 LDCs, the average farm size was under 1 hectare during 2000–2003, and for the LDCs as a group the average farm size was 0.69 hectares.

Thirdly, there are major inequalities in access to land resources and thus, even in apparently land-abundant countries where the land/labour ratio is apparently favourable, a significant share of the holdings are very small and a growing share of the population are virtually landless.

Against this background, urbanization is accelerating in the LDCs and a larger proportion of the population is seeking work outside agriculture. In 2000, 71 per cent of the labour force was engaged in agriculture and 75 per cent lived in rural areas. But the urbanization rate increased from 17 per cent in 1980 to 25 per cent in 2000, and the share of the population engaged in non-agricultural activities steadily increased from 21 per cent in 1980 to 29 per cent in 2000. These trends are widespread within the LDCs. In 1990, two thirds of the LDCs had less than one third of their population living in urban areas and less than one third of their economically active population engaged outside agriculture. But by 2010, less than one third of the LDCs will have this kind of economy and society.

Projections of the economically active population show that during 2000–2010, of the 89 million increase in that population, 49 million will be outside agriculture and 40 million within agriculture. This is a complete reversal of the pattern of the 1980s when 63 per cent of the increase in the economically active population was in agriculture. For the LDCs as a group it is the first decade in which the growth of the economically active population outside agriculture is expected to be greater than in agriculture. During the 1990s, a larger share of the growth of the economically active population was in agriculture.

The overall pattern of change for the LDCs as a group is strongly influenced by what is happening in Bangladesh. But in African LDCs, 46 per cent of the increase in the total economically active population is expected to be outside agriculture during 2000–2010 (as against 29 per cent in the 1980s) and in Asian LDCs other than Bangladesh, 45 per cent of the increase in the total economically active population is expected to be outside agriculture during the same period (as against 36 per cent in 1980s). The economically active population outside agriculture is projected to grow faster than the economically active population within agriculture during the decade 2000–2010 in almost half the LDCs (24 out of 50 countries). These countries include Benin, Chad, the Central African Republic, the Democratic Republic of the Congo, Equatorial Guinea, Lesotho, Liberia, Mauritania, Sierra Leone, Sudan, Togo and Zambia in Africa; Bangladesh, Myanmar and Yemen in Asia; and Cape Verde, Kiribati, Maldives, Samoa, Sao Tome and Principe, Tuvalu and Vanuatu within the group of island LDCs. The break with past trends is also apparent in Haiti. In many of the other LDCs this break is projected to occur during the decade 2011–2020.

These estimates are, of course, projections which may not be realized. Also, they rely on international data and so national estimates may vary. However, they define the essential dimensions of the problem of poverty reduction in the LDCs. This requires productive labour absorption in agriculture and also in non-agricultural sectors. This will be impossible without the development of productive capacities through capital accumulation, technological progress and structural change.

Constraints on the development of productive capacities

National and international policies to develop productive capacities in the LDCs should prioritize identifying and relaxing key constraints on capital accumulation, technological progress and structural change. This should be done on a country-by-country basis and adapted to local realities. However, the Report focuses on three constraints on the development of productive capacities which are likely to be important in a number of LDCs:

- Physical infrastructure;
- Institutional weaknesses — firms, financial systems and knowledge systems;
- The demand constraint.

Physical infrastructure

Most of the LDCs have the lowest and poorest-quality stock of transport, telecommunications and energy infrastructure in the world. The infrastructure divide is particularly important with respect to energy. The "electricity divide" has not received as much attention as the digital divide. But it is at least as significant — indeed, probably more significant — for economic growth and poverty reduction. A major constraint on the adoption within LDCs of mature modern technologies already available in developed and other developing countries is the low level of technological congruence between the LDCs and other countries. The low level of electrification is a central aspect of this lack of technological congruence and thus contributes to the maintenance of the technological gap.

The infrastructure divide between the LDCs, other developing countries and OECD countries is not only wide but also widening. This is particularly apparent for road infrastructure. Measured by its mileage, the stock of roads per capita in the LDCs was actually lower in 1999 (the latest year for which comprehensive data are available) than in 1990. The percentage of the total roads which are paved in the LDCs also declined   over the same period. The road stock per capita declined in both African and island LDCs, and the percentage of roads which are paved declined in African LDCs. In contrast, for the LDCs as a group, the number of fixed and mobile phone subscribers per 1,000 people increased eightfold between 1990 and 2002. But LDCs are still falling behind other developing countries and OECD countries, as there were more new subscribers in those last two country groups.

The low level and the poor quality of infrastructure stocks in the LDCs reflect poor maintenance of existing facilities and underinvestment in new facilities. This reflects declining public investment, the shift of ODA away from economic infrastructure towards social sectors, and limits to the interest of private investors in physical infrastructure in the LDCs. In real terms, ODA commitments for economic infrastructure declined by 51 per cent between 1992 and 2003. The decline in ODA committed to economic infrastructure was particularly marked in African LDCs. During the 1990s, there was an increase in private sector investment in energy and telecommunications. But private capital flows to transport have been much lower and mainly concentrated in Mozambique, where they have been associated with cross-border corridor development projects.

Closing the physical infrastructure divide between LDCs and other developing countries, one of the quantitative targets of the Brussels Programme of Action for the LDCs, will require increased public investment and a reversal of the downward trend in aid for economic infrastructure which a number of LDCs, particularly in Africa, have experienced in the period 1990–2003. Improved physical infrastructure can play an important role in reducing the cost and time factors with which exporters have to contend in international trade transactions. However, infrastructure investment should not only focus on investment in trade-related infrastructure. Rather, there is rather a need for a joined-up approach to infrastructure development which includes: (i) rural infrastructure and district-level links between rural areas and small towns; (ii) large-scale national infrastructure (such as trunk roads, transmission lines and port facilities); and (iii) cross-border regional infrastructure. Increased public investment in the first is important for agricultural productivity growth and the development of a market economy in rural areas, as well as the creation of rural non-farm employment. Increased public investment in the second is important for diversification and structural change, as well as international trade integration. Increased public investment in the third is important for regional integration.

Particular efforts should be made to promote electrification and to close the electricity divide between LDCs and other developing countries. Most modern technologies require electricity, and the current low levels of access to electricity increase costs for firms, reducing their available funds for investment, and are a basic source of the technological incongruence between the LDCs and the rest of the world which is hampering the acquisition of technologies. This Report also shows that access to electricity affects the composition of exports in developing countries, and that differences in the degree of diversification into manufactures exports are partly related to the degree of electrification.

Institutional weaknesses

There is now increasing emphasis on the importance of institutions for economic growth and poverty reduction. But the major focus is on State capacities and good governance. It is clear that State capacities are vital for effective formulation and implementation of policies, and good governance is certainly necessary. However, there is an equal need to focus on the nature of the private sector and the institutions within which entrepreneurship is embedded. From this perspective, the Report shows that most LDCs have serious institutional weaknesses with regard to their firms, financial systems and knowledge systems.

Firstly, the size distribution of enterprises within LDCs is generally characterized by a "missing middle" in which a multitude of informal micro-enterprises coexist with a few large firms, and there is weak development of formal sector SMEs, particularly medium-sized domestic firms. There are weak linkages between the large firms and other enterprises, and the life cycle of enterprises is stunted. Few informal micro-enterprises become formal sector enterprises. Moreover, small firms are often unable to grow even when they are efficient. There is also wide heterogeneity in firm performance, although it is often found that the large firms tend to be more productive than the small firms with regard to most productivity indicators.

Secondly, and closely related to the phenomenon of the "missing middle", both the domestic financial systems and the domestic knowledge systems are dualistic. The financial markets are characterized by an informal segment (including transactions between friends and relatives or small-scale group arrangements, as well as transactions conducted by moneylenders, traders and landlords), as well as by formal banks. The domestic knowledge system includes a modern knowledge system alongside a traditional knowledge system. Different types of enterprises are embedded within these different systems.

Thirdly, the domestic financial systems have large liquid reserves, but as a ratio of GDP, domestic credit loaned to the private sector is four times lower than in low- and middle-income countries (15 per cent as against 60 per cent). Moreover, it has declined in the aftermath of financial liberalization in many LDCs, particularly in African LDCs. During the same period, interest rate spreads have increased in LDCs, and the level of monetization has actually declined in African LDCs. Financial liberalization has simply failed to promote productive investment, as reflected in the poor delivery of credit to the private sector and to SMEs in particular. Banks are partly constrained because of the weak capacity of local entrepreneurs to formulate acceptable business plans and also because of weak contract enforcement. But at the same time, it is clear that the banks are very risk-averse and prefer to do business in the very safe areas of government bonds.

Fourthly, modern knowledge systems are vital for international competitiveness, but they are fragmented. Specialized creators of knowledge, such as research institutions, are not responsive to the demands of users. Evidence on the use of international standards within LDCs also suggests that there is a particular problem in terms of the extent to which the domestic knowledge systems are outward-looking and able to keep up with ever-rising international standards.

The development of productive capacities depends on the ability of an economy to create enterprises with a high propensity to invest, learn and innovate. SMEs are certainly important as they tend to use local inputs and thus are the agents that link local primary and manufacturing activities. They also provide employment for the local population. But an exclusive focus on SMEs is based on a static view of the development process. From a dynamic efficiency perspective, large-size firms are in a better position to generate the resources to achieve higher rates of capital formation, innovation, scale economies and the accompanying learning effects. Fostering linkages between large firms and SMEs is an important demand-side measure to complement the supply-side measures for SME development. Moreover, such inter-firm linkages can also facilitate knowledge transfers, technology transfer and technological upgrading. This suggests the need for an alternative policy framework based on supporting firm growth and expansion, the promotion of linkages between SMEs and large firms, the development of subcontracting relations, and the promotion of clustering and spatial agglomeration.

Overcoming bottlenecks in financing for the private sector should be a critical priority for policymakers in the LDCs. Without access to capital by the private sector, the potential for development of productive capacities cannot be achieved.

The importance of improving the financial systems in the LDCs is indeed widely recognized. However, new sources of financing urgently need to be identified and lessons may be drawn from the more successful cases in countries with deeper financial systems that are more responsive to the needs of the private sector. Historical experience suggests that a bank-based system is important at low levels of development. Possible financial institutions include the following:

- Loan guarantee schemes between the public and the private sector to facilitate access to bank credit for SMEs and large enterprises investing in technical change;
- Public development banks, particularly to create long-term financing;
- Value-chain lending in which lending to enterprises along a value-chain is coordinated;
- Innovative market-based financial instruments.

Knowledge systems are as important as financial systems in the development of productive capacities. Thus, improving domestic knowledge systems should complement efforts to improve the domestic financial systems. This involves not simply setting up special bodies oriented to creating knowledge which could be applied in production (such as research centres), but also creating bridging institutions with users and promoting linkages amongst the latter. For most LDCs the three most important sources for building their domestic knowledge base are education, foreign technology imports (through foreign licensing, FDI, turnkey plants and capital goods imports) and the mobility of experienced technical personnel. These are more important than seeking to increase levels of basic R&D. Investing in all levels of education, especially in technical skills and the building up of technological capabilities, is particularly important given the currently low levels of schooling which are found in most LDCs. Weak human resources make technology absorption difficult and slow down the technology catch-up process.

LDCs need to develop well-designed and coherent national technology learning strategies to increase access to technology and improve the effectiveness of imported technology, and to benefit from linking to global knowledge. There are major opportunities for blending modern and traditional knowledge in the areas of health and agriculture.

Demand constraints

The development of productive capacities cannot be achieved without addressing demand-side constraints as well as supply-side constraints. Yet demand as a source of growth has been generally neglected. Policies, and particularly aid inflows, which seek to engineer a supply-side fix for the weak productive capacities in the LDCs, without due attention to the dynamics of demand, are likely to fail. Inclusive development and poverty reduction require a development strategy which pays attention to the dynamics of domestic demand as well as external markets.

Evidence for a small but varied sample of LDCs shows that expansion of domestic demand has contributed most to their economic growth. Because domestic demand is such a large demand-side source of economic growth, its weak growth is a major constraint on the development of productive capacities in most LDCs. Sluggish domestic demand, which is associated with generalized and persistent poverty, is a central deficiency of the investment climate in the LDCs.

Because the share of agriculture in GDP and total employment is high in most LDCs, trends in domestic demand are closely related to what happens in the agricultural sector and also the nature of the linkages between agriculture and the rest of the economy. In this regard, the demand linkage effects of agricultural growth constitute an important growth and poverty reduction mechanism. In Bangladesh, it is possible to observe a virtuous circle in which demand stimulus from agricultural growth generates investment, entrepreneurship and employment in non-agricultural activities, particularly non-tradables. This virtuous circle is likely to be relevant in many LDCs and at the heart of efforts to create a more inclusive process of development which supports sustainable poverty reduction. Without the stimulus of domestic demand for non-tradables, it is difficult to envisage the productive absorption of labour outside agriculture. However, the effectiveness of this linkage dynamic depends on income distribution.

Although domestic demand makes a critical contribution to economic growth in the LDCs, exports also matter. There are various supply-side reasons for this. But exports also matter because economic growth and the full utilization of productive capacities are constrained through the balance of payments. Each component of demand has an import content which is essential for the continuation of ongoing economic activities and their expansion, and countries need foreign exchange to pay for imports. Analysis of the LDCs within this framework shows that export growth has made a positive contribution. But its contribution to relaxing the balance-of-payments constraint has been seriously reduced by declining terms of trade and currency depreciation. It is also clear that capital inflows and transfers have played an important role in the LDCs in alleviating the balance-of-payments constraint.

This implies that upgrading the export structure of the LDCs should be a priority. There is a place here for new forms of industrial policy, which have been elaborated recently in developed countries, based on a mixed market-based model, with private entrepreneurship and government working closely together in order to create strategic complementarities between public and private sector investment, and the State not picking winners but rather helping the private sector to discover and exploit economic potentials.

*   *   *   *   *

In addressing the issue of developing productive capacities in the least developed countries, it is necessary to maintain a balance between the constraints and the opportunities of the present situation. The evidence in this Report on the low level of development of productive capacities in most LDCs and on the weakness of processes of capital accumulation, technological progress and structural change is sobering. However, there are also major opportunities for rapid economic growth and substantial poverty reduction if constraints on the development of productive capacities can be relaxed in a systematic way, and underutilized productive resources and entrepreneurial capabilities can be harnessed for development. National Governments have the primary responsibility in this task. But both a favourable international enabling environment and enhanced international support for the LDCs are also necessary and can provide great benefits not simply for the LDCs but also for the world as a whole.

Dr. Supachai Panitchpakdi
Secretary-General of UNCTAD

Part One

RECENT ECONOMIC TRENDS AND UNLDC III DEVELOPMENT TARGETS

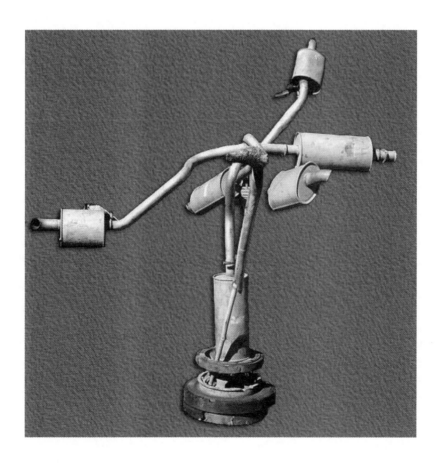

Recent Economic Trends

A. Introduction

This chapter examines trends in economic performance in the LDCs in 2003 and 2004, the latest years for which international data are available. It shows that the economic performance of the LDCs as a group continues to improve. The average GDP growth rate is the highest for two decades and merchandise exports are at record levels.

This good economic performance is partly due to favourable trends in oil-exporting LDCs, as a result of high oil prices. However, the improved growth performance is not limited to those countries. Higher non-oil commodity prices, particularly prices for minerals, have helped export growth in a number of LDCs. Moreover, there have been major increases in external finance, both ODA and FDI, flowing to the LDCs. Foreign capital inflows into the LDCs, like exports, are at record levels, and this has enabled increased investment.

Increases in both ODA and FDI are, however, geographically concentrated, with increases in ODA greatest in countries that have been affected by conflict, particularly Afghanistan and the Democratic Republic of the Congo, and FDI inflows focused on resource-rich oil and mineral economies. The heavy reliance on external sources for financing capital formation implies that the future sustainability of the recent growth and investment boom is not yet guaranteed. Rising international commodity prices are helping exports in a number of LDCs. But at the same time the combination of rising food prices and rising fuel prices is making many LDCs vulnerable, since they are net food importers as well as oil importers.

In 2004, the real GDP of the LDCs as a group grew by 5.9 per cent, which is the strongest growth performance that they have achieved over the last two decades.

B. Overall economic growth trends

In 2004, the real GDP of the LDCs as a group grew by 5.9 per cent, which is the strongest growth performance that they have achieved over the last two decades. This represents an acceleration of the growth rate by 1.6 percentage points compared with the 2003 level. As a result, in 2002–2004 the GDP performance of the LDC group accelerated to reach an average of 5.2 per cent per annum in real terms compared with 4.9 per cent in 2000–2002 and 4.4 per cent in 1998–2000. Nevertheless, the real GDP growth rate remained slower than that in the group of other developing countries, which stood at 6.7 per cent in 2004 and 5.1 per cent in 2003.

A regional breakdown shows that whereas the real average GDP growth rates of African and Asian LDCs were almost comparable in 2003 (4.5 per cent versus 4.8 per cent), this was no longer the case in 2004 when the real GDP growth rate of African LDCs exceeded that of Asian ones by 1.5 percentage points. The improvement of the growth performance of the African LDCs is also apparent if the comparison is made over a longer period. The real average annual GDP growth rate of African LDCs accelerated from 2.7 per cent per annum in the 1990s to 5.2 per cent per annum in 2000–2004. In Asian LDCs it actually decelerated from 5.7 per cent per annum to 4.7 per cent per annum between the two periods (see table 1).

Foreign capital inflows into the LDCs, like exports, are at record levels, however, highly geographically concentrated.

TABLE 1. REAL GDP AND REAL GDP PER CAPITA GROWTH RATES OF LDCs AND OTHER DEVELOPING COUNTRIES, 1990–2000, 2000–2002 AND 2002–2004

(Annual average, percentage)

	Real GDP growth					Real GDP per capita growth				
	1990–2000	2000–2002	2002–2004	2003	2004	1990–2000	2000-2002	2002–2004	2003	2004
LDCs	3.9	4.9	5.2	4.6	5.9	1.1	2.6	3.0	2.3	3.6
of which:										
Bangladesh	4.8	4.8	5.4	5.3	5.5	3.0	3.0	3.6	3.4	3.7
Other LDCs	3.5	4.9	5.2	4.4	6.0	0.5	2.4	2.8	1.9	3.7
African LDCs	2.7	5.2	5.5	4.5	6.5	0.0	2.7	3.1	2.1	4.2
Asian LDCs	5.7	4.6	4.9	4.8	5.0	2.8	2.6	2.9	2.8	3.0
Island LDCs[a]	..	2.2	4.2	3.4	5.0	..	-0.4	1.0	0.2	1.8
Other developing countries	4.9	3.0	5.9	5.1	6.7	3.2	1.7	4.6	3.8	5.4

Source: UNCTAD secretariat estimates based on World Bank, *World Development Indicators*, online data, December 2005.

Notes: Real GDP is measured in constant 2000 dollars.
No data were available for Afghanistan, Myanmar, Somalia or Tuvalu.
The group of other developing countries is composed of 69 countries for which real GDP data were available.
a During the 1990s no data were available for Maldives and Timor-Leste.

Data show that the real average GDP growth rate was consistently higher in the group of oil-exporting LDCs than in the non-oil-exporting LDCs in 2002, 2003 and 2004. In 2004, oil-exporting LDCs had an average real GDP growth rate of 7.9 per cent as compared with 5.3 per cent in the group of non-oil-exporting LDCs. But in the previous year the average real growth levels were 5.1 per cent and 4.5 per cent respectively. As a result, although oil-exporting LDCs drove the growth acceleration of the LDCs, the high growth rate of the LDC group in recent years is not solely the result of the high growth rate of oil-exporting LDCs, driven by high oil prices. In 2004, real GDP growth was 6 per cent or more in four oil-exporting LDCs and in 11 non-oil-exporting ones. Of those 15 LDCs, 12 are African LDCs.

The LDCs increased their already heavy reliance on external sources to finance their capital formation process in 2003 and 2004.

Table 2 shows the diversity of the LDCs' growth performance. In 2004, the real GDP per capita growth rate either declined or stagnated in 15 of the 46 LDCs for which data are available.

Despite the high real GDP growth performance of the LDCs, it should be noted, as shown in table 3, that the ratio of gross domestic savings to GDP remained at a depressed level in 2003 and even declined from 13.4 per cent in 2003 to 11 per cent in 2004. This does not compare favourably with the group of low- and middle-income countries, for which that ratio was more than twice as high as that for the LDCs in both years. The ratio of gross capital formation to GDP was also lower in the LDCs than in the group of low- and middle-income countries — by 4.1 and 5.6 percentage points respectively in 2003 and 2004.

Differences in the growth performance of the LDCs can be related to differences in access to external resources.

Whereas the resource gap deepened further, from -7.6 per cent in 2003 to -9.7 per cent in 2004 in the group of LDCs, the group of low- and middle-income countries showed an increasing resource surplus. Overall, this indicates that in contrast to the group of low- and middle-income countries, the LDCs as a group increased their already heavy reliance on external sources to finance their capital formation process in 2003 and 2004.

Differences in the growth performance of the LDCs can be related to differences in access to external resources associated with ODA, FDI and exports. Table 4 shows that the LDCs in which real GDP growth increased most in 2004 (group 1) are, on average, those for which the FDI and merchandise

TABLE 2. REAL GDP AND REAL GDP PER CAPITA GROWTH RATES OF LDCS, BY COUNTRY,
2000–2002, 2003 AND 2004

(Annual average, percentage)

	Real GDP growth			Real GDP per capita growth		
	2002–2004	2003	2004	2002–2004	2003	2004
Group 1 (2004 real GDP growth rate of 6% per cent and above)						
Chad[a]	20.7	11.3	31.0	17.4	8.2	27.4
Ethiopia	4.5	-3.7	13.4	2.4	-5.6	11.2
Angola[a]	7.3	3.4	11.2	4.0	0.4	7.7
Equatorial Guinea[a]	12.3	14.7	10.0	9.6	11.9	7.4
Maldives	8.6	8.4	8.8	6.2	6.0	6.5
Gambia	7.5	6.7	8.3	5.2	4.3	6.2
Mozambique	7.4	7.1	7.8	5.5	5.1	5.9
Sierra Leone	8.3	9.2	7.4	6.3	7.1	5.4
Mauritania	7.4	8.3	6.6	5.2	5.9	4.5
Dem. Rep. of the Congo	5.9	5.6	6.3	2.8	2.5	3.2
United Rep. of Tanzania	6.7	7.1	6.3	4.6	5.0	4.3
Cambodia	5.7	5.3	6.0	3.9	3.5	4.2
Sudan[a]	6.0	6.0	6.0	3.6	3.6	3.5
Lao People's Dem. Republic	5.7	5.3	6.0	3.3	2.9	3.6
Senegal	6.2	6.5	6.0	3.9	4.0	3.8
Group 2 (2004 real GDP growth rate of above 3% but below 6%)						
Uganda	5.2	4.7	5.7	2.5	1.9	3.1
Bangladesh	5.4	5.3	5.5	3.6	3.4	3.7
Burundi	2.1	-1.2	5.5	0.2	-3.1	3.5
Cape Verde	5.2	5.0	5.5	2.7	2.4	2.9
Madagascar	7.5	9.8	5.3	4.7	6.8	2.6
Bhutan	5.8	6.7	4.9	3.1	3.9	2.3
Zambia	4.9	5.1	4.6	3.4	3.5	3.2
Sao Tome and Principe	4.5	4.5	4.5	2.4	2.4	2.4
Guinea-Bissau	2.4	0.6	4.3	-0.5	-2.3	1.3
Burkina Faso	5.2	6.5	3.9	2.8	4.1	1.6
Malawi	4.1	4.4	3.8	2.0	2.3	1.8
Solomon Islands	4.4	5.1	3.8	1.3	2.0	0.7
Nepal	3.4	3.1	3.7	1.2	0.8	1.6
Rwanda	2.3	1.0	3.7	0.8	-1.8	3.5
Samoa	1.1	-1.0	3.2	0.3	-2.0	2.6
Lesotho	3.2	3.3	3.0	2.2	2.4	2.1
Djibouti	3.3	3.5	3.0	1.7	1.8	1.6
Togo	2.8	2.7	3.0	0.7	0.5	0.8
Vanuatu	2.7	2.4	3.0	0.4	0.2	0.7
Group 3 (2004 real GDP growth rate below 3%)						
Yemen[a]	2.9	3.1	2.7	-0.2	0.1	-0.4
Benin	3.3	3.9	2.7	0.7	1.3	0.2
Guinea	1.9	1.2	2.6	-0.2	-0.9	0.5
Mali	4.8	7.4	2.2	2.3	4.9	-0.3
Liberia	-16.1	-31.0	2.0	-18.0	-32.6	-0.2
Comoros	2.0	2.1	1.9	-0.4	-0.3	-0.5
Timor-Leste	-2.3	-6.2	1.8	-7.3	-11.0	-3.5
Kiribati	2.1	2.5	1.8	0.5	0.7	0.3
Eritrea	2.4	3.0	1.8	0.3	0.8	-0.2
Niger	3.1	5.3	0.9	0.2	2.3	-1.9
Central African Republic	-2.3	-5.4	0.9	-3.9	-6.9	-0.8
Haiti	-1.7	0.4	-3.8	-3.5	-1.4	-5.5

Source: UNCTAD secretariat estimates based on World Bank, *World Development Indicators*, online data, December 2005.

Notes: Real GDP is measured in constant 2000 dollars.
No data were available for Afghanistan, Myanmar, Somalia or Tuvalu.
a Oil-exporting LDCs.

TABLE 3. GROSS CAPITAL FORMATION AND GROSS DOMESTIC SAVINGS IN LDCs, 2000–2004

(Percentage of GDP)

	Gross capital formation			Gross domestic savings			Resource gap[a]		
	2000	*2003*	*2004*	*2000*	*2003*	*2004*	*2000*	*2003*	*2004*
Angola	12.7	12.8	11.6	63.0	36.7	..	-50.3	-23.9	..
Bangladesh	23.9	23.4	23.4	17.8	17.6	17.0	6.1	5.8	6.4
Benin	18.9	18.6	20.3	6.0	5.5	-1.3	12.9	13.2	21.6
Bhutan	48.4	..	..	19.5	..	..	28.8	..	..
Burkina Faso	22.7	18.7	19.1	6.5	3.9	4.8	16.2	14.8	14.3
Burundi	9.1	15.3	10.6	-5.7	4.3	-5.6	14.7	11.0	16.2
Cambodia	17.2	22.8	22.7	5.2	13.0	12.3	12.0	9.8	10.4
Cape Verde	19.7	20.2	21.6	-14.2	-16.0	-12.6	33.9	36.2	34.2
Central African Republic	10.8	6.0	6.9	7.8	11.9	..	3.1	-5.9	..
Chad	22.4	55.0	24.7	2.1	21.0	43.2	20.3	34.0	-18.5
Comoros	13.1	11.8	10.5	-1.4	0.6	..	14.5	11.1	..
Dem. Rep. of the Congo	3.5	13.7	17.6	4.8	..	..	-1.4	..	..
Djibouti	12.9	..	..	-5.3	..	..	18.2	..	..
Eritrea	31.9	22.4	21.8	-34.7	-62.9	-51.1	66.6	85.4	72.8
Ethiopia	15.9	20.5	19.8	0.9	1.0	1.3	15.0	19.4	18.6
Gambia	17.4	19.2	23.9	8.1	14.6	19.6	9.3	4.6	4.3
Guinea	22.0	9.9	10.5	16.8	7.4	8.6	5.1	2.5	1.9
Guinea-Bissau	11.3	12.4	12.4	-8.5	-1.1	4.0	19.8	13.5	8.4
Haiti	27.3	31.0	23.3	6.6	..	..	20.7	..	..
Lao PDR	21.1	22.0	18.9	16.8	20.5	..	4.3	1.5	..
Lesotho	42.2	44.3	41.1	-20.4	-24.1	-24.2	62.6	68.4	65.3
Liberia	..	8.7	13.5				..	8.7	13.5
Madagascar	15.0	17.9	24.4	7.7	7.8	8.8	7.3	10.1	15.5
Malawi	13.6	11.2	11.1	-2.8	-5.0	0.0	16.4	16.2	11.2
Maldives	26.3	..	..	44.2	51.4	..	-17.9	..	..
Mali	24.6	23.9	19.7	9.7	18.9	..	14.9	4.9	..
Mauritania	30.5	..	..	15.0	3.2	1.6	15.5	..	..
Mozambique	21.1	26.9	22.2	10.6	11.3	..	10.5	15.6	..
Myanmar	12.4	..	..	12.4	..	..	0.1	..	..
Nepal	24.3	25.8	..	15.2	13.7	12.9	9.1	12.1	..
Niger	11.4	14.2	15.9	3.5	5.0	7.6	7.9	9.2	8.3
Rwanda	17.5	18.4	20.8	1.4	1.1	..	16.1	17.3	..
Sao Tome and Principe	43.5	30.1	33.1	-6.0	-14.4	-17.9	49.5	44.5	51.0
Senegal	18.5	20.1	21.0	8.6	8.0	10.0	10.0	12.0	11.0
Sierra Leone	8.0	14.3	19.6	-8.2	-11.5	-10.7	16.2	25.8	30.3
Sudan	17.9	18.2	20.0	20.0	24.7	5.9	-2.1	-6.5	14.1
Timor-Leste	33.0	27.0	..	-50.0	..	..	83.0	..	..
Togo	17.8	18.9	18.0	-2.2	5.3	4.5	20.0	13.6	13.5
Uganda	19.8	20.7	21.7	7.9	6.6	7.9	11.9	14.0	13.8
United Rep. of Tanzania	17.6	18.6	19.2	9.3	9.5	..	8.3	9.1	..
Yemen	17.3	16.9	17.0	24.9	12.4	9.3	-7.6	4.4	7.7
Zambia	18.7	26.1	24.6	8.3	18.7	18.9	10.4	7.4	5.7
LDCs	19.5	21.1	20.7	13.7	13.4	11.0	-5.8	-7.6	-9.7
Low- and middle-income countries	24.4	25.1	26.3	25.2	26.7	27.1	0.8	1.6	0.8

Source: UNCTAD secretariat estimates based on World Bank, *World Development Indicators*, online data, December 2005.

Note: No data were available for Afghanistan, Equatorial Guinea, Kiribati, Solomon Islands, Somalia, Tuvalu and Vanuatu.

a Measured by gross capital formation % GDP less gross domestic savings % GDP.

TABLE 4. LDCs' RELIANCE ON EXTERNAL FINANCE AND MERCHANDISE EXPORTS, 2000 AND 2004

(Percentage of GDP)

	Net ODA			Net FDI			Merchandise exports		
	2000	*2004*	*% point change*	*2000*	*2004*	*% point change*	*2000*	*2004*	*% point change*
Group 1 (2004 real GDP growth rate of 6% per cent and above)									
Angola	3.4	5.7	2.3	9.6	10.2	0.6	86.8	67.4	-19.4
Cambodia	11.1	10.4	-0.7	4.1	2.9	-1.3	39.0	52.5	13.6
Chad	9.4	7.5	-1.9	8.3	11.2	2.9	13.2	36.1	23.0
Dem. Rep. of the Congo	4.3	27.6	23.4	0.5	13.7	13.2	17.7	21.5	3.8
Equatorial Guinea	1.6	0.9	-0.7	8.0	51.4	43.4	81.8	89.9	8.1
Ethiopia	10.6	22.6	12.0	2.1	6.7	4.7	7.4	7.3	-0.1
Gambia	11.7	15.3	3.6	10.3	14.5	4.1	3.6	4.8	1.3
Lao PDR	16.4	11.2	-5.2	2.0	0.7	-1.3	19.2	18.9	-0.3
Maldives	3.1	3.8	0.7	2.1	1.7	-0.4	17.5	22.8	5.4
Mauritania	22.6	13.3	-9.3	4.3	22.1	17.8	38.1	23.2	-14.9
Mozambique	23.8	22.2	-1.6	3.8	2.4	-1.4	9.9	16.7	6.8
Senegal	9.7	13.7	4.0	1.4	0.9	-0.5	21.0	20.0	-1.1
Sierra Leone	28.8	33.5	4.7	6.1	0.5	-5.7	2.1	12.9	10.9
Sudan	1.8	4.5	2.7	3.2	7.7	4.5	14.8	19.3	4.5
United Rep. of Tanzania	11.3	16.1	4.8	3.1	4.3	1.2	7.3	12.3	5.0
Group 2 (2004 real GDP growth rate of above 3% but below 6%)									
Bangladesh	2.6	2.5	-0.1	0.6	0.8	0.2	14.1	14.7	0.7
Bhutan	10.9	11.7	0.7	0.0	0.1	0.2	21.1	26.0	4.9
Burkina Faso	12.9	12.7	-0.3	0.9	0.7	-0.2	8.0	9.2	1.2
Burundi	13.7	53.4	39.8	1.7	0.5	-1.3	7.4	7.2	-0.2
Cape Verde	17.7	14.8	-2.9	6.1	2.2	-4.0	2.1	1.3	-0.8
Djibouti	12.9	9.8	-3.2	0.6	5.0	4.4	5.8	6.2	0.4
Guinea-Bissau	37.3	27.4	-9.9	0.3	1.8	1.5	28.8	28.9	0.1
Lesotho	4.3	7.5	3.2	3.7	3.8	0.1	25.6	43.3	17.7
Madagascar	8.3	28.3	20.0	2.1	1.0	-1.1	21.3	21.3	0.1
Malawi	25.6	26.3	0.7	1.5	0.9	-0.6	21.7	24.9	3.2
Nepal	7.1	6.4	-0.7	0.0	0.1	0.2	14.6	11.3	-3.4
Rwanda	17.8	25.4	7.6	0.4	0.6	0.1	2.9	5.3	2.4
Samoa	11.9	8.6	-3.2	-0.7	0.2	0.8	6.1	3.0	-3.0
Solomon Islands	22.9	50.8	27.9	0.5	-2.1	-2.5	21.7	41.4	19.7
Togo	5.3	3.0	-2.2	3.1	2.9	-0.2	34.6	31.0	-3.6
Uganda	13.9	17.0	3.1	3.1	3.5	0.4	7.8	9.4	1.6
Vanuatu	18.7	12.1	-6.6	8.3	6.9	-1.4	11.0	11.1	0.0
Zambia	24.6	20.1	-4.5	3.8	6.2	2.4	20.6	21.9	1.3
Group 3 (2004 real GDP growth rate below 3%)									
Benin	10.6	9.3	-1.3	2.6	1.5	-1.2	17.4	16.5	-0.9
Central African Republic	7.9	7.9	0.0	0.1	-1.0	-1.0	16.9	11.3	-5.6
Comoros	9.2	6.8	-2.4	0.0	0.5	0.5	3.4	3.8	0.4
Eritrea	27.8	28.1	0.3	4.4	3.2	-1.2	3.0	5.4	2.4
Guinea	4.9	8.0	3.1	0.3	2.9	2.5	21.4	18.0	-3.4
Haiti	5.3	6.9	1.6	0.3	0.2	-0.2	8.0	11.1	3.0
Mali	14.8	11.7	-3.2	3.4	3.7	0.3	22.7	23.1	0.3
Niger	11.7	17.4	5.7	0.5	0.6	0.2	15.7	12.0	-3.7
Yemen	2.8	2.0	-0.8	0.1	-0.2	-0.2	43.2	39.8	-3.4
Group 1	11.3	13.9	2.6	4.6	10.1	5.5	25.3	28.4	3.1
Group 2	14.9	18.8	3.9	2.0	1.9	-0.1	15.3	17.6	2.3
Group 3	10.6	10.9	0.3	1.3	1.3	0.0	16.9	15.7	-1.2

Source: UNCTAD secretariat estimates based on World Bank, *World Development Indicators*, online data, December 2005; and UNCTAD FDI/TNC database and *Handbook of Statistics, 2005*.

Notes: Insufficient data are available for Afghanistan, Kiribati, Myanmar, Somalia, Timor-Leste and Tuvalu.
Group averages are simple averages.
Liberia and Sao Tome and Principe are outliers and are therefore excluded from the estimates.

The extent to which the real GDP growth performance of LDCs will be sustained over time will also partly depend on the way in which ODA, FDI and exports are productively channelled in the economy.

exports to GDP ratio was highest in 2004 and increased most over the last five years. In contrast, the LDCs that on average displayed the lowest real GDP growth rate in 2004 (group 3) are those in which the ratio of FDI, net ODA and merchandise exports to GDP was lowest and increased least over the last five years. The countries in the middle of the spectrum (group 2) are those in which the net ODA to GDP ratio was highest and increased most between 2000 and 2004.

Overall, it is most likely that the high growth performance of the LDCs in 2004 was driven by the combination of positive trends in merchandise exports and external finance. The extent to which the real GDP growth performance of LDCs will be sustained over time will also partly depend on the way in which ODA, FDI and exports are productively channelled in the economy so as to contribute to the countries' capital formation process and to promote an inclusive form of growth.

C. Trends in merchandise trade

1. OVERALL PICTURE

UNCTAD merchandise trade data show that LDC revenues from merchandise exports totalled $57.8 billion in 2004. Compared with the 2002 and 2003 levels, this represents an additional $18.4 billion and $11.9 billion

TABLE 5. LDCS' EXPORTS, IMPORTS AND BALANCE IN MERCHANDISE TRADE, BY GROUP, 2000–2004

	$ millions				% change[a]			
	2001	*2002*	*2003*	*2004*	*2000– 2004*	*2001– 2002*	*2002– 2003*	*2003– 2004*
Merchandise exports								
LDCs	36 056	39 397	45 929	57 839	60.7	9.3	16.6	25.9
Oil-exporting LDCs	13 075	15 625	18 727	25 345	70.1	19.5	19.9	35.3
Non-oil-exporting LDCs	22 981	23 772	27 202	32 494	54.0	3.4	14.4	19.5
African LDCs	21 313	23 724	28 991	37 170	78.6	11.3	22.2	28.2
excluding oil-exporting LDCs	11 453	11 557	14 024	16 934	69.5	0.9	21.3	20.8
Asian LDCs	14 521	15 423	16 638	20 312	35.9	6.2	7.9	22.1
Island LDCs	223	252	301	357	48.8	13.0	19.4	18.6
Merchandise imports								
LDCs	46 308	47 867	56 474	64 435	49.8	3.4	18.0	14.1
Oil-exporting LDCs	8 564	9 290	11 068	13 267	80.1	8.5	19.1	19.9
Non-oil-exporting LDCs	37 744	38 577	45 406	51 168	43.5	2.2	17.7	12.7
African LDCs	26 831	28 546	34 251	40 929	69.9	6.4	20.0	19.5
excluding oil-exporting LDCs	34 193	34 757	41 082	45 487	38.4	1.6	18.2	10.7
Asian LDCs	18 373	18 167	20 875	21 896	22.4	-1.1	14.9	4.9
Island LDCs	1 105	1 154	1 346	1 610	53.2	4.4	16.6	19.6
Net trade								
LDCs	-10 252	-8 470	-10 545	-6 596	-6.1	-17.4	24.5	-37.4
Oil-exporting LDCs	4 511	6 335	7 659	12 078	60.3	40.4	20.9	57.7
Non-oil-exporting LDCs	-14 763	-14 805	-18 204	-18 674	28.3	0.3	23.0	2.6
African LDCs	-5 518	-4 822	-5 260	-3 759	14.9	-12.6	9.1	-28.5
excluding oil-exporting LDCs	-22 740	-23 200	-27 058	-28 553	24.9	2.0	16.6	5.5
Asian LDCs	-3 852	-2 744	-4 237	-1 584	-46.1	-28.8	54.4	-62.6
Island LDCs	- 882	- 902	-1 045	-1 253	54.5	2.3	15.9	19.9

Source: UNCTAD secretariat estimates based on UNCTAD, *Handbook of Statistics 2005.*

Notes: Estimates are based on a group of 49 LDCs for which data are available. No data are available for Timor-Leste. Chad is not included as an oil-exporting LDC in this table.

a Percentage change in trade values between initial year and end year.

respectively (see table 5). Despite this impressive performance, LDCs generated only 0.6 per cent of world merchandise exports. The four traditional oil-exporting LDCs — Angola, Equatorial Guinea, Sudan and Yemen — accounted for 52.7 per cent and 55.6 per cent of the 2003 and 2004 increases, respectively. The percentage of total LDC merchandise exports from those four economies increased steadily from 36.3 per cent in 2001 to 43.8 per cent in 2004. As a result of the lower rate of growth of the LDCs' total merchandise imports, the LDC trade deficit improved from -$10.5 billion in 2003 to -$6.6 billion in 2004. This improvement is, however, attributable almost exclusively to oil-exporting LDCs. If the latter are excluded, the LDC trade deficit worsened further, from -$18.2 billion in 2003 to -$18.6 billion in 2004. In fact, with the exception of Sudan, all oil-exporting LDCs have consistently displayed a trade surplus since 1999. Moreover, Chad, which started to export oil in the last quarter of 2003, first displayed a merchandise trade surplus in 2004. The merchandise trade balance worsened in 28, 35 and 33 LDCs in 2002, 2003 and 2004 respectively.

As shown in chart 1, five out of the six LDCs in which the value of merchandise exports increased most between 2003 and 2004 are oil exporters. The increasing oil price made a particularly strong contribution to this performance in 2004, when, according to UNCTAD secretariat estimates, the price index for crude petroleum rose by about 35 per cent. Despite the spectacular export performance of oil-exporting LDCs, it should be noted that non-oil-exporting LDCs also performed well in 2003 and 2004. In nominal terms, the merchandise export growth rate of the traditional oil-exporting LDCs averaged 19.9 per cent and 35.3 per cent respectively.[1] For their part, the non-oil-exporting LDCs displayed nominal rates of increase of 14.4 per cent and 19.5 per cent respectively.

Regional data show that, in 2003, African LDCs performed better than Asian ones, even excluding oil-exporting LDCs. But in 2004 the group of Asian LDCs outperformed the group of African non-oil-exporting LDCs (a nominal growth rate of 22.1 per cent versus 20.8 per cent). A breakdown by country shows that a few LDCs did not participate in the increase in the merchandise exports of this group of countries (see chart 1). Between 2002 and 2003, the value of exports actually decreased in nominal terms in the Central African Republic, The Gambia, Guinea, Mauritania, Myanmar and Somalia. Between 2003 and 2004 exports declined in Cape Verde, Eritrea, Liberia, Malawi and Samoa. In contrast, Angola, Bangladesh, Cambodia, Equatorial Guinea, Senegal, Sudan and Yemen were among the 10 best-performing LDCs during both periods in terms of the nominal value of exports. For Bangladesh, Cambodia and Senegal, this good performance is driven by exports of manufactures, while for the others it is driven by oil exports.

2. TRENDS IN INTERNATIONAL COMMODITY PRICES

The improved export performance of a large number of LDCs in 2003 and 2004 was supported by higher international commodity prices. Between 2002 and 2003 the average price indices of food, agricultural raw materials, and minerals, metals and ores increased by 3.9 per cent, 19.1 per cent and 12.6 per cent respectively. Between 2003 and 2004, the average price indices rose by 13.1 per cent for food and 39.8 per cent for minerals, metals and ores, whereas it rose by 9.8 per cent for agricultural raw materials. The crude petroleum price index increased by 15.8 per cent between 2002 and 2003 and by 30.7 per cent between 2003 and 2004.

The LDC trade deficit improved from -$10.5 billion in 2003 to -$6.6 billion in 2004. This improvement is, however, attributable almost exclusively to oil-exporting LDCs.

Despite the spectacular export performance of oil-exporting LDCs, it should be noted that non-oil-exporting LDCs also performed well in 2003 and 2004.

The improved export performance of a large number of LDCs in 2003 and 2004 was supported by higher international commodity prices in many commodities relevant to their exports.

CHART 1. NOMINAL CHANGE IN THE VALUE OF LDCs' MERCHANDISE EXPORT REVENUES, 2002–2003 AND 2003–2004
($ millions)

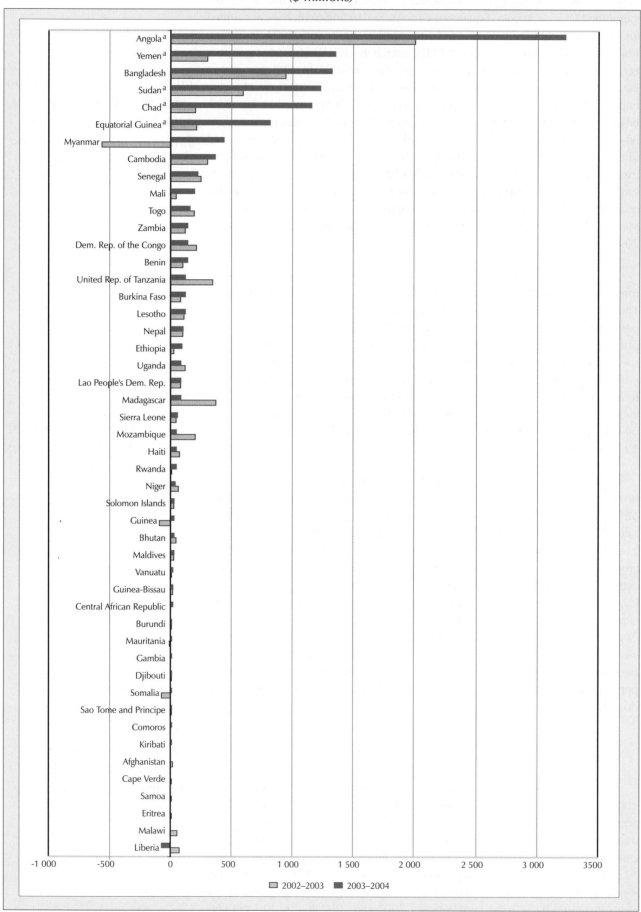

Source: UNCTAD secretariat estimates based on UNCTAD, *Handbook of Statistics 2005*.

Notes: Estimates are based on a group of 49 LDCs for which data are available. No data are available for Timor-Leste.

   a   These countries are oil-exporting LDCs. Chad started to export oil in the last quarter of 2003.

However, there is a very mixed trend that is affecting different LDCs in different ways. Available data on non-oil primary commodities that are of importance to LDC trade reveal that, compared with their levels in the year 2000, the price indices of coffee, tea, sugar and tobacco were actually lower in 2004. In contrast, it appears that between those two years, the price indices of cocoa, non-coniferous woods, copper, gold and crude petroleum increased by at least one third (see table 6).

TABLE 6. PRICE INDICES OF SELECTED PRIMARY COMMODITIES OF IMPORTANCE TO LDCs, 2001–2004
(Index, 2000=100)

	2001	2002	2003	2004
All food	100	103	107	121
Coffee (Arabicas)	72	72	74	93
Coffee (Robustas)	66	72	88	86
Cocoa	123	200	198	174
Tea	80	72	78	80
Sugar	106	84	87	88
Fish meal	118	147	148	157
Agricultural raw materials	96	94	112	123
Cotton	81	78	107	104
Non-coniferous woods	98	105	118	136
Tobacco	100	92	89	92
Minerals, metals and ores	89	87	98	137
Aluminium	93	87	92	111
Iron ore	105	103	112	132
Copper, Grade A	87	86	98	158
Copper, wire bars	87	86	97	153
Gold	97	111	130	147
Memo items:				
Crude petroleum	87	88	102	134
Unit value index of manufactured goods exported by developed countries	98	98	107	115

Source: UNCTAD secretariat estimates based on UNCTAD, *Commodity Price Bulletin,* various issues.

3. COMPOSITION OF MERCHANDISE TRADE

UNCTAD data show that in 2000–2003 primary commodities constituted almost two thirds of the merchandise exports of the LDCs as a group and over one third of their total merchandise imports. As illustrated in table 7, fuel exports were in 2000–2003 the leading source of total LDC export revenues and surpassed export receipts from manufactures, the second source of merchandise export receipts in the LDCs. In that period, fuel exports represented 40 per cent of the LDCs' total merchandise export receipts, while exports of manufactured goods averaged 33 per cent. Food items were in third position (14 per cent of total LDC merchandise exports), followed by agricultural raw materials (6 per cent) and minerals, metals and ores (5 per cent).

During the same period, the LDCs as a group had a trade surplus in fuels, agricultural raw materials and minerals, metals and ores. But the LDCs' trade surplus in fuels was driven by the few oil-exporting LDCs. The majority of the LDCs are likely to have been quite adversely affected by the recent surge in the price of oil. Petroleum products[2] imports accounted for 10.7 per cent of the LDCs' total merchandise imports bill in 2000–2003, compared with 8.9 per cent in the group of other developing countries.

The majority of the LDCs have been adversely affected by the recent surge in the price of oil which accounted for over 10.7 per cent of their total merchandise imports in 2000–2003.

TABLE 7. MERCHANDISE TRADE STRUCTURE IN LDCs, 2000–2003
(Sectors as per cent of exports, imports and net trade)

	% of total LDC exports	% of total LDC imports	% of LDC net trade
All food items	13.6	19.6	-38.6
Agricultural raw materials	6.0	2.5	8.6
Fuels	39.7	11.1	79.5
Metals and ores	5.3	1.2	11.5
Manufactured goods:	32.8	62.7	-157.5
Chemical products	1.6	9.3	-33.7
Other manufactured goods	29.6	27.6	-21.4
Machinery and transport equipment	1.6	25.8	-102.4
Unallocated	2.7	2.9	-3.6
Primary commodities	64.6	34.4	61.1
Non-fuel primary commodities	24.8	23.3	-18.5

Source: UNCTAD secretariat estimates based on UN COMTRADE.

Notes: No data are available for Timor-Leste.

Products have been classified by sector according to the SITC Revision 2 group (3-digit level). All food items include codes 0+1+22+4; agricultural raw materials include codes 2 less (22+27+28); fuels include codes 3; ores and metals include codes 27+28+68; manufactured goods include codes 5 to 8 less 68; chemical products include code 5 products; other manufactured goods include code 6+8 less 68 products; machinery and transport equipment include code 7 products. Primary commodities are the sum of all sectors with the exception of manufactured goods and unallocated goods. Non-fuel primary commodities are primary commodities excluding fuels.

Negative value means a deficit in the sector.

Interestingly, if fuels are excluded from the LDC trade basket, the LDCs were net primary commodity importers during 2000–2003. This non-fuel net primary import position has been apparent since 1998 and is explained by the deepening of the LDCs' deficit in food trade, which outweighed the LDCs' traditional trade surplus position in agricultural raw materials and in minerals, metals and ores. In contrast, the other developing countries (excluding China) remained net primary commodity exporters throughout the whole of the 1990–2003 period, even when fuel products are excluded.

Although food exports constituted 13.6 per cent of the LDCs' total exports in 2000–2003, the overwhelming majority of LDCs were net food-importing countries, with food imports averaging almost one fifth of their total imports. The group of other developing countries were less dependent on food trade, which accounted for 7 per cent of their total exports and imports respectively. It should be noted that the food import capacity of LDCs deteriorated drastically over the 1997–2003 period as the result of a substantial escalation of their food import bill. Between 2002 and 2003, the LDCs' food import bill increased by over $1 billion and reached $7.6 billion in the latter year, whereas the LDCs' food export receipts decreased by $0.2 billion and barely totalled $2.2 billion. The negative trend in the LDCs' food import capacity accelerated particularly in 2000–2001, which coincides with the beginning of the period of increasing food prices (see chart 2). Against this background, the short-term food price effects of the removal of agricultural export subsidies in OECD countries, agreed as part of the Doha negotiations, will need to be closely monitored.

If fuels are excluded from the LDC trade basket, the LDCs were net primary commodity importers during 2000–2003, resulting from deepening of the deficit in food trade.

Because they are net food importers, most of the LDCs are particularly vulnerable to swings in the prices of food items and to the financial terms attached to food imports (i.e. their concessionality level). This is particularly relevant for cereal products, which constituted over 40 per cent of the LDCs' total food imports in 2000–2003. The combination of rising food prices and rising fuel prices is likely to have a marked negative impact on the trade balance of LDCs.

CHART 2. LDCs FOOD IMPORT CAPACITY, 1990–2003
(Food export/food import)

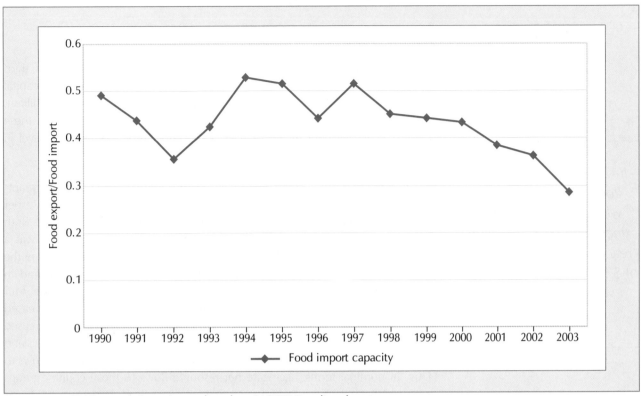

Source: UNCTAD secretariat estimates based on FAOSTAT, online data.
Note: Food includes animals.

Exports of manufactured goods, in particular capital-intensive manufactured goods, constitute a much smaller share of total LDC exports than of other developing countries' exports. In 2000–2003 the share of manufactured goods in total merchandise exports of LDCs was 33 per cent (22 per cent without Bangladesh). In contrast, during the same period, exports of manufactured goods generated 70 per cent of the merchandise export revenues of the group of other developing countries (66 per cent without China). The LDCs' manufactured exports were mainly composed of labour-intensive products, such as textiles, garments and footwear. In 2000–2003 these constituted 23 per cent of total LDC merchandise exports (11.8 per cent without Bangladesh). In contrast, the manufactured exports of the group of other developing countries were dominated by capital-intensive products such as machinery and transport equipment. These constituted 37 per cent of their total merchandise exports (versus 1.6 per cent in the LDCs). On the import side, machinery and transport equipment represented a much lower share of total merchandise imports in the LDCs than in the group of other developing countries. The ratio of capital goods imports to total imports averaged 25.8 per cent in the LDCs versus 42.4 per cent in the group of other developing countries in 2000–2003.

The LDCs' manufactured exports were mainly composed of labour-intensive products, such as textiles, garments and footwear, which constituted 23 per cent of total merchandise exports in 2000–2003.

Finally, it should be noted that despite the impressive export performance, the share of LDCs in world exports remains marginal both in aggregate and in major export sectors. In 2000–2003, the exports of LDCs as a group constituted 0.54 per cent of total world merchandise exports. LDC exports averaged 2 per cent of world fuel exports in 2000–2003, 1.8 per cent of world agricultural raw materials exports, 1 per cent of world food exports, 1 per cent of world exports of minerals, metals and ores and 0.2 per cent of world manufactures exports.

D. Trends in external finance

1. OVERALL PICTURE

Aggregate net foreign resource flows to LDCs increased in 2003[3] for the third consecutive year. It is estimated that between 2002 and 2003 long-term capital flows to the 46 LDCs for which data are available increased by $7.3 billion, reaching a new record level of $25.4 billion in 2003. As a result, in 2003, these flows were 40 per cent higher than in 2002, and almost double their level in 2000 (see table 8).

In 2003, long-term capital flows to the 46 LDCs for which data are available increased by $7.3 billion, reaching a new record level of $25.4 billion. This increase was concentrated in a few African LDCs.

This increase from 2002 to 2003 is mostly attributable to a large rise in grants disbursements and a large rise in FDI inflows. The former accounted for 72 per cent of the total increase, while the latter accounted for 16 per cent of it. Both increases were concentrated in a few African LDCs. In particular, there was a major jump in grants (debt relief in particular) to the Democratic Republic of the Congo, an increase in FDI inflows into Equatorial Guinea and Sudan and in publicly guaranteed private debt flows into Angola. Indeed, if those four countries (which were the four LDCs in which long-term capital flows increased most) are omitted, long-term capital flows to LDCs can be said to have increased only marginally (2.1 per cent) between 2002 and 2003.[4] Asian LDCs and island LDCs did not, on average, benefit from the increase in long-term capital flows to LDCs. In nominal terms, aggregate net resource flows to those country groups decreased by 0.8 per cent and 0.3 per cent respectively between 2002 and 2003.

TABLE 8. LONG-TERM NET CAPITAL FLOWS AND TRANSFERS TO LDCs, 2000–2003

	2000	2001	2002	2003	2000	2001	2002	2003
	($ millions)				(% of aggregate net resource flows)			
Aggregate net resource flows	**12 913**	**16 323**	**18 086**	**25 388**	**100**	**100**	**100**	**100**
Official net resource flows	9 201	9 747	12 371	17 672	71.3	59.7	68.4	69.6
Grants excluding tech. cooperation	7 331	7 234	9 296	14 528	56.8	44.3	51.4	57.2
Official debt flows	1 870	2 513	3 075	3 144	14.5	15.4	17.0	12.4
Bilateral	- 564	- 395	- 211	- 381	-4.4	-2.4	-1.2	-1.5
Bilateral concessional	- 478	- 396	- 152	- 196	-3.7	-2.4	-0.8	-0.8
Multilateral	2 434	2 908	3 285	3 525	18.8	17.8	18.2	13.9
Multilateral concessional	2 562	3 006	3 444	3 522	19.8	18.4	19.0	13.9
Private net resource flows	3 712	6 576	5 715	7 716	28.7	40.3	31.6	30.4
Foreign direct investment	4 074	6 372	6 119	7 260	31.6	39.0	33.8	28.6
Portfolio equity flows	2	7	7	2	0.0	0.0	0.0	0.0
Private debt flows	- 365	197	- 410	454	-2.8	1.2	-2.3	1.8
Private, non-guaranteed	- 49	49	- 51	- 45	-0.4	0.3	-0.3	-0.2
Private, publicly guaranteed	- 315	148	- 359	499	-2.4	0.9	-2.0	2.0
					(% of aggregate net transfers)			
Aggregate net transfers	**9 306**	**12 354**	**12 850**	**19 409**	**100**	**100**	**100**	**100**
Interest payments on long-term debt	980	833	1 080	1 143	10.5	6.7	8.4	5.9
Profit remittances on FDI	2 626	3 136	4 155	4 836	28.2	25.4	32.3	24.9
Memo item:								
IMF net flows	- 70	217	310	- 53	-0.8	1.8	2.4	-0.3
IMF, concessional net flows	58	366	597	51	0.6	3.0	4.6	0.3
IMF, non-concessional net flows	- 128	- 149	- 287	- 105	-1.4	-1.2	-2.2	-0.5
Debt forgiveness or reduction	- 912	-3 194	-3 467	-1 847	-9.8	-25.9	-27.0	-9.5

Source: UNCTAD secretariat estimates based on World Bank, *Global Development Finance 2005,* CD-ROM.

No data are available for Afghanistan, Kiribati, Timor-Leste or Tuvalu.

Official flows, the major source of long-term capital flows to LDCs, and grants in particular, accounted for 70 per cent and 57 per cent respectively of aggregate net resource flows to LDCs in 2003. This contrasts markedly with the situation regarding the other developing countries as a group, in which official net resource flows constituted only 6 per cent of their long-term capital flows and FDI accounted for 71 per cent of them. Three other major observations emerge from a comparative analysis of the structure of long-term capital flows to LDCs and other developing countries. First, the share of debt flows is much higher in LDCs (14.2 per cent in 2003) than in other developing countries (2.5 per cent). Second, multilateral creditors are the primary source of long-term debt flows in LDCs as opposed to other developing countries, where debt flows from multilateral creditors were negative in 2002 and 2003 and where private non-guaranteed debt flows are the leading component of long-term debt flows. Third, portfolio equity flows to LDCs are insignificant, whereas they constituted over 12 per cent of long-term capital flows to other developing countries in 2003. In other words, the main feature distinguishing the group of LDCs from that of other developing countries with respect to external finance is the increasingly higher reliance of the former on external finance and on official creditors in particular.

Official flows, and grants in particular, accounted for 70 per cent and 57 per cent respectively of aggregate net resource flows to LDCs in 2003.

The reliance of LDCs on external finance as measured by the ratio of aggregate net resource flows to GDP has increased significantly in recent years (see table 9). This ratio increased steadily from 7.8 per cent in 2000 to 12.7 per cent in 2003 in the group of 44 LDCs for which data are available. In contrast, it decreased from 3.5 per cent to 2.5 per cent between the same years in the group of other developing countries.[5] Thus, in 2003, in quantitative terms, the LDCs were over five times more dependent on long-term capital flows than other developing countries. A regional breakdown shows that the growing reliance of LDCs on external finance between 2000 and 2003 was driven by African LDCs, where the corresponding ratio increased from 10.8 per cent in 2000 to 18.9 per cent in 2003. In contrast, Asian LDCs and island LDCs were not only less but also decreasingly dependent on external flows.

The LDCs were over five times more dependent on long-term capital flows than other developing countries in 2003.

As a direct result of increasing long-term capital flows, aggregate net transfers to the group of 46 LDCs for which data are available grew by 51 per cent between 2002 and 2003 and by 109 per cent between 2000 and 2003. When the four African outliers mentioned above are excluded, aggregate net transfers can be said to have increased by 0.3 per cent and 25.5 per cent respectively. Omitting the Democratic Republic of the Congo, whose debt relief drove the impressive increase in grant disbursements to LDCs in 2003, the ratio of long-term interest payments to grants slightly decreased from 13.6 per cent to 10.9 per cent between 2000 and 2003, while the ratio of profit remittances to grants

TABLE 9. AGGREGATE NET RESOURCE FLOWS AS A SHARE OF GDP IN LDCs,
BY REGION, AND IN OTHER DEVELOPING COUNTRIES, 2001–2003

(Per cent)

	2000	2001	2002	2003
LDCs	7.8	9.6	10.1	12.7
African LDCs	10.8	13.6	14.7	18.9
Asian LDCs	3.5	3.7	3.1	2.9
Island LDCs	11.6	11.4	9.7	8.2
Other developing countries	3.5	3.2	2.4	2.5

Source: UNCTAD secretariat estimates based on World Bank, *Global Development Finance 2005*, CD-ROM, and World Bank, *World Development Indicators 2005*, CD-ROM.

Note: No data are available for Afghanistan, Kiribati, Myanmar, Somalia, Timor-Leste or Tuvalu.

increased from 36.5 per cent to 49.7 per cent between the same years. This means that in 2003 about 60 per cent of the amount of grants (excluding technical cooperation) disbursed to 45 LDCs were repatriated in the form of interest payments and profit remittances. In the four oil-exporting LDCs alone, namely Angola, Equatorial Guinea, Sudan and Yemen, the total amount of profit remittances on FDI was almost three times higher than that of grant disbursements (excluding technical cooperation) in 2003.

2. TRENDS IN AID FLOWS

In nominal terms, aid to LDCs actually doubled between 1999 and 2004.

According to the most recent data from OECD/DAC[6], net ODA to the group of 50 LDCs increased in 2004 to a record level of $24.9 billion. This increase was the continuation of an upward surge in aid to LDCs that began in 2000.[7] In nominal terms, aid to LDCs actually doubled between 1999 and 2004. During the period 1999–2004 the annual increase in real ODA to LDCs was four times faster than that to other developing countries. As a result, ODA disbursed to LDCs as a share of total ODA disbursed to all developing countries increased from 23.7 per cent in 1999 to 31.8 per cent in 2004.

Despite the impressive increase in aggregate ODA to LDCs over the period 1999–2004, it is important to note three features of the current situation. First, in real terms the increase has been less substantial. Net ODA to the group of LDCs from all donors actually decreased by 4.4 per cent between 2003 and 2004 in real terms, having increased by 14 per cent between 2002 and 2003. Moreover, real ODA per capita disbursed to LDCs was actually 13.5 per cent lower in 2000–2004 than in 1990–1994 (see charts 3a and 3b). Nevertheless, the upward surge in aid to LDCs since 2000 is one of the most important recent economic trends in LDCs.

Debt forgiveness, emergency aid, technical assistance and development food aid constituted 46.5 per cent of total net ODA disbursed to LDCs in 2004.

Second, an important feature of the recent upward surge in ODA to LDCs is that it is driven by debt forgiveness grants and emergency assistance grants. These grew by 22.6 per cent and 27.9 per cent per annum respectively in real terms between 1999 and 2004.[8] Taken together, debt forgiveness, emergency aid, technical assistance and development food aid constituted 46.5 per cent of total net ODA disbursed to LDCs in 2004 (see table 10). This was up from 37.5 per cent in 1995. In 2003 debt forgiveness grants accounted for almost one quarter of total net ODA disbursed to the LDCs. This ratio fell, however, to 15.1 per cent in 2004. Emergency assistance accounted for 10.5 per cent and 12.2 per cent of total ODA to LDCs in 2003 and 2004 respectively, while the share of technical cooperation was higher, having reached 17.2 per cent and 16.5 per cent respectively. Excluding debt forgiveness grants and emergency assistance, the share of technical cooperation to total net ODA to LDCs averaged 22.6 per cent in 2004 whilst net loan disbursements averaged only 17.3 per cent.

However, real ODA growth rates varied greatly by country.

Third, real ODA growth rates varied greatly by country (see table 11). ODA inflows increased by over 20 per cent per annum during this period in six LDCs, namely Afghanistan, Burundi, the Democratic Republic of the Congo, Lesotho, Sierra Leone and Sudan. All of these except Lesotho, are conflict-affected LDCs and the increases in ODA have mainly been driven by increases in debt relief and/or in emergency assistance. The increase in ODA was particularly marked in Afghanistan and the Democratic Republic of the Congo, where it increased by 79 per cent per annum and 93 per cent per annum respectively over the period 1999–2004. Indeed, 30 per cent of the increase in aid to LDCs in nominal terms can be attributed to increased aid flows to Afghanistan and the Democratic

CHART 3. NET ODA TO LDCs, 1990–2004

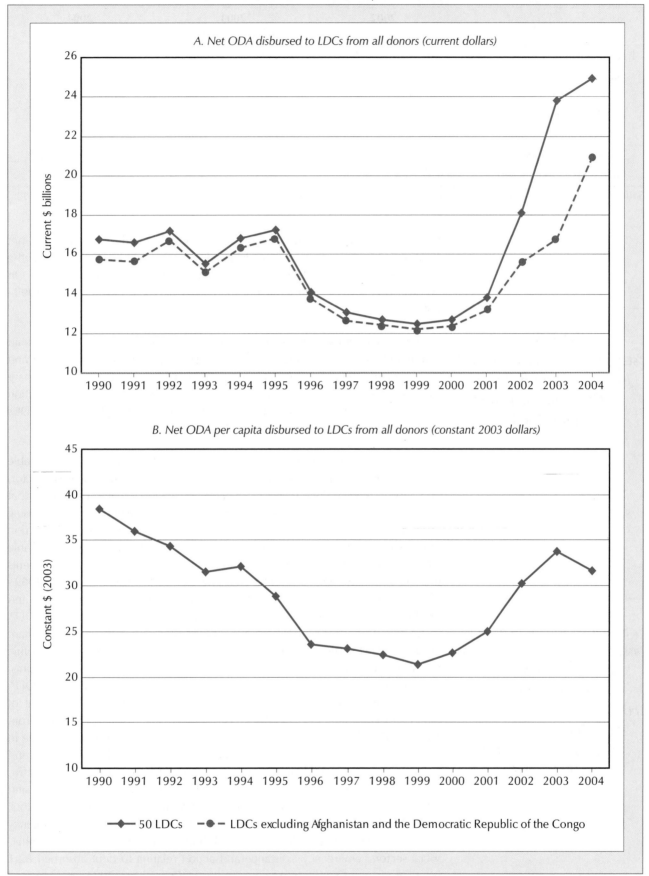

A. Net ODA disbursed to LDCs from all donors (current dollars)

B. Net ODA per capita disbursed to LDCs from all donors (constant 2003 dollars)

◆ 50 LDCs   ● LDCs excluding Afghanistan and the Democratic Republic of the Congo

Source: UNCTAD secretariat estimates based on OECD/DAC, *International Development Statistics*, online data, December 2005.

TABLE 10. NET ODA AND NET ODA PER CAPITA DISBURSED TO LDCs, FROM ALL DONORS, 2002–2004

	2002		2003		2004	
	$ million	$ per capita	$ million	$ per capita	$ million	$ per capita
Total net ODA	18 094	28.0	23 791	36.0	24 935	35.4
Grants	14 344	22.2	20 359	30.8	21 774	30.9
Emergency aid	1 760	2.7	2 497	3.8	3 053	4.3
Debt forgiveness grants	2 423	3.8	5 859	8.9	3 762	5.3
Technical cooperation	3 406	5.3	4 095	6.2	4 104	5.8
Development food aid	603	0.9	624	0.9	658	0.9
ODA (OA) loans total net	3 750	5.8	3 432	5.2	3 134	4.4

Source: UNCTAD secretariat estimates based on OECD/DAC, International Development Statistics, online data, December 2005.

Republic of the Congo (see chart 3a). But at the other end of the spectrum, net ODA inflows either stagnated or declined in real terms in almost half of the LDCs during the period 1999–2004, including in 9 of the 10 island LDCs.[9] On average, real ODA to the latter declined by 3 per cent per annum in 1999–2004.

Net ODA inflows either stagnated or declined in real terms in almost half of the LDCs during the period 1999–2004.

A regional comparison shows that the share of part A net ODA, that is aid committed to technical assistance, debt forgiveness, emergency assistance and development food aid, in total net ODA was greatest in African LDCs. This share was also very large in the group of island LDCs owing to the larger contribution of technical assistance in total net ODA disbursed to this group of 10 LDCs relative to that disbursed to African or Asian LDCs.

OECD/DAC data on ODA commitments (rather than disbursements) enable the disaggregation of those commitments to recipient countries by broad sector, and also by type of flow, that is grants and concessional loans. This shows that the upward surge in ODA has reinforced the trends whereby an increasing proportion of ODA is provided in the form of grants and a decreasing proportion of ODA is committed to economic infrastructure and productive sectors. Table 12 shows that grants represented 76 per cent of total net ODA commitments from all donors to LDCs in 2002–2004. This was up from 62 per cent in 1992–1994 and 68 per cent in 1999–2001. ODA for economic infrastructure and productive sectors actually declined from 32 per cent of total ODA commitments in 1999–2001 to 24 per cent in 2002–2004. This is half the share in 1992–1994. The decline in the share of ODA going to economic infrastructure and productive sectors is related to the shift from loans to grants, because a larger proportion of aid in these areas is financed by loans. ODA commitments to social infrastructure and services constituted 32 per cent of total ODA commitments to LDCs in 2002–2004. This was slightly down from 1999–2001, when the share stood at 33 per cent, but was a major increase in relation to the early 1990s, when the share of ODA to social infrastructure and services was less than half that to economic infrastructure and productive sectors. The fall in the share going to social sectors between 1999–2001 and 2002–2004 does not reflect a shift of donor priorities away from those sectors, but rather the increasing importance of action related to debt and emergency assistance, noted in the discussion of disbursements above. Taken together, social sectors, emergency assistance and action relating to debt absorbed 62.1 per cent of total ODA commitments to the LDCs in 2002–2004, as compared with 34.6 per cent in 1992–1994.

Social sectors, emergency assistance and action relating to debt absorbed 62.1 per cent of total ODA commitments to the LDCs in 2002–2004, as compared with 34.6 per cent in 1992–1994.

TABLE 11. SELECTED INDICATORS ON NET ODA DISBURSED TO LDCs, BY COUNTRY AND BY REGION, AND TO THE GROUP OF OTHER DEVELOPING COUNTRIES, BY ALL DONORS, 1995–2004

| | Real growth rate of net ODA (% per annum) | Level of Part A[a] net ODA (% total net ODA) | | Distribution of Part A net ODA (% total net ODA) | |
| | | | | Technical assistance | Remaining Part A net ODA[b] |
	1999–2004	1995–1999	2000–2004	2000–2004	
Afghanistan	79.2	81.6	54.5	20.1	34.4
Angola	17.0	54.6	44.3	12.7	31.6
Bangladesh	-0.5	38.6	42.0	18.6	23.3
Benin	4.9	33.7	44.0	27.1	16.9
Bhutan	2.0	37.7	31.5	30.5	1.0
Burkina Faso	5.4	32.1	36.6	19.5	17.1
Burundi	29.0	53.6	51.2	11.3	39.9
Cambodia	7.3	40.5	34.2	29.7	4.5
Cape Verde	-0.6	43.6	40.8	30.8	10.0
Central African Rep.	-9.0	38.2	50.9	34.2	16.6
Chad	9.5	27.1	33.2	16.3	16.9
Comoros	-0.3	49.1	50.2	40.5	9.7
Dem.Rep. of the Congo	93.0	64.1	74.6	5.6	69.1
Djibouti	-4.3	45.3	42.6	37.0	5.6
Equatorial Guinea	0.5	56.5	60.9	45.8	15.1
Eritrea	8.2	43.5	49.1	12.6	36.5
Ethiopia	19.8	39.9	43.5	12.2	31.3
Gambia	8.0	51.8	27.7	20.2	7.5
Guinea	2.0	26.4	53.8	25.0	28.8
Guinea-Bissau	4.9	39.8	46.4	19.2	27.2
Haiti	-5.1	51.9	70.7	44.9	25.8
Kiribati	-3.7	47.4	56.3	56.3	0.0
Laos	-2.6	30.2	31.8	28.6	3.2
Lesotho	21.0	37.0	22.3	18.9	3.4
Liberia	13.4	50.3	77.7	19.7	58.1
Madagascar	19.8	47.5	46.9	15.8	31.1
Malawi	-2.2	28.6	39.1	24.1	15.1
Maldives	-2.0	27.3	33.9	26.6	7.3
Mali	6.7	33.2	41.3	25.5	15.8
Mauritania	-5.2	25.7	42.4	14.9	27.5
Mozambique	5.2	56.2	46.9	15.6	31.4
Myanmar	5.3	80.7	70.4	43.1	27.3
Nepal	0.7	37.7	37.3	30.9	6.4
Niger	19.3	40.6	43.6	15.4	28.2
Rwanda	-0.6	52.9	35.2	21.8	13.4
Samoa	1.4	59.6	58.4	58.3	0.1
Sao Tome and Principe	-3.2	43.8	50.5	36.1	14.4
Senegal	5.9	44.6	57.8	30.5	27.3
Sierra Leone	25.0	40.8	43.4	13.4	30.0
Solomon Islands	7.2	47.9	66.6	64.5	2.1
Somalia	7.5	70.4	63.9	12.3	51.6
Sudan	27.6	75.0	69.2	10.7	58.5
Timor-Leste	-8.5	63.8	56.3	43.2	13.1
Togo	-9.0	39.2	75.0	52.1	22.8
Tuvalu	2.7	39.4	38.1	38.1	0.0
Uganda	6.5	30.6	32.1	18.3	13.7
United Rep. of Tanzania	8.5	32.0	36.0	11.8	24.2
Vanuatu	-7.4	59.5	66.7	65.9	0.8
Yemen	-11.9	29.2	30.5	15.0	15.5
Zambia	2.4	27.0	47.1	17.2	29.9
LDCs	12.5	40.9	47.4	18.4	29.0
African LDCs	13.7	40.7	48.4	16.2	34.9
Asian LDCs	10.8	40.7	43.1	22.9	10.9
LDC-SIDS	-3.0	47.5	53.4	44.8	8.6
Other developing countries	2.9	43.8	48.7	32.5	16.3

Source: UNCTAD secretariat estimates based on OECD/DAC, International Development Statistics, online data, December 2005.
  a   Part A net ODA is the sum of technical assistance, debt forgiveness, emergency assistance and development food aid.
  b   Remaining Part A net ODA is Part A net ODA excluding technical assistance.

TABLE 12. SECTORAL ALLOCATION OF ODA COMMITMENTS TO LDCS, FROM ALL DONORS,
1992–1994, 1999–2001 AND 2002–2004

(Percentage)

	Total ODA commitments to LDCs			Financed by grants			Financed by loans		
	1992–1994	1999–2001	2002–2004	1992–1994	1999–2001	2002–2004	1992–1994	1999–2001	2002–2004
Total	100.0	100.0	100.0	62	68	76	38	32	23
Social infrastructure and services	21.2	33.1	32.2	74	68	81	26	32	18
Action relating to debt	8.3	8.8	17.8	55	94	88	45	6	12
Emergency assistance	5.1	8.1	12.2	85	86	91	15	14	9
Economic infrastructure, production sector and multisector	47.9	32.3	23.5	52	52	57	48	47	41
Economic infrastructure	21.6	16.0	12.7	45	46	47	55	52	50
Production sector	15.6	8.7	5.5	56	61	60	43	38	37
Multisector	10.7	7.6	5.2	59	54	76	41	46	23
Commodity aid/ general programme assistance	16.7	16.5	13.5	72	73	67	28	27	33

Source: UNCTAD secretariat estimates based on OECD/DAC, *International Development Statistics*, online data , December 2005.

3. TRENDS IN FDI INFLOWS

Following a slight decrease in 2002, FDI inflows into the group of LDCs recovered dramatically in 2003, when they stood at over $10.4 billion, compared with $6.3 billion the preceding year. FDI inflows into LDCs further increased in 2004, when they reached a record level of $10.7 billion, which represents about 1.6 per cent of world FDI inflows (chart 4). In nominal terms, FDI inflows into LDCs increased by 63.6 per cent in 2003 and by 3.4 per cent in 2004. Between 2002 and 2004, FDI inflows into LDCs increased by 69.1 per cent. In 2004, the ratio of FDI to gross fixed capital formation averaged 20.8 per cent in the LDCs, which is twice as high as the share prevailing in the group of other developing countries.

FDI inflows into LDCs increased in 2004 to a record level of $10.7 billion. However, this represents only 1.6 per cent of world FDI inflows.

The data show that the distribution of FDI inflows into LDCs remain largely concentrated in resource-rich LDCs. The nominal change in the value of FDI inflows into LDCs was negligible in over half the countries for which data is available (see chart 5). Indeed, half of the increase in FDI inflows into LDCs between 2002 and 2004 occurred in the four traditional oil-exporting LDCs, namely Angola, Equatorial Guinea, Sudan and Yemen. In 2004, those four countries absorbed 48.6 per cent of total FDI inflows into the group of 50 LDCs. This ratio increases to 55.9 per cent if Chad and Mauritania, which recently received large oil-related FDI flows, are added to this list. In the same year, mineral-exporting LDCs attracted 12.7 per cent of the total FDI inflows into LDCs. Overall, about 70 per cent of FDI inflows into the group of LDCs was directed to oil- and mineral-exporting LDCs in 2004 (table 13).

FDI inflows into LDCs remain highly concentrated in resource-rich LDCs, which absorbed about 70 per cent of the total FDI inflows into the group.

The fact that FDI inflows into the LDCs increased less in 2004 than in 2003 is also related to changes in FDI inflows into oil-exporting LDCs. FDI flows to Angola in 2004 were $1.46 billion lower than in 2003 and flows to Chad were $234.5 billion lower.

Table 13 provides a further indication of the level of concentration of FDI into LDC economies and shows that the top 10 recipient LDCs absorbed 83.6 per cent of LDCs' FDI inflows in 2004. Those 10 countries were, in decreasing order of magnitude, Angola, Equatorial Guinea, Sudan, the Democratic Republic of the Congo, Myanmar, Ethiopia, Chad, the United Republic of Tanzania, Bangladesh and Zambia. With the exception of Bangladesh, the

Chart 4. FDI inflows into LDCs, 1990–2004

(In value and as a share of world FDI inflows)

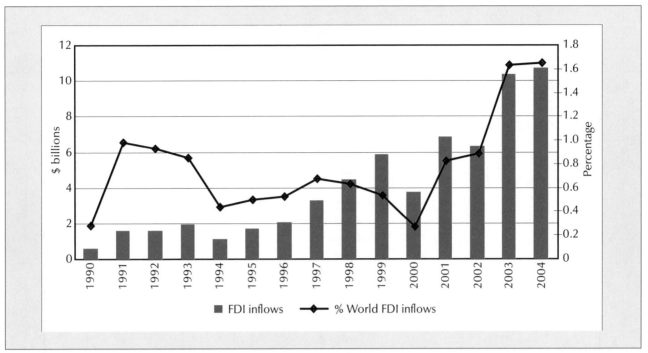

Source: UNCTAD secretariat estimates based on UNCTAD FDI/TNC database.
Note: No data are available for Kiribati.

Table 13. FDI inflows into LDCs, 2000–2004

	2000	2001	2002	2003	2004
In $ milions					
LDCs	3 758.1	6 839.8	6 333.2	10 352.6	10 723.0
Top 10	2 766.0	5 689.3	5 303.2	9 099.3	8 966.7
Rest of LDCs	992.2	1 150.5	1 030.0	1 253.3	1 756.3
Oil-exporting LDCs[a]+ Chad and Mauritania	1 539.9	4 352.1	3 852.0	7 216.8	5 979.9
Mineral-exporting LDCs[b]	223.8	201.6	241.4	427.8	1 366.2
Other LDCs	1 994.5	2 274.5	2 233.8	2 705.9	3 356.0
In %					
Top 10	73.6	83.2	83.7	87.9	83.6
Rest of LDCs	26.4	16.8	16.3	12.1	16.4
Oil-exporting LDCs[a]+ Chad and Mauritania	41.0	63.6	60.8	69.7	55.8
Mineral-exporting LDCs[b]	6.0	2.9	3.8	4.1	12.7
Other LDCs	53.1	33.3	35.3	26.1	31.3

Source: UNCTAD secretariat estimates based on UNCTAD FDI/TNC database.

Note: No data are available for Kiribati.
   a   The oil-exporting LDCs are Angola, Equatorial Guinea, Sudan and Yemen
   b   The mineral-exporting LDCs are the Central African Republic, Democratic Republic of the Congo, Guinea, Liberia, Niger, Sierra Leone and Zambia.

Democratic Republic of the Congo and Zambia, all the other countries were among the top 10 recipient LDCs throughout the whole period 2002–2004.

Evidence shows that between 2002 and 2004 FDI inflows into LDCs increased in all regions except the Pacific and Caribbean (see table 14). Annual data on FDI flows show the variability of these flows in all regions. In 2002–2003 and 2003–2004 FDI inflows into LDCs increased in nominal terms by 63.6 per cent and by 3.4 per cent respectively in the LDCs and by 4.5 per cent and 42.7 per cent respectively in the group of other developing countries. Within the group of LDCs, FDI inflows into African LDCs (where most of the resource-rich

CHART 5. NOMINAL CHANGE IN THE VALUE OF FDI INFLOWS INTO LDCS, 2002–2003 AND 2003–2004
($ millions)

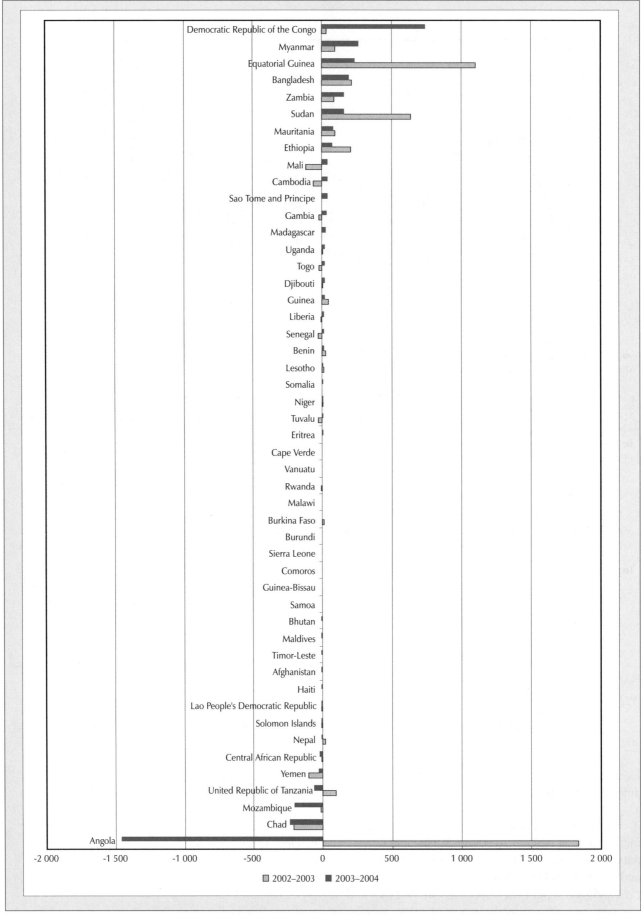

Source: UNCTAD secretariat estimates based on UNCTAD FDI/TNC database.

Note: No data are available for Kiribati.

TABLE 14. FDI INFLOWS INTO LDCs, BY REGION, 2000–2004

| | $ millions | | | | | % change | | | |
	2000	2001	2002	2003	2004	2001–2002	2002–2003	2003–2004	2002–2004
LDCs	3 758.1	6 828.2	6 327.2	10 350.6	10 702.1	-7.3	63.6	3.4	69.1
African LDCs	3 035.8	6 118.4	5 765.2	9 624.3	9 496.2	-5.8	66.9	-1.3	64.7
Asian LDCs	689.9	697.2	524.0	704.5	1 173.3	-24.8	34.4	66.5	123.9
Pacific and Caribbean island LDCs	32.4	12.6	38.1	21.7	32.5	202.8	-42.9	49.6	-14.5

Source: UNCTAD secretariat estimates based on UNCTAD FDI/TNC database.

Note: In this table, small island LDCs are not presented as a distinct group and are therefore included in their respective regions.

LDCs are concentrated) grew by 66.9 per cent in 2002–2003 but decreased by 1.3 per cent in 2003–2004. In comparison, FDI inflows into Asian LDCs increased during both periods. It should be noted, however, that FDI inflows into the Lao People's Democratic Republic and Yemen declined during those two consecutive years.

E. Trends in external debt

Following a downward trend between 1998 and 2001, and despite a large reduction in their debt arrears, the LDCs' total debt stock increased in 2003[10] for the second consecutive year and reached in 2003 a record level of $158.9 billion, which represents a $12 billion increase over the 2002 level and a $20.8 billion increase over the 2001 level. Data on debt by creditor status show that, between 1990 and 2003, the share of debt stock from multilateral creditors in total debt stock increased significantly in the LDCs, whereas that of debt stock from bilateral creditors decreased. In 2003, multilateral debt constituted over 46 per cent of LDCs' total debt stock, compared with about 27 per cent in 1990 (chart 6). In fact, multilateral debt stock first exceeded bilateral debt stock in 1999, that is, since the inception of the enhanced HIPC Initiative[11]. Overall, almost 80 per cent of the increase in the LDCs' total debt stock between 2001 and 2003 is attributed to an increase in their multilateral debt stock. A regional breakdown shows that the trend in the LDCs' external debt stock has been driven by African LDCs, which accounted for 72.8 per cent of the LDCs' total debt stock in 2003, down from 76.7 per cent in 1998. Country data show that debt stock increased between 2001 and 2003 in all of the countries of the group of 46 LDCs for which data are available except the Democratic Republic of the Congo, which was granted $10 billion of debt relief under the enhanced HIPC Initiative and received almost half of this in 2003.

The LDCs' total debt stock increased in 2003 reaching a record level of $158.9 billion, which represents a $20.8 billion increase over the 2001 level.

Table 15 contains data on recent trends in four debt burden indicators for the LDCs and for the group of other developing countries, namely the debt stock to GDP ratio, the debt stock to exports of goods and services, income and workers' remittances ratio, the total debt service paid to exports of goods and services, income and workers' remittances ratio, and the present value of debt to GNI ratio. The data clearly show that the debt burden in the group of LDCs is about twice as great as the debt burden of other developing countries for three of the four indicators. The exception is debt service paid as a ratio of exports of goods and services, income and workers' remittances. This is less than half for the group of LDCs than for the other developing countries.

The low ratio of debt service paid to exports is, however, somewhat deceptive. It certainly reflects the good export performance of the LDCs in part. But also it arises because of the difficulty which a number of LDCs still have in

CHART 6. TRENDS IN THE LDC TOTAL DEBT STOCK, BY STATUS OF OFFICIAL CREDITORS, 1990–2003
($ billions)

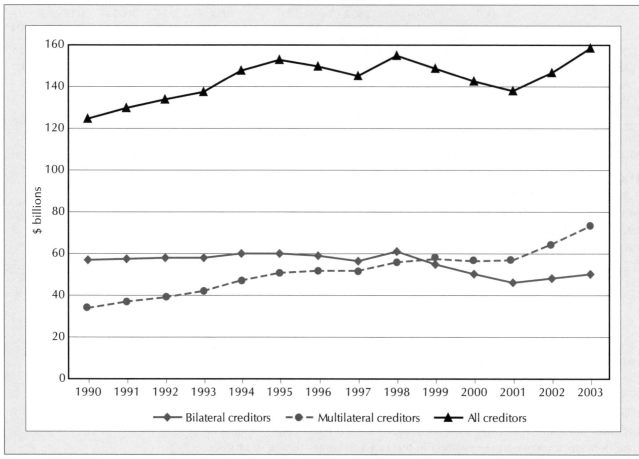

Source: UNCTAD secretariat estimates based on World Bank, *Global Development Finance 2005,* CD-ROM.

Note: Estimates are based on the 46 LDCs for which data are available. No data are available for Afghanistan, Kiribati, Timor-Leste or Tuvalu.

keeping up with contractual debt service payments. According to the Global Development Finance database, principal arrears on long-term debt were equivalent to 38 per cent of exports of goods and services, income and workers' remittances in the group of LDCs in 2003, as compared with 2.7 per cent in the group of other developing countries. Similarly, in the same year, the ratio of interest arrears to exports of goods and services, income and workers' remittances averaged 20.2 per cent in the LDCs versus 1.5 per cent in the group of other developing countries.

The debt burden in the group of LDCs is about double the debt burden of other developing countries.

A regional breakdown shows that the debt burden is much greater in African LDCs than in Asian LDCs. Despite the recent increase in the LDCs' total debt stock as outlined earlier, data show that relative to their GDP or to their exports of goods and services, income and workers' remittances, the debt burden of the group of LDCs improved between 2001 and 2003, a fact that suggests sizeable improvements in the LDCs' GDP and foreign exchange revenues between those years. As shown in table 15, this improvement in the LDC debt burden is mainly attributable to African LDCs. In Asian LDCs the debt burden continued to increase between 2001 and 2003.

In assessing these debt indicators, particular attention should be paid to the trends in workers' remittances in the LDCs. Relative to GNI, those remittances increased steadily in the LDCs and in the group of other developing countries during the period 1999–2003, reaching 4.8 per cent in the former group and 1.9 per cent in the latter in 2003. The increase in this ratio has been particularly impressive in the Asian LDCs, where workers' remittances averaged 7 per cent

TABLE 15. EXTERNAL DEBT BURDEN INDICATORS AND WORKERS' REMITTANCES IN LDCS, BY COUNTRY AND BY REGION, AND IN THE GROUP OF OTHER DEVELOPING COUNTRIES, 1999–2003

(Percentage)

	Total debt stock						Total debt service paid			Present value of debt			Workers remittances		
	% GDP			% exports of goods and services, income and workers' remittances			% exports of goods and services, income and workers' remittances			% GNI			% GNI		
	2001	2002	2003	2001	2002	2003	2001	2002	2003	2001	2002	2003	2001	2002	2003
Angola	97.5	82.2	73.5	136.6	108.1	108.1	22.7	16.3	14.9	142.0	120.5	101.7	0.0	0.0	0.0
Bangladesh	32.5	35.9	36.2	169.4	173.1	168.5	7.5	7.4	6.0	20.1	22.3	25.1	4.3	5.7	5.8
Benin	70.0	68.1	52.6	264.5	..	..	7.9	..	..	36.2	36.1	28.2	3.6	3.1	2.4
Bhutan	49.5	62.6	60.6	178.2	272.7	..	4.2	4.6		57.4	72.3	73.9	0.0	0.0	0.0
Burkina Faso	54.7	50.9	44.1	483.1	493.4	397.3	13.3	14.9	11.2	26.2	16.2	19.5	1.8	1.6	1.2
Burundi	155.2	191.7	219.9	2 313.5	3 157.5	2 950.6	49.7	61.1	65.8	95.1	115.1	150.4	0.0	0.0	0.0
Cambodia	72.8	72.5	74.3	119.1	114.9	114.5	1.0	0.9	0.9	66.5	67.7	70.2	3.7	3.7	3.4
Cape Verde	65.6	67.1	60.2	141.9	144.7	125.7	5.5	7.6	5.7	42.3	47.6	50.9	14.9	14.0	11.7
Central African Republic	85.0	101.8	110.8	..	..	..	..	..	..	54.6	77.9	154.9	0.0	0.0	0.0
Chad	66.3	64.0	57.5	..	..	..	..	..	..	41.5	36.8	44.9	0.0	0.0	0.0
Comoros	110.6	109.2	89.1	..	..	..	..	..	..	81.8	85.4	79.5	5.4	4.8	3.7
Dem. Rep. of the Congo	236.0	181.3	197.0	..	..	..	..	..	..	250.6	184.9	150.2	0.0	0.0	0.0
Djibouti	45.8	56.6	63.4	..	..	..	..	..	..	31.1	37.6	43.7	0.0	0.0	0.0
Equatorial Guinea	14.0	12.3	11.0	..	..	..	..	..	..	43.9	..	..	0.0	0.0	0.0
Eritrea	61.6	82.5	84.5	300.5	403.5	758.9	4.9	7.3	14.1	28.8	38.8	46.8	0.0	0.0	0.0
Ethiopia	88.0	107.5	107.5	565.2	585.4	537.4	18.0	7.6	6.8	45.1	62.9	24.4	0.3	0.5	0.7
Gambia	116.5	154.9	159.1	..	..	..	..	..	..	66.0	77.5	90.4	7.6	9.5	10.8
Guinea	107.0	106.0	95.2	381.1	414.6	398.9	12.3	15.2	15.1	55.3	46.8	58.7	0.3	0.5	3.1
Guinea-Bissau	335.8	343.5	312.2	862.7	879.0	794.7	30.1	13.8	16.2	213.4	235.5	245.8	5.5	9.2	7.9
Haiti	34.8	36.0	44.8	117.3	113.7	102.1	2.4	2.5	4.1	20.8	22.7	28.6	17.3	19.5	27.9
Lao PDR	142.6	155.0	134.1	516.4	614.3	591.3	9.0	10.3	10.3	81.0	84.7	90.6	0.1	0.1	0.0
Lesotho	77.9	89.2	62.0	107.6	113.1	93.2	12.3	11.7	8.8	38.4	44.4	47.3	22.2	20.5	13.3
Liberia	404.9	413.7	580.6	1 416.1	1 125.1	1 751.4	0.5	0.4	0.1	489.4	561.3	646.2	0.0	0.0	0.0
Madagascar	91.8	102.7	90.6	319.3	614.0	431.1	5.2	8.7	6.1	51.3	33.3	31.0	0.2	0.4	0.3
Malawi	152.8	154.9	182.9	537.5	608.5	677.9	8.0	6.3	7.7	87.3	50.7	108.1	0.1	0.1	0.1
Maldives	37.6	42.4	39.3	49.7	54.2	47.5	4.6	4.4	3.6	30.6	34.1	34.7	0.3	0.3	0.4
Mali	110.9	84.8	72.3	297.5	234.8	..	8.3	6.9		57.2	46.8	42.4	3.6	4.4	3.3
Mauritania	238.2	228.9	215.8	..	..	..	..	..	..	148.7	56.2	72.6	0.2	0.2	0.2
Mozambique	132.8	132.4	114.1	425.5	433.4	388.2	8.5	6.9	6.9	26.5	26.8	38.1	1.3	1.6	1.7
Myanmar	..	..	..	191.4	216.8	253.0	2.8	3.7	4.2				..	..	..
Nepal	48.6	53.4	55.6	201.0	180.2	173.7	6.9	6.2	6.0	29.1	30.9	37.7	2.6	12.2	13.4
Niger	81.7	82.9	77.5	..	..	..	..	..	..	53.8	26.1	25.5	0.4	0.4	0.3
Rwanda	75.5	83.9	94.1	718.8	970.8	1 044.8	10.3	11.5	14.4	37.3	39.7	57.5	0.5	0.4	0.4
Samoa	86.0	97.4	136.3	..	..	..	..	..	..	59.9	70.2	122.1	19.2	18.7	17.0
Sao Tome and Principe	655.4	622.8	567.4	1 876.7	1 738.7	1 586.6	24.6	25.0	31.0	232.5	252.6	314.2	2.3	2.2	2.0
Senegal	79.5	81.8	68.0	212.1	218.4	188.2	12.3	11.6	10.4	53.6	52.9	36.4	6.7	7.1	5.4
Sierra Leone	172.9	184.9	203.2	1 413.2	1 168.5	789.0	104.6	17.5	12.4	125.5	102.6	118.2	1.0	2.9	3.4
Solomon Islands	65.9	73.1	73.5	..	..	..	..	..	..	37.8	50.1	59.6	0.8	0.8	0.8
Somalia	..	..	..	..	..	..	..	..	..				..	..	..
Sudan	113.2	106.6	98.3	626.2	532.0	459.6	2.3	0.8	0.9	136.7	129.7	120.4	6.1	6.9	7.5
Togo	105.9	107.5	97.1	277.6	253.1	203.1	6.4	2.1	1.9	73.2	87.1	91.1	5.4	7.2	6.1
Uganda	65.7	68.1	72.3	353.5	359.3	385.8	4.7	6.3	7.1	20.0	22.3	32.6	8.7	6.5	4.8
United Rep. of Tanzania	71.7	75.1	73.0	447.9	446.7	421.4	10.2	6.7	5.1	15.0	18.8	22.2	0.1	0.1	0.1
Vanuatu	32.5	38.6	33.5	41.6	72.9	65.0	0.9	1.5	1.4	16.5	24.7	28.1	24.5	3.5	3.2
Yemen	53.3	52.3	49.6	101.6	100.2	95.7	5.2	3.3	3.1	43.6	39.9	40.4	14.6	14.0	12.6
Zambia	155.9	161.7	148.2	512.9	525.1	459.6	11.3	25.4	27.8	127.1	127.3	121.1	0.0	0.0	0.0
LDCs	77.5	77.9	74.9	251.4	247.8	238.9	9.3	8.1	7.5	56.9	55.2	54.1	4.1	4.8	4.8
African LDCs	102.6	99.8	94.0	336.5	322.5	304.1	12.8	10.7	9.9	79.1	73.8	69.0	3.1	3.2	3.2
Asian LDCs	41.9	44.9	44.7	161.1	165.3	165.3	5.6	5.2	4.7	28.0	29.6	32.5	5.3	7.0	7.0
LDC-SIDS	74.0	78.7	75.3	107.1	119.3	104.6	4.5	5.4	4.5	45.9	52.8	60.8	9.4	7.0	6.2
Other developing countries	34.2	34.8	33.3	116.4	108.2	96.9	19.4	18.0	17.0	34.5	33.5	35.8	1.4	1.7	1.9

Source: UNCTAD secretariat estimates based on World Bank, *Global Development Finance 2005*, CD-ROM, and *World Development Indicators 2005*, CD-ROM.

Notes: Averages are weighted by the denominator and are subject to data availability.
Data are systematically not available for Afghanistan, Kiribati, Timor-Leste and Tuvalu.

of GNI in 2003, compared with 5 per cent in 1999. The corresponding ratio increased to a lesser extent — from 2.6 per cent to 3.2 per cent — in African LDCs between the same years. The heavy and increasing reliance of Asian LDCs on workers' remittances was, however, not sufficient to reverse the increase in those countries' ratio of debt stock to exports of goods and services, income and workers' remittances between 2001 and 2003. The overall higher level of reliance of LDCs on workers' remittances implies that the outcome of the multilateral trade negotiations on Mode 4 (movement of natural persons) of GATS (General Agreement on Trade in Services) may be of particular interest to those countries.

F. Conclusions

The economic performance of the LDCs as a group continues to improve. The average GDP growth rate in 2004 was the highest for two decades. This was underpinned by record levels of merchandise exports and record levels of capital inflows, particularly in the form of grants and FDI. Most of the oil-exporting LDCs did particularly well, benefiting from higher oil prices in 2004 especially. But the good economic performance was not confined to those countries. Real GDP growth was 6 per cent or more in 15 LDCs in 2004, including 11 LDCs which do not export oil.

Within this overall growth performance the trend towards increasing divergence amongst the LDCs, which first emerged in the early 1990s, has continued. Real GDP per capita stagnated or declined in 2004 in 14 out of 46 LDCs for which data are available.

This divergence is partly related to the differential access to external finance. Both FDI inflows and ODA grants, the two major elements driving the surge in capital inflows, were highly concentrated. Ten LDCs absorbed 84 per cent of FDI inflows in 2004. In nominal terms, aid actually doubled between 1999 and 2004. But 30 per cent of this increase was absorbed by Afghanistan and the Democratic Republic of the Congo. For other countries, the nominal increase in aid was much smaller. Indeed, it either stagnated or declined in real terms in almost half of the LDCs during the same period, including 9 out of the 10 island LDCs.

Another issue of concern is the sustainability of the recent economic performance. Growth in the LDCs remains highly dependent on commodity prices, trends in external finance and preferences for exports of manufactured goods. The ratio of gross domestic savings to GDP, which is already much lower than in other developing countries, actually declined from 13.4 per cent in 2003 to 11 per cent in 2004. During that period, the LDCs' reliance on external finance savings to finance capital formation increased. Many LDCs are also particularly vulnerable because they are net importers of both food and oil. The combination of price increases in these sectors can considerably worsen their persistent trade deficits.

The sustainability of the recent growth performance will depend in particular on the extent to which existing and additional ODA and FDI are channelled into productive investment, both private and public, and support increased domestic savings, structural change and an upgrading and diversification of productive capacities. Unfortunately, a large share of the increase in ODA is attributable to debt relief and emergency assistance, which together accounted for 35 per cent of total net ODA disbursed to LDCs in 2003 and 27 per cent disbursed in 2004.

While the economic performance of the LDCs as a group continues to improve, the trend towards increasing divergence amongst them also continues.

This divergence is partly related to the differential access to external finance.

The sustainability of the recent growth performance will depend in particular on the extent to which existing and additional resources are channelled into productive investment, both private and public.

FDI inflows remain oriented towards exploiting extractive sectors. The external debt stock of the LDCs continues to increase in spite of major debt relief measures. In 2003, interest payments and profit remittances were equivalent to about 60 per cent of the value of grants received (excluding technical cooperation).

Finally, economic growth will not be sustainable unless it leads to improvements in human well-being that are socially inclusive. Progress in relation to a number of social indicators is considered in the next chapter.

Notes

1. If Chad, a recent oil-exporting LDC is added, merchandise exports in the five LDCs increased by 20.9 per cent in 2003 and 40.7 per cent in 2004, while those of the rest of the LDCs increased by 13.7 per cent and 15.4 per cent respectively.

2. These are crude petroleum, refined petroleum products and residual petroleum products.

3. At the time of writing, 2003 was the latest year for which data from the World Bank's Global Development Finance database were available.

4. Excluding those four countries, LDC dependence on external finance as measured by the ratio of long-term capital flows to GDP, increased from 8.5 per cent of GDP in 2000 to 9.3 per cent of GDP in 2003.

5. Calculations are based on a group of 62 countries for which data are available. When Angola, the Democratic Republic of the Congo, Equatorial Guinea and Sudan are excluded, the LDC dependence on external finance as measured by the ratio of long-term capital flows to GDP can be said to have increased from 8.5 per cent of GDP in 2000 to 9.3 per cent of GDP in 2003.

6. Development Assistance Committee (DAC) of the Organization for Economic Co-operation and Development (OECD).

7. In real terms during 1999–2004, ODA to LDCs increased by 12.5 per cent per annum. When Afghanistan and the Democratic Republic of the Congo, which in 2000–2004 absorbed 16 per cent of total net ODA disbursed to the 50 LDCs, are excluded, the average annual growth rate in net ODA disbursed to the 48 remaining LDCs is reduced to 6.7 per cent per annum in real terms. In Afghanistan, net ODA increased by 79.2 per cent per annum during the period 1999–2004 mainly as a result of an unprecedented and sustained increase in emergency assistance and technical cooperation. In the Democratic Republic of the Congo, the 93 per cent per annum increase in real net ODA is attributed to a surge in debt forgiveness grants, particularly in 2003, when debt forgiveness amounted to $4.46 billion, up from $160 million in 2002.

8. If Afghanistan and the Democratic Republic of the Congo are excluded, the rate of increase was 5 per cent and 25.2 per cent per annum respectively.

9. Net ODA growth is regarded as having stagnated if in real terms it was lower or about equivalent to the population growth of the recipient country.

10. At the time of writing, 2003 was the latest year for which debt data were available in the World Bank's Global Development Finance database.

11. The Heavily Indebted Poor Country (HIPC) Initiative is a comprehensive approach to debt reduction of heavily indebted poor countries pursuing IMF- and World Bank-supported adjustment and reform programmes. The Initiative was first launched in 1996 and it was enhanced following a review in 1999.

Progress Towards UNLDC III Development Targets

Chapter

2

A. Introduction

In May 2001, a new Programme of Action for the Least Developed Countries for the Decade 2001–2010 (POA) was agreed at the Third United Nations Conference on the Least Developed Countries (UNLDC III). The Programme of Action is intended as "a framework for a strong global partnership to accelerate sustained economic growth and sustainable development in LDCs, to end marginalization by eradicating poverty, inequality and deprivation in these countries, and to enable them to integrate beneficially into the global economy" (United Nations, 2001: para. 4). Partnership is founded on mutual commitments by LDCs and their development partners to undertake concrete actions in seven areas:

(i)   Fostering a people-centred policy framework;

(ii)   Good governance at national and international levels;

(iii)   Building human and institutional capacities;

(iv)   Building productive capacities to make globalization work for LDCs;

(v)   Enhancing the role of trade in development;

(vi)   Reducing vulnerability and protecting the environment;

(vii)   Mobilizing financial resources.

An important feature of the Programme of Action is that it includes quantified, time-bound development targets. The inclusion of these targets is important as it is now easier to monitor the success of the Programme.

An important feature of the Programme of Action is that it includes quantified, time-bound development targets.

This chapter describes the progress which has been made in relation to a number of the quantified development targets of the Programme of Action. Some of these targets overlap with the development targets associated with the Millennium Development Goals (MDGs). However, there are also differences between the MDGs and the UNLDC III targets (see box 1). The targets considered in the present chapter are the following:

(i)   Growth and investment targets;

(ii)   Poverty reduction targets;

(iii)   Human development targets;

(iv)   Transport and communications infrastructure development targets;

(v)   ODA, debt relief and market access targets;

(vi)   Progress towards graduation from the LDC category (for which there are defined and quantifiable thresholds).

The chapter updates and extends earlier assessments of where the LDCs and their development partners stand in relation to the POA targets in UNCTAD (2001), UNCTAD (2002: part I, chapter 2) and UNCTAD (2004: part I, chapter 2, annex 1).

BOX 1. HOW DO THE UNLDC III TARGETS DIFFER FROM THE MILLENNIUM DEVELOPMENT GOALS?

UNLDC III was held after the UN Millennium Summit and thus the POA includes the major development goals that were written into the Millennium Declaration (United Nations, 2000). However, the UNLDC III targets differ from the MDGs in two major ways.

First, the POA targets go beyond the MDGs by including macroeconomic variables, notably a target growth rate and investment rate, and more far-reaching targets on international trade and physical infrastructure, in particular with respect to transport and communications.

Second, the UNLDC III targets are frequently formulated more ambitiously than the MDGs. For instance, UNLDC III goals are to combat not only hunger, but also malnutrition, especially amongst pregnant women and pre-school children (similar to MDG 1); to promote not only universal primary education, but also computer literacy, especially in junior and high schools and universities, and adult literacy, particularly for women (similar to MDGs 2 and 3); not only to reduce the maternal mortality rate, but also to increase the share of women with access to prenatal and maternal health care services (similar to MDG 5); and not only to halt the spread of HIV/AIDS, but also to actually reverse its spread, particularly in the most affected countries (similar to MDG 6). The Programme of Action also highlights how to achieve education and health-related development goals, namely through equitable access to basic and continuing education for all, including adults, and through unrestricted access by all to the primary health care system, including unrestricted access to the widest possible range of safe, effective, affordable and accepted family planning and contraceptive methods.

A problem with the POA targets that go beyond the MDGs is that they are often not yet specified in a way that enables them to be monitored. Monitoring is impeded by both a lack of agreed indicators and a lack of base years against which progress can be measured. A major effort is required in order to make the quantitative targets of the Programme of Action monitorable, and also to ensure that they are consistent with the MDGs.

There has been a major statistical effort to monitor the MDGs and create an institutional consensus on how they should be monitored. There may therefore be a tendency to use progress towards achieving the MDGs as a basis for monitoring progress towards achieving POA targets. However, neglect of the targets that are specific to the POA would be undesirable. Development in the LDCs requires not only improvements in social areas but also a substantial improvement in productive capacities and economic growth, which depends on higher levels of investment, better infrastructure and trade.

Source: Herrmann (2003).

B. Growth and investment targets

The Programme of Action includes growth and investment targets for the group of LDCs, specifically that "LDCs, with the support of their development partners, will strive to attain a GDP growth rate of at least 7 per cent per annum and increase the ratio of investment to GDP to 25 per cent per annum" (United Nations, 2001: para. 6). Since the start of the POA, growth rates and investment ratios have been improving in many LDCs. As shown in chapter 1, the year 2004 was an exceptionally positive year for the LDCs in terms of GDP growth. However, in aggregate, the LDC performance with respect to these targets is falling behind.

Between 2001 and 2004, only 6 out of the 46 LDCs for which data are available were able to meet or exceed the Programme of Action target of an average annual growth rate of 7 per cent per annum.

Between 2001 and 2004, only 6 out of the 46 LDCs for which data are available were able to meet or exceed an average annual growth rate of 7 per cent per annum. These include three countries which are (or are becoming) oil exporters — Angola, Chad and Equatorial Guinea — together with Maldives, Mozambique and Sierra Leone. Over the same period, 11 LDCs were on track, growing between 5 and 7 per cent per annum; 8 LDCs were, on average, growing moderately (between 3.5 and 5 per cent per annum) but were under the target rate; 16 LDCs were growing at less than half the target rate, which was barely sufficient to ensure positive GDP per capita growth; and finally, GDP was declining in the remaining 5 countries.

With respect to the POA investment target, out of 39 LDCs for which data are available, Bhutan, Chad, Eritrea, Haiti, Lesotho, Maldives, Mozambique, Nepal, Sao Tome and Principe, and Timor-Leste achieved or exceeded an investment/GDP ratio of 25 per cent per annum during the period 2001–2004. Eight LDCs were on track for achieving the target, with average annual gross capital formation rates of between 20 and 25 per cent of GDP; 10 had average annual investment rates of between 17 and 20 per cent; and a last subgroup of 11 LDCs exhibited low levels of gross capital formation.

C. Poverty reduction targets

The Programme of Action states that the "The overarching goal of the Programme of Action is to make substantial progress toward halving the proportion of people living in extreme poverty and suffering from hunger by 2015 and promote the sustainable development of the LDCs" (United Nations, 2001: para. 6). However, identifying the progress which LDCs have made in meeting the poverty reduction goal through household survey data is very difficult (see box 2).

If the past trend continues, the number of people living in poverty in the LDCs will increase from 334 million in 2000 to 471 million in 2010.

In past LDC Reports UNCTAD has argued that, given the paucity of good household-survey-based estimates of poverty over time in the LDCs, it would be advisable to use national-accounts-based estimates of the incidence of poverty. UNCTAD estimates in the *Least Developed Countries Report 2002* suggest that the incidence of poverty did not decline in the 1990s in the LDCs as a group and has remained at 50 per cent of the total population (UNCTAD, 2002: part II, chapter 1). If this past trend continues, the number of people living in poverty in the LDCs will increase from 334 million in 2000 to 471 million in 2010 (UNCTAD, 2004: 222).

National-accounts estimates of poverty such as these have given rise to lively debate, and some reject their validity, arguing that national-accounts household consumption estimates are too flawed and too broadly specified to give an

---

Box 2. What do household survey data show about poverty trends in LDCs?

Box table 1 sets out household-survey-based estimates of the proportion of the population living on less than $1 a day in the LDCs using the international poverty line (1993 PPP $), and also the proportion of the population living in poverty according to nationally defined poverty lines reported internationally. The data are drawn from the MDG statistical indicators website and the World Bank online poverty database (PovcalNet).

These sources provide the most comprehensive coverage of household-survey-based estimates of poverty. However, it is clear that the data are not sufficient to provide a clear picture of the situation across all LDCs. There are only 30 LDCs for which there are poverty estimates. Moreover, it is possible to estimate a rate of change in the incidence of poverty using the international poverty line in only 14 LDCs, and using the national poverty line in only 10 LDCs.

The data suggest that poverty trends within the LDCs are very mixed. The incidence of poverty is declining during those periods for which there are data in 6 out of 14 LDCs using the international poverty line and in 7 out of 10 LDCs using the national poverty line.

Drawing any conclusions from these data is even more difficult because there is an inconsistency between the trends that appear when the international poverty line is used and those that appear when the national poverty line is used. In the case of seven LDCs where data are available for both poverty lines, the trend in the incidence of poverty is in a different direction (positive or negative) for the international poverty line compared with the national poverty line. In most cases this reflects the fact that the poverty rates are estimated for different periods during the 1990s. However, the inconsistency means that it is impossible to construct a coherent view of poverty trends in the LDCs in the 1990s using these data.

Box 2 (contd.)

BOX TABLE 1. POVERTY ESTIMATES FOR LDCS ACCORDING TO INTERNATIONAL AND NATIONAL POVERTY LINES

	International poverty line: % of population below $1[a] per day consumption				National poverty line: % of population below national poverty line			
	Year	Latest poverty estimate	Period	Rate of change per annum	Year	Latest poverty estimate	Period	Rate of change per annum
Bangladesh	2000	36	1996–2000	2.3	2000	50	1996–2000	-0.3
Benin					1995	33		
Burkina Faso	1998	45	1994–1998	-4.5	1998	45	1994–1998	0.2
Burundi	1998	55	1992–1998	1.7				
Cambodia	1997	34			1997	36	1994–1997	-1.0
Central African Republic	1993	67						
Chad					1996	64		
Djibouti					1996	45		
Ethiopia	1995	31	1995–2000	-1.6	1996	46		
Eritrea					1994	53		
Gambia	2000	26	1998–2000	-1.7				
Guinea					1994	40		
Guinea-Bissau					1991	49		
Haiti	2001	67						
Lao People's Dem. Rep.	1997	26	1992–1997	3.6	1998	39	1993–1998	-1.3
Lesotho	1995	36	1993–1995	-3.5				
Madagascar	2001	61	1999–2001	6.0	1999	71	1997–1999	-1.0
Malawi	1997	42			1998	65	1991–1998	1.6
Mali	1994	72			1998	64		
Mauritania	2000	26	1995–2000	-0.6	2000	46	1996–2000	-0.9
Mozambique	1996	38			1997	69		
Nepal	1995	39			1996	42		
Niger	1995	61	1992–1995	6.3	1993	63		
Rwanda	2000	52			1993	51		
Sierra Leone					2004	70		
Senegal	1994	22	1991–1994	-7.7	1992	33		
Uganda	1999	85	1996–1999	-0.3	1997	44	1993–1997	-2.8
United Rep. of Tanzania	1991	49			2001	36	1991–2001	-0.3
Yemen	1998	16	1992–1998	2.0	1998	42		
Zambia	1998	64	1998–1996	4.5	1998	73	1996–1998	1.9

Source: UNCTAD secretariat estimates based on World Bank, *World Development Indicators 2005,* CD-ROM, PovcalNet and United Nations Statistics Division.

a Measured in 1993 purchasing power parity.

accurate picture of household poverty.[1] However, as stated in the *LDC Report 2002,* national-accounts-based poverty estimates "offer as plausible poverty estimates as purely household-survey-based estimates" (UNCTAD, 2002: 47). On pragmatic grounds, the only way in which it will be possible to monitor poverty trends in the LDCs as a group will be to use national accounts data, used as sensitively as possible and with an awareness of its flaws.

With this in view, chart 7 shows the real average annual growth rates for private consumption per capita in 27 LDCs for which data are available during the period 2001–2003. Private consumption per capita is falling in eight of the LDCs and is growing at less than 0.5 per cent per annum in a further three countries. Without data on income distribution changes it is impossible to say definitely that falling private consumption per capita implies increasing poverty. But in the LDCs there is a very close long-term relationship between increases in average private consumption per capita and the incidence of poverty

CHART 7. PRIVATE CONSUMPTION PER CAPITA AND GDP PER CAPITA IN LDCs, 2001–2003
(Annual average growth rates)

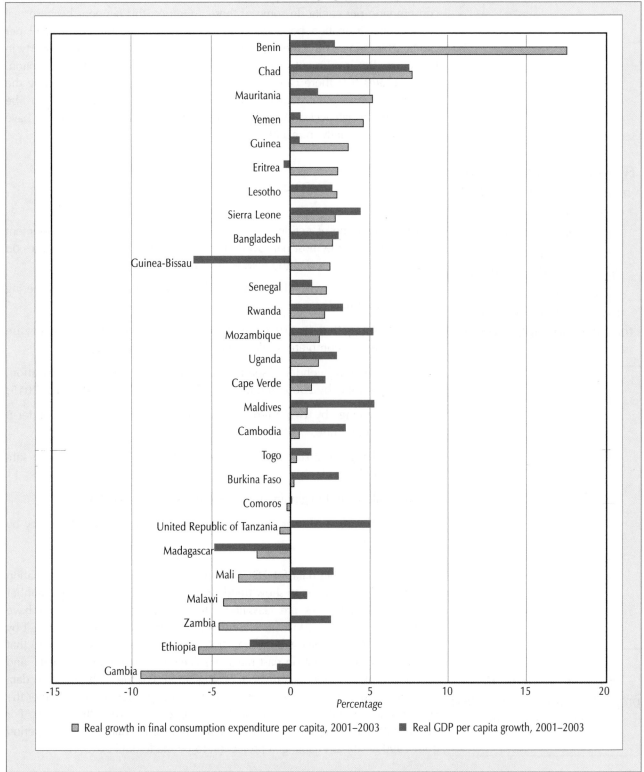

Source: UNCTAD secretariat estimates based on World Bank, *World Development Indicators* 2005, CD-ROM.

(UNCTAD, 2002: part 2, chapter 3). There is thus a strong probability that the incidence of poverty is increasing in these countries.

Chart 7 also includes evidence of real GDP per capita growth rates. In general, private consumption per capita is increasing in LDCs with increasing GDP per capita, and decreasing in LDCs with decreasing GDP per capita. However, this is not always the case. There are a number of countries —

Comoros, Malawi, Mali, the United Republic of Tanzania and Zambia — in which positive GDP per capita growth is associated with declining private consumption per capita. In some of these countries, this happens because real gross capital formation per capita has been increasing faster than GDP per capita. This is increasing the capacity to produce goods and reduce poverty in the future. But investment is occurring at the expense of current consumption. This indicates that there can be a short-term trade-off between achieving the UNLDC III investment target and poverty reduction target.[2] This can be attenuated through access to foreign savings, which, as shown in chapter 1, have increased significantly in recent years.

D. Human development targets

The Programme of Action includes a large number of human development targets, which for the most part overlap with the MDGs. This section focuses on progress towards achieving the following seven targets:

(i) Halving, between 1990 and 2015, the proportion of people suffering from hunger;

(ii) Ensuring that, by 2015, children everywhere, boys and girls alike, are able to   complete a full course of primary schooling;

(iii) Eliminating gender disparity in primary and secondary education, preferably by 2005, and at all levels of education no later than 2015;

(iv) Reducing, by two thirds, between 1990 and 2015, the under-5 mortality rate;

(v) Halving, by 2015, the proportion of people without access to safe drinking water;

(vi) Halting and beginning to reverse the spread of HIV/AIDS;

(vii) Achieving a 50 per cent improvement in levels of adult literacy by 2015.[3]

Although available data for LDCs are patchy, there is sufficient information on the first five indicators to show trends from 1990 to 2003 for a large number of LDCs. The countries are classified into four groups: (i) those that have achieved the target by 2003; (ii) those that are on track to achieve the target by 2015 if the rate of progress between 1990 and 2003 continues; (iii) those that are making progress, but on past rates, are likely to miss the 2015 targets; and (iv) those in which there is a reversal or stagnation. For the sixth indicator, data are available only for 2001 and 2003, and thus it is possible to see whether the HIV prevalence rate is increasing or decreasing only between those years. For the seventh indicator, data on adult literacy rates are available for the period from 1990 to 2002, enabling a projection to be made until 2015.

Table 16 summarizes the trends for the first five indicators. It shows that even though no LDC has yet managed to *reduce by half the proportion of the population that is undernourished*, of the 34 LDCs covered, approximately one third have made great strides towards reductions since the beginning of the 1990s. The cases of Angola, Chad, Haiti, Malawi and Mozambique are notable. The proportion of undernourished people in those countries fell by between 24 and 17 per cent from 1990 to 2002, having been over 50 per cent in 1990.

Nevertheless, it is a matter of concern that there is very slow progress, stagnation or reversals in 21 of those LDCs. In 11 of them, the proportion of

Even though no LDC has yet managed to reduce by half the proportion of the population that is undernourished, approximately one third have made great strides towards reductions since the beginning of the 1990s.

But in 11 of them, the proportion of undernourished people is increasing.

undernourished people is increasing. The Democratic Republic of the Congo and Burundi exemplify this situation: the proportion of undernourished people in those countries increased by 40 and 20 per cent respectively between 1990 and 2002. It is unlikely that, at current levels of progress, this set of countries will achieve the hunger target by the 2015 deadline.

With respect to the *primary education target*, with full data available only for 26 LDCs, Cape Verde is the only LDC to have achieved the target. Nine more LDCs were on track to meet the 2015 deadline. Guinea managed to increase net primary enrolment rates by 40 per cent between 1990 and 2003. However, the majority of LDCs have low levels of progress towards meeting the primary education target. Furthermore, any assessment of progress needs to take into account great disparities in initial enrolment rates. Island and, generally, Asian LDCs had initial primary enrolment ratios of above 70 per cent and in some cases above 90 per cent. Although the experience of African LDCs varies, with some countries having initial enrolment rates of as low as 8 per cent and others as high as 79 per cent, the average initial proportion of enrolment in 1990 in African LDCs is much lower than for the other two LDC groupings.

Improvement towards *eliminating gender disparities* in primary education has been relatively good, with 10 LDCs (out of 36 for which data are available) having achieved the target, and 9 others considered to be on track to achieve it by 2015. For example, the ratio between girls' and boys' primary enrolment increased from 35 per cent in 1990 to 69 per cent in 2003 in Yemen, and during the same period from 68 per cent to 98 per cent in Gambia, from 47 per cent to 77 per cent in Guinea and from 60 per cent to 89 per cent in Nepal. However, approximately half of LDCs for which data are available are experiencing low levels of progress.

Progress towards reducing levels of *child mortality* in LDCs is very slow in over 80 per cent of the cases for which data are available, and several LDCs are experiencing setbacks. Only 11 LDCs are on track to meet the target. Impressive reductions have been made by Bhutan, Guinea, Mozambique and the Lao People's Democratic Republic.

The Central African Republic, Myanmar and the United Republic of Tanzania have met the target of decreasing by half the proportion of the population without *sustainable access to water*. Between 1990 and 2002, access in those countries increased from 38 per cent to 73 per cent, from 48 per cent to 80 per cent and from 48 per cent to 75 per cent respectively. Of the remaining LDCs for which data were available, 10 were on track to meet the 2015 deadline, 16 were progressing very slowly and 5 were experiencing stagnation or reversals.

Many of the LDCs have been particularly badly affected by the HIV/AIDS epidemic. According to data from UNAIDS (2004), by the end of 2003:

- 28 per cent of the estimated global population of adults and children in the world and 27 per cent of all the world's adult infected population lived in the LDCs.

- 32 per cent of the world's women with HIV were living in the LDCs.

- 45 per cent of the world's children (aged 0–14) with HIV were living in the LDCs.

- An estimated 34 per cent of AIDS deaths (children and adults) occurred in the LDCs.

- 43 per cent of children orphaned by HIV/AIDS lived in the LDCs.

The majority of LDCs have low levels of progress towards meeting the primary education target.

With respect to the primary education target, 10 out of 26 LDCs have achieved or are on track to meet the 2015 deadline.

Improvement towards eliminating gender disparities in primary education has been relatively good.

Progress towards reducing levels of child mortality in LDCs is very slow and only 11 LDCs are on track to meet the target.

TABLE 16. PROGRESS TOWARDS ACHIEVEMENT OF SELECTED HUMAN DEVELOPMENT TARGETS IN THE LDCS, 1990–2003[a]

Target	Data availability	Achieved by 2003	Achievable by 2015	Low progress	Reversal/ stagnation
Hunger	**34 LDCs**		**13** Angola Benin Cambodia Chad Guinea Haiti Lao People's Dem. Rep. Lesotho Malawi Mauritania Mozambique Myanmar Togo	**9** Bangladesh Burkina Faso Central African Rep. Nepal Niger Rwanda Somalia Sudan Uganda	**12** Afghanistan Burundi Dem. Rep.of Congo Gambia Liberia Madagascar Mali Senegal Sierra Leone United Rep. of Tanzania Yemen Zambia
Primary education	**26 LDCs**	**1** Cape Verde	**9** Cambodia Gambia Guinea Lao People's Dem. Rep. Lesotho Mauritania Rwanda Togo Vanuatu	**14** Bangladesh Burkina Faso Burundi Chad Eritrea Ethiopia Madagascar Maldives Mali Mozambique Niger Senegal United Rep. of Tanzania Yemen	**2** Zambia Myanmar[b]
Gender equality in education	**36 LDCs**	**10** Bangladesh Lesotho Madagascar Maldives Myanmar Rwanda Samoa United Rep. of Tanzania Vanuatu Uganda	**9** Cambodia Gambia Guinea Malawi Mauritania Senegal Togo Yemen Nepal	**14** Benin Burkina Faso Cape Verde Central African Rep. Chad Comoros Djibouti Ethiopia Lao People's Dem. Rep. Mali Mozambique Niger Sudan Zambia	**3** Afghanistan Burundi Eritrea
Child mortality	**50 LDCs**		**11** Bangladesh Bhutan Cape Verde Comoros Eritrea Lao People's Dem. Rep. Maldives Nepal Samoa Solomon Islands Vanuatu	**24** Benin Djibouti East Timor Equatorial Guinea Ethiopia Gambia Guinea Guinea-Bissau Haiti Kiribati Lesotho Madagascar Malawi Mali Mozambique Myanmar	**15** Afghanistan Angola Burkina Faso Burundi Cambodia Central African Republic Chad Dem. Rep. of Congo Liberia Mauritania Rwanda Sao Tome and Principe Somalia United Rep. of Tanzania Zambia

Table 16 (contd.)

Target	Data availability	Achieved by 2003	Achievable by 2015	Low progress	Reversal/ stagnation
Child mortality (contd..)				Niger Senegal Sierra Leone Sudan Togo Tuvalu Uganda Yemen	
Access to water	34 LDCs	**3** Central African Republic Myanmar United Rep. of Tanzania	**10** Angola Burundi Comoros Eritrea Haiti Kiribati Malawi Mauritania Nepal Rwanda	**16** Bangladesh Benin Burkina Faso Chad Dem. Rep. of the Congo Djibouti Guinea Liberia Madagascar Mali Niger Senegal Sudan Togo Uganda Zambia	**5** Ethiopia Maldives Samoa Vanuatu Yemen

Source: UNCTAD secretariat estimates based on UNDP Human Development Report Office: direct communication.

a   The quantitative variables used to monitor the targets on hunger, primary education, gender equality in education, child mortality and access to safe water are: undernourished people as a percentage of total population, the net primary school enrolment ratio, the ratio between girls' and boys' primary enrolment (gender parity index), the under-5 child mortality rate (per 1,000 live births) and the percentage of people with access to improved water sources, respectively.
To estimate progress towards achievement, data for the following years were used: for the hunger target: 1990/1992 and 2000/2002, for the primary education target: 1990/1991 and 2002/2003, for gender equality in education: 1991 and 2003, for child mortality: 1990 and 2003, and for access to water: 1990 and 2002. Projections are based on the assumption that annual average rates of change between 1990 (or the nearest year) and 2003 (or the nearest year) will continue until 2015.

b   Achieved in 2000, but has since experienced a reversal.

Table 17 summarizes recent progress in terms of *HIV prevalence* in the 32 LDCs for which data are available.[4] HIV prevalence rates for those aged 15–49 were increasing in 13 LDCs, stagnant in 9 LDCs and decreasing in 10 LDCs between 2001 and 2003. UNCTAD (2004: part 1, chapter 2) discusses the major economic and social impacts of the epidemic in the LDCs. Unless further progress is made on this front, it is unlikely that the target will be met by 2015.

Table 18 summarizes progress towards the POA *adult literacy target*, which has been estimated by assuming that the target is to increase adult literacy by 50 per cent above the 2001 level by the year 2015. From the table it is apparent that if the trend that prevailed from 1990 to 2001 continues until 2015, only one LDC — Mali — will be lagging far behind in terms of achieving this target. Only three LDCs are on track, but the majority of those for which there are data should increase their adult literacy rates by over 33 per cent.

The majority of LDCs should increase their adult literacy rates by over 33 per cent above the 2001 level by the year 2015.

TABLE 17. HIV PREVALENCE RATE AND DIRECTION OF CHANGE IN LDCS, 2001 AND 2003
(Prevalence rate: percentage of 15–49 age group)

	2001	2003	Direction of change
Burundi	6.2	6.0	decreasing
Cambodia	2.7	2.6	decreasing
Chad	4.9	4.8	decreasing
Eritrea	2.8	2.7	decreasing
Lesotho	29.6	28.9	decreasing
Malawi	14.3	14.2	decreasing
Togo	4.3	4.1	decreasing
Uganda	5.1	4.1	decreasing
United Republic of Tanzania	9.0	8.8	decreasing
Zambia	16.7	16.5	decreasing
Benin	1.9	1.9	stagnant
Burkina Faso	4.2	4.2	stagnant
Central African Republic	13.5	13.5	stagnant
Democratic Republic of the Congo	4.2	4.2	stagnant
Gambia	1.2	1.2	stagnant
Lao People's Democratic Republic	0.1	0.1	stagnant
Mali	1.9	1.9	stagnant
Senegal	0.8	0.8	stagnant
Rwanda	5.1	5.1	stagnant
Angola	3.7	3.9	increasing
Djibouti	2.8	2.9	increasing
Guinea	2.8	3.2	increasing
Haiti	5.5	5.6	increasing
Liberia	5.1	5.9	increasing
Madagascar	1.3	1.7	increasing
Mauritania	0.5	0.6	increasing
Mozambique	12.1	12.2	increasing
Myanmar	1.0	1.2	increasing
Nepal	0.4	0.5	increasing
Niger	1.1	1.2	increasing
Ethiopia	4.1	4.4	increasing
Sudan	1.9	2.3	increasing

Source: UNAIDS estimates; UN Statistics Division.

E. Transport and communications infrastructure development targets

The Programme of Action contains the following six infrastructure-related targets:

The Programme of Action contains six infrastructure-related targets.

"(a) Increasing road networks or connections in LDCs to the current level of other developing countries and urban road capacities, including sewerage and other related facilities, by 2010;

(b) Modernizing and expanding ports and airports and their ancillary facilities to enhance their capacities by 2010;

(c) Modernizing and expanding railway connections and facilities, increasing their capacities to the level of those in other developing countries by the end of the decade;

(d) Increasing LDCs' communication networks, including telecommunication and postal services, and improving access of the poor to such services in urban and rural areas to reach the current levels in other developing countries;

TABLE 18. PROGRESS OF LDCs TOWARDS ACHIEVEMENT OF ADULT LITERACY TARGET, 1990, 2001 AND 2015

(Adult literacy rate: percentage of population aged 15 and above)

	1990	2001	2015 target	2015 expected[a]
Bangladesh	34	41	61	49
Benin	26	39	58	54
Burundi	37	49	74	65
Cambodia	62	69	100	77
Cape Verde	64	75	100	89
Central African Republic	33	49	73	68
Chad	28	44	66	65
Comoros	54	56	84	59
Ethiopia	29	40	60	55
Haiti	40	51	76	65
Lao People's Dem. Rep.	57	66	98	77
Lesotho	78	81	100	86
Liberia	39	55	82	75
Malawi	52	61	91	73
Maldives	95	97	100	100
Mali	19	19	29	19
Mauritania	35	41	61	48
Mozambique	33	45	68	60
Myanmar	81	85	100	90
Nepal	30	43	64	59
Niger	11	17	25	23
Rwanda	53	68	100	87
Samoa	98	99	100	100
Senegal	28	38	57	51
Sudan	46	59	88	75
Togo	44	58	88	76
Uganda	56	68	100	83
United Rep. of Tanzania	63	76	100	93
Yemen	33	48	71	67
Zambia	68	79	100	93

Source: UNCTAD secretariat estimates and projections based on *World Development Indicators 2005*, CD-ROM.

a   The expected adult literacy rate in 2015 is calculated assuming that rates of progress between 1990 and 2001 will have continued between 2001 and 2015.

(e) Increasing computer literacy among students in higher institutions and universities by 50 per cent and in junior and high schools by 25 per cent by 2015;

(f) Increasing average telephone density to 5 main lines per 100 inhabitants and Internet connections to 10 users per 100 inhabitants by the year 2010" (United Nations, 2001: para. 43).

To assess the LDCs' progress in achieving goals (a) and (f), it has been assumed that these goals specifically aim at bringing, by 2010, the LDCs to the level that other developing countries (ODCs) had in 2001.

The unavailability of data seriously limits the extent of the analysis. Except for goals (a) and (f), there are too few observations to permit comparison. With regard to goal (a) lack of recent data meant that evaluation was based on growth rates in the 1990s to the most recent year, which were then projected to the year 2010. The estimated values, which assume that the growth rates before the

Programme of Action will be maintained, are then compared with the corresponding 2001 value in other developing countries. For goal (f), more recent data is available, and evaluation of progress is based on estimating the average annual growth rate experienced by the LDCs over the period 2001-2003 and making projections for the year 2010.

Table 19 shows the progress of each LDC towards the achievement of goals (a) and (f). The following conclusions can be drawn:

- Island LDCs have better transport and communications infrastructures than the remaining LDCs and seem more likely to achieve the POA goals.

- Regarding the transport infrastructure goal, 16 LDCs are on track for achieving by 2010 the same length of roads per capita as ODCs had in 2001, against 17 LDCs that are far behind. When a measure of infrastructure quality, for example paved roads, is taken into account, a different picture emerges: 24 LDCs are far behind, 5 have achieved the goal and only 1 is on track. This shows that it is not sufficient to increase the length of the road network when roads are of poor quality and barely usable.

- The digital divide is not likely to be closed before 2010. The majority of the LDCs are far behind as regards the goals of having 5 main telephone lines and 10 Internet users per 100 inhabitants by 2010. It is interesting to note that in the case of the number of Internet users, 21 LDCs are on track for achieving the goal, on the assumption that the growth rate of the period 2001–2004 is maintained until 2010.

16 LDCs are on track for achieving by 2010 the same length of roads per capita as ODCs had in 2001, against 17 LDCs that are far behind.

F. ODA, debt relief and market access targets for development partners

1. QUANTITY OF AID

Under commitment 7 of the Programme of Action, "Mobilizing financial resources", it is stated, *inter alia,* that "Donor countries will implement the following actions that they committed to at the second United Nations Conference on the Least Developed Countries as soon as possible:

(a) Donor countries providing more than 0.20 per cent of their GNP as ODA to LDCs: continue to do so and increase their efforts;

(b) Other donor countries which have met the 0.15 target: undertake to reach 0.20 per cent expeditiously;

(c) All other donor countries which have committed themselves to the 0.15 per cent target: reaffirm their commitment and undertake either to achieve the target within the next five years or to make their best efforts to accelerate their endeavours to reach the target;

(d) During the period of the Programme of Action, the other donor countries: exercise individual best efforts to increase their ODA to LDCs with the effect that collectively their assistance to LDCs will significantly increase" (United Nations, 2001: para. 83).

The digital divide is not likely to be closed before 2010. The majority of the LDCs are far behind as regards the goals of having 5 main telephone lines and 10 Internet users per 100 inhabitants by 2010.

TABLE 19. PROGRESS OF LDCs TOWARDS POA TRANSPORT AND COMMUNICATIONS INFRASTRUCTURE TARGETS, 2010

(Before and after the Brussels conference)

	Transport target		Communications infrastructure target	
	Roads *km/000 people*	*Paved roads* *km/000 people*	*Telephone mainlines* *per 100 people*	*Internet users* *per 100 people*
Afghanistan	Far behind	Far behind	Far behind	On track
Angola	Lagging	Slipping back	Far behind	On track
Bangladesh	Far behind	Far behind	Far behind	Far behind
Benin	Far behind	Far behind	Far behind	On track
Bhutan	On track	Achieved	Slipping back	Far behind
Burkina Faso	Far behind	Slipping back	Far behind	Far behind
Burundi	..	..	Far behind	Far behind
Cambodia	Slipping back	Far behind	Far behind	Far behind
Cape Verde	Far behind	Achieved	Achieved	On track
Central African Republic	On track	Far behind	Far behind	Far behind
Chad	On track	Far behind	Far behind	On track
Comoros	..	..	Lagging	On track
Dem. Rep. of the Congo	..	..	Slipping back	Far behind
Djibouti	On track	Far behind	Far behind	On track
Equatorial Guinea	On track	..	Far behind	On track
Eritrea	Far behind	Far behind	Far behind	Far behind
Ethiopia	Far behind	Slipping back	Far behind	Far behind
Gambia	Far behind	Far behind	Lagging	On track
Guinea	On track	Far behind	Far behind	On track
Guinea-Bissau	Lagging	Far behind	Far behind	On track
Haiti	Far behind	Far behind	Lagging	On track
Kiribati	..	..	On track	Far behind
Lao PDR	On track	Achieved	Far behind	Far behind
Lesotho	On track	Far behind	On track	On track
Liberia	On track	Far behind	Slipping back	Far behind
Madagascar	On track	Slipping back	Slipping back	Far behind
Malawi	On track	Lagging	Far behind	Far behind
Maldives	..	..	Achieved	On track
Mali	Far behind	Far behind	Far behind	Far behind
Mauritania	Lagging	Far behind	Lagging	Far behind
Mozambique	Far behind	Far behind	Slipping back	On track
Myanmar	Far behind	Far behind	Far behind	Far behind
Nepal	Far behind	Slipping back	Far behind	Far behind
Niger	Slipping back	Slipping back	Far behind	Far behind
Rwanda	Far behind	Slipping back	Slipping back	Far behind
Samoa	..	Achieved	On track	On track
Sao Tome and Principe	..	Achieved	On track	Achieved
Senegal	Far behind	Far behind	Slipping back	On track
Sierra Leone	Slipping back	Slipping back	Far behind	Far behind
Solomon Islands	On track	Far behind	Slipping back	Far behind
Somalia	Lagging	Far behind	On track	Far behind
Sudan	Far behind	Far behind	On track	On track
Timor-Leste	..	..	..	..
Togo	Far behind	Far behind	Far behind	Far behind
Uganda	..	..	Far behind	Far behind
United Rep. of Tanzania	On track	Slipping back	Slipping back	On track
Vanuatu	On track	On track	Slipping back	Far behind
Yemen	On track	Far behind	On track	On track
Zambia	On track	Lagging	Slipping back	On track

Source: UNCTAD secretariat estimates and projections based on World Bank, *World Development Indicators 2005*, CD-ROM, and *World Telecommunications Indicators 2005,* CD-ROM.

Note: The gap with respect to the other developing countries for the first goal (i.e. goal A) was calculated by applying the average annual growth rate of the period 1990–1999 to the latest available year and by making projections until the year 2010. The following nomenclature is used:

"Achieved" (the country is already at the same level as the ODC average); "On track" (the country has already attained 95 per cent of the ODC average); "Lagging" (the country has achieved between 75 and 94 per cent of the ODC average); "Far behind" (the country has achieved between 0 and 74 per cent of the ODC average); "Slipping back" (the country's level worsened during the 1990s).

The progress towards the achievement of the latest goal (i.e. goal E) was estimated by applying the average annual growth rates of the period 2001–2004 to the latest available figure and by making projections until the year 2010.

As table 20 shows, seven DAC member countries, namely Belgium, Denmark, Ireland, Luxembourg, Netherlands, Norway and Sweden met the POA target of making net ODA disbursements equivalent to 0.20 per cent of their respective GNI in 2003. In 2004, Portugal, Norway, Luxembourg, Denmark, the Netherlands, Sweden and Ireland achieved the target. In 2004, Belgium and France met the 0.15 per cent target (0.18 per cent and 0.15 per cent of GNI respectively). The combined EU member States' contributions, which accounted for 63.6 per cent of total ODA disbursements to LDCs in 2004, decreased slightly from 0.13 to 0.12 as a percentage of GNI between 2003 and 2004, but represent an increase over the 2000–2001 period (0.09 per cent in 2001 and 0.10 per cent in 2002).

Among the DAC member countries, the United States continues to be the leading donor to the LDCs in absolute terms, accounting for 19.2 per cent of total DAC net aid disbursements to LDCs in 2004. Nevertheless, the United States' ODA to LDCs as a share of GNI increased only marginally — to 0.04 per cent in 2003 and 2004, up from 0.03 per cent in 2002. France became the second largest DAC donor to LDCs in absolute terms in 2004.

Seven DAC member countries met the POA target of making net ODA disbursements equivalent to 0.20 per cent of their respective GNI in 2003.

TABLE 20. NET AID DISBURSEMENTS FROM OECD/DAC MEMBER COUNTRIES TO LDCs,[a] AND ODA UNTYING RATIO OF ODA TO LDCs, 2003 AND 2004

(Ranked in descending order of % of donors' GNI)

	$ millions	% of total DAC	% of donor's total	% of donor's GNI	$ millions	% of total DAC	% of donor's total	% of donor's GNI	ODA untying ratio[b]
		2003				*2004*			*2004*
Portugal	205	0.9	64	0.14	878	3.7	85	0.53	0.99
Norway	801	3.6	39	0.36	837	3.6	38	0.33	1.00
Luxembourg	65	0.3	34	0.27	87	0.4	37	0.31	1.00
Denmark	673	3.0	38	0.32	735	3.1	36	0.31	0.80
Netherlands	981	4.4	25	0.20	1 453	6.2	35	0.25	0.96
Sweden	822	3.7	34	0.27	762	3.2	28	0.22	0.98
Ireland	266	1.2	53	0.21	322	1.4	53	0.21	1.00
Belgium	1 088	4.9	59	0.35	645	2.7	44	0.18	0.99
France	2 965	13.3	41	0.16	3 169	13.5	37	0.15	0.85
United Kingdom	2 273	10.2	36	0.12	2 988	12.7	38	0.14	1.00
Switzerland	405	1.8	31	0.12	399	1.7	26	0.11	0.95
Germany	2 508	11.3	37	0.10	2 312	9.8	31	0.08	0.66
Finland	183	0.8	33	0.11	153	0.6	23	0.08	1.00
Canada	634	2.9	31	0.07	702	3.0	27	0.07	0.76
New Zealand	45	0.2	27	0.06	65	0.3	31	0.07	0.36
Australia	259	1.2	21	0.05	350	1.5	24	0.06	0.91
Austria	169	0.8	33	0.07	168	0.7	25	0.06	0.68
Italy	1 104	5.0	45	0.08	788	3.4	32	0.05	0.80
Spain	342	1.5	17	0.04	424	1.8	17	0.04	0.95
United States	4 474	20.1	27	0.04	4 504	19.2	23	0.04	0.03
Japan	1 922	8.6	22	0.04	1 684	7.2	19	0.04	0.81
Greece	55	0.2	15	0.03	65	0.3	14	0.03	0.41
Total DAC	22 237	100.0	32	0.08	23 490	100.0	30	0.08	0.68
of which:									
EU Members	13 697	61.6	37	0.13	14 949	63.6	35	0.12	..

Source: UNCTAD secretariat estimates based on OECD/DAC online data and, for untying ratio, OECD (2006).

a   Including imputed multilateral flows, i.e. making allowance for contributions through multilateral organizations, calculated using the geographical distribution of multilateral disbursements for the year of reference.

b   The bilateral LDC ODA untying ratio is the following: untied bilateral LDC ODA divided by total bilateral LDC ODA (commitments basis).

In terms of volume, net ODA disbursements from DAC member countries to LDCs almost doubled in 2004 in comparison with the 2001 levels (rising from $12,019 million in 2001 to $23,490 million in 2004). The aid effort of all DAC member countries, as measured by the ODA to GNI ratio, stood at 0.08 in both 2003 and 2004, having increased from 0.06 in 2002. Nevertheless, in global terms, the ODA to GNI ratio still remains below the ODA targets for the LDCs in the Programme of Action.

2. THE UNTYING OF AID

With regard to improving the effectiveness of aid to the LDCs, the Brussels Programme of Action includes a commitment on the part of donor countries to implement the 2001 OECD/DAC Recommendation on Untying Official Development Assistance to the Least Developed Countries (DCD/DAC (2001)12/FINAL). This entered into force on 1 January 2002.

The bilateral LDC ODA untying ratio continues to rise... and most Members have untied their aid beyond the requirements of the Recommendation.

As shown in table 20, the bilateral LDC ODA untying ratio continues to rise. The average bilateral ODA untying ratio to the LDCs for the composite of DAC Members in 2004 surpassed the Members' agreed reference point, 0.60. It is further reported in the 2006 OECD/DAC progress report that, "In 2005, the implementation of the Recommendation continued to proceed well, ... and most Members have untied their aid beyond the requirements of the Recommendation" (OECD, 2006: 2-3).

Furthermore, according to the 2006 progress report:

- All Members had implemented the coverage provisions of the Recommendation.

- In response to the Paris Declaration and calls from major international conferences to increase the share of aid that is untied, the DAC has discussed "approaches to extend the benefits of untied aid, especially in terms of improved aid effectiveness and greater value for money". (OECD: 2006: 7). One of the actions adopted includes: the elimination of coverage thresholds in order to improve effort-sharing among donors; these provisions are expected to enter into force on 1 July 2006.

The process of untying aid towards LDCs has been evolving at a rapid pace, and there seems to be consensus that further untying would further contribute to the aid effectiveness agenda.

- Although technical cooperation is excluded from the coverage of the Recommendations, a further step taken involves "studying the possibilities for untying procurement related technical cooperation" (OECD, 2006:8). Notwithstanding, in 2004, Australia adopted a policy of untying technical cooperation to the LDCs.

- In 2005, the European Community adopted two new regulations on access to EC external assistance, in which all aid to the LDCs will be untied. With the new adopted regulation "all expertise, e.g. technical cooperation, will be untied and based on the dual criteria of quality and price" (OECD, 2006: 3), and food aid will additionally be untied.

In sum, the process of untying aid towards LDCs has been evolving at a rapid pace, and there seems to be consensus that further untying would further contribute to the aid effectiveness agenda.

3. Debt relief

The Programme of Action highlights a number of key measures to be taken in relation to debt relief and debt management on the part of the LDCs and their development partners. The cornerstone of action by development partners is the effective implementation of the enhanced HIPC Initiative.

Thirty LDCs are currently identified as potentially eligible to receive debt relief under the enhanced HIPC Initiative. As of August 2005, 22 of those countries had reached decision point and 13 had reached completion point in the HIPC process (see table 21).[5] Most countries reached decision point in the year 2000. Since May 2001, only four more LDCs have reached decision point. But over this period 12 LDCs have reached completion point, including eight, namely Benin, Ethiopia, Madagascar, Mali, Niger, Rwanda, Senegal and Zambia, since 2003.

In 2004, the "sunset clause" of the enhanced HIPC Initiative was extended until the end of 2006. This will allow additional countries to qualify under the enhanced HIPC Initiative if income and indebtedness criteria are satisfied utilizing end-of-2004 data. On the basis of analysis by the IMF and the IDA, 10 LDCs have estimated debt burden indicators above the enhanced HIPC Initiative thresholds. These include seven LDCs which were already recognized as potential beneficiaries of the Initiative but which had not yet reached decision point — the Central African Republic, Comoros, the Lao People's Democratic Republic, Liberia, Somalia, Sudan and Togo — and also Eritrea, Haiti and Nepal. Two LDCs (Afghanistan and Cape Verde) have ratios below the enhanced HIPC Initiative thresholds, and in the case of three LDCs incomplete data have not allowed a final assessment to be made. These countries are Bangladesh and Bhutan, and also Myanmar, which was already identified as potentially eligible. It is therefore possible that up to 5 more LDCs may be added to the 30 LDCs currently on the list of HIPCs.

In net present value terms, the LDC-HIPCs that have reached completion point have received committed debt relief equivalent to $14.2 billion, 60 per cent of which has been received by Ethiopia, Mozambique, the United Republic of Tanzania and Zambia. The LDC-HIPCs that have reached decision points have received $9.7 billion, 65 per cent of which has been received by the Democratic Republic of the Congo.

Table 21 shows how a key indicator of the debt burden, namely the ratio of debt service paid to government revenue, changed in those countries between 2000 and 2004. The ratio decreased in 17 out of the 22 LDCs-HIPC that had reached decision point before September 2005. The five exceptions, where debt service paid to government revenue has increased despite debt relief, are Burundi, the Democratic Republic of the Congo, the Gambia, Mozambique and Zambia. In the 22 LDCs that have reached decision point the ratio of debt service paid to government revenue declined from 22.3 per cent in 2000 to 16.6 per cent in 2004. The decrease was even more pronounced in the 13 completion point LDC-HIPCs. But the average ratio of debt service to government revenue was still just over 10 per cent in 2004.

This indicates that although debt relief has led to considerable improvements in the debt situation of those LDCs that have reached completion point, the debt problem has not been completely resolved. In countries struggling to develop infrastructure and meet human development goals, the fiscal burden of debt remains significant. It is in this context that additional measures to cancel bilateral and multilateral debt, which are also identified as desirable in the

As of August 2005, 22 LDCs had reached decision point and 13 had reached completion point in the HIPC process.

In those LDCs that have reached completion point, the debt problem has not been completely resolved... It is in this context that additional measures to cancel bilateral and multilateral debt, which are also identified as desirable in the Programme of Action, become important.

TABLE 21. RATIO OF DEBT SERVICE TO GOVERNMENT REVENUE IN SELECTED LDC-HIPCs, 2000–2004

	Date of approval of		Debt service paid as a % of government revenue				
	Decision point	*Completion point*	*2000*	*2001*	*2002*	*2003*	*2004*
Benin	July 2000	March 2003	14.6	9.4	7.8	5.4	5.4
Burkina Faso	July 2000	April 2002	18.5	11.4	10.3	8.1	5.8
Ethiopia	November 2001	April 2004	10.2	15.5	8.9	6.4	8
Madagascar	December 2000	October 2004	13.9	9.8	14.3	9.3	11.9
Mali	September 2000	March 2003	20.9	12.9	12.5	9.1	9.8
Mauritania	March 2000	June 2002	36.1	40.2	20.9	15.6	12.6
Mozambique	April 2000	September 2001	4.1	6.7	12.3	11.6	6.5
Niger	December 2000	April 2004	14.5	18.8	23	9.3	6.8
Rwanda	December 2000	April 2005	23.4	11.8	8.1	7.2	7.1
Senegal	June 2000	April 2004	21.8	19.6	16.5	13.8	8.1
Uganda	March 2000	May 2000	15.3	9.3	8.6	8.6	10.5
United Rep. of Tanzania	April 2000	November 2001	16.1	8.3	8	6.8	7.7
Zambia	December 2000	April 2005	29.3	21.7	18.3	23.6	37.6
Burundi	August 2005		16.5	11.9	22.7	22.3	69.7
Chad	May 2001		29.4	9.3	18.6	14.9	12.4
Dem. Rep. of the Congo	July 2003		..	..	8.2	21	13.6
Gambia	December 2000		26.6	26.3	43.2	22	34
Guinea	December 2000		33.1	18.5	19.7	18.1	16.7
Guinea-Bissau	December 2000		31.3	1.2	6.9	12.8	28.2
Malawi	December 2000		36.1	25.7	18.6	28.6	17.4
Sao Tome and Principe	December 2000		38.7	46.4	39.2	36.6	18.6
Sierra Leone	March 2002		44.4	88.6	19.2	12.7	28

Source: International Monetary Fund and International Development Association, Heavily Indebted Poor Countries (HIPC) Initiative: Status of implementation, prepared by the staffs of the IMF and World Bank, 19 August, 2005.

Note: 2004 figures preliminary.

Programme of Action, become important. In this regard, the debt cancellation decision, for African LDCs that had already reached HIPC completion points, agreed at the G8 Gleneagles Summit in July 2005 and endorsed at the September IMF/World Bank meetings is a positive development.

4. MARKET ACCESS

The Programme of Action recognizes the importance of trade for the LDCs and addresses a number of trade-related policy issues, including the heavy dependence of LDCs on a narrow range of primary commodity exports, the need for improved special and differential treatment, and weaknesses in supply capacities. With regard to market access, there is a specific quantifiable target — duty-free and quota-free market access for all LDCs' products to the markets of developed countries — progress on which can be monitored.[6]

In 2003, the latest year for which data are available, 80.5 per cent of total developed country imports by value (excluding arms) from LDCs were admitted duty-free and quota-free. This represents an increase of three percentage points over 2001. Excluding arms and oil, 72.1 per cent of LDC imports entered duty-free (table 22), an increase of almost two percentage points over 2001.

Excluding arms and oil, 72.1 per cent of LDC imports entered duty-free, an increase of almost two percentage points over 2001.

There have been a number of initiatives, since 2001, by the Quad countries (Canada, the European Union, Japan and the United States) to offer quota- and duty-free market access for an increasing range of LDC products.[7] However, if oil and arms are excluded, the proportion of total developed country imports from LDCs that are admitted duty-free actually fell between 1996 and 2003. As table 22 shows, it is developing countries other than LDCs that have in practice seen the greatest increase in the share of their imports into developed country

TABLE 22. PROPORTION OF TOTAL DEVELOPED COUNTRY IMPORTS (BY VALUE) FROM DEVELOPING COUNTRIES AND LEAST DEVELOPED COUNTRIES ADMITTED FREE OF DUTY, 1996, 2001, 2002 AND 2003

	1996	2001	2002	2003
Excluding arms				
Developing countries	48.2	62.6	64.8	69.7
LDCs	70.3	77.5	78	80.5
Excluding arms and oil				
Developing countries	44.7	60.2	63.4	63.9
LDCs	77.4	70.4	69.2	72.1

Source: UNCTAD-WTO estimates compiled by UNCTAD and WTO in consultation with the World Bank, based on WTO Integrated Database and complemented by ITC Market Access Map and UNCTAD Trade Analysis and Information System (TRAINS), CD-ROM (Geneva, annual).

The effective benefits of market access will depend on whether sensitive products are included... and on simple and transparent rules of origin, as well as efforts to increase export supply capacity.

markets that are admitted duty-free. A likely reason for this, given the new market access initiatives in favour of LDCs, is the greater supply capacity of the other developing countries.

At the Sixth WTO Ministerial Conference, held in Hong Kong (China), in December 2005 it was agreed that developed country Members, and developing country Members in a position to do so, should "provide duty-free and quota-free market access on a lasting basis, for all products originating from all LDCs by 2008 or no later than the start of the implementation period in a manner that ensures stability, security and predictability" and "ensure that preferential rules of origin applicable to imports from LDCs are transparent and simple, and contribute to facilitating market access", and that "Members facing difficulties at this time to provide market access as set out above shall provide duty-free and quota-free market access for at least 97 per cent of products originating from LDCs, defined at the tariff line level, by 2008 or no later than the start of the implementation period" (Hong Kong Declaration, Annex F).

Whether this will enhance effective market access for the LDCs will depend on whether sensitive products such as textiles, rice, dairy products and fish are included. If they are not, the Hong Kong commitment will only guarantee the current level of duty-free and quote-free market access. Also, the effective benefits of market access will depend on simple and transparent rules of origin, as well as efforts to increase export supply capacity.

G. Progress towards graduation from LDC status

The Programme of Action considers graduation from LDC status to be one of the criteria for judging the success of its implementation.

The Programme of Action for the Least Developed Countries for the Decade 2001–2010 considers graduation from LDC status to be one of the criteria for judging the success of its implementation. The principle of graduation was adopted in 1991 by the Committee for Development Planning (now the Committee for Development Policy), a group of independent experts appointed by the Economic and Social Council (ECOSOC) and responsible, inter alia, for the triennial review of the list of LDCs.

The graduation criteria are conceptually similar to the criteria for placing countries on the list: a low-income criterion, a human capital weakness criterion and an economic vulnerability criterion. The graduation methodology is based on specific quantitative thresholds for the aggregate or composite indicators relevant to those criteria: gross national income per capita, the Human Assets Index (HAI) and the Economic Vulnerability Index (EVI) respectively (see box 3).

The 2003 review of the list led the Committee for Development Policy to recommend the graduation of Cape Verde and Maldives, two countries that were meeting graduation thresholds under the low-income and human capital weakness criteria while remaining economically vulnerable. The General Assembly's decision that these two countries would eventually be removed from the list was adopted in 2004, a few days before Maldives was struck by the tsunami of 26 December. The major economic setback suffered by Maldives as a result of this natural disaster led the General Assembly, in 2005, to grant it an exceptional three-year moratorium before the regular three-year grace period towards graduation actually began. This now takes to early 2011 the expected date of Maldives' graduation from LDC status. Meanwhile, Cape Verde would normally graduate from the list in early 2008.

Samoa was deemed to be eligible for graduation in 2003, when the country met two graduation thresholds (those relevant to the low-income and human capital weakness criteria). This eligibility was confirmed at the time of the 2006 review of the list, which led the CDP to recommend Samoa's graduation. The latter will take place, unless conditions change, in early 2010. Eligibility for graduation in accordance with the graduation rule was noted by the CDP, in 2006, for three other LDCs, namely, Kiribati, Tuvalu and Vanuatu.

BOX 3. THE METHODOLOGY FOR REVIEWING GRADUATION FROM LDC STATUS

Box table 2 shows the specific quantitative thresholds for the aggregate or composite indicators used to decide admission to and graduation from the LDC list.

For each of these indicators, there is a margin between the threshold for adding a country and the threshold for graduating a country. This margin is considered to be a reasonable estimate of the additional socio-economic progress that ought to be observed in the relevant country once the latter has risen above the threshold below which a country would be added to the list: the graduating country is expected not only to exceed the thresholds for inclusion, also to exceed them by a standard margin. This rule warrants the robustness of the assumption that a graduating country must be undergoing structural progress, and it removes the risk of graduation being dictated by temporary or insignificant economic circumstances.

Two other fundamental aspects of the graduation rule also warrant structural progress in the graduating country: (i) at least two of the three graduation criteria must be met for the country to be found eligible for graduation, whereas a symmetrical application of the inclusion and graduation rule would have implied that only one criterion had ceased to be met, since all three criteria should be met for a country to be added to the list; (ii) after eligibility for graduation has been observed once on the occasion of a review of the list, full qualification for graduation will not be recognized until the relevant graduation criteria have been met again in a second consecutive review of the list.

If a recommendation to graduate a country in accordance with the above rule is endorsed by ECOSOC and the United Nations General Assembly, actual graduation will in principle take place after a three-year moratorium. This pre-graduation period was instituted by the General Assembly in December 2004 as a grace period to enable the graduating country to negotiate with its development partners a "smooth transition" strategy. By using the notion of "smooth transition" to prevent graduation from disturbing the development process, the UN encourages the development partners of LDCs to ensure that the loss of concessionary treatment, if inevitable, will take place in a gradual, non-disturbing manner.

An important amendment to the graduation rule was introduced by the Committee for Development Policy in 2005 (and applied for the first time in 2006) in the light of the atypical case of Equatorial Guinea. The Committee decided that in the event that a country would meet only the graduation threshold relevant to the low-income criterion, and would do so with a substantial margin above the graduation line, that country would be regarded as eligible for graduation as if it had met two graduation criteria. The rationale for this amendment, as set out by the CDP, was founded on the assumption that a country that is suddenly enjoying financial comfort (notably in the context of oil exports) has acquired a capacity to remedy, without exceptional external support, the structural weaknesses that are measured through the other two criteria. The Committee decided that this exceptional rule would apply whenever the gross national income per capita is more than twice as high as the relevant graduation threshold. In the case of Equatorial Guinea, as shown in box chart 1, the ratio to the graduation threshold was nearly 4 (see also box charts 2 and 3). The Committee therefore found the country eligible for graduation, and subject to the regular time frame under the graduation rule, which implies, unless conditions change, a loss of LDC status for Equatorial Guinea in early 2013.

Box 3 (contd.)

BOX TABLE 2. EVOLUTION IN THE UN'S CRITERIA FOR REVIEWING THE LIST OF LDCs, AS AT 2006

Criteria used before 2000 to review the list of LDCs	Criteria used in 2003 to review the list of LDCs	Criteria used in 2006 to review the list of LDCs
Low-income criterion: *Per capita gross domestic product (GDP):* 3-year (1993–1995) average (under $800 for addition cases; above $900 for graduation cases)	**Low-income criterion:** *Per capita gross national income (GNI):* 3-year (1999–2001) average (under $750 for addition cases; above $900 for graduation cases)	**Low-income criterion:** *Per capita gross national income (GNI):* 3-year (2002–2004) average (under $750 for addition cases; above $900 for graduation cases)
"Quality of life" criterion: *Augmented Physical Quality of Life Index (APQLI):* Composite index based on the following four indicators: * average per capita daily calorie consumption * life expectancy at birth * combined primary and secondary school enrolment rate * adult literacy rate	**Human assets weakness criterion:** *Human Assets Index (HAI):* Composite index based on the following four indicators: * average per capita daily calorie consumption as % of relevant minimum requirements * under-5 child mortality rate * gross secondary school enrolment rate * adult literacy rate	**Human assets weakness criterion:** *Human Assets Index (HAI):* Composite index based on the following four indicators: * percentage of population undernourished * under-5 child mortality rate * gross secondary school enrolment rate * adult literacy rate
Economic diversification criterion: *Economic Diversification Index (EDI):* Composite index based on the following four indicators: * share of manufacturing in GDP * share of labour in industry * per capita electricity consumption * export concentration index	**Economic vulnerability criterion:** *Economic Vulnerability Index (EVI):* Composite index based on the following five indicators: * index of instability of agricultural production * index of instability of exports of goods and services * share of manufacturing and modern services in GDP * merchandise export concentration index * population (in log.) A variant formulation of the EVI, with the proportion of population displaced by natural disasters as an additional component, was also considered.	**Economic vulnerability criterion:** *Economic Vulnerability Index (EVI):* Composite index based on the following seven indicators: * index of instability of agricultural production * proportion of population displaced by natural disasters * index of instability of exports of goods and services * share of agriculture, forestry and fisheries in GDP * merchandise export concentration index * population (in log.) * index of remoteness
For graduation cases: A country would be recommended for immediate graduation if it had met at least two of the three criteria (subject to a margin between the thresholds for addition to, and graduation from, the list of LDCs) in at least two consecutive triennial reviews of the list. However, the CDP would not consider a graduation case unless a vulnerability profile of the country was made available to it.	**For graduation cases:** A country could be recommended for immediate graduation if it had met at-least two of the three criteria (subject to a margin between the thresholds for addition to, and graduation from, the list of LDCs) in at least two consecutive triennial reviews of the list.	**For graduation cases:** A recommendation to graduate a country can be made by the CDP on the basis of the same graduation rule, but actual graduation will not take place before a three-year grace period beginning after the General Assembly has decided to endorse the recommendation (after ECOSOC itself has endorsed it) has elapsed, in accordance with General Assembly resolution 59/209 of 20 December 2004.

Source: Methodology summary by UNCTAD secretariat.

Box 3 (contd.)

BOX CHART 1. LOW INCOME CRITERION (AVERAGE GROSS NATIONAL INCOME PER CAPITA, 2002–2004)

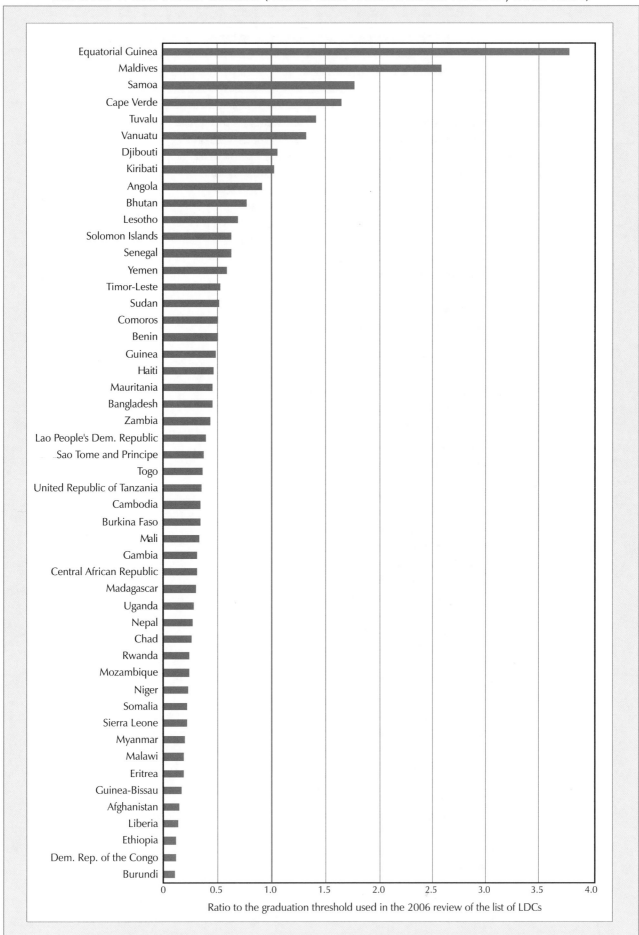

Source: UNCTAD secretariat estimates, based on data provided by the UN Committee for Development Policy (2006).

Box 3 (contd.)

BOX CHART 2. WEAK HUMAN ASSETS CRITERION (HUMAN ASSETS INDEX)

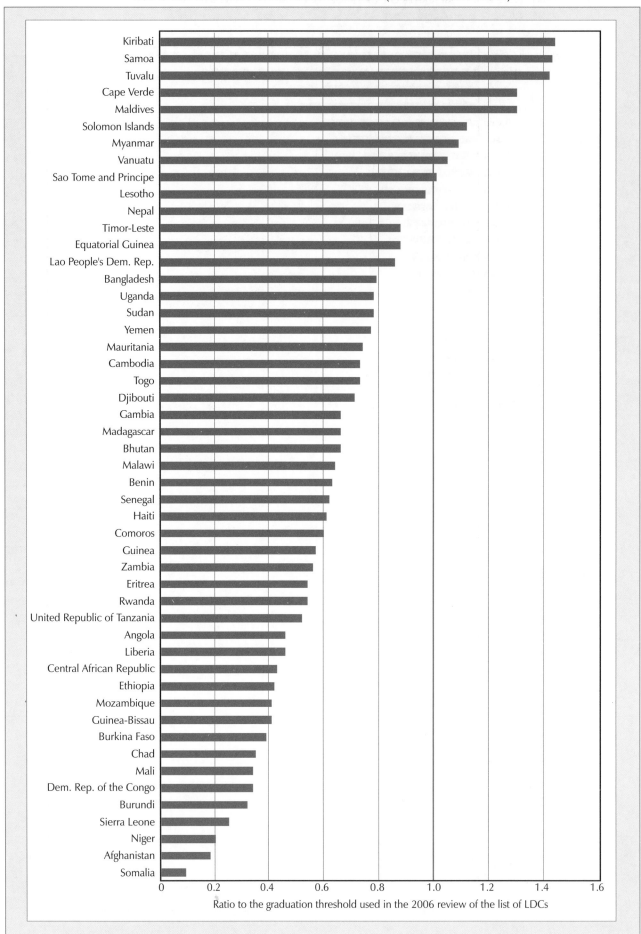

Ratio to the graduation threshold used in the 2006 review of the list of LDCs

Source: Same as for box chart 1.

Box 3 (contd.)

BOX CHART 3. ECONOMIC VULNERABILITY CRITERION (ECONOMIC VULNERABILITY INDEX)

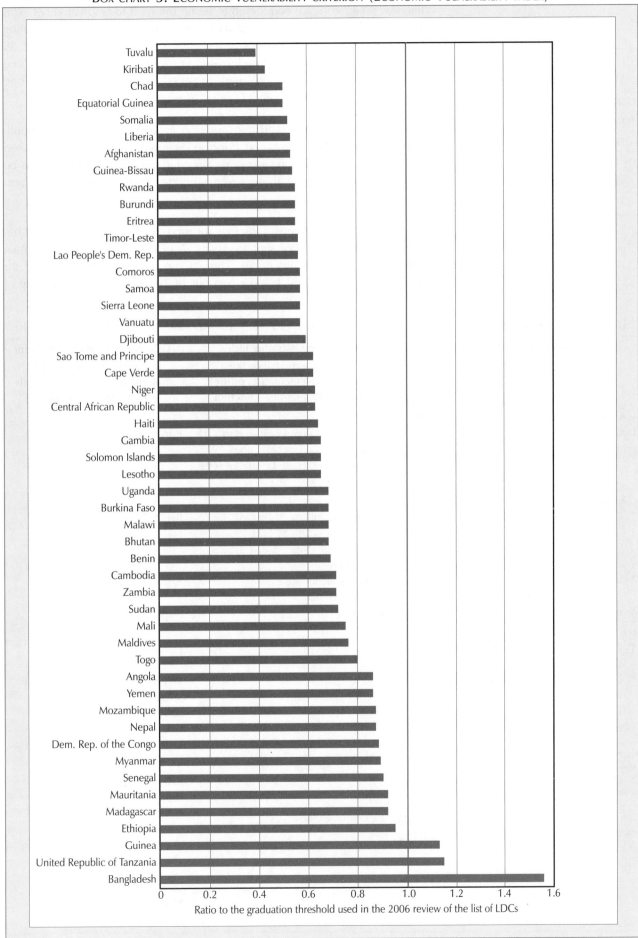

Ratio to the graduation threshold used in the 2006 review of the list of LDCs

Source: Same as for box chart 1.

While seven countries are considered to be on the road to graduation between 2008 and 2013, over 70 per cent of all LDCs were not meeting any graduation criterion.

Table 23 summarizes the pattern of LDCs' progress towards graduation. While seven countries are considered to be on the road to graduation between 2008 and 2013, over 70 per cent of all LDCs (36 out of 50) were not meeting any graduation criterion at the time of the 2006 review of the list. Of these 36 countries, 10 had demonstrated no long-term progress towards any of the three graduation thresholds, while 17 had recorded some progress under one criterion, 7 under two criteria and 2 under three criteria.

Seven LDCs met one graduation criterion in 2006 (Bangladesh, Djibouti, Guinea, Myanmar, Sao Tome and Principe, Solomon Islands and the United Republic of Tanzania). Progress towards a second graduation threshold can be expected in only three of those seven countries (Bangladesh, Djibouti and Myanmar).

In short, on current trends, prospects for progress towards graduation in the foreseeable future are very slim in nearly 7 LDCs out of 10, and remain insignificant in nearly 2 out of 10. There is, to a varying extent, scope for eventual graduation in one LDC or two out of 10. Also, a vertical reading of

TABLE 23. CLASSIFICATION OF THE LDCS ACCORDING TO THEIR PROGRESS TOWARD GRADUATION THRESHOLDS, 2006

Classification of LDCs	LDCs demonstrating little or no progress since the start of implementation of the Brussels Programme of Action	LDCs demonstrating significant progress since the start of implementation of the Brussels Programme of Action
LDCs meeting no graduation criterion in 2006: LDCs demonstrating no long-term progress under any criterion	Afghanistan, Central African Rep., Chad, Dem. Rep. of the Congo, Guinea-Bissau, Haiti, Liberia, Senegal, Sierra Leone	Burkina Faso
LDCs demonstrating some long-term progress: * under one criterion	Burundi, Cambodia, Comoros, Gambia, Lao PDR, Malawi, Mozambique, Niger, Somalia, Togo, Zambia	Benin, Ethiopia, Lesotho, Mali, Sudan, Timor-Leste
* under two criteria	Madagascar, Rwanda Uganda, Yemen	Angola, Bhutan, Mauritania,
* under three criteria	Eritrea	Nepal
LDCs meeting only one graduation criterion in 2006: * LDCs meeting the graduation criterion relevant to low income		Djibouti
* LDCs meeting the graduation criterion relevant to weak human assets * LDCs meeting the graduation criterion relevant to economic vulnerability		Myanmar, Sao Tome and Principe, Solomon Islands Bangladesh, Guinea, United Rep. of Tanzania
LDCs meeting two graduation criteria in 2006: * LDCs found eligible for graduation in 2013 * LDCs qualifying for graduation in 2010		Kiribati, Tuvalu, Vanuatu Samoa
LDC found eligible for graduation in 2013 though meeting only one graduation criterion in 2006 (exception to the rule)	Equatorial Guinea	
LDCs earmarked for graduation: * Graduation normally expected in 2008 * Graduation normally expected in 2011		Cape Verde Maldives
LDC already graduated		Botswana (1994)

Source: UNCTAD secretariat estimates.

table 23 reveals that over half of all LDCs (27 out of 50) have demonstrated significant progress towards graduation since implementation of the Programme of Action started. Whether or not this is due to implementation of the latter or to other factors requires further research.

H. Conclusion

The most striking feature of progress towards the UNLDC III targets since 2001 is the strong engagement of development partners in meeting commitments with respect to aid, debt relief and market access. In contrast to the 1990s, when aid to LDCs fell sharply and debt relief initiatives were very limited, there has been a significant increase in aid and important progress on debt relief. These efforts to increase development finance for the LDCs have been complemented with new initiatives to improve market access.

The most striking feature of progress towards the UNLDC III targets since 2001 is the strong engagement of development partners in meeting commitments with respect to aid, debt relief and market access.

Aid inflows have still not reached the levels commensurate with the aid-to-GNI targets in the POA. However, recent trends are a major turnaround from the 1990s. During that decade, many LDCs engaged in significant and far-reaching economic reforms, including extensive trade liberalization, financial liberalization and privatization. But in real per capita terms, aid fell by 45 per cent between 1990 and 1998 (UNCTAD, 2000).

Growth rates and investment ratios in the LDCs have not yet achieved the ambitious targets of the POA. However, the growth and investment performance in the LDC group as a whole was better during the period 2001–2004 than during the 1990s.

However, aid inflows have still not reached the levels commensurate with the aid-to-GNI targets in the POA.

There are nevertheless certain disturbing features in progress made so far towards the UNLDC III targets.

First, there are growing divergences amongst the LDCs in terms of growth performance. Eighteen out of the 42 LDCs for which data are available have been unable to achieve per capita growth rates of more than 1.0 per cent per annum during the period 2001–2004, which is far too low to have a serious effect on the extreme poverty in which about half the population of LDCs live. Similarly, half of the LDCs are on track to achieve the road infrastructure target, with the length of roads per capita in 2010 equivalent to that in other developing countries in 2001 if past trends continue. But at the same time, the other half of the LDCs are far behind, and even more so if the quality of roads (in terms of the percentage paved) is taken into account. This weak performance has important negative consequences for production and trade, and also for human welfare.

Half of the 42 LDCs for which data are available have been unable to achieve per capita growth rates of more than 0.5 per cent per annum, which is far too low to have a serious effect on the extreme poverty in which about half the population of LDCs live.

Second, progress towards human development goals is very mixed. Although often slow, more progress is being made in human development dimensions that are directly affected by the quantity and quality of public services (primary education, gender equity in education and access to water) than with regard to those that are the outcome of both public services and levels of household income (hunger and child mortality).

Third, an important feature of the LDCs' situation is their economic vulnerability and, in view of this, it is unclear to what extent the recent improvement will prove to be sustainable. The effects of very high recent oil prices, for example, are not evident given the years for which data are available.

The sustainability of economic and social progress in the LDCs will ultimately depend on building up their productive base.

The sustainability of economic and social progress in the LDCs will ultimately depend on building up their productive base so that they can increasingly rely on domestic resource mobilization and private rather than official sources of external finance, and can compete in international markets without special market access preferences. The POA targets wisely have a wider reach than the MDGs, emphasizing the importance of developing productive capacities. Ultimately, the increased external resources being provided by development partners will not translate into sustained economic and social progress unless development finance for LDCs continues to be scaled up, to be complemented with more effective trade development measures and to be linked to efforts to develop domestic productive capacities. It is this last issue that will be considered in the next part of the Report.

Notes

1. For the debate on this, see Deaton (2003) and Ravallion (2001). Karshenas (2004) offers a unified view which seeks to use all the information in both household surveys and national accounts.

2. On the trade-off between increased investment and poverty reduction in LDCs, see Storm (2005).

3. This is a Programme of Action target which is not an MDG.

4. The main Millennium indicators used to track progress in this area are the following: HIV prevalence among pregnant women aged 15–24 years, condom use rate of the contraceptive prevalence rate, condom use at last high-risk sex, percentage of population aged 15-24 years with comprehensive correct knowledge of HIV/AIDS, the contraceptive prevalence rate, and the ratio of school attendance of orphans to school attendance of non-orphans aged 10–14 years. However, data for these indicators are very sparse for the group of LDCs; therefore, the indicator used for the analysis is that of the HIV prevalence rate in the population aged 15–49.

5. For discussion of the HIPC process, including the significance of the decision point and completion points, see UNCTAD (2000).

6. The overall goal on market access is more complex, as follows: "Improving preferential market access for LDCs by working towards the objective of duty-free and quota -free market access for all LDCs' products. This will apply in the markets of developed countries. Improvements in market access for LDCs should be granted on a secure and predictable basis. They should be combined with simplified rules of origin that provide transparency and predictability so as to help ensure that LDCs benefit from the market access granted, and multi-donor programmes, such as the Integrated Framework for Trade-related Technical Assistance (IF), to upgrade LDCs' production and export capacities and capabilities. Consideration should also be given to proposals for developing countries to contribute to improved market access for LDCs' exports" (United Nations, 2001: para. 68).

7. Just before UNLDC III, the EU introduced the Everything But Arms Initiative to benefit LDCs. Other developed countries followed this lead. Canada and Japan have expanded the market access preferences that they provide to the LDCs, and the United States has, through the African Growth and Opportunity Act, expanded market access preferences that it provides to a number of African countries, including LDCs. LDCs in the Asia-Pacific region continue to benefit from preferential market access to the United States under the Generalized System of Preferences, and Haiti, the only LDC in the Latin American and Caribbean region, continues to benefit from preferential market access to the United States under the Caribbean Basin Initiative. In addition, there are other developed countries and advanced developing countries that provide market access preferences for LDCs. For a discussion of the different initiatives, see UNCTAD (2003, 2004, 2005).

References

Deaton, A. (2003). Measuring poverty in a growing world (or measuring growth in a poor world), NBER Working Paper Series, Working Paper 9822, National Bureau of Economic Research, Cambridge, Mass.

Herrmann, M. (2003). Millennium Development Goals and LDC-specific development goals: An assessment of differences and recommendations towards harmonization, mimeo.

IMF/IDA (2005). Heavily Indebted Poor Countries (HIPC) Initiative: Status of implementation, prepared by the staffs of the IMF and World Bank, 19 August.

Karshenas, M. (2004). Global poverty estimates and the millennium goals: Towards a unified framework, Employment Strategy Paper No. 5, International Labour Office, Geneva.

OECD (2006). Implementing the 2001 DAC Recommendation on Untying ODA to the Least Developed Countries, 2006 Progress Report to the High Level Meeting, DCD/DAC, Paris.

Ravallion, M. (2001). Measuring aggregate welfare in developing countries: How well do national accounts and surveys agree? World Bank Policy Research Working Paper No. 2665, World Bank, Washington, DC.

Storm, S (2005). Development, trade or aid? UN views on trade, growth and poverty. *Development and Change*, 36 (6), 1239-1261.

UNAIDS (2004), *2004 Report on the Global AIDS Epidemic*, UNAIDS/04.16E Joint United Nations Programme on HIV/AIDS, Geneva.

United Nations (2000). Millennium Declaration, Resolution 55/2, General Assembly, Official Records, 55th session, Supp. No. 49. A/RES/55/49, New York.

United Nations (2001). Programme of Action for the Least Developed Countries for the Decade 2001–2010, 8 June, A/CONF.191/11.

UNCTAD (2000). *The Least Developed Countries Report 2000*, United Nations publication, sales no. E.00.II.D.21, Geneva and New York.

UNCTAD (2002). *The Least Developed Countries Report 2002*, United Nations publication, sales no. E.02.II.D.13, Geneva and New York.

UNCTAD (2003). Main recent initiatives in favour of least developed countries in the area of preferential market access: Preliminary impact assessment, TD/B/50/5, Geneva.

UNCTAD (2004). *The Least Developed Countries Report 2004*, United Nations publication, sales no. E.04.II.D.27, Geneva and New York.

UNCTAD (2005). Erosion of preferences for least developed countries: Assessment of effects and mitigation options, TD/B/52/4, Geneva.

Part Two
DEVELOPING PRODUCTIVE CAPACITIES

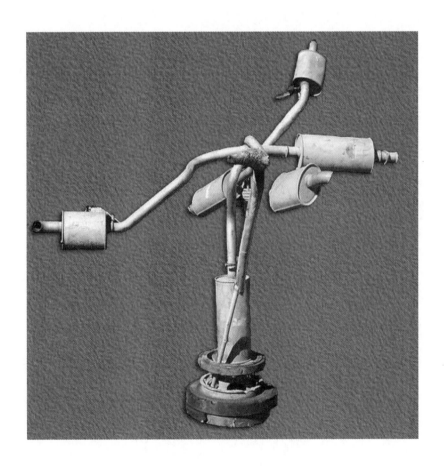

What are
Productive Capacities?
How do They Develop?
Why do They Matter?

A. Introduction

In most LDCs absolute poverty is all-pervasive. The majority of the population is living at or below income levels which are barely sufficient to meet their basic needs. UNCTAD estimates suggest that at the end of the 1990s about 50 per cent of the population living in the LDCs were living on less than a dollar a day, and that if the trends of the 1990s persist, the number of people living on less than a dollar a day in those countries can be expected to increase from 334 million in 2000 to 471 million in 2010 (UNCTAD, 2004). In theory, it would be possible to go a long way to eradicating this extreme poverty by redirecting present international aid to the LDCs into direct cash transfers provided to the population living on less than a dollar a day. But such international welfarism, even if it were feasible, is not a sustainable solution. People need to be able to make their own way in the world through their work and creativity, and to define their horizon of individual freedom through their own activity. For this to occur, productive employment opportunities must expand in the LDCs.

The population of working age within the LDCs is growing very rapidly. Between 2000 and 2010 it will increase by almost 30 per cent (UNCTAD, 2004). These people could try to seek work in other countries. Indeed, this is becoming an increasingly important source of livelihood for more and more LDC citizens. However, other countries are often reluctant to admit workers who are unskilled. Without some kind of change in the regime governing international migration and without the faster expansion of productive employment in the LDCs, the majority of new entrants into the labour force are thus faced with the stark choice between poverty at home and social exclusion abroad as illegal international migrants.

The only way to reduce poverty in the LDCs without resort to international welfarism or international migration is through the development of the productive capacities of the LDCs and the concomitant expansion of productive employment opportunities within them. The importance of developing productive capacities for economic growth and poverty reduction is evident in the development experience of developing countries which have managed to achieve sustained and substantial poverty reduction over the last 30 years. The hallmark of their policies is that they have consciously sought to promote economic growth and have done so through deliberate policies which have aimed at developing domestic productive capacities. This has involved efforts to promote investment, innovation and structural transformation (see UNCTAD, 1994, 1996, 2003; World Bank, 2005a: 80–92). Increased agricultural productivity, accelerated industrialization and building up of international competitiveness in tradable sectors have all been basic objectives which have been pursued in a step-by-step way focusing on real economy targets. This has not been undertaken as an end in itself, but with a view to improving the living standards of the population, to reducing mass poverty and, in the end, to

The only way to reduce poverty in the LDCs without resort to international welfarism or international migration is through the development of the productive capacities of the LDCs and the concomitant expansion of productive employment opportunities within them.

ensuring political stability and enhancing the effective sovereignty of the nation State.

The importance of developing productive capacities for economic growth and poverty reduction is also increasingly being recognized in international policy:

- The Brussels Programme of Action for the LDCs identifies the development of productive capacities as one of the seven major commitments and the key to ensuring that LDCs benefit from globalization rather than suffer further socio-economic marginalization (United Nations, 2001).

- UNIDO, working with NEPAD, has initiated the African Productive Capacity Initiative as the centrepiece of its approach to strengthening the productive base of African economies (UNIDO, 2003).

- In its important report *Economic Growth in the 1990s: Lessons from a Decade of Reform*, the World Bank has argued that the growth impact of reforms in the 1990s was smaller than expected because "the policy focus of the 1990s enabled better use of productive capacity but did not provide sufficient incentives for expanding capacity" and that in going forward more emphasis needs to be placed on the incentives needed to expand productive capacity and on the forces underlying economic growth (World Bank, 2005a: 10).

- ECLAC has placed productive development at the centre of its policy proposals for achieving accelerated economic growth with equity, publishing *Productive Development in Open Economies* in 2004 as the latest in a series of important reports on the subject, which began with *Changing Production Patterns with Social Equity* (1990).

- UNIDO (2005) has emphasized the importance of building technological capabilities for catching up and for sustained poverty reduction.

This Report is in a similar vein. It builds on earlier work by UNCTAD on the development dynamics of the few developing countries, mostly East Asian, which have successfully started, sustained and accelerated development (referred to above), as well as on the empirical findings and arguments of the last two LDC Reports. These two Reports analysed the nature and dynamics of poverty in LDCs (UNCTAD, 2002), and argued that the underdevelopment of productive capacities is the missing link between the expanding international trade which many LDCs have achieved in recent years and the sustained poverty reduction which remains elusive in most of them (UNCTAD, 2004). The present Report seeks to take this analysis forward in three ways:

- It describes the current status of productive capacities in LDCs and analyses how they are developing (chapters 2, 3 and 4).

- It discusses three basic constraints on the development of productive capacities in the LDCs — physical infrastructure (chapter 5), institutions (chapter 6) and the stimulus of demand (chapter 7).

- It sets out some general policy implications (chapter 8).

This analysis is intended to provide a better substantive basis for the design of international and national policies to promote economic growth and poverty reduction within the LDCs. It should also support the achievement of a key commitment of the Brussels Programme of Action for the LDCs during the decade 2001–2010, namely to develop productive capacities.

The Brussels Programme of Action for the LDCs identifies the development of productive capacities as one of the seven major commitments and the key to ensuring that LDCs benefit from globalization rather than suffer further socio-economic marginalization.

The present chapter sets out the basic conceptual framework for the Report and discusses why the subject is important for policymakers. It specifies the way in which the notion of productive capacities is defined in this Report (section B) and also the analytical framework which is used to understand how productive capacities develop (section C). Section D examines the value added for policymakers of a focus on productive capacities, both for promoting economic growth and ensuring that growth is poverty-reducing. The last section summarizes the key points of the chapter.

B. What are productive capacities?

Although the term "productive capacities" is increasingly used in international development policy circles, there is no accepted definition of what it is (see box 4).[1] This Report adopts a broad definition of productive capacities, congruent with the approach to productive capacities within the Programme of Action for the Least Developed Countries (United Nations, 2001). This focuses on both structural and supply-side constraints, and encompasses physical infrastructure, technology, enterprise development and energy, as well as specific sectoral challenges in relation to agriculture and agro-industries, manufacturing and mining, rural development and food security, and sustainable tourism. The broad approach avoids the trap of fixing on certain types of ingredients of the production process (for example, machinery and equipment, physical infrastructure, human resource development, technological capabilities) as magic bullets for economic growth and poverty reduction. It also avoids predetermining which types of economic activities (such as exports or manufacturing) should be the focal concern of policy attention in developing productive capacities. Priorities will vary according to country circumstances and the sequence of development processes.

Although the term "productive capacities" is increasingly used in international development policy circles, there is no accepted definition of what it is.

To avoid the dangers of a partial definition, this Report defines productive capacities as *the productive resources, entrepreneurial capabilities and production linkages which together determine the capacity of a country to produce goods and services and enable it to grow and develop.*

Within market economies, production is mainly affected through capable entrepreneurs mobilizing productive resources and intermediate inputs to produce outputs which can profitably meet present and expected future demand. At any given moment, the potential output of an economy is the maximum aggregate supply of goods and services that can be achieved if all productive resources and entrepreneurial capabilities are utilized efficiently and to the fullest degree. When productive capacities are underemployed or are being inefficiently utilized, it is possible for an increase in output to occur through resource reallocation or inducing a higher rate of utilization of existing resources and capabilities. However, sustained economic growth requires the expansion and development, as well as fuller utilization, of productive capacities. The potential (full-capacity) growth rate of an economy over time is defined by the growth and development of productive capacities. But this growth rate will not be achieved unless productive capacities are not only created but also used. This depends on demand-side factors, and for tradable goods and services it requires that production takes place in a competitive manner.

This Report defines productive capacities as the productive resources, entrepreneurial capabilities and production linkages which together determine the capacity of a country to produce goods and services and enable it to grow and develop.

The three basic elements of productive capacities as defined in this Report are productive resources, entrepreneurial capabilities, and production linkages (see chart 8).

BOX 4. ALTERNATIVE DEFINITIONS OF CAPACITIES AND CAPABILITIES IN RELATION TO PRODUCTION, TRADE AND DEVELOPMENT

In everyday language, the terms "capacity" and "capability" are often used interchangeably to refer to the ability to do something. In international policy discussions, these words have been linked to various phenomena, including production capabilities, supply capabilities, technological capabilities, industrial capabilities, social capabilities, productive capacities, productive capacity (in the singular), production capacity, trade capacity and supply capacity. This semantic proliferation reflects the fact that different analysts are focusing on different aspects of the problem of productive capacities. Some equate the development of productive capacities with the development of export supply capacities, others with the development of manufacturing industries. For some, productive capacity is a question of the maximum output of the physical plant, equipment and buildings which constitute a factory, or the capacity of physical infrastructure facilities on which production depends, whilst for others the focus of capacity-building is training and human resource development. Others again identify the development of productive capacities with the development of technological capabilities – the ability of enterprises to master, adapt and improve on existing technologies, as well as to design new products and processes. Yet others equate the development of productive capacities with investing in people through improvements in health, education and nutrition.

The definitions set out below, mostly taken from official documents, are intended to illustrate profusion of terminology and the range of uses of terminology related to the notion of productive capacities. They encompass some definitions which are trade-centric (that is, they equate productive capacities with export supply capacities) – for example, WTO; some which are industry-focused – for example, UNIDO; some which are focused on human capacities – for example, the Commission for Africa Report; UNDP; some which mix trade and production (NEPAD African Productive Capacity Initiative; EU/ACP Partnership Agreements); and some which are broad-based (UNLDC III POA). This Report uses a broad definition which is set out in the main text.

UNLDC III POA: "The capacity of LDCs to accelerate growth and sustainable development is impeded by various structural and supply-side constraints. Among these constraints are low productivity; insufficient financial resources; inadequate physical and social infrastructure; lack of skilled human resources; degradation of the environment; weak institutional capacities, including trade support services, in both public and private sectors; low technological capacity; lack of an enabling environment to support entrepreneurship and promote public and private partnership; and lack of access of the poor, particularly women, to productive resources and services.....A paramount objective of the actions by LDCs and their development partners should be to continue to strengthen productive capacities by overcoming structural constraints" (United Nations, 2001: 31).

NEPAD Africa Productive Capacity Initiative: "We define productive capacity as the ability, first, to produce goods that meet the quality requirements of present markets and second to upgrade in order to tap future markets. Rising productive capacity will ensure a sustainable participation in the new global production system based on production networks...Productive capacity is a function of six factors...the skill levels of workers, infrastructure, the availability of intermediate inputs, available technology, actual patterns of joint action and benchmarking practice. Other issues influence these six factors and, if dealt with positively, can enhance productive capacity" (UNIDO, 2003: 4).

UNIDO Industrial Development Report 2004: "The key to raising productivity to competitive levels lies in improving industrial capabilities. But what are industrial capabilities? They are not production capacities in the sense of physical plant, equipment and buildings; it is relatively easy to acquire or build capacity, at least if financial resources are available. Capability — the ability to operate capacity competitively — requires something more: the tacit, knowledge, skills and experience related to specific technologies that are collected by enterprises and cannot be imported or bought in. The process involves creating new skills, partly by formal education, but usually, more importantly, by training and experience of new technologies. It requires obtaining technical information, assimilating it and improving it. It entails institutional rather than individual capital, with new managerial and organizational methods, new ways of storing and disseminating information and of managing internal hierarchies. It also needs interaction between enterprises — firms do not learn on their own — and between enterprises and support institutions. Finally it requires the factor markets that provide skills, technology, finance, export marketing and infrastructure to respond to the new needs of enterprises" (UNIDO, 2004: box 1).

EU/ACP Economic Partnership Agreements: In this context, supply-side constraints have been defined as "serious constraints faced by local enterprises in producing goods competitively as a result of the developing nature of the economies of which they form a part...Effectively addressing these supply-side constraints is a fundamental challenge in promoting the structural transformation of ACP economies, so that investment is promoted, more value is added locally and more jobs and income earning opportunities are created to enable people to work their way out of poverty" (European Research Office, p.1, 2004).

WTO: "Supply-side constraints refer to impediments to the development of capacity to produce goods and services competitively and to the ability to get them to markets at a reasonable cost. Such a broad definition covers a wide scope

Box 4 (contd.)

of issues impeding the LDCs' participation in international trade. The issues range from physical infrastructure, customs, trade support services and human and institutional capacity to technological requirements, the provision of public utilities and macroeconomic frameworks…What is common among the above-mentioned supply-side issues, although different in nature, is that they raise the transaction costs for businessmen [sic] in LDCs to engage in trade. This cost comes in addition to the market barriers imposed on their products at the borders, such as tariffs, thereby reducing competitiveness in export markets… Supply-side constraints are often mentioned together with the lack of or need for export diversification. Dependence on a few commodities is a typical feature of LDCs' export profile and is closely associated with their weak supply-side capacities. Overcoming supply-side weakness is a precondition for developing and diversifying a sustainable export portfolio." (WTO, 2004: 1–3).

Commission for Africa 2005: Capacity is "The ability of individuals, organisations and societies to perform functions, solve problems and set and achieve their own objectives. In a development context, 'capacity development' refers to investment in people, institutions, and practices that will, together, enable that country to achieve its development objectives" (Commission for Africa, 2005: 389).

Fukuda-Parr et al., 2002 (UNDP): "Capacity development" is understood in this context as a process of human resource development, "a process by which individuals, groups, institutions and societies increase their abilities to (1) perform core functions, solve problems and define and achieve objectives; and (2) understand and deal with their development needs in a broad context and in a sustainable manner" (Fukuda-Parr et al., 2002).

CHART 8. THE THREE BASIC ELEMENTS OF PRODUCTIVE CAPACITIES

Productive capacities

Productive resources
- Natural resources
- Human resources
- Financial capital
- Physical capital

Entrepreneurial capabilities
- Core competencies
- Technological capabilities

Production linkages
- Backward and forward linkages
- Flows of information and exchange of experience
- Resource flows (human capital, financial capital)
- Territorial production clusters
- Global value-chains
- Links between FDI and domestic entrepreneurs
- Links between large firms and SMEs

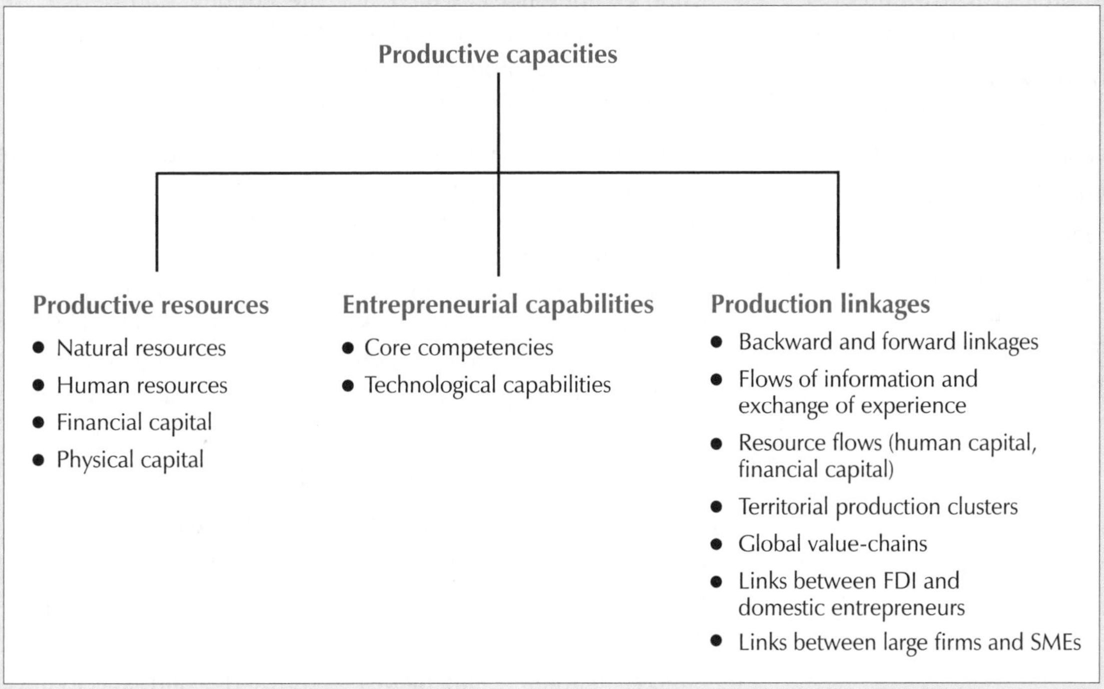

Productive resources are factors of production. They include the following:

- Natural resources, including quantity and quality of agricultural land, water resources, energy resources, mineral deposits, forestry and fishery resources, biodiversity and landscape quality;

- Human resources — the quantity and quality of labour, including the level of education, health, nutrition and skills;

- Financial capital resources — the availability and cost of financial capital to finance production, investment and innovation;

- Physical capital resources — the stock of tools, machinery and equipment available to producers, as well as the physical infrastructure which provides a range of services to producers, including transportation, power, telecommunications, water supply and sanitation, and irrigation.

The mix of factors that are used in production vary from one economic activity to another. Some of the factors of production are mobile between countries, whilst others are not.

Entrepreneurial capabilities are the skills, knowledge and information which enterprises have, firstly, to mobilize productive resources in order to transform inputs into outputs which can competitively meet present and future demand, and, secondly, to invest, to innovate, to upgrade products and their quality, and even to create markets. Capabilities, as defined in this Report, refer to an attribute of economic agents. Within the literature, entrepreneurial capabilities are sometimes defined as "firm capabilities". But this term is not appropriate within the LDC context because many enterprises are household-based and not constituted as separate legal entities independently from the household members that own and manage them.

Entrepreneurial capabilities are the skills, knowledge and information which enterprises have, firstly, to mobilize productive resources in order to transform inputs into outputs and, secondly, to invest, to innovate, to upgrade products and their quality, and even to create markets.

Entrepreneurial capabilities are a matter of knowing what to do and how to do it to produce and compete. They encompass the following:

- Core competences, which are the routine knowledge, skills and information to operate established facilities or use existing agricultural land, including production management, quality control, repair and maintenance of physical capital, and marketing;

- Technological capabilities (or dynamic capabilities), which refer to the ability to build and reconfigure competences to increase productivity, competitiveness and profitability, and to address a changing external environment in terms of supply and demand conditions. Technological capabilities have been specified in various ways (e.g. Dahlman and Westphal, 1983; Dahlman, Ross-Larsen and Pack, 1986; Amsden, 2001; Lall, 1992, 2004). A useful list, originally drawn up in UNCTAD, identifies five major kinds of technological capabilities, namely:

(a) Investment capabilities — knowledge and skills used to identify and execute projects to expand physical facilities;

(b) Incremental innovation capabilities — knowledge and skills used to continuously improve and adapt products and processes through incremental innovation, adaptive engineering and organizational adjustments;

(c) Strategic marketing capabilities — knowledge and skills to develop new markets and improve the enterprise's competitive advantage;

(d) Linkage capabilities — knowledge and skills associated with the transfer of technology within the enterprise, from one enterprise to another and between the enterprise and the domestic science and technology institutions;

(e) Radical innovation capabilities — knowledge and skill required for the creation of new technology — that is, major changes in the design and core features of products and production processes (Ernst, Ganiatos and Mytelka, 1998: 17–23).

Technological capabilities are particularly important as they are the basis for the creativity, flexibility and dynamism of an economy.

Success in the mobilization of productive resources and the exercise of entrepreneurial capabilities cannot be divorced from the wider production systems within which economic agents are embedded. Thus the third element of the productive capacities of a country is the *production linkages* between enterprises and between different types of economic activity.

Production linkages take different forms, including the following:

- Flows of goods and services, which may take the form of backward and forward linkages (which for a particular enterprise or activity refer to links with suppliers and links with buyers respectively);

- Flows of information and knowledge between enterprises, which occur through interactions with customers and suppliers as well as collaborative relations between geographically clustered enterprises;

- Flows of productive resources amongst enterprises, which may include short-term credit relations associated with sales and purchases, as well as movement of skilled workers.

Production linkages include linkages between enterprises of different sizes and linkages amongst enterprises of similar sizes (e.g. amongst SMEs), and can take the form of outsourcing and subcontracting relations. In open economies, production linkages for tradable goods can be international in their scope, with domestic enterprises linked to global value-chains (Gereffi, 1999; UNIDO, 2002: chapter 6; Kaplinsky, Morris and Readman, 2002). They also encompass linkages between foreign-owned and domestically-owned enterprises located within the country. Production linkages may also be territorially clustered. Such production clusters can be defined as "a sectoral and/or geographical concentration of enterprises engaged in the same or closely related activities with substantial and cumulative external economies of agglomeration and specialization (through the presence of producers, suppliers, specialized labour and sector specific related services) and capable of taking joint action to seek collective efficiency" (Ramos, 1998: 108).

Production linkages have been identified as being particularly important within manufacturing industries (Hirschman, 1958; Chenery, Robinson and Syrquin, 1986). However, linkages are also important for the agricultural sector, where commercial production depends on links between farmers and input suppliers and output buyers, where the availability of infrastructure services affects production and transaction costs, and where the linkages between agriculture and non-agricultural activities are critically important during the process of economic development (Fei and Ranis, 1997). The various production complementarities to which all kinds of production linkages give rise mean that the competitiveness of particular activities and individual enterprises depends not only on the productive resources and entrepreneurial capabilities within those activities and enterprises but also on the competitiveness of the production system as a whole (Porter, 1990).

Productive resources, entrepreneurial capabilities and production linkages together determine not only the overall capacity of a country to produce goods and services, but also what goods and services a country can produce. The reason for this is that productive capacities are not always generic — rather, they are often activity-specific.

Finance capital is malleable and can be allocated to different uses and activities. But once it is transformed into physical capital, in the form of a factory with physical plant, machinery and equipment producing particular goods, it is

The various production complementarities to which all kinds of production linkages give rise mean that the competitiveness of particular activities and individual enterprises depends not only on the productive resources and entrepreneurial capabilities within those activities and enterprises but also on the competitiveness of the production system as a whole.

Productive capacities are not always generic — rather, they are often activity-specific.

difficult to use that stock of capital to produce something else. A textile factory cannot be used to produce cement, and cocoa trees cannot be used to grow coffee.[2] Human capital accumulated in one domain also cannot always be applied in another domain. There are of course some levels of skill, such as literacy and numeracy, which are generic. But without training, a farm worker who is skilled in producing maize will not be able to produce shirts. Even physical infrastructure cannot be regarded as a wholly economy-wide facility. A rural road built in one locality will serve the farmers in that locality and not others.

Technological learning is also activity-specific, with different technologies requiring a different breadth of skills and knowledge. Some need a narrow range of specialization and others a broad one. Technological capabilities acquired in one activity may be applied in related and linked activities, but they are not always easily transferable. Production linkages are also to some extent activity-specific, related to the technical characteristics of products and production processes.

C. How do productive capacities develop?

For policymakers, what productive capacities are matters less than what they can become.

The productive capacities of a country constitute a potentiality for production and economic growth. As noted earlier, at any given moment, they set a ceiling to how much an economy can produce. But more important than this static potential is the dynamic potential which arises from the fact that productive resources, entrepreneurial capabilities and production linkages are not simply given but are created and transformed over time. As this occurs, the potential output of an economy increases, thus making economic growth possible.

Of course, countries do have different natural factor endowments. But natural resources have no economic value until this is perceived and realized through the application of capital and knowledge. What constitutes natural resource abundance or natural resource scarcity can be transformed by technology. Capital and knowledge accumulate through economic activity, and labour is educated, trained and developed through production experience. For policymakers, what productive capacities *are* matters less than what they can *become*.

How productive capacities develop can be conceptualized in various ways. This Report draws eclectically on the analytical insights of various theories of economic growth which are concerned with the long-term development of productive capacities (see box 5). These theories suggest that:

- The core processes through which productive capacities develop are capital accumulation, technological progress and structural change.

- The sustained development of productive capacities occurs through a process of cumulative causation in which the development of productive capacities and the growth of demand mutually reinforce each other.

- The development and utilization of productive capacities within a country are strongly influenced by the degree and form of its integration into the global economy as well as national and international institutions.

This conceptualization is illustrated schematically in chart 9.

BOX 5. ANALYTICAL FOUNDATIONS OF THE REPORT

This Report draws eclectically on the analytical insights of the following bodies of knowledge:

- The work of the first generation of development economists in the 1950s and 1960s, most notably the Lewis model of economic growth with unlimited supplies of labour (Lewis, 1954) and Albert Hirschmann (1958) on linkages. Ros (2000) provides an important formal elaboration of this work as well as a synthesis with some insights deriving from neoclassical and endogenous growth theory.

- The analyses of Kalecki (1969) and Kaldor (1967, 1981), which emphasize the importance of aggregate and intersectoral demand for economic growth, and also post-Keynesian growth models which identify the balance-of-payments constraint as a key determinant of growth rate differences between countries (see McCombie and Thirlwall, 2004).

- Various structuralist analyses of economic growth, including empirical descriptions of recurrent patterns of economic growth and structural change (Chenery, Robinson and Syrquin, 1986), the work of Latin American structuralists of the 1950s on ways in which integration into the global economy affected national development and the work of the Latin American neo-structuralists of the 1990s who have updated these ideas to take account of the policy failures which led to the collapse in the 1980s and subsequent economic reform and the weak response to economic reforms (Sunkel, 1993; Ocampo, 2005).

- Analyses based on an evolutionary approach to economic growth, which, following Schumpeter's insights, emphasize the importance of entrepreneurship and technological capabilities for economic growth — see, in particular, Nelson and Winter (1974, 1982) and much empirical analysis deriving from that approach.

These bodies of knowledge are generally neglected within current development policy analysis.[1] However, they offer a particularly fruitful terrain for analysing the development of productive capacities and also the relationship between productive capacities, economic growth and poverty reduction. Their value is also being enhanced at the present moment as analysts are seeking to synthesize the macroeconomic insights of post-Keynesian growth analysis with the microeconomic insights on technological capability-building of neo-Schumpeterian and evolutionary economics (see Llerena and Lorentz, 2004a, 2004b), and also to apply this new synthesis to understand the specific policy problems of developing countries (see Ocampo, 2005; Cimoli, 2005; Cimoli, Primi and Pugno, 2005). This work has not yet, however, been applied to illuminate development policy issues within the LDCs. This Report seeks to do so.

[1] Exceptions to this generalization are the following: (i) UNIDO's analyses of industrial development (see, in particular, UNIDO, 2005); (ii) the series of reports by ECLAC since 1990 which examine the problem of promoting productive development with social equity in open economies (see ECLAC, 2004); and (iii) UNCTAD's analyses of the policies underlying East Asian development success, notably through the animation of an investment–profits–export nexus (see UNCTAD, 1994, 1996).

CHART 9. HOW PRODUCTIVE CAPACITIES DEVELOP

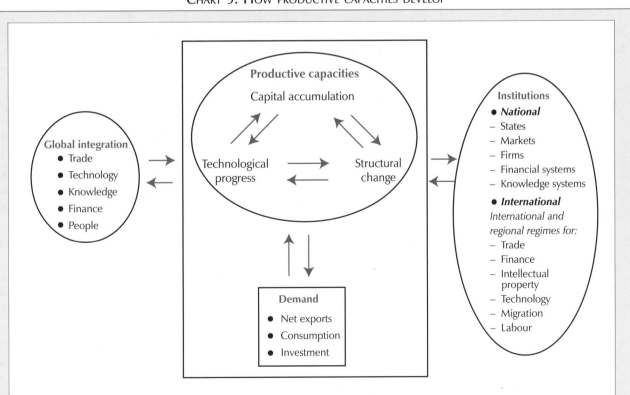

1. The core processes

Productive capacities develop within a country through three closely interrelated processes: capital accumulation, technological progress and structural change. Each of these processes is related to the three basic elements of productive capacities identified in section B. Capital accumulation is related to changes in the supply of productive resources. Technological progress is related to the development of technological capabilities. Structural change is related to changes in the types and density of the production linkages within an economy.

Capital accumulation is the process of increasing capital stocks of various kinds through investment. This involves physical capital formation, which increases stocks of plant, machinery and equipment used by firms and farms as well as supporting economic and social infrastructure facilities; human capital formation, which depends in particular on public expenditure on health and education; and the sustainable use of renewable and non-renewable environmental assets to maintain natural capital or to ensure that the expansion of produced capital is faster than the depletion of natural capital. Investment in human development, as inscribed in the targets for human well-being within the Millennium Development Goals and advocated by the UN Millennium Project (2005), is an important part of developing productive capacities. But the process of developing productive resources cannot be limited to this activity.

Technological progress is the process of introducing new goods and services, new or improved methods, equipment or skills to produce goods and services, and new and improved forms of organizing production through innovation. Innovation is the application of knowledge in production. It requires technological capabilities, which can be defined as the knowledge, experience and skills needed to introduce new products, new production processes and forms of organizing production, or to improve old ones. The development of technological capabilities can be described as a process of technological learning.

Structural change is the change in the inter- and intrasectoral composition of production, the pattern of inter- and intrasectoral linkages and the pattern of linkages amongst enterprises. There are strong empirical regularities between the increase in the potential output of an economy and changes in its production structure. This was recognized by Adam Smith, who wrote about the importance of an increasing division of labour for the wealth of nations. But increasing output per worker within an economy has historically been associated with a decline in the proportion of the labour employed in agriculture and a rise in the proportion employed in industry, particularly manufacturing, and services, together with a shift within broad sectors towards activities which use more capital and skills. There has also been a general tendency for the production linkages within a country to become denser and more "roundabout" as a higher proportion of output is sold to other producers rather than final users (Chenery, Robinson and Syrquin, 1986).

Capital accumulation, technological progress and structural change are all closely interrelated. New technologies are often embodied in machinery and equipment, and thus much innovation requires fixed capital investment (physical capital formation). Human capital formation is also necessary in order to improve the skills base, which is an essential foundation for technological learning. The potential profits associated with innovation are also a major incentive for investment, and the realization of such profits is an important

Productive capacities develop within a country through three closely interrelated processes: capital accumulation, technological progress and structural change.

Investment in human development is an important part of developing productive capacities.

source to finance further investment and innovation. Investment and innovation are also the proximate causes of structural change, a process of creative destruction in which some activities and sectors develop whilst others are destroyed.

Structural change also affects the potential for further investment and innovation. One reason for this is that not all activities have the same potential to create and develop productive capacities through investment and innovation. In short, there are dynamic products, leading sectors or "high quality" activities which are active determinants of growth momentum or, as it is put colloquially, "engines of growth". Another (related) reason is that production complementarities amongst activities, sectors and enterprises can set in train dynamic production linkage effects. These are stimuli to investment and innovation in particular sectors and enterprises which emanate from investment and innovation in other sectors and enterprises.

Dynamic activities (engines of growth) have been identified on various criteria (see, for example, Reinert, 1995). These include (i) demand characteristics, in particular whether there is a high income elasticity of demand for products; (ii) competitive environment, in particular whether markets are imperfectly competitive (and therefore can yield high profits) or perfectly competitive; and (iii) potential for technological progress and the development of a dynamic investment–profits nexus. But an important basic feature which differentiates more dynamic from less dynamic activities is whether they are subject to increasing returns or diminishing returns (Reinert, 2004). In diminishing returns activities, as labour is added to a fixed factor (such as land in the case of agriculture), the added output of each additional worker falls. In increasing returns activities, labour productivity and per capita income rise as output and employment expands, whilst in diminishing returns activities they fall. Mechanisms through which increasing returns occur include: economies of scale or scope, in which unit costs decrease with increases in the scale of production; learning-by-doing, in which productivity increases according to cumulative production experience; productivity growth based on an increasing division of labour and specialization; and strong dynamic linkage effects.

Dynamic production linkage effects occur through demand-side relationships and supply-side relationships. On the demand side, the multiplier effects of export growth depend very much on domestic production linkages. They are very small if the export sector operates as an enclave and also if there are high propensities to import. The supply-side effects of production complementarities work through a range of mechanisms, including the positive externalities that different economic agents generate among themselves through cost reductions made possible by economies of scale in production or lower transport and transaction costs (economies of agglomeration), or through the induced provision of more specialized inputs or services (economies of specialization), or through the externalities generated by the sharing of knowledge and the development of human capital that can move among firms (technological or knowledge spillovers) (Ocampo, 2005: 18).

The fact that economic activities are not all alike in their potential for further development of productive capacities and that there are dynamic inducement effects associated with production linkages has the important corollary that production structure is not simply a passive outcome of the growth process, but rather an active determinant of growth potential. This is why structural transformation, which itself reflects the past path of development of productive capacities within an economy, is so important for the future potential

The fact that economic activities are not all alike in their potential for further development of productive capacities and that there are dynamic inducement effects associated with production linkages has the important corollary that production structure is not simply a passive outcome of the growth process, but rather an active determinant of growth potential.

development of productive capacities. However, the existence of qualitative difference amongst activities creates difficult policy challenges for Governments. In essence, the dilemma they must address is how to promote structural transformation and thus harness the potential positive growth effects of dynamic activities without falling into the multiple traps of "picking winners".

2. CUMULATIVE CAUSATION, DEMAND AND THE DEVELOPMENT OF PRODUCTIVE CAPACITIES

Capital accumulation, technological progress and structural change are cumulative processes in which investment, innovation and the production structure at one point in time create the conditions for further investment, innovation and structural change. Within capitalist forms of production, business profits are the major incentive for investment, and at the same time profits are an important source for financing investment as well as an outcome of investment. Capital accumulation accelerates if there is a strong investment–profits nexus in which businesses constantly reinvest in order to increase profits and investment. Technological learning is similarly cumulative and path-dependent, with earlier knowledge, skills and experience providing the basis for the emergence of new capabilities. But these processes will not occur automatically by themselves or continue in some mechanical fashion for ever. The sustained development of productive capacities occurs when there is a virtuous process of cumulative causation in which the development of productive capacities and the growth of demand mutually reinforce each other (Myrdal, 1957; Kaldor, 1967, 1981; Hirschman, 1958).

The sustained development of productive capacities occurs when there is a virtuous process of cumulative causation in which the development of productive capacities and the growth of demand mutually reinforce each other.

The importance of demand in the development of productive capacities reflects the fact that productive capacities create only a potentiality for production and growth. At any point in time, existing productive capacities set a ceiling to actual output. But the existence of that ceiling does not mean that existing productive capacities will be fully utilized. Whether the potential inherent in any given set of productive capacities is realized or not depends on demand-side factors. This is an obvious point which can be easily conceptualized once it is realized that there is a difference between the creation of new productive capacities and their utilization, and that decisions to create productive capacities through investment and innovation are based on profit expectations and hence demand expectations. But it requires rejection of the mainstream assumptions that savings automatically creates investment, that productive resources are invariably fully employed and that demand adjusts passively to accommodate supply (see León-Ledesma and Thirlwall, 2002).

Introducing demand into the picture does not mean that there are no supply constraints. In fact, as indicated earlier, at any point in time supply constraints set a ceiling to actual output. But both the level of utilization of productive capacities and their development over time must also take account of demand constraints and the growth of demand.

Demand growth originates from three sources: domestic consumption, domestic investment and net exports (i.e. exports minus imports). Exports are a particularly important component of demand for two reasons. Firstly, whereas both consumption demand and investment demand depend on national income, export demand is autonomously determined. Secondly, both consumption demand and investment demand have an import component and without export earnings, domestic demand will have to be constrained to ensure balance-of-payments equilibrium (Thirlwall, 2002: 53). Within poor countries, exports are even more important as the underdevelopment of their production structures means that they have to import most intermediate inputs and capital goods. But the importance of exports does not mean that domestic sources of demand can be neglected in a growth process. Michael Porter, in his business-focused analysis of international competitiveness; identifies *home demand* conditions as one of the four basic determinants of international competitiveness in particular industries (Porter, 1990: 86–100). Classic work identifying recurrent patterns of economic development also has found that in small countries at early stages of development, domestic demand growth is typically the source of over 75 per cent of economic growth (Chenery, Robinson and Syrquin, 1986).

The way in which the development of productive capacities and the growth of demand can be linked in a virtuous circle of cumulative causation is shown in simplified form in chart 10. In that chart, increased productive capacities are associated with an increase in average productivity. Growth of productivity has three basic causal links to growth of demand. Firstly, it can increase competitiveness and thus net exports. Secondly, it can increase profits, which stimulate investment — the second component of demand — which in itself can lead to further increases in productivity. Thirdly, it increases real wages and also real incomes within household enterprises (both smallholder farms and urban informal-sector enterprises). This increases consumption, which may also be supplemented by use of profits for consumption, although this will reduce the intensity of the link between profits and investment. A further possible causal link (which is left out of the chart) is through the increased fiscal space which

Exports are a particularly important component of demand, but the importance of exports does not mean that domestic sources of demand can be neglected in a growth process.

CHART **10.** LINKS BETWEEN THE DEVELOPMENT OF PRODUCTIVE CAPACITIES AND GROWTH OF DEMAND

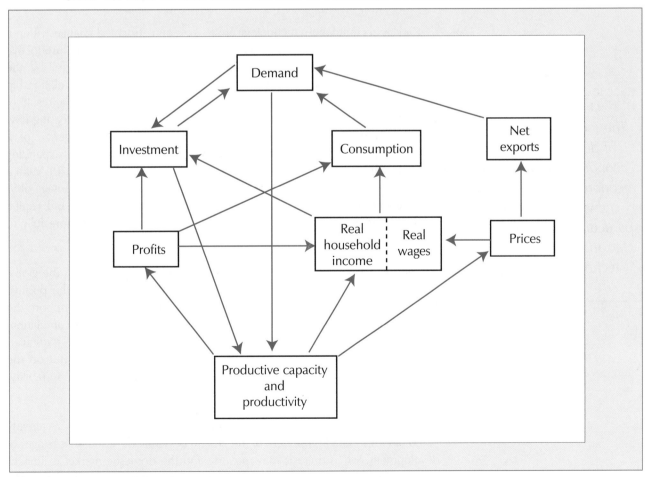

Source: Based on Castellacci (2001).

Governments can achieve through the expansion of the productive base and productivity. This enables increased public investment, which can be important for crowding in private investment, as well as increased government consumption expenditure, which can also help to improve the living standards of the population and further encourage the growth of consumption.

Whilst the growth of productivity stimulates the growth of demand, the growth of demand, in turn, stimulates the development of productive capacities and productivity growth. This occurs most simply through the full utilization of productive capacities and the incentives for investment and innovation which growing demand creates. But in addition to this there are possibilities for various increasing returns to scale as market demand expands, as well as the dynamic production linkage effects discussed earlier.

Sustaining a positive process of cumulative causation between the development of productive capacities and the growth of demand creates difficult dilemmas. Within more advanced economies, the central issue has been the division of value added between profits, which animate investment demand, and wages, which animate private consumption. Within poor developing economies which have an industrial sector but where the major part of the population is still engaged in agriculture, the central issue has been the problem of mobilizing savings from the agricultural sector without undermining incentives for expanded agricultural production and without squeezing the domestic demand for industrial output, which must, of necessity, come primarily from agricultural household incomes.

3. The importance of global integration

Capital accumulation, technological progress and structural change within a country, as well as the relationship between the development of productive capacities and the growth of demand, are all strongly influenced by the relationship of the country with the rest of the world.

Capital accumulation, technological progress and structural change within a country, as well as the relationship between the development of productive capacities and the growth of demand, are all strongly influenced by the relationship of the country with the rest of the world. This external relationship has become increasingly important over the last thirty years as a result of globalization and liberalization. Globalization has involved "an increasing flow of goods and resources across national borders and the emergence of a complementary set of organizational structures to manage the expanding network of international activity and transactions" (UNCTAD, 1997: 70). With a view to becoming part of this process and also in order to take advantage of it, Governments have at the same time undertaken increasing trade and capital account liberalization. This has opened their national economies more fully to the influence of external factors.

The increasing integration of developing national economies into the global economy has brought both new opportunities, in particular, enhanced access to markets, knowledge, technology and capital.

The increasing integration of developing national economies into the global economy has brought both new opportunities and new risks. On the positive side, there are various ways in which global integration can support the development of productive capacities through capital accumulation, technological progress and structural change. These include, in particular, enhanced access to markets, knowledge, technology and capital. But on the negative side, globalization has been associated with increasing instability, exclusion and inequality.

Focusing on the positive side, exporting to international markets is, as already noted, an important component of the growth of demand. At the initial stages of development, when there is mass poverty and the domestic market is limited, exporting enables natural resources and labour resources, hitherto underutilized owing to domestic demand constraints, to be productively mobilized. With a progressive upgrading of export composition towards more knowledge-, skill- and capital-intensive products, together with strong domestic production linkages effects associated with export activities, exporting can also accelerate a process of structural change which increases the overall productivity of an economy. There is the possibility of a virtuous circle in which fast export growth leads to fast output growth; fast output growth leads to fast productivity growth (through the increasing returns mechanisms discussed earlier); and fast productivity growth leads to increased competitiveness.

Enhanced access to knowledge and modern technologies already being used in other countries can also enable latecomer economies to achieve significant productivity increases without having to reinvent continually. This is particularly important for very poor countries because the potential for technological progress is actually greatest in the countries which are furthest behind the technological frontier. Exporting can facilitate the acquisition of modern technologies through links with buyers and also because a major channel for technology transfer to developing countries, particularly the poorest ones, is through imports of machinery and equipment. Foreign direct investment can also serve as an important channel of technology acquisition under the right circumstances.

Enhanced access to foreign capital can also boost capital accumulation. This is particularly important in very poor countries which are trapped in a vicious circle in which low levels of domestic investment are associated with low productivity and low domestic savings. In these circumstances, access to foreign savings can play a catalytic role in starting a virtuous circle of economic growth and domestic resource mobilization. Once this has been started, foreign capital can also permit a faster rate of growth of private consumption and poverty reduction without the degree of belt-tightening which would be necessary if the national economy was closed and thus economic growth was thus wholly financed out of domestic savings. Foreign direct investment can be a particularly important source of foreign capital as it comes bundled with important entrepreneurial capabilities.

Although the opportunities provided by globalization and liberalization are sizable and significant, it has become increasingly clear since the mid-1990s that there are also significant risks associated with these processes.

Although the opportunities provided by globalization and liberalization are sizable and significant, it has become increasingly clear since the mid-1990s that there are also significant risks associated with these processes.

In this regard, financial globalization has been associated with the increasing instability of economic growth in a number of countries as a result of the intense boom-and-bust cycles associated with surges of short-term capital inflows followed by surges of short-term capital outflows (UNCTAD, 2003: figure 4.2). In these cases, the associated volatility in exchange rates and macroeconomic instability have seriously reduced domestic capital accumulation and also led Governments to keep increasing volumes of resources tied up in foreign exchange reserves designed to prevent speculation. However, the poorest countries have not experienced the kind of hot surges and sudden withdrawals that have characterized emerging market economies in Latin America and East Asia. For them the problem has been their effective exclusion from international capital markets and the concomitant need to rely heavily on official resource inflows as a source of foreign savings.

Globalization has also been a very uneven process in which very poor countries, in particular, have experienced marginalization (World Bank, 2002; Sachs, 2000; Ghose, 2003). With the globalization of competition, the minimum requirements in terms of capital resources, sophisticated technology and human skills for competing in more open and sophisticated markets have risen for some products. Even in basic commodity markets, buyers within commodity chains have upgraded their volume, reliability and quality criteria for purchasing, and these more stringent market requirements have called for ever larger investments to enter or stay in markets (Gibbon, 2001). The globalization of production systems, in which different stages of the production process are located in different countries, has also been associated with different countries playing different roles in a hierarchical production system which is split into different activities with different levels of technological sophistication and different potentials for dynamic learning through technology spillovers. Countries may thus get locked in to a particular level of technological sophistication, depending on their position in the hierarchical production network (Henderson, 1989).

Globalization has also been a very uneven process in which very poor countries, in particular, have experienced marginalization.

It has also been shown that the uneven nature of globalization processes has been associated with increasing inter-country inequality, as well as a widening gap between the richest and poorest countries (Svedberg, 2004; Milanovic, 2005). Exclusion from global markets, technology and capital has also not been total but rather associated with partial incorporation. Within many countries, there has been an increasing momentum towards a dualistic production structure in which productivity improves in a few enterprises and activities which are effectively linked to the rest of the world, but these enterprises and activities have few links with the domestic economy (Cimoli, Primi and Pugno, 2005). This is a particular problem within very poor countries, where export sectors, for example in large-scale commercial farms, mines, tourism and labour-intensive manufacturing located within an export-processing zone, function as economic enclaves (UNCTAD, 2004). As inequality increases within countries and economic opportunities are insufficient to meet the needs of the educated population, there has been an increasing brain drain, which further diminishes the human capacity to take advantage of the manifold opportunities which globalization could bring.

Within many countries, there has been an increasing momentum towards a dualistic production structure in which productivity improves in a few enterprises and activities which are effectively linked to the rest of the world, but these enterprises and activities have few links with the domestic economy.

4. THE IMPORTANCE OF INSTITUTIONS

The balance between the opportunities and the risks that globalization brings in relation to the development of productive capacities depends to a large extent on the policies which a country adopts to manage the integration of the national economy with the global economy, as well as the nature of national and international institutions. The term "institutions" will be understood here to refer, using a distinction made by Douglas North (1990), to both the institutional environment (the set of political, social and legal ground rules that establish the basis for production, exchange and distribution – for example, systems of property rights) and institutional arrangements (regular relationships amongst economic agents which govern the way in which they cooperate and compete). The latter can be formalized through the establishment of organizations (such as firms) or entail looser relationships governed by informal rules and recurrent relationships.

The national institutions which matter for the development of productive capacities are various. They encompass, for example, the social values which govern attitudes towards capital accumulation and technological progress that are embodied in diverse cultures, as well as the household and wider gender institutions which govern how the social relations of production are integrated with the social relations of reproduction. But within this Report the focus will be upon economic institutions, in particular the following:

- Markets — the degree of development or underdevelopment of product and factor markets, as well as their degree of competitiveness;

- States — which (i) govern the background rules for market exchange, provide the physical infrastructure and other public goods, including macroeconomic stability, required for a modern market economy; (ii) support the development of entrepreneurial capabilities and also coordination mechanisms required to ensure joint commitment amongst linked economic agents and activities, and (iii) affect the availability and cost of various productive resources, including finance capital, human capital and natural resources;

- Firms — which are the basic locus of investment and innovation and necessary institutions to realize the creative potential of the market;

- Non-market coordinating mechanisms (such as business associations) associated with production linkages, including between economic agents or activities whose production is already interlinked or can be potentially interlinked;

- Financial systems — which are critical for realizing potentially profitable investment opportunities and processes of capital accumulation;

- Knowledge systems — the set of institutions which enable or constrain processes of technological learning and the development of capabilities which underlie innovation.

For rapid capital accumulation and technological progress the nature of the relationship between the entrepreneurial class and the State is very important. But this is a question of the nature of the private sector as much as it is of the nature of good governance. In very poor countries in particular, the problem is that markets are underdeveloped and there are very few firms. In this situation the policy challenge is not to get the Government out of the way on the assumption that a capitalist market economy is already in existence and that the problem is to make it work better by removing excessive government regulation. The policy challenge is to create markets.[3]

With globalization and liberalization, international institutions also matter for capital accumulation, technological progress and structural changes within countries. Critically important are the international regimes governing private capital flows and aid, technology transfer and intellectual property rights, and international migration, both globally and regionally. The nature of these international regimes has an important role to play in enhancing the opportunities provided by globalization and reducing its risks. They are generally characterized by asymmetries which constrain and enable different countries to a different extent. These asymmetries are a result of the relative power of different States to ensure that the interests of the economic groups which they represent are reflected within them. Improving both national and international institutions is an important policy pressure point to promote the development of productive capacities within LDCs.

For rapid capital accumulation and technological progress the nature of the relationship between the entrepreneurial class and the State is very important. But this is a question of the nature of the private sector as much as it is of the nature of good governance.

With globalization and liberalization, international institutions also matter. Critically important are the international regimes governing private capital flows and aid, technology transfer and intellectual property rights, and international migration, both globally and regionally.

D. The value added for policymakers of a focus on productive capacities

There are two general reasons why the focus on productive capacities is important for policymakers:

- Firstly, it provides a better understanding of how to promote economic growth — how to start it, to sustain it and to accelerate it.

- Secondly, it provides a better understanding of the links between economic growth and poverty reduction, why some forms of economic growth are more poverty-reducing than others, and thus how to ensure that economic growth supports the objective of poverty reduction.

1. PRODUCTIVE CAPACITIES AND ECONOMIC GROWTH

The focus on productive capacities provides a better understanding of economic growth because the expansion, development and utilization of productive capacities are at the heart of processes of economic growth. This is implicitly recognized by both neoclassical and endogenous growth theories which analyse growth using an aggregate production function which expresses the relationship between aggregate output on the one hand and stocks of factor inputs (productive resources in our terminology) and their productivity on the other hand. However, these bodies of knowledge generally do not use the notion of "productive capacities". The term "productive capacities" is explicitly used, rather, within various theories of economic growth which are currently neglected in development policy analysis. These theories are those already introduced above, which in this Report provide the basis for understanding how productive capacities develop (see box 5). They go beyond the identification of the relative importance of supply-side ingredients of economic growth and seek to get behind the abstract aggregates of the neoclassical growth models — capital (K), labour (L) and total factor productivity. By focusing on the reality of production they lead to a different understanding of growth processes from that provided by the mainstream models, which can help policymakers, particularly in poor countries, gain a better view of how to start, sustain and accelerate economic growth.

The recognition that supply-side constraints are a matter of both supply conditions and demand conditions can lead to much improved policy.

One important insight which can be derived from these theories is that both supply-side and demand-side factors are important in the analysis of economic growth. This makes it possible to explain what animates capital accumulation, innovation and structural change. The recognition that "supply-side constraints" are a matter of both supply conditions and demand conditions can lead to much improved policy. Within very poor countries which are highly aid-dependent, it shifts attention from promoting an illusory supply-side aid fix (for example, to remedy deficient infrastructure) to considering how relaxing supply-side constraints can be part of a process of reinforcing domestic processes of economic growth founded on the interaction between the development of productive capacities and the growth of demand.

A second key insight for policymakers that can be derived from these theories is that productive capacities are not wholly generic but rather also activity-specific and enterprise-specific. From this perspective, the growing economy is not seen as an "inflating balloon" (as Ocampo, 2005, has vividly put it) in which increasing supplies of factors of production and a steady flow of technological progress smoothly increase aggregate GDP. Rather than being an outcome of economy-wide processes, economic growth is understood as being affected by the sectoral composition of the economy, as well as by the interactions between macro-processes, structural dynamics and the exercise of entrepreneurship at the micro-level.

A third important insight is that growing economies do not necessarily follow a steady-state growth rate in which productive resources are always fully utilized and there is full employment. Rather, the possibility of underutilization of resources and a gap between the potential (full-capacity) growth rate and the actual growth rate are recognized. This leads to a more complete analysis of growth processes which includes the role of demand as well as supply, as indicated above. Moreover, it facilitates analysis of the links between growth and poverty in all situations where underemployment of labour are central causes of poverty. Within most developing countries, and particularly in the least developed countries, this issue is the heart of the matter.

The development of productive capacities is an evolutionary process in which certain prerequisites have to be in place before other developments can take place.

Fourthly, a further insight from these growth theories is that the development of productive capacities is a cumulative, step-by-step process in which what is possible at any given moment depends on the past path and current state of development. This idea (which some economists call "path dependence") is intuitively quite obvious, but it is quite different from the assumption that the economy is always in, or rapidly moving towards, equilibrium. The step-by-step view of the growth process is important for the policymaker because it implies that sequencing issues are central to development strategies and the development of productive capacities is an evolutionary process in which certain prerequisites have to be in place before other developments can take place.

2. PRODUCTIVE CAPACITIES AND POVERTY REDUCTION

The focus on productive capacities provides a better understanding of poverty reduction firstly because economic growth is a necessary condition for the reduction of poverty. But the focus on productive capacities can also provide a better understanding of the extent to which economic growth is poverty-reducing. For many developing countries the extent to which improved economic growth performance is failing to lead to improved human well-being for poorer citizens has become a major concern. It is this concern which has led to the propagation of the notion of "pro-poor growth" as an important policy objective (World Bank, 2005b). But what pro-poor growth means is highly contested and how to achieve it remain elusive (see box 6). A focus on productive capacities can illuminate this issue.

For many developing countries the extent to which improved economic growth performance is failing to lead to improved human well-being for poorer citizens has become a major concern.

Chart 11 is a schematic representation of the key links between economic growth, productive capacities and poverty reduction. On the left-hand side of the chart, there is the virtuous circle between the development of productive capacities and economic growth. On the one hand, economic growth provides a demand-side stimulus for the development and fuller utilization of productive capacities. On the other hand, the development of productive capacities releases supply-side constraints, thus enabling faster growth. But on the right-hand side of the chart, there are further feedback loops between the development and utilization of productive capacities on the one hand, and poverty reduction on the other hand, and vice versa.

The development of productive capacities can lead to poverty reduction through three major mechanisms. Firstly, it enables the progressive absorption of the unemployed and underemployed into expanding economic activities with higher productivity (Islam, 2004). As productivity increases, earnings can also

Box 6. Productive capacities, pro-poor growth and inclusive development

The notion of pro-poor growth has become pivotally important within the design of poverty reduction strategies. It promises a way of getting beyond the limits of a microeconomic approach to poverty analysis divorced from the macroeconomic setting on the one hand and an over-simplistic view that growth is always and invariably good for the poor on the other hand.

The microeconomic approach to poverty analysis adopts the household as the basic unit of analysis, divides the population into poor and non-poor on the basis of a chosen income or consumption poverty line, and then focuses on the characteristics which distinguish the poor from the non-poor. These correlates of poverty (which may include such factors as food production as the major occupation, illiteracy, living in a female-headed household and living in a remote location) can then be seen as causes of poverty and as factors which policy must seek to address. But the problem is that such micro-analysis is divorced from the broader macroeconomic context. The efficacy of policies based on such observed relationships depends on whether or not relationships in aggregate are the same as those observed at the individual level.

Linking such poverty diagnoses to the macro-context is a difficult task and thus analyses of the causes of poverty have turned to the other end of the problem by focusing on the links between economic growth and poverty reduction. However, the bold assertion that "economic growth is good for the poor" has not proved to be robust. The notion of pro-poor growth recognizes that economic growth is a necessary but not sufficient condition for poverty reduction and seeks to identify the conditions and policies under which economic growth is more poverty-reducing or less poverty-reducing.

There is, however, no agreement on what pro-poor growth actually is (see Kraay, 2005; Ravallion, 2004; World Bank, 2005b). Some argue that any economic growth which reduces poverty is pro-poor growth. Others suggest that economic growth is pro-poor if the income share of the poor increases. In this formulation, pro-poor growth is a particular type of inequality-reducing growth. Others suggest that economic growth is pro-poor if the rate of income growth of the poor accelerates. This can occur with increasing inequality (and falling income shares of the poor) if the income growth of the poor accelerates more slowly than the income growth of the non-poor.

A common feature of these three definitions of pro-poor growth is that they are founded on a statistical approach to poverty analysis which is based on the statistical relationships between economic growth, income inequality and poverty. From a statistical point of view, the strength of the impact of economic growth on poverty reduction can certainly be "explained" in terms of the arithmetic relationships between rising average incomes and changes in income distribution (Bourguignon, 2003). But empirical work on pro-poor growth shows that to get behind these statistical relationships it is necessary to consider the dynamics of production structures, the nature of technological choices, the level of utilization of productive resources, in particular unemployment and underemployment of labour, and patterns of productive growth and access to productive assets (World Bank, 2005b). In short, the growth–poverty relationship is endogenous to the growth process and depends on the way in which productive capacities expand, develop and are utilized.

It is possible to get a different view of the relationship between economic growth and poverty reduction by shifting from a statistical approach to poverty analysis to what Graham Pyatt has called a "structuralist approach to poverty analysis" (Pyatt, 2001). Such an approach, as elaborated by Pyatt, is founded on the view that household living standards are primarily based on the generation and sustainability of jobs and livelihoods. The starting point for poverty analysis should thus be an analysis of how people make a living, which in turn depends on the structure of the economy and its relationships with the rest of the world (for an extended discussion see UNCTAD, 2002: box 16, p. 192). Islam (2004) has also argued that pro-poor growth should be seen as a process in which economic growth, development of productive capacities and expansion of productive employment opportunities reinforce each other in a cumulative virtuous circle.

The present Report adopts a structuralist approach to poverty analysis (in Pyatt's sense) and argues that the development and utilization of productive capacities are at the heart of processes of poverty reduction. This is what pro-poor growth should be about. But given the ambiguities surrounding that term, this Report, like earlier LDC Reports, prefers to speak of "inclusive development" to describe an economic growth process which is broad-based and socially inclusive.

CHART 11. THE RELATIONSHIP BETWEEN ECONOMIC GROWTH, PRODUCTIVE CAPACITIES AND POVERTY REDUCTION

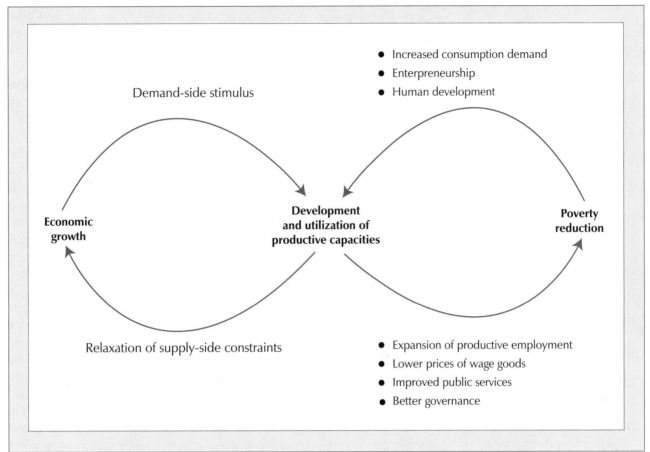

rise, although in conditions where there is surplus labour the key effect will occur through the expansion of employment opportunities rather than rising real wage rates. The extent to which the development and fuller utilization of productive capacities will lead to poverty reduction depends on the employment potential of this change, in terms of the number of new employment opportunities and the increase in labour productivity, as well as the extent to which the poor are able to integrate into the growth process by getting access to the new jobs and livelihoods. Secondly, the development of productive capacities can lead to the lowering of the prices of wage goods, particularly food prices, and the reduction in instability in those prices. This is an important mechanism for raising real incomes and poverty reduction. Thirdly, the strengthening of the productive base of an economy can enable increased government revenue. This allows improved public services and also better governance, both of which further support poverty reduction.

The link between productive capacities and good governance is important as good governance is essential for wealth creation, poverty reduction and political stability. There are certainly instances of inadequate governance which arise from rapacious leadership in very poor countries. But as well as bad volition, lack of financial resources and lack of capacity, which are partly due to lack of financial resources, are key sources of inadequate governance (UN Millennium Project, 2005). How is it possible, for example, to have financial accountability when government cannot attract competent accountants owing to low salaries? Good governance requires a competent and adequately paid civil service, judiciary and police force; adequate communication and information technology; equipment and training for a reliable police force; and modern technological capabilities for customs authorities to secure borders. In countries with weak productive capacities and a low GDP per capita, governance is likely

Developing productive capacities is essential for increasing the fiscal space which is essential for improving governance.

to be constantly underfunded and it will be difficult to provide the services expected of a modern State in a globalizing world. Developing productive capacities is essential for increasing the fiscal space which is essential for improving governance.

Through these mechanisms the development of productive capacities supports poverty reduction. But as chart 11 shows, poverty reduction in turn supports the development and utilization of productive capacities. Firstly, higher incomes and earnings allow poor people to spend more on education, health, nutrition and skills formation (Islam, 2004). Secondly, poverty reduction increases consumption demand and thus acts as a stimulus to the full utilization and further development of productive capacities. This effect of poverty reduction is not so relevant within economies where poverty is a phenomenon which affects a minority of the population. But where there is mass poverty, rising real incomes of the poor is a major channel of expansion of aggregate demand. As the chart shows, this depends on employment expansion with rising productivity. Thirdly, poverty reduction acts to promote productive entrepreneurship.

This feedback loop exists because people living at a bare subsistence minimum cannot take entrepreneurial risks because it is a matter of life and death for them. Instead they have to focus on low-risk activities which are at the same time low-return activities. These may involve, for example, avoiding price fluctuations in markets by sticking to a certain level of subsistence food production or reducing risk by getting involved in multiple, low-productivity livelihoods without specializing. All-pervasive and life-threatening insecurity also adversely affects entrepreneurship as it leads to short-termism and can reinforce the predatory behaviour which is associated with unproductive entrepreneurship.

The virtuous circle between the development of productive capacities and poverty reduction can reinforce the virtuous circle between the development of productive capacities and economic growth.

Thus the virtuous circle between the development of productive capacities and poverty reduction can reinforce the virtuous circle between the development of productive capacities and economic growth. It must be stressed that this is not likely to be a straightforward, uninterrupted or conflict-free process. There can be, for example, a trade-off between employment expansion and productivity growth. For example, it would be possible to build an irrigation ditch with crude tools employing many people working at low labour productivity with very low remuneration or with machines working at high labour productivity. For any given rate of economic growth, the higher the rate of labour productivity growth, the lower the rate of growth of employment. Moreover, there is a trade-off between increases in consumer demand and increase in household savings. But the chart identifies the major channels through which the development and utilization of productive capacities support a process of pro-poor growth and inclusive development.

Ideally, policymakers should seek to start, sustain and accelerate a cumulative process in which the development of productive capacities, based on investment, innovation and structural change, and the growth of demand mutually reinforce each other. Inclusive development (or pro-poor growth) will be achieved if this is done in such a way that productive employment expands, prices of wage goods fall and fiscal space is expanded. Poverty reduction will in turn reinforce the development of productive capacities through its impact on human development, entrepreneurship and consumption demand. This will in turn reinforce economic growth.

F. Conclusions

This chapter has four basic messages.

Firstly, although the term "productive capacities" is increasingly used in development policy discussions, there is no accepted definition of what it is. Rather, there is a profusion of overlapping concepts. This Report adopts a broad approach to defining productive capacities. This does not limit it to certain types of ingredients of production (for example, physical infrastructure or human resources) or to certain types of economic activity (such as exports or manufactures). Productive capacities are defined as the productive resources, entrepreneurial capabilities and production linkages which together determine the capacity of a country to produce goods and services and enable it to grow and develop.

Secondly, as with the definition of the term, there is no accepted approach to analysing how productive capacities develop. This Report adopts an eclectic analytical framework based on the insights of various theories of economic growth which are currently neglected within development policy. These theories emphasize the importance for economic growth of technological capabilities, entrepreneurship and the dynamics of production structures, and they also view economic growth as a cumulative process based on the interaction between supply-side and demand-side factors.

Thirdly, drawing on these theories, this Report suggests that:

- The core processes through which productive capacities develop are capital accumulation, technological progress and structural change;

- The sustained development of productive capacities occurs through a process of cumulative causation in which the development of productive capacities and the growth of demand mutually reinforce each other;

- The development and utilization of productive capacities within a country are strongly influenced by the degree and form of its integration into the global economy as well as by national and international institutions.

Fourthly, by focusing on the promotion of economic growth through the development and full utilization of productive capacities, policymakers in LDCs can design more effective poverty reduction strategies and their development partners can provide more effective international support for LDCs. The focus on productive capacities will not only help policymakers to start, sustain and accelerate economic growth, but also ensure that economic growth is more poverty-reducing.

This requires a better understanding of the current status of productive capacities within the LDCs, of how they are developing (or not) and of key constraints on the development of productive capacities. The main body of this Report undertakes this analysis, whilst the final chapter draws some general policy implications for the LDCs and their development partners.

By focusing on the promotion of economic growth through the development and full utilization of productive capacities, policymakers in LDCs can design more effective poverty reduction strategies and their development partners can provide more effective international support for LDCs.

Notes

1. King and Palmer (2005) provide an extended discussion of the use of the term "capacity" in international cooperation.
2. This has important implications for the role of investment in achieving effective structural adjustment. See Griffin (2005).
3. This is at the heart of the analysis of economic reforms in the 1990s by Japanese economists — see notably Ishikawa (1998) and Ohno (1998), as well as their alternative paradigm, the Economic Systems Approach, which seeks to promote, in a unified way, the development of productive capacities (human resources, equipment, technology), the enhancement of organizations and institutions, and structural change (composition of output and allocation of resources) (Yanagihara, 1997: 11).

References

Amsden, A. (2001). *The Rise of "the Rest": Challenges to the West from Late-Industrializing Economies*. Oxford University Press, Oxford.

Bourguignon, F. (2003). The growth elasticity of poverty reduction: Explaining heterogeneity across countries and time periods. In Eicher, T. and Turnovski, S. (eds.), *Inequality and Growth: Theory and Policy Implications*, Cambridge, Mass., MIT Press.

Castellacci, F. (2001). A "technology gap approach to cumulative growth": Toward an integrated model. Empirical evidence for Spain, 1960–1997. Paper presented at the Druid Academy Winter Conference, Copenhagen, 18–20 January 2001.

Chenery, H., Robinson, S. and Syrquin, M. (1986). *Industrialization and Growth: A Comparative Study*. World Bank, Washington DC.

Cimoli, M. (2005). Trade openness and technology gaps in Latin America: A low-growth trap. In: Ocampo, J.A. (ed.), *Beyond Reforms: Structural Dynamics and Macroeconomic Vulnerability*, Stanford Economics and Finance, Stanford Universty Press and the World Bank, Washington DC.

Cimoli, M., Primi, A. and Pugno, M. (2005). An enclave-led model of growth: The structural problem of informality persistence in Latin America. Paper presented at the GRADE Workshop "A Micro Approach to Poverty Analysis", University of Trento, Italy, February 2005.

Commission for Africa (2005). *Our Common Interest*. Report of the Commission for Africa, March 2005.

Dahlman, C. and Westphal, L.E. (1983). The transfer of technology – issues in the acquisition of technological capability by developing countries. *Finance and Development*, December.

Dahlman, C., Ross Larsen, B. and Westphal L.E. (1987). Managing technological development: Lessons from newly industrializing countries, *World Development*, 15 (6): 759–775.

ECLAC (1990). *Changing Production Patterns with Social Equity*. Economic Commission for Latin America and the Caribbean, Santiago, Chile. Sales No. E.90.II.G.6.

ECLAC (2004). *Productive Development in Open Economies*. Thirtieth Session of Economic Commission for Latin America and the Caribbean, San Juan, Puerto Rico, 28 June–2 July 2004, LC/G.2247.

Ernst, D., Ganiatos, T. and Mytelka, L. (eds.) (1998). *Technological Capabilities and Export Success in Asia*. Routledge, London and New York.

European Research Office (2004). The issue of supply side constraints in Africa — EU trade. EPA Watch, October.

Fei, J.C. and Ranis, G. (1997). *Growth and Development from an Evolutionary Perspective*. Blackwell Publishers, United Kingdom.

Fukuda-Parr, S., Lopes, C. and Malik, K. (2002). *Capacity for Development: New Solutions for Old Problems*. Earthscan and UNDP, New York.

Gereffi, G. (1999). International trade and industrial up-grading in the apparel commodity chain, *Journal of International Economics*, 48 (1): 37–70.

Ghose, A.K. (2003). *Jobs and Incomes in a Globalizing World*, ILO, Geneva.

Gibbon, P. (2001). Upgrading primary production: A global commodity chain approach, *World Development*, 29 (2): 345–363.

Griffin, K. (2005). Relative prices and investment: An essay on resource allocation. International Poverty Centre, Working Paper No. 4, January 2005, UNDP, Brasilia, Brazil.

Henderson, J. (1989). *Globalization of High Technology Production: Society, Space and Semiconductors in the Re-structuring of the Modern World*. Routledge, London.

Hirschman, A. O. (1958). *The Strategy of Economic Development*. Norton, New York.

Ishikawa, S. (1998). Underdevelopment of the market economy and the limits of economic liberalism. Chapter 6 in Ohno, K. and Ohno, I. (eds.), *Japanese Views on Economic Development: Diverse Paths to the Market*. Routledge, London and New York.

Islam, R. (2004). The nexus of economic growth, employment and poverty reduction: An empirical analysis, ILO Issues in Employment and Poverty Discussion Paper, 14, International Labour Office, Geneva.

Kaldor, N. (1967). *Strategic Factors in Economic Development*. Cornell University Press, Ithaca, New York.

Kaldor, N. (1981). The role of increasing returns, technical progress and cumulative causation in the theory of international trade and economic growth, *Economie Appliquée*, 34 (4): 593–617.

Kaplinsky, R., Morris, M. and Readman, J. (2002). The globalization of product markets and immiserizing growth: Lessons from the South African furniture industry, *World Development*, 30 (7): 1159–1177.

Kalecki, M. (1969). *Theory of economic dynamics*, New York: Augustus M. Kelley. (The original edition was published in 1952.)

King, K. and Palmer, R. (2005). Skills, capacities and knowledge in the least developed countries: New challenges for development cooperation. Background paper prepared for *The Least Developed Countries Report 2006*.

Kraay, A. (2005). When is growth pro-poor? Cross-country evidence. World Bank Policy Research Working Paper No. 3225, March, Washington, DC.

Lall, S. (1992). Technological capabilities and industrialization, *World Development*, 20 (2): 165–186.

Lall, S. (2004). Stimulating industrial competitiveness in Sub-Saharan Africa: Lessons from East Asia on the role of FDI and technology acquisition. Paper prepared for the World Bank for the NEPAD/TICAD Conference on Asia-Africa Trade and Investment. Tokyo International Conference on African Development 31October–2 November 2004.

León-Ledesma, M. and Thirlwall, A.P. (2002). The endogeneity of the natural rate of growth, *Cambridge Journal of Economics*, 26(4): 2002.

Lewis, W.A. (1954). Economic development with unlimited supplies of labour, *Manchester School of Economic and Social Studies*, May.

Llerena, P. and Lorentz, A. (2004a). Alternative theories on economic growth and the co-evolution of macro-dynamics and technological change: A survey. LEM Working Paper Series. 2003/27, Sant'Anna School of Advanced Studies, Pisa, Italy.

Llerena, P. and Lorentz, A. (2004b). Cumulative causation and evolutionary micro-founded technical change: A growth model with integrated economies. LEM Working Paper Series, 2003/05. Sant'Anna School of Advanced Studies, Pisa, Italy.

McCombie, J.S.L. and Thirlwall, A.P. (2004). *Essays on Balance of Payments Constrained Growth*. Routledge, London.

Milanovic, B. (2005). *Worlds Apart: Measuring International and Global Inequality*, Princeton University Press, Princeton, USA.

Myrdal, G. (1957). *Rich Lands and Poor Lands*. Harper Brothers, New York.

Nelson, R.R. and Winter, S.G. (1974). Neoclassical vs. evolutionary theories of economic growth: Critique and prospectus, *The Economic Journal*, 84, (336): 886–905.

Nelson, R.R. and Winter, S.G. (1982). *An Evolutionary Theory of Economic Change*, Cambridge, Mass., Harvard University Press

Nelson, R.R. (1998). The agenda for growth theory: A different point of view. *Cambridge Journal of Economics*, 22 (4): 497–520.

North, D. (1990). *Institutions, Institutional Change and Economic Performance*. Cambridge University Press, Cambridge.

Ocampo, J.A. (2005). The quest for dynamic efficiency: Structural dynamics and economic growth in developing countries. In: Ocampo, J. A. (ed.) *Beyond Reforms: Structural Dynamics and Macroeconomic Vulnerability*, Stanford Economics and Finance, Stanford University Press and the World Bank, Washington DC.

Ohno, K. (1998). Overview: Creating the Market Economy. Chapter 1 in Ohno, K. and Ohno, I. (eds.), *Japanese Views on Economic Development: Diverse Paths to the Market*. Routledge, London and New York.

Porter, M. (1990). *The Competitive Advantage of Nations*, Macmillan, London and Basingstoke.

Pyatt, G. (1999). Poverty versus the poor. In: Pyatt, G.F. and Ward, M. (eds.), *Identifying the Poor*, IOS/ISI, Amsterdam/Voorburg.

Pyatt, G. (2001). An alternative approach to poverty analysis, valedictory address at the Institute for Social Studies, The Hague, mimeo.

Ramos, J. (1998). A development strategy founded on natural resource-based production clusters. *CEPAL Review*, 66: 105–127.

Ravallion, M. (2004). Pro-poor growth: A primer, Policy Research Working Paper 3242, World Bank, Washington DC.

Reinert, E. (2004). Globalization in the periphery as a Morgenthau Plan: The Underdevelopment of Mongolia in the 1990s. Chapter 6 in Reinert, E. (ed.), *Globalization, Economic Development and Inequality*, Edward Elgar, Cheltenham, UK, and Northhampton, Mass., USA.

Reinert, E. (1995). Competitiveness and its predecessors: A 500-year cross-national perspective, *Structural Change and Economic Dynamics*, 6: 23–42.

Ros, J. (2000). *Development Theory and the Economics of Growth*. University of Michigan Press, Ann Arbor, Michigan, USA.

Sachs, J.D. (2000). Globalization and patterns of economic development, *Weltwirtschafts Archiv Review of Economics*, 136 (4): 579–600.

Sunkel, O. (ed.) (1993). *Development from Within: Toward a Neostructuralist Approach for Latin America*. Lynne Rienner Publishers, Boulder, Colorado, and London.

Svedberg, P. (2004). World income distribution: Which way? *World Development*, 40 (5): 1–32.

Thirlwall, A.P. (2002). *The Nature of Economic Growth: An Alternative Framework for Understanding the Performance of Nations*. Edward Elgar, Cheltenham, UK, and Northampton, Mass., USA.

United Nations (2001). *Programme of Action for LDCs* , A/CONF.191/11, New York.

UNCTAD (1994). *Trade and Development Report 1994,* Part Two, Chapter I. The visible hand and the industrialization of East Asia. United Nations publication, sales no. E.94.II.D.26.

UNCTAD (1996). *Trade and Development Report 1996,* Part Two: Rethinking development strategies: Some lessons from the East Asian experience. United Nations publication, sales no. E.96.II.D.6.

UNCTAD (1997). *Trade and Development Report 1997.* Globalization, Distribution and Growth. United Nations publication, sales no. E.97.II.D.8.

UNCTAD (2002). *The Least Developed Countries Report 2002: Escaping the Poverty Trap,* United Nations publication, sales no. E.02.II.D.13.

UNCTAD (2003). *Trade and Development Report 2003,* Part II: Capital Accumulation, Economic Growth and Structural Change. United Nations publication, sales no. E.03.II.D.7.

UNCTAD (2004). *The Least Developed Countries Report 2004: Linking International Trade with Poverty Reduction.* United Nations publication, sales no. E.04.II.D.27.

UNIDO (2002). *Industrial Development Report 2002/2003. Competing through Innovation and Learning.* UNIDO, Vienna.

UNIDO (2003). *African Productive Capacity Initiative: From Vision to Action.* Paper prepared for the Conference of African Ministers of Industry (CAMI). Vienna, 28 November 2003.

UNIDO (2004). *Industrial Development Report 2005. Industrialization, Environment and the Millennium Development Goals in Sub-Saharan Africa: The New Frontier of the Fight Against Poverty.* UNIDO, Vienna.

UNIDO (2005). *Industrial Development Report 2005. Capability Building for Catching-up: Historical, Empirical and Policy Dimensions.* UNIDO, Vienna.

UN Millennium Project (2005). *Investing in Development: A Practical Plan to Achieve the Millennium Development Goals.* New York.

World Trade Organization (2004). Assistance to address supply-side constraints. Sub-Committee on Least Developed Countries. (WT/COMTD/LDC/W/33: pp.1–3).

World Bank (2002). *Globalization, Growth and Poverty: Building an Inclusive World Economy*, World Bank and Oxford University Press, New York, and Washington DC.

World Bank (2005a). *Economic Growth in the 1990s: Learning from a Decade of Reform*. World Bank, Washington DC.

World Bank (2005b). *Pro-poor Growth in the 1990s: Lessons and Insights from 14 Countries*. World Bank, Washington DC.

World Trade Organization (2004). Assistance to address supply-side constraints. Sub-Committee on Least Developed Countries (WT/COMTD/LDC/W/33: pp.1–3).

Yanagihara, T. (1997). Economic system approach and its applicability. Chapter 1 in Yanagihara, T. and Sambommatsu, S. (Eds.), *East Asian Development Experience: Economic Systems Approach and Its Applicability*, Institute of Developing Economies, Tokyo.

Economic Growth and Capital Accumulation

Chapter 2

A. Introduction

The core processes through which productive capacities develop are capital accumulation, technological progress and structural change. This chapter and the next one examine how these processes are working in the LDCs. Although they are closely interrelated, the present chapter focuses, for analytical purposes, on capital accumulation, whilst the next one examines technological progress and structural change. The working of all three processes within the LDCs is strongly affected by the degree and form of integration of the LDCs with the global economy. Thus, the analysis in the present chapter discusses the extent to which external capital flows, including both ODA and FDI, hinder or facilitate domestic capital accumulation, and includes estimates of the brain drain from the LDCs, whilst the next chapter includes discussion of trade integration. The nature of institutions also affects how these core processes work within the LDCs, but this issue is discussed in chapter 6.

The first section of the present chapter (section B) provides an overall framework for the discussion of the two chapters by comparing the actual growth rates of the LDCs in the past with the potential GDP growth rates which the LDCs could achieve if the productivity of their labour force was increased in ways which are feasible for late-developing countries and if their growing labour force was fully employed. The comparison shows that there is a major opportunity for accelerated economic growth in the LDCs through the development and full utilization of productive capacities. But to realize this opportunity, strong constraints on capital accumulation, technological progress and structural change must be overcome. Increased investment, encompassing both physical and human capital formation, and increased effort in building technological capabilities are both required. Moreover, exports must grow sufficiently fast to finance the necessary imports for developing productive capacities and sustaining accelerated economic growth.

After section B, the rest of the chapter focuses on processes of capital accumulation. Sections C and D examine trends in physical and human capital formation in the LDCs respectively.[1] Section E discusses the limits and potential for domestic resource mobilization, whilst section F discusses the relationship between external resource inflows, particularly in the form of ODA and FDI, and domestic capital accumulation processes. The concluding section summarizes the main messages of the chapter.

There is a major opportunity for accelerated economic growth in the LDCs through the development and full utilization of productive capacities.

B. Economic growth in the LDCs: Potential versus actual

1. THE GROWTH POTENTIAL OF THE LDCs

The least developed countries have the potential to achieve very high rates of economic growth and to reduce poverty rapidly. The high growth potential of very poor countries can be explained in different ways. For example, it has been argued that poor countries should grow more rapidly than rich ones because of diminishing returns to capital in capital-abundant rich countries. This is at the

It is not utopian to imagine that the least developed countries could achieve the rapid growth rates which some very poor countries have already achieved.

heart of the neo-classical growth model formalized by Solow (1956). Economic historians, on the other hand, have focused on the potential for technological latecomers to achieve rapid economic progress because they are "technologically backward", in the sense of being behind the global technological frontier, and thus they can innovate by adopting existing technologies rather than have to invent from scratch (Gerschenkron, 1962). However, the best evidence of the high growth potential of very poor countries is the economic performance of the handful of developing countries, most notably the newly industrializing economies in East Asia, which have managed to sustain rapid economic growth over a number of decades and thereby reduce poverty drastically.

It is not utopian to imagine that the least developed countries could achieve the rapid growth rates which some very poor countries have already achieved. This section presents an analytical framework and empirical estimates of how fast LDCs could grow during the period 2002–2015. The analytical framework adopted is a modified and extended version of a catching-up model proposed by Taylor and Rada (2005) for the analysis of the growth potential of several developing regions. It draws on the methodology used for the analysis of the growth prospects of Mexico and Central America (Ros, 2006), and is based on Ros (2005a), who applies this methodology for 23 LDCs for which the necessary data are available.

In the catching-up model the potential growth rate is estimated assuming that there is full employment of the labour force and that a number of sources of potential labour productivity growth within poor countries are exploited. Thus, potential GDP growth rate is estimated as a function of the labour force growth and the potential labour productivity growth rate (see box 7). Following Taylor and Rada (2005), the analysis identifies three major factors as determinants of potential labour productivity growth. These factors reflect both the heterodox and orthodox traditions in the analysis of the growth potential. They are as follows:

Simulations were made for two scenarios — a fast catch-up scenario and a slow catch-up scenario — based on different assumptions regarding the ability to take advantage of the technological gap between LDCs and other developing countries.

1. The effects of increasing returns to scale in industrial sectors of the economy. Here it is assumed that the overall labour productivity growth rate responds to the GDP growth rate with a 'Verdoorn elasticity', which varies according to the structure of the economy. The term 'Verdoorn elasticity' is used as Verdoorn was the first economist to identify empirically the tendency for a fast growth of manufacturing output to induce a fast rate of labour productivity in manufacturing as a result of static and dynamic returns to scale — Verdoorn's Law (see McCombie, Pugno and Soro, 2003).

2. The effects of human capital accumulation. Here it is assumed that a more rapid increase in educational level (rather than a higher level) will lead to a higher productivity growth rate.

3. The effects of technological backwardness. Here it is assumed that the size of the gap between the income level of a given country and the prevailing level in more developed countries is related to productivity growth rates associated with technological catch-up. This can be explained, following Gerschenkron (1962), as the result of the "advantages of backwardness", or can be seen as the result of a convergence process in a neoclassical growth model.

The potential growth rate can be derived from projections of the growth of the labour force and assumptions regarding the values of parameters related to these three factors. Simulations were made for two scenarios — a fast catch-up scenario and a slow catch-up scenario — based on different assumptions regarding the ability to take advantage of the technological gap between LDCs and other developing countries (see box 7).

Box 7. A catching-up model for the LDCs

On the basis of Taylor and Rada (2005) and on Ros (2006), Ros (2005a) developed a model to analyse the growth potential of the least developed countries. It relies on an identity on the basis of which the potential GDP growth rate (y*) is equal to the labour force growth rate (l*) and also on the potential labour productivity growth rate (r), in other words:

$$y* = l* + \rho \qquad (1)$$

where $\rho = \rho o + \gamma y + \eta h + G$ (2)

The potential labour productivity growth rate (ρ) is determined by (i) the autonomous rate of productivity growth (ρo); (ii) the impact of the Verdoorn elasticity (γ) on GDP growth (y); (iii) the effect of human capital accumulation (h), whereby the rate of the increase in educational level leads to a productivity growth rate according to the parameter η; and (iv) the extent of technological backwardness (G), assumed to be equal to the gap between a country's income level and the one prevailing in more developed countries.[1]

Combining (1) with (2) gives the following:

$$y* = A + B G \qquad (3)$$

where: $A = [1/(1-\gamma)] (l* + \rho o + \eta h)$

   $B = 1/(1-\gamma)$

Term G is an inverse function of the "income gap", $I = (Y/P)_{ldc}/(Y/P)_{odc}$, between per capita income in the LDCs and the per capita income of other developing countries, such that when $I = 1$, a situation in which there is no income gap between LDC and ODC, productivity growth arising from the catching up process is nil.

The precise speed of catch-up associated with the income gap is specified with a parameter E as follows:

$$G = E(1- lo)$$

where lo is the initial value of I

The higher the value for parameter E, the faster the rate of technological catch-up.

In estimating the potential growth rates of the LDCs in the sample for the period 2002–2015, a number of assumptions were made.

Firstly, the labour force grows at the same rate as the population aged 15–64. This assumes that there is no change in the labour force participation rates. Any upward trend in the women's participation rate will be offset by a reduction in the rate among school-aged youth.

Secondly, countries are grouped according to their major export specialization – agricultural exporters, oil and mineral exporters, manufactures exporters and services exporters — and apparent historical estimates were made of Verdoorn elasticities (the relationship between output growth and labour productivity growth). Manufactures exporters show the highest Verdoorn elasticity (0.27) and oil and mineral exporters the lowest (0.08), with agricultural exporters (0.11) and service exporters (0.16) falling somewhere in between.

Thirdly, human capital accumulation in the LDCs is estimated on the basis of the growth of the educational level index used in the UNDP *Human Development Report* (a weighted average of the literacy rate and enrolment in the three levels of education). The assumption made is that, with few exceptions, the rate of human capital accumulation is the same in all the LDCs in the sample, such that by 2015 the educational index converges towards today's average level of education in developing countries. This implies a rather high rate of human capital accumulation (2.4 per cent per year). The exceptions are Cape Verde (h = 1.8 per cent), Maldives (h = 0.3 per cent) and Sao Tome and Principe (h = 1.7 per cent), with relatively high initial educational indexes, which are assumed to converge towards today's average level of education in high human development countries. Labour productivity growth is assumed to respond to human capital growth with a parameter of 0.5 (η). This is based on Ros (2000) who finds this parameter for a sample of developing and developed countries.[2]

Fourthly, two scenarios are assumed with regard to the effect of the income gap on technological catch-up — a slow catch-up scenario and a fast catch-up scenario. In the slow catch-up scenario, the value of the parameter E, which governs the speed of catch-up associated with any given income gap, is 0.013, which is equivalent to the historical experience of the LDCs in the sample during the period 1980–2003. In the fast catch-up scenario, the parameter E is set equal to 0.04, which assumes that GDP per capita in the LDCs will converge towards the average level in other developing countries at a rate equal to one third the rate at which Japan converged towards developed country levels in the post-war period.[3] The growth of per capita income in developing countries is assumed to be 2.8 per cent per year (the value recorded for the period 1990–2002).

Source: Ros (2005a).

[1] The technological backwardness can be seen as an "advantage" (Gerschenkron, 1962) or as a result of a convergence process in a neoclassical growth model.

[2] Maddison's estimate (1995) ($\eta = 1$) is more optimistic.

[3] See Taylor and Rada (2005). There are two exceptions — Cape Verde and Maldives — with levels of per capita income in 2002 higher than the developing country average. These two countries are assumed to converge towards the world average.

The results of the simulations for the two catch-up scenarios are presented in table 24. For comparison, the table also presents actual GDP and per capita GDP growth rates for 1990–2003. Several observations can be made on the basis of the table.

First, the potential GDP growth rate of the LDCs in the fast catch-up scenario is 7.5 per cent per annum (table 24). This growth rate is similar to the type of catch-up growth rates which China and India are now achieving, and which newly industrializing economies such as the Republic of Korea, Thailand and Malaysia sustained in the past. It also meets the rate of growth which the Brussels Programme of Action declares the LDCs, with the support of the development partners, should strive to attain.[2] Moreover, it is a growth rate which would enable the realization of one of the aspirations of the "Spirit of Monterrey" declaration which emerged from the Heads of State retreat at the Financing for Development Conference held in Monterrey in 2002. This stated as follows: "We undertake to assist the world's poorest countries to double the size of their economies within a decade, in order to achieve the MDGs (Millennium Development Goals)".

The potential GDP growth rate of the LDCs in the fast catch-up scenario is 7.5 per cent per annum... which meets the target growth rate of the Brussels Programme of Action.

TABLE 24. PROJECTIONS OF POTENTIAL GROWTH OF GDP AND GDP PER CAPITA IN SELECTED LDCS AND INCOME GAP RELATIVE TO OTHER DEVELOPING COUNTRIES

	GDP growth (% per annum)			Per capita GDP growth (% per annum)			Income gap[a] (%)		
	1990–2003 Actual growth rate	2002–2015 Potential growth rate		1990–2003 Actual growth rate	2002–2015 Potential growth rate		2002 Actual gap	2015 Potential gap	
		Slow catch-up scenario	Fast catch-up scenario		Slow catch-up scenario	Fast catch-up scenario		Slow catch-up scenario	Fast catch-up scenario
Angola	3.2	5.2	6.7	0.3	2.3	3.7	53	50	59
Bangladesh	4.9	5.6	7.9	2.6	3.8	6.0	42	48	62
Benin	5.0	5.8	8.3	2.2	3.3	5.7	26	28	37
Bhutan	6.7	5.3	7.1	4.6	2.8	4.5	49	49	60
Burkina Faso	4.2	5.7	8.3	1.3	2.7	5.1	27	27	36
Cape Verde	5.9	5.3	6.4	3.8	3.5	4.5	64[d]		
Eritrea	3.7[b]	6.4	9.2	1.4	3.5	6.1	22	24	32
Ethiopia	4.3	5.6	8.3	1.4	3.2	5.8	19	20	27
Guinea	4.2	5.2	6.8	1.7	2.7	4.2	52	51	62
Guinea Bissau	0.4	5.9	8.8	-2.6	3.0	5.7	18	18	26
Haiti	-0.1	4.6	6.8	-2.2	3.3	5.4	40	43	55
Lao PDR	6.3	6.0	8.3	4.0	3.9	6.1	42	48	63
Malawi	3.0	5.0	8.0	1.0	3.1	6.0	14	15	21
Maldives	7.1[c]	4.7	6.1	4.2	1.8	3.0	61[d]		
Mali	4.9	6.3	9.0	2.1	3.1	5.5	23	24	32
Mozambique	7.0	5.1	8.0	4.4	3.6	6.4	26	29	40
Rwanda	2.3	4.9	7.3	-0.5	2.8	5.0	31	31	41
Sao Tome and Principe	2.2	5.4	7.7	-0.4	3.1	5.2	32	33	43
Uganda	6.8	5.9	8.3	3.8	2.3	4.5	34	32	42
United Rep. of Tanzania	3.7	5.3	8.3	1.0	3.5	6.4	14	15	22
Vanuatu	2.6	5.3	6.5	-0.1	3.1	4.2	71	74	84
Yemen	5.8	6.6	9.3	1.8	3.0	5.4	21	22	29
Zambia	1.4	4.3	6.8	-0.8	2.9	5.3	21	21	29
Simple average	4.1	5.5	7.5	1.5	3.1	5.2	32[e]	33	43[e]

Source: Ros (2005a).

Note: For explanation of growth scenarios see text and box 1 of the chapter.
        a GDP per capita in LDCs as percentage of GDP per capita in other developing countries.
        b 1992–2003; c 1995–2003; d Relative to world average; e Excludes Cape Verde and Maldives.

With the potential growth rates which are possible within the fast catch-up scenario, potential GDP per capita would grow at 5.2 per cent per annum on average, which would enable substantial and rapid poverty reduction given that economic growth is founded on full employment and growth of labour productivity. In the slow catch-up scenario, potential GDP growth would be slower, but nevertheless potential GDP per capita would grow at 3.1 per cent per annum, enabling substantial poverty reduction.

Second, in the fast catch-up scenario potential growth rates of both total GDP and per capita GDP in the period 2002–2015 are much higher than in the period 1990–2003. For the whole sample of countries potential GDP growth during 2002–2015 is on average 3.4 percentage points higher than in the period 1990–2003 and potential per capita GDP growth is 3.7 points higher. Potential GDP growth is higher than in the past in all but one country (Maldives) and per capita GDP growth is higher in all but two countries (Bhutan and Maldives).

In the slow catch-up scenario, potential GDP growth rates are significantly lower (by two percentage points) than in the first scenario but still higher than in the period 1990–2003 (by 1.4 percentage points). However, even in this slow catch-up scenario, potential per capita GDP growth is 1.6 percentage points higher than in the period 1990–2003. In this case, potential GDP growth and potential per capita GDP growth are higher than in 1990–2003 in all but six countries (Bhutan, Cape Verde, Lao People's Democractic Republic, Maldives, Mozambique and Uganda).

Third, the highest growth rates are found in the poorest LDCs. For example, in the fast catch-up scenario all but one of the LDCs with below average incomes have above average potential GDP growth rates and all but three LDCs with above average potential GDP growth rates have below average incomes. This is an indication of the important role that the assumptions about technological catch-up are playing in the simulations. It also implies that there will be a process of convergence amongst LDCs as GDP per capita differentials amongst them diminish and also between the LDCs and other developing countries. In the fast catch-up scenario, assuming that the growth rate of GDP per capita in other developing countries continues at the same rate as the period 1990–2002, the GDP per capita of the least developed countries would be expected to rise from 32 per cent of the average in other developing countries in 2002 to 43 per cent of that average in 2015 (see table 24). Of course, this process of convergence would be much slower in the slow catch-up scenario. The income gap between the LDCs and other developing countries would decrease by less than one percentage point, and in fact the income level in a few LDCs (Angola, Guinea and Uganda) tends to diverge from the average income level prevailing in developing countries.

Fourth, the highest potential growth rates of per capita GDP are found among the manufactures exporters (3.7 per cent to 6.0 per cent), followed by the agricultural exporters (3.0 per cent to 5.5 per cent), the oil and mineral exporters (2.7 per cent to 4.7 per cent) and the services exporters (2.8 per cent to 3.9 per cent). The contrast between the manufacturing exporters on the one hand and the oil and mineral exporters on the other reflects the role of returns to scale in the growth simulations since the highest "Verdoorn elasticity" is estimated to exist in the manufactures exporters and the lowest "Verdoorn elasticity" in the oil and mineral exporters.[3] The relatively low rates of potential growth of the services exporters are due to their relatively high income levels and as a result the reduced scope for technological catching-up effects.

In the fast catch-up scenario, potential GDP growth during 2002–2015 is on average 3.4 percentage points higher than in the period 1990–2003 and potential per capita GDP growth is 3.7 points higher.

In the slow catch-up scenario, potential GDP growth rates are significantly lower than in the first scenario but still higher than in the period 1990–2003.

These growth scenarios are obviously sensitive to the assumptions which have been made with regard to key parameters. But the assumptions are empirically grounded in the experience of either least developed countries or developing countries. They thus provide a realistic indication of what a full employment growth path for the LDCs could look like if productive capacities were developed. The estimates indicate that there are major opportunities for increased growth rates. However, for these opportunities to be realized, various constraints on the achievement of the potential growth rates must be addressed.

Achieving these potential growth rates will first of all require substantially increased investment rates (see box 8). These must be financed from substantially increased domestic savings, or substantially increased external resource inflows, or some combination of the two. Accelerated export growth will also be necessary in order to pay for the increased imports which will be required for sustaining faster economic growth. There will also need to be increased technological effort to acquire and use modern technologies in use in other countries. The full-employment output growth trajectory will not be achieved if investment demand falls short of the investment requirements. Macroeconomic policies will thus need to ensure macroeconomic stability, which is vital for investment expectations, and also to create an environment in which there are strong demand-side incentives to invest.

Achieving these potential growth rates will be possible only if key constraints on the development of productive capacities are addressed.

Realizing the potential growth rates outlined in these scenarios, and particularly the fast catch-up scenario which conforms to the aspirations of the Brussels Programme of Action, will be possible only if key constraints on the development of productive capacities are addressed. These constraints are very strong in the LDCs, and they are also interlocking to create vicious circles of persistent mass poverty and underdevelopment. If the growing labour force is not being fully employed and also not being equipped with more skills, capital and technology to increase productivity, the negative effects of fast population growth can quite simply swamp any potential positive effects of a faster labour force growth on the overall potential growth rate. The policy challenge is to relax key constraints in order to break down the vicious circles of poverty and underdevelopment and to start and sustain the potential growth rates which these catch-up scenarios suggest are achievable.

BOX 8. INVESTMENT REQUIREMENTS FOR POTENTIAL CATCH-UP GROWTH RATES

This box extends the catch-up model introduced in the main text by estimating the investment rates required in order to achieve the potential growth rates which are achievable under the fast and slow catch-up growth scenarios.

The required investment rates as a share of GDP are estimated on the basis of assumptions regarding the rate of capital depreciation (which is assumed to be 10 per cent per annum) and the marginal capital–output ratio. The latter varies between countries and may be expected to change over time. But in the present analysis it is assumed to be 3.2, which is the trimmed average for the sample of LDCs for the period 1990–2003. The required gross investment rate $(I/Y)^*$ is estimated as the net investment required plus the rate of depreciation, with the required net investment rate being the potential growth rate multiplied by the capital–output ratio.[1] The assumption that the average productivity of capital is the same in all countries and remains the same is obviously a simplification. But it is difficult to identify a better method of estimating the ratios of capital to potential output — which is what is ideally required. The problem with using country-specific capital–output ratios is that these estimates are very sensitive to the rate of capacity utilization, and there are no data on changes in capacity utilization to adjust the country–specific estimates.

Using these assumptions, box table 3 shows estimates of the gross investment rates, $(I/Y)^*$, required in order to achieve the potential growth rate in the LDCs for the period 2002–2015 together with the average investment rate observed during the period 1990–2003. The estimates are given for both the slow and the fast catch-up scenarios.

As can be seen from the table, achieving the potential growth rate will require increasing investment well above the levels recorded in the 1990–2003 period. The average investment requirement for the slow catch-up scenario is 28 per cent of GDP, whilst the average investment rate for the fast catch-up scenario is 35 per cent. For the sample as a whole, it implies an additional investment effort of over 4 percentage points of GDP in the slow convergence scenario and of almost 12 percentage points of GDP in the fast convergence scenario. The results — which, to emphasize again, depend

Box 8 (contd.)

BOX TABLE 3. INVESTMENT REQUIREMENTS TO ACHIEVE ESTIMATED POTENTIAL GROWTH RATES
(Percentage of GDP)

	Actual investment rate (a)	Investment requirement rate (b)		% point change (b-a)	
		Slow catch-up scenario	Fast catch-up scenario	Slow catch-up scenario	Fast catch-up scenario
	1990–2003	*2003–2015*		*2003–2015*	
Angola	32.5	26.6	31.4	-5.9	-1.1
Bangladesh	21.1	27.9	35.3	6.8	14.2
Benin	17.6	28.6	36.6	11.0	19.0
Bhutan	45.5[a]	27.0	32.7	-18.5	-12.8
Burkina Faso	21.2	28.2	36.6	7.0	15.4
Cape Verde	24.7	27.0	30.5	2.3	5.8
Eritrea	27.0[b]	30.5	39.4	3.5	12.4
Ethiopia	16.7	27.9	36.6	11.2	19.9
Guinea	17.9	26.6	31.8	8.7	13.9
Guinea Bissau	17.1	28.9	38.2	11.8	21.1
Haiti	24.6	24.7	31.8	0.1	7.2
Lao PDR	21.4[c]	29.2	36.6	7.8	15.2
Malawi	10.3	26.0	35.6	15.7	25.3
Maldives	29.9	25.0	29.5	-4.9	-0.4
Mali	22.5	30.2	38.8	7.7	16.3
Mozambique	29.3	26.3	35.6	-3.0	6.3
Rwanda	16.7	25.7	33.4	9.0	16.7
Sao Tome and Principe	38.0	27.3	34.6	-10.7	-3.4
Uganda	18.0	28.9	36.6	10.9	18.6
United Rep. of Tanzania	18.1	27.0	36.6	8.9	18.5
Vanuatu	..	27.0	30.8	..	..
Yemen	20.2	31.1	39.8	10.9	19.6
Zambia	20.1	23.8	31.8	3.7	11.7
Simple average	23.2	27.5	34.8[d]	4.3	11.8

Source: Ros (2005a).

a 1990-2002; *b* 1992-2003; *c* 1995-2003; *d* Excludes Vanuatu.

on the assumptions — imply that the additional investment effort will be particularly great in Benin, Ethiopia, Guinea-Bissau, Malawi, Rwanda, Uganda, the United Republic of Tanzania, and Yemen. In all but four countries (Angola, Bhutan, Maldives, and Sao Tome and Principe) the average investment requirements are above historical levels (average of the slow and fast catch-up scenarios). It is worth noting that three of these four exceptions (Angola, Bhutan, and Sao Tome and Principe) have relatively low investment requirements because the assumed capital–output ratio is well below the actual capital–output ratio recorded over the period 1990–2003 (the actual capital–output ratios are 7.0, 5.4 and 12.7 respectively).

It is possible to extend the analysis further by considering the extent to which domestic savings are sufficient to finance the higher level of investment, given past inflows of foreign savings. The results (which are not shown) indicate that domestic savings will have to be 5 percentage points higher than they were in 2000–2003 for the slow catch-up scenario and as much as 12 percentage points higher for the fast catch-up scenario. The additional savings effort, which is required even for the slow catch-up scenario, will be difficult to achieve. But if one assumes that domestic savings do not increase, financing the investment requirements for catch-up growth will require a similar major increase in resource inflows from abroad as a share of GDP.

Although these results depend on the assumptions of the scenarios, the findings have two important implications. Firstly, within most LDCs low domestic savings rates are the key constraint on achieving fast catch-up economic growth through the development of productive capacities. Ros (2005b) identifies this as the most ubiquitous constraint on attaining the higher potential growth rates of the catch-up scenarios. Secondly, there is a need for a combination of increased domestic savings and increased external resource inflows to support the realization of the growth potential of the LDCs.

Source: Ros (2005a).

[1] The capital depreciation rate follows from the assumption that the rate of depreciation as a fraction of the capital stock is 3 per cent (the estimate in Mankiw, Romer and Weil, 1992) and that the capital–output ratio is 3.2 per cent. The trimmed average excludes the two highest and two lowest values of the ratio in the sample.

2. Actual growth experience of the LDCs

The analysis above shows that the potential growth rates which LDCs could be expected to achieve are higher than the actual growth rates which occurred during the period 1990–2003. But the gap between the potential and the actual is considerably larger if one takes a longer time perspective. Between 1980 and 2003, real GDP per capita grew at only 0.72 per cent per annum for the group of LDCs as a whole. The overall growth rate over the period was slower than in other developing countries. The gap between the GDP per capita of the LDC group and other developing countries was actually greater in 2003 than in 1980.

Between 1980 and 2003, real GDP per capita grew at only 0.72 per cent per annum for the group of LDCs as a whole.

Within this long-term performance, there are significant differences in economic performance amongst the LDCs. Table 25 classifies the LDCs into three groups — converging economies, weak-growth economies and regressing economies — according to their growth performance over the period 1980–2003. The converging economies are those in which real GDP per capita exceeded 2.15 per cent per annum over the period, which was the average annual real GDP per capita growth rate in high-income OECD countries over that period. The weak-growth economies are those in which the average annual real GDP per capita growth rate was below this rate over this period, but still positive. The regressing economies are those in which the average annual real GDP per capita growth rate was negative over the period. As can be seen from the table, amongst the 41 LDCs for which data are available, there are 9 converging economies, 15 weak-growth economies and 17 regressing economies. Only 2 of the weak-growth economies — Guinea and Sudan — achieved a real GDP per capita growth rate which was greater than 1.26 per cent per annum, the average in other developing countries over the period 1980–2003.

Closer analysis of the year-to-year changes which have occurred in the LDCs over the period 1980–2003, shows more complex patterns of economic growth which are characterized by periods of sustained economic growth, economic crises in which there are often quite severe output losses, and economic recoveries of varying strengths and completeness.[4] From this perspective, the LDCs actual growth performance has three major features.

Over the period 1980–2003, 21 out of 40 LDCs have experienced severe growth collapses, 12 experienced severe output losses in the 1980s but managed to recover subsequently and 7 LDCs have been able to sustain steady growth.

- Very few LDCs have been able to sustain steady growth and have not experienced economic crises with significant output losses.

- About half the LDCs have experienced severe growth collapses, which are defined here as a situation in which output losses have been sufficiently large and the subsequent economic recovery so weak or delayed that their GDP per capita is below the level it was in the 1970s or early 1980s.[5]

- Some LDCs experienced severe output losses in the 1980s but managed to recover subsequently, thus contributing to an improvement in the overall growth performance of the LDCs as a group after 1990.

For 40 LDCs for which data are available (see annex charts to this chapter), there are only 7 which have experienced steadily sustained growth — Bangladesh, Bhutan, Burkina Faso, Cape Verde, the Lao People's Democratic Republic, Lesotho and Nepal. All the other LDCs have experienced economic contractions of varying length and severity since achieving political independence. Of the 7 countries, Bhutan, Cape Verde and the Lao People's Democratic Republic are the only ones in which actual growth rates in the period 1990–2003 reached the potential growth rates in the scenarios above. Moreover, amongst this group, although Burkina Faso has not experienced a major prolonged negative shock, growth of GDP per capita was slow in both the 1980s and the 1990s.

TABLE 25. REAL GDP PER CAPITA GROWTH RATES OF LDCs, 1980–2003
(Percentage per annum)

	Growth rate
Converging economies	
Bangladesh	2.2
Bhutan	4.0
Cape Verde[a]	3.0
Equatorial Guinea[b]	11.2
Lao People's Democratic Republic[c]	3.3
Lesotho	2.9
Mozambique	2.3
Nepal	2.4
Uganda[d]	2.7
Weak-growth economies	
Benin	0.7
Burkina Faso	1.2
Chad	0.8
Ethiopia[a]	0.1
Guinea[e]	1.5
Kiribati	1.1
Malawi	0.4
Mali	0.6
Mauritania	0.7
Samoa	1.1
Senegal	0.4
Solomon Islands	0.4
Sudan	1.8
United Republic of Tanzania[f]	0.8
Vanuatu	0.2
Regressing economies	
Angola	-1.1
Burundi	-1.7
Central African Republic	-1.2
Comoros	-1.0
Democratic Republic of the Congo	-5.7
Djibouti	-4.2
Gambia	-0.4
Guinea-Bissau	-0.4
Haiti	-2.9
Liberia	-9.6
Madagascar	-1.3
Niger	-1.8
Rwanda	-1.2
Sao Tome and Principe[e]	-0.6
Sierra Leone	-4.3
Togo	-0.8
Zambia	-1.7

Source: UNCTAD secretariat estimates based on World Bank, *World Development Indicators 2005*.

Note: LDCs with recent data only have the following real GDP per capita growth rates:
Cambodia 4.02 (1993–2003); Eritrea 1.04 (1992–2003); Maldives 4.65 (1995–2003); Yemen 2.42 (1995–2003).
a 1981–2003; *b* 1985–2003; *c* 1984–2003; *d* 1982–2003; *e* 1986–2003; *f* 1988–2000.

Of the 33 LDCs which have experienced economic crises with major output losses, there are only 12 whose GDP per capita is now higher than it was at its peak in the 1970s or early 1980s. These countries include a number of high-performing economies such as Mozambique and Uganda which have grown rapidly after economic collapse (see chart 12). During the 1990s, these countries were also, like Bhutan, Cape Verde and the Lao People's Democratic Republic,

CHART 12. TRENDS IN REAL GDP PER CAPITA IN SELECTED LDCS
(Constant 2000 $)

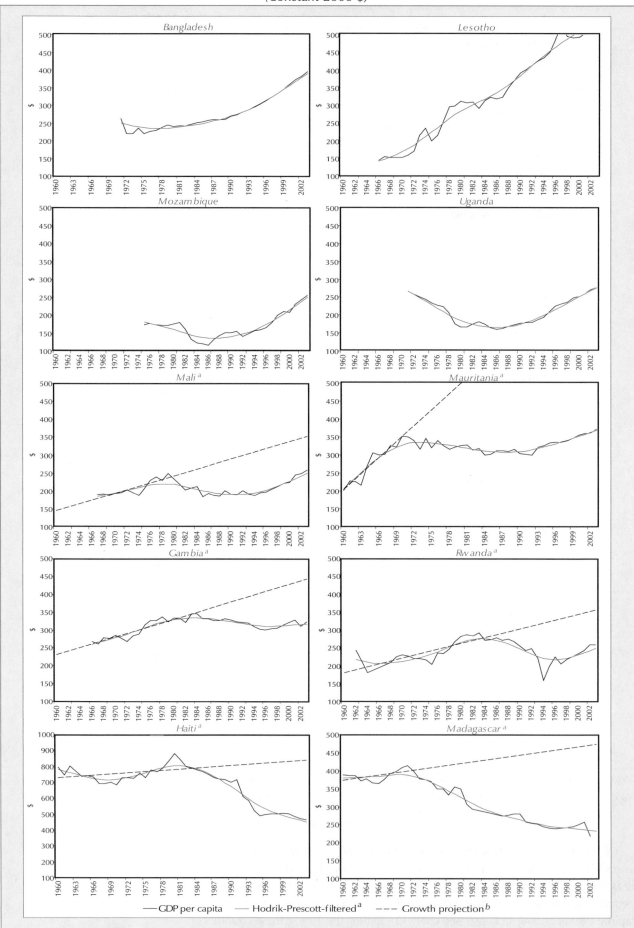

———— GDP per capita   —— Hodrik-Prescott-filtered[a]   – – – Growth projection[b]

Source: UNCTAD secretariat estimates based on World Bank, *World Development Indicators 2005*, CD-ROM.
   a   Hodrik-Prescott filter was used to identify long-term trends in GDP per capita and remove short-term fluctuations.
   b   Growth projections are based on the trends before major negative economic shocks.

growing at rates similar to their potential growth rates as estimated in the scenarios above.

The other 21 LDCs — that is, just over half of the countries for which data are available — have experienced growth collapses in the sense that their GDP per capita in 2003 was lower than it had been between 20 and 30 years earlier. Eleven out of these 21 LDCs have simply not recovered at all from the growth collapse. In some of these countries, such as Haiti and Madagascar, economic contraction continues. However, amongst the other 10, there are a number of countries, such as Gambia and Rwanda, whose growth record since the mid-1990s has been good but which still have not recovered to achieve earlier levels of GDP per capita (see chart 12).

Finally, although a few LDCs have achieved higher growth rates after economic crisis than before, the more common tendency is for their growth rates to be lower afterwards. They do not conform to a V-shaped recovery in which there is a growth acceleration following the output loss and the post-crisis growth rate then returns to the pre-crisis growth rate.[6] Instead, the negative shocks not only derail economic growth, but also have a longer-term negative impact on actual growth rates. Even amongst those countries which have achieved their earlier peak GDP per capita, there are cases, such as Mali and Mauritania, which have been unable to regain the growth rates which they had before economic collapse (see chart 12). It is this slowness of post-collapse growth rates which, together with the severity of the growth collapse, explains why many countries have not been able to achieve again their earlier income per capita. Out of 17 countries for which one can reconstruct a pre-collapse growth rate, the post-collapse growth rate is slower in 14 countries.

There are a few LDCs which have managed to achieve the sustained high growth rates which the potential growth scenarios indicate are attainable for the LDCs. However, in most of them, GDP per capita is not much higher, or is even lower, than it was at its peak in the 1970s or early 1980s.

To summarize, there are a few LDCs which have managed to achieve the sustained high growth rates which historical experience suggests should be possible for very poor countries and which the potential growth scenarios discussed above indicate are attainable for the LDCs. In most of them, GDP per capita is not much higher, or is even lower, than it was at its peak in the 1970s or early 1980s. Generally, the economic stagnation or regression of the LDCs is not due to the fact that they have not experienced any economic growth whatsoever. Rather, they have grown, sometimes rapidly, but have been unable to sustain that growth. These empirical regularities support the idea that many LDCs are caught in a poverty trap (see box 9). But they suggest that a key feature of the trap is vulnerability to economic crises and negative output shocks, and the consequences of such vulnerability.

The potential for rapid economic growth certainly exists in very poor countries. But realizing this potential requires that the vicious circles which create an interlocking set of constraints be addressed and that the foundation for sustained economic growth be laid.

Box 9. Does recent evidence support the idea that poor countries are enmeshed in a poverty trap?

In the LDC Report 2002, UNCTAD argued that many LDCs were caught in an international poverty trap in which an interlocking complex of domestic and international vicious circles led to economic stagnation and persistent poverty. The importance of country-level poverty traps for understanding the persistence of extreme poverty has also been strongly argued for sub-Saharan Africa (see Sachs et al., 2004) and made central to the policy recommendations of the UN Millennium Project Report entitled *Investing in Development* (UN Millennium Project, 2005). However, there have also been critiques of this idea. Both Easterly (2005) and Kraay and Raddatz (2005) have argued that there is no empirical evidence for the existence of poverty traps. Does this mean that the idea of the poverty trap is no longer valid?

Close examination of the evidence of Easterly and of Kraay and Raddatz suggests that this conclusion would be premature. The nature of the poverty trap is formally specified in Sachs et al. (2004) in a neoclassical model which includes low productivity of capital because minimum thresholds of capital (particularly infrastructure) per worker are not attained, low domestic savings rates and high population growth rates. Kraay and Raddatz test for the existence of a poverty trap by examining whether the savings and productivity functions behave empirically in the way that Sachs et al. suggest in their model of Africa's poverty trap. Even though they find that evidence does not conform to the conditions required for a poverty trap as specified by Sachs et al., they do find that an economy in which consumption is close to subsistence can exhibit low savings rates and low growth for a significant period of time (p. 14). In effect, although countries are not stuck in a poverty trap in the sense defined by the mechanisms within Sachs' formal model, Kraay and Raddatz state that the growth dynamics of these countries may well conform to "something that looks like a poverty trap over the medium term" (p. 14). In effect, there is a poverty trap, but its nature does not conform to that specified by Sachs et al.

Easterly, in contrast, tests for the existence of a poverty trap by asking the following: do the poorest countries have significantly lower per capita growth than the rest, and is their growth zero? What he finds is that the answer depends on the time period. Taking per capita growth from 1950–2001, 1950–75 and 1975–2001 for the poorest fifth of the countries at the start of each period, he finds no evidence for a poverty trap as he defines it. But the growth rate of the poorest fifth is not statistically distinguishable from zero in the period 1980–2001; and in the period 1985–2001, it is also not significantly different from zero and is statistically significantly lower than the growth rate of all the other countries. This actually indicates the existence of a poverty trap.

However, he rejects this as supporting the idea of a poverty trap since almost a third of the poorest countries were richer in 1950 than 1985 (and thus "had gotten into poverty by declining from above rather than being stuck in it from below", p. 11). He also rejects the idea of the poverty trap as specified in the UN Millennium Project since he argues that it is linked to a case for increased aid. He finds that in the last period, when there is empirical evidence of the poverty trap, the poorest countries actually received more aid. Thus, he suggests that they cannot be caught in a poverty trap of the type which Sachs et al. and the UN Millennium Project are talking about.

Whilst the conclusions of these two studies must be read carefully and closely, it should be noted that recent research has deepened understanding of the nature of poverty traps within which the poorest countries are enmeshed. Cerra and Saxena (2005) show that if one focuses solely on periods of expansion the poor countries can actually catch up with the rich as they experience stronger expansions. However, because the poor countries have more frequent and deeper recessions than initially rich countries, the long-term result is divergence between the richer countries and the poorer countries, and also a situation in which, over the long term and despite spurts of rapid growth, output per capita may be the same as it was 30–40 years earlier (see box chart 4). Ros (2005b) shows that the form of integration into the world economy is a source of growth collapse. Analysing the different frequency of growth collapses since the 1960s in developing countries classified according to their initial GDP per capita (1960), economic size, resource abundance, export specialization and inequality, he finds that:

• In terms of initial income level, the major divide is between the low- and low-middle-income countries on the one hand, and the high-middle and high-income countries on the other hand, with growth collapses much more frequent in the former group. Fifty-nine per cent of the low-income countries and 59 per cent of the low-middle-income countries experienced growth collapses.

• The incidence of growth collapses is much greater in small economies than in large economies.

• Collapses in natural-resource-rich economies are more frequent than in natural-resource-poor economies, and they are particularly more frequent in economies which specialize in mineral and oil exports.

• Fifty-two per cent of high-inequality and 55 per cent of medium-inequality countries experienced growth collapses, but none of the low-inequality countries did so.

As Ros puts it, "These processes of growth collapse reflect the combined influence of unequal income distribution and the pattern of specialization, as determined by the abundance of natural resources and the size of the economy" (Ros, 2005a: 228).

Box 9 (contd.)

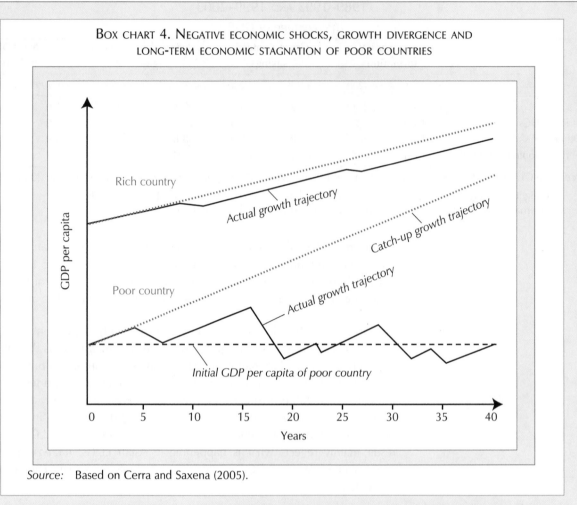

BOX CHART 4. NEGATIVE ECONOMIC SHOCKS, GROWTH DIVERGENCE AND
LONG-TERM ECONOMIC STAGNATION OF POOR COUNTRIES

Source: Based on Cerra and Saxena (2005).

To summarize, the weight of the recent evidence does not undermine the notion that countries can get stuck in a poverty trap; rather it reinforces it. But the nature of the poverty trap needs to be understood in a way which incorporates the vulnerability of poor countries to negative shocks and growth collapses. Also, it is clear that the form of integration into the world economy, which is central to the UNCTAD analysis of the poverty trap but not part of the Sachs et al. and UN Millennium Project analysis, should be included as a critical aspect of the poverty trap.

C. Trends in physical capital formation

Increased investment is essential for achieving the potential GDP growth rates which are possible in the LDCs. It is through such increased investment that technological progress and structural change will be possible, productive capacities will develop and the LDC economies will become less vulnerable to negative shocks and growth collapses. Investment rates have actually increased over the last 15 years. As table 26 shows, the ratio of gross capital formation to GDP for the LDCs for which data are available increased from 16.6 per cent during 1989–1993 to 22 per cent during 1999–2003. However, the level of investment is still below the average level in other developing countries. It is also below the investment target of the Brussels Programme of Action for the LDCs (25 per cent of GDP). In addition, it is still well below the investment requirements of either the slow catch-up scenarios or the fast catch-up scenarios discussed above.

Increased investment is essential for achieving the potential GDP growth rates which are possible in the LDCs.

Within this average improved performance there is much diversity amongst the LDCs. The ratio of gross capital formation to GDP actually worsened in one third of the LDCs for which data are available. Whether it improved or not is

TABLE 26. GROSS CAPITAL FORMATION AND DOMESTIC SAVINGS IN LDCS AND OTHER DEVELOPING COUNTRIES, 1989–1993 AND 1999–2003

(Percentage of GDP)

	Gross capital formation		Gross domestic savings		External resource gap[a]		Net FDI inflows	
	1989–1993	*1999–2003*	*1989–1993*	*1999–2003*	*1989–1993*	*1999–2003*	*1989–1993*	*1999–2003*
LDCs	16.6	22.0	7.2	13.6	-9.4	-8.4	1.0	2.6
African LDCs	15.8	21.5	5.8	10.6	-10.0	-10.9	1.0	4.6
Other LDCs	17.8	22.5	9.2	17.0	-8.6	-5.5	0.9	0.3
Other developing countries	24.8	25.2	24.5	26.4	-0.3	1.2	1.2	2.8

Source: UNCTAD secretariat estimates based on World Bank, *World Development Indicators,* online data, May 2005.

Note: Weighted averages for 28 LDCs and 84 other developing countries for which data are available.

 a External resource gap is gross domestic savings minus gross capital formation.

closely related to the form of trade integration with the global economy. It improved substantially in the manufactures- and oil-exporting LDCs. But it worsened in one quarter of the agricultural-exporting LDCs, half of the mineral-exporting LDCs and all the service-exporting LDCs for which data are available.

Capital formation in the LDCs also remains highly dependent on external finance. For the LDCs as a group, the resource gap (measured as the difference between gross capital formation and gross domestic savings) was 8.4 per cent of GDP in 1999–2003, which implies that external finance supported nearly 40 per cent of capital formation in the LDCs. In contrast, it was only 1 per cent of GDP in other developing countries. During the 1990s, an increasing proportion of capital formation was financed by domestic savings in the LDCs. But this result mainly reflects what is happening in Asian LDCs. Increasing levels of investment in African LDCs are largely attributable to foreign capital inflows, particularly FDI.

For the LDCs as a group, the resource gap was 8.4 per cent of GDP in 1999–2003, which implies that external finance supported nearly 40 per cent of capital formation in the LDCs.

It is possible to decompose data on gross fixed capital formation into public fixed investment, domestic private fixed investment and foreign direct investment for 12 LDCs during the 1990s (chart 13). A number of significant patterns are revealed:

- Public investment was very low in most LDCs in the sample, exceeding 10 per cent of GDP in only 4 of the 12 countries (two barely) in the early 1990s and only 3 in the late 1990s;

- Public investment was also in general declining during the 1990s. It decreased as a share of GDP between the first half of the 1990s and the second half of the 1990s in 8 out of the 12 LDCs;

- Domestic private investment is even weaker than public investment in the majority of the countries in this sample. Domestic private investment as a share of GDP exceeded public investment in only 5 countries in the first half of the 1990s and only 3 countries in the second half of the 1990s;

- Domestic private investment became *less* important in animating capital formation in the 1990s. Domestic private investment as a share of GDP declined in 8 out of the 12 LDCs in the sample;

- The foreign private sector became *more* important in animating capital formation in the 1990s. FDI as a share of GDP increased in 10 out of the 12 LDCs. Nevertheless, the ratio of domestic private investment to GDP remained higher than the ratio of FDI to GDP in all the LDCs except two — Cambodia and Malawi.

CHART 13. COMPOSITION OF GROSS FIXED CAPITAL FORMATION IN SELECTED LDCs, 1990–1995 AND 1995–2000
(Percentage of GDP)

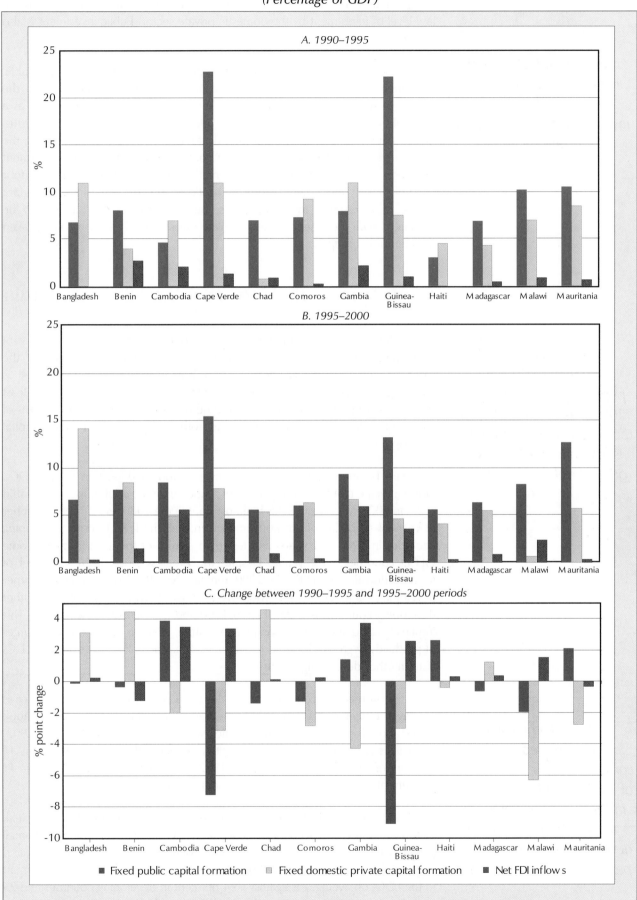

Source: UNCTAD secretariat estimates based on World Bank data (direct communication) and *World Development Indicators 2005*, CD-ROM.

Note: Gross fixed capital formation has been disaggregated into three components: gross fixed public capital formation, gross fixed domestic private capital formation and FDI. The sum of gross fixed domestic private capital formation and net FDI inflows equals gross fixed private capital formation.

Although this is a small sample, these patterns are very significant. They suggest that an important feature of the investment process in the LDCs is the low level of investment by the domestic private sector. Public investment is also very low.

On face value, the data indicate few positive associations between public investment, domestic private investment and FDI. There are *no* LDCs in the sample in which both public and domestic private investment are higher as a share of GDP in the second half of the 1990s than in the first half of the 1990s. In four countries where the domestic private investment to GDP ratio rises, the public investment ratio falls, and in four countries where the public investment ratio rises, the domestic private investment ratio falls. In the remaining four countries, both ratios fall. Rising FDI inflows are an increasingly important source of investment for many LDCs, but they too do not appear to be associated with increased domestic private investment. This issue will be taken up later in this chapter.

An important feature of the investment process in the LDCs is the low level of investment by the domestic private sector.

D. Human capital formation and the brain drain

Human capital formation is an important part of the process of developing productive capacities. Indeed, the potential growth rates in the catch-up model assume significant rates of human capital formation as well as requiring increased physical capital formation. At the present time, least developed countries seriously lag behind other developing countries in terms of levels of educational attainment and other aspects of human capital development.

Chart 14 shows estimates of the level of formal education within LDCs. These indicate that the average years of schooling of the adult population within LDCs in 2000 was 3 years. This is almost double the 1980 level. But the number of years of schooling of the population were half the level in other developing countries in 2000 (7.1 years) and less than a third of the level in high-income OECD countries (11.4 years). Despite the progress since 1980, the level of formal education in LDCs in 2000 remains less than what it was in other developing countries in 1960. Moreover, the gap between the LDCs and other developing countries is wider than in 1960 and is progressively widening.[7] This implies that the rate of human capital formation, which is one of the key sources of productivity growth in the catch-up model, has actually been slower in LDCs than in other developing countries.

The average years of schooling of the adult population within LDCs in 2000 was 3 years. Despite the progress since 1980, this is less than what it was in other developing countries in 1960.

An immediate consequence of the short period of school attendance is low levels of literacy. As table 27 shows, it is estimated that 32 per cent of adult males and 56 per cent of adult females were illiterate in the LDCs in 2002. Youth illiteracy rates are equally stark. It is estimated that in the same year, 34 per cent of the total population aged 15–24 were illiterate and as much as 41 per cent of the female population in that age group.

In 2001, technical and vocational education constituted only 2.6 per cent of total secondary enrolment in the LDCs on average, as against 10.4 per cent in developing countries and 25 per cent in OECD countries.

Various other indicators of technical skill creation provide an equally bleak picture. Enrolment in secondary technical and vocational education is a small percentage of total secondary school enrolments. In 2001, technical and vocational education constituted only 2.6 per cent of total secondary enrolment in the LDCs on average, as against 10.4 per cent in developing countries and 25 per cent in OECD countries (King and Palmer, 2005). Enrolment in tertiary technical subjects is also very low. The main reason for this is that enrolment in tertiary education in the LDCs in general is much lower than in other developing

CHART 14. AVERAGE NUMBER OF YEARS OF SCHOOLING IN LDCS AND OTHER DEVELOPING COUNTRIES, 1960–2010

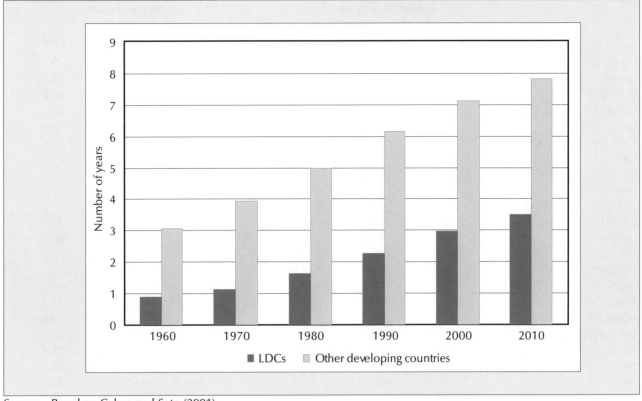

Source: Based on Cohen and Soto (2001).

countries and OECD countries. In recent years, only 6 per cent of the population aged 20–24 in LDCs were enrolled in tertiary education, compared with 23 per cent in other developing countries and 57 per cent in high-income OECD countries (see table 28). Within tertiary enrolment, the share of enrolments in science and agriculture in LDCs is at approximately the same levels as in other developing countries and OECD countries. But the share of engineering enrolments within tertiary enrolment is just over half the level in other developing countries. Tertiary-level enrolments, particularly in technical subjects, are important for developing the managerial and technical skills to use modern technologies efficiently and to adapt imported technologies for local conditions. This indicates a major gap in the general competences that provide the basis for technological capabilities.

The length of formal education is, of course, not the ideal measure of skills. It ignores the quality of education, as well as on-the-job learning and other forms of training. There are no internationally comparable data on these latter processes of skill formation. However, the nature of the production structure is likely to exacerbate the skills gap. The small size of the manufacturing sector (which will be discussed in the next chapter) means that entrepreneurs and the labour force have little manufacturing experience, a fact which is of crucial significance with regard to the ability to introduce new manufacturing industries. Also, the fact that most people are employed in household enterprises, either small-scale agriculture or the urban informal sector, means that there are definite limits to on-the-job learning in the context of work. There are, for example, highly developed traditional apprenticeship training systems within the informal sector (Atchoarena and Delluc, 2001). But whilst these can serve the needs of the informal economy well, they are not immediately relevant for mass factory production, or applicable without extension advice to modern techniques of intensification of agricultural production.

In recent years, only 6 per cent of the population aged 20–24 in LDCs were enrolled in tertiary education, compared with 23 per cent in other developing countries and 57 per cent in high-income OECD countries... The share of engineering enrolments within tertiary enrolment is just over half the level in other developing countries.

TABLE 27. ADULT AND YOUTH LITERACY RATES IN LDCs, BY GENDER, 2002

	Adult literacy rate (% of people aged 15 and above)			Youth literacy rate (% of people aged 15-24)		
	Female	Male	Total	Female	Male	Total
Bangladesh	31.4	50.3	41.1	41.1	57.8	49.7
Benin	25.5	54.8	39.8	38.5	72.7	55.5
Burundi	43.6	57.7	50.4	65.1	67.2	66.1
Cambodia	59.3	80.8	69.4	75.9	84.5	80.3
Cape Verde	68.0	85.4	75.7	86.3	92.0	89.1
Central African Republic[a]	33.5	64.7	48.6	46.9	70.3	58.5
Chad	37.5	54.5	45.8	64.0	75.8	69.9
Comoros	49.1	63.5	56.2	52.2	65.6	59.0
Ethiopia	33.8	49.2	41.5	51.8	63.0	57.4
Haiti	50.0	53.8	51.9	66.5	65.8	66.2
Lao PDR	55.5	77.4	66.4	72.7	85.8	79.3
Lesotho[b]	90.3	73.7	81.4	98.5	82.7	90.5
Liberia	39.3	72.3	55.9	55.4	86.3	70.8
Malawi	48.7	75.5	61.8	62.8	81.9	72.5
Maldives	97.2	97.3	97.2	99.2	99.1	99.2
Mali[a]	11.9	26.7	19.0	16.9	32.3	24.2
Mauritania	31.3	51.5	41.2	41.8	57.4	49.6
Mozambique	31.4	62.3	46.5	49.2	76.6	62.8
Myanmar	81.4	89.2	85.3	91.1	91.6	91.4
Nepal	26.4	61.6	44.0	46.0	78.1	62.7
Niger	9.3	25.1	17.1	15.1	34.0	24.5
Rwanda	63.4	75.3	69.2	83.6	86.3	84.9
Samoa	98.4	98.9	98.7	99.5	99.4	99.5
Senegal	29.7	49.0	39.3	44.5	61.3	52.9
Sudan	49.1	70.8	59.9	74.2	83.9	79.1
Togo	45.4	74.3	59.6	66.6	88.3	77.4
Uganda	59.2	78.8	68.9	74.0	86.3	80.2
United Rep. of Tanzania	69.2	85.2	77.1	89.4	93.8	91.6
Yemen	28.5	69.5	49.0	50.9	84.3	67.9
Zambia	73.8	86.3	79.9	86.9	91.5	89.2
LDCs	44.4	67.6	53.8	59.1	72.6	65.6

Source: UNCTAD secretariat estimates based on World Bank, *World Development Indicators* 2005, CD-ROM.
       a 2000 data; b 2001 data.

TABLE 28. INDICATORS OF EDUCATIONAL ENROLMENT IN TECHNICAL SUBJECTS IN LDCs, OTHER DEVELOPING COUNTRIES AND OECD COUNTRIES, RECENT YEARS[a]

(Percentage)

	LDCs	Other developing countries	OECD countries
Enrolment in technical and vocational education as % of secondary school enrolment	2.6	10.4[b]	24.8[c]
Percentage of population aged below 20 -24 enrolled in tertiary education	5.9	23.2	56.9
Of which:			
Science	10.0	10.5	10.8
Engineering	7.5	13.2	14.3
Agriculture	4.0	2.5	1.9

Source: King and Palmer (2005) and Knell (2006).
       a Data on enrolment in technical vocational education are for 2001; data on tertiary education are averages for the school years between 1998/1999 and 2002/2003.
       b All developing countries.
       c OECD countries excluding Ireland, Poland, New Zealand and United States, for which data are not available.

An important feature of the process of human capital formation in the LDCs is that there is a strong propensity for skilled workers to seek work outside the country. This can, of course, be a source of remittances and new skills, and the possibility of out-migration may increase incentives for education. But this "brain drain" seriously diminishes a key component of the human capital stock of the LDCs.[8]

It is difficult to have a comprehensive picture of this phenomenon because of lack of data on emigration from least developed countries to other developing countries. However, there are now estimates of the intensity of the brain drain from developing countries to OECD countries (Docquier and Mafouk, 2004). Using this new database, it is possible to estimate the number of high-skill workers (those with tertiary education — 13 years of schooling and above) born in each LDC who were working in OECD countries in 1990 and 2000. On this basis, "emigration rates" from individual LDCs to OECD countries, which are defined as the fraction of the total stock of high-skill workers of a particular LDC working in OECD countries, can be estimated.

About one in five of the high-skill workers (persons with tertiary education) born in LDCs were working in OECD countries in 2000.

From table 29, which presents the results, a number of key points stand out:

- About one in five of the high-skill workers (persons with tertiary education) born in LDCs were working in OECD countries in 2000.

- This was slightly higher than the proportion in 1990, but the intensity of the brain drain was increasing in almost all of the LDCs, and in some significantly.

- The intensity of the brain drain from the LDCs as a group is slightly less than that of the brain drain from other developing countries. Whilst 21.4 per cent of the high-skill workers born in LDCs were working in OECD countries, 22.9 per cent of the high-skill workers born in other developing countries were working in OECD countries.

- The rates of out-migration rate of high-skill workers to OECD countries are much lower for Asian LDCs (12.4 per cent) than for African and island LDCs (21.9 per cent and 26.8 per cent respectively).

- The intensity of the brain drain from African and Asian LDCs to OECD countries increased significantly in the 1990s. The rate of emigration of high-skill workers from African LDCs increased by about one quarter and the rate for Asian LDCs by one third. The rate of emigration of high-skill workers from the island LDCs to OECD countries decreased significantly in the 1990s, but from very high levels in 1990 (44 per cent).

In the 1990s, the rate of out-migration of high-skill workers from African LDCs increased by about one quarter and the rate for Asian LDCs by one third.

Within these general averages, there is much variation. For almost half the LDCs (23 countries) the intensity of the brain drain exceeds 20 per cent. For 12 LDCs, more than one in three of the high-skill workers born in the country were working in OECD countries in 2000, namely Angola (emigration rate of 33 per cent), Cape Verde (68 per cent), Eritrea (34 per cent), The Gambia (63 per cent), Haiti (84 per cent), the Lao People's Democratic Republic (37 per cent), Liberia (44 per cent), Mozambique (45 per cent), Samoa (76 per cent), Sierra Leone (53 per cent), Somalia (33 per cent) and Uganda (36 per cent). The intensity of the brain drain is a particularly severe problem in island LDCs, small countries and countries which have experienced severe civil conflict. But emigration rates from island LDCs in 2000 were lower than in 1990 in 5 out of the 9 island LDCs. Leaving aside the island LDCs, there are only three LDCs where the emigration rate declined by more than one percentage point between 1990 and 2000 — the Democratic Republic of the Congo, Gambia and Uganda.

TABLE 29. EMIGRATION RATES FOR HIGH-SKILLED WORKERS[a] FROM LDCs TO OECD COUNTRIES, 1990 AND 2000
(Per cent of total high-skilled workforce)

	1990 (a)	2000 (b)	% point change (b-a)
Afghanistan	13.5	23.3	9.8
Angola	4.6	33.0	28.4
Bangladesh	2.1	4.3	2.3
Benin	7.3	11.3	4.0
Bhutan	0.7	0.6	-0.1
Burkina Faso	1.5	2.6	1.1
Burundi	9.5	8.5	-1.0
Cambodia	15.6	18.3	2.7
Cape Verde	56.8	67.5	10.7
Central African Republic	4.0	7.1	3.0
Chad	2.1	2.4	0.3
Comoros	7.0	21.2	14.1
Dem. Rep. of the Congo	21.0	13.7	-7.3
Djibouti	7.6	11.0	3.3
East Timor	..	15.5	15.5
Equatorial Guinea	1.1	13.0	11.9
Eritrea	0.0	34.0	34.0
Ethiopia	8.0	10.1	2.0
Gambia	80.4	63.3	-17.1
Guinea	13.4	11.3	-2.2
Guinea-Bissau	9.3	24.4	15.1
Haiti	78.6	83.6	5.0
Kiribati	68.5	23.1	-45.4
Lao PDR	29.9	37.4	7.5
Lesotho	10.4	4.3	-6.1
Liberia	32.4	45.0	12.6
Madagascar	5.7	7.6	1.9
Malawi	16.8	18.7	1.9
Maldives	1.2	1.2	0.0
Mali	8.2	15.0	6.8
Mauritania	2.8	11.8	9.0
Mozambique	26.6	45.1	18.5
Myanmar	4.3	4.0	-0.2
Nepal	1.8	5.3	3.5
Niger	6.4	6.0	-0.5
Rwanda	17.3	26.0	8.6
Samoa	96.7	76.4	-20.4
Sao Tome and Principe	3.6	22.0	18.3
Senegal	12.3	17.7	5.4
Sierra Leone	34.2	52.5	18.3
Solomon Islands	39.2	6.4	-32.9
Somalia	17.4	32.7	15.3
Sudan	5.2	6.9	1.7
Togo	11.1	18.7	7.7
Tuvalu	74.6	27.1	-47.5
Uganda	44.2	35.6	-8.6
United Rep. of Tanzania	11.6	12.4	0.7
Vanuatu	48.2	8.2	-40.1
Yemen	5.5	6.0	0.5
Zambia	16.7	16.8	0.0
LDCs	20.3	21.4	1.0
African LDCs	16.5	21.9	5.4
Asian LDCs	9.2	12.4	3.2
Island LDCs	44.0	26.8	-17.2
Other developing countries	26.6	22.8	-3.8
Developed countries	11.0	10.4	-0.7

Source: Docquier and Marfouk (2004). *International Migration by Educational Attainment (1990–2000),* release 1.1.
     a High-skilled workers are those with tertiary education (13 years and above).

E. The limits and potential for domestic resource mobilization[9]

The rate of physical and human capital accumulation is inadequate in most LDCs for three basic reasons. Firstly, the domestic resources available for financing physical and human capital formation are very limited. Secondly, the surplus that does exist is not being channelled sufficiently into productive investment to create a virtuous circle of expanding capital accumulation. Thirdly, external capital inflows are not adequately supporting processes of domestic capital accumulation. The present section and the next one examine the first and the last of these reasons respectively. The weaknesses of financial systems within the LDCs also critically affect both the magnitude of the investible surplus and the extent to which the latter is channeled into productive investment; but this institutional issue will be discussed in chapter 6.

1. Low domestic savings

Gross domestic savings were equivalent to 13.6 per cent of the GDP of the LDCs for which data are available in 1999–2003 (see table 26 above). Although this was a significant improvement from 10 years earlier, the domestic savings rate was only about half the savings rate in other developing countries. The domestic savings rate in this period was particularly low in African LDCs – only 10.6 per cent of GDP.

With such a low domestic savings rate it is impossible to achieve the investment rates required for economic growth and poverty reduction without resort to external finance. The domestic savings rates are far below the rates required for financing domestically the investment rates for either the slow or the fast catch-up growth scenarios discussed above. Indeed, without external resource inflows, the average domestic savings rate for the LDCs as a group is actually insufficient for economic growth to take place at all. The UN Millennium Project estimates that the average domestic savings rate in the LDCs during 1980–2000 was just 6.7 per cent of GDP, and without external resource inflows GDP per capita in the LDCs would have declined by 3.1 per cent per annum even if all these domestic resources had been invested efficiently (UN Millennium Project, 2005: table 3.11).[10] If the same analysis is applied with the higher domestic savings rate of 13.6 per cent of GDP that pertained in 1999–2003 and a slower population growth rate (2.4 per cent per annum rather than 2.5 per cent), it will be seen that domestic savings in the LDCs are still too low to achieve economic growth on their own. Without access to external savings, the real GDP per capita of the LDCs as a group would have declined by 0.66 per cent per annum during 1999–2003 even if all domestic savings had been efficiently invested.

An even starker picture emerges if one estimates "genuine savings rates" which adjust the savings rate from national accounts to take account of depletion of environmental resources. This adjustment is important for LDCs because their economies are generally so heavily dependent on natural resources. For the LDCs for which data are available, it is apparent that average genuine savings rates did not increase between 1990 and 2003. Genuine savings remained at below 5 per cent of GNI for most of the 1990s (chart 15). In 2003, the rate of genuine savings in the LDCs was about half the level in low- and middle-income countries, although it had been about the same in 1990. Genuine savings are also estimated on the basis of gross national savings, which include ODA grants. If the genuine savings rates are further adjusted to take out

Gross domestic savings were equivalent to 13.6 per cent of the GDP of the LDCs... This is far below the rates required for financing domestically the investment rates for either the slow catch-up growth scenario or the fast catch-up growth scenario.

CHART 15. GENUINE SAVINGS[a] IN LDCs AND LOW- AND MIDDLE-INCOME COUNTRIES, 1986–2003

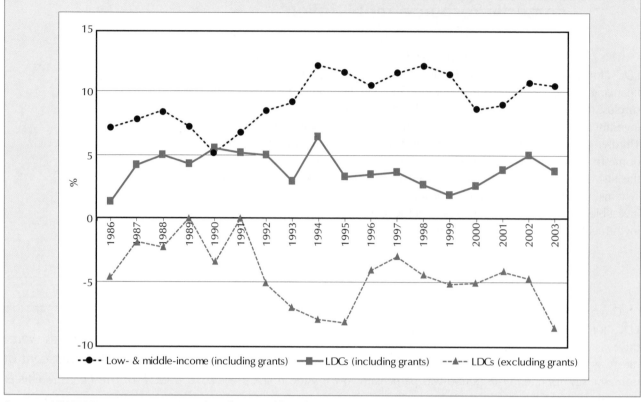

Source: UNCTAD secretariat estimates based on World Bank, *World Development Indicators* and *Global Development Finance*, online data, November 2005.

Note: Based on 26 LDCs for which data are available.

a   For definition of genuine savings, see text.

For 17 LDCs, there are only three in which tax revenue exceeds 15 per cent of GDP and it is below 10 per cent of GDP in 7 countries.

this external capital inflow, this seriously reduces the estimate of genuine savings in the LDCs. The adjusted genuine savings are actually negative in the LDCs in all years between 1991 and 2003. There is also a declining trend.

Thus, although the growth performance of the LDCs as a group improved considerably in the 1990s, their domestic productive resource base — as measured by genuine savings without ODA grants — has been shrinking. This raises serious questions about the sustainability of the recent acceleration of economic growth, which is apparent in the growth experience discussed in the present chapter and also the most recent growth trends discussed in part I of this Report.

2. LOW GOVERNMENT REVENUES

Government revenues are also very low in most LDCs. Some are able to collect major resource rents, notably on oil and minerals, but also, in the case of island LDCs, through fishing licences. However, most LDCs raise revenue domestically mainly through taxation. For 17 LDCs for which recent data on public finances are available, there are only three in which tax revenue exceeds 15 per cent of GDP and it is below 10 per cent of GDP in 7 countries (table 30). This is very low, compared with other developing countries and developed countries. Recent calculations, for example, indicate that tax revenue as a share of GDP is 18 per cent on average in developing countries and 38 per cent in developed countries (McKinley, 2005).

TABLE 30. GOVERNMENT FINANCE IN SELECTED LDCs
(Percentage of GDP)

	Period [a]	Government revenue	Tax revenue	Non–tax revenue [b] (excluding grants)	Grants	Government expenditure
Bangladesh	2001–2003	10.9	7.8	2.3	0.9	9.1
Bhutan	2001–2003	38.8	10.8	11.9	16.2	21.2
Burundi	1998–1999	15.4	14.5	0.9	..	19.9
Dem. Rep. of the Congo	2001–2002	6.1	5.0	1.0	..	6.3
Ethiopia	1998–1999	19.9	12.9	6.1	0.9	21.5
Guinea	1998–1999	16.2	10.8	0.7	4.6	12.8
Maldives	2001–2003	32.6	13.0	17.8	1.9	25.9
Myanmar	1996–1999	6.7	3.5	3.2	..	..
Nepal	2001–2003	13.1	9.4	2.1	1.7	..
Rwanda	1990–1992	9.9	8.7	1.2	..	13.1
Senegal	1999–2001	19.6	17.0	0.7	1.8	13.9
Sierra Leone	1998–1999	11.1	7.0	0.2	3.9	17.3
Sudan	1998–1999	7.5	6.2	1.3	..	7.1
Uganda	2000–2002	18.8	11.2	0.3	7.3	18.0
Vanuatu	1997–1999	23.9	20.0	4.0	..	23.5
Yemen	1998–1999	29.1	10.9	17.6	0.5	25.3
Zambia	1998–1999	25.0	18.1	0.6	6.3	19.2

Source: UNCTAD secretariat estimates based on IMF, *Governmental Financial Statistics March 2005* and World Bank, *World Development Indicators* online data, May 2005.

a   Most recent period available.
b   Non-tax revenue (excluding grants) include property income, sales of goods and services, fines penalties and forfeits and voluntary transfers other than grants.

There are certainly important problems of taxation administration which have to be addressed within the LDCs. However, their low tax base should not be seen exclusively as a result of lack of taxation effort or tax reform. A good indication of this is the fact that at least 28 LDCs have introduced value-added taxes, including 24 since 1990. These major reforms, introduced as part of structural adjustment programmes and later within PRSPs, are often partly designed to offset the adverse tax consequences of trade liberalization. But wider evidence shows that whilst they can do so in high-income countries, VAT has been able to compensate for only 45–60 per cent of the revenue lost from trade liberalization in middle-income countries and only about 30 per cent of the revenue lost from trade liberalization in low-income countries (Baunsgaard and Keen, 2004).

The low level of taxation revenue limits the level of government expenditure in all the LDCs which do not have access to resources rents.

The low level of taxation revenue limits the level of government expenditure in all the LDCs which do not have access to resources rents. The extent of this limitation is shown in chart 16. During 2000–2003, government final consumption expenditure was equivalent to about 10 per cent of GDP in the LDCs for which data are available. This is six percentage points below the level in other developing countries. However, because of very low GDP per capita in the LDCs, these shares translate into very little public expenditure per capita. In fact, during 2000–2003, government final consumption expenditure in the LDCs was only $26 per capita compared with $186 per capita in other developing countries. As a result, current public expenditure on health is very low in per capita terms within the LDCs. During 2000–2002, LDCs on average spent $13 per head per annum on public health expenditure, in contrast to an average of $75 per head per annum in other developing countries, and $2,908 in high-income OECD countries.

During 2000–2003, government final consumption expenditure in the LDCs as a group was only $26 per capita compared with $186 per capita in other developing countries.

CHART 16. GOVERNMENT FINAL CONSUMPTION EXPENDITURE IN LDCS AND OTHER DEVELOPING COUNTRIES, 2000–2003

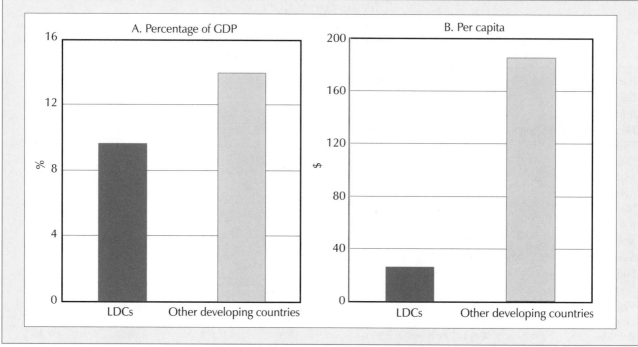

Source: UNCTAD secretariat estimates based on World Bank, *World Development Indicators 2005*, CD-ROM.
Notes: Group averages are weighted averages.
Calculations are based on a group of 39 LDCs and 68 other developing countries for which data were available.

3. THE POTENTIAL FOR DOMESTIC RESOURCE MOBILIZATION

There are various reasons why domestic savings rates and government revenues are low in the LDCs, most obviously because of generalized mass poverty. Because the average income per capita is so low in the LDCs, a large proportion of the population survives on incomes which are barely sufficient to meet their basic physical needs. The ability to save and also to raise revenue through taxes is thus highly constrained.[11] Dependency ratios (the number of dependants per working person in each household) are also high and this further dampens the capacity to save.

However, the strong limitation on the *current capacity* to save and raise government revenue does not mean that there is a low *potential* for domestic resource mobilization. The contrary is in fact the case. The underdevelopment of the LDC economies has the corollary that there are hidden and underutilized resources that could be tapped to finance increased investment. In thinking about the potential for domestic resource mobilization within the LDCs, it is necessary to have a dynamic perspective which identifies how this potential can be realized. As Albert Hirschman (1958:5) put it, "Development depends not so much on finding optimal combinations for given resources and factors of production as on calling forth and enlisting for development purposes resources and abilities that are hidden, scattered and badly utilized".

The potential for domestic resource mobilization is high within the LDCs for a number of reasons.

Firstly, the level of monetization of the LDC economies is very low. In 2003, the money supply was just 31 per cent of GDP compared with almost 80 per cent in other developing countries (David, 2005). The weak monetization levels are related to weak financial systems (see chapter 6). But they also reflect the continuing subsistence orientation of agriculture, where the main form of

> *The strong limitation on the current capacity to save and raise government revenue does not mean that there is a low potential for domestic resource mobilization.*

savings is often physical rather than financial assets and where part of agricultural output is consumed within the household and not monetized. The intensification of commercial agriculture and the development of the market economy within rural areas could, together with the development of rural financial institutions in which farmers can, with confidence, deposit savings, lead to significant savings mobilization.

Secondly, as will be discussed in chapter 4, a significant proportion of the labour force within LDCs is either underemployed or has very low productivity as they work applying their raw labour with rudimentary tools and equipment and poor infrastructural facilities. Most agricultural production and a significant part of non-agricultural production are also organized on the basis of household enterprises. When production is organized in this way and productivity is very low, there is often surplus labour. This does not necessarily mean that the marginal productivity of labour is zero or negative, or that labour is totally redundant. Rather, there is surplus labour in the sense that some individuals receive more than the marginal product of the labour. This is likely to occur whenever the marginal product of labour is unable to meet subsistence requirements and when individual earnings are based on institutional sharing norms within the household (Fei and Ranis, 1997; Ranis, 1997).

The existence of surplus labour means that there are some direct opportunities for physical capital formation in rural areas through mobilizing labour for simple infrastructure projects (Griffin, 1996, Griffin and Brenner, 2000).[12] However, beyond this, with fuller and more productive employment for the labour force, domestic savings can be expected to increase. This is indeed apparent in the historical experience of the LDCs. The evidence shows that as income levels rise, there is a high propensity to save within the LDCs. Moreover, the propensity to save is actually higher than in other developing countries (see UNCTAD, 2000: 36–37).

Thirdly, the potential for domestic resource mobilization is high because the domestic capitalist corporate sector of the economy is as yet underdeveloped in most LDCs. This is the mirror image of the importance of household enterprises within the private sector of LDCs. But it has important implications because business savings are a key component of domestic savings. As W.A. Lewis put it in the mid-1950s: "If we ask why the less developed countries save so small, the answer is not that they are so poor but because their capitalist sector is so small" (Lewis, 1955). The evidence shows that a defining feature of the most successful East Asian developing economies has been their ability to raise their domestic savings ratios by increasing business savings (not simply household savings). In the initial stages of the development process the mobilization of the agricultural surplus was important. But after this initial stage the engine of the development of productive capacities was the creation of a strong investment–profits nexus in which expected profits provided the incentive for investment and realized profits were both an outcome of investment and a source for further investment (Akyüz and Gore, 1996). Evidence from Investment Climate Surveys also shows that this is relevant in LDCs. Retained profits are the source of 80 per cent of the working capital and 71 per cent of the new investment in Ugandan manufacturing firms, and 74 per cent of the working capital and 63 per cent of the new investment in Eritrean manufacturing firms (World Bank, 2004: appendix 4, p. 133).

Fourthly, the potential for domestic resource mobilization is high within the LDCs because there is latent entrepreneurship which can be harnessed into productive channels to support the expansion of productive investment and

The level of monetization of the LDC economies is very low. In 2003, the money supply was just 31 per cent of GDP compared with almost 80 per cent in other developing countries.

As income levels rise, there is a high propensity to save within the LDCs.

There is latent entrepreneurship which can be harnessed into productive channels to support the expansion of productive investment and employment.

employment. This requires both macroeconomic stability and household-level economic security. At the present moment, all-pervasive economic insecurity at the household level associated with generalized poverty adversely affects entrepreneurship as it leads to short-termism and limits risk-taking. The existence of production complementarities which render individual investment decision dependent on the decisions of others, together with weak coordinating devices which can enable positive linkage effects, is another reason why entrepreneurial capabilities remain latent. In addition, there are incentives for unproductive (or destructive) entrepreneurial activities, which exist when entrepreneurs establish illegal barriers to entry or engage in predatory behaviour based on monopoly position which can stem from political favours (Baumol, 1990). A major policy challenge is not simply to foster entrepreneuship but also to bring about a switch from unproductive entrepreneuship to productive entrepreneurship.

The low level of financial resources is partly due to the low level of income. But it also reflects weak investment incentives and the lack of profitable investment opportunities.

Fifthly, there is an important potential for domestic resource mobilization which is associated with how the small stratum of rich individuals within LDCs use their wealth. How these people deploy their wealth can make an important difference to the savings-investment process. If their savings are used for productive investment within the country, it will facilitate strong domestic capital accumulation.[13] Many highly-qualified individuals have also migrated to work in other countries, and ensuring that their financial resources could return is yet another avenue for resource mobilization.

In summary, the low level of financial resources is partly due to the low level of income. But it also reflects weak investment incentives and the lack of profitable investment opportunities. If investment increases, there are significant possibilities for increased domestic resource mobilization based on increased monetization of the economy, the mobilization of surplus labour, a shift away from household to corporate financing of investment, the mobilization of entrepreneurship which is latent because of all-pervasive economic insecurity and weak coordination mechanisms to address production complementarities, the turning of unproductive entrepreneurship into productive entrepreneurship, and the increased deployment of the resources of the small stratum of the rich for productive investment within the LDCs. Comparison of the contrasting investment and savings performance of LDCs classified according to their growth experience suggests that these potentials for domestic resource mobilization are not imaginary. Some LDCs have significantly increased both domestic savings and investment in a virtuous circle (box 10).

Box 10. Economic growth and capital accumulation: Diversity amongst LDCs

There is much diversity in the performance of LDCs in terms of capital accumulation. This is quite closely related to the diversity in actual growth performance discussed in this chapter. In order to clarify the relationship, trends in savings, investment and foreign resource inflows were examined in the three groups of LDCs identified in the main text according to their long-term growth performance: converging economies, weak-growth economies and regressing economies. Oil-exporting LDCs (Angola, Equatorial Guinea, Sudan and Yemen) and island LDCs were removed from the sample as they have rather specific patterns of change.

This left the following countries[1] for which there were data:

• Converging economies: Bangladesh, Bhutan, Nepal, Mozambique and Uganda;

• Weak-growth economies: Benin, Burkina Faso, Chad, Ethiopia, Mali, Mauritania, Senegal and Malawi;

• Regressing economies: Burundi, Central African Republic, Democratic Republic of the Congo, Gambia, Guinea-Bissau, Haiti, Madagascar, Niger, Rwanda, Sierra Leone, Togo and Zambia.

There are major differences between these three groups of countries in terms of the rates of physical capital formation and its financing. At the start of the 1980s, there was not that much difference in the investment rates in the three groups of countries. In the converging economies gross capital formation constituted 18 per cent of GDP compared with 16 per cent in the weak-growth economies and 17 per cent in the regressing economies. But in the converging economies, the

Box table 4. Resource availability and investment as percentage of GDP in LDCs and LDCs subgroups with different growth experiences, 1980–1984, 1989–1993 and 1999–2003
(Percentage of GDP)

	Gross capital formation			Gross domestic savings			ODA Grants			Foreign direct investment		
	1980–1984	1989–1993	1999–2003	1980–1984	1989–1993	1999–2003	1980–1984	1989–1993	1999–2003	1980–1984	1989–1993	1999–2003
Converging economies												
Bangladesh	16.6	17.2	23.0	6.3	11.2	17.5	3.7	2.7	1.2	0.0	0.0	0.3
Bhutan	37.4	37.7	48.7	8.0	26.1	26.9	2.7	10.9	5.9	0.0	0.2	0.0
Mozambique	10.3	23.4	32.6	-5.9	-7.0	12.8	3.2	32.1	22.5	0.0	0.8	7.7
Nepal	18.3	20.6	23.8	10.0	9.8	14.2	2.9	4.2	3.3	0.0	0.0	0.0
Uganda	7.6	13.6	19.7	2.6	0.8	6.7	3.4	7.1	7.5	0.0	0.3	2.8
Weak growth economies												
Benin	17.8	14.1	18.3	-2.8	1.2	5.5	2.5	7.4	5.2	0.1	3.6	1.8
Burkina Faso	15.7	18.6	20.1	-5.9	5.5	5.4	5.4	6.8	7.3	0.1	0.1	0.4
Chad	3.3	9.5	42.1	-3.2	-5.1	18.8	6.4	7.2	4.6	0.2	0.6	26.7
Ethiopia	13.6	11.5	18.3	6.5	4.7	1.9	2.6	7.6	8.8	0.0	0.0	1.1
Malawi	19.9	20.4	9.3	13.5	7.3	-4.8	3.9	12.5	13.7	0.8	0.1	1.5
Mali	14.6	22.2	22.4	-0.6	5.8	15.3	7.0	7.9	7.4	0.3	0.0	3.8
Mauritania	28.4	19.2	32.9	-4.2	7.1	8.7	8.8	11.9	17.3	1.7	0.7	9.4
Senegal	12.4	13.3	19.2	-3.6	8.2	9.4	3.6	6.6	4.4	0.6	0.4	1.7
Regressing economies												
Burundi	17.4	15.3	9.7	3.0	-3.2	-2.5	4.5	10.8	16.7	0.4	0.1	0.4
Central African Republic	9.1	11.7	14.6	-3.4	1.1	10.5	6.7	6.1	5.2	0.8	-0.3	0.4
Dem. Rep of the Congo	9.6	7.3	6.9	8.4	7.1	5.6	0.7	2.7	22.7	-0.1	0.0	1.6
Gambia	22.6	21.6	18.4	5.4	8.8	12.0	12.2	13.8	4.3	0.2	2.6	11.4
Guinea-Bissau	28.3	35.5	13.3	-1.9	3.6	-7.9	23.3	19.8	25.6	0.3	1.2	1.2
Haiti	16.9	12.0	27.2	6.2	3.5	4.5	2.6	4.0	2.5	0.5	0.0	0.3
Madagascar	10.6	12.3	16.3	0.5	3.8	9.2	1.3	7.9	3.8	0.1	0.6	1.2
Niger	18.4	8.6	12.6	7.6	4.1	4.5	4.1	9.6	7.3	0.7	0.7	0.7
Rwanda	15.3	14.8	18.4	4.9	3.3	1.3	5.0	7.4	11.1	1.2	0.3	0.3
Sierra Leone	15.1	8.7	7.9	4.1	9.6	-10.3	1.9	7.9	22.6	0.0	1.3	1.5
Togo	22.6	17.2	17.7	17.6	7.9	1.8	2.5	5.8	2.5	1.4	0.3	3.0
Zambia	17.9	13.1	21.4	12.8	7.4	12.9	2.1	14.0	11.0	0.6	4.4	3.0
LDCs	16.8	16.8	20.6	3.4	5.3	7.2	4.9	9.4	9.8	0.4	0.7	3.3
Converging economies	18.0	22.5	29.6	4.2	8.2	15.6	3.2	11.4	8.1	0.0	0.3	2.2
Weak-growth economies	15.7	16.1	22.8	0.0	4.3	7.5	5.0	8.5	8.6	0.5	0.7	5.8
Regressing economies	17.0	14.8	15.4	5.4	4.7	3.5	5.6	9.1	11.3	0.5	0.9	2.1

Source: UNCTAD secretariat estimates based on World Bank, *World Development Indicators and Global Development Finance,* online data May 2005.
Note: Group averages are simple averages.

Box 10 (contd.)

investment rate had increased to 23 per cent in the period 1989–1993 and 30 per cent in the period 1999–2003. At the other end of the spectrum, the average investment rate within the regressing economies declined from 17 per cent in 1980–1984 to 15 per cent in 1999–2003. Investment rates increased between 1980–1984 and 1999–2003 in all the converging economies. But they declined in 7 out of 12 regressing economies.

In association with this increase in investment in the converging economies, gross domestic savings increased from 4 per cent of GDP in 1980–1984 to 8 per cent in 1989–1993 and 16 per cent in 1999–2003. In contrast, the savings rate, which actually started higher in the regressing economies than the converging economies, fell from 5 per cent to 4 per cent of GDP from the early 1980s to 1999–2003.

The weak-growth economies fall between these trends. Gross capital formation as a share of GDP does not change in the 1980s, but increases from 16 per cent in 1989–1993 and to 23 per cent in 1999–2003. This level is 6 percentage points higher than the average of the regressing economies but 7 percentage points lower than the converging economies. The domestic savings rate does not fall in the weak-growth economies as it does, on average, in the regressing economies. But the growth of investment in the 1990s is not matched, as in the converging economies, by a strongly rising domestic savings ratio. It increases from 0 per cent in 1980–1984 to 4 per cent in 1989–1993 and to 8 per cent in 1999–2003.

Although the converging economies have a strong domestic savings effort, external resources are still important for their investment processes. The domestic savings–investment gap was about 14 per cent of GDP during each of the three periods. In contrast, the domestic savings–investment gap is somewhat smaller (10 to 12 per cent of GDP) in the regressing economies. Once again the weak-growth economies are in an intermediate position. Their reliance on external resources as measured by the savings–investment gap somewhat decreased between 1980–1984 and 1989–1993, but increased in the subsequent period. But the increase in gross capital formation as a percentage of GDP from 1989–1993 to 1999–2003 is driven by an increase in external resources rather than an increase in the domestic savings rate.

It is also possible to identify trends in FDI and ODA grants as a share of GDP in these countries. This shows that in the period 1999–2003, FDI increased its contribution to gross capital formation in all groups of countries, but was insignificant in the two earlier periods. FDI is also most important as a share of GDP in the weak-growth economies. On average, three-quarters of the increase in the rate of capital formation in these countries can be attributed to increased FDI inflows. With regard to grants, it is clear that during the 1980s grants as a share of GDP increased significantly in all three country groups. However, their share subsequently decreased in the group of converging economies. In contrast, grants are increasing as a share of GDP in both the weak-growth and the regressing economies, although at a lower pace than previously.

These results show that it is possible for LDCs to achieve expanded domestic capital accumulation with a mix of increased domestic resource mobilization and external resource inflows.

[1] This includes all the countries for which data were available except Lesotho, which is treated as an outlier because, unlike in all the other countries, domestic consumption far exceeded GDP in all these periods.

F. External resource inflows and domestic capital accumulation

External finance can play an important catalytic role in kick-starting and supporting a virtuous cycle of domestic resource mobilization.

Realizing these potentials for domestic resource mobilization will certainly be difficult, given the all-pervasive extreme poverty and economic insecurity within LDCs. In these circumstances, external finance can play an important catalytic role in kick-starting and supporting a virtuous cycle of domestic resource mobilization in which expanding investment opportunities generate increased savings and increased savings in turn finance increased investment. Both ODA and FDI inflows are important. They can directly finance investment, and also, as will be discussed in chapter 7, play a significant role in relaxing balance-of-payments constraints on economic growth. But in practice there are various problems which mean that both these types of external resource inflows are not generally playing the catalytic financing role which they could play in expanded domestic capital accumulation.

1. ODA AND DOMESTIC ACCUMULATION AND BUDGETARY PROCESSES

ODA is particularly important. For the LDCs as a group, 67 per cent of aggregate net resource flows to the LDCs in 2000–2003 were official flows compared with 4 per cent in other developing countries.[14] But a major problem with capital formation processes within LDCs is that there are features of the current aid regime which interfere with a strong positive relationship between ODA inflows and domestic processes of capital accumulation in the LDCs.

Firstly, since the early 1990s an increasing proportion of the aid flows to the LDCs has been provided in ways which mean that they are not directly available to finance capital formation. In 2000–2003, almost half of the total ODA disbursements to the LDCs were directed to debt relief, emergency assistance, technical cooperation and development food aid. This was up from one third of total ODA to the LDCs in 1992–1995 (chart 17A).[15]

Secondly, a sectoral breakdown shows that the share of ODA committed to LDCs which is directed towards economic infrastructure and production-oriented sectors has declined significantly. Between 1992–1995 and 2000–2003, ODA commitments to economic infrastructure and production-oriented sectors, as defined in chart 17B, declined from 45 per cent to 26 per cent of the total commitments of all donors to LDCs. If one focuses solely on aid commitments to production sectors (agriculture, industry, mining, construction, trade and tourism) it is apparent that this constituted only 6.8 per cent of total aid commitments in the period 2000–2003. ODA commitments to banking and financial services accounted for only 1 per cent of total aid commitments in 2000–2003.

> *ODA is particularly important. For the LDCs as a group, 67 per cent of aggregate net resource flows to the LDCs in 2000–2003 were official flows compared with 4 per cent in other developing countries.*

> *ODA commitments to economic infrastructure and production-oriented sectors declined from 45 per cent to 26 per cent of the total commitments of all donors to LDCs.*

CHART 17. THE COMPOSITION OF ODA COMMITMENTS TO LDCS BY ALL DONORS, 1992–1995 AND 2000–2003

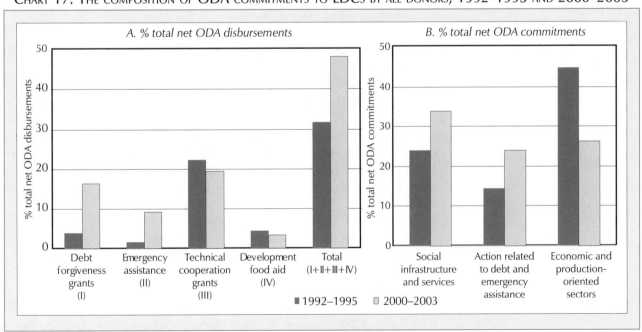

Source: Source: Calculations based on OECD/DAC *International Aid Statistics*, online data.

Notes: All donors comprise bilateral donors (DAC and non-DAC donor countries) and multilateral donors.
"*Social infrastructure and services*" comprises: education, health, population programmes, water supply and sanitation, government and civil society, other social infrastructure and services.
"*Economic and production-oriented sectors*" comprises: production sectors (agriculture, industry, mining, construction, trade, tourism and multisector),economic infrastructure, transport and storage, communication, energy, banking and financial services.

Thirdly, the extent to which aid inflows have expanded the fiscal space of Governments has been reduced by a number of features of the way in which aid is provided.[16] These are discussed in detail in LDC Report 2000 (chapter 5). They include the following:

- *The unpredictability and volatility of aid.* Long-term analysis of aid inflows to LDCs over the period 1970–1998 shows that foreign aid has been more volatile than extremely volatile export revenues; there is little correlation between variations in aid and variations in government revenue and export revenue; and variations in foreign aid have not acted to counteract other shocks. As a consequence, "the volatility of aid inflows has contributed to macro-economic instability" (UNCTAD, 2000: 181).

- *Lack of coordination of the aid system and the low degree of integration of the aid system into the local economic and administrative structures.* This has severely eroded State capacities. This is particularly evident in the high transaction costs associated with multiple donors and also the internal brain drain from the public sector to donor projects.[17] This has been exacerbated by the reduction of the public sector wage bill, which has eroded the real value of public salaries, together with the creation of parallel management structures for donor projects. These have interacted in a vicious cycle in which the more that State administrative capacities have eroded, the more donors have needed parallel structures to get things done.

- *The fiscal squeeze on current expenditures.* This occurred through conditionality on the level of current government expenditure, together with increased capital expenditures associated with aid projects which create future spending needs which have to be met from current expenditures. The increase in debt service payments from aid loans is one aspect of this problem.

The PRSP process tends to pay greater attention to direct poverty reduction than to indirect poverty reduction through the development of productive capacities.

The PRSP approach has sought to overcome these problems by seeking to link aid to national development strategies. The tendency to provide more aid in the form of budgetary support, together with debt relief in HIPC-LDCs, has also reduced the fiscal squeeze. However, the progress which has been made in terms of change in the behaviour of donors at the country level has been less than expected (see, for example, Driscoll and Evans, 2004; World Bank Operations Evaluation Department, 2004; World Bank/IMF 2005: 37–41). Moreover, whilst the changes may have improved aid delivery somewhat, they have imparted a particular bias to the way in which ODA supports capital formation.

This is the fourth key issue in terms of the relationship between aid and domestic accumulation and budgetary processes. The PRSP process tends to pay greater attention to direct poverty reduction than to indirect poverty reduction through the development of productive capacities. There has been a shift towards a greater focus on economic growth in the PRSPs since 2002 (UNCTAD, 2004: chapter 7). Nevertheless, there remain deep problems concerning how social sectors and productive sectors are integrated in PRSPs. As Driscoll and Evans (2004) observe:

- "Most PRSs have yet to deliver a fully integrated strategy in which the quality of social sector plans are matched by those for the productive sectors."

- "Underlying policy processes in the productive sectors are often particularly weak…The PRS emphasis on centralized national or sectoral expenditure targets tends to limit the focus to support for the local enabling environment or the provision of 'soft' services such as extension and technology to rural or informal sector producers."

- "Under pressure to demonstrate results, many donors have opted for quick wins of targeted social sector spending instead of seeking to address the paucity of analytical work on pro-poor growth, and support longer-term government action to bring it about." (pp. 7–8).

More emphasis is now being placed on the need to tie the PRSs with the long-term development vision of each country and also to link goals and targets to clear public actions designed to achieve them (World Bank/IMF, 2005). However, the orientation towards social targets and away from production and employment has possibly been exacerbated by the dominance of social sector targets and the marginal position of employment in the Millennium Development Goals.

A further important aspect of the development model underlying the poverty reduction strategies is the way in which economic growth is supposed to be promoted. Essentially, it is expected that this will occur through the deepening of economic reforms. Second-generation reforms pay more attention to governance issues and the investment climate, and they also seek to achieve more effective and more pro-poor public expenditure. But it remains to be seen how effective these second-generation reforms will be in addressing the interlocking structural constraints which most LDCs face and supporting the development of productive capacities, which is essential for achieving both high and sustainable rates of economic growth.

The failure of the first-generation reforms to increase domestic savings and investment sufficiently has been recognized as one of their critical weaknesses (World Bank, 2005; Griffin, 2005). It is for this reason that improving the investment climate is now being stressed. But currently, there is a tendency to shrink the notion of the investment climate in two ways: firstly, to equate it with government policies and regulations directly shaping opportunities and incentives of firms (rather than enterprises in general); and secondly, to associate less government with a better investment climate. Narrowing the idea of the investment climate in this way seriously diminishes the analytical and policy value of the concept. It is clear that improving the investment climate has been central in successful developing countries. But the good investment climate which they managed to promote was not associated with less government; rather, it entailed public action which recognized the heterogeneity of enterprise-level capabilities and sought pro-actively to upgrade them, and it also sought to manage a progressive transformation of production structures. Also, it was associated with a macroeconomic framework which was not geared simply to stabilization but also to promoting rapid capital accumulation by providing investment incentives.

The final issue which is also becoming increasingly relevant is the way in which conditions regarding good governance are being attached to aid inflows (Hoppenbrouwer, 2005). Government effectiveness is certainly vital for developing productive capacities. But it is possible that governance-related conditions for access to aid will undermine the effectiveness of aid. This can occur if the notion of good governance is defined in a way that prescribes a certain role for government in managing an economy rather than in a way that specifies standards of bureaucratic competence and administrative capability per se. The problem with the former approach is that it may assume a role for government which is not appropriate in particular countries and at particular times within the development process. Good governance will ultimately be possible only if government finances are sufficiently strong to enable adequate

The orientation towards social targets and away from production and employment has possibly been exacerbated by the dominance of social sector targets and the marginal position of employment in the Millennium Development Goals.

The failure of the first-generation reforms to increase domestic savings and investment sufficiently has been recognized as one of their critical weaknesses. It is for this reason that improving the investment climate is now being stressed.

expenditure on administration, law and order, and the provision of the services of a modern State. This ultimately requires the development of productive capacities to build up the revenue base of the domestic economy.

2. FDI AND DOMESTIC PRIVATE CAPITAL ACCUMULATION

The other major form of external finance which is important to the LDCs is FDI inflows. The way in which FDI affects domestic capital formation is, like the links between aid and domestic capital formation, a complex issue. It needs to take account of the fact that export-oriented FDI might work differently from FDI which is seeking to serve domestic markets, and that FDI seeking to exploit natural resources might have different effects from FDI in manufactures and services. As with aid, its effectiveness will also depend on domestic policies which integrate FDI into domestic development processes. Finally, it must be recognized that the definition of FDI includes both greenfield investment and acquisition of existing assets through takeovers. This makes it difficult to analyse precisely the relationship between FDI and domestic capital formation.

Good governance ultimately requires the development of productive capacities to build up the revenue base of the domestic economy.

Empirical studies show that there is often a significant relationship between FDI and domestic investment, but that the relationship may be one in which FDI crowds out domestic investment as frequently as it crowds in domestic investment (Agosin and Mayer, 2000; Kumar and Pradhan, 2002; Ghose, 2004). Chart 18 presents evidence on changes in levels of FDI and domestic fixed private capital formation between the first half of the 1990s and the second half of the 1990s in 12 LDCs for which it was possible to obtain data. This shows, as noted earlier in the chapter, that FDI as a share of GDP has increased in 10 out of the 12 countries. But in all five countries where the FDI/GDP ratio increased

CHART 18. CHANGES IN NET FDI INFLOWS AND DOMESTIC PRIVATE INVESTMENT AS A PER CENT OF GDP
IN SELECTED LDCS BETWEEN 1990–1995 AND 1995–2000
(Change in percentage points)

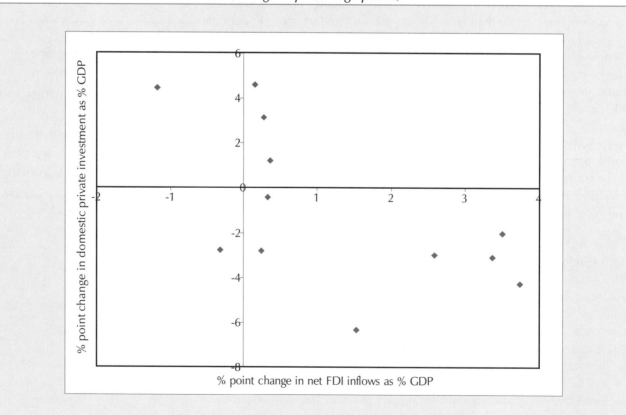

Source: UNCTAD secretariat estimates based on World Bank data (direct communication) and UNCTAD FDI/TNC data.

by over one percentage point between the first half and the second half of the 1990s, the ratio of domestic private investment to GDP fell by two percentage points or more. There are only three countries in which an increasing FDI/GDP ratio is associated with an increasing private domestic investment/GDP ratio.

It is difficult to identify what precisely is behind these tendencies, and the sample size is small. However, the data suggest that foreign investment has not had strong positive linkages effects that have generated higher levels of private domestic investment. As analysed in the last LDC Report, growth based on exports of oil, minerals, or manufactures produced in EPZs, which in all cases has been highly dependent on FDI, has often been an isolated enclave within the LDC national economies. Elaborating policies which can foster positive linkages between FDI and domestic private sector is a major challenge.

F. Conclusions

In addressing the issue of developing productive capacities in the least developed countries, it is necessary to maintain a balance between the constraints and the opportunities that characterize the present situation. Focusing on the multiple and interlocking constraints can lead to a paralysing sense of pessimism and an overwhelming sense of dependence on external aid. But there are in practice major opportunities for rapid economic growth and substantial poverty reduction if these constraints can be relaxed in a systematic way. Moreover, there are important hidden and underutilized productive resources and entrepreneurial capabilities that can support the development of productive capacities from within.

This chapter has shown how fast LDCs could grow if their labour force were to be fully employed and various potential sources of labour productivity growth, which are available to all very poor countries, were exploited. The analysis indicates that the growth rate target of more than 7 per cent, which is part of the Brussels Programme of Action for the LDCs, is achievable. But this requires a fast catch-up growth scenario in which there is development, as well as full and efficient utilization, of productive capacities. In particular, it requires full employment of the labour force, faster human capital accumulation, faster acquisition and absorption of technologies already in use in other countries, and structural change to enable increasing returns to scale.

Increased investment is essential for achieving the potential GDP growth rates which are possible in the LDCs. It is through such increased investment that technological progress and structural change will be possible and productive capacities will develop. But despite improvements in the 1990s, capital formation was still only 22 per cent of GDP in the LDCs as a group in 1999–2003 and domestic private investment was particularly weak. Capital formation in the LDCs is far below the rate which is estimated to be required for the fast catch-up scenario (35 per cent of GDP) and also below that required for a slow catch-up scenario in which technological acquisition occurs more slowly than in the fast catch-up scenario. A further concern is that actual rates of human capital formation in the LDCs in the 1990s were slower than in other developing countries. The average years of schooling of the adult population in the LDCs was three years in 2000, which was the same as the level in other developing countries in 1960. Enrolment rates in secondary technical and vocational education and also tertiary enrolment rates in engineering are much lower on average in LDCs than in other developing countries. The brain drain is also increasing in many LDCs. In 2000, one in five of the stock of "high-skill workers"

Elaborating policies which can foster positive linkages between FDI and domestic private sector is a major challenge.

The analysis indicates that the growth rate target of more than 7 per cent, which is part of the Brussels Programme of Action for the LDCs, is achievable, if constraints on the productive capacities can be relaxed in a systematic way.

in the LDCs, defined as those with tertiary education (13 years of schooling or above), were working in OECD countries.

The inadequate rates of physical and human capital formation reflect weaknesses in domestic resource mobilization to finance capital formation, as well as weaknesses in the way in which external capital inflows are supporting domestic processes of capital accumulation. Gross domestic savings rose to 13.6 per cent of GDP in 1999–2003. But with this savings rate it is not only impossible to achieve the investment rates required by the catch-up scenarios without external capital inflows, but also impossible even to achieve positive rates of GDP per capita growth. Estimates of genuine savings, which take account of capital depreciation and natural resource depletion, also indicate that, without ODA grants, there were negative savings for all years between 1991 and 2003, and that the genuine savings rate, without ODA grants, was also declining. Government revenue and expenditure are also low, particularly in countries which do not have access to mineral resource rents. During 2000–2003, government final consumption expenditure in the LDCs was equivalent to $26 per capita compared with $186 per capita in other developing countries.

Mass poverty means that there are considerable limits to the current capacity to save and raise government revenue within the LDCs. However, this does not mean that there is a low potential for domestic resource mobilization. In practice, the contrary is true as the underdevelopment of the LDC economies has the corollary that there are hidden and underutilized resources. If investment increases there are significant possibilities for increased domestic resource mobilization based on increased monetization of the economy, the mobilization of surplus labour, a shift away from household to corporate financing of investment, the mobilization of latent entrepreneurship and turning unproductive into productive entrepreneurship, and the increased deployment of the resources of the small stratum of the rich for productive investment within the LDCs. Comparison of the contrasting investment and savings performance of LDCs classified according to their growth experience indicates that some LDCs have significantly increased both domestic savings and investment in a virtuous circle.

Recent growth accelerations in the LDCs will not be sustainable unless ODA inflows enhance increased domestic savings and investment and thus reduce aid dependence. The recent surge in aid to LDCs should be linked to policies which promote economic growth by explicitly developing their productive capacities.

External capital inflows can play an important catalytic role in kick-starting and supporting such a virtuous cycle of domestic resource mobilization in which expanding profitable investment opportunities generate increased savings and increased savings in turn finance increased investment. There is a major opportunity here because since 2000 the sharp decline in ODA to LDCs which occurred during the 1990s has been reversed, and FDI inflows into LDCs, though geographically concentrated, are also increasing. But the limited evidence suggests that FDI inflows are not crowding in domestic private investment. Moreover, there are various features of the current aid regime which imply that ODA is not playing a catalytic role in boosting domestic resource mobilization and expanded domestic capital accumulation. These are related to: the composition of aid which is oriented away from physical capital formation and productive sectors; bias towards social sectors away from production and employment within PRSPs; and conditionality which prescribes a certain role for government in managing an economy which is not adapted necessarily well to the structural weaknesses and enterprise heterogeneity within the LDCs. Recent growth accelerations in the LDCs will not be sustainable unless ODA inflows enhance increased domestic savings and investment and thus reduce aid dependence. The recent surge in aid to LDCs should be linked to policies which promote economic growth by explicitly developing their productive capacities.

ANNEX CHART 1. LONG-TERM TRENDS IN GDP PER CAPITA IN LDCs
(Constant 2000 $)

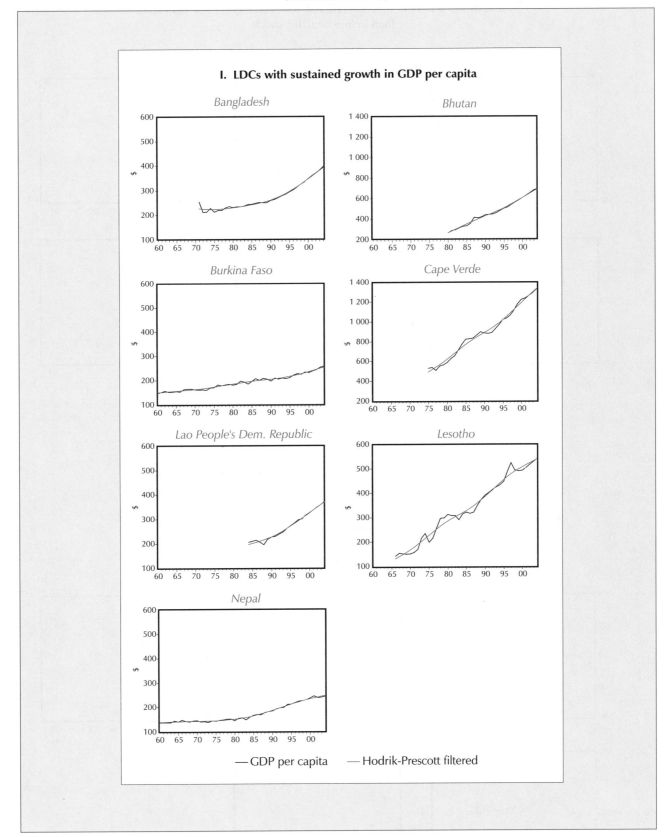

I. LDCs with sustained growth in GDP per capita

—GDP per capita   —Hodrik-Prescott filtered

Annex chart 1 (contd.)

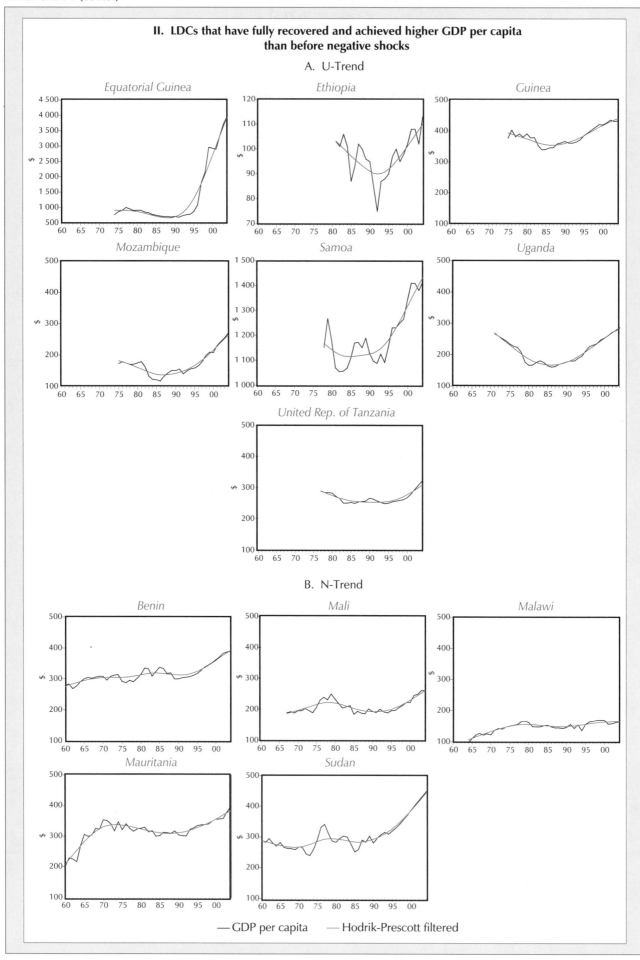

II. LDCs that have fully recovered and achieved higher GDP per capita than before negative shocks

A. U-Trend

Equatorial Guinea   *Ethiopia*   *Guinea*

Mozambique   *Samoa*   *Uganda*

United Rep. of Tanzania

B. N-Trend

Benin   *Mali*   *Malawi*

Mauritania   *Sudan*

— GDP per capita   — Hodrik-Prescott filtered

Annex chart 1 (contd.)

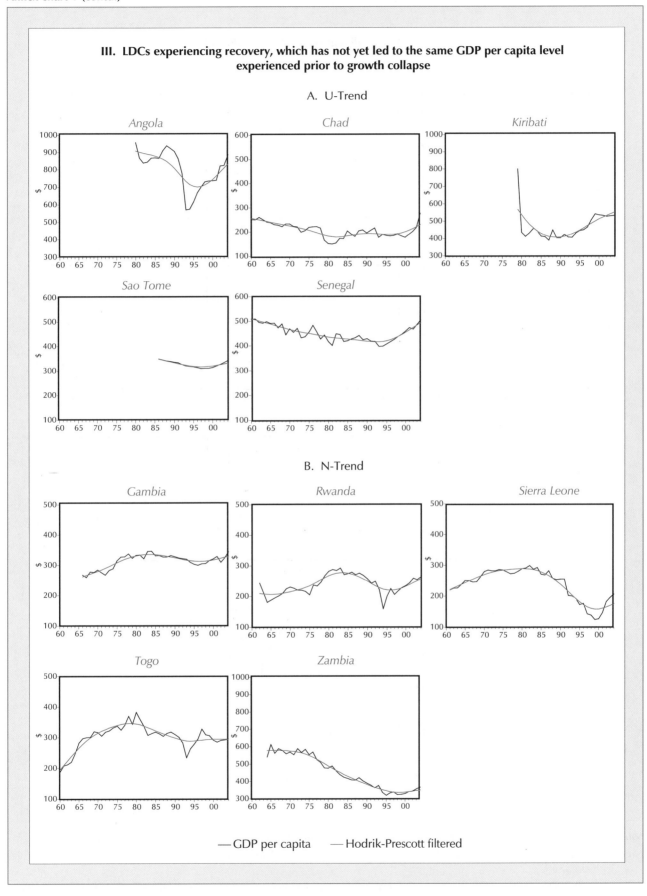

III. LDCs experiencing recovery, which has not yet led to the same GDP per capita level experienced prior to growth collapse

A. U-Trend

B. N-Trend

—GDP per capita   — Hodrik-Prescott filtered

Annex chart 1 (contd.)

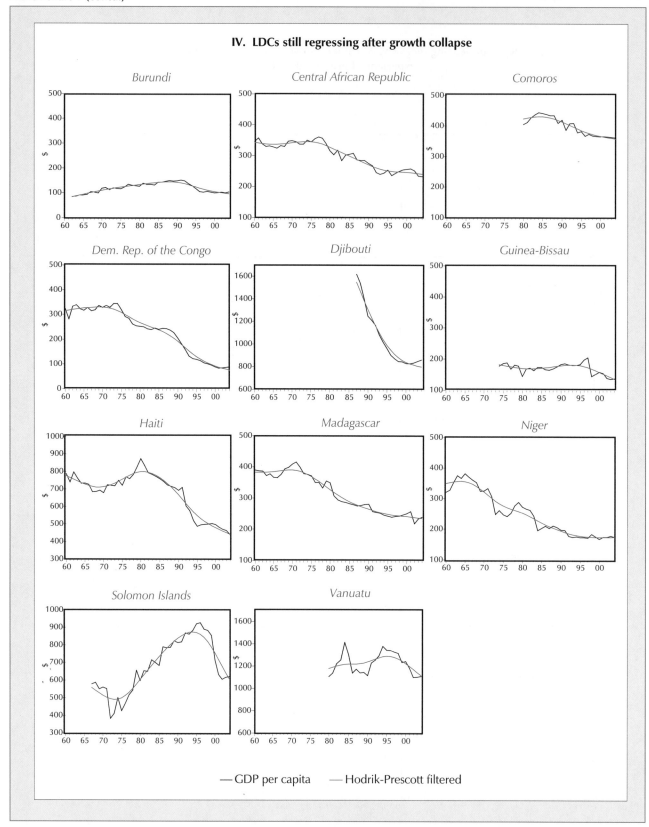

IV. LDCs still regressing after growth collapse

Source: UNCTAD secretariat estimates based on World Bank, *World Development Indicators 2005*, CD-ROM.

Notes: Aiming at highlighting the domestic trend in real GDP per capita, while accounting for the sample diversity, different scales were used.

Real GDP per capita was reconstructed by applying the growth rates of real GDP per capita obtained from the United Nations Statistical Division for the following countries: (1975-1980) for Cape Verde, (1974-1984) for Equatorial Guinea, (1975-1985) for Guinea, (1975-1979) for Mozambique, (1977-1987) for the United Republic of Tanzania and (1971-1981) for Uganda.

a   Data refers to GDP per capita. Starting date coincides with political independence or the earliest year for which data are available.

Notes

1. Ideally, the analysis should include discussion of trends in natural capital. Some estimates of genuine savings (i.e. savings which take account of natural resource depletion) are given, and they show that this is a serious issue. But natural capital is not treated here for lack of space. Atkinson (2005) provides a first overview of the environmental assets of the LDCs.

2. In the Programme of Action, the target is a GDP growth rate of "at least 7 per cent per annum" (United Nations, 2001: para. 6)

3. It should be recalled that the term "Verdoorn elasticity" is being used here to refer to the assumed relationships between economic growth rate and the labour productivity growth rate which is estimated on historical experience. Verdoorn's Law itself would not predict that there would be any such elasticity except in the manufactures-exporting LDCs.

4. Many analysts are now rejecting the idea that one can undertake growth analysis by identifying a single average growth rate over a long span of time and then relate it to a set of country characteristics and policies. They show that growth is not a steady process. See, for example, Rodrik (1999), Pritchett (2000), Hausmann, Pritchett and Rodrik (2004), Ros (2005b), Cerra and Saxena (2005) and Jerzmanowski (2006).

5. This is the same definition of a severe growth collapse as Ros (2005b).

6. For theoretical explanations of these different responses of output to negative shocks, see Cerra and Saxena (2005).

7. These statistics are based on Cohen and Soto (2001). An alternative (and actually more widely used) database (Barro and Lee, 2000) shows that in 1999, the level of formal schooling in LDCs was actually lower than these data indicate (2 years and 4 months).

8. For an overview of the different effects of international migration, see Ozden and Schiff (2006).

9. The term "domestic resource mobilization" is used here to refer to mobilization of financial resources through increases in domestic savings and government revenue.

10. In this calculation, the capital/output ratio is assumed to be 3 and the rate of depreciation 2.8 per cent per annum. The population growth rate in the LDCs during the period is estimated at 2.5 per cent per annum.

11. For a discussion of the macroeconomic and development impact of generalized poverty, in which a majority of the population lives at a bare subsistence level, see Steger (2000).

12. As Griffin (1996) puts it, "In many instances investment requires little more than the direct application of labour: digging an irrigation or drainage ditch; planting a tea garden, coffee bushes or fruit trees; clearing, leveling or terracing a field; constructing a wall, animal shelter or home out of earth bricks. Whether a household will expend the labour on such tasks depends on whether it is worthwhile or profitable. If there is plenty of slack in the labour market, e.g. in the form of seasonal rural unemployment, potentially profitable investments can be 'financed' not by consuming less (i.e. saving) but by working longer. That is, surplus labour at the level of the household can be used to finance household level investment projects. The problem is not how to save more but how to create investment opportunities. If there is an abundance of investment opportunities, the problem of savings will take care of itself" (p. 22).

13. In his discussion of the structural features of LDCs, Ignacy Sachs writes that "although the present rate of savings in LDCs is very low, the rate of extracted surplus is quite substantial; but this surplus partly flows abroad through adverse terms of trade and debt servicing; besides it finances the conspicuous consumption of urban elites, often supports the plethoric public administration and the patriarchal state; in other words, the extracted surplus is misallocated" (Sachs, 2004: 1803).

14. Private capital flows to LDCs are increasing. But the only type of such flows that is significant for the LDCs is FDI and these flows are concentrated in oil- and mineral-exporting LDCs. The LDCs are effectively excluded from raising loans on international capital markets because of their perceived risk, weak (or non-existent) credit ratings and the requirements of official debt relief processes. The contribution of private debt flows to total resources flows in LDCs never exceeded 2 per cent throughout 1990–2003.

15. For an important discussion of the relationship between the composition of aid and its impact, see Clemens, Radelet and Bhavnani (2004).

16. The fiscal impact of aid is the subject of a growing literature. Major issues, as well as empirical results for some LDCs, are usefully summarized in ODI (2004), and Heller (2005) provides an overview of issues related to expanding "fiscal space".

17. Ghani, Lockhart and Carnahan (2005) cite the case of the internal brain drain from government offices to bilateral and multilateral agencies in Afghanistan. Approximately 280,000 civil servants work in the government bureaucracy, earning $50 per month, while approximately 50,000 Afghan nationals work for NGOs, the UN and bilateral and

multilateral agencies, where support staff can earn up to $1,000 per month. Not surprisingly, the national civil servants seek work in the international sector, thus undermining the capacity of the Government to carry out its functions.

References

Agosin, M. and Mayer, J. (2000). Foreign investment in developing countries: Does it crowd in domestic investment? UNCTAD Discussion Papers, no. 146, Geneva.

Akyuz, Y. and Gore, C.G. (1996). The investment profits nexus in East Asian industrialization, *World Development*, 24(3), 461–470.

Atchoarena, D. and Delluc, A. (2001). Revisiting technical and vocational education in sub-Saharan Africa: An update on trends, innovations, and challenges. IIEP/Prg. DA/01.320. International Institute for Educational Planning, Paris.

Atkinson, A. (2005). Current state and recent trends in natural resource endowment in the least developed countries. Background paper prepared for the *Least Developed Countries Report 2006*, UNCTAD, Geneva.

Barro, R.J. and Lee, J.W. (2000). International data on educational attainment: Updates and implications. CID Working Paper No. 42, Center for International Development at Harvard University, Mass.

Baumol, W.J. (1990). Entrepreneurship: Productive, unproductive and destructive. *Journal of Political Economy*, vol. XXVIII: 1708–1715.

Baunsgaard, T. and Keen, M. (2004). Tax revenue and trade liberalization. (Draft). Fiscal Affairs Department, International Monetary Fund, Washington DC.

Cerra, V. and Saxena, S. (2005). Growth dynamics: The myth of economic recovery. IMF Working Paper WP/05/147, International Monetary Fund, Washington, DC.

Clemens, M., Radelet, S. and Bhavnani, R. (2004). Counting chickens when they hatch: The short term effect of aid on growth. Working Paper No. 44, Center for Global Development, Washington DC.

Cohen, D. and Soto, M. (2001). Growth and human capital: good data, good results. Discussion Paper No. 3025, Centre for Economic Policy Research, London.

David, M. (2005). The LDC domestic financial sector. Background paper prepared for *The Least Developed Countries Report 2006*, UNCTAD, Geneva.

Docquier, F. and Marfouk, A. (2004). Measuring the international mobility of skilled workers (1990–2000): Release 1.0. World Bank Policy Research, Washington DC.

Driscoll, R. and Evans, A. (2004). Second generation poverty reduction strategies. Paper prepared for the PRSP Monitoring and Synthesis Project, Overseas Development Institute, London.

Easterly, W. (2005). Reliving the '50s: The big push, poverty traps, and takeoffs in economic development. Working Paper No. 65, Center for Global Development, New York University.

Fei, J.C. and Ranis, G. (1997). *Growth and Development from an Evolutionary Perspective*, Blackwell Publishers, UK.

Gerschenkron, A. (1962). *Economic Backwardness in Historical Perspective*. Cambridge, Mass., Harvard University Press.

Ghani, A., Lockhart C. and Carnahan, M. (2005). Closing the sovereignty gap: An approach to state-building. Overseas Development Institute, Working Paper 253, London.

Ghose, A.K. (2004). Capital inflows and investment in developing countries. Employment Strategy Papers, International Labour Office, Geneva.

Griffin, K. (1996). Macroeconomic reform and employment: An investment-led strategy of structural adjustment in sub-Saharan Africa. Issues in Development Discussion, Paper No. 16, International Labour Office, Geneva.

Griffin, K. and Brenner, M.D. (2000). Domestic resource mobilization and enterprise development in sub-Saharan Africa. In Griffin, K. (2000). *Studies in Development Strategy and Systemic Transformation*. London, Macmillan.

Hausmann, R., Pritchett, L. and Rodrik, D. (2004). Growth accelerations. NBER Working Paper no. 10566, Washington, DC.

Heller, P.S. (2005). Understanding fiscal space. IMF Policy Discussion Paper, PDP/05/4, International Monetary Fund, Washington, DC.

Hirschman, A.O. (1958). *The Strategy of Economic Development*. New Haven, Yale University Press.

Hoppenbrouwer, I.S. (2005). Governance in LDCs and selectivity in aid allocation. Background paper prepared for *The Least Developed Countries Report 2006*, UNCTAD, Geneva.

Jerzmanowski, M. (2006). Empirics of hills, plateaus, mountains and plains: A Markov-switching approach to growth. *Journal of Development Economics*. (forthcoming).

King, K. and Palmer, R. (2005). Capacities, skills and knowledge in the least developed countries: New challenges for development cooperation. Background paper prepared for the *Least Developed Countries Report 2006*.

Knell, M. (2006). Uneven technological accumulation and growth in the least developed countries. Background paper prepared for *The Least Developed Countries Report 2006*, UNCTAD, Geneva.

Kraay, A. and Raddatz, C. (2005). Poverty traps, aid and growth. World Bank Policy Research Working Paper 3631, Washington, DC.

Kumar, N. and Pradhan, J. (2002). Foreign direct investment, externalities and economic growth in developing countries: Some empirical explorations and implications for WTO negotiations on investment. RIS Discussion Paper No. 27, New Delhi, Research and Information System for the Non-Aligned and other Developing Countries.

Lewis, W.A. (1955). *The Theory of Economic Growth*. Allen and Unwin, London.

Maddison, A. (1995). *Monitoring the World Economy, 1820–1992*. Organisation for Economic Cooperation and Development, Paris.

Mankiw, G., Romer, D. and Weil, D. (1992). A contribution to the empirics of economic growth. *Quarterly Journal of Economics*, 107: 407–437.

McCombie, J., Pugno. M. and Soro, B. (eds.) (2003). *Productivity growth and economic performance: Essays in Verdoorn's Law*. Palgrave Macmillan, London.

McKinley, T. (2005). Economic alternatives for Sub-Saharan Africa: "Poverty traps", MDG-based strategies and accelerated capital accumulation. UNDP draft paper for the G-24 Meeting, 15–16 September 2005, New York.

Overseas Development Institute (2004). What can the fiscal impact of aid tell us about aid effectiveness? ESAU Briefing Paper, No. 4, London.

Ozden, C. and Schiff, M. (2006). *International Migration, Remittances and the Brain Drain*, World Bank and Macmillan, Basingstoke, UK.

Pritchett, L. (2000). Understanding patterns of economic growth: Searching for hills among plateaus, mountains and plains. *World Bank Economic Review*, 14(2): 221–250.

Ranis, G. (1997). The micro-economics of "surplus labor". Center Discussion Paper No. 772, Economic Growth Center, Yale University, New Haven, Conn.

Rodrik, D. (1999). Where did all the growth go? External shocks, social conflict, and growth collapses, *Journal of Economic Growth*, 4 (4): 385–412.

Ros. J. (2000). *Development Theory and the Economics of Growth*, Ann Arbor, MI, University of Michigan Press.

Ros, J. (2005a). Growth prospects and constraints in LDCs. Background paper for *The Least Developed Countries Report 2006*, UNCTAD, Geneva.

Ros, J. (2005b). Growth collapses. In: Ocampo, J.A. (ed.) Beyond Reforms, Structural Dynamics and Macroeconomic Vulnerability. Latin American Development Forum Series, United Nations Economic Commission for Latin America and the Caribbean Washington, DC.

Ros, J. (2006). Changing growth constraints in Northern Latin America. In Solimano, A. (ed.), *Vanishing growth in Latin America. The late 20th century experience*, Edward Elgar, London.

Sachs, I. (2004). From poverty trap to inclusive development in LDCs. *Economic and Political Weekly*, 39 (18): 1802–1811.

Sachs, J. et al. (2004). Ending Africa's poverty trap, *Brookings Papers on Economic Activity*, 1: 117–240.

Solow, R. (1956). A contribution to the theory of economic growth. *Quarterly Journal of Economics*, 70, 65–94.

Steger, T.M. (2000). Economic growth with subsistence consumption. *Journal of Development Economics*, 62: 343–361.

Taylor, L. and Rada, C. (2005). Can the poor countries catch up? Sources of growth accounting gives weak convergence for the early 21st century, New School of Social Research, New York, mimeo.

United Nations (2001). Programme of Action for the Least Developed Countries for the Decade 2001–2010. A/CONF.191.11.

UN Millennium Project (2005). *Investing in Development: A Practical Plan to Achieve the Millennium Development Goals*. New York.

UNCTAD (2000). *The Least Developed Countries Report 2000: Aid, Private Capital Flows and External Debt – The Challenge of Financing Development in the LDCs*. United Nations publication, sales no. E.00.II.D.21, Geneva and New York.

UNCTAD (2004). *The Least Developed Countries Report 2004, Linking International Trade with Poverty Reduction*, United Nations publication, sales no. E.04.II.D.27, Geneva and New York.

World Bank (2004). Competing in the global economy: An investment climate assessment for Uganda. Washington, DC.

World Bank Operations Evaluation Department (2004). The Poverty Reduction Strategy Initiative: An independent evaluation of the World Bank's support through 2003. World Bank, Washington, DC.

World Bank (2005). *Economic Growth in the 1990s: Learning from a Decade of Reform*. World Bank, Washington, DC.

World Bank/IMF (2005). 2005 Review of the PRS approach: Balancing accountabilities and scaling up results. Washington, DC.

Technological Progress, Structural Change and Trade Integration

Chapter

3

A. Introduction

Productive capacities do not only develop through capital accumulation, but also through technological progress and structural change. Technological progress usually requires investment because much technology is embodied in machinery and other kinds of capital equipment. However, it also requires knowledge and know-how which people and organizations acquire through learning, and which are embodied in procedures and institutional arrangements. In particular, technological progress will not take place without technological capabilities — the skills, information and experience to build and reconfigure core production competences through new investment, incremental and radical product and process innovation and the development of new markets and linkages.

Within development policy analysis there is quite a sharp divide between those who emphasize the importance of capital accumulation as the key to development and those who emphasize knowledge accumulation, technological capabilities and learning. Nelson and Pack (1999), for example, distinguish two explanations of the growth of the Asian Newly Industrializing Economies (NIEs) – accumulation theories, which emphasize the role of physical and human capital accumulation, and assimilation theories, which emphasize the importance of learning in identifying, adapting and operating imported technologies. But this divide is artificial. In reality both processes are important and interrelated. Within LDCs, the development of productive capacities requires both capital accumulation and knowledge accumulation.

The development of productive capacities requires both capital accumulation and knowledge accumulation.

Technological progress occurs through innovation which, following Schumpeter (1942), can best be defined as: (i) the introduction of new goods and services, or of new qualities of goods and services; (ii) the development of new production methods, or new marketing strategies; (iii) the opening-up of new markets; (iv) the discovery of new sources of raw materials or exploitation of previously known resources; and (v) the establishment of new industrial structures in a given sector. Whenever firms undertake activities which are new to them, even if it is not new to their competitors, to their countries or to the world, it is a risky process. But if it is successful, a technology may become more and more widely adopted. Various incremental innovations normally occur in the innovation diffusion process. These involve minor increases in technical efficiency, productivity and precision in production processes, or changes in products to achieve better quality, reduce costs or widen their range of uses. But the end-result of this process is intra-sectoral productivity growth and economy-wide structural change, as well as changes in the form of trade integration of a country as enterprises acquire international competitiveness in the production of more skill- and technology-intensive goods and services.

In the most successful developing economies which have achieved fast rates of catch-up growth, economic growth has been associated with a structural transformation. This has occurred as successive waves of economic activity which are new to the country have been introduced and diffused. Agricultural productivity growth has usually occurred at the initial stages of the growth process. However, agriculture has become progressively less important and manufacturing and services have become relatively more important as a share of GDP and source of employment. There has also been a shift from less to more technology-, skill- and capital-intensive activities both within and across sectors. Moreover, there has been a progressive shift in the export structure as enterprises located within the country acquire the technological capabilities necessary to compete internationally.

In the most successful developing economies which have achieved fast rates of catch-up growth, economic growth has been associated with a structural transformation... and a shift from less to more technology-, skill- and capital-intensive activities both within and across sectors.

This chapter provides an overview of patterns of structural change, trade integration and the development of technological capabilities in the LDCs. Section B provides an overview of trends in production structure, labour productivity and trade integration in the LDCs. The evidence shows that for LDCs as a whole there has been very little structural change since 1980, the productivity gap between the LDCs and other developing countries is widening and most LDCs remain focused on primary commodity exports. However, there are significant differences amongst the LDCs. Section C examines whether differences in growth performance are related to patterns of structural change and trade integration. Section D thus completes the analysis by examining the level and trends in technological learning in LDCs. The general lack of structural change, productivity growth and international competitiveness is a manifestation of weak technological capabilities. But this section deepens the analysis by examining indicators of technological effort. Data are very patchy and the section therefore draws on evidence from Investment Climate Surveys conducted in the LDCs. The conclusion summarizes the main points of the chapter.

B. Trends in production structure, labour productivity and trade integration

The economies of most of the LDCs continue to be dominated by agriculture and petty service activities.

The present section identifies trends in production structure using data from various sources, including World Bank, the UN Statistical Division (UNSD), UNIDO and FAO, and trends in trade structure using UN COMTRADE data. The data are far from ideal. Indeed, it is striking how difficult it is to get dtailed internationally comparable data on what LDCs produce and how people within LDCs earn a living. The analysis which follows is based on a careful assessment of differences in data sources and comparative analysis to ensure that the arguments presented in this chapter are robust with regard to the particular selection of data sources (see box 11). It is also limited to the relatively broad level of sectoral disaggregation which the data allow.

1. Trends in production structure

There has been little structural change in the LDCs as a group over the past twenty-five years. The economies of most of the LDCs continue to be dominated by agriculture and petty service activities. Both industrial activities and services are becoming slowly more important for the LDC group as a whole. The types of industrial activities which are expanding are mining, the exploitation of crude oil and, in the same cases, the generation of hydropower; and the types of services which are expanding are petty trade and commercial services. However, within this overall pattern of structural stasis there are considerable differences amongst the trends in different LDCs.

Box 11. Data on production and labour in least developed countries

Internationally comparable data on value added in least developed countries is provided by two principle sources, namely the United Nations Statistical Division (UNSD) and the World Bank's *World Development Indicators* (WDI). Both databases provide value-added data for the three principal economic sectors, namely agriculture, industry and services, and both databases also provide value-added data for the manufacturing sector. The two datasets have their advantages and disadvantages. The UNSD database, unlike WDI data, provides value-added data for sub-sectors of the industrial sector, and provides value-added data for the main sub-sectors of the services sector. But a major shortcoming of the UNSD database, compared with the WDI data, is that it does not provide value-added data in constant dollars for one of the main economic sectors, namely the industrial sector. As one of the objectives of this report was to conduct a trend analysis of structural change, value added data in constant dollars was indispensable, especially for the principal sectors of the economies. As the available data for the LDCs has not allowed for the estimation of reliable deflators for the industrial sector, this report has based its analysis on value-added data provided by WDI rather then UNSD, even though this choice implies accepting a smaller country coverage.

But the differences between the two datasets are not only limited to the disaggregation of data, the availability of deflators and the coverage of countries. There are also marked differences between the two datasets as regards the actual level of value added. The two datasets show considerable differences in the level of value added for the group of LDCs, but also for a good number of individual LDCs. But the differences in value added cannot be systematically linked to individual countries. Furthermore, the differences in value added cannot systematically be linked to the use of deflators. In some cases, conversion of the data into constant dollars exacerbates the differences, but in others the conversion into constant dollars actually minimizes these differences.

The United Nations Industrial Development Organization (UNIDO) publishes value added data for sub-sectors of the manufacturing sector. This data shows: the technology intensity of manufacturing activities; employment by manufacturing activities; and gross fixed capital formation by manufacturing activities. The data therefore does not only make it possible to estimate the level of manufacturing value-added, but also to evaluate the nature of manufacturing activities. The basic problem as far as the LDCs are concerned is that the country coverage is very weak, and that the available data are not very reliable. Data on employment and gross fixed capital formation associated with individual manufacturing activities was only available for seven LDCs out of a sample of 50 LDCs for the period between the early 1980s to the late 1990s. Furthermore, there are large discrepancies between total manufacturing value-added, as presented by UNIDO, and total manufacturing value-added as presented by either UNSD or WDI. Due to these data issues, this report focuses on value added in two categories, namely the category of resource-intensive and low-technology manufacturing activities and the category of medium- and high-technology manufacturing activities. Value-added data for these categories is presented only as a share of total manufacturing value-added.

In addition to the difficulties with production data, there are considerable difficulties with employment data. While UNIDO collects employment data for the manufacturing sector, the International Labour Organization (ILO) collects employment data for all principal economic sectors. The ILO database, however, has a very weak coverage of the LDCs. Long-term employment trends by economic activities can be observed for only 7 LDCs out of a sample of 50 LDCs. Some of the LDCs for which the ILO provides employment data are the same as the LDCs for which UNIDO has collected employment data. Where employment in the manufacturing sector is concerned, these two data sources show considerable differences. The weak coverage of countries and the discrepancies between available employment data make it difficult to conduct a trend analysis of employment or labour productivity by economic sectors. This report therefore estimates employment changes on the basis of changes in the size of the economically active population.

Data on the economically active population may be used as a proxy for employment as they include both people that are formally employed, but also persons who are informally employed. It includes everybody who works to make a living and formally or informally contributes to output. According to ILO's definition (ILO LABORSTA online, January 2006) it includes all those "who furnish the supply of labour for the production of goods and services during a specified time-reference period", namely employers; self-employed workers; salaried employees; wage earners; unpaid workers, people assisting in a family, farm or business operation; members of producers' cooperatives; and members of the armed forces (see ILO LABORSTA online, January 2006). The same definition is also used by FAO (FAOSTAT online January 2006). Those that are economically active at a given point in time are also referred to as the labour force. In this analysis, the term economically active population is therefore used interchangeably with the term labour force.

Data on the economically active population in the LDCs is provided in three principal sources, namely the ILO, the WDI and the Food and Agriculture Organization (FAO). All three data sources have a good coverage of the LDCs, but there are also some discrepancies between them. The largest discrepancies are apparent between FAO and WDI data on the one hand, and ILO data on the other; the discrepancies are small between FAO data and WDI data. Another important difference between the datasets is that unlike ILO and the WDI database, which provide data on the economi-

Box 11 (contd.)

cally active population only for the economy as a whole, the FAO provides a breakdown of the data for the agricultural and the non-agricultural sectors. This report uses the FAO database. It is only by using the FAO database that it is possible to show changes in the structure of employment between the agricultural and the non-agricultural sector and changes in labour productivity in the agricultural and non-agricultural sectors. While the WDI database does not provide the data to estimate labour productivity in the agricultural or non-agricultural sectors, the WDI database does provide an estimate of labor productivity in the agricultural sector. The estimated level of agricultural labour productivity provided by WDI is lower than our estimate of agricultural labour productivity based on FAO data. A comparison between estimates of the level of economy-wide labour productivity using FAO data and estimates using ILO data indicated that the latter were 10 per cent higher on average. However, the labour productivity trends were the same for both data sources.

Source: Herrmann (2006).

CHART 19. DISTRIBUTION OF VALUE ADDED AMONG PRINCIPAL ECONOMIC SECTORS OF LDCs, OTHER DEVELOPING
COUNTRIES AND DEVELOPED COUNTRIES, 1980–1983, 1990–1993 AND 2000–2003
(Percentage of total value-added, average)

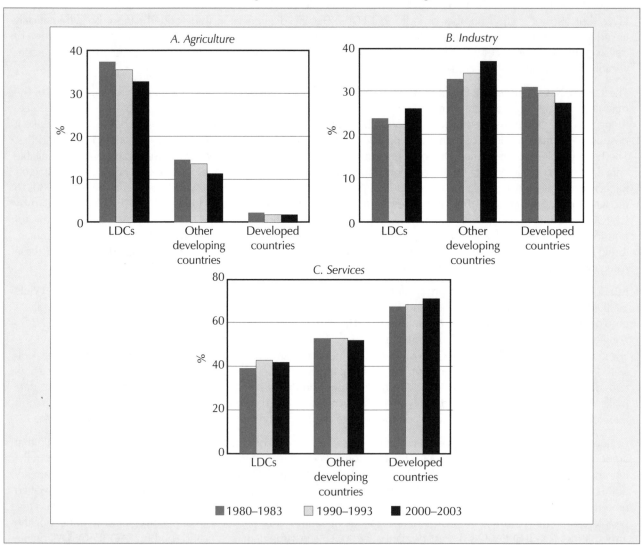

Source: UNCTAD secretariat estimates based on World Bank, *World Development Indicators 2005*, CD-ROM.

Note: Shares are calculated based on constant 2000 dollars. Averages are weighted. Group values are based on a sample of 64 other developing countries and 22 developed countries.

Chart 19 shows the share of agriculture, industry and services in total value-added in LDCs, other developing countries and developed countries in 1980–1983, 1990–1993 and 2000–2003. In 2000–2003:

- Agriculture contributed 33 per cent of total value-added of the LDCs compared with 11 per cent in other developing countries, and 2 per cent in developed countries;

- Industry contributed 26 per cent of total value-added of the LDCs compared with 37 per cent in other developing countries and 27 per cent in developed countries;

- Services contributed 42 per cent of total value-added of the LDCs compared with 52 per cent in other developing countries, and 71 per cent in developed countries.

The share of agriculture in GDP[1] is declining slowly in the LDCs — down four percentage points in 2000–2003 from 37 per cent in 1980–1983; whilst the share in industry and services in GDP is rising slowly — with industrial share rising (in rounded numbers) by three percentage points from 23 per cent in 1980–1983 and the services share rising by three percentage points from 39 per cent in 1980–1983.

At this broad level of aggregation, the extent of structural change (measured as percentage point changes) is not that much different from that which has occurred within other developing countries. However, more disaggregated analysis which examines differences amongst the LDCs (see table 31), and also breaks down the industrial sector (which includes manufacturing activities and also non-manufacturing activities, namely construction, utilities and mining) and the services sector, gives a more nuanced picture.

Although the share of industrial value-added within GDP has increased for the group of LDCs as a whole, this is mainly attributable to the increase of mining, oil extraction and hydroelectric power.

(a) Agriculture

The overall slow decline in the relative share of agriculture disguises a complex pattern in which agriculture is rising as a share of GDP in some LDCs, whilst falling in others, sometimes quickly. The share of agriculture in GDP rose between 1980–1983 and 2000–2003 in more than one-third of the LDCs for which there are data (13 out of 35 countries). Within the 22 LDCs in which the contribution of agriculture decreased, there are 5 LDCs in which the agricultural sector as a share of total value added contracted by more than one third of its 1980–1983 level. In four of these LDCs (Angola, Bhutan, Equatorial Guinea and Lesotho), the relatively large contraction of the agricultural sector is attributable to a relatively large expansion of the industrial sector, mainly oil exploitation, hydroelectric power and, in the case of Lesotho, some manufacturing industries; in one of these LDCs (Kiribati), it is attributable to a relatively large expansion of the services sector, especially in tourist activities.

(b) Industry

Although the share of industrial value-added within GDP has increased for the group of LDCs as a whole, this is mainly attributable to the increase of mining, oil extraction and hydroelectric power. The share of manufacturing activities in GDP is much lower in LDCs than in other developing countries, and is also increasing much more slowly than within other developing countries. It increased from 9 to 11 per cent of GDP in the LDCs as compared with an increase from 17 to 23 per cent in the other developing countries between 1980–1983 and 2000–2003. Within manufacturing activities, the share of medium- and high-technology manufactures is also lower and growing more slowly in LDCs than in other developing countries. The share of medium- and high-technology manufactures increased from 13 to 16 per cent in the LDCs between 1980–1983 and 2000–2003, whilst it increased from 24 to 28 per cent in other developing countries and from 46 to 51 per cent in developed countries over the same period (chart 20).

The share of industrial value-added within GDP has fallen in more than one-third of the LDCs between 1980–1983 and 2000–2003.

The overall increase in the share of industrial value-added within GDP also disguises significant differences between the LDCs. The share has fallen in more

TABLE 31. SHARE OF VALUE ADDED IN PRINCIPAL ECONOMIC SECTORS IN LDCs AND LDC SUBGROUPS, 1980–1983 AND 2000–2003

(percentage of total value added, average)

	Agriculture		Industry		Manufacturing		Services	
	1980–1983	2000–2003	1980–1983	2000–2003	1980–1983	2000–2003	1980–1983	2000–2003
Afghanistan	..	56	..	21	..	..	..	24
Angola	10	6	57	74	8	3	33	20
Bangladesh	33	24	17	26	11	16	50	50
Benin	25	36	13	14	6	9	62	49
Bhutan	57	34	19	38	5	8	24	27
Burkina Faso	32	32	19	16	16	11	49	52
Burundi	52	49	22	21	..	..	26	30
Cambodia	..	37	..	26	..	19	..	36
Cape Verde	16	12	17	18	10	9	66	71
Central African Republic	43	59	21	21	9	10	36	20
Chad	40	38	12	16	..	..	48	46
Comoros	27	46	8	13	2	5	65	41
Dem. Rep. of the Congo	29	62	37	21	..	..	34	17
Djibouti	..	4	..	14	..	3	..	82
Equatorial Guinea	55	6	25	89	..	..	20	5
Eritrea	..	15	..	24	..	12	..	61
Ethiopia	59	47	11	10	..	..	29	43
Gambia	39	32	13	14	5	5	48	54
Guinea	23	24	35	36	..	4	42	40
Guinea-Bissau	48	57	19	14	15	11	33	29
Haiti	34	28	26	17	18	8	40	55
Kiribati	30	17	8	10	2	1	62	73
Lao PDR	62	51	12	25	7	18	26	25
Lesotho	27	17	29	42	10	18	43	40
Madagascar	27	30	14	14	13	12	58	56
Malawi	30	37	20	16	16	11	50	47
Mali	44	41	14	23	4	3	42	36
Mauritania	24	20	29	30	18	9	47	50
Mozambique	32	27	24	28	..	15	44	45
Nepal	54	42	13	22	4	9	34	37
Niger	32	39	20	17	7	7	48	44
Rwanda	35	43	30	21	22	11	35	37
Samoa	..	14	..	26	..	16	..	60
Sao Tome and Principe	..	20	..	17	..	4	..	63
Senegal	23	18	17	21	11	13	60	61
Sierra Leone	54	47	29	34	..	..	17	19
Sudan	36	41	20	20	11	8	44	39
Togo	23	35	21	19	7	9	57	46
Uganda	51	36	11	21	5	10	37	43
United Rep. of Tanzania	..	45	..	16	..	8	..	39
Vanuatu	19	15	12	10	3	4	69	75
Yemen	..	14	..	46	..	5	..	39
Zambia	15	21	36	27	8	12	49	52
LDCs	37	33	23	26	9	11	39	42

Source: UNCTAD secretariat estimates based on World Bank, *World Development Indicators 2005*, CD-ROM.

Note: Shares are calculated based on constant 2000 dollars.
Other LDCs were not included due to lack of data.

than one-third of the LDCs for which there are data (14 out of 35 countries) between 1980–1983 and 2000–2003. Much of the increase in industrial value-added, both manufacturing and non-manufacturing, is concentrated in a few LDCs. Sixty per cent of the increase in industrial value-added of the LDCs as a group is concentrated in four countries — Angola, Bangladesh, Equatorial Guinea and Yemen. If these four LDCs are omitted from the sample, the share of industrial activities in GDP hardly changed within LDCs between 1980–1983 and 2000–2003, increasing by just one percentage point. Three of these

CHART 20. DISTRIBUTION OF VALUE ADDED WITHIN THE INDUSTRIAL SECTOR OF LDCS,
OTHER DEVELOPING COUNTRIES AND DEVELOPED COUNTRIES, 1980–1983, 1990–1993 AND 2000–2003[a]
(Percentage)

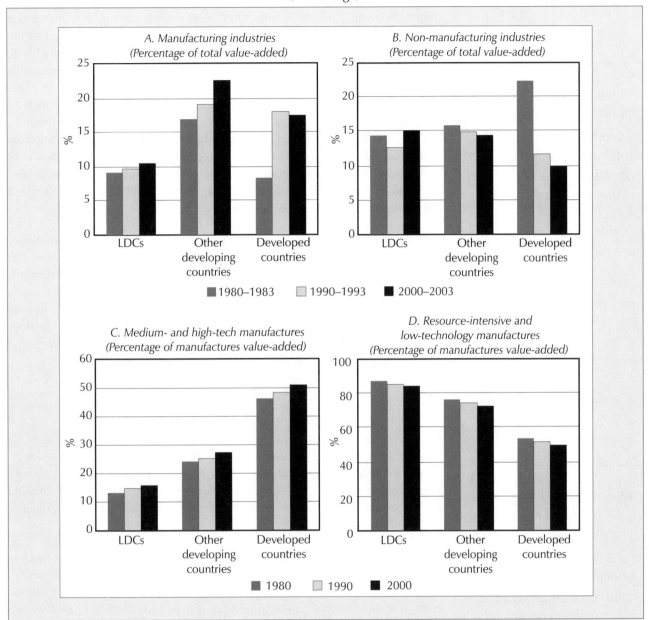

Source: UNCTAD secretariat estimates based on World Bank, *World Development Indicators 2005*, CD-ROM; UNIDO (2005).

Note: For classification of medium- and high-technology manufactures, and resource-intensive and low-technology manufactures see UNIDO (2005).

For charts A and B, group values are based on a sample of 64 other developing countries and 22 developed countries. For charts C and D, group values are based on a sample of 27 LDCs, 72 other developing countries and 33 developed countries.

Between 1990 and 2000 medium- and high-tech manufactures of LDCs increased by 1.2 percentage points if Senegal is included, and increased by only 0.6 percentage points if Senegal is not included in the sample.

a   Data on medium- and high-tech mamufactures and resource-intensive and low-tech manufactures are available only for 1980, 1990 and 2000.

countries — Angola, Equatorial Guinea and Yemen — are oil exporters and extractive industrial activities have been the largest economic sector in terms of value-added since 1990–1993. In contrast, the major industrial activity in Bangladesh is manufacturing.

Whilst the LDC group as a whole has seen a relatively modest increase of manufacturing value-added, there is considerable unevenness in this process. Bangladesh accounted for 38 per cent of the manufacturing value-added in the LDC group in 2000–2003. Between 1990–1993 and 2000–2003, half of the total increase in manufacturing value-added in the LDC group as a whole was attributable to the growth of manufacturing in Bangladesh. Many of the LDCs individually have seen a considerable contraction of manufacturing value-added. Between 1990–1993 and 2000–2003 manufacturing value added as a share of total value-added declined in 19 out of 36 LDCs for which data are available and stagnated in two LDCs (chart 21). Many of the countries that have seen a decline of manufacturing value-added, have seen a relatively large decline, measured as a share of their total value added. Out of the 19 LDCs there are 15 LDCs where manufacturing value added declined by more than 10 per cent of total value added vis-à-vis the 1990–1993 level; out of these 15 LDCs, there are 10 LDCs in which manufacturing value-added declined by more than 20 per cent of total value added vis-à-vis the same base period of 1990–1993. Measured in constant dollar terms manufacturing value-added declined in absolute terms in seven out of the 19 LDCs and it remained unchanged in one of these LDCs.

Many LDCs have, moreover, not only experienced a decline in the relative size of the manufacturing sector, but also a decline in the relative importance of medium- and high-technology manufactures. On the basis of UNIDO data it is apparent that between 1990 and 2000, a total of 14 out of 25 LDCs saw a decline of their share of medium- and high-technology manufactures in total manufactures. The slight increase of the share of medium- and high-technology manufactures in total manufacturing value-added for the LDC group noted above is largely attributable to a single country, Senegal.

(c) Services

Within most LDCs, services make the largest contribution to GDP. But the services sector in LDCs has two major characteristics. Firstly, most of the LDCs have a very weak specialization in advanced commerce-support services, including financial intermediation and business promotion and support. Secondly, many of the LDCs have experienced a large relative and absolute decline of state administrative services, including public administration, defense and compulsory social security.

Chart 22, which draws on UNSD data, shows the share of different types of services within total services value-added in LDCs, other developing countries and developed countries in 1980–1983, 1990–1993 and 2000–2002. From the chart, it is apparent that basic commercial services have become relatively more important within the LDCs between 1980–1983 and 2000–2002, whilst they declined in importance in both other developing countries and developed countries. In the latter period they contributed almost 20 percentage points more of services value-added in the LDCs than in other developing countries. Human development services also increased as a share of services value-added in the LDCs over the same period, and they were around the same share as other developing countries in 2000–2002. Advanced commerce-oriented services are relatively less important than in other developing countries and they contracted between 1980–1983 and 2000–2002. Finally, state administrative services declined from 17 to 9 per cent of services value-added in the LDCs, which was the opposite trend to other developing countries where there was a slight increase from 13 to 14 per cent of services value-added.

Although state administrative services absorbed a much larger share of GDP in the LDCs than in other developing countries and developed countries at the start of the 1980s, this situation was completely reversed 20 years later. In 2000–2002, only 3.5 per cent of GDP was devoted to state administrative services in

> *Between 1990–1993 and 2000–2003 manufacturing value added as a share of total value-added declined in 19 out of 36 LDCs and stagnated in two LDCs.*

> *Within most LDCs, services make the largest contribution to GDP. But most of the LDCs have a very weak specialization in advanced commerce-support services, and have experienced a large decline of state administrative services.*

CHART 21. CHANGE IN SHARE OF MANUFACTURING VALUE ADDED IN TOTAL VALUE-ADDED
BETWEEN 1990–1993 AND 2000–2003

(Percentage point change)

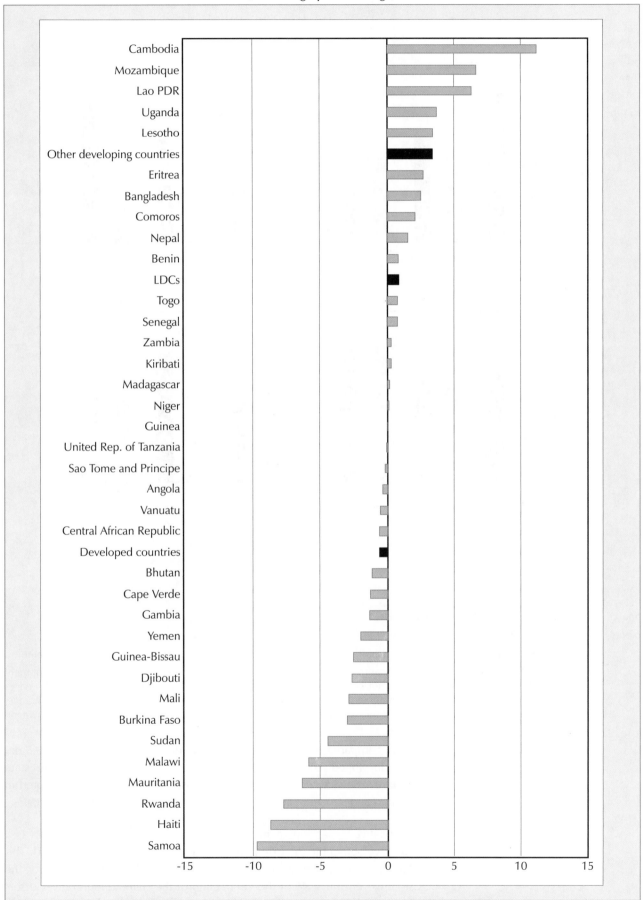

Source: UNCTAD secretariat estimates based on World Bank, *World Development Indicators 2005*, CD-ROM.

Note: Shares are calculated based on data in constant 2000 dollars.
            Group of other developing countries includes 67 countries; group of developed countries includes 22 countries.

CHART 22. DISTRIBUTION OF VALUE ADDED WITHIN THE SERVICE SECTOR OF LDCS, OTHER DEVELOPING COUNTRIES
AND DEVELOPED COUNTRIES, 1980–1983, 1990–1993 AND 2000–2002
(Percentage of services value-added)

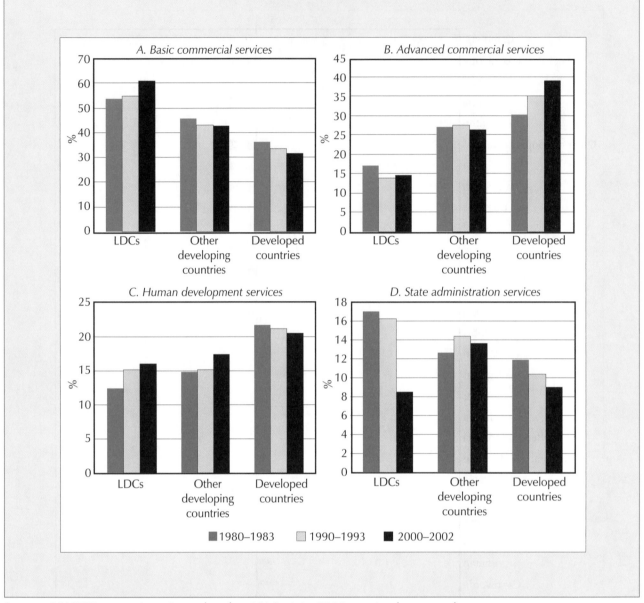

Source: .UNCTAD secretariat estimates based on UN Statistics Division national accounts data.

Note: Shares are calculated based on data in constant 2000 dollars. Averages are weighted.

The group of other developing countries includes 67 countries; the group of developed countries includes 22 countries.

Services include State administrative (public administration, defence and compulsory social security), human development services (education, health, social work, other community, social and personal services), advanced commercial services (financial intermediation, real estate, renting and business activities) and basic commercial services (transport, storage, communication, wholesale, retail, gastronomy, and personal household services). For this clasification see Herrmann (2006).

the LDCs, compared with 7.1 per cent in other developing countries and 6.5 per cent in developed countries. The relatively large contraction of the state administrative service sector in the LDCs is associated with policies adopted in stabilization and structural adjustment programmes in the 1980s and 1990s.

The relative expansion of human development services in the LDCs is a positive development to the extent that the quality of those services is good. This development will contribute to improving the weak human resources of the LDCs. However, the scale of the contraction of the state administrative sectors can have negative consequences in LDCs, particularly as they had already weak state capacities to begin with.

This evidence highlights the fact that the pattern of structural change in most LDCs has been relatively weak compared with the changes in other developing countries. Moreover they show that for most LDCs, the type of structural transformation which has occurred in the most successful developing countries is not occurring. De-industrialization, in the sense that manufacturing value-added is declining as a share of GDP, is occurring in many LDCs. The share of medium- and high-technology manufacturing activities is only increasing very slowly, and instead of an increasing specialization in high value-added service sector activities, what is actually occurring is a shift away from specialization in these sectors.

Productivity growth has been slow for the LDCs as a group.

2. Trends in labour productivity

Not only has the pattern of structural change been weak within the LDCs but the available data also indicate that productivity growth has been slow for the LDCs as a group, and that the productivity gap between the LDCs and other developing countries is widening.

The available international data do not allow a detailed sectoral analysis. However, FAO provides estimates of the number of people working in agriculture and non-agriculture, and on the basis of these estimates it is possible to identify labour productivity in these two broad sectors and trends over time. According to this data, value-added per worker in 2000–2003 was just 20 per cent of the level in other developing countries and 1 per cent of the level in developed countries (table 32).

In 2000–2003, agricultural labour productivity in the LDCs was just 46 per cent of the level in other developing countries and non-agricultural labour productivity was just 23 per cent.

One reason for the low level of labour productivity is the fact that a large share of the working population is engaged in agriculture in the LDCs. In 2000–2003, 70 per cent of the economically active population was engaged in agriculture in the LDCs, as against 52 per cent in other developing countries, and 3 per cent in the developed countries. In all countries, labour productivity in the agricultural sector tends to be below the national average, and thus, other things being equal, the larger the share of the labour force in agriculture the lower the overall labour productivity. However, a much more important reason for the productivity gap between the LDCs and other country groups is that labour productivity is lower in the LDCs within both agriculture and non-agricultural activities. As table 32 shows that in 2000–2003:

- Agricultural labour productivity in LDCs was just 46 per cent of the level in other developing countries, and less than 1 per cent of the level in developed countries;

- For non-agriculture, productivity in the LDCs was just 23 per cent of the level in other developing countries, and 2 per cent compared with that in developed countries.

The productivity gap between LDCs, other developing countries and developed countries widened in both agriculture and non-agriculture sectors.

Not only is the productivity gap between LDCs and other developing countries and developed countries very wide, it is also widening over time. Chart 23 shows that labour productivity in the LDCs as a group remained almost unchanged in the 1980s and early 1990s. Despite a subsequent increase, it was only 18 per cent higher in 2003 than in 1983. In contrast, over the same period, labour productivity increased by 41 per cent in other developing countries and by 62 per cent in developed countries.

The lackluster performance in productivity growth in the LDCs is apparent in both agriculture and non-agriculture. The productivity gap between LDCs, other

TABLE 32. SECTORAL DISTRIBUTION OF LABOUR FORCE AND INTER-SECTORAL LABOUR PRODUCTIVITY IN LDCs, 1980–1983 AND 2000–2003

| | Labour force[a] in agriculture % total labour force | | Labour productivity[b] | | | | | |
| | | | in agriculture | | in non-agriculture | | economy-wide | |
	1980–1983	2000–2003	1980–1983	2000–2003	1980–1983	2000–2003	1980–1983	2000–2003
Afghanistan	72	66	239	251	556	398	327	300
Angola	76	71	..	148	..	..	..	..
Bangladesh	71	54	223	307	1 147	1 125	487	682
Benin	67	53	264	572	..	..	..	..
Bhutan	94	94	127	185	1 634	5 242	212	504
Burkina Faso	92	92	128	165	2 871	3 919	341	457
Burundi	93	90	118	104	1 316	958	205	188
Cambodia	75	70	..	294	..	1 117	..	545
Cape Verde	36	22	..	1 630	..	..	..	..
Central African Republic	84	71	281	400	1 933	691	545	483
Chad	87	74	151	214	1 532	1 000	327	421
Comoros	80	73	305	367	..	1 025	..	545
Dem. Rep. of the Congo	71	62	221	198	1 256	195	520	197
Djibouti	84	78	..	69	..	6 298	..	1 441
Equatorial Guinea	78	70	..	712	..	24 086	..	7 789
Eritrea	..	77	..	63	..	1 211	..	326
Ethiopia	..	82	..	123	..	622	..	214
Gambia	84	79	290	233	2 349	1 784	618	566
Guinea	90	83	..	221	..	3 499	..	769
Guinea-Bissau	87	82	185	249	..	873	..	358
Haiti	70	62	803	473	3 696	1 919	1 658	1 029
Kiribati	35	27	1 125	727	1 338	1 332	1 264	1 169
Lao PDR	79	76	..	457	..	1 414	..	684
Lesotho	41	39	452	509	875	1 533	699	1 135
Liberia	76	67	..	..	..	..	..	..
Madagascar	81	74	181	177	2 043	1 156	534	436
Malawi	87	82	89	122	1 435	965	262	271
Maldives	48	21	..	..	..	..	..	..
Mali	88	80	172	223	1 664	1 274	344	432
Mauritania	69	53	207	283	1 465	1 219	597	727
Mozambique	84	81	..	133	..	1 542	278	401
Myanmar	75	70	..	..	..	..	..	..
Nepal	94	93	163	207	2 097	3 817	284	462
Niger	91	87	189	168	3 863	1 727	518	365
Rwanda	93	91	220	220	4 250	2 439	518	429
Samoa	48	34	..	1 729	..	5 338	..	4 125
Sao Tome and Principe	74	63	..	223	..	1 639	..	752
Senegal	80	73	275	264	3 122	2 885	840	965
Sierra Leone	69	61	532	282	910	507	648	369
Solomon Islands	79	73	..	..	..	..	..	..
Somalia	78	70	..	..	..	..	..	..
Sudan	72	60	378	680	1 633	1 434	732	984
Timor-Leste	85	81	..	263	..	..	..	..
Togo	68	59	275	402	1 583	937	690	622
Uganda	87	79	202	228	1 307	1 547	349	500
United Rep. of Tanzania	86	80	..	278	..	1 371	..	499
Vanuatu	48	36	1 000	1 096	4 530	3 373	2 833	2 559
Yemen	69	49	..	495	..	2 695	..	1 620
Zambia	76	68	185	207	3 362	1 743	958	692
LDCs	79	70	239	273	1 319	1 204	495	554
Other developing countries	64	52	408	599	4 248	5 145	1 789	2 765
Developed countries	7	3	11 608	28 013	38 766	52 887	36 761	52 067

Source: UNCTAD secretariat estimates based on World Bank, *World Development Indicators 2005*, CD-ROM; and FAO, FAOSTAT online, December 2005.

Note: Labour productivity was calculated using value-added data are in constant 2000 dollars.

a   The labour force is the economically active population.

b   Labour productivity in agriculture, non-agriculture and economy-wide is the ratio between value added and the economically active population in respective sectors.

CHART 23. CHANGE OF AGRICULTURAL, NON-AGRICULTURAL AND ECONOMY-WIDE LABOUR PRODUCTIVITY
IN LDCs, OTHER DEVELOPING COUNTRIES AND DEVELOPED COUNTRIES, 1983–2003

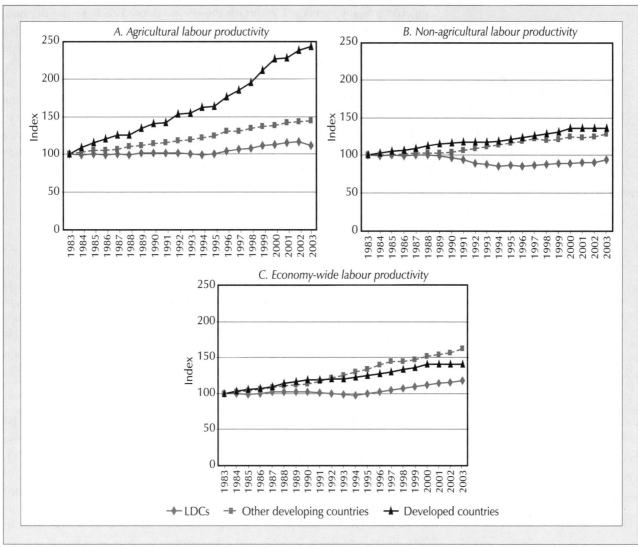

Source: UNCTAD secretariat estimates based on World Bank, *World Development Indicators* 2005, CD-ROM; and FAO, FAOSTAT online, December 2005.

Note: Group of other developing countries includes 67 countries; group of developed countries includes 22 countries; averages are weighted.
Indices are calculated based on data in constant 2000 dollars.
Labour productivity is ratio of value-added and economically-active population in respective sectors.

developing countries and developed countries widened in both sectors. But whereas agricultural labour productivity increased slightly within the LDCs during the period 1983–2003, non-agricultural labour productivity actually decreased. Chart 23 shows that between 1983 and 2003:

- Value-added per worker in agriculture within the LDCs increased by only 11 per cent;

- Value-added per worker in non-agriculture actually declined by 6 per cent.

Both these trends are widespread amongst LDCs (table 32). Between 1980–1983 and 2000–2003:

- Agricultural labour productivity rose, albeit slightly in most cases, in over two-thirds of the LDCs for which data are available (19 out of 29 countries)

- Non-agricultural labour productivity declined in four-fifths of the LDCs for which data are available (21 out of 26 countries).

Although agricultural labour productivity rose, albeit slightly in most cases, in over two-thirds of the LDCs, non-agricultural labour productivity declined in four-fifths of the LDCs.

The finding that non-agricultural value-added per worker is actually declining in the LDCs as a group and also within four-fifths of those for which data are available is highly significant. Although there is no data to disaggregate the non-agricultural sector, this decline is related to the nature of structural change taking place in most LDCs noted above in which the increasing share of industry in GDP is mainly based on mining industries and oil extraction, manufacturing value-added is declining as a share of GDP in many LDCs and there has been an expansion of petty services. Population is growing rapidly and the share of the economically active population seeking work outside agriculture has risen from 21 per cent in 1980-1983 to 30 per cent in 2000–2003. But most LDCs have found it difficult to generate the jobs to employ them productively. This issue will be explored further in the next chapter.

3. TRENDS IN TRADE INTEGRATION

The goods and services which the LDCs can supply competitively to world markets are ultimately limited by the goods and services which they can produce and how efficient they are in producing them.

The goods and services which the LDCs can supply competitively to world markets are ultimately limited by the goods and services which they can produce and how efficient they are in producing them. Given the scale of the productivity gap identified above, it is not surprising to find that the participation of LDCs in world trade is marginal, despite improvements since the early 1990s (see UNCTAD 2002; 2004). In 2000–2003, when their share of the world population was 10.6 per cent, the LDC share in world exports of goods and services was 0.5 per cent, and their share in world imports of goods and services was 0.7.

Even if LDCs exported all their output, their share of world exports of goods and services would only be 2.4 per cent.

However, the marginal position of the LDCs in world trade cannot be attributed to a low level of integration of the national economies of these countries in the world economy, or to a lack of "openness".[2] In 2000–2003, exports and imports of goods and services constituted 52 per cent of the GDP of the LDC group as whole (table 33). If the trade/GDP ratio is taken as an indicator of the "openness" of an economy, then the LDCs as a group are as "open" as high-income OECD countries (which had a trade/GDP ratio of 49 per cent in 2000–2003), and more "open" than low-income countries as a group (43 per cent).

The LDCs have a low share of world trade because they have a low share of world output. Although comparable to the world average and the level in high-income OECD countries, the export/GDP of the LDCs (22 per cent in 2000–2003) is slightly lower than in low- and middle-income countries (30 per cent). But even if the export orientation of the LDCs increased to the same level as low- and middle-income countries in 2000–2003, their share of world exports of goods and services would only increase to 0.8 per cent. Indeed, even if they exported all their output, their share of world exports of goods and services would only be 2.4 per cent. The development of export supply capacities cannot be divorced from the improvement of productive capacities in general.

The development of export supply capacities cannot be divorced from the improvement of productive capacities in general.

The importance of productive capacities for the development of export supply capacities applies as much to the composition of exports as it does to the volume of exports. In this regard, just as the production structure of the LDCs is strongly oriented to the exploitation of natural resources, so the export structure is strongly oriented to exploitation of natural resources.

Focusing on merchandise exports, chart 24 shows that in 2000–2003, primary commodities constituted 70 per cent of the total merchandise exports.[3] Oil exports from Angola, Chad (since 2003), Equatorial Guinea, Sudan (since

TABLE 33. LEVEL OF TRADE INTEGRATION OF LDCs AND OTHER COUNTRY GROUPS,
1980–1983, 1990–1993 AND 2000–2003

(Percentage of GDP)

	1980–1983	1990–1993	2000–2003
LDCs			
A. Total trade (B+C)	35.7	37.0	52.3
B. Exports of goods and services	11.9	13.5	22.1
C. Imports of goods and services	23.8	23.5	30.2
D. Trade balance (B-C)	-11.9	-10.0	-8.1
Low-income countries			
A. Total trade (B+C)	24.6	31.7	43.4
B. Exports of goods and services	9.7	14.3	20.7
C. Imports of goods and services	14.9	17.3	22.7
D. Trade balance (B-C)	-5.1	-3.0	-2.0
Low and middle income countries			
A. Total trade (B+C)	33.4	43.7	58.4
B. Exports of goods and services	16.4	21.6	30.1
C. Imports of goods and services	17.0	22.1	28.3
D. Trade balance (B-C)	-0.5	-0.5	1.8
High-income OECD countries			
A. Total trade (B+C)	36.0	34.2	43.5
B. Exports of goods and services	17.6	17.1	21.4
C. Imports of goods and services	18.4	17.1	22.0
D. Trade balance (B-C)	-0.8	0.0	-0.6
World			
A. Total trade (B+C)	37.8	38.4	48.5
B. Exports of goods and services	18.6	19.2	24.2
C. Imports of goods and services	19.2	19.2	24.3
D. Trade balance (B-C)	-0.6	-0.1	-0.1

Source: UNCTAD secreteriat estimates based on World Bank, *World Development Indicators 2005*, CD-ROM.

2000) and Yemen constitute more than half the primary commodity exports, with the remainder divided more or less equally between minerals and agricultural products. Exports of manufactured goods constituted thirty per cent of total merchandise exports in 2000–2003.

An important feature of the trends in the merchandise export composition of the LDCs is that manufactures exports have been increasing. In 1980–1983, manufactured exports constituted only 13 per cent of total merchandise exports for the LDCs as a group. However, the shift away from primary commodities into manufactures is occurring much more slowly than in other developing countries and has not gone as far. Between 1980–1983 and 2000–2003, the share of manufactures in total merchandise exports of other developing countries increased from 33 to 70 per cent (chart 24).

On top of this, the increase in manufactures exports in the LDCs has been driven by low-skill labour-intensive products, particularly garments. This is a major difference between the LDCs and other developing countries. As chart 25 shows, the greatest increase in the latter group of countries has been in medium- and high-technology exports whilst the greatest increase in the LDCs has been in labour- and resource-intensive exports. In 2000–2003, clothing exports constituted 21 per cent of the merchandise exports of the LDCs. Most of these have developed through various trade preference regimes, mainly associated with the now-defunct Agreement on Clothing and Textiles or special preferences geared towards LDCs. Medium- and high-technology manufactured goods

The shift away from primary commodities into manufactures is occurring much more slowly than in other developing countries and has not gone as far... and has been driven by low-skill labour-intensive products, particularly garments.

CHART 24. COMPOSITION OF MERCHANDISE EXPORTS IN LDCS AND OTHER DEVELOPING COUNTRIES,
1980–1983 AND 2000–2003
(Percentage of total merchandise exports)[a]

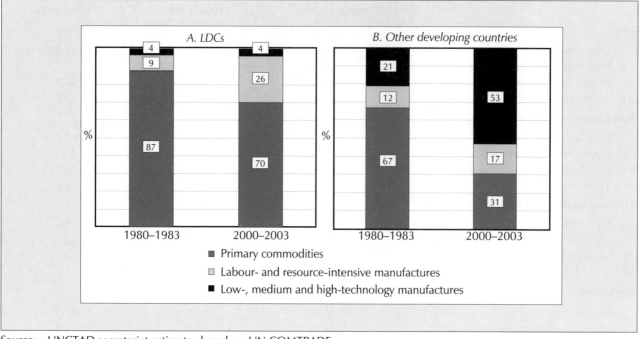

Source: UNCTAD secretariat estimates based on UN COMTRADE.

Note: Other manufactures includes low-, medium and high-technology manufactures. For classification, see note 3 to text.

   a   The charts exclude other manufactures and products not classified elsewhere. These constitute an insignificant share.

exports were less than 3 per cent of total merchandise trade of LDCs in 2000–2003, whilst they constituted 40 per cent of those of other developing countries.

The expansion of manufactured exports has also been concentrated within a few LDCs (chart 26). This is apparent if the LDCs are classified according to their major export specialization.[4] For the agricultural exporters, exports of manufactured goods only increased from 6 to 10 per cent of total merchandise exports between 1980–1983 and 2000–2003, whilst in mineral exporters exports of manufactured goods only increased from 6 to 14 per cent of total merchandise exports. In contrast, the group of LDCs classified as manufactures exporters started with a much higher share of manufactures in total exports (37 per cent in 1980–1983). But by 2000–2003 this had increased to 76 per cent. However, within this group of LDCs medium- and high-technology manufactures exports have not expanded. For this group, 62 per cent of total merchandise exports is composed of clothing and accessories.

The only positive sign of upgrading in the composition of commodity exports has been a shift, within unprocessed agricultural products, from static to more dynamic products.

These data show that there has been little diversification out of primary commodity exports in most LDCs. But a further significant trend is that there has been very mixed pattern with regard to upgrading *within* primary commodity exports. For the LDCs as a group, the share of processed minerals and metals within total mineral and metal exports fell from 35 to 28 per cent between 1980–1983 and 2000–2003 (chart 27). Within agricultural exports, there has been a fall in processing before export for agricultural goods. The share of processed agricultural goods within total agricultural exports decreased from 23 per cent in 1980–1983 to 18 per cent in 2000–2003. The only positive sign of upgrading in the composition of commodity exports has been a shift, within unprocessed agricultural products, from static to more dynamic products.[5] The share of dynamic agricultural products within total agricultural exports increased from 19 per cent in 1980–1983 to 39 per cent in 2000–2003. The most

CHART 25. TRENDS IN MERCHANDISE EXPORTS[a] CLASSIFIED ACCORDING TO TECHNOLOGY INTENSITY FOR LDCS AND OTHER DEVELOPING COUNTRIES, 1980–2003

(Index 1980 = 100)

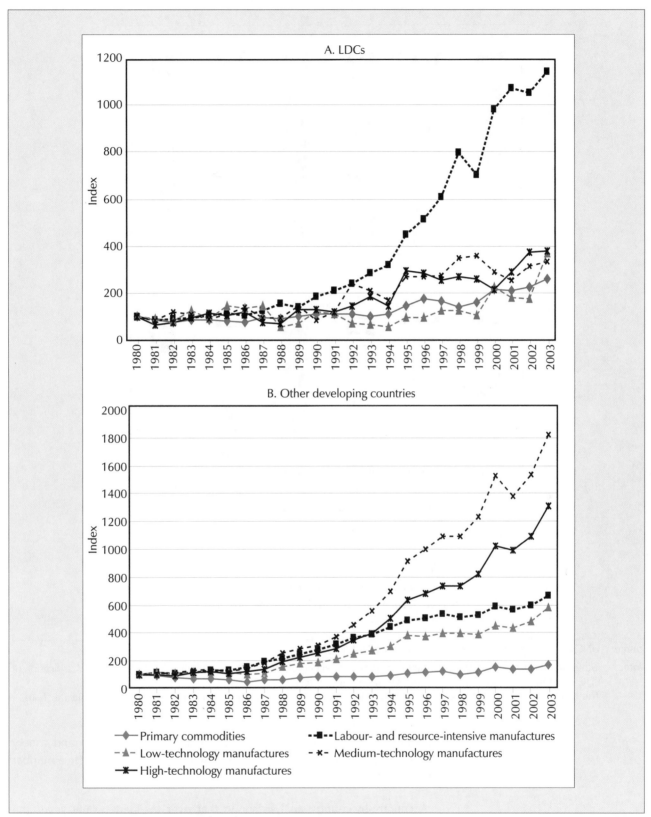

Source: UNCTAD secretariat estimates based on UN COMTRADE.

a   Trends are based on value of exports in current dollars.

CHART 26. COMPOSITION OF MERCHANDISE EXPORTS IN LDC SUBGROUPS
CLASSIFIED BY EXPORT SPECIALIZATION, 1980–1983 AND 2000–2003
(Percentage of total merchandise exports)[a]

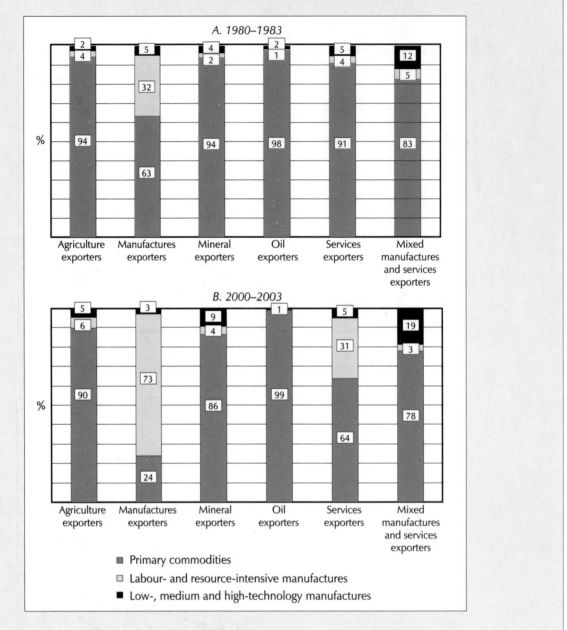

Source: UNCTAD secretariat estimates based on UN COMTRADE.

Note: Other manufactures includes low technology, medium technology and high technology manufactures. For classification of
          LDC subgroups by export specialization, see note 4 to the text.
   a   The charts exclude other manufactures and products not classified elsewhere. These constitute an insignificant share.

important dynamic agricultural products are fresh or frozen fish and fishery
products and spices. But exports of the former have been unstable in a number
of LDCs (see box 12).

A country-by-country analysis shows that over the past twenty years, the
number of commodities exported has increased over time for the majority of
LDCs (28 out of 44). There are two noteworthy examples of large increase in the
number of products exported,   classified at the SITC 3 digit level: Myanmar has
seen its number of commodities increase from 59 in the early 1980s to 104 in
2000–2003, while in the case of the United Republic of Tanzania the increase

CHART 27. LDC EXPORTS OF AGRICULTURAL GOODS AND PROCESSED MINERALS,
1980–1983, 1990–1993 AND 2000–2003
(Percentage)

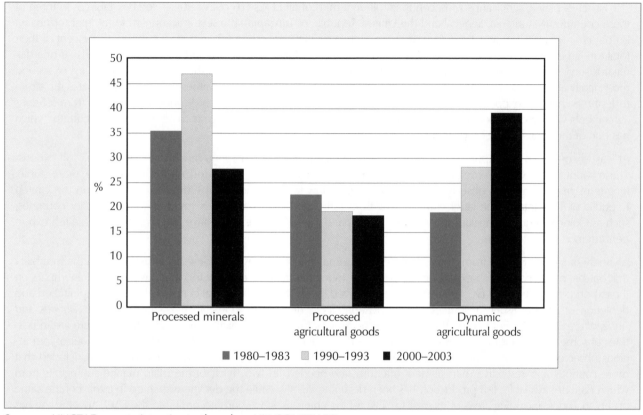

Source: UNCTAD secretariat estimates based on UN COMTRADE.

Note: Exports of processed minerals have been calculated as a share of total exports of minerals and metals, while exports of processed and of dynamic agricultural goods have been calculated as a share of total agricultural goods. Exports of minerals do not include oil and oil-related exports.
For definition of dynamism, see text.

has been from 56 to 104 (see table 34). Four conflict-affected countries have experienced the greatest fall in the number of commodities exported, namely Afghanistan, the Democratic Republic of the Congo, Sierra Leone and Sudan. In spite of the increase, the number of commodities exported by the LDCs (43) remains low when compared with the average of 123 commodities exported by the other developing countries in 2003.[6]

Focusing on the top five export products, it is apparent that the major exports of many LDCs (32 out of the 44 countries for which data are available) included more dynamic products in 2000–2003 than in 1980–1983 (table 34). However, for most LDCs, with the exception of those who have diversified into manufactures, the most important export products still rank low in terms of their market dynamism. Also, the export structure of the LDCs is not only composed of few commodities, but its dynamic components, excluding manufactures, are concentrated on products that seem to be the same for all LDCs, namely spices, fish and fishery products.

The export structure of the LDCs is not only composed of few commodities, but its dynamic components are concentrated on products that seem to be the same for all LDCs, namely spices, fish and fishery products.

Box 12. Fish Exports from LDCs

Fisheries play a significant socio-economic role in a third of all LDCs (16 out of 50) — see box table 5. In three of these countries (Mauritania, Senegal and the United Republic of Tanzania), the sector accounted for at least (or nearly) 20 per cent of total exports of goods and services, while six LDCs relied on fish exports for about 10 per cent of their total foreign exchange earnings (Samoa, Uganda, Mozambique, Kiribati, Maldives and the Solomon Islands). If one disregards service exports and considers the structure of merchandise exports only, fisheries have been the first or second most significant source of export earnings in 10 LDCs, among which are four countries where fish dominates the structure of merchandise exports: Tanzania, Senegal, Samoa and Maldives. In addition, licence fees/royalties from fisheries agreements with foreign operators have been the main source of foreign exchange earnings in Kiribati, a country which has one of the largest exclusive economic zones of all LDCs.

At least six of the 16 fish-exporting LDCs represented in the table have undergone much instability in their fish exports. These countries are Cape Verde, The Gambia, Madagascar, Mauritania, Uganda and Yemen. Meanwhile, more stable, long-term growth has been observed in Eritrea (from very low levels in the mid-1990s), Mozambique and the United Republic of Tanzania. In the latter country, growth in fish exports was particularly rapid after 2000. Other countries, such as Guinea, Senegal, Bangladesh, Maldives, Samoa and the Solomon Islands, have had a relatively stable fish export performance in the long run.

A variety of factors, ranging from domestic issues to external influences beyond domestic control, explain the instability that has been observed in fish exports in some LDCs. Among the main external factors that have also had an impact on the export performance of LDCs are the changes observed in fish stocks. The global concern about overexploitation and depletion of marine fishery resources has implications for a number of LDCs. In the *State of World Fisheries and Aquaculture 2004*, the FAO noted that "the status of skipjack tuna stocks is highly uncertain, although there are indications of some potential for increases in catches in the Pacific and Indian oceans…". It stated that in three out of four regions observed, "at least 70 per cent of fish stocks are already fully exploited or overexploited", and concluded that more cautious and restrictive management measures are needed. In two thirds of the main marine subregions from which data are available, fish production has been declining slightly, while the decline was sharp in a third of the same observed zones, including areas of interest to LDC fishing enterprises. In short, according to the FAO, "overfishing has been a main contributory factor in some cases, [while] … adverse or highly variable environmental conditions" have also played a negative role.

Box table 5. LDCs in which fisheries are an important socio-economic sector

	Export value in 2003 ($ million)	Broad evolution in relevant exports over the last two decades	Percentage of total exports of goods and services in 2003	Ranking of fisheries among all merchandise exports	Ranking of fisheries among all export sectors
Bangladesh	338.9	Peaks in 1995 and 2000, stability after 2000	4.3	2	2
Cape Verde	0.7	Large fluctuations since 1985	0.3	3	7
Eritrea	1.5	Higher export performance since 2000 than in the 1990s	1.3	4	7
Gambia	2.9	Large fluctuations since 1985	2.0	3	6
Guinea	24.4	Relatively stable export performance	3.3	5	6
Kiribati	2.6	Stability since 1995	9.8	2	3[a]
Madagascar	82.1	Large fluctuations since 1985	7.3	4	4
Maldives	53.7	Peak in 1998, stability at lower levels after 2000	9.8	1	2[b]
Mauritania	143.4	Sharp decline in the 1990s, recovery since 2000	39.4	2	2
Mozambique	117.9	Long-term growth since 1985	10.0	2	2[c]
Samoa	9.7	Peak in 1999, relative stability in subsequent years	12.8	1	2
Senegal	295.9	Peak in 1996, decrease since 2000	19.6	1	1
Solomon Islands	12.4	Peak in 1997, substantial decline then stability afterwards	9.5	2	4
Uganda	90.5	Large fluctuations since 1995	10.9	2	3
U. R. of Tanzania	350.2	Growth in the 1990s, rapid increase after 2000	22.3	1	2
Yemen	66.5	Sharp fluctuations since 1980	1.6	3	4

Source: UNCTAD secretariat estimates based on UN COMTRADE.
   a   Besides the domestic fishing sector, the first source of foreign exchange earnings in Kiribati, in 2003, were licence fees/royalties from fisheries agreements with foreign operators.
   b   Licence fees/royalties from fisheries agreements were the fifth largest source of foreign exchange earnings in Maldives in 2003.
   c   Licence fees/royalties from fisheries agreements were the seventh largest source of foreign exchange earnings in Mozambique in 2003.

TABLE 34. EXPORTED GOODS BY TYPE AND DYNAMISM IN THE LDCs, 1980–1983 AND 2000–2003

	Type of export product[a]		Average rank of first 5 products[b]		Number of commodities exported		Dynamic agricultural goods as % of total primary exports		Processed goods as % of total primary exports[c]	
	1980–1983	2000–2003	1980–1983	2000–2003	1980–1983	2000–2003	1980–1983	2000–2003	1980–1983	2000–2003
Afghanistan	MAN	SAG	164	175	58	29	30.3	34.4	34.9	30.7
Angola	MIN	MIN	149	85	34	51	0.3	0.5	0.2	0.1
Bangladesh	MAN	MAN	110	33	49	95	25.2	73.3	2.9	0.7
Benin	SAG	SAG	191	146	21	41	25.8	25.7	31.9	8.3
Bhutan	DAG	MAN	95	106	17	35	43.9	15.0	22.3	22.9
Burkina Faso	SAG	SAG	171	159	29	58	6.0	4.5	8.3	5.8
Burundi	MIN	SAG	163	196	18	11	0.4	0.7	2.8	13.0
Cambodia	SAG	MAN	149	59	29	66	3.8	14.3	2.7	23.2
Cape Verde	DAG	MIN	118	52	13	15	25.4	35.2	5.0	32.7
Central African Republic	SAG	MIN	164	173	18	12	0.1	0.1	8.4	3.0
Chad	SAG	SAG	155	124	11	26	1.3	0.3	6.3	1.7
Comoros	DAG	DAG	106	108	10	5	88.9	99.7	0.8	0.0
Dem. Rep. of the Congo	MIN	MIN	166	140	61	37	3.4	0.1	8.5	1.4
Djibouti	MIN	MIN	130	143	36	56	10.0	23.7	27.2	26.4
Equatorial Guinea	SAG	MIN	195	142	11	18	0.4	0.8	0.7	0.1
Eritrea	..	SAG	..	135	..	27	..	23.3	..	48.7
Ethiopia	..	SAG	..	136	..	33	..	9.3	..	6.8
Gambia	SAG	DAG	148	121	17	24	32.6	55.4	34.7	31.1
Guinea	MIN	MIN	166	152	41	35	1.9	0.9	1.6	1.2
Guinea-Bissau	SAG	MIN	167	134	16	11	32.5	63.2	6.5	0.3
Haiti	SAG	MAN	108	33	60	49	15.4	48.4	19.2	12.6
Kiribati	SAG	DAG	161	117	11	8	19.6	53.7	7.9	0.2
Lao People's Dem. Rep.	SAG	SAG	159	100	24	48	1.7	1.8	9.6	37.8
Lesotho	..	MAN	..	53	..	34	..	5.2	..	78.8
Liberia	..	..	..	..	24	10	0.9	0.1	1.7	1.8
Madagascar	SAG	DAG	143	76	48	86	38.8	80.7	3.6	10.4
Malawi	SAG	SAG	197	165	55	56	3.0	3.2	21.0	17.0
Maldives	DAG	DAG	118	80	15	10	66.8	93.3	16.7	21.8
Mali	SAG	SAG	172	145	29	..	9.7	2.4	12.1	2.9
Mauritania	MIN	DAG	131	139	20	40	35.2	52.9	17.4	2.5
Mozambique	SAG	MIN	161	122	61	79	20.8	21.4	18.8	5.5
Myanmar	SAG	MIN	150	97	59	104	14.6	28.1	42.8	12.0
Nepal	MAN	MAN	142	84	37	63	27.6	61.2	38.3	63.8
Niger	MIN	MIN	189	113	44	42	4.4	13.5	8.3	6.7
Rwanda	SAG	SAG	176	192	14	10	0.9	0.1	6.4	1.6
Samoa	SAG	MAN	144	74	16	20	38.9	85.2	30.9	22.9
Sao Tome and Principe	SAG	SAG	131	152	9	8	0.2	5.8	0.1	1.6
Senegal	MIN	DAG	151	114	88	123	35.3	44.4	28.5	22.4
Sierra Leone	MIN	SAG	154	100	29	13	14.8	0.0	4.9	0.1
Solomon Islands	SAG	SAG	141	154	18	25	43.8	24.9	31.9	10.1
Somalia	SAG	SAG	163	132	21	46	24.5	17.9	11.6	10.6
Sudan	SAG	MIN	175	188	61	43	10.4	2.9	18.6	1.8
Timor-Leste	MAN	..	83	..	14	..	19.3	..	13.5	..
Togo	MIN	MAN	195	178	35	71	0.5	12.3	1.5	17.4
Tuvalu	MAN	MAN	111	67	5	31	0.1	1.0	0.0	1.7
Uganda	SAG	SAG	145	166	35	78	0.4	20.7	2.4	7.6
United Rep. of Tanzania	SAG	MIN	193	126	56	102	18.0	38.0	6.8	6.9
Vanuatu	SAG	SAG	177	129	10	15	3.6	22.2	0.9	9.7
Yemen	..	MIN	..	143	..	83	..	2.9	..	1.2
Zambia	MIN	MIN	146	125	69	103	0.4	2.3	3.8	7.0
LDC	..	..	152	122	32	43	17.4	25.0	12.7	13.4

Source: UNCTAD secretariat estimates based on UN COMTRADE and UNCTAD (2005).

a   The types of export product are classified into mineral products (MIN), manufacture products (MAN), static agricultural goods (SAG), and dynamic agricultural goods (DAG), based on the first five most exported merchandise goods.

b   The product ranking, according to export dynamism, was taken from UNCTAD (2002). It was estimated by taking the products at the 3-digits level, SITC Rev. 2, whose export growth, calculated from 1980 to 1998, has led to products being ranked in decreasing order (from the highest to the lowest). There is a maximum of 225 products.

c   Exports of processed goods do not include oil or oil-related exports.

C. Economic growth, structural change and trade integration

Given the diversity in growth performance and in patterns of structural change and of trade integration amongst the LDCs, an important question which arises is whether or not there is a relationship between economic growth and structural change, and between economic growth and trade integration. This section explores this relationship by examining the differences between LDCs which have been classified (see chapter 2) as : (1) converging economies — those in which real GDP per capita grew at more than 2.15 per cent per annum from 1980–2003; (2) weak growth economies — those in which annual average growth of real GDP per capita was positive, but below this level over the same period; and (3) regressing economies — those in which annual average growth of real GDP per capita was negative during the period 1980–2003. Oil-exporting LDCs (Angola, Equatorial Guinea, Sudan and Yemen) and island LDCs were taken out of the sample as they have rather specific patterns of change. This left the following countries:

- Converging economies: Bangladesh, Bhutan, Lao People's Democratic Republic, Lesotho, Nepal, Mozambique and Uganda;

- Weak-growth economies: Benin, Burkina Faso, Chad, Ethiopia, Guinea, Malawi, Mali, Mauritania and Senegal;

- Regressing economies: Burundi, Central African Republic, Democratic Republic of Congo, Gambia, Guinea-Bissau, Haiti, Madagascar, Niger, Rwanda, Sierra Leone, Togo and Zambia.

The analysis in the following sections is based on this list of countries, although the precise sample for the analysis of structural change differs slightly from that for trade integration owing to data availability.

A country specializing in increasing returns activities will naturally have a higher growth of output than countries specializing in diminishing returns activities, and in this sense structure and structural change will matter for economic growth.

1. ECONOMIC GROWTH AND STRUCTURAL CHANGE

The orthodox neo-classical growth model is an aggregate one-sector model, with constant returns to scale, and diminishing returns to the factors of production. Capital, labour and GDP rises as a result of increases in the labour force, capital accumulation and technical progress. The structure of the economy does not matter. There is no distinction between the different production characteristics of sectors, so that no one sector is regarded as more important than another. The effect of resource shifts between sectors is included as part of technical progress or total factor productivity growth; and in the long run, in a competitive environment, productivity is assumed to equalise across sectors.

In practice, however, different activities have different production characteristics, and by aggregating them into a single production function, important insights into the dynamics of growth are lost. An important distinction needs to be made between diminishing returns activities, on the one hand, and increasing returns activities, on the other. A country specializing in increasing returns activities will naturally have a higher growth of output than countries specializing in diminishing returns activities, and in this sense structure and structural change will matter for economic growth.

In general, land-based activities such as agricultural products and minerals are subject to diminishing returns and also have a low income elasticity of demand, while manufacturing activities are generally produced under conditions of increasing returns and have a higher income elasticity of demand. Service activities vary according to whether they are petty service activities to be found in the urban sector of poor countries, or sophisticated producer services that support the industrial sector of rich countries. Historically, income per capita started to rise rapidly in the now-prosperous countries as resources switched from agriculture to industry; nowadays, there is a close association across countries between the level of per capita income and the share of resources devoted to manufacturing industries and the services associated with them. There is also a close association across countries between the growth of per capita income and the growth of manufacturing industry, or more accurately the growth of living standards and the excess of manufacturing output growth over non-manufacturing output growth. In other words, living standards are growing fast where the share of manufacturing output in total output is rising, i.e. in the so-called newly-industrializing economies.

The association between the growth of GDP and the growth of the manufacturing sector is known in the literature as Kaldor's growth laws, after Kaldor put forward the hypothesis of manufacturing as the engine of growth in two lectures in the 1960s (Kaldor, 1966 and 1967). The basis of the argument is two-fold. First, a fast growth of manufacturing output induces a fast rate of growth of labour productivity *within* manufacturing industries because of static and dynamic increasing returns. Static returns relate mainly to the economies of large-scale production, while dynamic returns relate to induced capital accumulation embodied technical progress and learning by doing. All these efforts are captured by Verdoorn's Law named after the economist who discovered a relationship across countries of eastern Europe between manufacturing output growth and labour productivity growth (Verdoorn, 1949). Second, a fast growth of manufacturing output induces a fast rate of growth of labour productivity *outside* of industry because in agriculture and petty services there are diminishing returns to labour, so that as labour is absorbed from those sectors into industry, the average product of labour rises. A fast rate of growth of manufacturing output thus has two important productivity effects, both of which contribute to a fast rate of growth of GDP.[7]

In order to clarify the relationship between economic growth and structural change among the LDCs, chart 28 shows the differences in the pattern of structural change and productivity growth within converging economies, weak-growth economies and regressing economies between 1980–1983 and 2000–2003. From the chart, it is clear that there are significant differences between the pattern of structural change and growth performance in the LDCs.

Firstly, the share of agricultural value-added in GDP has fallen on average by ten percentage points in the converging economies. In contrast, within the regressing economies it rose by six percentage points. The agricultural value-added share declined in each of the converging economies and rose in 8 out of the 11 regressing economies. The weak-growth economies fall between these two extremes. The share of agricultural value-added in GDP increased by one percentage point on average, but it declined — but not by as much as in the converging economies — in 5 out of the 8 weak-growth economies.

Secondly, the share of industrial value-added in GDP increased on average by nine percentage points in the converging economies and declined by four percentage points on average in regressing economies. Once again, the weak-growth economies are between these two extremes. Industrial value-added increased by one percentage point over the same period.

The share of agricultural value-added in GDP has fallen on average by ten percentage points in the converging economies. Within the regressing economies it rose by six percentage points.

The share of industrial value-added in GDP increased on average by nine percentage points in the converging economies and declined by four percentage points on average in regressing economies.

CHART 28. CHANGE OF VALUE-ADDED TO LABOUR FORCE AND LABOUR PRODUCTIVITY IN LDCs
CLASSIFIED ACCORDING TO LONG-TERM GROWTH PERFORMANCE, BETWEEN 1980–1983 AND 2000–2003

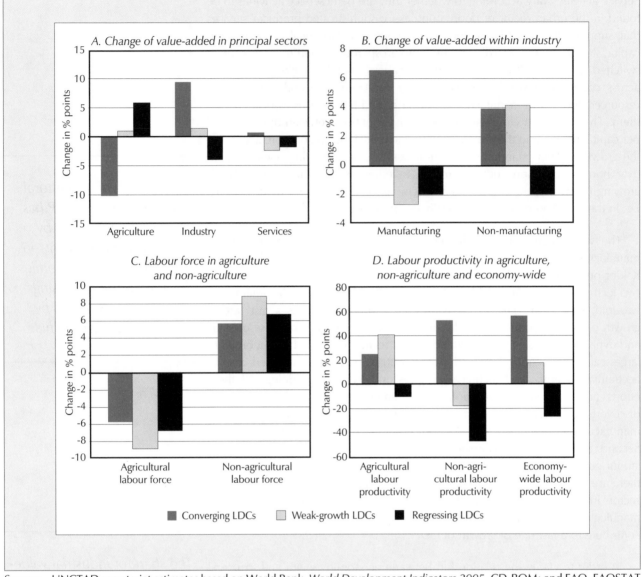

Source: UNCTAD secretariat estimates based on World Bank, *World Development Indicators 2005*, CD-ROM; and FAO, FAOSTAT online, December 2005.

Note: Converging LDCs: Bangladesh,Lao PDR, Lestho,Mozambique, Nepal and Uganda; Weak-growth LDCs: Benin, Burkina Faso, Chad, Guinea, Malawi, Mali, Mauritania, Senegal; Regressing LDCs: Burundi, Cetral African Republic, Democratic Republic of the Congo, Gambia, Guinea-Bissau, Haiti, Madagascar, Niger, Rwanda, Sierra leone, Togo and Zambia). The samples with data on manufactures and non-manufactures are smaller. They do not include Mozambique, Chad, Guinea, Burundi, Democratic Republic of the Congo or Sierra Leone.
Calculations were based on data in constant 2000 dollars.

The share of manufacturing value-added increased in the converging economies.

Thirdly, the share of manufacturing value-added increased by seven percentage points on average in the converging economies. Moreover, the manufacturing value-added share increased in each of the converging economies. In contrast, the manufacturing value-added share decreased by three percentage points in the weak growth economies and two percentage points in the regressing economies. During the 1990s, the manufacturing value-added share declined, or was stagnant, in 13 out of 16 weak-growth or regressing economies for which there is data.

Fourthly, there was little difference between the country groups in terms of the change in the share of services in GDP. It grew slightly in the converging economies and fell slightly in the weak-growth and regressing economies.

A further difference amongst the three groups is that the share of the economically active population in agriculture tended to decline more slowly in the converging economies than in the other economies. On average, this share fell by 6 percentage points in the converging economies, and by nine and seven percentage points in the weak-growth and regressing economies, respectively.

Finally, turning to the trends in labour productivity, there are again clear differences amongst the three groups. As chart 28d shows:

- Between 1980–1983 and 2000–2003, labour productivity increased by 56 per cent on average in the converging economies. It also increased in the weak-growth economies, but more slowly — by 18 per cent. However, it fell by 27 per cent on average in the regressing economies.

- Within the converging economies, labour productivity increased within both agriculture and non-agriculture, more strongly in the latter than the former.

- Within the weak-growth economies, labour productivity increased within agriculture but declined in non-agriculture. The increase in agricultural productivity was actually greater than in converging economies (by 41 per cent as against 25 per cent).

- Within the regressing economies, labour productivity fell in agriculture and non-agriculture. The decline in non-agricultural labour productivity was stronger than in the weak-growth economies (48 per cent as against 18 per cent).

From these patterns it seems clear that the dynamics of production structure matter for economic growth in the LDCs.

From these patterns it seems clear that the dynamics of production structure matter for economic growth in the LDCs. Just as within other developing countries, industrialization, and in particular the expansion of manufacturing activities, is characteristic of the LDCs which have experienced the highest and most sustained economic growth. Moreover, de-industrialization, understood here as a decline in the share of manufacturing activities in GDP, and also an increase in the share of agriculture in GDP, are characteristic features of economic regression.

2. Economic growth and trade integration

It is possible to deepen the analysis of the comparative growth performance of the LDCs by considering how this is related to the level and form of trade integration. Chart 29 summarizes the differences amongst the three groups of countries — converging, weak-growth and regressing economies — in terms of key trade indicators. At a theoretical level, it is expected that the relation between trade and economic growth will depend on the nature of the goods exported. Different goods have different income elasticities of demand, which will affect how fast the demand for them grows in the world market as world income and trade grows. Primary commodities typically have an income elasticity lower than unity (Engel's Law), while manufactured goods and traded services have an income elasticity of demand greater than unity. But within each sector, income elasticities will also differ according to the type of goods: whether they are low value-added or high value-added; whether they are niche products in the case of agricultural commodities, and where they lie on the ladder of technical sophistication in the case of manufactures. Countries which export traditional commodities are likely to have a slow growth of exports and output than countries which have acquired dynamic comparative advantage and shifted their trade structure in the direction of niche markets and higher value-

It is expected that the relation between trade and economic growth will depend on the nature of the goods exported.

Chart 29. Trade indicators for LDC subgroups classified according to long-term growth performance, 1980–1983 and 2000–2003

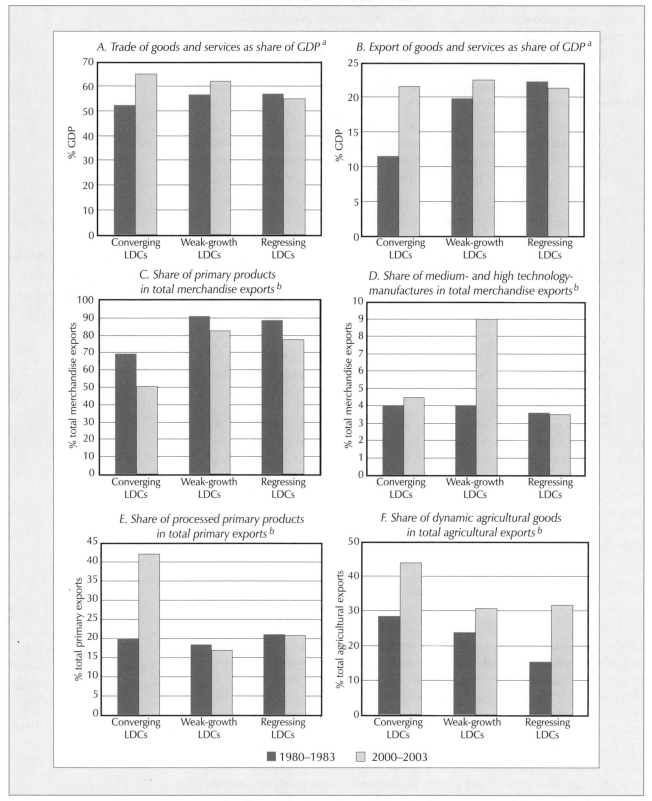

A. Trade of goods and services as share of GDP [a]

B. Export of goods and services as share of GDP [a]

C. Share of primary products in total merchandise exports [b]

D. Share of medium- and high technology-manufactures in total merchandise exports [b]

E. Share of processed primary products in total primary exports [b]

F. Share of dynamic agricultural goods in total agricultural exports [b]

■ 1980–1983   □ 2000–2003

Source: UNCTAD secretariat estimates based on UN COMTRADE and World Bank, *World Development Indicators 2005*, CD-ROM.

a   Converging LDCs include: Bangladesh, Bhutan, Lesotho, Mozambique, Nepal and Uganda. Weak-growth LDCs include: Benin,Burkina Faso, Chad, Ethiopia, Malawi, Mali, Mauritania, Senegal. Regressing LDCs include: Burundi, Central African Republic, Democratic Republic of the Congo, Gambia, Guinea-Bissau, Haiti, Madagascar, Niger, Rwanda, Sierra Leone, Togo and Zambia.

b   Converging LDCs include: Bangladesh, Bhutan, Lao PDR, Mozambique, Nepal and Uganda. Weak-growth LDCs include: Benin,Burkina Faso, Chad, Guinea, Ethiopia, Malawi, Mali, Mauritania and Senegal. Regressing LDCs include: Burundi, Central African Republic, Democratic Republic of the Congo, Gambia, Guinea-Bissau, Haiti, Madagascar, Niger, Rwanda,Togo and Zambia.

added manufactures. The evidence below for the LDCs supports these predictions.

The results show that between 1980–1983 and 2000–2003, the share of trade in GDP increased by 13 percentage points in converging economies, by six percentage points in the weak-growth economies and declined in regressing economies (see chart 29A). This picture fits well with the conventional wisdom that increasing trade orientation is good for growth. However, it is necessary to point out that there is also an important difference between the three groups of countries in terms of the initial level of trade integration. Both the weak-growth and regressing LDCs had higher trade/GDP ratios in 1980–1983 than the converging LDCs. If the trade/GDP ratio is used as an index of the openness of the economy, it is the economies which were initially more "open" (in the sense of trade integration with the global economy), which subsequently did worse in terms of growth performance. But it is the economies which increased their "openness" (in the same sense) most over the 20-year period which did best. This is not a paradox because the more open countries were initially more dependent on primary commodities (see below).

The trends in the export/GDP ratio underlie and mirror changes in the trade/GDP ratio. But to underline the importance of the initial degree of trade integration, it is worth noting that the export/GDP share in 1980–1983 in the converging economies was 12 per cent compared with 20 per cent in weak-growth economies and 22 per cent in the regressing economies. In the latter group, the export/GDP was slightly lower in 2000–2003 than in 1980–1983. In weak-growth economies it increased by only 2 percentage points, whilst in the converging economies it doubled to 22 per cent of GDP.

With regard to the share of manufactures in total merchandise exports, the converging economies start with a much higher share in 1980–1983 than the other two groups of countries — 31 per cent of total merchandise exports as against 9 per cent in the weak growth economies and 11 per cent in regressing economies. By 2000–2003 primary products had become less important in all groups. But the shift to manufactures went furthest fastest in the converging LDCs. By that period, manufactures constituted 49 per cent of total merchandise exports in the converging economies, compared with 17 per cent on average in the weak-growth economies and 22 per cent in the regressing economies. Interestingly the regressing economies include two countries – Haiti and Madagascar — which have successfully developed clothing manufactures exports through Export Processing Zones (EPZs). This reflects the fact that it is possible to expand manufacturing exports without much expansion of domestic value-added, as export production involves assembly or limited processing of imported inputs (see UNCTAD 2002). It is therefore clear that although the converging economies have tended to shift their composition of exports out of primary commodities towards manufactures, this is not a magic solution and will not, in itself, ensure sustained economic growth.

Turning to the composition of primary commodity exports, there are two clear trends which indicate that the converging LDCs have not simply been diversifying into manufactures but also upgrading the composition of their primary commodity exports.

Firstly, the share of processed products in total primary exports of the converging economies increased from 20 per cent in 1980–1983 to 42 per cent in 2000–2003. Over the same period, the share remained constant at 21 per

Since 1980 the share of trade in GDP increased by 13 percentage points in converging economies, by six percentage points in the weak-growth economies and declined in regressing economies.

Although the converging economies have tended to shift their composition of exports out of primary commodities towards manufactures, this is not a magic solution and will not, in itself, ensure sustained economic growth.

cent in the regressing economies and decreased by 1 percentage point in the weak growth economies.

Secondly and in contrast, there is little difference between the performance of the country groups in terms of the shift from static to dynamic agricultural exports. The share of dynamic agricultural products in total agricultural exports increased on average in all country groups, including in the regressing LDCs. In 2000–2003, these products constituted 44 per cent in the converging economies, compared with 31 per cent in weak-growth LDCs and 32 per cent in the regressing economies.

Diversification away from primary commodity exports towards manufactured exports, as well as upgrading within primary commodity exports has proceeded further and faster, in the converging economies.

To summarize, the converging economies have switched towards more processed and more dynamic agricultural goods, while the regressing economies have switched towards more dynamic agricultural products but the processing of primary products before export has not changed. These patterns show that the converging economies have not only been characterized by greater structural change than the other countries and rising labour productivity in both agriculture and non-agriculture, but they are also characterized by a greater increase in trade orientation and export orientation than the other groups. In addition, diversification away from primary commodity exports towards manufactured exports, as well as upgrading within primary commodity exports has proceeded further and faster in this group of countries. Thus, within the converging economies, the pattern of trade integration has reinforced the pattern of structural change.

However, the development of manufactured exports is not a magic bullet for development success. Even in the converging economies it is apparent that there is still a mismatch between the production structure and the trade structure, suggesting that whereas the growth of manufacturing exports has occurred, this process may be, as discussed more generally in UNCTAD (2004), weakly linked to the rest of the economy. Some of the regressing economies have actually successfully developed manufactured exports but this has not been associated with structural change and economic growth, and assembly activities with few local technological capabilities can easily collapse. Moreover, it is clear that in 1980 many of the weak-growth and regressing LDCs started with a much higher level of integration with the global economy and also greater export orientation than the converging economies. Thus, whilst changes in the level of trade integration are related to growth performance, the actual level is not.

The overall lack of structural change, the very slow rate of productivity growth and the limited range of goods in which LDCs are internationally competitive are all symptomatic of a lack of technological learning and innovation within LDCs.

D. Processes of technological learning

The overall lack of structural change, the very slow rate of productivity growth and the limited range of goods in which LDCs are internationally competitive are all symptomatic of a lack of technological learning and innovation within LDCs. The patterns of production and trade not only indicate that the level of accumulation of knowledge-based assets is generally low, but there is also regression rather than accumulation in these assets in many LDCs.

The rest of this section focuses more closely on the processes of technological learning which underlie innovation. It is these processes which, together with capital accumulation, are at the heart of structural change and international competitiveness. Developing productive capacities in the LDCs will entail addressing the constraints on technological learning as much as the constraints on capital accumulation.

1. TECHNOLOGICAL LEARNING TRAJECTORIES IN LDCs

Technological learning is the process of acquiring and mastering the information and skills that enable enterprises to operate physical plant and equipment efficiently and competitively, as well as the information and skills to raise quality and to introduce new products and production processes. This is not a simple process. As Lall (2005a: 11) has put it:

"Whilst technological hardware (equipment, designs, patents and so on) *is* available to all countries, just importing hardware does not ensure that it is used efficiently. This is because the disembodied elements of technology ("tacit" knowledge) cannot be transferred like physical products. Technical knowledge is difficult to locate, price and evaluate. Its transfer cannot be embodied in equipment or instructions, designs or blueprints. Unlike the sale of a good, where the transaction is complete when physical delivery has taken place, the successful transfer of technology is a prolonged process, involving local learning to complete the transaction. The embodied elements can be used at best operative levels only if they are complemented by a number of *tacit* elements that must be developed locally. The need for learning exists in all cases, even when the seller provides assistance, though the costs vary by technology, firm and country".

There are important differences between the technological learning trajectories of countries at different levels of development and this implies that the necessary technological capabilities change as countries develop.

Lall (2004) summarizes the ten general features of technological learning as follows: (1) it is real and significant process which is primarily conscious and purposive rather than automatic and passive; (2) there is limited information on technical alternatives and learning involves risk, uncertainty and costs; (3) enterprises may not even know how to learn; (4) learning is path-dependent and cumulative; (5) different technologies differ in their learning requirements and so the learning process is highly technology specific; (6) learning occurs through external sources as well as internal activities; (7) it involves effort at all levels of the enterprise and is not limited to R&D; (8) it becomes increasingly costly as enterprises acquire a deeper understanding of technology; (9) it requires inter-linkages between suppliers and customers; and (10) it takes place through interactions both within and between countries.

However, there are also important differences between the technological learning trajectories of countries at different levels of development and this implies that the necessary technological capabilities change as countries develop. Within OECD countries, high levels of R&D investment are at the heart of technological learning. However, technological learning and technical change in the LDCs takes place primarily by using and improving technologies that already exist in advanced industrial countries or other developing countries. Key technological capabilities are related to: the acquisition of mature technologies, including simple assembly, product specification, production know-how, technical personnel and components and parts; the ability to undertake incremental innovations to adapt technologies to local conditions; the ability to develop new markets through close links with customers and strategic management of marketing functions; and to develop linkages with other enterprises, public research organizations and technology transfer agencies. For most LDCs, the three most important sources of building their endogenous knowledge-base are likely to be education and strengthening of the skills base; foreign technology transfer; and the mobility of experienced technical personnel. Importation of foreign technology, reverse engineering of existing mature foreign products, and the mobility of experienced technical and managerial engineering personnel can be harnessed to bring about effective adoption and diffusion of imported technologies to their economies.

For most LDCs, the three most important sources of building their endogenous knowledge-base are likely to be education and strengthening of the skills base; foreign technology transfer; and the mobility of experienced technical personnel.

The relative importance of different channels through which firms acquire and improve technology in LDCs and in other developing countries is shown in table 35. This evidence is based on the World Bank's Investment Climate Assessments (ICA) and includes data for 12 LDCs and 21 other developing countries. From this data, it is clear that capital investment in new machinery and equipment is the most important source of technological acquisition in both LDCs and other developing countries. In the LDCs, 45 per cent of the firms report the investment in new machinery and equipment as the most important source of technological acquisition. Overall, almost two-thirds of the firms report new machinery and equipment as either the first-most, second-most or third-most important source. This result has an important corollary that there is a close association between capital investment and technological learning. The low levels of capital investment described in the previous chapter are directly related to low levels of technological learning.

In the LDCs, 45 per cent of the firms report that investment in new machinery and equipment is the most important source of technological acquisition.

Key personnel is the second most important channel of technology acquisition within the LDCs, whereas in other developing countries internal R&D is reported as the second most important channel. Compared with capital investment, fewer firms report these two sources as their most important source of technology acquisition. Only 14 per cent of LDC firms report key personnel as the most important source of technology acquisition, and only 11 per cent report R&D. The differences between LDCs and other developing countries in the proportion of firms reporting these as their most important source of technology acquisition are not great. However, if one adds up the firms reporting key personnel as their first-most, second-most and third-most important source of technology acquisition, it is apparent that 55 per cent regard key personnel as important in the LDCs, as against only 43 per cent in other developing countries.

These trends reflect expectations. However, table 35 also suggests significant weaknesses in the process of technology acquisition and diffusion within the LDCs.

Firstly, licensing from domestic or international sources and transfers from a parent company in LDCs are both negligible sources of technology acquisition.

TABLE 35. RELATIVE IMPORTANCE OF DIFFERENT CHANNELS OF TECHNOLOGY ACQUISITIONS IN LDCS AND OTHER DEVELOPING COUNTRIES, VARIOUS YEARS

	Share of companies in LDCs that considered it...			Share of companies in other developing countries that considered it...		
	Most important channel	*Second most important channel*	*Third most important channel*	*Most important channel*	*Second most important channel*	*Third most important channel*
New machinery or equipment	45.0	11.5	9.5	44.3	13.0	9.9
Key personnel	13.7	26.6	14.1	12.2	19.6	10.7
Collaboration with customers	11.3	13.3	15.9	7.6	12.2	12.7
Internal R&D	11.3	15.8	14.9	13.6	19.0	15.1
Trade Fairs	5.8	10.0	12.7	6.9	11.4	15.0
Collaboration with suppliers	3.8	5.4	7.7	4.3	9.3	11.9
Transferred from parent company	2.3	2.2	2.7	3.2	2.9	2.9
Consultants	2.1	4.9	7.9	2.5	4.1	8.2
Licensing from international sources	1.6	2.7	3.8	1.9	2.5	2.8
Licensing from domestic sources	1.6	3.5	3.4	1.5	2.2	2.3
Business or industry associations	1.3	3.1	5.5	1.7	2.8	6.2
Universities, public institutions	0.4	1.0	2.0	0.5	1.2	2.4

Source: Knell (2006) based on World Bank, Investment Climate Surveys, online, December 2005.

Only 1.6 per cent of firms in LDCs report licensing from international sources as the most important source of technology acquisition. Only 2.3 per cent report transfer from a parent company as the most important source of technology acquisition. The latter figure may partly reflect sampling design of the ICA surveys. However, it suggests that although foreign firms do, as we shall later see, undertake more internal R&D and use more foreign-licenced technology than domestic firms in the LDCs, the direct transfer of technology to LDCs through transnational corporations is of relatively minor importance in this sample of countries.[8]

Secondly, universities and public institutions are currently under-utilized in the process of technology acquisition in LDCs. They are reported as the first-most, second-most and third-most important sources of technology acquisition by only 3.4 per cent of the firms. This same disconnect between public technology institutions and private sector enterprise is also apparent in other developing countries.

The institutional context for technological learning and innovation is weak in the LDCs.

Thirdly, one would expect that collaboration amongst firms would be a very important source of technology acquisition in a low-income setting. For LDCs, it is apparent that collaboration with customers is indeed important, and if we take collaboration with customers and suppliers together, 15 per cent of the firms report that they are the most important source of technology acquisition. But this too seems low because in the LDC context, knowledge acquired from external sources is likely to be a critical component of technological learning.

Fourthly, consultants are a very minor channel of technology acquisition by private firms in LDCs. Given the important role of consultants in technical cooperation, this suggests that there is a major disconnect between aid in the form of technical cooperation and the development of private sector technological capabilities.

What these data suggest is that both firm-level learning capabilities and the institutional context for technological learning and innovation is weak in the LDCs. The development of technological capabilities depends in part on the extent of linkages amongst economic agents, as well as with specialized organizations such as public research bodies which are generating knowledge. The nature of the domestic knowledge systems in the LDCs will be addressed in chapter 6.

Gross expenditure on R&D in 2003 was 0.2 per cent of GDP in the LDCs.

2. INDICATORS OF TECHNOLOGICAL EFFORT

There is now an expanding literature on the measurement of technological capabilities and the knowledge assets of countries (Archibugi and Coco 2004; 2005). Widely-used indicators include R&D expenditure, number of scientists and engineers, licensing fees and number of publications in scientific journals. Care must be taken in interpreting these data as they do not capture the full range of innovative activities in LDCs, in particular incremental innovation. However, they provide the only internationally comparable data to measure the extent of the knowledge divide in terms of technological capabilities.

Table 36 summarizes where LDCs stand in relation to other developing countries and developed countries with regard to some traditional indicators of technological effort. From the table, it is clear that:

- R&D expenditure in both LDCs and other developing countries is very low when compared with OECD countries. Gross expenditure on R&D

TABLE 36. INDICATORS OF TECHNOLOGICAL EFFORTS IN LDCs, OTHER DEVELOPING COUNTRIES AND DEVELOPED COUNTRIES

	LDCs	Other developing countries	Developed countries
Total R&D expenditures as share of GDP in 2003[a]	0.2	0.3	2.2
Researchers & scientists per million population in 2003[a]	176	662	7144
Scientific & technical publications, sum 1990–1999			
Number	7 788	479 837	4 841 762
Share in world total (%)[b]	0.1	8.5	86.0
Utility patents[c], sum 1991–2004			
Number	20	14 824	1 823 019
Share in world total (%)[b]	0.0	0.8	99.0

Source: Knell (2006).

Note: Gross expenditures on research and development as share of GDP is based on 11 LDCs; researchers and scientists per million population is based on 16 LDCs.
   a   Or latest available year.
   b   Shares in world total do not add up to 100 per cent because transition economies are not shown in the table.
   c   Utility patents include patents for inventions, but do not include design patents, plant patents, re-issue patents, etc.

Only 7 per cent of the domestic firms in LDCs license foreign technology and only 21 per cent of domestic firms in LDCs use a website for business.

in 2003 (or the latest available year) was 0.2 per cent of GDP in the LDCs and 0.3 per cent of GDP in other developing countries, compared with 2.2 per cent of GDP in OECD countries.

• The number of researchers and scientists engaged in R&D activities per million population in the LDCs in 2003 (or the nearest year) are just 27 per cent the level in other developing countries and 2 per cent the level in OECD countries

• During the period 1990-1999, only 0.1 per cent of the scientific and technical journal articles in physics, biology, chemistry, mathematics, clinical medicine, biomedical research, engineering and technology and earth and space sciences originated in LDCs

• Between 1991 and 2004, only 20 US patents were granted to citizens from LDCs compared with 14,824 to citizens from other developing countries and 1.8 million to citizens from OECD countries.

These statistics show there is a major knowledge divide within the global economy. However, it would be wrong to infer that innovation and problem-solving is not occurring in the LDCs. There are many incremental innovations with significance for domestic needs that are not being captured by these traditional indicators. This is especially the case for "invisible" process innovations. These can only be measured through field research and also indicators of sales, productivity and profitability.

Chart 30 includes some firm-level data from the Investment Climate Surveys. These differentiate between the technological effort of domestic firms and foreign firms in both LDCs and other developing countries. In all cases, the indicators of technological effort are lower in the LDCs than in other developing countries, and they are lower in domestic firms than in foreign firms. It is striking that average expenditure by domestic firms in the LDCs on R&D as a percentage of sales is almost zero. More worrying still is the fact that only 7 per cent of the domestic firms in LDCs license foreign technology. Only 21 per cent of domestic firms in LDCs also use a website for business. This is less than half the proportion of foreign-owned firms who use a website for business; domestic firms in LDCs also lag behind domestic firms in other developing countries.

CHART 30. DIFFERENCES IN TECHNOLOGICAL EFFORT IN LDCS AND OTHER DEVELOPING COUNTRIES
BY FOREIGN AND DOMESTIC COMPANIES, VARIOUS YEARS[a]

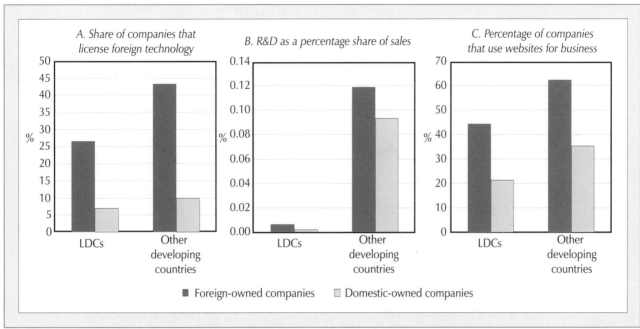

Source: Knell (2006) based on World Bank, *Investment Climate Surveys*, online, December 2005.

Note: Investment Climate Surveys were conducted between 2000 and 2005.

   a   The group of other developing countries includes 21 countries; the group of LDCs includes 12 countries for which data are available, namely Bangladesh (2002), Bhutan (2001), Cambodia (2003), Eritrea (2002), Ethiopia (2002), Madagascar (2005), Mali (2003), Nepal (2000), Senegal (2003), Uganda (2003), United Republic of Tanzania (2003) and Zambia (2002).

Given the importance of capital investment for technology acquisition, imports of machinery and equipment are a good indicator of technological effort in the LDCs. Chart 31 shows machinery and equipment imports into LDCs and other developing countries between 1980 and 2003 using two indicators of technological effort: machinery and equipment imports as share of GDP and machinery and equipment imports per capita.

From this chart it is clear that:

*   As a share of GDP, machinery and equipment imports into LDCs in the period 2000–2003 were lower than those into other developing countries (3 per cent versus 4.8 per cent of GDP) and the gap between the two groups of countries has widened since the early 1980s (when machinery and equipment imports to LDCs were 2.9 per cent of GDP, while those to other developing countries was 3.3 per cent).

*   In real per capita terms, machinery and equipment imports into LDCs during 2000–2003 were at almost the same level as 1980. Real capital goods imports per capita were about $10 per capita (in 1990 US$), which was seven times lower than real capital goods imports of other developing countries.

In real per capita terms, machinery and equipment imports into LDCs during 2000–2003 were at almost the same level as 1980.

Disaggregating the trends between converging economies, weak growth economies and regressing economies, it is apparent that there is a sharp fall in machinery and equipment imports into regressing LDCs, both as a share of GDP and per capita (chart 31 E and 31F). But significantly, no strong upward trend can be discerned in such imports in the converging economies. In real terms machinery and equipment imports per capita stood at the same level in the converging economies in 2003 as they were in 1985. This suggests weaknesses in the development of technological capabilities in the converging economies, and that these LDCs may be vulnerable to setbacks as a result of intensifying competition with other developing countries. Case studies of garment exports in

CHART 31. MACHINERY IMPORTS PER CAPITA[a] AND AS A SHARE OF GDP
IN LDCs, LDC SUBGROUPS AND OTHER DEVELOPING COUNTRIES, 1980–2003
(Constant $ and percentage of GDP)

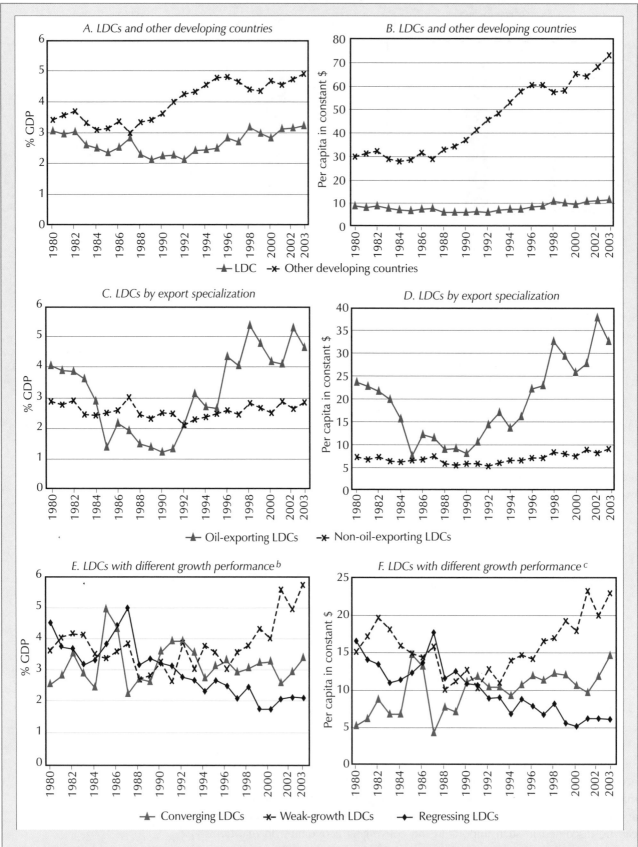

Source: UNCTAD secretariat estimates based on UN COMTRADE; and World Bank, *World Development Indicators 2005*, CD-ROM.
    a   Machinery imports per capita are in constant 2000 dollars. The GDP deflator, in dollars, was used to convert the series into real terms.
    b   Converging LDCs include: Bangladesh, Bhutan, Mozambique, Nepal and Uganda. Weak-growth LDCs include: Benin, Burkina Faso, Chad, Malawi, Mali, Mauritania and Senegal. Regressing LDCs include: Burundi, Central African Republic, Democratic Republic of the Congo, Gambia, Guinea-Bissau, Haiti, Madagascar, Niger, Rwanda, Sierra Leone, Togo and Zambia.
    c   Converging LDCs include: Bangladesh, Bhutan, Lao PDR, Mozambique, Nepal, Uganda. Weak growth LDCs include: Benin, Burkina Faso, Chad, Guinea, Malawi, Mali, Mauritania, Senegal. Regressing LDCs include: Burundi, Central African Republic, Democratic Republic of the Congo, Gambia, Guinea-Bissau, Haiti, Madagascar, Niger, Rwanda, Togo and Zambia.

Lesotho and also Cambodia indeed confirm these weaknesses and the vulnerability to competition (Lall 2005; Rasiah 2006). The strongest upward trend in terms of machinery and equipment imports is apparent in the weak-growth economies. This probably reflects the fact that it is in these economies that increasing investment has been most strongly driven by FDI (see previous chapter).

It is impossible to differentiate the relative importance of domestic and foreign firms in capital goods imports. However, it is apparent that there is a close association between countries which have received the highest levels of FDI inflows and countries in which capital goods imports have risen as a share of GDP and in per capita terms. An important feature of the trends in capital goods imports to LDCs, and a reflection of the role of FDI, is that the oil-exporting LDCs experienced significant increases in the 1990s. Thus, whilst the capital goods imports to oil-exporting LDCs rose from $7 per capita to $33 per capita (in 1990 US $) from 1990 to 2003, those into non-oil exporting LDCs only increased from $6 to $10. Amongst non-oil exporting African LDCs, capital goods imports were not only smaller in per capita terms but accounted for a smaller share of GDP in 2000–2003 than they were in 1980–1983.

Amongst non-oil exporting African LDCs, capital goods imports were not only smaller in per capita terms but accounted for a smaller share of GDP in 2000–2003 than they were in 1980–1983.

Most of the data above refer to firms engaged in industrial activities and services. However, given the importance of agriculture in many LDC economies, agricultural research and development, and also extension activities to link research findings with farmers, are particularly important aspects of technological effort. Data on this is also patchy. However, table 37 gathers

TABLE 37. PUBLIC AGRICULTURAL RESEARCH EXPENDITURES IN SELECTED LDCs,
1980–1989, 1990–1999 AND 2000–2001

	Public research expenditures							
	1993, $ million			Change	*Percentage of agricultural GDP*			Change
	Average				Average			
	1980–1989 (a)	1990–1999 (b)	2000–2001	(b-a)	1980–1989 (a)	1990–1999 (b)	2000–2001	(b-a)
Burkina Faso	4.0	7.9	..	3.9	0.6	0.9	..	0.4
Burundi	..	3.3	1.5	..	..	0.7	0.4	..
Cape Verde	1.7	1.9	..	0.2	3.5	4.1	..	0.7
Ethiopia	6.6	9.9	13.6	3.3	0.3	0.3	0.4	0.0
Guinea	..	4.4	3.5	..	..	0.6	0.3	..
Lesotho	0.8	0.8	..	-0.1	0.7	0.6	..	-0.1
Madagascar	5.8	5.3	2.6	-0.5	0.6	0.6	0.3	0.0
Malawi	10.4	11.0	..	0.6	1.6	1.4	..	-0.2
Mali	12.1	11.3	..	-0.8	1.3	1.0	..	-0.3
Mauritania	..	1.9	2.4	..	..	0.8	1.0	..
Niger	5.7	5.6	..	-0.1	0.7	0.7	..	0.0
Rwanda	4.3	3.9	..	-0.5	0.5	0.6	..	0.0
Senegal	23.6	15.2	..	-8.4	2.6	1.4	..	-1.1
Sudan	8.7	9.0	7.9	0.3	0.5	0.1	0.2	-0.4
Togo	5.8	4.3	4.2	-1.5	1.4	0.8	0.6	-0.6
Uganda	..	7.8	10.2	..	..	0.4	0.5	..
United Rep. of Tanzania	..	6.5	8.5	..	..	0.3	0.4	..
Yemen	..	16.2	..	..	..	0.5	..	..
Zambia	11.7	11.6	..	-0.2	2.8	2.2	..	-0.6

Source: UNCTAD secretariat estimates based on CGIAR, ASTI database online, February 2006; and World Bank, *World Development Indicators 2005,* CD-ROM.

available data on public expenditure on agricultural research and development in African LDCs for which data is available.

From this table it is clear that for this sample of countries public expenditure on agricultural R&D declined in real terms in the 1980s and also in the 1990s in many countries. This reflects the fact that in Africa rapid growth of spending on agricultural R&D in the 1960s — a post-independence period of institution-building underwritten with development aid — gradually gave way to the debt crisis in the 1980s and curbs on government spending and waning donor support in the 1990s (Pardey and Beintema 2001: 3). Today, despite relatively high returns on investments in agricultural research, investment in agricultural research and development remains very low.

E. Conclusions

This chapter has described and analysed the trends in production structure, labour productivity and trade integration in the LDCs, and examined the processes of technological learning which, together with capital accumulation, underlie structural transformation, productivity growth and international competitiveness.

The chapter has shown that for the LDCs as a group there has been little structural change and the productivity gap between the LDCs and other developing countries and developed countries is increasing. The share of agriculture in GDP in the LDCs is declining slowly (from 37 per cent in 1980–1983 to 33 per cent in 2000–2003). Both industrial and service activities are expanding. But much of the increase in industrial value-added is concentrated in a few LDCs and the type of industrial activities which are expanding most in the LDCs are mining industries, the exploitation of crude oil and, in come cases, the generation of hydroelectric power, rather than manufacturing. Moreover, the type of services which are expanding most are low value-added petty trade and commercial services.

The data show that, on average, it requires 5 workers in the LDCs to produce what one worker produces in other developing countries, and 94 LDC workers to produce what one worker produces in developed countries in 2000–2003. Worse still, the productivity gap is widening. Labour productivity in the LDCs as a group in 2000–2003 was just 12 per cent higher than in 1980–1983, whilst it increased by 55 per cent on average in other developing countries. Significantly, although agricultural value-added per agricultural worker rose slightly in the LDCs, non-agricultural value-added per non-agricultural worker actually declined by 9 per cent between 1980–1983 and 2000–2003. Non-agricultural labour productivity declined in four fifths of the LDCs for which data are available over this period, indicating that there is a widespread and major problem in productively absorbing labour outside agriculture.

The goods and services which the LDCs can supply competitively to world markets are ultimately limited by the goods and services which they can produce and how efficiently they are in producing them. This is the basic source of the marginalization of the LDCs in world trade. Even if they exported all their output, the LDCs' share of world exports of goods and services would be only 2.4 per cent, even though their share of world population is 10.6 per cent. Moreover, just as the production structure of the LDCs is strongly oriented to exploit natural resources, so their export structure is also strongly oriented in that way. The capacity to export manufactures is increasing in the LDCs. But this is

Despite relatively high returns on investments in agricultural research, investment in agricultural research and development remains very low.

Labour productivity in the LDCs as a group in 2000–2003 was just 12 per cent higher than in 1980–1983.

occurring much more slowly than in other developing countries, it is also concentrated in only a few countries, and has thus far limited mainly to low-skill, labour-intensive products, particularly garments, with low learning potential and weak domestic linkages, rather than in the medium- and high-technology exports.

Structural change, productivity growth and trade integration cannot be divorced from patterns of economic growth. With this in view, the chapter has analysed whether there are differences between LDCs according to their growth performance. Using the classification of the LDCs as converging, weak-growth and regressing economies introduced in the previous chapter, important patterns emerge. In short, the converging economies are characterized by: (i) a decline in the share of agriculture in GDP; (ii) an increase in manufacturing value-added; (iii) rising labour productivity in both agriculture and non-agricultural sectors; (iv) an increase in the share of trade in GDP; and (v) an increase in the share of manufactures exports in merchandise exports. In the regressing economies: (i) the share of agriculture in GDP is rising; (ii) de-industrialization, in the sense of a declining share of manufactures in GDP, is occurring; (iii) labour productivity is declining in both agricultural and non-agriculture; (iv) trade is declining as a share of GDP; and (v) although manufactures exports are increasing as a share of total merchandise exports, this is occurring much more slowly than in the converging economies.

This analysis shows that the LDC experience does not diverge from the classic long-term patterns of structural transformation which has been found when sustained economic growth occurs (see Clark 1957, Kuznets 1966; Syrquin and Chenery1989). The dynamics of production structure are closely associated with economic growth performance. In the previous chapter, it was shown that the converging economies did significantly better than the weak-growth economies and regressing economies in terms of their domestic savings mobilization and investment effort. It is also now clear that structural transformation has been greater in these countries.

The patterns of production and trade indicate that the level of accumulation of knowledge-based assets is generally low. But there is also regression rather than accumulation in these assets in many LDCs.

The overall lack of structural change, the very slow rate of productivity growth and the limited range of goods in which LDCs are internationally competitive are all symptomatic of a lack of technological learning and innovation within LDCs. The patterns of production and trade indicate that the level of accumulation of knowledge-based assets is generally low. But there is also regression rather than accumulation in these assets in many LDCs. Using traditional indicators of technological effort (such as R&D, patenting, numbers of scientists and researchers and publications), it is apparent that there is a major knowledge divide between the LDCs, other developing countries and developed countries. These statistics do not represent the full picture as they do not capture types of innovation and dimensions of innovativeness which are relevant for very poor countries. But firm-level data also identifies deficiencies in technological capabilities. Significantly, this appears to be an area of weakness even in converging economies.

Within rich countries, an increasing proportion of production is now within what is called the knowledge economy, i.e. they are based on the manipulation of ideas and knowledge rather than material objects. But the knowledge intensity of production within the global economy is high not only in high-technology sectors, creative industries and producer services. It is also increasing within primary production and low-skill manufactures. For this reason, knowledge accumulation and the development of technological capabilities is as important for the LDCs as it is for rich countries. International competitiveness in

For the LDCs, the weak development of technological capabilities together with weaknesses of capital accumulation reinforce each other and threaten the marginalization of the LDCs within the global economy.

the global economy is increasingly based on knowledge and innovation rather than on price and cost. As this occurs the divide between rich and poor countries in terms of their stock of knowledge assets and learning capabilities is becoming increasingly important as an obstacle to development and poverty reduction. For the LDCs, the weak development of technological capabilities together with weaknesses of capital accumulation reinforce each other and threaten the marginalization of the LDCs within the global economy. Yet, as discussed in the growth model at the start of the previous chapter, the availability of technologies already in use in other countries offers a major opportunity for catch-up growth.

This chapter completes the discussion of the core processes through which productive capacities develop — capital accumulation, technological progress and structural change. The next chapter extends the analysis by considering the implications of the slow rate of capital accumulation and technological progress, as well as the weak pattern of structural change for poverty. It does so by focusing more closely on the labour productivity trends identified in this chapter, as well as the ability of the LDCs to absorb their growing labour force productively both within and outside agriculture.

Notes

1. For semantic simplicity the text throughout this chapter refers to sectoral shares in GDP. The estimates are based on shares in total value-added.

2. The term "openness" within trade and development analysis refers both to a type of trade policy regime or the degree of trade orientation (see UNCTAD 2002: Box 9). It is used in the latter sense here. However, as shown in the LDC Report 2004, most LDCs have also undertaken extensive trade liberalization.

3. For this estimate, primary products correspond to categories 0-4 plus items 524 (radioactive and associated materials), 667 (precious stones), 68 (non-ferrous metals), 941 (live and zoo animals) and 971 (gold). This classification of primary products differs slightly from that used in Part I of this Report (and also earlier LDC Reports). The inclusion of items 524, 667, 941 and 971 means that the share of primary commodities in total merchandise exports is slightly higher than the estimate in Part I. The commodity classification is based on Wood and Mayer (1998) and UNCTAD (1998), and is used throughout this section.

4. This classification is based on the LDC export structure of the late 1990s: (i) Agricultural exporters: Afghanistan, Benin, Bhutan, Burkina Faso, Burundi, Chad, Eritrea, Ethiopia, Guinea-Bissau, Kiribati, Malawi, Mali, Mauritania, Rwanda, Sao Tome and Principe, Solomon Islands, Somalia, Togo, Uganda and the United Republic of Tanzania; (ii) Mineral exporters: Central African Republic, Democratic Republic of Congo, Guinea, Liberia, Niger, Sierra Leone and Zambia; (iii) Oil exporters: Angola, Equatorial Guinea, Sudan and Yemen; (iv) manufactures exporters: Bangladesh, Cambodia, Haiti, Lao People's Democratic Republic, Lesotho, Madagascar, Myanmar and Nepal; (v) Service exporters: Cape Verde, Comoros, Djibouti, Gambia, Maldives, Samoa, Tuvalu and Vanuatu; and (vi) Mixed manufactures and services exporters: Mozambique and Senegal (UNCTAD, 2004, p. 24).

5. The distinction between static and dynamic agricultural goods is drawn from Wood and Mayer (1998). Dynamic agricultural goods are those with an income elasticity of demand greater than one.

6. The number of commodities exported include only those products that are greater than $100,000 or more than 0.3 per cent of the country's total exports. (UNCTAD, *Handbook of Statistics*, 2005)

7. Since Kaldor first enunciated his growth laws in the mid-1960s there has been a mass of empirical evidence supporting them (see, for example, surveys by Thirlwall, 1983; McCombie, Pugno and Soro, 2003). A recent study has tested these laws across 45 countries including 27 LDCs in Africa (Wells and Thirlwall, 2003).

8. It is of course important in those LDCs in which FDI inflows are concentrated, particularly oil-exporting LDCs.

References

Archibugi, D. and Coco, A. (2004). A new indicator of technological capabilities for developed and developing countries. *World Development*, 32(4): 629–654.

Archibugi, D. and Coco, A. (2005). Measuring technological capabilities at the country level: A survey and a menu for choice. *Research Policy*, 34(2): 175–194.

Clark, C. (1957). *The Conditions of Economic Progress*. Macmillan, London.

FAO (2004). *The State of World Fisheries and Aquaculture 2004*. FAO, Rome.

Herrmann, M. (2006). Structural changes in labour-surplus economies: Evidence from least developed countries. Bakground paper prepared for *The Least Developed Countries Report 2006*, UNCTAD, Geneva.

Lall, S. (2004). Re-inventing industrial strategy: the role of government policy in building industrial competitiveness. G-24 Discussion Paper Series No.28, UNCTAD, Geneva.

Lall, S. (2005a). Is African industry competing? QEH Working Paper Series No.121, Queen Elizabeth House, Oxford University.

Lall, S. (2005b). FDI, AGOA and manufactured exports by a landlocked, least developed African economy: Lesotho, *Journal of Development Studies*, Vol. 41(6): 998–1022.

Kaldor, N. (1966). *Causes of the Slow Rate of Economic Growth of the United Kingdom*, Cambridge: Cambridge University Press.

Kaldor, N. (1967). *Strategic Factors in Economic Development*, Ithaca, NY: Cornwell University.

Knell, M. (2006). Uneven technological accumulation and growth in the least developed countries. Background paper prepared for *The Least Developed Countries Report 2006*, UNCTAD, Geneva.

Kuznets (1966). *Modern Economic Growth*, Yale University Press, New Haven, Conn.

McCombie, J., M. Pugno, and B. Soro (eds.) (2003). *Productivity Growth and Economic Performance: Essays in Verdoorn's Law*. London: Palgrave Macmillan.

Nelson, R. and Pack, H. (1999). The Asian miracle and modern growth theory. *Economic Journal*, 109 (457): 416–436.

Pardey, P.G. and Beintema, N.M. (2001). Slow magic: Agricultural R&D a century after Mendel. Agricultural Science and Technology Indicators Initiative, International Food Policy Research Institute, Washington, DC.

Rasiah, R. (2006). Sustaining development through garment exports in Cambodia. Background paper prepared for *The Least Developed Countries Report 2006*, UNCTAD, Geneva.

Schumpeter, J. (1942). *Capitalism, Socialism and Democracy*. London, Unwin, third edition, 1950, New York, Harper and Row.

Syrquin, M. and Chenery, H. (1989). Patterns of development 1950–1985. World Bank Discussion paper no. 41, World Bank, Washington, DC.

Thirlwall, A.P. (1983). Symposium on Kaldor's Growth Laws, *Journal of Post Keynesian Economics*, Spring.

UNCTAD (2002a). *The Least Developed Countries Report 2002, Escaping the Poverty Trap*, United Nations publication, sales no. E.02.II.D.13, Geneva and New York.

UNCTAD (2002b). *The Trade and Development Report, 2002: Developing countries in World Trade*. United Nations publication sales no. E.02.II.D.2, Geneva and New York.

UNCTAD (2004). *The Least Developed Countries Report 2004: Linking International Trade with Poverty Reduction*. United Nations publication, sales no. E.04.II.D.27, Geneva and New York.

UNCTAD (2005). *Handbook of Statistics*, United Nations publication, sales no. E/F.05.II.D.29, Geneva and New York.

UNIDO (2005). *Industrial Development Report 2005: Capability building for catching-up. Historical, empirical and policy dimensions*. UNIDO, Vienna.

Verdoorn, P. J. (1949). Fattori che Regolano lo Sviluppo della Produttivitá del Lavoro, *L'Industria*, No. 1.

Wells, H. and A.P. Thirlwall (2003). Testing Kaldor's Growth Laws across the Countries of Africa, *African Development Review*, 15(2–3): 89–105.

Wood, A. and Mayer, J. (1998). Africa's export structure in a comparative perspective . Study No. 4, African Development in a Comparative Perspective. (http://www.ids.ac.uk./ids/global.strat1.html).

Labour Supply and the Lack of Productive Employment

A. Introduction

The labour force is an important productive resource of the LDCs, and a key challenge which they face in developing their productive capacities is to ensure that it is more fully and productively employed. In almost all the LDCs there is an imbalance between the rate of growth of the labour force, which is very rapid owing to population growth, and the rate of capital accumulation and technological progress, which as shown in the previous two chapters, is generally slow. As a result, most workers have to earn their living using their raw labour, with rudimentary tools and equipment, little education and training, and poor infrastructure. Labour productivity is low and there is widespread underemployment.

This is the basic cause of persistent mass poverty in the LDCs. In most of the LDCs extreme poverty is not mainly associated with outright unemployment; rather, it arises because the labour force is generally working for very low incomes which are insufficient to raise household living standards above the poverty line. There are two proximate causes of poverty in this situation: (i) underemployment, and (ii) low returns to labour (Osmani, 2005). Underemployment is most clearly discernible in situations in which persons work less than full-time in terms of the total number of hours a week and days a year. But "disguised underemployment" is also possible in the sense that a person apparently works full-time, but at a very low intensity, within a household enterprise (such as a family farm or a petty trading business) in which work and income are shared amongst household members. However, even when they work full-time and high-intensity, many workers in the LDCs are able to achieve only low returns for their labour. Again, following Osmani (2005), this situation arises for the following reasons: (i) because these workers compete with potential entrants who have very low reservation wages (unemployed and underemployed who constitute a pool of surplus labour); (ii) because of low productivity (owing to poor skills, poor technology or inadequate complementary factors); and (iii) owing to adverse terms of trade (low product prices or high input costs).

Creating productive employment opportunities for the expanding labour force is a major economic and social problem for most LDCs. However, this problem is also a major economic opportunity. If the latent energies and enterprise of underutilized labour are harnessed, it should be possible not only to reduce poverty but also to accelerate economic growth. As discussed in chapter 2, high growth rates can be achieved in very poor countries through investment and innovation in activities with increasing returns and strong linkage effects. In successful developing countries this process has been sustained by an elastic supply of labour and capital for those dynamic sectors of the economy (Ros, 2000). In the LDC context, the potential for such a high elasticity of supply of labour is present owing to high rates of underemployment and the concentration of workers in low-productivity activities. The underemployed labour working in low-productivity activities is an immense underutilized

The labour force is an important productive resource of the LDCs, and a key challenge which they face in developing their productive capacities is to ensure that it is more fully and productively employed.

High growth rates can be achieved in very poor countries through investment and innovation in activities with increasing returns and strong linkage effects.

productive resource which can provide the foundation for high and sustained growth within the LDCs if the growing labour supply is linked to processes of capital accumulation and technological progress.

The previous chapter showed that labour productivity within the LDCs was very low and growing slowly. There was also a very widespread pattern in which labour productivity outside agriculture was falling within the LDCs. This chapter seeks to deepen the understanding of these trends by examining trends in labour supply and in employment opportunities within agriculture and outside agriculture. Some of the analysis draws on international data on labour supply and agriculture. However, most of the evidence relies on case-study material. Although this does not encompass the full range of situations within the LDCs, it illustrates the dimensions of the problem of generating productive employment opportunities which most LDCs now face.

The chapter begins (section B) by looking at the growth and changing locus (both rural–urban location and sectoral composition) of the labour force in the LDCs. Section C discusses opportunities for the productive employment of labour within agriculture. These are changing as the land frontier is being reached and farm sizes are becoming smaller, whilst extreme poverty means that many households simply do not have the means to increase productivity through sustainable intensification. Section D discusses opportunities for the productive employment of labour outside agriculture. Here the basic trend is one in which formal employment opportunities are not expanding fast enough to absorb the economically active population outside agriculture, and there is a proliferation of survivalist, low-productivity informal sector enterprises and high levels of urban underemployment. Section E summarizes the basic messages of the chapter.

The underemployed labour working in low-productivity activities is an immense underutilized productive resource which can provide the foundation for high and sustained growth within the LDCs if the growing labour supply is linked to processes of capital accumulation and technological progress.

B. The growth and changing locus of the labour force

The dearth of available data makes it difficult to describe conditions of labour supply in detail in the LDCs.[1] Following the approach in the previous chapter, the description here is based on FAO estimates of the economically active population. These are used as they enable a breakdown into the labour force in agriculture and in non-agricultural sectors of the economy, the latter encompassing all economic activities outside agriculture (mining, construction, utilities, manufactures and various kinds of services). The economically active population is defined as those who furnish the supply of labour for the production of goods and services during the specified reference period, namely employers, self-employed workers, salaried employees, wage earners, casual day-workers, unpaid workers assisting in a family farm or business operation, members of producers cooperatives and members of the armed forces (see FAOSTAT online). The terms "economically active population" and "labour force" will be used interchangeably throughout this chapter.

Between 1990 and 2000, the labour force of the LDCs increased by 71 million, and it is expected to grow between 2000 and 2010 by a further 89 million to reach 401 million.

According to the FAO estimates, the total labour force of the LDCs was 312 million people in 2000. Between 1990 and 2000, the labour force increased by 71 million, and is expected to grow between 2000 and 2010 by a further 89 million to reach 401 million (chart 32). A large share of the increment in the total labour force between 2000 and 2010 (22 per cent), will occur in Bangladesh.[2] However, all LDCs are experiencing large growth in their labour force during the present decade. For 36 out of 50 LDCs for which data are available, the labour force is expected to increase by over 25 per cent.

CHART 32. THE GROWTH AND CHANGING LOCUS OF THE LABOUR FORCE IN LDCs, 1980–2010

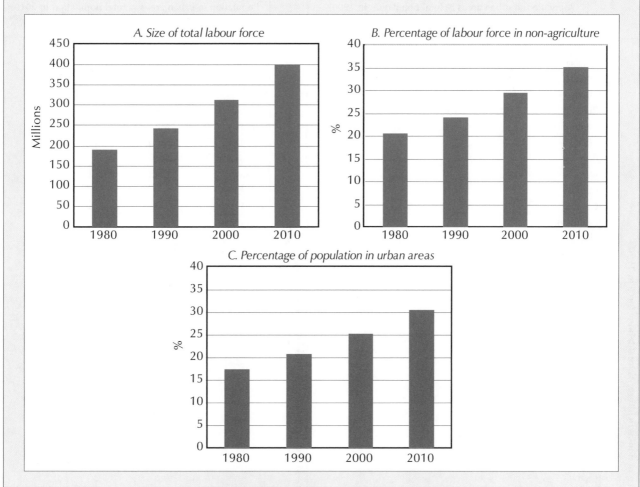

Source: UNCTAD secretariat estimates based on FAO, FAOSTAT, online, December 2005.

Note: The labour force is the economically active population.

Chart 32 also shows past trends and future projections of the share of the labour force in non-agricultural activities and the distribution of the population between urban centres and rural areas. In 2000, 71 per cent of the labour force was engaged in agriculture and 75 per cent lived in rural areas. But the urbanization rate increased from 17 per cent in 1980 to 25 per cent in 2000, and the share of the population engaged in non-agricultural activities steadily increased from 21 per cent in 1980 to 29 per cent in 2000.

These trends are widespread within the LDCs. Table 38 summarizes the projected shift from 1990 to 2010 in individual countries. In 1990, two thirds of the LDCs had less than one third of their population living in urban areas and less than one third of their economically active population engaged outside agriculture. But by 2010, less than one third of the LDCs will have this kind of economy and society.

The broad contours of change in the LDCs are thus clear. Within almost all LDCs, the population is not only growing rapidly but also urbanizing rapidly from very low levels. The combination of these factors is making the current decade a critical decade with regard to the employment situation within the LDCs. More people than ever before are seeking work. But in addition to this, an increasing proportion of the labour force is working or seeking work outside agriculture.

In 2000, 71 per cent of the labour force was engaged in agriculture and 75 per cent lived in rural areas, but the urbanization rate increased from 17 per cent in 1980 to 25 per cent in 2000.

TABLE 38. CHANGING LOCUS OF THE LABOUR FORCE IN LDCs, 1990 AND 2010

		Population in urban areas % total population in 1990				Population in urban areas % total population in 2010		
		0–33%	34–66%	67–100%		0–33%	34–66%	67–100%
Labour force in non-agriculture, % total labour force in 1990	0–33%	Afghanistan Angola Bhutan Burkina Faso Burundi Cambodia Chad Comoros Dem. Rep.of the Congo Gambia Guinea Guinea-Bissau Haiti Lao PDR Madagascar Malawi Mali Mozambique Myanmar Nepal Niger Rwanda Sierra Leone Solomon Islands Somalia Sudan Timor-Leste Uganda United Rep. of Tanzania	Central African Rep. Equatorial Guinea Liberia Sao Tome & Principe Senegal Zambia	Djibouti	Labour force in non-agriculture, % total labour force in 2010 — 0–33%	Bhutan Burkina Faso Burundi Eritrea Ethiopia Gambia Lao PDR Madagascar Malawi Nepal Niger Rwanda Solomon Islands Timor-Leste Uganda	Angola Comoros Guinea Guinea-Bissau Mali Mozambique Myanmar Senegal United Rep. of Tanzania	Djibouti
	34–66%	Bangladesh Lesotho Samoa Togo Vanuatu Yemen	Benin Mauritania		34–66%	Afghanistan Bangladesh Cambodia Chad Lesotho Yemen	Benin Central Afr. Rep. Dem. Rep. of Congo Equatorial Guinea Haiti Liberia Sao Tome & Principe Sierra Leone Somalia Sudan Togo Zambia	Mauritania
	67–100%	Maldives	Cape Verde Kiribati Tuvalu		67–100%	Maldives Samoa Vanuatu	Cape Verde Tuvalu Kiribati	

Source and Note: As for chart 32.

It is important to emphasize that agriculture will still be the major source of livelihood in the LDCs by 2010. The combination of the rate of growth of the economically active population and the rate of decline in the share in the total economically active population in agriculture means that the economically active population in agriculture is expected to continue to rise during the current decade. It is projected to increase in 2010 to 260 million people as against 141 million in non-agricultural activities.

However, projections of economically active population show that during 2000–2010, of the 89 million increase in the economically active population, 49 million will be outside agriculture and 40 million in agriculture (chart 33). This is a complete reversal of the pattern of the 1980s, when 63 per cent of the increase in the economically active population was in agriculture. For the LDCs as a group it is the first decade in which the growth of the economically active population outside agriculture is expected to be greater than in agriculture. During the 1990s, a larger share of the growth of the economically active population was in agriculture.

The overall pattern of change for the LDCs as a group is strongly influenced by what is happening in Bangladesh. But in African LDCs, 46 per cent of the increase in the total economically active population is expected to be outside agriculture during 2000–2010 (as against 29 per cent in the 1980s), and in Asian LDCs other than Bangladesh 45 per cent of the increase in the total economically active population is expected to be outside agriculture during the same period (as against 36 per cent in 1980s) (chart 33). The economically active population outside agriculture is projected to grow faster than the economically active population in agriculture during the decade 2000–2010 in almost half the LDCs (24 out of 50 countries). These countries include Benin, Chad, the Central African Republic, the Democratic Republic of the Congo, Equatorial Guinea, Lesotho, Liberia, Mauritania, Sierra Leone, Sudan, Togo and Zambia in Africa; Bangladesh, Myanmar and Yemen in Asia; and Cape Verde, Kiribati, Maldives, Samoa, Sao Tome and Principe, Tuvalu and Vanuatu within the group of island LDCs. The break with past trends is also apparent in Haiti. In many of the other LDCs this break is projected to occur during the decade 2011–2020.

These estimates are, of course, projections which may not be realized. They rely on international data and so national estimates may vary. However, they define the essential dimensions of the problem of poverty reduction in the LDCs. This requires productive labour absorption both in agriculture and in non-agricultural sectors. The current configuration of growth of the labour force, urbanization and the increasing proportion of the population working outside agriculture mean that the latter challenge cannot now be neglected. Poverty reduction requires the employment creation in both the agricultural and non-agricultural sectors.

Productive labour absorption can be said to occur when there are "employment changes in the economically active population that increase the average productivity of those in work, without increasing open unemployment and without average productivity falling in major production branches or groupings" (Gurrieri and Sáinz, 2003: 151). In ECLAC studies, where this concept has been used widely, productive absorption has generally been associated with the movement of economically active population from the agricultural sector to urban sectors (particularly industry), from manual to non-manual occupations and from the informal to the formal sector, and with reductions in the productivity gaps among these occupational groups or sectors, or between primitive parts of given sectors and their modern parts. The term "spurious labour absorption" has been used for employment changes in the economically active population that reduce the average productivity of a major occupational group. In the present analysis, the term "productive labour absorption" will be used to refer to both agriculture and non-agriculture. The challenge facing the LDCs is to ensure that the growth of the economically active population is associated with productive labour absorption in both these broad sectors of the economy.

For the LDCs as a group, 2000–2010 is the first decade in which the growth of the economically active population outside agriculture is expected to be greater than in agriculture.

The challenge facing the LDCs is to ensure that the growth of the economically active population is associated with productive labour absorption in both agriculture and non-agriculture sectors.

CHART 33. INCREASE OF AGRICULTURAL AND NON-AGRICULTURAL LABOUR FORCE IN LDCs AND LDC SUBGROUPS, FOR THE DECADES 1980–1990, 1990–2000 AND 2000–2010

(Millions of persons)

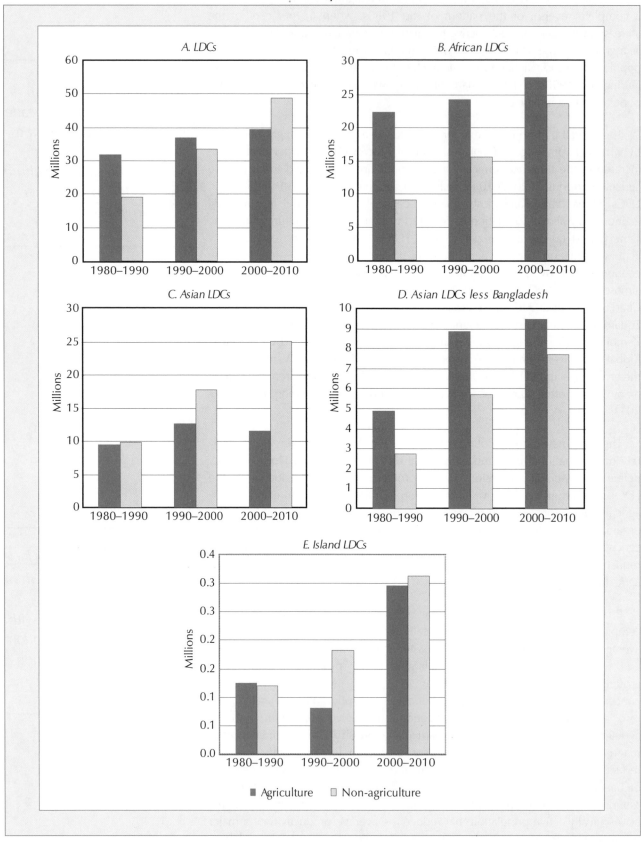

Source and Note: As for chart 32.

C. The changing relationship between land and labour

As shown in the previous chapter, agriculture is the major source of employment in most LDCs. Agriculture encompasses farming, forestry and fisheries, and for some LDCs, particularly island LDCs, fisheries play a significant economic role. But for most LDCs, farming is the most important of these three activities, and thus opportunities for productive employment depend critically on the relationship between land and labour.

1. LAND ABUNDANCE OR LAND SCARCITY?

The most important way in which labour has found productive work within LDCs over the last twenty-five years has been through agricultural land expansion. As shown above, during the 1980s and 1990s the increase in the economically active population was greatest in agriculture. But in addition, most of the expansion of agricultural output associated with this increase in the agricultural labour force is attributable to expansion of the cultivated area rather than increases in yields. Available FAO estimates indicate that in the 1980s, area expansion accounted for 77 per cent of the growth in cereal production in the LDCs, 77 per cent of the growth in roots and tubers production, 35 per cent of the growth of cotton production and 85 per cent of the growth of oil crop production. In the 1990s, area expansion accounted for 72 per cent of the growth in cereal production in the LDCs, 81 per cent of the growth in roots and tubers production, 80 per cent of the growth of cotton production, 105 per cent of the growth of oil crop production (yields declined) and 84 per cent of the growth of pulses production (FAO, 2002: table 5).

This process can continue to the extent that there is an unused agricultural land frontier. In this regard, the situation varies considerably amongst the LDCs. However, FAO (2002: 12) argues that "most have considerable unexploited potential in agriculture, thanks to their factor endowment in land, water, climate, the scope for utilizing their human resources and improving on their so far limited use of modern farming methods".

Estimates for the mid-1990s suggest that for half of the LDCs for which data are available less than 40 per cent of potential arable land was actually being used (table 39). Potential arable land is defined here as areas which are suitable for cultivation in terms of soil suitability and availability of water (rainfall or irrigation), and includes lands currently under forest or wetlands which are protected and not available for agriculture. The level of utilization of potential arable land is particularly low in the humid zone of central Africa. But at the other end of the spectrum there are small group of LDCs (Burundi, Haiti, Yemen, Lesotho, Eritrea, Afghanistan and Rwanda) which have exploited almost all their potential arable land, as well as a few others (Bangladesh, Togo, Uganda and Somalia) which have relatively limited potential arable land to exploit. Significantly, available data show that water resources are also underutilized in many LDCs.[3]

These overall indicators suggest that abundance of unutilized agricultural land resources is a basic characteristic of many LDCs. However, the idea that LDCs are land abundant must be qualified in at least three ways.

Firstly, as more and more arable land is being brought into cultivation in the LDCs, there is increasing dependence on fragile lands (such as arid regions,

The most important way in which labour has found productive work within LDCs over the last twenty-five years has been through agricultural land expansion.

This process can continue to the extent that there is an unused agricultural land frontier. In the mid-1990s, in half of the LDCs less than 40 per cent of potential arable land was actually being used.

TABLE 39. INDICATORS OF AGRICULTURAL LAND RESOURCES IN LDCS

	Land in use (% of potential arable land)	Population on fragile land (% of total population)	Irrigated land (% of total agricultural land)	Agricultural land per agricultural worker[a] (hectares per worker)			Total fertilizers consumption (kilograms per hectare)	
	1994	1994	2000–2003	1980–1983	2000–2003	% change between 1980–1983 and 2000–2003	1980–1983	2000–2002
African LDCs and Haiti								
Angola	6	30-50	0.1	1.2	0.8	-33.3	3.1	0.1
Benin	26	30-50	0.4	1.4	1.8	28.6	1.9	13.9
Burkina Faso	24	50-70	0.2	0.8	0.8	0.0	3.3	3.0
Burundi	130	20-30	0.9	0.6	0.4	-33.3	1.3	2.4
Central African Republic	6	30-50	0.0	1.9	1.6	-15.8	0.5	0.3
Chad	15	30-50	0.1	1.6	1.3	-18.8	1.3	4.9
Dem. Rep. of Congo	3	50-70	0.0	0.8	0.6	-25.0	1.1	0.6
Djibouti	..	..	0.1	0.0	0.0	0.0	..	..
Equatorial Guinea	..	30-50		2.7	1.7	-37.0	0.1	0.0
Eritrea	201	>70	0.3	..	0.4	..	..	11.8
Ethiopia	40	30-50	0.9	..	0.5	..	..	13.5
Gambia	22	30-50	0.3	0.6	0.6	0.0	11.4	2.6
Guinea	20	30-50	0.8	0.5	0.5	0.0	0.4	1.9
Guinea-Bissau	10	20-30	1.5	1.0	1.1	10.0	2.5	4.4
Haiti	151	30-50	5.8	0.6	0.5	-16.7	3.2	12.8
Lesotho	160	30-50	0.1	1.4	1.2	-14.3	15.3	30.6
Liberia	7	20-30	0.1	1.0	0.7	-30.0	5.3	0.0
Madagascar	10	30-20	3.9	0.8	0.6	-25.0	3.7	2.6
Malawi	51	..	1.3	0.6	0.5	-16.7	21.3	37.7
Mali	10	50-70	0.7	0.6	1.0	66.7	5.4	8.8
Mauritania	66	30-50	0.1	0.4	0.8	100.0	2.0	3.9
Mozambique	4	20-30	0.2	0.6	0.6	0.0	9.4	5.0
Niger	..	>70	0.2	3.9	3.2	-17.9	0.3	0.3
Rwanda	259	30-50	0.5	0.4	0.3	-25.0	0.5	3.8
Senegal	..	30-50	1.4	1.1	0.8	-27.3	8.6	13.7
Sierra Leone	35	30-50	1.1	0.6	0.6	0.0	3.3	0.4
Somalia	90	50-70	0.5	0.4	0.4	0.0	1.5	0.5
Sudan	14	50-70	1.4	2.3	2.2	-4.3	5.6	3.9
Togo	83	20-30	0.2	2.6	2.2	-15.4	1.3	7.1
Uganda	84	30-50	0.1	1.0	0.8	-20.0	0.1	1.0
United Rep. of Tanzania	16	30-50	0.4	0.5	0.3	-40.0	7.2	2.5
Zambia	14	20-30	0.4	2.5	1.7	-32.0	15.3	8.4
Asian LDCs								
Afghanistan	207	50-70	7.1	1.8	1.30	-27.8	6.4	1.8
Bangladesh	71	..	49.5	0.3	0.2	-33.3	49.8	165.1
Bhutan	..	>70	7.3	0.2	0.1	-50.0	1.1	0.0
Cambodia	49	20-30	5.1	0.8	0.8	0.0	5.1	0.0
Lao People's Dem. Rep	22	50-30	9.4	0.6	0.5	-16.7	2.7	8.7
Myanmar	35	20-30	17.3	0.8	0.6	-25.0	13.8	13.7
Nepal	65	30-50	27.5	0.3	0.2	-33.3	12.4	31.8
Yemen	156	>70	2.9	0.8	0.6	-25.0	8.8	8.8
Island LDCs								
Cape Verde	..	>70	4.1	1.2	1.2	0.0	0.8	4.1
Comoros	..	30-50		0.6	0.5	-16.7	0.0	2.3
Kiribati	..	..		4.6	3.7	-19.6	0.0	0.0
Maldives	..	..		0.2	0.4	100.0	0.0	0.0
Samoa	..	..		4.6	6.1	32.6	1.2	35.6
Sao Tome and Principe	..	..	18.4	1.2	1.2	0.0	0.0	0.0
Solomon Islands	..	30-50		0.6	0.4	-33.3	0.0	0.0
Timor Leste	..	..		0.5	0.6	20.0	0.0	0.0
Tuvalu	..	..		2.0	2.0	0.0	0.0	0.0
Vanuatu	..	30-50		4.2	3.3	-21.4	0.0	0.0

Source: UNCTAD secretariat estimates based on FAO, FAOSTAT online, December 2005.

a Agricultural land is annual and permanent crops land; agricultural labor force is economically active population in agriculture.

steep slopes and fragile soils). For a sample of 39 LDCs for which data are available, it is estimated that there are 11 in which over 50 per cent of the population live on fragile lands and 31 in which over 30 per cent of the population live on fragile lands (World Bank, 2003: table 4.3) (see table 39). This is likely to become a major problem because extreme poverty can make it difficult for many households to use sustainable agricultural practices, and thus there are problems of land degradation and declining soil fertility.

Secondly, even though new land is being brought into cultivation within the LDCs, the agricultural labour force is growing faster than the expansion of the land area under crop cultivation. This is evident from the fact that the land under crop cultivation per person engaged in agriculture is generally declining. There are only 7 LDCs in which this ratio is clearly increasing, including 4 island LDCs plus Benin, Mali and Mauritania (table 39). For the LDCs as a group, the average size of the cultivated holding per economically active agriculturalist has fallen by 29 per cent over the last 40 years, compared with 18 per cent in the other developing countries. If this ratio is taken as a rough proxy of farm size, it is evident that in 33 out of the 50 LDCs the average farm size was under 1 hectare during the decade 2000–2003, and for the LDCs as a group average farm size was 0.69 hectares.

Thirdly, there are major inequalities in access to land resources and thus, even in apparently land-abundant countries where the land/labour ratio is apparently favourable, a significant share of the holdings are very small.

2. INEQUALITY IN LAND ACCESS

The issue of access to land resources is very complex because of the diversity of the land tenure situation. This includes private ownership; communal systems in which access to land is controlled by a group which allocates land in a particular area to individuals or households; and landlord–tenant relations, which may be based on a fixed rent for the use of the land or various types of sharecropping arrangements. Within African LDCs, where women have a very significant role in agricultural production, the gendered nature of modes of access to and control of land resources is also particularly important (see Gore, 1994). However, the basic situation in most LDCs is that as the rural population increases and the richer households accumulate land through market transactions, access to productive land becomes more and more restricted. This is not necessarily manifested in landlessness. But the poorest households have effective access to so little land that they can barely scratch a subsistence living through agriculture on their own holding.

Recent analysis has shown the smallholder land distribution in five African LDCs – Ethiopia, Rwanda, Malawi, Mozambique and Zambia (Jayne et al., 2003). The first three countries are land-scarce and the last two are land-abundant, and thus the data are indicative of the range of situations within African LDCs. These data, which exclude landless households and also agribusinesses, show that:

- On a per capita basis, farm sizes are very small, ranging from 0.16 hectares in "land-scarce" Rwanda to 0.56 hectares in "land-abundant" Zambia.

- There is significant inequality in land access in both land-scarce and land-abundant countries. The Gini coefficient of land per capita is equal to or exceeds 0.50 in all five countries.

However, the idea that LDCs are land abundant must be qualified in at least three ways. There is increasing dependence on fragile lands... The agricultural labour force is growing faster than the expansion of the land area under crop cultivation...

... and there are major inequalities in access to land resources and thus, even in apparently land-abundant countries where the land/ labour ratio is apparently favourable, a significant share of the holdings is very small.

- The top 25 per cent of the population (in terms of land access) have access to more than 1 hectare per capita in land-abundant Mozambique and Zambia, but only 0.58 hectare per capita in Ethiopia, 0.43 hectares per capita in Rwanda and 0.60 hectares per capita in Malawi.

- In both land-abundant and land-scarce countries, the bottom 75 per cent of the population (in terms of land access) have access to less than 0.26 hectares per capita.

- The bottom 25 per cent of the population (in terms of land access) are approaching landlessness in all five countries, with access to less than 0.12 and 0.10 hectares per capita in "land-abundant" Zambia and Mozambique, respectively, and 0.02, 0.03 and 0.08 hectares per capita in Rwanda, Ethiopia and Malawi, respectively (table 40).

In "land-scarce" areas within African LDCs, there is a "Malthusian trap" in which land tenure is "under unendurable stress".

These surveys do not generally permit analysis of trends over time. But there are good data available showing trends in land access in Rwanda between 1984 and 2000 (table 40). These show that over this 16-year period household land access (use rights plus rented land) declined by 57 per cent, from 0.28 to 0.16 hectares per capita. Mean land access of the top 25 per cent of the households in terms of land access declined from 0.62 to 0.43 hectares per capita, whilst it declined from 0.07 to 0.02 hectares per capita for the bottom quartile. As a consequence, the gap between the land access of the top and bottom quartiles in terms of land access widened from a ninefold difference to a 21-fold difference in 2000 (Jayne et al., 2003: 265). These trends have rightly been described as a "Malthusian trap" in which land tenure is "under unendurable stress" (André and Platteau, 1996/1997). Although extreme, the trends are quite illustrative of what is happening in "land-scarce" areas within African LDCs.

The analysis unfortunately does not extend to other LDCs. However, data from Bangladesh, Cambodia, Haiti and Nepal indicate high levels of land inequality, with about 70 per cent of households having access to less than 1 hectare of land.

- In *Bangladesh*, survey estimates show that in 2000-2001, only 17 per cent of the farm households operated over 1 hectare of land. The average farm size was 0.65 hectares, which, with the level of land productivity prevailing at the time, could meet only about 70 per cent of basic human needs. For poor households, the average farm size per household was 0.29 hectares (Hossain, 2004: 8–9).

- In *Cambodia*, survey estimates for the late 1990s vary, but the main trend indicates that only 75–80 per cent of rural households with land had less than 1 hectare, and that 11–17 per cent of rural households

TABLE 40. ACCESS TO LAND OF SMALLHOLDERS IN SELECTED AFRICAN LDCS

	Survey year	Land access per capita by income quartiles (Hectares)				Average land access per capita	Average land access per household	Gini coefficients	
		1	2	3	4	Hectares	Hectares	Hectare per capita	Hectare per household
Ethiopia	1995	0.03	0.12	0.22	0.58	0.24	1.17	0.55	0.55
Rwanda	1984	0.07	0.15	0.26	0.62	0.28	1.20	...	...
Rwanda	2000	0.02	0.06	0.13	0.43	0.16	0.71	0.54	0.54
Malawi	2000	0.08	0.15	0.25	0.60	0.22	0.99	...	...
Zambia	2000	0.12	0.26	0.26	1.36	0.56	2.76	0.50	0.44
Mozambique	1996	0.10	0.23	0.23	1.16	0.48	2.10	0.51	0.45

Source: Based on Jayne et al. (2003).

were landless. The average land holding is estimated at between 1 and 1.3 hectares per household (Boreak, 2000: chapter 6).

- In *Haiti*, the average farm holding is 1.8 hectares and 50 per cent of the holdings are less than 1 hectare (Government of Haiti, 2005: 18, and table 8).

- In *Nepal*, 47 per cent of the agricultural land holdings were less than 0.5 hectares and 74 per cent were less than 1 hectare in 2001 (National Census of Agriculture, quoted in UNDP, 2004: 25).

To summarize, most LDCs have underutilized agricultural land potential. But the available data indicate that inequality in access to land means that a large share of agricultural households have very small farms even in "land-abundant" LDCs.

3. TRENDS IN LAND PRODUCTIVITY

Farmers could make a reasonable living with quite small holdings if land productivity is high. But in most LDCs agricultural yields are low and also growing very slowly.

Table 41 summarizes annual average yields for some important food and export crops in the LDCs and other developing countries between 1980–1983 and 2000–2003. What is striking is that:

- Although cereal yields increased within the LDCs between these decades, they were increasing much more slowly than in other developing countries.

- For fibre crops, fruits, nuts and sugar yields were actually lower in 2000–2003 than in 1980–1983, and for two other food crops, oil-bearing crops and pulses yields were almost stagnant.

- With regard to export crops, yields have increased more, with the exception of sugar.

Estimates of agricultural yields in the LDCs in the period 2000–2003 show that cereal yields were just over about half the level in other developing countries, and yields for some other basic food crops (oil-bearing crops and vegetables) were less than half those in other developing countries (table 41). Moreover, rather than catching up with other developing countries in terms of agricultural yields, the LDCs as a group have been falling behind. Cereal yields fell from 63 per cent of the level in other developing countries in 1980–1983 to 53 per cent in 2000–2003. Yields of export crops within the LDCs (where land productivity has generally grown the most) are also even falling relative to other developing countries for all commodity groups except pepper and tobacco.

The poor performance of the LDCs is related to low levels of investment in agricultural land, particularly irrigation, and also low levels of use of modern inputs, particularly fertilizers. There are differences amongst the LDCs in this regard, with Asian LDCs performing much better than African LDCs. As chart 34 shows, only 7 per cent of agricultural land in the African LDCs was irrigated in 2000–2003, a level which was not much more than the level in the 1960s. In contrast, the proportion of agricultural land area which is irrigated in Asian LDCs increased from 10 per cent in the 1960s to 30 per cent in 2000–2003. The irrigated land area increased particularly strongly in Bangladesh (from 7 per cent to 53 per cent), but also in the Lao People's Democratic Republic, Myanmar and Nepal.

Farmers could make a reasonable living with quite small holdings if land productivity is high. But in most LDCs agricultural yields are low and also growing very slowly.

The poor performance of the LDCs is related to low levels of investment in agricultural land, particularly irrigation, and low levels of use of modern inputs, particularly fertilizers.

TABLE 41. AGRICULTURAL LAND PRODUCTIVITY IN LDCS AND OTHER DEVELOPING COUNTRIES,
1980–1983 AND 2000–2003

(Hectograms per hectare)

	Period average		% change
	1980–1983	*2000–2003*	*1980–1983 and 2000–2003*
LDCs			
Cereals	13 285	16 142	21.5
Fibre crops	5 069	4 906	-3.2
Fruits	59 902	57 462	-4.1
Nuts	7 919	6 359	-19.7
Oil-bearing crops	2 187	2 171	-0.7
Pulses	5 943	6 004	1.0
Roots and tubers	..	..	..
Vegetables	63 927	76 130	19.1
Cocoa	2 431	2 524	3.8
Coffee	4 250	5 337	25.6
Cotton	6 561	8 411	28.2
Pepper	5 301	7 791	47.0
Sugar	457 010	439 167	-3.9
Tobacco	8 608	10 579	22.9
Other developing countries			
Cereals	21 192	30 392	43.4
Fibre crops	4 506	6 801	50.9
Fruits	91 836	100 286	9.2
Nuts	9 881	10 689	8.2
Oil-bearing crops	3 089	5 709	84.8
Pulses	6 199	7 035	13.5
Roots and tubers	117 396	136 572	16.3
Vegetables	114 746	166 080	44.7
Cocoa	3 565	4 782	34.2
Coffee	5 519	7 610	37.9
Cotton	3 779	7 366	94.9
Pepper	7 169	7 167	0.0
Sugar	576 345	654 660	13.6
Tobacco	13 335	15 836	18.8

Source: As for chart 34.

Note: Cotton is included in fibre crops. All other products and product groups add up to total primary crops.

There is much heterogeneity amongst smallholders in terms of land productivity.

With regard to fertilizer use, which represents the major purchased input of farmers in LDCs, fertilizer consumption per hectare was 44 kilograms per hectare in Asian LDCs compared with 7 kilograms in African LDCs in 2000–2003. The more detailed picture of fertilizer trends in LDCs by country (see table 39) shows that between 1980–1983 and 2000–2003 fertilizer consumption per hectare fell in as many African LDCs as it increased. One reason for this is the withdrawal of fertilizer subsidies and the failure of private traders selling fertilizer to enter the market in many rural areas following the dismantling of State marketing boards.[4]

As with access to land, there is much heterogeneity amongst smallholders in terms of land productivity. Yields are strongly influenced by the high incidence of extreme poverty, which means that farmers simply cannot afford to purchase the necessary inputs to increase or even maintain yields. Evidence from Uganda, the United Republic of Tanzania and Malawi shows that agricultural yields are much higher for richer smallholders than for poorer ones (Ellis, 2004; 2005). Net farm output per hectare for the richest 25 per cent of households was between three and six times higher that that in the poorest 25 per cent. The richest

CHART 34. IRRIGATION AND FERTILIZER CONSUMPTION IN LDCs, LDC SUBGROUPS AND OTHER COUNTRY GROUPS, 1960s, 1970s, 1980s, 1990s AND 2000–2003[a]

(Period averages)

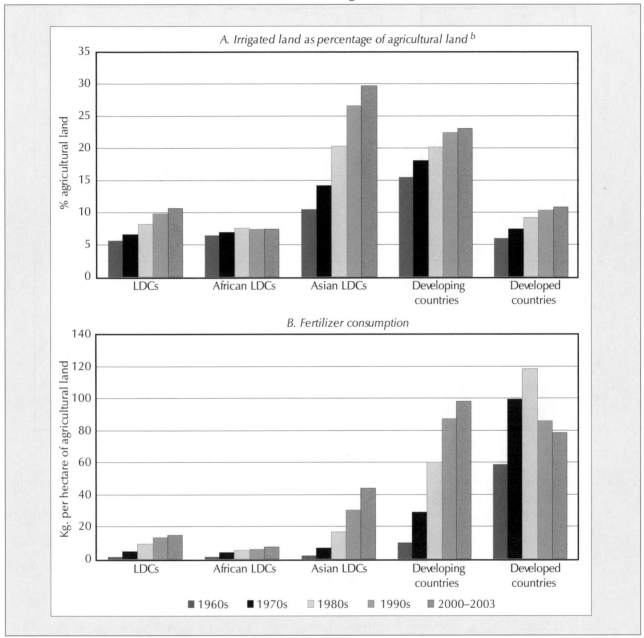

Source: UNCTAD secretariat estimates based on FAO, FAOSTAT online, March 2006.

   a   The 1960s do not include 1961 and fertilizer consumption is 2000–2002.

   b   Agricultural land area is area of arable land and land under permanent crops.

households also derived a much higher share of their total household income from off-farm activities, a fact that indicates a positive link (for these households at least) between engagement in off-farm activities and agricultural productivity. Similar patterns are found in Nepal (Acharya, 2004), where the value of farm output per hectare of poor households is about half that of the non-poor households (see chart 35).

In situations where many farmers have access to little land and are unable to purchase inputs to increase or maintain yields, strong pressures leading to environmental degradation may arise. As shown in UNCTAD (2002: 92–97), this can be part of a downward spiral of impoverishment in which the

Yields are strongly influenced by the high incidence of extreme poverty, which means that farmers simply cannot afford to purchase the necessary inputs to increase or even maintain yields.

CHART 35. LAND PRODUCTIVITY, INCOME INEQUALITY AND POVERTY IN SELECTED LDCS

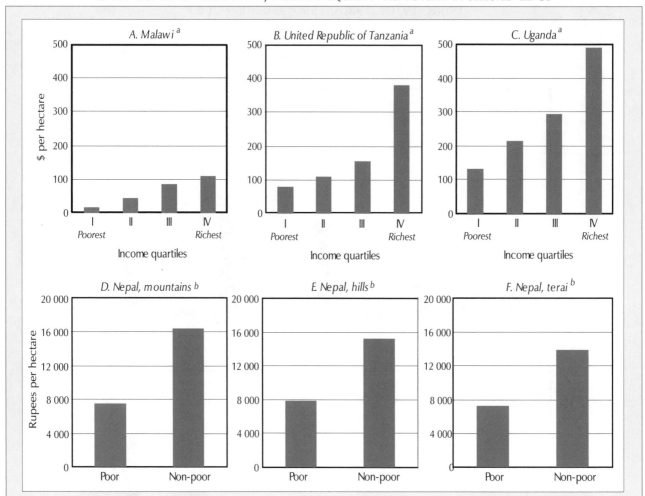

Source: Based on Ellis and Freeman (2004) for Malawi, Uganda and United Republic of Tanzania; and Acharya (2004) for Nepal.
   a   Based on survey data of 2001 and 2002;
   b   Charts for Nepal are based on data from the early 1990s: Mountains, hills and terai are regions with different agricultural potential.

productivity of agricultural assets declines as people eat into the natural capital on which their livelihoods are based in order to survive.

4. THE LIMITS OF PRODUCTIVE LABOUR ABSORPTION WITHIN AGRICULTURE

Up to now, the growth of yields, though slow, has been fast enough to offset the decline in land per person working in agriculture. In the future it is going to become increasingly difficult for more LDCs to absorb labour productively within agriculture.

Trends in agricultural labour productivity are the outcome of trends in land per person working within agriculture and trends in agricultural yields (output per unit of land). Up to now, the expansion of the land frontier, together with slow growth of yields, has made possible the productive absorption of labour within agriculture in most LDCs. The average farm size has generally been falling as the population working in agriculture has expanded faster than the area under cultivation. In most cases, the growth of yields, though slow, has been fast enough to offset the decline in land per person working in agriculture. But there are already some LDCs where the productive absorption of labour within agriculture is not occurring. Moreover, in the future it is going to become increasingly difficult for more and more LDCs to absorb labour productively within agriculture.

Chart 36 shows overall trends in the growth of labour productivity and employment in agriculture from 1980–1983 to 2000–2003 in the LDCs, other developing countries and developed countries. The countries fall into distinct

CHART 36. CHANGE OF LABOUR FORCE AND LABOUR PRODUCTIVITY IN AGRICULTURE, IN LDCs, OTHER DEVELOPING
COUNTRIES AND DEVELOPED COUNTRIES BETWEEN 1980–1983 AND 2000–2003

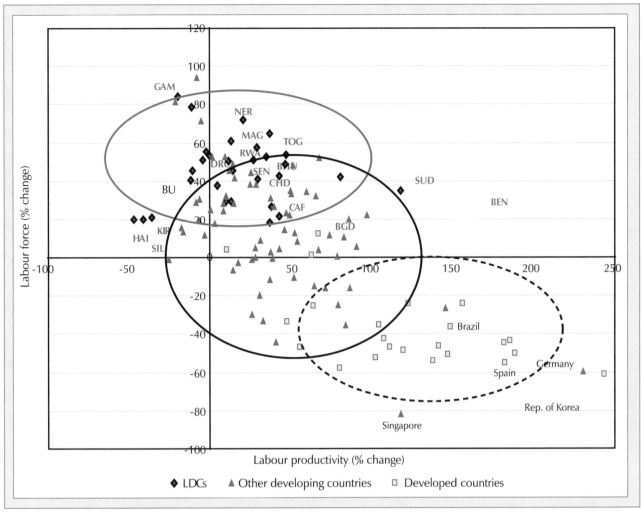

Source: UNCTAD secretariat estimates based on World Bank, *World Development Indicators 2005*, CD-ROM, and FAO, FAOSTAT
          online, December 2005.

Notes: Value-added data are in constant 2000 dollars; labour productivity is estimated by value-added in agriculture divided by
          labour force in agriculture; labour force is the economically active population.

          BGD: Bangladesh; BEN: Benin; BHU: Bhutan; BDI: Burundi; CAF: Central African Republic; CHD: Chad; DRC: Dem. Rep.
          of the Congo; GAM: Gambia; HAI: Haiti; KIR: Kiribati; MAG: Madagascar; NER: Niger; RWA: Rwanda; SEN: Senegal; SIL:
          Sierra Leone; SUD: Sudan; TOG: Togo.

groups. The developed countries are almost all characterized by declining
absolute numbers of people working in agriculture and the highest rates of
agricultural productivity growth. Most of the developing countries have slower
rates of agricultural productivity growth (with Brazil and the Republic of Korea
being notable exceptions) than the developed countries. In two thirds of the
developing countries, this is combined with rising absolute numbers of people
working in agriculture and in one thirds it is combined with falling numbers. The
LDCs stand out in that in all cases they have rising absolute numbers in
agriculture. Also, although some LDCs overlap with some of the other
developing countries, they have the slowest rates of agricultural productivity
growth.

From chart 36 it is also evident that in one third of the LDCs, as employment
in agriculture has been growing since the early 1980s, agricultural labour
productivity has been falling. This is also happening in a few of the other
developing countries. But the majority of the cases are LDCs.

*In one third of the LDCs,
as employment in agriculture
has been growing since the
early 1980s, agricultural
labour productivity
has been falling.*

These average trends also mask the effects of inequality in land access and in yields. As shown above, in a sample of countries representative of land-abundant and land-scarce LDCs within Africa, the bottom 75 per cent of the small farm-households in terms of land access have access to less than 0.26 hectares per capita. Moreover, the most disadvantaged 25 per cent of the small farmers in terms of land access are virtually landless in both land-abundant and land-scarce countries, a pattern which is also found in a number of Asian LDCs and in Haiti. In addition, there are major productivity gaps amongst smallholders, as noted earlier.

It is the combination of limited access to land and low productivity which is at the root of the precariousness of many rural lives in Africa.

Taken together, the combination of access to very little land and of low yields means that the poorest farmers are simply too asset-poor to make a good living from farming. Their farms provide a bare subsistence, with most of the physical output of food crops being retained for home consumption rather than sold in the market. It is this combination of limited access to land and low productivity which is at the root of the precariousness of many rural lives in Africa, evident in the way in which poor weather conditions are associated with widespread hunger and famine. Moreover, it leads to a situation in which the poor tend to diversify their sources of livelihood out of own-farm agriculture into various forms of local casual work, notably for the small stratum of richer farmers. For example, in the studies of smallholder land distribution referred to earlier, off-farm income contributes as much as 39 per cent and 35 per cent of household income of the 25 per cent of the farmers with least access to land in Zambia and Rwanda respectively, although the shares are lower in Ethiopia (8 per cent) and Zambia (13 per cent) (Jayne et al., 2003: table 5). There is also increasing reliance of remittances as younger and male household members move to urban centres to seek a living.

In the future as the agricultural frontier closes within more and more LDCs and the possibility of increasing agricultural production through area expansion diminishes, it is going to be increasingly difficult to absorb labour within agriculture unless there is a switch to a more intensive pattern of agricultural growth. The gap between agricultural yields within LDCs and other developing countries suggests that there is the potential for major agricultural productivity gains within the LDCs. However, sustainable intensification will be difficult to achieve for the poorest farmers, for whom the lack of productive asset holdings creates poverty traps (see Barrett, Carter and Little, 2006).

Productive employment opportunities are growing too slowly outside agriculture to absorb the increasing labour force seeking work away from the farm.

With the trade liberalization which has taken place in the LDCs too, farmers must also compete with more efficient farmers elsewhere in the world. Given the huge gaps in both agricultural land per person working in agriculture between the LDCs, other developing countries and developed countries, as well as widening productivity gaps, this is a daunting prospect. As noted earlier, for the LDCs as a group the average amount of agricultural land per person working in agriculture during 2000–2003 was 0.69 hectares. This compares with 13.1 hectares per economically active person in agriculture in developed countries. The global playing-field within agriculture is being levelled, but the capacities of players in these different worlds are far apart.

D. The informal sector and urban underemployment

The fact that it is becoming more difficult to absorb labour productively within agriculture does not matter in itself. But the challenge facing most LDCs is that at the same time as this is occurring, productive employment opportunities are growing too slowly outside agriculture to absorb the increasing labour force seeking work away from the farm. As the previous chapter showed, labour is not being productively absorbed outside agriculture in four-fifths of the LDCs. The numbers of people seeking work outside agriculture is increasing, but the labour productivity outside agriculture is declining.

Further country-level empirical research is necessary in order to show what is behind this ubiquitous trend.[5] However, in most LDCs the most likely explanation is that employment opportunities in formal sector enterprises are not expanding fast enough to absorb the growing non-agricultural labour force, and as a consequence the importance of employment in informal sector enterprises as a share of non-agricultural employment is increasing. Labour productivity within informal sector enterprises is on average lower than labour productivity within formal sector enterprises. Thus, as the share of the economically active population working outside agriculture which is also working within informal sector enterprises increases, so the non-agricultural labour productivity falls. This is the phenomenon of "spurious" rather than productive labour absorption referred to above.

Employment opportunities in formal sector enterprises are not expanding fast enough to absorb the growing non-agricultural labour force, and as a consequence the importance of employment in informal sector enterprises as a share of non-agricultural employment is increasing.

There is, of course, some heterogeneity amongst informal sector enterprises, with some having much higher productivity and greater dynamic potential than others (Ranis and Stewart, 1999). This is an issue to which we shall return in chapter 7, as there are certain conditions, which are related to the stimulus of domestic demand, in which informal sector enterprises can play an important role in both productivity growth and employment creation. But most employment within informal sector enterprises in most of the LDCs consists of very small survivalist activities for which there are low entry requirements in terms of capital and professional qualifications. The scale of operation is small; capital equipment is rudimentary and skills are basic; and often the enterprise is run by the person who started it, sometimes with unpaid family members who share their earnings. Often the work involves petty services of various kinds, buying and reselling tiny quantities of goods, usually catering to the poorer sections of the population.

1. THE IMPORTANCE OF EMPLOYMENT IN INFORMAL SECTOR ENTERPRISES IN LDCs

It is very difficult to obtain the data which show the informalization of employment (see box 13). But cross-sectional data confirm the pre-eminent importance of employment in informal sector enterprises as a share within non-agricultural employment in LDCs, as well as the labour productivity gap between formal and informal enterprises and the extent of underemployment within labour markets. Moreover, the little evidence available on employment trends over time supports the thesis that as the share of non-agricultural employment in total employment increases, so the share of employment in informal sector enterprises within non-agricultural employment also increases.

Most employment within informal sector enterprises in most of the LDCs consists of very small survivalist activities for which there are low entry requirements in terms of capital and professional qualifications.

Table 42 brings together available estimates of the importance of informal sector enterprises in LDCs in terms of employment and output. For most of the countries, employment in informal sector enterprises constitutes 70–80 per cent of non-agricultural employment. In output terms, the informal sector is not so predominant. It contributes 40–50 per cent of non-agricultural GDP within the LDCs for which data are available.

This shows that value added per worker in informal enterprises is on average lower than that in formal enterprises. The table includes imputed estimates of

---

Box 13. Informal sector and informal employment

The concepts of the informal sector and informal employment are now understood in different ways (Hussmanns, 2004).

Following the definition in the 1993 System of National Accounts, the distinction between the formal and the informal sector refers to different kinds of production units or enterprises. These are not grouped according to their branch of activity (manufacturing, services) but according to certain characteristics which they have in common. The formal sector is constituted by corporations and quasi-corporations and the informal sector is constituted by household enterprises which "are not constituted as separate legal entities independently of the household or of household members that own them, and no complete set of accounts are available which could permit a clear distinction between the production activities of the enterprises and the other activities of their owners". Many informal sector enterprises are owned and operated by individual household members or by several members of the same household. But informal sector enterprises also include micro-enterprises which employ one of more employees on a continuous basis, but which are below a certain size threshold (which may be defined differently in different countries, but which is often fewer than five employees) and are not legally registered.

Informal employment is now regarded as not totally synonymous with persons working within informal sector enterprises. In 2002, the ILO adopted a concept of informal employment which included (i) persons working in informal sector enterprises, and (ii) wage employment in formal enterprises which is not regulated, stable and protected, including casual and day labourers, domestic workers, industrial outworkers (including home workers), unregistered or undeclared workers and some subset of temporary and part-time workers (Chen, 2005).

This new concept can provide a richer picture of employment relationships than a dualistic division between employment in formal and informal sector enterprises, and also a complete view of what the process of informalization of an economy entails. However, there are, in practice, too few comparative data currently available for this approach to be applied within the LDCs. The discussion in this chapter thus focuses on employment within informal sector enterprises.

For an extended discussion on the conceptualization and measurement of the informal sector and informal employment, see Charmes (1998, 2000, 2002), Schneider (2002), ILO (2002), Flodman Becker (2004), the Delhi Group on Informal Sector Statistics (2004), Hussmanns (2004), Chen (2005), and Havinga and Vu (2005). Overviews of the size of the informal sector in Africa and Asia are found in Xaba, Horn and Motala (2002) and Nural Amin (2002), whilst the relationship between gender and informal employment is discussed in ILO (2002) and UNIFEM (2005).

Table 42. Contribution of informal sector to total non-agricultural employment and GDP in selected LDCs

	Year of estimate	Share of informal sector employment in total non-agricultural employment (%)	Contribution of informal sector to non-agricultural GDP (%)	Memo: Imputed labour productivity gap[a] (formal sector/ informal sector)
African LDCs				
Benin	1993	93	43	17.0
Burkina Faso	1992	77	..	6.0
Chad	1993	74	45	3.6
Guinea	1994–2000	72	..	
Mali	1989	79	42	5.1
Mauritania	1989	75	14	18.6
Mozambique	1994	74	45	3.5
Niger	1995	..	59	..
United Rep. of Tanzania	1991	..	43	..
Senegal	1991	76	41	4.5
Zambia	1998	58	20	1.9
Asian LDCs				
Bangladesh	1995/96	68	..	..
Nepal	1998/99	73	..	..

Source: Based on Nural Amin 2002; Charmes 1998, 2000, 2002; Delhi Group 2004; ILO 2002.

a   Imputed labour productivity gap is estimated by dividing the formal sector GDP per formal sector worker by the informal sector GDP per informal sector worker.

the average labour productivity gap outside agriculture between the formal and informal sector based on their shares in non-agricultural employment and GDP. For most countries, non-agricultural labour productivity in the formal sector is four to five times higher than in the informal sector. This productivity gap is similar in magnitude to estimates obtained through more precise survey methods in other developing countries (see ILO, 2004).

There are little data on trends over time. But in sub-Saharan Africa, Kingdon, Sandefur and Teal (2005a: 3–4) suggest that the key trends are the following: (i) the level of wage employment has increased in absolute terms, but failed to keep pace with a growing labour force, and (ii) the share of the informal sector in total employment has grown rapidly. They also find that African economies with high unemployment rates have relatively small informal sectors, a fact which suggests that both informality and unemployment are manifestations of excess labour supply.

Available data from the United Republic of Tanzania indicate that between 1991/92 and 2000/01 the non-agricultural labour force grew by 2.26 million, but wage employment outside agriculture grew by only 172,000. In Uganda between 1992 and 1999/2000, the non-agricultural labour force is estimated to have expanded by 428,000, but wage employment by 82,000 (Kingdon, Sandefur and Teal, 2005b). Charmes (2002) indicates that 93 per cent of the new employment in sub-Saharan Africa in general is informal. Ethiopia is one LDC in which open unemployment rates are very high in urban areas. Estimates suggest that 39 per cent of the urban labour force was unemployed in 1994 and 30 per cent in 1997 (Kingdon, Sandefur and Teal, 2005b). This phenomenon is related to young people searching for jobs, particularly in the public sector, with long waiting times (Serneels, 2004).

In Burkina Faso, only 5 per cent of males and 3 per cent of females found their first paid job in the private formal sector in 2000.

A unique longitudinal study which has examined young people's access to labour markets in 1980, 1990 and 2000 in the major cities of Burkina Faso also shows increasing informalization (Calvès and Schoumaker, 2004). In 1980, 23 per cent of male 15–24 year olds found their first paid job in formal employment. In 1990, this figure had fallen to 15 per cent, and by 2000 it was only 8 per cent. Only 5 per cent of males and 3 per cent of females found their first paid job in the private formal sector in 2000.

2. URBAN LABOUR MARKETS IN THE WEAK-GROWTH ECONOMIES

Recent surveys in West Africa provide a more detailed and comparable picture of urban labour markets within a number of LDCs (Brilleau, Roubaud and Torelli, 2005). The surveys were undertaken in seven countries in 2001–2002 and include information on employment conditions in the following LDC capital cities: Bamako (Mali), Cotonou (Benin), Dakar (Senegal), Lomé (Togo), Niamey (Niger) and Ouagadougou (Burkina Faso). The focus here will be on four countries which, using the classification of chapter two, can be classified as "weak-growth economies" — Benin, Burkina Faso, Mali and Senegal.

These are not the best-performing LDC economies. But since 1990, the economic performance of these countries has been comparatively good. Burkina Faso has not experienced a growth collapse; Benin and Mali grew rapidly enough in the 1990s to recover from growth collapses of the 1980s; and Senegal has grown rapidly since 1995. However, as the data below show, despite rising GDP per capita, the generation of productive and remunerative employment opportunities in the capital cities of these countries has been difficult.

With the focus on these four economies, a number of features of the labour markets of their capital cities can be underlined.

Firstly, informal enterprises are the major source of employment in all the cities, providing 77 per cent of employment on average.[6] On average, only 12 per cent of employed persons are in private formal enterprises in the four capitals. In Cotonou, less than 10 per cent of employed persons are in private formal sector enterprises (table 43).

In these cities, incomes in informal sector enterprises are just over one third of those in private formal sector enterprises.

Secondly, average monthly incomes in informal enterprises are much lower than average incomes in private formal sector enterprises, and average incomes in private formal sector enterprises are much lower than average incomes in public administration and public enterprise. On average, incomes in informal sector enterprises are just over one third those in private formal sector enterprises, and incomes in public administration and public enterprises are about 25 per cent and 40 per cent higher respectively than in formal private sector enterprises (table 43).

TABLE 43. STRUCTURE OF EMPLOYMENT AND INCOME IN URBAN LABOUR MARKETS OF SELECTED AFRICAN LDCs, 2000–2001

	Cotonou (Benin)	Ouagadougou (Burkina Faso)	Bamako (Mali)	Dakar (Senegal)	Average
Employment (% of employed population)					
Public administration	6.3	10.4	7.5	5.7	7.5
Public entreprises	2.2	2.3	2.5	1.8	2.2
Formal private entreprises	9.9	11.8	11.4	15.0	12.0
Informal Private entreprises	80.3	73.4	77.5	76.4	76.9
Entreprises Associatives	1.3	2.1	1.1	1.1	1.4
Income (monthly average in 1000 CFA franc)[a]					
Public administration	89.5	94.7	89.4	149.7	105.8
Public entreprises	122.2	100.0	140.2	134.6	124.3
Formal private entreprises	65.6	73.5	92.6	111.0	85.7
Informal private entreprises	26.5	20.4	37.5	38.4	30.7

Source: Based on Brilleau, Roubaud and Torelli (2005).

Note: ·The private formal sector includes private formal entreprises and associated entreprises.

a Communaute financière africaine franc.

TABLE 44. DISTRIBUTION OF INCOME AMONGST DIFFERENT OCCUPATIONAL GROUPS IN URBAN LABOUR MARKET IN SELECTED AFRICAN LDCs, 2000–2001

(Average monthly income in CFA 1,000)

	Cotonou (Benin)	Ouagadougou (Burkina Faso)	Bamako (Mali)	Dakar (Senegal)	Average
Public sector					
Managers	124.3	135.1	119.6	201.8	145.2
Employees/workers	64.0	66.0	62.7	99.3	73.0
Apprentices/family help	25.3	30.5	35.3	57.6	37.2
Formal private sector					
Managers	97.8	172.5	157.6	238.6	166.6
Employees/workers	49.9	55.0	52.4	87.9	61.3
Apprentices/family help	17.8	19.8	27.3	40.1	26.3
Informal sector					
Managers	56.9	59.0	77.0	110.8	75.9
Self-employed	32.3	23.2	40.2	50.0	36.4
Employees/workers	29.6	28.7	39.5	44.3	35.5
Apprentices/family help	3.7	8.4	11.1	12.7	9.0

Source: As for table 43.

Thirdly, there is much variation between monthly incomes within the different sectors according to occupational status (table 44). Managers within the formal sector have the highest monthly incomes in all the cities. The self-employed within the informal sector have incomes which are roughly half those of employees in private sector enterprises, and workers and employees in informal sector enterprises earn less than that in all the cities except Ouagadougou. The level of incomes within the informal sector means that there is a close association between employment in informal sector enterprises and urban poverty.

Fourthly, unemployment exists in all four cities. According to the ILO definition of unemployment, the average unemployment rate is 10 per cent. Ouagadougou has the highest unemployment rate (15.4 per cent) and Cotonou (5.5 per cent) the lowest. Using a broader definition of unemployment which includes discouraged workers, the average unemployment rate is 15 per cent, with more than one in five of the economically active population in Ouagadougou unemployed (table 45).

Finally, there are very high rates of underemployment in all four cities. With regard to visible underemployment, measured by those who work less than 35 hours per week, 14 per cent of employed persons are underemployed. In Ouagadougou, the visible underemployment rate is 10.6 per cent of employed persons, whilst in Bamako it is 17.1 per cent. Underemployment can also be invisible in the sense that people work long hours but with unusually low productivity. Within the surveys, an attempt is made to estimate such "invisible underemployment" by estimating the proportion of employed persons with incomes below the national minimum wage. According to this definition, 58 per cent of employed persons are on average invisibly underemployed in the four cities, ranging from a high of two thirds of employed persons in Ouagadougou to a low of 45 per cent in Bamako (table 45).

It is apparent that for the four cities in these weak-growth economies two thirds of the economically active population (employed persons plus unemployed) are either unemployed or invisibly underemployed.

When these estimates are added to the earlier estimates of unemployment, it is apparent that for the four capital cities in these weak-growth economies two thirds of the economically active population (employed persons plus unemployed) are either unemployed or invisibly underemployed. In the best case, Bamako, six out of ten economically active persons are either unemployed or underemployed; in the worst case, Ouagadougou, almost three quarters of the economically active population are in this situation.

It is possible to quibble over definitions of unemployment and underemployment. However, what these statistics lay bare is the fact that underemployment and very low incomes are major problems in these urban labour markets, and this situation is closely related to lack of formal sector employment.

TABLE 45. UNEMPLOYMENT AND UNDEREMPLOYMENT IN URBAN LABOUR MARKETS
OF SELECTED AFRICAN LDCs, 2000–2001

(Percentage of employed population)

	Cotonou (Benin)	Ouagadougou (Burkina Faso)	Bamako (Mali)	Dakar (Senegal)	Average
Unemployment rate:					
ILO definition	5.5	15.4	7.1	11.7	9.9
Enlarged definition	6.8	22.4	12.5	18.9	15.2
Visible underemployment rate	13.4	10.6	17.1	16.2	14.3
Invisible underemployment rate	61.1	66.5	45.4	57.8	57.7
Global Unemployment Rate	69.2	73.0	58.8	69.4	67.6

Source: As for table 43.

Note: For definition of variables, see text.

These case studies have been highlighted here as they are regarded as being typical of economies which have experienced weak growth. As the data in chapter 2 showed, the growth performance of many of the LDCs has been poorer than that of these case-study countries, and thus one may infer that the labour market conditions are likely to be worse. However, there are a few LDCs which have experienced higher growth. In these economies, it is possible to create a virtuous circle between expansion of the formal sector and a shift towards higher productivity and more remunerative activities in the informal economy. The nature of this virtuous circle, which is closely related to the opportunities created by expanding demand, will be examined in chapter 7.

E. Conclusions

In African LDCs, 46 per cent of the increase in the economically active population during 2000–2010 is expected to occur outside agriculture, whilst in Asian LDCs other than Bangladesh, 45 per cent of the increase will occur outside agriculture.

The basic message of this chapter is that the present decade is a decade of transition for many LDCs. In the past, the growth of the labour force in agriculture was always greater than the growth of the labour force outside agriculture. But in 2000–2010, the growth of the economically active population seeking work outside agriculture is expected to exceed the growth of the economically active population seeking work within agriculture in 24 out of 50 countries. For the LDC group as whole, this is the first decade in which the growth of the economically active population outside agriculture will exceed the growth of that in agriculture. The overall trend is strongly influenced by what is happening in Bangladesh. But, in African LDCs, 46 per cent of the increase in the economically active population is expected to occur outside agriculture, whilst in Asian LDCs other than Bangladesh, 45 per cent of the increase will occur outside agriculture.

This transition is associated with increasing urbanization within LDCs. However, it also reflects the fact that the traditional mechanism through which the increasing labour supply has been employed within LDCs is becoming more and more circumscribed. That mechanism has consisted in bringing more land into agricultural cultivation. In the past, this has made possible the productive absorption of labour, even though agricultural productivity has been increasing very slowly. However, there is a general tendency for agricultural land per worker to be decreasing and a larger share of the population to be focused on fragile lands. Moreover, even in land-abundant countries, inequalities in land access mean that the poorest smallholders have little access to land. This means that whatever the "pull" factors driving urbanization, there is going to be an increasing number of "push" factors as more and more people find it difficult to achieve a satisfactory living from agriculture.

LDCs need to shift from an extensive pattern of agricultural growth (based on expansion of the area of cultivation) to an intensive pattern of agricultural growth based on increasing yields and sustainable intensification.

There remain under-exploited agricultural resources in many of the LDCs (for example, pharmaceutical drugs from plants and the potential to produce biofuels; see Sachs, 2005). The agricultural productivity gap between LDCs and other developing countries also means that there are major opportunities to increase productivity in agriculture. Against this background many LDCs need to shift from an extensive pattern of agricultural growth (based on expansion of the area of cultivation) to an intensive pattern of agricultural growth based on increasing yields and sustainable intensification. But this will be hard to achieve amongst the asset-poor smallholders, as it requires more working capital and private investment by smallholders. It will also require increased public investment in better rural infrastructure and agricultural research and development, as well as improved markets for production inputs, agricultural output and seasonal finance. Moreover, it will be necessary to create more productive employment outside agriculture, in both rural and urban areas, as well.

The problem facing most LDCs is that not only are they finding it difficult to increase agricultural productivity, but also that they have a severe problem in absorbing the expanding labour force outside agriculture productively. A general tendency in most LDCs is that labour productivity outside agriculture is declining. This reflects the inability to create sufficient formal jobs and the proliferation of employment in marginal petty trade and services activities. The labour force is growing outside agriculture, but it is not being productively employed. The key policy issue which arises is: can current policies rectify these trends and, if not, what is the alternative?

Sustainable agricultural intensification and the creation of productive off-farm employment will require increased capital accumulation and technological learning as well as innovation in new sectors to create structural change. The next three chapters focus on three key constraints on such development of productive capacities — infrastructure, institutions, and the lack of incentives provided by effective demand — before turning to the policy implications.

Sustainable agricultural intensification and the creation of productive off-farm employment will require increased capital accumulation and technological learning as well as innovation in new sectors to create structural change.

Notes

1. For a discussion of the severe limitations of data on labour supply in sub-Saharan Africa, see Sender, Cramer and Oya (2005). With regard to Asia, the Asian Development Bank (2005: 5) emphasizes that the main problem there is lack of comparability of data across countries owing to differences in the scope and coverage of labour force surveys, the reference population, the reference period for which labour force status is determined, and the definitions of labour force status.
2. This reflects the size of Bangladesh which, in 2000, accounted for 22 per cent of the total labour force.
3. Atkinson (2005), using data of the University of Kassels ranking 140 countries according to the proportion of their territory suffering from severe water stress, indicates that most LDCs rank low on the list. Exceptions are Nepal, Niger, Sudan, Somalia, Ethiopia and Bangladesh.
4. For a full discussion of trends, see Crawford et al. (2003).
5. ILO has initiated a number of studies which explore the nexus between growth, employment and poverty in a programme of work which is ongoing and, in part, being conducted in collaboration with UNDP and supported by SIDA. These studies include a number of LDCs, notably Bangladesh (Muqtada, 2003; Rahman and Islam, 2003; Islam, 2004), Ethiopia (Demeke, Guta and Ferede, 2003; Denu, Tekeste and van der Deijl, 2005), Uganda (Kabann et al., 2003) and Mozambique (Bruck and van der Broeck, 2006). Comparative analysis remains difficult because of differences in definitions and comparability between labour force surveys (see Khan, 2005). But the evidence of the country-level studies confirms the importance of the creation of productive employment as an essential link between economic growth at the macro-level and poverty reduction at the household level (Islam, 2004; Osmani, 2005).
6. Informal sector enterprises are defined in this context as production units without formal administrative registration or formal written accounts.

References

Acharya, S. (2004). Measuring and analyzing poverty (with a particular reference to the case of Nepal). *European Journal of Comparative Economics*, 1 (2): 195–215.

André, C. and Platteau, J.P. (1996/1997). Land tenure under unendurable stress: Rwanda caught in the Malthusian trap. Cahiers de la Faculté des Sciences Economiques et Sociales de Namur, Série Recherche No. 164, Namur, Belgium.

Asian Development Bank (2005). *Labor Markets in Asia: Promoting Full, Productive, and Decent Employment.* Manila.

Atkinson, A. (2005). Current state and recent trends in natural resource endowment in the least developed countries. Background paper prepared for the *Least Developed Countries Report 2006*, UNCTAD, Geneva.

Barrett, C.B., Carter, M.R. and Little, P. D. (2006). Understanding and reducing persistent poverty in Africa: Introduction to a special issue. *Journal of Development Studies*.

Boreak, S. (2000). Land ownership, sales and concentration in Cambodia: A preliminary review of secondary data and primary data from four recent surveys. Cambodia Development Resource Institute, Working Paper 16.

Brilleau, A., Roubaud, F. and Torelli, C. (2005). L'emploi, le chômage et les conditions d'activité. Enquête 1-2-3 phase 1, STATECO 99: 41–86.

Bruck, T. and van der Broeck, K. (2006). Growth, employment and poverty in Mozambique. Issues in Employment and Poverty Discussion Paper No. 21, ILO, Geneva.

Calvès, A.E. and Schoumaker, B. (2004). Deteriorating economic context and changing patterns of youth employment in urban Burkina Faso: 1980–2000. *World Development*, 32(8): 1341–1354.

Charmes, J. (1998). Women working in the informal sector in Africa: New methods and new data. Paper prepared for the United Nations Statistics Division, the Gender and Development Programme of the UNDP and the project "Women in Informal Employment: Globalizing and Organizing" (WIEGO).

Charmes, J. (2000). The contribution of informal sector to GDP in developing countries: Assessment, estimates, methods, orientations for the future. 4th Meeting of the Delhi Group on Informal Sector Statistics, Geneva, 28–30 August 2000.

Charmes, J. (2002). Estimation and survey methods for the informal sector. University of Versailles, Versailles, France.

Chen, M.A. (2005). Rethinking the informal economy: Linkages with the formal economy and the formal regulatory environment. Study presented at the EGDI-WIDER Conference on Unlocking Human Potential — Linking the Informal and Formal Sectors, Helsinki, 17–18 September 2004. Research Paper No. 2005/10. EGDI and UNU-WIDER.

Crawford, E. et al (2003). Input use and market development in sub-Saharan Africa: An overview. *Food Policy,* 28: 277–292.

Delhi Group on Informal Sector Statistics (2004). Sub-Committee on Statistics, First Session, Bangkok, 18–20 February 2004.

Demeke, M. Guta, F. and Ferede, T. (2003). Growth, employment, poverty and policies in Ethiopia. Issues in Employment and Poverty Discussion Paper No. 21, ILO, Geneva.

Denu, B., Tekeste, A. and van der Deijl, H. (2005). Characteristics and determinants of youth unemployment, underemployment and inadequate employment in Ethiopia. Employment Strategy Papers, 2005/07, ILO, Geneva.

Ellis, F. (2004). Occupational diversification in developing countries and the implications for agricultural policy. Programme of Advisory and Support Services to DFID (PASS), Project No. WB0207.

Ellis, F. (2005). Small-farms, livelihood diversification and rural-urban transitions: Strategic issues in sub-Saharan Africa. Paper prepared for Research Workshop on the Future of Small Farms organized by the International Food Policy Research Institute (IFPRI) and the Overseas Development Institute (ODI), London, 26–29 June 2005.

FAO (2002). The role of agriculture in the development of LDCs and their integration into the world economy, FAO, Rome.

Flodman Becker, K. (2004). The informal economy. Fact finding study. Department for Infrastructure and Economic Co-operation, SIDA, Sweden.

Gore, C.G. (1994). Social exclusion and Africa south of the Sahara: A review of the literature. International Institute for Labour Studies Discussion Paper 62, ILO, Geneva.

Gurrieri, A. and Sáinz, P. (2003). Employment and structural mobility: Revisiting a Prebischian theme. *CEPAL Review,* 80, August 2003, ECLAC, Santiago.

Government of Haiti (2005). Développement rural en Haïti: Diagnostic et Axes d'Intervention – Rapport de Synthèse. Report prepared by the Ministère de l'Agriculture, des Ressources Naturelles et du Développement Rural and by the World Bank.

Havinga, I. and Vu, V. (2005). Informal sector in the 1993 system of national accounts. Discussion paper prepared for the UNSD/ESCAP Workshop on the 1993 SNA Update, Bangkok, April 2005. ESCAP, Bangkok.

Hossain (2004). Poverty alleviation through agriculture and rural development in Bangladesh. Centre for Policy Dialogue, Paper 39. Dhaka, Bangladesh.

Hussmanns, R. (2004). Measuring the informal economy: From employment in the informal sector to informal employment. Working Paper No. 53, Bureau of Statistics, ILO, Geneva.

ILO (2002). Women and men in the informal economy: A statistical picture. Employment Sector, International Labour Office, Geneva.

ILO (2004). *World Employment Report 2004-05, Employment, Productivity and Poverty Reduction*, International Labour Office, Geneva.

Islam, R. (2004). The nexus between economic growth, employment and poverty reduction: An empirical analysis. Issues in Employment and Poverty Discussion Paper No. 14, ILO, Geneva.

Jayne, T.S. et al. (2003). Smallholder income and land distribution in Africa: Implications for poverty reduction strategies. *Food Policy,* 28, 253–275.

Kabann, I.B. et al. (2003). Economic growth, employment and pro-poor policies in Uganda. Issues in Employment and Poverty Discussion Papers, No. 16, ILO, Geneva.

Khan, A.R. (2005). Growth, employment and poverty: An analysis of the vital nexus based on some recent UNDP and ILO/SIDA studies. Issues in Employment and Poverty Discussion Paper No. 19, ILO, Geneva.

Kingdon, G., Sandefur, J. and Teal, F. (2005a). Labour market flexibility, wages and incomes in sub-Saharan Africa in the 1990s. Centre for the Study of African Economies, Department of Economics, University of Oxford, UK.

Kingdon, G., Sandefur, J. and Teal, F. (2005b). Patterns of labour demand in sub-Saharan Africa: A review paper. Africa region — employment issues — regional stocktaking review. Centre for the Study of African Economies, Department of Economics, University of Oxford, UK.

Muqtada, M. (2003). Promotion of employment and decent work in Bangladesh: Macroeconomic and labour policy considerations. Employment Strategy Department, International Labour Organization, Geneva.

Nural Amin, A.T.M. (2002). The informal sector in Asia from the decent work perspective. Series on the Informal Economy, 4, ILO, Geneva.

Osmani, S.R. (2005). *The Employment Nexus between Growth and Poverty: An Asian Perspective.* SIDA Studies, Stockholm.

Rahman, R.I. and Nabiul Islam, K. (2003). Employment poverty linkages: Bangladesh. Issues in Employment and Poverty Discussion Paper No. 10, ILO, Geneva.

Ranis, G. and Stewart, F. (1999). V-goods and the role of the urban informal sector in development. *Economic Development and Cultural Change,* 47(2): 259–288.

Ros. J. (2000). *Development Theory and the Economics of Growth*. University of Michigan Press, Ann Arbor, MI, USA.

Sachs, I. (2005). Expensive oil: For least developed countries a Quidproquo of a curse and blessing in disguise. Background paper prepared for the *Least Developed Countries Report 2006*, UNCTAD, Geneva.

Schneider, F. (2002). Size and measurement of the informal economy in 110 countries around the world. Paper presented at a Workshop of the Australian National Tax Centre, Canberra, Australia, 17 July 2002.

Sender, J., Cramer, C. and Oya, C. (2005). Unequal prospects: Disparities in the quantity and quality of labour supply in sub-Saharan Africa. African Studies Centre Working Paper 62, Leiden.

Serneels, P. (2004). The nature of unemployment in urban Ethiopia. Centre for the Study of African Economies, Oxford University, UK.

UNCTAD (2002). *The Least Developed Countries Report 2002: Escaping the Poverty Trap*. United Nations publication, sales no. E.02.II.D.13, Geneva and New York.

UNDP (2004). *The Macro-Economics of Poverty Reduction in Nepal,* New York.

UNIFEM (2005). *Progress of the World's Women: Women, Work and Poverty*, New York, UNIFEM.

World Bank (2003). *World Development Report 2003: Sustainable Development in a Dynamic World.* Washington, DC.

Xaba, J., Horn, P. and Motala, S. (2002). Informal sector in sub-Saharan Africa. Series on the Informal Economy, 10, ILO, Geneva.

The Infrastructure Divide

A. Introduction

Poor physical infrastructure is a major constraint on faster economic growth, substantial poverty reduction and the development of productive capacities in the LDCs. Physical infrastructure encompasses a diverse range of structures, equipment and facilities, including the following: power, plants, transmission lines and distribution lines; telephone exchanges, telephone lines and transmitting facilities for mobile phones; roads, railways, bridges, harbours and airports; dams, reservoirs, water pipes, water treatment plants and sewers; and garbage dumps and incinerators for solid waste collection and disposal. The mere existence of these structures and facilities does not bring economic benefits or contribute to human welfare. But the services made possible by the stock of physical infrastructure increase the productivity of other productive resources (land, machinery and equipment, and labour) and are essential for the exercise of entrepreneurial capabilities and the development of production linkages. They contribute to increasing enterprise-level productivity and profitability by reducing input costs, removing supply bottlenecks which lead to capacity underutilization and augmenting the productivity of other factors of production. Infrastructure investment can also play a catalytic role in crowding in investments in directly productive activities because it opens up new investment opportunities for entrepreneurs. Infrastructure services can also contribute to household welfare (for example, through releasing time previously spent in fetching water) and enhance access to schools, health centres and jobs.

New infrastructure investment has some immediate beneficial effects by creating demand for labour and construction materials. But the major positive effects of such investment on enterprise performance often take longer and are not automatic. They depend firstly on the efficient operation of physical facilities and their maintenance. Furthermore, the beneficial effects of infrastructure will not occur automatically if there are other strong constraints on firm-level investment and profitability. The services generated by new infrastructure will not have positive effects on productivity and investment if domestic entrepreneurship is oriented to unproductive activities; if institutions, particularly financial and knowledge systems, constrain investment and innovation; or if the demand stimulus which animates investment in general is weak. Infrastructure services will also not have positive effects if the financing of investment in physical infrastructure facilities or the provision of infrastructure services is done in such a way that it causes macroeconomic instability or limits the availability of financial capital for the private sector, or undermines private sector incentives. Investment in physical infrastructure should thus be seen as part of a wider package of policy measures to develop productive capacities within LDCs. It is a necessary basis for developing modern production within a global economy. But it is not sufficient for that.

This chapter discusses three types of physical infrastructure which are critical for economic growth, structural change, better trade integration and more productive employment within the LDCs — namely, transport, energy and telecommunications. It focuses on the physical facilities rather than the organization of infrastructure services. Although the latter issue is vital for realizing the benefits of infrastructure investment, infrastructure services simply cannot exist without the physical facilities.

Poor physical infrastructure is a major constraint on faster economic growth, substantial poverty reduction and the development of productive capacities in the LDCs.

Investment in physical infrastructure should be seen as a part of a wider package of policy measures to develop productive capacities within LDCs.

The chapter is divided into three major sections. Section B provides an overview of the level and trends in the infrastructure stock in the LDCs. Section C focuses on trends in infrastructure financing, including trends in public investment, ODA and private investment. Section D completes the analysis by examining the mechanisms through which increased public investment and ODA in infrastructure can support the further development of productive capacities in the LDCs. It examines rural infrastructure, large-scale national infrastructure and cross-border infrastructure, and includes discussion of the links between infrastructure investment and international trade. Section E summarizes the main points of the chapter.

B. Physical infrastructure in LDCs: Current status and recent trends

1. THE MAGNITUDE OF THE INFRASTRUCTURE DIVIDE

Available data on transport, energy and telecommunications indicate that most of the LDCs have the worst stock of physical infrastructure in the world.

The world's infrastructure stock has been valued at about $15 trillion. Of this total, about 60 per cent is in high-income countries, 28 per cent in middle-income countries and 13 per cent in low-income countries. (Fay and Yepes, 2003) There are no estimates of the proportion of the world's infrastructure stock in the LDCs. But available data on transport, energy and telecommunications indicate that most of the LDCs have the worst stock of physical infrastructure in the world.

Chart 37 shows the latest available data for some basic indicators of provision of transport, telecommunications and energy infrastructure. It shows that:

- In 1999, the length of roads per square kilometre and per capita were about half the level in other developing countries and the per capita road stock was one fifth of the level in OECD countries.

- In 2003, telephone mainlines and fixed and mobile phones per 1,000 people were 11 per cent of their level in other developing countries and 3 per cent of their level in OECD countries.

- In 2002, electricity consumption per capita in the LDCs was 7 per cent of the level in other developing countries, and 1.6 per cent of the level in OECD countries. Only 16 per cent of the LDC population are estimated to have had access to electricity in that year, compared with 53 per cent in other developing countries and 99 per cent in OECD countries.

The quantity of investment in infrastructure facilities is the lowest in the LDCs, and the quality of infrastructure services is the poorest.

Not only is the quantity of investment in infrastructure facilities lowest in the LDCs, but also the quality of infrastructure services is the poorest. As chart 38 shows:

- In 1999, only 22 per cent of LDC roads were paved compared with 43 per cent in other developing countries and 88 per cent in OECD countries.

- In 2003, there were 65 telephone faults reported for every 100 telephone mainlines, twice the level in other developing countries and 8 times the level in OECD countries.

- In 2003, the cost of Internet access per month was almost 3 times the monthly GNI per capita in the LDCs compared with one third of monthly

CHART 37. SELECTED INDICATORS OF AVAILABILITY OF TRANSPORT, TELECOMMUNICATION AND ENERGY INFRASTRUCTURE IN LDCs, OTHER DEVELOPING COUNTRIES AND OECD COUNTRIES

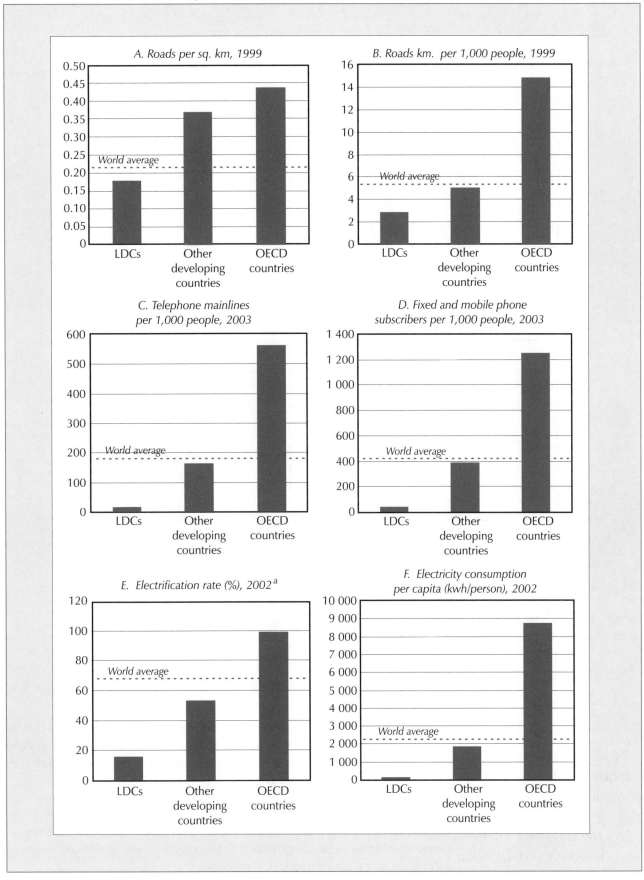

Source: UNCTAD secretariat estimates based on World Bank, *World Development Indicators 2005*, CD-ROM; IEA, *World Energy Outlook 2004*, CD-ROM.
Note: Averages are simple averages.
  a Electrification rate is defined as the percentage of the population with access to electricity.

CHART 38. SELECTED INDICATORS OF THE QUALITY OF TRANSPORT, TELECOMMUNICATION AND ENERGY INFRASTRUCTURE IN LDCS, OTHER DEVELOPING COUNTRIES AND OECD COUNTRIES

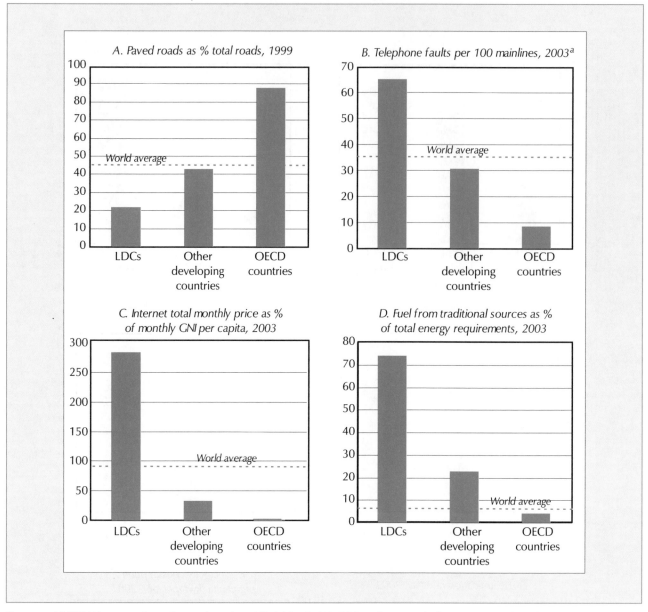

Source   UNCTAD secretariat estimates based on World Bank, *World Development Indicators 2005*, CD-ROM.

Note: Averages are simple averages.

     a   Defined as the number of reported faults per 100 mainlines.

GNI per capita in other developing countries and just one per cent of monthly GNI per capita in OECD countries.

- Within the LDCs, 74 per cent of total energy requirements were met by traditional sources (charcoal and firewood) rather than coal, oil, gas and electricity as compared with 23 per cent in other developing countries and 4 per cent in OECD countries.

74 per cent of total energy requirements were met by traditional sources and 20 per cent of total electricity output in the LDCs was lost in transmission and distribution.

Data available for 14 LDCs also show that on average, in the period 1999–2001, 20 per cent of total electricity output in the LDCs was lost in transmission and distribution, compared with 13 per cent in low- and middle-income countries and 6 per cent in OECD countries.

Chart 39 shows the nature of the infrastructure divide between LDCs and other developing countries. Using various indicators it ranks all developing countries, including the LDCs, from those with the best infrastructure to those

CHART 39. RANKING OF DEVELOPING COUNTRIES[a] ACCORDING TO THEIR INFRASTRUCTURE PROVISIONS

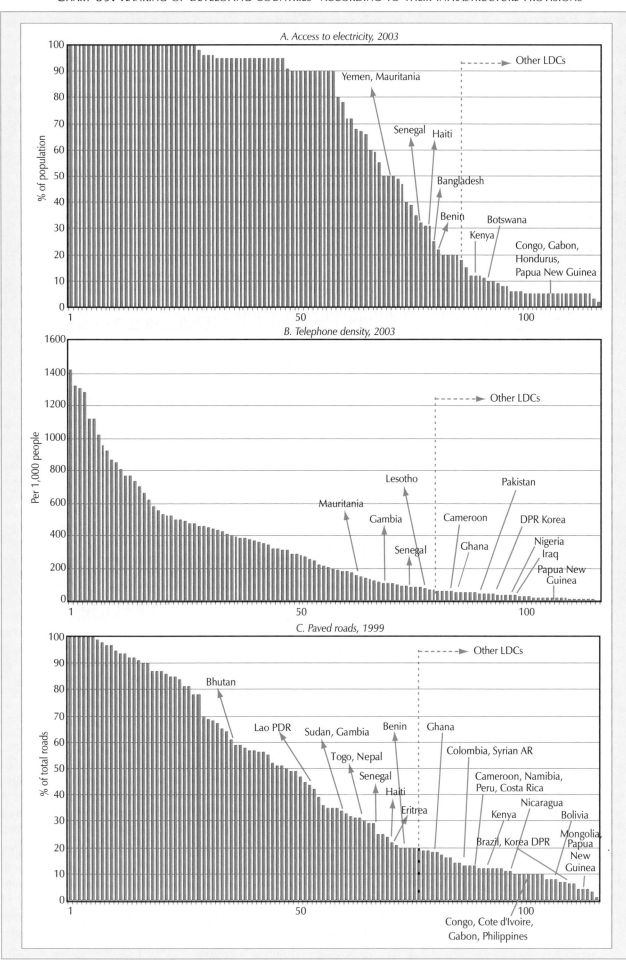

Chart 39 (contd.)

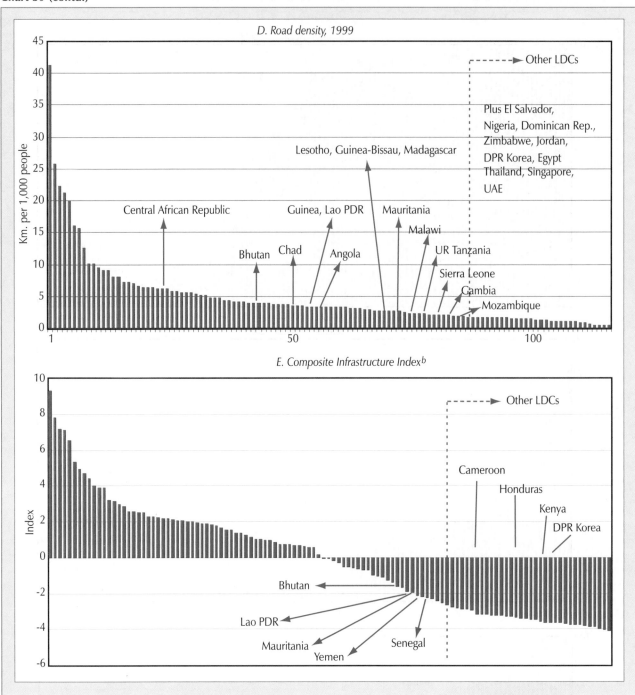

Source: Borgatti (2005a).

  a   Transition economies have been included in the sample.

  b   Based on latest available data.

with the worst infrastructure. Most of the LDCs are at the bottom of the ranking, although it is clear that on some of these indicators (notably length of roads per 1,000 people and the share of the road network which is paved) there are a number of other developing countries which have infrastructure that is as bad as that of most of the LDCs, and that there are a number of other developing countries that have better infrastructure than most of the LDCs. Chart 39E shows the results of a composite infrastructure index constructed on the basis of all indicators.[1] Twenty-seven of the 31 LDCs included in the sample are located between 80th and 115th (the last) place in the ranking, with the exception of Bhutan, the Lao People's Democratic Republic, Mauritania and Yemen. All the LDCs are below the sample average and are located in the bottom 40 per cent of all the developing countries considered (for fuller discussion see Borgatti, 2005a).

The shape of these charts is also striking. For roads per capita, telephone mainlines per capita and paved roads as a percentage of all roads, infrastructure provision declines gently after an initial drop from the best-provided developing countries. But for access to electricity there is a sharp drop from the top half of the sample, in which over 90 per cent of the population have access to electricity, to the bottom quarter of the countries, in which most of the LDCs are clustered. In the latter countries, less than 10 per cent of the population has access to electricity. This "electricity divide" has not received the attention that the digital divide has received (see box 14). But it is at least as significant, and probably more significant, for economic growth, poverty reduction and the development of productive capacities in the LDCs.

The "electricity divide" has not received the attention that the digital divide has received.

BOX 14. LDCs AND THE DIGITAL DIVIDE: THE UNCTAD ICT DIFFUSION INDEX

The UNCTAD ICT Diffusion Index measures the digital divide on the basis of the following three dimensions of ICT development: (i) connectivity, which measures the extent of telecommunications infrastructure development; (ii) access, which measures the opportunity to take advantage of being connected; and (iii) policy, which measures the level of competition in telecommunication and the Internet service provider market. Specific indicators have been used to assess and measure each of the three components. Connectivity is measured by the number of Internet hosts per capita, the number of PCs per capita, the number of telephone main lines per capita and the number of mobile subscribers per capita. Access is measured by the estimated number of Internet users, the adult literacy rate, the cost of a local call and GDP per capita in purchasing power parity terms. Policy is measured by the presence of Internet exchanges, and the levels of competition in telecommunications and Internet service provider markets. The ICT Diffusion Index is obtained by estimating the value achieved in a country as a proportion of a maximum reference value and then calculating an average of the scores for each indicator and for each dimension.

Box chart 5 shows where LDCs, other developing countries and OECD countries stand in the ICT Diffusion Index and also its different dimensions. From the box chart 5, it is clear that the area in which the LDCs lag behind most is connectivity — that is, the level of telecommunications infrastructure development.

BOX CHART 5. ICT DIFFUSION INDEX FOR LDCs, OTHER DEVELOPING COUNTRIES AND OECD COUNTRIES, 2002

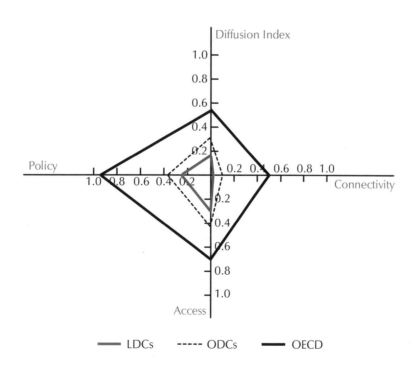

Source: UNCTAD secretariat estimates based on UNCTAD (2005).

Amongst the LDCs, Maldives stands out as having a higher degree of ICT readiness than the other LDCs. Its ICT Diffusion Index (0.3565) is twice as high as that for the LDC average (0.1778). The level of competitiveness in the domestic telecommunications sector is low in most LDCs, with some notable exceptions, namely Guinea-Bissau, Madagascar,

Box 14 (contd.)

Malawi and Sudan. Interestingly, in spite of its relatively high policy index, Guinea-Bissau has the lowest ICT diffusion ranking amongst the 165 countries considered.

Data are available to show how the ICT diffusion ranking of 19 LDCs changed between 1995 and 2002 (box table 6). It is apparent that the majority of the LDCs are losing ground with respect to other developing countries and developed countries. Sixteen of the 19 LDCs show a decline in their ranking, whilst the ranking improves in only three LDCs, namely Sierra Leone, Maldives and the Central African Republic. In terms of ICT diffusion ranking, Lesotho, the United Republic of Tanzania, Madagascar and Malawi lost over 50 positions over the period 1995–2002.

From these data it is apparent that despite a fast-growing mobile phone network in many LDCs, these countries are still falling behind other developing countries in terms of ICT readiness. The digital divide and the electricity divide reinforce each other and result in a lack of technological congruence with the rest of the world, which is a major barrier to the acquisition of modern technologies for mass production.

BOX TABLE 6. CHANGES IN THE ICT DIFFUSION RANKINGS FOR SELECTED LDCs[a]
BETWEEN 1995 AND 2002

	1995 ranking (a)	2002 ranking (b)	Difference (b-a)
Angola	114	143	29
Bangladesh	107	145	38
Burkina Faso	140	159	19
Cambodia	105	119	14
Cape Verde	63	87	24
Central African Republic	156	144	-12
Chad	138	155	17
Djibouti	113	147	34
Lesotho	64	117	53
Madagascar	80	131	51
Malawi	88	138	50
Maldives	86	50	-36
Mali	132	157	25
Rwanda	89	134	45
Sierra Leone	150	103	-47
Sudan	99	129	30
Uganda	144	154	10
United Rep. of Tanzania	76	165	89
Yemen	102	136	34

Source: UNCTAD, 2005b (table 3, p. 8).

a   These rankings are available for 165 countries in 2002, and for 154 countries in 1995. The closer to the bottom rank, the worse the ICT diffusion.

2. DIFFERENCES AMONGST LDCs

African LDCs are below the LDC average for every indicator of infrastructure access and quality of the service.

Although the LDCs are, as group, much worse off than other developing countries, there are also significant differences amongst the LDCs. Island LDCs have better physical infrastructure than either African or Asian LDCs. African LDCs are below the LDC average on almost every indicator of physical infrastructure and its quality. The length of roads per square kilometre is particularly low in the African LDCs (0.12 kilometres per square kilometre in 1999 compared with 0.29 in Asian LDCs and 0.33 in island LDCs).[2] In terms of the electrification rate, only 14 per cent of the population had access to electricity in 2002 in African LDCs compared with 21 per cent in Asian LDCs. Moreover, only 15 per cent of the roads were paved in African LDCs compared with 27 per cent in Asian LDCs and 49 per cent in island LDCs. African LDCs are below the LDC average for every indicator of infrastructure access and quality of the service. They have, however, the same roads per capita and a higher number of fixed and mobile phone subscribers than Asian LDCs (table 46).

TABLE 46. INDICATORS OF THE STATUS OF TRANSPORT, TELECOMMUNICATION AND ENERGY INFRASTRUCTURE
IN AFRICAN, ASIAN AND ISLAND LDCs, MOST RECENT YEARS

	Year[a]	African LDCs[b]	Asian LDCs	Island LDCs
Roads per sq. km	1999	0.1	0.3	0.3
Roads per 1,000 people	1999	2.7	2.7	3.9
Telephone mainlines per 1,000 people	2003	9.0	13.4	61.2
Fixed and mobile phone sub. per 1,000 people	2003	33.0	27.2	111.7
Electrification rate (%)[b]	2002	14.2	21.3	..
Telephone faults per 100 mainlines[b]	2003	61.9	116.5[c]	48.4
Paved roads % total roads	1999	15.5	26.7	48.5
Internet monthly price % monthly GNI per capita	2003	355.0	130.1	131.5
Energy consumption per capita (Kwh/per person)	2002	148.4	105.9	..
Energy from traditional sources(% of total energy requirements)	2002	78.5	68.0	..

Source: UNCTAD secretariat estimates based on World Bank, *World Development Indicators 2005*, CD-ROM; International Energy
         Agency, *World Energy Outlook 2004*; UN *Energy Statistics Yearbook 2004*, CD-ROM.

a   Most recent year for which data are available.
b   For definitions, see charts 37 and 38.
c   This is due to the way the series is calculated. The humber of telephone faults per 100 mainlines is calculated by dividing
    the total number of reported faults for the year by the total number of mainlines in operation, and multiplying by 100.

A more detailed picture of the diversity amongst LDCs was obtained through
statistical analysis which classifies 31 LDCs for which data are available
according to their physical infrastructure using the indicators in chart 39.[3] This
analysis identifies three groups of countries:

- Relatively good infrastructure amongst the LDCs — Benin, Bhutan,
  Gambia, Haiti, Lao People's Democratic Republic, Lesotho, Mauritania,
  Senegal, Sudan, Togo, and Yemen;

- Average infrastructure amongst the LDCs — Bangladesh, Burkina Faso,
  Cambodia, Eritrea, Ethiopia, Malawi, Mali, Mozambique, Nepal, Niger,
  Rwanda, Sierra Leone, Uganda and United Republic of Tanzania;

- Relatively bad infrastructure amongst the LDCs — Angola, Central
  African Republic, Chad, Guinea, Guinea-Bissau, and Madagascar
  (Borgatti, 2005a).

The fastest-growing LDCs had relatively good or average physical infrastructure.

The LDCs in the cluster with the relatively bad infrastructure amongst the
LDCs are large African countries with a low population density. Some of them
have also experienced civil conflicts. Both Angola, which has been an oil-
exporter for a long time, and Chad, which started exporting oil in late 2003, are
in this group. The cluster with relatively good infrastructure includes a number of
LDCs which have the highest urbanization rates within the group (for example,
Mauritania and Senegal, with 62 per cent and 50 per cent of the total
population living in urban centres in 2003). The fastest-growing LDCs had
relatively good or average physical infrastructure, whilst those LDCs with
relatively bad infrastructure are economies which have either weak growth or
are regressing economically.

During the 1990s the infrastructure divide between the LDCs, other developing countries and OECD countries was widening.

3. TRENDS IN INFRASTRUCTURE PROVISION

Lack of data make it difficult to analyse trends in infrastructure provision in
detail.[4] However, during the 1990s the infrastructure divide between the LDCs,
other developing countries and OECD countries was widening (table 47). This is
particularly apparent for road infrastructure. Measured by length of the network,
the stock of roads per capita in the LDCs was actually lower in 1999 (the latest
year for which comprehensive data are available) than in 1990. The percentage
of paved roads in the LDCs also declined over the same period. The road stock

Table 47. Changes in infrastructure in LDCs, other developing countries and OECD countries, between 1990 and 2003

	Year[a]	LDCs	ODCs	OECD
Roads				
Per sq. km.	1990	0.1	0.2	0.4
	1999	0.2	0.4	0.4
Per 1,000 people	1990	3.1	3.1	15.1
	1999	2.9	5.1	14.9
Paved % total roads	1990	23.0	38.5	72.8
	1999	22.0	43.2	88.0
Fixed and mobile phone subscribers (per 1,000 people)	1990	6.2	86.6	478.0
	2003	45.1	390.5	1254.7
Telephone faults (per 100 mainlines)	1992	148.7	78.9	16.0
	2003	65.0	30.7	8.5
Electricity consumption per capita (kwh/person)	1990	104.0	1153.8	7187.6
	2002	136.3	1870.1	8769.3
Fuel from traditional sources (% of total energy requirements)	1990	77.5	25.8	4.8
	2002	74.2	22.9	4.1

Source: UNCTAD secretariat estimates based on World Bank, *World Devleopment Indicators 2005*, CD-ROM; UN *Energy Statistics Yearbook,* 1993 and 2004; IEA, *World Energy Outlook 2004.*

a   Or closest available year.

The poor infrastructure stocks of the LDCs reflect inadequate maintenance of existing infrastructure and under-investment in new infrastructure.

per capita declined in both African and island LDCs, and the percentage of roads which are paved declined in African LDCs. In contrast, for the LDCs as a group, the number of fixed and mobile phone subscribers per 1,000 people increased eightfold between 1990 and 2002. But LDCs are still falling behind other developing countries and OECD countries as there were more new subscribers in these country groups. The gap has also increased for electricity consumption per capita. But the difference in the share of total energy requirements supplied by traditional fuel between LDCs and other developing countries has interestingly stayed constant over time. This suggests very little change in the diversification process towards non-traditional sources of energy in both the LDCs and other developing countries.

Focusing on differences amongst the LDCs (chart 40), the data show that in terms of the length of the network the situation as regards road stock and paved road stock per capita worsened in many LDCs during the period 1990–1999. In contrast, the data on telecommunications infrastructure show a dramatic improvement between 1990 and 2002 in all LDCs.

C. Financing infrastructure investment

While the private sector has financed some economic infrastructure in the LDCs, it has not filled the gap created by declining public investment and ODA.

The poor infrastructure stocks of the LDCs reflect inadequate maintenance of existing infrastructure and under-investment in new infrastructure. These two features are a particular manifestation of the general problem outlined in chapter 2, with few domestic resources being available to finance investment of any kind. The share of resources allocated to economic infrastructure also declined (i) as Governments reduced such expenditure to balance budgets in the context of first-generation economic reforms, and (ii) as donors switched their aid to social sectors, thus allowing the volume of aid for economic infrastructure to decline sharply in real terms. As the Commission for Africa (2005) has observed for sub-Saharan Africa in general, "This was a policy mistake founded in a new dogma of the 1980s and 1990s asserting that infrastructure would now be financed by the private sector" (p. 234). In practice, although the private sector has financed some economic infrastructure in the LDCs, it has not filled the gap created by declining public investment and ODA.

CHART 40. CHANGES IN TRANSPORT AND TELECOMMUNICATIONS INFRASTRUCTURE PROVISIONS IN LDCs
BETWEEN 1990 AND 2002[a]

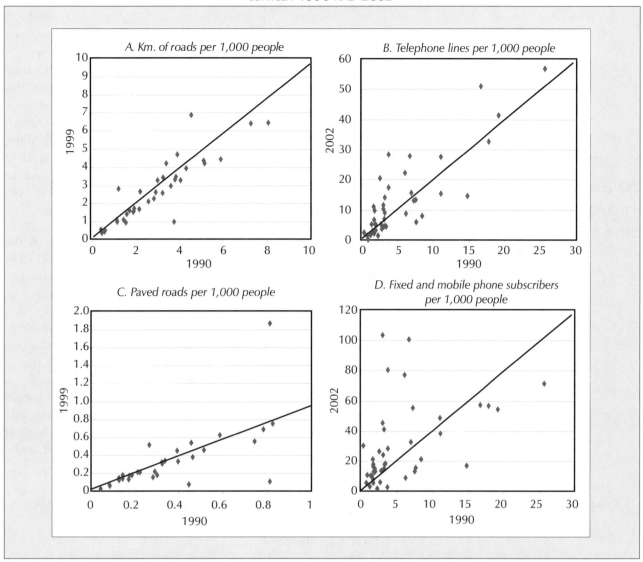

Source: UNCTAD secretariat estimates based on World Bank, *World Development Indicators 2005*, CD-ROM.

Note: Cape Verde has been excluded from the charts on paved roads, telephone mainlines and fixed and mobile phone subscribers, while Maldives has been excluded from the last two only.

  a Data on roads and paved roads refer to the year 1999, while the remaining data refer to the year 2002.

According to Torero and Chowdhury (2005), over the period from 1980 to 1998, infrastructure spending decreased from 6 to 4 per cent of total government expenditure in Africa, from 12 to 5 per cent in Asia and from 11 to 6 per cent in Latin America. Although there are no equivalent figures available for LDCs, data available for 13 LDCs[5] during the second half of the 1990s show that 5 of them spent less than 1 per cent of GDP on economic infrastructure and 7 of them spent less than 2 per cent. In 5 of the 13 LDCs, public expenditure on energy, transport and communications is one third of the level of social sector expenditure on education, housing, health and social protection.[6]

This orientation towards social sector expenditure is also evident in ODA trends. For the LDCs, this is the primary source of financing for infrastructure. But during the 1990s, there was a strong shift in resource allocation away from economic infrastructure towards social infrastructure and services. Between 1992 and 2003, aid for social infrastructure and services to LDCs increased by 14.6 per cent per annum in nominal terms, while aid for economic infrastructure increased by a mere 3 per cent over the whole period. In real

During the 1990s, there was a strong shift in resource allocation away from economic infrastructure towards social infrastructure and services.

terms, aid flows commitments to LDCs for economic infrastructure in 2003 were 51 per cent lower than in 1992.

The fall in ODA allocated to economic infrastructure was particularly marked in African LDCs, which in 2003 experienced a fall in real terms equivalent to 68 per cent of the ODA received in 1992. Chart 41 shows that Asian LDCs have experienced a less substantial fall in their ODA for economic infrastructure. This resulted in the Asian LDCs receiving in 2003 an inflow of ODA for economic infrastructure which was one third higher than the amount received by African LDCs. This last group of LDCs appears to be the greatest loser as a result of this shift: ODA flows for economic infrastructure going to African LDCs in 1992 were double those going to Asian LDCs. On the other hand, aid flows for social infrastructure have more than doubled over the same reference period in both African and Asian LDCs, and have increased fivefold in the island LDCs.

In theory, it might be expected that the private sector would fill the infrastructure financing gap which was created as public investment and ODA for economic infrastructure declined. But although private finance can contribute to infrastructure investment and offers a potential new source of investment finance, physical infrastructure often has the characteristics of a public good. Consumption by one user does not reduce the supply available to others, and users cannot be prevented from consuming the good. There are also sometimes indivisibilities in the scale of infrastructure facilities, and thus a minimum initial investment, which can be quite large, is required in order to establish such facilities. In addition, the benefits of infrastructure investment often depend on the existence of a broad network, and creating all the links which make this network effective will involve a minimum threshold level of investment. For all these reasons physical infrastructure is likely to be under supplied if left to private investors alone.

The decline in ODA allocated to economic infrastructure was particularly marked in African LDCs.

CHART 41. CHANGE IN BILATERAL DAC AID COMMITMENTS TO ECONOMIC AND SOCIAL INFRASTRUCTURE IN LDCS BETWEEN 1992 AND 2003

(Percentage increase)

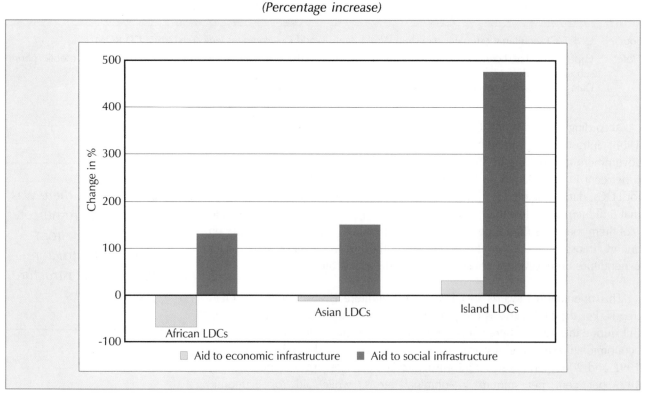

Source: UNCTAD secretariat estimates based on OECD/CDE database online, March 2006.

Private investment in infrastructure in the LDCs has certainly increased (see chart 42). But there are limits to the types of assets and countries to which it is attracted. In general, infrastructure investments which are attractive to private capital are ones in which there is a growing market and scope for monopolistic power. Where it is difficult to restrict access to the services generated by infrastructure facilities, they are unattractive to private financing. There has thus been a sustained increase in private sector investment in telecommunications, particularly in building the light and cost-effective infrastructure required for mobile phones, and also electricity-generating plants. Within the transport sector, private capital inflows have been much smaller and focused on infrastructure projects for which (a) access can be limited (as in airports, tunnels, bridges and major highways); (b) the projected volume of traffic is high (container ports, rail freight and a few trunk roads); (c) the generation of cash is expected to be reliable; and (e) foreign exchange earnings are possible.

Telecommunications and energy constituted 90 per cent of private investment infrastructure in 10 out of the 14 years and of that over 70 per cent was absorbed by African LDCs.

During the period 1990–2003, telecommunications and energy constituted 90 per cent of private investment infrastructure in 10 out of the 14 years for which data are available (chart 42). Private investment in transport infrastructure has been not only much lower but also much more highly concentrated geographically. During the period from 1993 to 2003, Mozambique absorbed 59 per cent of private capital flows to transport in the LDCs. From 1999 to 2003 over 70 per cent of the private investments in energy and telecommunications were absorbed by African LDCs. This marks a clear change from the previous period, 1992–1998, when the majority of private flows were invested in Asian LDCs.

CHART 42. PRIVATE INVESTMENT IN INFRASTRUCTURE PROJECTS IN THE LDCs, 1990–2003
($ millions)

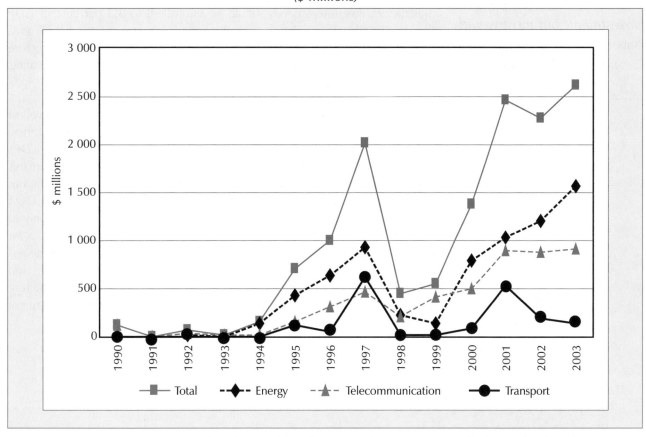

Source: UNCTAD secretariat estimates based on World Bank, Private Infrastructure Project database online, March 2006.

Note: Based on a varying sample of LDCs, which include a maximum of 31 LDCs.

Foreign investment interest in infrastructure is limited by high levels of indebtedness and instability of foreign exchange earnings.

Some of the financing needs could be met from private investment, but most would have to be financed by public investment and ODA.

Foreign investment interest in infrastructure in LDCs is also limited by various structural weaknesses, notably high levels of indebtedness and instability of foreign exchange earnings associated with commodity dependence, both of which have a negative influence on credit ratings and increase uncertainty regarding future profit remittances whatever the legal framework. Small countries also face a catch-22 situation. On the one hand, large projects are considered risky because they can dominate economic performance and profit remittances can become too large in relation to available foreign exchange. On the other hand, small projects (those costing less than several hundred million dollars) are not big enough to justify the high development costs of project finance.

There is now a consensus on the need to increase ODA for physical infrastructure, and a realization that private finance can at best play a complementary role in infrastructure investment. This is evident in the World Bank's Infrastructure Action Plan, launched in July 2003 to revitalize the World Bank Group's support for meeting unmet infrastructure investment needs, as well as in the Commission for Africa Report (2005), the Asian Development Bank et al. (2005) and Faye et al. (2004). Estimates of future financing needs for infrastructure investment vary.[7] But if one assumes that estimates for low-income countries can be applied to the LDCs, annual infrastructure investment needs have been roughly estimated to be equivalent to between 7.5 per cent and 9 per cent of GDP (Briceño-Garmendia, Estache and Shafik, 2004). This includes new investment and operations and maintenance requirements, including the main networks (roads, rail, electricity, water and sanitation, telecommunications). A preliminary estimate of the investment needed to meet the Programme of Action transport and telecommunications infrastructure target (which is to increase, by 2010, the stock of such infrastructure in LDCs to the level which other developing countries had in 2000) suggests that annual infrastructure investment needs should be equivalent to 3.3 per cent of GDP (Borgatti, 2005b). This is lower than the other estimates as it is based on a different methodology (calculating unit costs to upgrade the LDCs' infrastructure to the level of the other developing countries in 2000) and ignores elements such as energy, water and sanitation included in other estimates.

The infrastructure investment required is a major increase over past levels of investment. For low-income countries, it implies an increase from historical levels of 4 per cent of GDP. The financing gap is likely to be larger in the LDCs on the basis of historical levels of public investment presented earlier in this chapter. Some of the financing needs could be met from private investment, but most would have to be financed by public investment and ODA. In 2004 ODA for transport, telecommunications and energy infrastructure amounted only to $1 billion. This was equivalent to 0.5 per cent of the LDCs' GDP. This is far below the estimated infrastructure investment needs, even for achieving the less comprehensive POA targets required with regard to transport and telecommunications. Private investment in these types of infrastructure contributed a further $0.4 billion. But together ODA and private investment were equivalent to only 0.7 per cent of the LDCs' GDP in 2004.

D. The benefits of public investment and ODA in physical infrastructure in the LDCs

This section examines the benefits which can accrue from increased public investment and ODA in economic infrastructure in the LDCs. It focuses on three levels of infrastructure investment:

- Rural infrastructure, particularly rural roads, which is required at the local and district level;

- Large-scale national transport, communications and power infrastructure (such as trunk roads and major electricity transmission lines), which benefit different regions of a country and not simply specific localities or regions;

- Large-scale cross-border infrastructure.

These different levels of investment — rural, national and cross-border — are distinguished here as they bring different types of benefits. Rural infrastructure is particularly important for enhancing agrarian commercialization and productivity growth, as well as for fostering rural growth linkages between agricultural and non-agricultural activities in small towns. Large-scale national infrastructure is important for the growth of the formal, non-farm economy and fostering structural change and progressive international trade integration. Large-scale cross-border infrastructure supports regional integration, as well as the transit trade of landlocked countries.

In a comprehensive approach to the development of economic infrastructure, all these levels would be included. That is to say, a "joined-up approach" to infrastructure development is necessary. National and cross-border infrastructure which supports international trade is essential. But on its own, it will exacerbate structural heterogeneity, dualism and an enclave pattern of development within a country. Similarly, feeder roads in isolated rural localities are essential for facilitating the market access of small farmers. But unless these feeder roads link to an efficient national transport network connecting major urban centres, their impact will be limited.

National and cross-border infrastructure which supports international trade is essential. But on its own, it will exacerbate structural heterogeneity, dualism and an enclave pattern of development within a country.

1. RURAL INFRASTRUCTURE

The low productivity and partial subsistence orientation of agriculture in most LDCs are closely related to lack of local market access, which is related to poor rural transport infrastructure. Smallholder producers are usually enmeshed to some degree within product and labour markets, selling and buying foodstuffs throughout the year on a seasonal basis, producing cash crops for exports, hiring labour, working for other farmers on a casual basis and seeking off-farm employment. However, their degree of engagement with the market economy is often limited because production for the market has high transaction costs and risks. In terms of production costs, it may be rational for the farmer to specialize in high-value export or food crops. But the high transport costs of getting agricultural produce to market, coupled with uncertainty about the prices which will prevail at the moment of sale, and the costs and risks of buying foodstuffs with the earnings from the sale all lead farm households to stick to low-yielding staples to meet their basic subsistence needs (see Omamo, 1998a, 1998b).

The low productivity and subsistence orientation of agriculture are closely related to poor rural transport infrastructure.

These costs and risks are related mainly to poor local-level transport systems. The problem is particularly marked in African LDCs (Hayami and Platteau, 1996). Rural road densities are very low; and much of the rural road network is

With very poor roads, the availability of transport capacity is also a problem.

of low quality, with some rural roads becoming temporarily impassable in the rainy season. Estimates for 11 African LDCs indicate that, in 6 of these countries, over two thirds of the total rural population live 2 kilometres away from an all-season passable road, and in 10 out of the 11 countries more than one third of the rural population face this level of inaccessibility as regards good road facilities (see chart 43). With very poor roads, the availability of transport capacity is also a problem, and there is a notable underdevelopment of intermediate forms of transport such as carts, donkeys and bicycles, which can considerably relax rural transport constraints.

In poor rural areas, lack of incentives to specialize and invest reinforces a stagnant rural economy in which poor infrastructure, weak market access and thin markets for agricultural inputs and output and finance, high costs of information, weak technological development and weak market institutions all reinforce each other in a low-level equilibrium trap (Kydd and Dorward, 2003). These areas are featured by "a business environment characterized by weak information (on prices, on new technologies and on other potential market players), difficult and weak contract enforcement, high risks (not only in production and prices but also in access to inputs and markets and in enforcing contracts) and…costs that buyers and sellers incur in protecting themselves against risks of transactions failing (due to absence of suppliers or buyers)" (Kydd and Dorward, 2003: 8).

CHART 43. ACCESSIBILITY OF ROAD NETWORKS[a] FOR RURAL POPULATION IN SELECTED LDCS AND OTHER COUNTRY GROUPS
(Percentage of population)

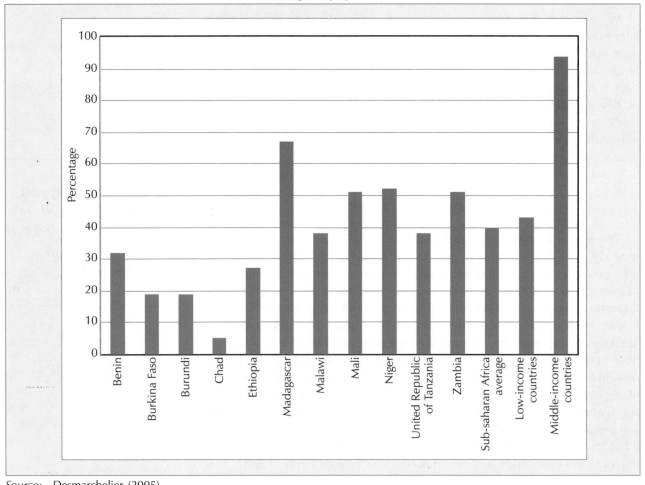

Source: Desmarchelier (2005).

a   Percentage of rural people who live within 2 km of an all-season passable road as a proportion of the total rural population. Latest available year.

High transport costs also mean that many agricultural products are effectively non-tradable not simply internationally but also nationally. The scale of local production is then limited by the local market demand, which is low because of the weak development of the local market economy. When surplus crops are produced (because of favourable weather conditions) they may simply rot in the fields.

This is a daunting complex of interrelated constraints. However, public investment targeted to improve rural infrastructure is essential for escaping this trap. Investment should not only improve rural feeder roads, but also seek to focus key economic and social infrastructure on small market centres and market towns, and foster linkages between these small urban centres and the rural areas. The lower transport costs and risks resulting from improved infrastructure can open up new frontiers in areas with higher agricultural potential in which production was previously economically unviable because of physical isolation, as well as convert some non-tradables into tradables in already-settled areas. This vent-for-surplus can also be enhanced to the extent that improved infrastructure increases market competition by encouraging more buyers and sellers. The linkages between rural areas and small towns can also open up opportunities for local and district-level off-farm employment, which can increase the incomes of rural households. Finally, the process of rural road construction itself can also bring positive demand-side effects if maximum use is made of local materials, labour and methods of construction (Tajgman and de Veen, 1998; Bentall, Beusch and de Veen, 1999).

High transport costs mean that many agricultural products are effectively non-tradable not simply internationally but also nationally. The scale of local production is limited by the local market demand.

Public investment in rural infrastructure is a particularly important component of policies to promote agricultural intensification through the adoption of high-yielding varieties. Analysis of successful Green Revolutions shows that different policies are important at different stages of agricultural intensification (chart 44). In the first phase, it is important to "establish the

CHART 44. POLICY PHASES TO SUPPORT AGRICULTURAL TRANSFORMATION IN FAVOURED AREAS

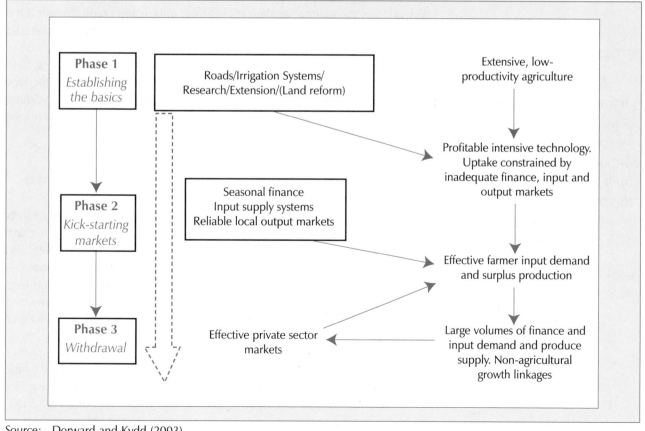

Source: Dorward and Kydd (2003).

basics" for the adoption of new technologies through investment in rural infrastructure, including roads and irrigation systems, and research and extension. In the second phase, it is important to "kick-start markets" through government interventions to enable a broad spectrum of farmers, not simply the large ones, to have access to seasonal finance and inputs, and output markets at low cost and risk. As the volumes of credit and input demand and of produce supply increase, transaction costs and risks will fall and so in the third phase, it is important that the Government withdraws from public action in these markets and lets the private sector take over (Dorward et al., 2004).

Improved rural infrastructure is at the heart of building a market economy in rural areas where the population is still partially subsistence-oriented.

Evidence which quantifies the marginal returns to different kinds of public spending during different decades of the Green Revolution in India supports this pattern (Fan, Hazell and Thorat, 1999; Dorward et al., 2004, 32–36). In the 1960s, the highest returns in terms of increased agricultural output from public spending were derived from road and education investments. In the 1970s, the returns to most of these investments and subsides declined, but road investments, education, fertilizer subsidies and agricultural R&D all provided relatively good returns. In the 1980s, fertilizer subsidies provided much lower returns than earlier. But roads, education, credit subsidies and agricultural R&D still yielded relatively good returns. Finally, in the 1990s, the returns from all forms of public spending were lower and only roads and agricultural R&D still yielded relatively good returns. Significantly, the policies which yield the highest returns in terms of agricultural production growth are also estimated to provide the highest returns in terms of numbers of people lifted out of poverty. There is little comparative evidence for the LDCs. However, studies on the returns to public spending in Uganda and the United Republic of Tanzania indicate that investment in agricultural R&D, roads and education provide the highest returns in terms of agricultural output and productivity gains (see box 15).

From this discussion, it is clear that one should not look upon rural infrastructure investment as a quick fix which will solve all problems. It needs to be complemented with other policies which provide agricultural R&D and which address institutional weaknesses in input, output and credit markets if it is to be successful. However, improved rural infrastructure, including local feeder roads as well as links to small market centres and small towns, is at the heart of building a market economy in rural areas where the population is still partially subsistence-oriented. Moreover it is an essential first stage in promoting the type of agricultural intensification which characterizes Green Revolutions. Without the rural infrastructure basics in place, the supply response to agricultural pricing reforms has inevitably been less than expected.

Large-scale national infrastructure provides the foundations on which economic growth for the formal, non-farm economy is built as it not only increases the productivity of firms but generates significant structural changes.

2. The linkage effects of large-scale national infrastructure

Whilst small-scale rural infrastructure is vital for agricultural productivity growth and commercialization, large-scale national infrastructure — national trunk roads connecting major urban centres, national power plants and transmission lines, and the infrastructure for fixed-line or mobile telephones — "provides the foundations on which economic growth for the formal, non-farm economy is built" (GRIPS, 2003: 84). It increases the productivity of firms and also can generate significant structural changes in national and regional economies.

There is greater potential for attracting private investment within some elements of large-scale infrastructure, particularly as noted above for telecommunications and electricity-generating power plants. However, public investment is still necessary because large-scale infrastructure can have

BOX 15. RETURNS TO PUBLIC INVESTMENT IN UGANDA AND THE UNITED REPUBLIC OF TANZANIA

Fan et al. (2004; 2005) have conducted studies on Uganda and the United Republic of Tanzania, which examine benefit-cost ratios for different types of public investments in different regions of each country. Both studies show that investment in agricultural research and development has the highest benefit-cost ratio and that investments in roads were associated with the second highest benefit-cost ratio, followed by education (see box table 7).

In addition, the studies indicate that investment in agricultural research and development has the strongest poverty-reduction effects. But evidence was mixed on poverty-reduction effects regarding roads and education. In the United Republic of Tanzania, where the studies focused on roads in general, the poverty-reduction effect of education was considerably higher than the poverty-reduction effect of roads. In Uganda, however, where the study focused on different types of roads, the poverty-reduction effect of feeder roads was more than twice as high as the poverty-reduction effects of education. But while the study on Uganda showed a relatively high poverty-reduction effect for feeder roads (i.e. relatively low-grade roads), it showed a relatively small poverty-reduction effect for murram and tarmac roads (i.e. relatively high-grade roads). Along the same lines, other studies on infrastructure development have highlighted the fact that the poverty-reduction effect of basic rural infrastructure projects tends to be higher than the poverty-reduction effect of more sophisticated rural infrastructure projects (Asian Development Bank et al., 2005). This has to do with the relatively high labour intensity of basic infrastructure projects, which leads to more off-farm employment opportunities and higher household incomes, especially for the duration of the projects.

BOX TABLE 7. BENEFIT-COST RATIO AND POVERTY-REDUCTION EFFECTS OF ALTERNATIVE PUBLIC INVESTMENTS IN UGANDA AND THE UNITED REPUBLIC OF TANZANIA

	Fiscal year/ year of evaluation	Agriculture research	Roads/ feeder roads	Education	Health
Benefit-cost ratio					
Uganda	1999	12.4	7.2	2.7	0.9
United Rep. of Tanzania	2000/2001	12.5	9.1	9.0	..
Number of poor people lifted above poverty line per million shillings					
Uganda	1999	58.4	33.8	12.8	4.6
United Rep. of Tanzania	2000/2001	40.4	26.5	43.1	..

Source: Fan, Zhang and Rao (2004); Fan, Nyange and Rao (2005).

Note: Unlike the study on Tanzania, the study on Uganda assessed the impact of different types of roads. The road-related data in the table refers to feeder roads.

Unlike the study on the United Republic of Tanzania also examined investment in electricity, but data were too limited to permit precise conclusions. That study did not investigate the effects of investment in health.

significant positive externalities which mean that the social returns from infrastructure investment are much higher than the private returns.

The linkage effects of large-scale infrastructure occur through both supply-side and demand-side effects (chart 45). On the supply side, large-scale infrastructure lowers costs of inputs, makes existing businesses more profitable, opens up new opportunities and enables economic actors to respond to new types of demand in different places. This can generate investment, both foreign and domestic, which leads to higher industrial growth and output and the creation of factory employment, which in turn, through the procurement of local inputs, and expansion of supporting industries and of related services, lead to greater economic growth, employment creation and higher incomes. The improved infrastructure services can also activate regional economies, improving the productivity of existing agriculture, opening up greater opportunities for non-farm business and promoting more diversified agriculture.

The linkage effects of large-scale infrastructure occur through both supply-side and demand-side effects.

The increase in the reliability of electricity is likely to be particularly important for the development of the non-agricultural economy, affecting both investment and innovation levels. An analysis of Ugandan firms, for example,

CHART 45. LINKAGES BETWEEN LARGE-SCALE INFRASTRUCTURE, GROWTH AND POVERTY REDUCTION

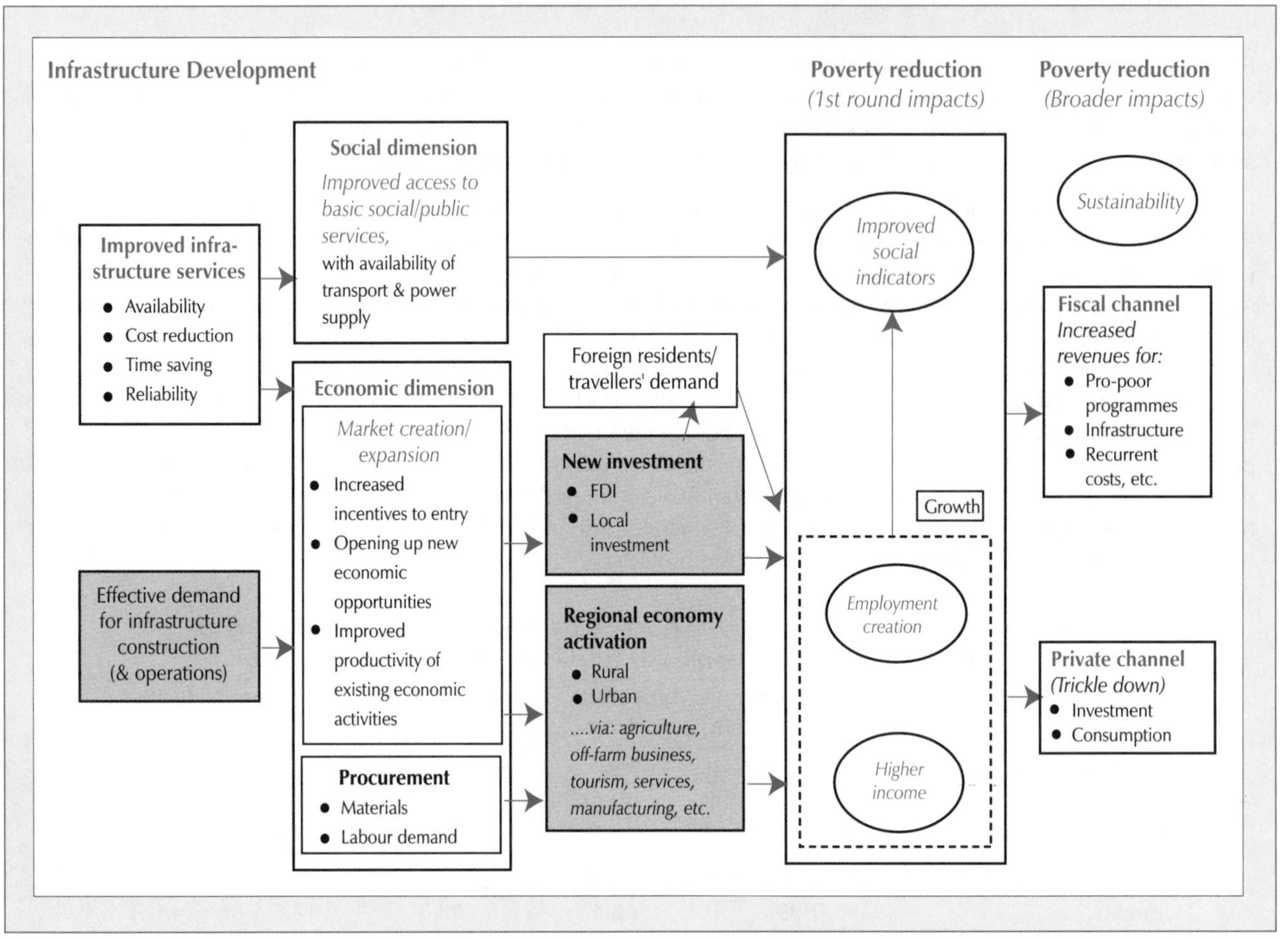

Infrastructure Development

Poverty reduction
(1st round impacts)

Poverty reduction
(Broader impacts)

Social dimension
Improved access to basic social/public services,
with availability of transport & power supply

Improved infra-structure services
- Availability
- Cost reduction
- Time saving
- Reliability

Economic dimension

Market creation/ expansion
- Increased incentives to entry
- Opening up new economic opportunities
- Improved productivity of existing economic activities

Effective demand for infrastructure construction (& operations)

Procurement
- Materials
- Labour demand

Foreign residents/ travellers' demand

New investment
- FDI
- Local investment

Regional economy activation
- Rural
- Urban
....via: agriculture, off-farm business, tourism, services, manufacturing, etc.

Improved social indicators

Growth

Employment creation

Higher income

Sustainability

Fiscal channel
Increased revenues for:
- Pro-poor programmes
- Infrastructure
- Recurrent costs, etc.

Private channel
(Trickle down)
- Investment
- Consumption

Source: GRIPS (2003).

The low level of access to electricity within LDCs is likely to be a major reason for the lack of technological congruence which hinders the acquisition and use of modern technologies.

shows that for firms without their own electricity generator, there is a clear relationship between their investment rate and the number of days lost to production due to power cuts. The greater the number of days lost due to power outages, the lower the investment rate. But even firms which have invested in their own generator lose out as it is estimated that they invest, on average, 25 per cent of their total investment funds in generators (Reinikka and Svensson, 2002). The low level of access to electricity within LDCs is also likely to be a major reason for the lack of technological congruence which hinders the acquisition and use of modern technologies (see part II, chapter 3).

On the demand side, effective demand from public works during construction can generate jobs and income during the construction period both directly and indirectly through the procurement of local materials, inputs and services. The growth of the local construction sector is one important outcome.

These supply-side and demand-side effects can also have broader impacts. The increased level of economic activity increases fiscal revenues. Moreover, private spending from increased incomes and employment generates further multiplier effects, whose magnitude depends on the extent to which new income is spent on domestically produced goods and services. Both these channels can reinforce the poverty-reducing impact of investment in large-scale infrastructure, which can also be attributed to the higher incomes and employment as well as better physical access to social facilities.

The case of Viet Nam illustrates many of these linkages and also how quickly it is possible, with commitment, to reverse poor infrastructure (GRIPS, 2003). Expansion of the electricity network has enabled the country to sustain high economic growth rates at an annual average of 7.5 per cent and to meet the rising demand for electricity of the order of 10–19 per cent per annum. The proportion of people using electricity as a source of lighting in the North rose from 47 per cent in 1993 to 80 per cent in 2002, whilst in the South the proportion rose from 22 per cent to 82 per cent over the same period. Similarly a major project to rehabilitate National Highway No. 1, the only road that links the Mekong Delta at the southern end of Viet Nam with the rest of the country has resulted in travel times between the capital, Ho Chi Minh City, and the Mekong Delta being cut by one third. This has enabled the economic activation of the Mekong Delta economy.

3. THE INTERNATIONAL TRADE EFFECTS OF INFRASTRUCTURE INVESTMENT

One further important impact of public investment in large-scale national and rural infrastructure is that it reduces the costs of international trade. Parts of the large-scale national infrastructure, such as seaport and airport facilities, can be identified as being specifically related to international trade. However, economic activity which uses infrastructure can be oriented to different markets — local, national, regional and international – and thus it is difficult to isolate that part of the infrastructure which is specifically related to international trade. What constitutes investment in "international trade-related infrastructure" should thus not be too narrowly defined. For example, rural feeder roads may be important in enabling a vent-for-surplus in certain cash crops.

Trade performance and competitiveness are affected by both international transport costs and internal transport costs.

Trade performance and competitiveness are affected by both international transport costs (the costs of moving goods between countries) and internal transport costs (the costs of moving goods within a country). High transport costs for moving goods from the production point to their destination can price producers out of export markets. This is particularly relevant in natural-resource-based and labour-intensive activities, where transport costs represent a large share of the final price of the products. Lengthy transport times also have negative effects. Hummels (2001) estimated that each extra day of shipping time reduces the probability of trade by 1 per cent for all goods, and by 1.5 per cent for manufactures. High transport costs for imports inflate the prices of imported goods, including food, capital goods, intermediate inputs and fuel, and this increases the cost of production. This has particularly negative consequences for the competitiveness of manufactured exports which use imported inputs (Livingstone, 1987). Radelet and Sachs (1998) argue that the inflated costs of capital goods also dampen the incentive to invest and reduce the financial surplus available for investment. Payments to foreign carriers for transport services can also have significant balance-of-payments effects. Landlocked African countries have to face freight costs that absorb 30 per cent of export earnings, compared with 11 per cent if Africa is considered as a whole (Amjadi and Yeats, 1995).

Landlocked African countries face freight costs that absorb up to 30 per cent of export earnings, compared with 11 per cent in Africa.

The available evidence suggests that LDCs, and particularly landlocked African LDCs, face high transport costs (UNCTAD, 1999). A recent estimate of the transport and insurance costs faced by the LDCs exporting to the United States shows that they amounted to some 6 per cent of total imports (valued f.o.b at US ports) and that these costs were higher than import tariffs for all product groups except beverages (Borgatti, 2005b). But the extent to which this is attributable to poor infrastructure is difficult to identify. The low volume of exports limits their ability to achieve economies of scale in transport. For landlocked LDCs, high transport costs are related to geographical disadvantages and the difficulties of establishing cross-border transit systems, including both physical infrastructure and related services.

The low volume of exports limits their ability to achieve economies of scale in transport.

One of the few attempts to estimate how transport infrastructure affects trade volume was made by Limão and Venables (2001). They found that improving infrastructure from the 50th percentile to the top 25th percentile of the sample of countries increases the volume of trade by 68 per cent and that it would be equivalent to bringing a country 2,005 kilometres closer to other countries (p. 13).

Much of the research relating infrastructure to trade has focused on the effects of high transport costs on the volume on trade. But the availability of power, and particularly electricity, is important for the composition of trade. Box 16 extends analyses which have been made of how the share of manufactures within merchandise exports is related to the land abundance and skill abundance (measured by level of schooling of the population) of countries. Within these analyses, countries with a high ratio of land to skills tend to be more specialized in primary commodity exports, whilst countries with high skills to land ratios tend to be more specialized in manufactures. However, electricity availability also seems to be important. The inclusion of electricity as a factor of production shows that an increase in electricity production is closely correlated

---

Box 16. Energy infrastructure and the composition of merchandise exports

Wood and Berge (1997) tested the hypothesis that countries with high skill/land ratios tend to export manufactures, while those with a low skill/land ratio tend to specialize in the production of primary products. They conclude that African and Latin American countries will not be able to follow or replicate East Asia's export performance because they have a ratio of skill to land that is too low to give them a comparative advantage in manufactures. Owens and Wood (1997) included processed primary products in the analysis and found that the chances of developing countries replicating the East Asian export miracle have been improved for some of those countries only, and that the least developed countries are likely to be excluded. Their models account for only three factors of production, namely skills, land and labour force.

The "augmented" Wood and Berge (1997) model adds electricity production, a proxy for energy infrastructure, to the above three factors of production, in the original model. Three dummy variables have also been used in the model to test the impact that electricity production would have on three separate groups of countries: the LDCs, the ODCs and the developed countries. The estimated equation is:

$$\left(X_m / X_p\right)_i = \alpha + \gamma h_i - \delta n_i + \beta e_i + \sigma e_i \times D_c + \varepsilon$$

where X_m is export of manufactures

X_p is export of primary products

h represents the years of schooling per worker

n represents land per worker

e represents electricity production per worker

i identifies the countries

D_c identifies the dummy variables for the LDCs, the other developing countries and developed countries.

The export data are taken from the UN COMTRADE database, electricity production is taken from UN Energy Statistics, and land, labour force and number of pupils in secondary school (used as a proxy for skill) are taken from the World Bank's *World Development Indicators 2005*. X_m is calculated by taking the exports of manufactures, chapters 5 to 8 less chapter 68 of the SITC revision 2, while X_p is calculated by taking the exports of agricultural goods, SITC, chapters 0 to 4 plus chapter 68. Export figures include estimates calculated by UNCTAD. All variables are in logs.

Owing to the high positive correlation between electricity and skills, a variance inflation factor model was used to remove the collinearity problem.

The model was run for the full period 1990–2001 and for two sub-periods: 1990–1995 and 1998–2001. The results of the cross-county regressions are listed in box table 8. As expected, $\gamma > 0$, $\delta < 0$, $\beta > 0$, $\sigma > 0$.

Box 16 (contd.)

BOX TABLE 8. ESTIMATION RESULTS OF THE "AUGMENTED" WOOD AND BERGE MODEL			
	1990–2001	**1990–1995**	**1998–2001**
LDCs			
C	-3.55*	-4.90***	-4.27***
e_i	0.36*	0.51***	0.47***
n_i	-0.19***	-0.21***	-0.14**
h_i	0.14	0.10	-0.10
$e_i * D_{LDC}$	-0.04	-0.02	0.002
Adj. R^2	0.24	0.27	0.17
F-statistics	10.04***	10.74***	7.07***
Log-likelihood	-208.62	-195.91	-219.78
Other developing countries			
c	-3.35**	-3.57***	-3.57***
e_i	0.42***	0.48***	0.48***
n_i	-0.21***	-0.17**	-0.17**
h_i	0.10	-0.07	-0.08
$e_i * D_{ODC}$	-0.11***	-0.13***	-0.13***
Adj. R^2	0.29	0.23	0.23
F-statistics	12.3***	9.63***	9.63***
Log-likelihood	-205.25	-215.68	-215.68
Developed countries			
c	-3.35**	-4.45***	-3.57***
e_i	0.30*	0.43***	0.35***
n_i	-0.21***	-0.23***	-0.17**
h_i	0.10	0.07	-0.08
$e_i * D_{Developed}$	0.11***	0.10**	0.13***
Adj. R^2	0.29	0.30	0.23
F-statistics	12.3***	12.4***	9.63***
Log-likelihood	-205.25	-193.51	-215.68
No. of countries	**114**	**106**	**115**

Notes: * 10 per cent significance level; ** 5 per cent significance level; *** 1 per cent significance level. All variables used in the regression are per worker and in logs. The estimations are White heteroskedasticity-consistent.

     a Residuals from a Variance Inflation Factor model with electricity as dependent variable and skills as independent variable.

The coefficients for land and electricity are significant, while the coefficient for skills is insignificant.[1] Box table 9 shows that the elasticity for electricity is positive and that it has decreased for the other developing countries and developed economies over time, while it has remained constant in the LDCs. This shows that the elasticity for electricity production in the recent period is higher for the LDCs than for the other developing countries; and this indicates that an increase in electricity production would increase LDCs' exports of manufactures more than for the other developing countries.

BOX TABLE 9. ELECTRICITY ELASTICITY, 1990–2001, 1990–1995, 1998–2001			
	1990–2001	**1990–1995**	**1998–2001**
LDCs	0.327	0.496	0.471
ODCs	0.303	0.426	0.347
Developed countries	0.416	0.527	0.476

In absolute terms, the slope coefficients for both land and electricity per worker were larger in the sub-period 1990–1995 than they were in 1998–2001 for the three groups. This could be explained by the large increase in the log (labour force) that occurred during the periods 1990–1995 and 1998–2001.

The elasticity for electricity is higher than that for land for the three groups of countries. This implies that an increase in electricity production pushes up the *Xm/Xp* ratio by more than a rise in land would push it down, leading therefore to a net increase in the export of manufactures versus the exports of primary goods. Although this net effect has decreased over time for the three groups of countries, its net impact on *Xm/Xp* for the LDCs is the greatest of the country groups considered.

Source: Borgatti (2005c).

    1. Although a likelihood ratio omission test showed that the skill variable could be safely removed from the sample at 5 per cent significance level, it was kept in the model since its exclusion would not have much affected the statistical significance of the model.

The Least Developed Countries Report 2006

with an increase in the manufactures share of merchandise exports (see box 16). This finding is significant as it implies that energy infrastructure is as important as transport infrastructure for trade development.

4. LARGE-SCALE CROSS-BORDER INFRASTRUCTURE

Investment in cross-border infrastructure is also important for LDCs. This applies particularly to landlocked LDCs whose transit trade is affected by cross-border infrastructure. However, cross-border regional infrastructure is also important in general for encouraging regional trade (Ndulu, Kritzinger-van Niekerk and Reinikka, 2005). Regional cooperation in transport infrastructure financing can also be important for reducing infrastructure financing requirements and mobilizing financial resources (UNCTAD, 1999).

An important innovation for this is the corridor development approach adopted in Southern Africa. This approach seeks to address the fact that transport development is a chicken-and-egg problem at low income levels. On the one hand, infrastructure investment may not be economically viable until economic activity justifies it by creating a demand for transport. On the other hand, economic activity cannot emerge and develop unless there are adequate transport facilities and traffic flows on a scale sufficient to achieve economies of scale and competitiveness in transport services. The corridor approach addresses this problem by seeking to concentrate industrial investment projects within selected corridors connecting inland production areas to ports at the same time as infrastructure investment takes place. The synchronous development of directly productive activity and infrastructure ensures a revenue stream which renders infrastructure investment attractive to private business. At the same time, the infrastructure investment attracts economic activity and helps to promote the agglomeration process. Government policy aims to attract "anchor investment" which ensures the basic viability of infrastructure investments and then seeks to attract other investment. Special attention is paid in this process to small and medium-sized enterprises, which deepen the production cluster.

The Maputo corridor, which links Maputo to Johannesburg, has been particularly successful in attracting private sector investment projects, which in 1997 constituted over 60 per cent of total transport-related projects in Africa (UNCTAD, 1999). This corridor covers the development of roads, railways, border posts and ports and runs through two very productive regions in Southern Africa. It has increased trade between South Africa and Mozambique as well as traffic of Southern African goods through the renovated ports of Maputo and Matola (Horne, 2004).

Another example of a successful cross-border transport corridor is the one created in the Greater Mekong Subregion (GMS) to facilitate intraregional flows of goods and services between Viet Nam, Thailand, Cambodia, the Lao People's Democratic Republic, Myanmar and a number of Chinese provinces. The transport corridors that are in the process of being created include a highway between Phnom Penh and Ho Chi Minh City, and two (North–South and East–West) transport corridors to better link the countries in the region. As the new transport infrastructure projects were built, cross-border transport agreements were signed in order to harmonize customs procedures, visa requirements and other administrative costs. Even though the transport corridor within the GMS is due to be completed by 2007, trade and FDI inflows have already increased (Fujimura, 2004).

An increase in electricity production is closely correlated with an increase in the manufactures share of merchandise exports implying that the energy infrastructure is as important as transport infrastructure for trade development.

Investment in cross-border infrastructure is particularly important for landlocked LDCs.

The Maputo corridor, which links Maputo to Johannesburg, has been particularly successful in attracting private sector investment. It covers the development of roads, railways, border posts and ports.

E. Conclusions

This chapter has shown that there is an infrastructure divide between the LDCs, other developing countries and OECD countries. Most of the LDCs have the lowest and poorest-quality stock of transport, telecommunications and energy infrastructure in the world. The infrastructure divide is particularly important with respect to energy. The "electricity divide" has not received as much attention as the digital divide. But it is at least as significant — indeed, probably more significant — for economic growth and poverty reduction. A major constraint on the adoption within LDCs of mature modern technologies already available in developed and other developing countries is a low level of technological congruence between the LDCs and other countries. The low level of electrification is a central aspect of this lack of technological congruence and thus contributes to the maintenance of the technological gap.

The infrastructure divide between the LDCs, other developing countries and OECD countries is not only wide but also widening.

The infrastructure divide between the LDCs, other developing countries and OECD countries is not only wide but also widening. This is particularly apparent for road infrastructure. Measured by the length of the network, the stock of roads per capita in the LDCs was actually lower in 1999 (the latest year for which comprehensive data are available) than in 1990. The percentage of the total roads which are paved in the LDCs also declined over the same period. The road stock per capita declined in both African and island LDCs, and percentage of the roads which are paved declined in African LDCs. In contrast, for the LDCs as a group, the number of fixed and mobile phone subscribers per 1,000 people increased eightfold between 1990 and 2002. But LDCs are still falling behind other developing countries and OECD countries as there were more new subscribers in these last two country groups.

ODA commitments for economic infrastructure declined by 51 per cent in real terms between 1992 and 2003.

The low level and the poor quality of infrastructure stocks in the LDCs reflect weak maintenance of existing facilities and underinvestment in new facilities. This reflects declining public investment, the shift of ODA away from economic infrastructure towards social sectors, and limits to the interest of private investors in physical infrastructure in the LDCs. In real terms, ODA commitments for economic infrastructure declined by 51 per cent between 1992 and 2003. The decline in ODA committed to economic infrastructure was particularly marked in African LDCs. During the 1990s, there was an increase in private sector investment in energy and telecommunications. But private capital flows to transport have been much lower and mainly concentrated in Mozambique, where they have been associated with cross-border corridor development projects.

Global estimates of future financing needs for infrastructure investment in developing countries vary according to their assumptions. But available estimates for low-income countries suggest that the LDCs will need annual infrastructure investment, including new investment and maintenance costs, equivalent to between 7.5 per cent and 9 per cent of GDP. A preliminary estimate of the transport and communications investment needed to meet the Programme of Action's infrastructure target (which is to increase, by 2010, the stock of infrastructure in LDCs in these types of infrastructure to the level which other developing countries had in 2000) suggests that annual infrastructure investment needs should be equivalent to 3.3 per cent of GDP.

LDCs will need annual infrastructure investment, including new investment and maintenance costs, equivalent to between 7.5 per cent and 9 per cent of GDP.

An increased level of ODA inflows is required in order to meet these investment needs. Private finance can make a useful contribution to infrastructure investment in public–private partnerships, where the profit motive can be reconciled with the national interest. However, the small scale of private flows in relation to requirements, and limits on the types of assets and countries to which it is attracted, mean that private finance will at best be a supplement to public investment programmes and ODA, rather than an independent solution to infrastructure financing, as was sometimes assumed in the 1990s. In 2004, ODA commitments for economic infrastructure amounted to $1 billion and private capital inflows for energy, telecommunications and transport amounted to $0.4 billion. Together this was equivalent to 0.7 per cent of their GDP. This is far below the estimated infrastructure investment needs, even for achieving the less comprehensive POA targets required with regard to transport and telecommunications.

Increased public investment and ODA in physical infrastructure can play an important role in supporting the development of the international trade of LDCs. With improved transport and communications infrastructure, transport costs and time can be reduced, thus enabling increased trade volumes. However, this chapter also shows that investment in electricity is significantly correlated with export composition. Diversification into manufactures exports in LDCs is likely to be facilitated by closing the electricity divide with the rest of the world.

However, it is important that increased public investment and ODA in physical infrastructure within the LDCs do not focus on trade-related infrastructure alone. The best results from increased public investment and ODA are likely to come from a "joined-up" approach to the development of infrastructure in which international trade-related infrastructure forms an integral part. Such an approach should encompass the development of rural infrastructure, large-scale national infrastructure and cross-border infrastructure. Rural infrastructure is vital for agricultural commercialization and productivity growth and the development of local off-farm activities. Large-scale national infrastructure is vital for enabling economic diversification, the exercise of entrepreneurial capabilities and the development of production linkages as well as international trade. Cross-border infrastructure can reduce financing requirements, open new trading opportunities in intraregional trade and provide the basis for better transit facilitation for landlocked LDCs.

Diversification into manufactures exports in LDCs is likely to be facilitated by closing the electricity divide with the rest of the world.

The best results from increased public investment and ODA are likely to come from a "joined-up" approach to the development of infrastructure in which international trade-related infrastructure forms an integral part.

Notes

1. The composite infrastructure index is constructed by (i) normalizing the indicators for access to electricity, telephone density per 1,000 people, paved roads as a percentage of total roads and road density per square kilometre so that for each indicator the mean is zero and the variance is one, and (ii) summing up the normalized data with equal weighting for each infrastructure indicator.

2. This partly reflects low population density in the African LDCs. But studies which have sought to adjust for this factor show that African countries generally have a poorer rural road infrastructure (see Spencer, 1994).

3. The statistical analysis is a non-hierarchical K-means cluster analysis which classifies countries according to their similarity or dissimilarity on multiple indicators.

4. The efforts by Estache and Goicoechea (2005) in providing a snapshot of the infrastructure sector at the end of 2004 are notable, although they do not fill all the gaps. Certain series suffer from data unavailability problems more than others. Transport statistics are plagued with data unavailability problems and energy statistics are totally rudimentary, but data on telecommunications are readily available for a large number of LDCs.

5. Bangladesh, Bhutan, Burundi, Democratic Republic of the Congo, Ethiopia, Madagascar, Maldives, Myanmar, Nepal, Uganda, Vanuatu, Yemen, and Zambia.

6. These figures are based on IMF (2004).

7. Using the MDG targeted 7 per cent growth rate, Estache (2004) found that sub-Saharan Africa requires investment of the order of $20 billion per year in 2005–2015, including both capital and maintenance expenditures. Fay and Yepes (2003) estimate an annual infrastructure investment need for sub-Saharan Africa equivalent to $13 billion per year in new investment and $13 billion per year in maintenance costs between 2000 and 2010. World Bank (2000) estimates an infrastructure financing need of $18 billion per year to improve infrastructure services and competitiveness in sub-Saharan Africa.

References

Amjadi, A. and Yeats, A.J. (1995). Have transport costs contributed to the relative decline of sub-Saharan African exports? Working Paper No. 1559, Development Economics Research Group on International Trade, The World Bank Group, Washington, DC.

Asian Development Bank, Japan Bank for International Reconstruction and World Bank (2005). Connecting East Asia: A new framework for infrastructure (http://www.adb.org/Projects/Infrastructure-Development/Infrastructure-study.pdf).

Bentall, P., Beusch, A. and de Veen, J. (1999). Employment-intensive infrastructure programmes: Capacity building for contracting in the construction sector. ILO, Geneva (http://www.ilo.org/public/english/support/publ/xtextcon.htm#b581x).

Borgatti, L. (2005a). Status of infrastructure in the LDCs: A cluster analysis. Background paper prepared for *The Least Developed Countries Report 2006*, UNCTAD, Geneva.

Borgatti, L. (2005b). Transport costs and infrastructure needs in the LDCs. Background paper prepared for *The Least Developed Countries Report 2006*, UNCTAD, Geneva.

Borgatti, L. (2005c). The electricity challenge. Background paper prepared for *The Least Developed Countries Report 2006*, UNCTAD, Geneva.

Briceño-Garmendia, C., Estache, A. and Shafik, N. (2004). Infrastructure services in developing countries: Access, quality, costs and policy reform. World Bank Policy Research Working Paper 3468, Washington, DC.

Commission for Africa (2005). *Our Common Interest*. Report of the Commission for Africa, (www.commissionforafrica.org/english/report/introduction.htlm).

Desmarchelier, A. (2005). Trade logistics indicators: The SSATP transport indicator initiative. Transport Forum, Washington, DC, 9 March 2005.

Dorward, A. et al. (2004). Institutions and economic policies for pro-poor agricultural growth. DSGD Discussion Paper No. 15, International Food Policy Research Institute, Washington, DC.

Dorward, A. and Kydd, J. (2005). Making agricultural market systems work for the poor: promoting effective, efficient and accessible coordination and exchange. ADB Workshop, 15–16 February 2005, Manila. (http//www.dfid.gov.uk/news/files/trade_news/adb-workshop.asp).

Estache, A. (2004). What's the state of Africa's infrastructure? Quantitative snapshots. World Bank Background Paper prepared for the Commission for Africa, OECD-POVNET Infrastructure Task Force and 2nd World Bank-IMF Global Monitoring Report.

Estache, A. and Goicoechea, A. (2005). A "research" database on infrastructure economic performance. World Bank Policy Research Working Paper No. 3643, Washington, DC.

Fan, S., Hazell, P. and Thorat, S. (1999). Linkages between government spending, growth and poverty reduction in rural India. Research Report 110, International Food Policy Research Institute, Washington, DC.

Fan, S., Zhang, X. and Rao, N. (2004). Public expenditure, growth and poverty reduction in rural Uganda. DSGD Discussion Paper No. 4, International Food Policy Research Institute, Washington, DC.

Fan, S., Nyange, D. and Rao, N. (2005). Public investment and poverty reduction in Tanzania: Evidence from household survey data. DSGD Discussion Paper No. 18, International Food Policy Research Institute, Washington, DC.

Fay, M.and Yepes, T. (2003). Investing in infrastructure: What is needed from 2000 to 2010? World Bank Policy Research Working Paper No. 3102, Washington, DC.

Faye, M.L. et al. (2004). The challenges facing landlocked developing countries. *Journal of Human Development*, 5 (1): 31–68.

Fujimura, M. (2004). Cross-border transport infrastructure, regional integration and development. ADB Institute Discussion Paper No. 16, Asian Development Bank, Manila.

GRIPS Development Forum (2003). Linking economic growth and poverty reduction. Large-scale infrastructure in the context of Vietnam's CPRGS (http://www.grips.ac.jp/forum/pdf03/infra_paper/LinkingEcoGrowth.pdf).

Hayami, Y. and Platteau J-Ph. (1996). Resource endowments and agricultural development: Africa vs. Asia. Prepared for the IEA Round Table Conference "The Institutional Foundation of Economic Development in East Asia", Tokyo, 16–19 December 1996.

Horne, B. (2004). Experience of private sector stakeholders working together on the Maputo Corridor to the transit port of Maputo. Presented at the UNCTAD Expert Meeting in Geneva, 26 November 2004.

Hummels, D. (2001). Time as a trade barrier. GTAP Working Paper No. 18, University of Purdue, Indiana, USA. (http://ideas.repec.org/p/gta/workpp/1152.html).

Kydd, J. and Dorward, A. (2003). Implications of market and coordination failures for rural development in least developed countries. Paper presented at the Development Studies Association Annual Conference, Strathclyde University, Glasgow, 10–12 September 2003.

Limão, N. and Venables, A.J. (2001). Infrastructure, geographical disadvantage, transport costs and trade. *World Bank Economic Review 2001*, Washington, DC.

Livingstone, I. (1987). International transport costs and industrial development in least developed countries. *Industry and Development*, 19.

Ndulu, B., Kritzinger-van Niekerk, L. and Reinikka, R. (2005). Infrastructure, regional integration and growth in sub-Saharan Africa. Africa in the World Economy: The National Regional and International Challenges, Fondad, The Hague.

Omamo, S.W. (1998a). Farm-to-market transaction costs and specialization in small-scale agriculture: Explorations with a non-separable household model, *Journal of Development Studies*, 35 (2): 152–163.

Omamo, S.W. (1998b). Transport costs and smallholder cropping choices: An application to Siaya District, Kenya. *American Journal of Agricultural Economics*, 80 (2): 116–123.

Owens, T. and Wood, A. (1997). Export-oriented industrialization through primary processing? *World Development*, 25(9): 1453–1470.

Radelet, S. and Sachs, J. (1998). Shipping costs, manufactured exports and economic growth. Paper presented at the American Economic Association Meeting, Harvard University, Mass., USA.

Reinikka, R. and Svensson, J. (2002). Coping with poor public capital. *Journal of Development Economics*, 69 (1): 51–69.

Spencer, D.S.C. (1994). Infrastructure and technology constraints to agricultural development in the humid and sub-humid tropics of Africa. Environment and Production Technology Division Discussion Paper No. 3, International Food Policy Research Institute, Washington, DC.

Tajgman, D. and de Veen, J. (1998). Employment-intensive infrastructure programmes: Labour policies and practices. ILO, Geneva (http://www.ilo.org/public/english/support/publ/xtextcon.htm#b581x).

Torero, M. and Chowdhury, S. (2005). Increasing access to infrastructure for Africa's rural poor. 2020 Africa Conference Brief 16, International Food Policy Research Institute, Washington, DC.

UNCTAD (1999). UNCTAD's contribution to the implementation of the United Nations new agenda for the development of Africa in the 1990s: African transport infrastructure, trade and competitiveness. TD/B/46/10, Geneva.

UNCTAD (2005). *The Digital Divide: ICT Development Indices Report 2004*. UNCTAD/ITE/IPC/2005/4, Geneva.

Wood, A. and Berge, K. (1997). Exporting manufactures: Human resources, natural resources and trade policy, *Journal of Development Studies*, 34 (1): 35–59.

World Bank (2000). *Can Africa reclaim the 21st century?* Washington, DC.

Institutional Weaknesses: Firms, Financial Systems and Knowledge Systems

A. Introduction

The development of productive capacities within a country is strongly influenced by institutions which enable or constrain processes of capital accumulation, technological progress and structural change. The institutions which matter include both the institutional environment — the set of fundamental political, social and legal ground rules (such as property rights) that establish the basis for production, exchange and distribution — and institutional arrangements – the regular relationships amongst economic agents and related informal rules which govern the ways in which they cooperate and compete. The latter are sometimes strengthened through the establishment of formal organizations, such as firms or trade unions, or they may exist as looser recurrent patterns of interaction amongst agents and formal organizations.

A large range of institutions matter for the development of productive capacities. For example, cultural values with regard to the position of women in society can have a major influence on labour supply, and attitudes towards money, consumption and wealth can have a major influence on capital accumulation. With globalization, international regimes governing trade, finance, investment, technology, knowledge and the movement of people have also become increasingly important for the development of productive capacities within countries.

Within development policy debate, there is increasing recognition of the importance of institutions for economic growth and poverty reduction (Rodrik, 2004; Acemoglu, Johnson and Robinson, 2004). Within countries which are highly aid-dependent, attention has focused particularly on the quality of national governance. This focus is closely related to the legitimate desire of donors to ensure that aid and debt relief are well used. However, good governance has also been specified in a particular way which is associated with the policy agenda of freeing the private sector from government restraints and allowing greater room for market forces.

This Report recognizes the importance of good governance (see chapter 8) and the central role which the private sector must play in development of productive capacities. However, institutional prescriptions must be adapted to the prevailing characteristics of national economies. Accordingly, there is a need for a much closer examination of the nature of the private sector within LDCs and the institutions within which entrepreneurship is embedded. As shown earlier in the Report, an important feature of the LDCs is that a large part of production is still organized on a household basis. Market institutions are also underdeveloped in an LDC context (Ishikawa, 1998). If policy reform is undertaken in this context on the assumption that the elements characteristic of a functioning market economy need only to be freed from government interference in order to exist, it is likely to have unexpected and disappointing consequences. The policy problem is rather to develop a capitalist market economy and to ensure that this is organized in a way which supports the achievement of national development and poverty reduction objectives.

Chapter 6

Within development policy debate, there is increasing recognition of the importance of institutions for economic growth and poverty reduction. However, institutional prescriptions must be adapted to the prevailing characteristics of national economies.

There is a need for a much closer examination of the nature of the private sector within LDCs and the institutions within which entrepreneurship is embedded.

This chapter focuses on the nature of the domestic private sector within LDCs and the key institutions which support investment and innovation – the firm, domestic financial systems and domestic knowledge systems. Section B discusses the nature of the firm in the LDCs by drawing on the results of the World Bank Investment Climate Assessment Surveys and also the Research Programme in Enterprise Development (RPED) of the World Bank. Section C analyses the domestic financial systems of the LDCs, whilst section D analyses domestic knowledge systems. A basic argument of this Report is that both financial systems and knowledge systems matter for the development of productive capacities. The former are vital for the investment process, whilst the latter are vital for the innovation process. Section E summarizes the main messages of the chapter.

B. Firms in LDCs

The development of productive capacities is not an abstract process but occurs through the exercise of entrepreneurship. Entrepreneurship is the act of creating value by seizing opportunities through risk-taking and the mobilization of human, social, financial and physical capital. The critical institution within which entrepreneurship is exercised is the firm (box 17), although it does not operate in a vacuum. Its activities are enabled or constrained by the institutional matrix within which it is operating, including financial and innovation systems.

Firms are a locus for investment and learning. They are critical institutions for realizing the creative potential of the market. Success in the development of productive capacities depends on the existence of firms which are capable of investing and innovating. A dynamic economy is one which has the ability to create such firms.

In this perspective, a critical constraint on the development of productive capacities within the LDCs is the nature of their firms. Survey evidence is still patchy. But it is possible to identify three broad tendencies which analysts repeatedly find in country studies. They are the following:

- The size distribution of enterprises within most LDCs has a "missing middle" and the life cycle of small firms tends to be stunted.

- There is much heterogeneity in firms' performance within countries, with a strong tendency for large firms to be more productive, investment-oriented and innovative than small firms.

- There are some linkages between formal sector and informal sector enterprises, but they are often weak.

These features are not necessarily unique to LDCs. The evidence on firm performance suggests that small market size, price volatility, subsistence demand patterns and weak supporting institutions result in similar patterns in other developing countries (Tybout, 2000). But, to the extent that these features are more prevalent in LDCs, their enterprise structure is likely to be even more skewed.

1. The "missing middle" and stunted life cycle of firms

The "missing middle" refers to the weak development of formal sector small and medium- sized enterprises (SMEs), particularly medium-sized domestic firms. At one end of the size distribution, there are a multitude of informal

---

Firms are critical institutions for realizing the creative potential of the market. Success in the development of productive capacities depends on the existence of firms which are capable of investing and innovating.

The size distribution of enterprises within most LDCs has a "missing middle" and the life cycle of small firms tends to be stunted.

The "missing middle" refers to the weak development of formal sector small and medium- sized enterprises (SMEs), particularly medium-sized domestic firms.

BOX 17. THE FIRM AS A LOCUS OF LEARNING AND AGENT OF MARKET CREATION

Following Williamson (1983), firms are interpreted in this chapter as non-market institutions or hierarchies that operate with bounded rationality in the face of uncertainty. Unlike the neoclassical theory that treats the firm as a "black box" of technological relations (represented through cost functions), which minimizes costs while maximizing profits, the new institutionalist school, in which prominent authors such as Coase, Williamson and North argue that there are initially two types of governance structures: the market and hierarchy. The market is primal. The firm as a hierarchy, emerges only when the transaction costs of economic coordination within the firm (to make) are lower than those of doing business in the market (to buy).

The firm follows routines, that consist of operating characteristics and competences that determine what the firm does in the short run; investment rules which determine the firm's investment behaviour; and search routines that determine its survival and expansion (including organizing R&D and innovation), (Nelson and Winter, 1982). Search routines are limited by past history and are thus path-dependent. The market is essentially a selection mechanism that separates the "wheat from the chaff" (Nelson and Winter, 1982). But, the extended neo-Schumpeterian perspective interprets the firm as a learning, evolutionary institution that blurs the boundary between the firm and the market over time, essentially adopting a dynamic approach to market creation and development (see Dosi, Teece and Winter, 1992). Building on the Austrian theories of the firm, they interpret the market process as constantly changing and creating novel combinations among different economic agents. As such, the market itself is a creative process bringing into existence new innovations, new consumer goods and new ways of doing things. The central agents in this process are firms that realize the creative potential of the market (Schumpeter, 1947).

But unlike the market, the firm employs conscious coordination of the "visible hand" (Chandler, 1977; Schapiro, 1991). In this respect, it fulfils the following essential functions: (i) it stores knowledge (including tacit knowledge); (ii) it reproduces that knowledge and calls forth new entrants or shares it with other firms; and (iii) it establishes trust and cooperation. Tacit knowledge refers to knowledge developed from direct experience and action in contrast to explicit knowledge which can be codified and formally written-down.

To the extent that these three conditions are satisfied, the firm can be said to represent a continuum of relations that develop over time through productive experience and thereby realises what Kaldor called the "creative role of markets" (1967).

Given the experience-based nature of technological capabilities acquired from learning-by-doing, firms must draw on their internal capabilities and creativity in order to produce and develop new products and processes. Tacit knowledge needs to be acquired; it cannot be bought, imported or borrowed. Equally, change and innovation depend on cooperation between various (and possibly conflicting) groups within the production process itself, particularly management and labour, over and above what is normally stipulated in employment contracts. Innovation requires flexibility in employment contracts that pure market-based contracts cannot spell out or accommodate. In order to create an environment that allows interactive learning to occur, firms must share information, and this implies a closeness and continuity of relations.

The firm provides an important forum for discussing and codifying the necessary changes and adaptations to work routines and industrial relations more generally, which are essential if technical change and innovation are to evolve in a satisfactory manner. In all these respects, the firm therefore provides an important forum for long-term learning activities (benefiting from external economies resulting from experience accumulated over time) and strategic decision-making, the importance of which has been greatly underestimated. By creating a context in which a convergent interest in innovation could develop, the firm complements its role in providing the degree of insurance against risk and failure faced by producers in the highly volatile and uncertain markets that technical change itself generates.

This notion of the activist entrepreneurial firm echoes Penrose's (1959) description of the firm as a bundle of physical and human resources engaged in a collection of complementary activities which create wealth by producing one or more than one product which can be used by other firms as inputs into their production processes or by the final consumer for consumption. Moreover, the firm is always operating in an environment which challenges its ability to match the performance of other firms by seeking to reduce unit costs but also by creating new products or continuously improving its existing products. Furthermore, the firm acts as a depository of experiential, practical and tacit knowledge.

Innovative activity must draw on as wide a variety of capabilities as possible, which may not be formalized or codified but require trust and cooperation if appropriate responses are to be forthcoming. Lundvall proposes the notion of organized markets as an intermediate mode of governance between markets and hierarchies characterized by a network of user–producer relationships. Organized markets constitute selective and lasting relationships between users and producers, involving not only traditional market elements such as price, commodity and sale, but also the exchange of qualitative information, common codes of information and conduct, and sometimes even direct cooperation (Lundvall, 1988). This description of the firm as embodying collective entrepreneurship within the context of an organized market is better able to accommodate the dynamic interpretation of technical change referred to earlier. The Schumpeterian innovator is by definition a productive entrepreneur who shapes the economic environment in a creative way.

Source: Kozul-Wright, 2000.

micro-enterprises, most of which are characterized by the use of basic and traditional technologies and cater to the needs of restricted and relatively small local markets. As shown in chapter 4, although these enterprises account for important proportions of employment, they are generally characterized by lower levels of aggregate productivity. At the other end of the spectrum, there are a few large firms, which are mainly capital-intensive, resource-based, import-dependent or assembly-oriented. These firms are often wholly or minority-owned foreign affiliates, or state-owned enterprises. These large firms are not large by international standards, but they dominate the business landscape within most LDCs. Between these two extremes, there are very few formal sector SMEs.

Although the "missing middle" is widely accepted (see UNCTAD, 2001; Commission for Africa Report, 2005; Kauffmann, 2005), it is in practice difficult to get data on a country-by-country basis to substantiate the pattern. A major challenge for comparisons amongst countries is the lack of standardized definition of micro, small, medium and large enterprises across countries. According to ILO estimates, the contribution of formal sector SMEs to GDP in high-income countries is almost double that in low-income countries, over 40 per cent as against 20 per cent respectively, and the contribution of those SMEs to employment in high-income countries, which is over 60 per cent, is similarly double that in low-income countries (ILO, 2004).

The life cycles of enterprises are stunted in two ways. Firstly, informal sector enterprises rarely develop into formal sector firms. Secondly, small firms do not generally evolve into larger firm size classes.

Within Asia, Bangladesh seems to have a more important formal SME sector in terms of its contribution to value added. Although there are serious controversies with regard to their importance, various sources suggest that they contribute between 45 and 50 per cent of total manufacturing value-added (Bangladesh Enterprise Institute, 2004, based on estimates from the Asian Development Bank, the World Bank and the Bangladeshi Planning Commission). But in African LDCs, surveys find that a few large firms contribute the most to manufacturing value-added. According to Albaladejo and Schmitz (2000), SMEs in Africa can be classified into subsistence micro-enterprises and growth-oriented SMEs. The former are informal sector enterprises, which typically employ fewer than five workers, in most cases just one person, and which also use unpaid family labour. They are mainly labour-intensive activities that are characterized by very low entry barriers and minor rents, and employment is dominated by women. Examples of the most common trades include street-selling and home-based subcontracted work. Growth-oriented SMEs are mainly concentrated in the 5–19 worker-size category, but may include some micro-enterprises. They are usually formal sector enterprises, but may include some informal sector enterprises. They predominate in resource-based sectors, but more successful growth-oriented SMEs are in capital-intensive sectors and in some more technologically developed sectors (i.e. ICTs, garment design), and exhibit greater growth potential than subsistence micro-enterprises. They tend to serve domestic markets but also international markets (particularly regional). It is the weak development of these growth-oriented SMEs which constitutes the phenomenon of the "missing middle".

There is little evidence to suggest that entry or exit is a problem for small firms (see, for example, Elhiraika and Nkuunziza, 2005). Empirical evidence on African countries tends to corroborate the fact that the rate of new enterprise establishment is very high (Mead and Liedholm, 1998), but so is the exit rate for small firms in particular. It has been estimated that 50 per cent of start-ups fail in the first three years (ibid.). Moreover, the life cycles of enterprises are stunted in two ways. Firstly, informal sector enterprises rarely develop into formal sector firms. Albaladejo and Schmitz (2000), estimate that in Africa less than 1 per cent of subsistence-oriented micro-enterprises develop into growth-oriented SMEs. Secondly, small firms do not generally evolve into larger firm size classes (Harding, Soderbom and Teal, 2004; Van Biesebroeck, 2005; Liedholm, 2001).

The typical life cycle of firms — in which firms are usually small when they are set up and a select few then evolve from small into medium- and then large-size firms — does not seem to be occurring. Small firms are unable to grow and attain minimum efficient production size. New entrants tend to be small and have below average productivity levels and higher exit rates than the large firms. Within sub-Saharan Africa, it has been estimated that only 7 per cent of the new micro-enterprises grow to the medium or large size. Further evidence shows that in sub-Saharan Africa transition between size classes is extremely rare and most firms remain in their initial size categories. Moreover, the probability that the firm will remain in the same size category greatly increases with firm size. Many large-size firms in fact start out as large and tend not to drop below medium size (Van Biesebroeck, 2005).

Small firms are unable to grow and attain minimum efficient production sizes.

Contrary to conventional wisdom, these firm dynamics do not necessarily imply that in the LDCs the market selection process does not "prune out" inefficient firms. On the contrary, there is evidence to support the perspective that markets may indeed be very competitive as regards "pruning-out" less efficient firms. However, that "churning" process may be so strong that it may not permit new entrants to acquire the requisite technological capacities for manufacturing, thus imposing high costs on entrepreneurs for acquiring them independently (Shiferaw, 2005). Shiferaw (2005) finds that medium-sized firms in Ethiopia were between 40 and 50 per cent more productive than small enterprises, on average, while large enterprises were found to be between 65 and 80 per cent more efficient, on average. But at the same time the large firms are significantly less likely to exit and to survive longer even when they exhibit weak productivity performance (Mead and Liedholm, 1998; Van Biesebroeck, 2005).

Risk and volatility, access to credit, weak technological capabilities, and access to knowledge, entrepreneurial capabilities and labour force skills, are major obstacles to firm-level expansion in poor countries.

What factors are constraining normal growth dynamics at the firm level in LDCs? A set of standard constraints, including risk and volatility, access to credit, weak technological capabilities, and access to knowledge, entrepreneurial capabilities and labour force skills, are known to pose major obstacles to firm-level expansion in poor countries. The fact that these same factors are strongly correlated with investment performance and productivity would certainly suggest how small firms can get stuck in a perverse business environment (Van Biesebroeck, 2005). In environments in which business information collection mechanisms are not well developed, the perception of greater creditworthiness that tends to accompany larger size may help larger firms access credit more easily (Bigsten et al. 2003). Furthermore, larger firms are found to be more capable of overcoming the legal and financial obstacles faced by all firms on account of their negotiating power, and tend to display lower relative levels of dependence on the local economy owing to their greater levels of access to foreign finance, technology and external markets. Finally, larger-sized firms are found to generally be able to overcome more easily bottlenecks arising from the non-existence or failure of adequate public support mechanisms that would otherwise constrain their growth.

The inability to tap into capital markets or to face very high rates on borrowing undermines investment, and leads SMEs to operate with much less capital per worker than the larger firms.

Small firms in LDCs certainly do have difficulty in accessing credit markets (see Bigsten and Soderbom, 2005 and also section C of this chapter). The inability to tap into capital markets or to face very high rates on borrowing undermines investment, and leads SMEs to operate with much less capital per worker than the larger firms. By contrast, larger firms have more access to formal credit (see Bigsten and Soderbom, 2005), and since they are more productive and have greater investment propensities than the SMEs, they are better placed to improve their productivity performance.

Enabling network-building among firms is a further crucial component in successful firm evolution. Membership of a cohesive network is a very important determinant of size at entry in the case of Africa, for example (Biggs and Shah, 2005). This in turn has an important influence on future firm prospects, pointing to the importance of social capital (network externalities) in the enterprise survival process. The lack of formal market institutions to support private sector activities and underdeveloped markets in several LDCs are major business impediments, increasing the "extraordinarily high costs of searching, screening, and deterring opportunism" (Biggs and Shah, 2005: 7). Firms create "architectures of relational contracts that substitute for failed or non-existent formal institutions and economize on search and screening costs" (Biggs and Shah, 2006: 6). But it has been observed in Africa that these business networks are often organized around ethnicity (Ranja, 2003; Mengistae, 2001; Ramachandran and Shah, 1999; Fafchamps, 1999). The business networks provide support for the "insiders", but make it difficult for "outsiders" to enter particular activities or markets.

The lack of formal market institutions to support private sector activities and underdeveloped markets in several LDCs are major business impediments.

While relying on ethnic or cultural networks is a common strategy worldwide, exclusive dependence on such networks cannot be an adequate substitute for an appropriate institutional environment that can support and generate productive entrepreneurship. Prevailing investment patterns suggest that much investment finance in Africa is derived from family sources, thereby reinforcing ethnically or culturally based entrepreneurial links. Almost exclusive reliance on ethnic networks in providing resources for productive investment can be unreliable and insufficient. Networks can also limit competition and lead to unproductive entrepreneurial activities.[1]

An important obstacle to growth identified in the firm-level studies was the inadequate size of the market and an inelastic demand for the output of many firms.

An important obstacle to growth identified in the firm-level studies was the inadequate size of the market and an inelastic demand for the output of many firms. This can in turn impose a major constraint on investment in SMEs, which is reinforced by scarcity of credit (Van Biesebroeck, 2005). Exports can provide only a partial solution to lack of demand by expanding the potential market and facilitating the repayment of (trade) credit (Van Biesebroeck, 2005). Unsurprisingly, smaller firms have a much lower propensity to export than larger firms. However, larger firms may face particularly daunting obstacles in expanding abroad. In the first place, wages appear to be higher in larger firms than would be expected from a skill premium. To remain competitive would require productivity to rise equally strongly with firm size. However, this does not often appear to be the case. The squeeze on firms can become even larger in the face of high infrastructure costs. Indeed, high transaction costs appears to be a major bottleneck in many poor countries. From this perspective, many larger firms in LDCs do not appear capable of expanding beyond the size threshold needed to become competitive on world markets.

Many larger firms in LDCs do not appear capable of expanding beyond the size threshold needed to become competitive on world markets.

2. FIRM HETEROGENEITY AND THE PRODUCTIVITY DIVIDE BETWEEN SMALL AND LARGE FIRMS

Data on enterprise performance within LDCs can be obtained from Investment Climate Assessments for: Bangladesh, Benin, Bhutan, Cambodia, Eritrea, Mali, Madagascar, Mozambique, Nepal, the United Republic of Tanzania, Uganda, and Zambia.[2] These indicate major weaknesses in the average economic performance of firms in both African and Asian LDCs. Within African LDCs, capacity utilization rates are relatively low by international standards – generally ranging from 50 to 60 per cent, although Senegal is higher (see chart 46). Capital intensity tends to be high, although capital productivity tends to be relatively low (particularly in the cases of Eritrea and Zambia). This may be due to a combination of factors, most notably the age and quality of capital equipment. Enterprises also operate with relatively high unit labour costs.[3] In the United Republic of Tanzania, Uganda, and Zambia, for example, average unit labour costs for all firms included in the surveys were 0.39, 0.39 and 0.41 US dollars as against 0.32 and 0.27 US dollars in China and India respectively (World Bank, 2004a: table 2.6). In Asian LDCs, capacity utilization rates are similar to those in African LDCs in both Bhutan and Nepal, although they are higher in Bangladesh. Median investment rates are also below estimated depreciation rates in Bhutan and Nepal, a fact which indicates that the capital stock is being depleted faster than it is being replaced.[4]

The most striking feature of the enterprise performance in the LDCs is the high level of firm heterogeneity.

However, the most striking feature of the enterprise performance in the LDCs is the high level of firm heterogeneity, which has been identified as a key finding from the RPED studies in Africa (Bigsten and Soderbom, 2005) as well as in the Investment Climate Assessment Surveys in Asia. Firm heterogeneity means that, within the overall performance, there is much variety in outcomes and some firms are doing much better than others, both within and between sectors. In African LDCs, foreign ownership, export orientation and education of enterprises' managers have significant impacts on productivity measures, investment rates and turnover. Foreign-owned firms and exporting firms tend to perform better than domestically-owned firms and those which do not export. In

CHART 46. CAPACITY UTILIZATION IN FORMAL MANUFACTURING SECTOR ENTERPRISES IN SELECTED LDCs

(Median, percentage of total production capacity)

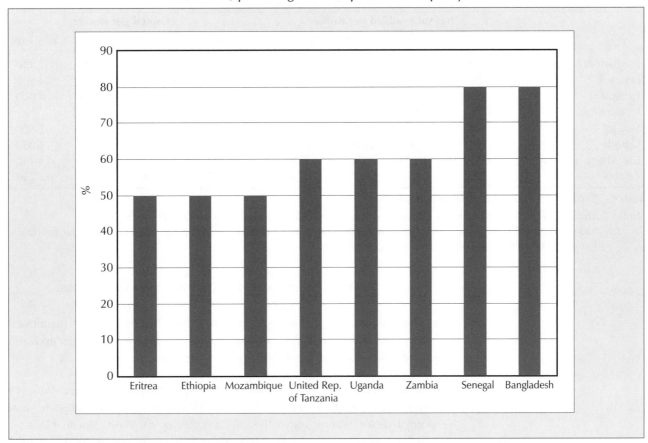

Source: Based on Eifert, Gelb and Ramachandran (2005).

Note: This chart uses Investment Climate Assessment data for surveys conducted from 2000 to 2004.

Asian LDCs, there are also wide disparities in productivity performance between export sectors and non-export sectors, with firms in export sectors performing substantially better in terms of sales growth, investment growth and employment growth in comparison with non-exporting firms.

A recurrent finding with regard to the heterogeneity of firm performance is that large firms tend to be more productive than small firms on measures of labour productivity, capital productivity and total factor productivity (Mazumdar and Mazaheri, 2003; Van Biesebroeck, 2005; Mead and Liedholm, 1998). Table 48 provides an overview of value-added per employee, a frequently used measure of labour productivity, as well as capital/worker, a measure for capital intensity for selected LDCs, based on the World Bank´s Investment Climate Assessments, which measure mainly manufacturing firm performance across several countries using survey data. The table shows that in all the countries labour productivity in medium-sized firms is higher than in small firms, and that in all countries except Bangladesh and Eritrea, labour productivity in large firms is also higher than in small firms. Labour productivity in the large firms is between 50 per cent and almost four times higher than in the small firms, although in five out of the eight cases labour productivity in medium-sized firms is higher than in large firms. This reversal of the pattern is even stronger with regard to labour productivity differences between the large and very large firms – labour productivity is only higher in the very large firms in the United Republic of Tanzania and Zambia. Capital per worker also increases between small and large firms in all countries in the sample except Bangladesh. As with labour productivity differences, the very large firms may or may not have greater capital per worker than the large firms (see table 48).

Large firms tend to be more productive than small firms on measures of labour productivity, capital productivity and total factor productivity.

TABLE 48. Net value-added per worker and capital per worker, by firm size, in selected LDCs
(Median in dollars)

	Net value-added per worker[a]				Capital per worker			
	Small	*Medium*	*Large*	*Very large*	*Small*	*Medium*	*Large*	*Very large*
Bangladesh	1 300	1 650	1 200	1 150	1 450	1 650	800	1 150
Eritrea	2 450	5 450	2 000	1 600	17 700	52 050	52 650	14 500
Ethiopia	550	750	1 050	650	2 450	3 750	4 600	4 400
Mozambique	1 250	2 800	2 200	..	6 200	5 600	12 250	..
Senegal	7 500	17 100	15 600	14 500	6 900	11 300	11 950	1 000
Uganda	1 000	1 600	4 800	950	1 550	4 700	8 850	1 050
United Rep. of Tanzania	1 850	4 200	3 400	6 800	5 900	4 750	13 250	13 150
Zambia	800	950	1 250	2 500	9 650	14 000	6 700	13 750

Source: Based on Eifert, Gelb and Ramachandran (2005).

Note: This table is based on Investment Climate Assessment surveys conducted from 2000 to 2004.

a Net value-added is the gross value of sales minus the cost of raw materials and estimated indirect costs of production. For definition of indirect costs of production, see source.

3. Linkages between informal and formal enterprises

The limitations of the skewed size distribution of enterprises is manifested through the lack of linkages between large firms and formal SMEs and also between formal sector and informal sector enterprises.

Once again there are few data on these phenomena. However, table 49 provides some evidence on the extent of linkages between formal sector and informal sector enterprises in the capital cities of six West African LDCs — Bamako, Cotonou, Dakar, Lomé, Niamey and Ouagadougou in 2000 and 2001 (Brilleau et al., 2005). This shows that:

TABLE 49. LINKAGES OF INFORMAL SECTOR ENTERPRISES WITH FORMAL SECTOR ENTERPRISES
IN THE CAPITAL CITIES OF SELECTED WEST AFRICAN LDCS

	Cotonou (Benin)	Ougadougou (Burkina Faso)	Bamako (Mali)	Niamey (Niger)	Dakar (Senegal)	Lomé (Togo)	Average
Source of raw material inputs of the informal sector (% of the total value of raw material inputs).							
Formal commercial	27.4	14.8	14.0	4.3	9.8	7.1	12.9
Informal commercial	62.1	76.5	83.1	90.0	79.9	85.6	79.5
Others	10.5	8.7	2.8	5.7	10.3	7.3	7.6
Users of output produced by informal sector (% sales revenue)							
Formal sector	10.2	10.3	6.8	3.7	8.2	6.8	7.7
Informal sector	30.3	22.0	25.8	12.6	10.2	17.6	19.8
Households	56.4	67.6	66.4	82.7	81.2	73.7	71.3
Foreigners	3.1	0.1	1.0	1.0	0.4	1.9	1.3
Major sources of competition for the informal sector (% total informal sector enterprises)							
Formal commercial	3.2	4.2	7.9	6.2	3.7	4.1	4.9
Formal non-commercial	6.8	2.6	4.9	3.4	3.1	3.0	4.0
Informal commercial	61.7	57.6	64.3	71.5	57.8	66.9	63.3
Informal non-commercial	24.6	15.9	23.0	18.7	22.1	14.8	19.9
Other	3.7	19.8	0.0	0.0	13.3	11.3	8.0

Source: Based on Brilleau et al. (2005).

- There are few backward linkages from informal sector enterprises to formal sector enterprises. On average, only 12.9 per cent of the material inputs of the informal sector enterprises in these cities was procured from formal sector enterprises. In five of the six cities less than 15 per cent of the material inputs were procured from formal sector enterprises. But Cotonou stands out as an exception, with 27 per cent of the material inputs of informal sector enterprises procured from formal sector enterprises.

- The outputs of informal sector enterprises are generally not sold to formal sector enterprises. On average, only 7.7 per cent of the sales of informal sector enterprises are to formal sector enterprises. The highest share of sales to formal sector enterprises is in Cotonou and Ouagadougou (10.2 per cent and 10.3 per cent respectively).

- Formal sector and informal sector enterprises do not compete. In all countries, less than 13 per cent of informal sector enterprises identify formal sector enterprises as a source of competition. On average, 83.2 per cent of informal sector enterprises identify other informal sector enterprises as their competitors.

The limitations of the skewed size distribution of enterprises is manifested through the lack of linkages between large firms and formal SMEs and also between formal sector and informal sector enterprises.

These results suggest a segmented production system in which there are weak linkages between different types of enterprises and also little competition amongst them. However, there may be positive consumption linkages between the growth of formal sector enterprises and the incomes of those working in them, and demand for output of informal sector enterprises from households. Evidence in Burkina Faso shows that in particular localities, the growth of the formal and informal sectors was positively correlated (Grimm and Günther, 2005).

Not all informal sector enterprises are subsistence SMEs; some are growth-oriented. In this regard, Ranis and Stewart (1999) usefully differentiate between traditional and modernizing informal sector enterprises. The former have very low capitalization, low labour productivity and low incomes, very small size (three or fewer workers) and static technology. The latter are more capital-intensive, usually larger in size (as many as 10 workers) and have more dynamic technology. It is this segment of the informal sector which is part of what Albaladejo and Schmitz (2000) call "growth-oriented SMEs". The modernizing informal sector enterprises are likely to be more closely linked to formal sector

Not all informal sector enterprises are subsistence SMEs, but some are growth-oriented.

enterprises. They produce consumer goods which may compete with formal sector goods, as well as intermediate products and simple capital goods which meet the informal sector needs but also partly respond to the demands of the formal sector. Within the informal sector it is these enterprises which have the potential to become firms in the formal sector.

Within dynamic Asian economies it is apparent that these types of informal enterprises have played an important economic role (Ranis and Stewart, 1999, and see also the next chapter). But it is difficult to say how important they are within the LDCs.

C. Domestic financial systems

1. THE CHANGING POLICY ENVIRONMENT

The nature of the domestic financial systems is critical for the processes of enterprise development and the development of productive capacities in the LDCs. This is widely recognized and after achieving their political independence, many LDCs sought to establish development finance institutions and targeted credit schemes. These were often funded and assisted by foreign aid agencies, and designed to provide credit to priority sectors or specialized concessionary services in rural areas. Governments played a major role in determining credit flows through a system of subsidies, interest-rate ceilings, policy-based credit allocation, high reserve requirements and restricting entry into banking and capital account transactions (UNCTAD, 1996).

In the economic crises during the late 1970s and early 1980s, the inherent weaknesses of LDCs financial institutions were further exposed and the response was to switch from a policy of financial repression to financial liberalization.

These financial policies were often unsuccessful and hindered the development of financial institutions. As Nissanke (2001: 347) has put it with regard to Africa, in terms which are relevant for African LDCs, "Commercial viability was largely prevented by the dictates of government policy objectives and political goals. This history of political interference undoubtedly impaired their risk-handling capacity. Banks failed to develop the capacity for risk assessment and for monitoring loan portfolios, and savings mobilization was not actively pursued. There was neither active liquidity and liability management nor any incentive to increase efficiency, often resulting in increased costs for financial intermediations. Financial repression discouraged banks from investing in information capital, crucial for the development of financial systems. In dealing with the idiosyncratic risks of private borrowers, banks were burdened by problems caused by costly and imperfect information — adverse selection, moral hazard and contract enforcement".

In the economic crises which most LDCs faced in the late 1970s and early 1980s, the inherent weaknesses of financial institutions were further exposed and the response was to switch from a policy of financial repression to financial liberalization, usually as part of stabilization and structural adjustment programmes. There are no systematic data on the extent of this process of financial policy reform. But available data show that Bangladesh, Burundi, Madagascar, Malawi, Nepal, Sierra Leone and the United Republic of Tanzania initiated their financial liberalization process in the second half of the 1980s whereas Haiti, Uganda and Zambia proceeded in the first half of the 1990s (Glick and Hutchinson, 2002). These trends are indicative of a broader movement. Gelbard and Leite (1999), for example, provide data on the status of financial liberalization in 24 LDCs, which indicate that 23 had "repressed" financial systems in 1987, whilst only 4 had such systems in 1997.

Financial liberalization aimed at enhancing the efficiency of financial intermediation and strengthening financial regulation (i.e. reducing the allocative regulation of financial markets), thus targeting increases in deposits (savings mobilization), in the quality of the investment portfolio and in economic growth. The main policy components of financial liberalization in LDCs included reform and liberalization of interest rates, introduction of market-based instruments of money markets (i.e. a switch from direct monetary-policy instruments such as interest rate controls and credit ceilings to indirect monetary instruments such as auction of treasury bonds), removal of sectoral credit directives and of restrictions on the types of activities financial institutions can undertake, liberalization of restrictions on the entry of private-sector and/or foreign institutions into domestic financial markets, privatization of government-owned financial institutions and restructuring/liquidation of banks (UNCTAD, 1996).

The financial reforms have contributed to somewhat increased competition within the financial sector and to the establishment of a more prudential regulation system. However, although the pace and extent of financial liberalization differ greatly from country to country, the evidence, which will be discussed below, suggests that the introduction of market-oriented policies within the financial sector of LDCs did not bring about the expected benefits. The LDC financial sector not only remained undiversified, bank-dominated and weakly competitive, but also developed an alternative mode of credit rationing focusing on short-term profitability instead of long-term productive investment. In other words, the LDC financial sector, and the banking sector in particular, did not act as an engine for private sector development in the aftermath of financial liberalization. Financial liberalization simply failed to promote productive investment in LDCs, as reflected by the poor delivery of credit to the private sector and to SMEs in particular. In the context of high information asymmetry, weak contract enforcement, weak capacity to monitor and assess risk, and a tradition of weak loan repayment, the behaviour of formal lenders is by and large dominated by an extremely high perception of risk, at the expense of enterprise development and employment creation.

The introduction of market-oriented policies within the financial sector of LDCs did not bring about the expected benefits.

2. TRENDS IN FINANCIAL INTERMEDIATION

This section shows the evidence of trends in financial intermediation in LDCs since the early 1980s. For comparative purposes, the trends in low- and middle-income countries or in other developing countries are also presented.

The first general indicator of financial depth is the level of monetization.[5] Data show that the monetization level prevailing in the group of LDCs still lags far behind that of the group of other developing countries. In the group of LDCs, the M2 to GDP ratio increased by only six percentage points between 1986 and 2003. In contrast, the same ratio increased by 43 percentage points in the group of other developing countries over that period. In 2003, money supply did not reach 31 per cent of GDP in LDCs as compared with almost 80 per cent of GDP in the group of other developing countries, with the share of interest-bearing and longer-maturity holdings to GDP being almost three times lower in LDCs (18 per cent) than in other developing countries (51 per cent). As a result, in 2003 the LDC ratio of M2 to GDP was still lower than the one displayed by the group of other developing countries in the early 1980s. The trends in the monetization level of the LDCs tend to indicate that, on average, financial deepening did not occur in this group of countries in the aftermath of financial liberalization. As outlined in box 18, there were distinct patterns of monetization

The trends in the monetization level of the LDCs tend to indicate that, on average, financial deepening did not occur in this group of countries in the aftermath of financial liberalization.

BOX 18. LEVEL AND STRUCTURE OF MONETIZATION IN LDCs

Trends in the monetization structure[1] of both LDCs and other developing countries show that since the mid-1980s a growing proportion of money supply has been in the form of quasi-money (see box chart 6). The share of quasi-money first exceeded that of money (M1) in 1993 in the group of LDCs as compared with as from 1986 in the group of other developing countries, thus indicating that in the period preceding the implementation of financial reforms the LDC economies were already at a much earlier stage of financial development than the group of other developing countries. In 2003, however, the structure of monetization of both LDCs and other developing countries was comparable to that of the group of developed countries, with quasi-money contributing to 60 to 65 per cent of total money supply in all three groups of countries. In disaggregating the group of LDCs by region, data show that these results have mainly been driven by Asian LDCs. In African LDCs, despite an increasing trend in the proportion of quasi-money, the share of M1 was in 2003 still higher than that of quasi-money. This observation may simply indicate that, on average, improvements in the use and delivery of financial services were much slower in African LDCs than in Asian LDCs in the aftermath of financial liberalization.

BOX CHART 6. THE STRUCTURE AND LEVEL OF MONETIZATION IN LDC SUBGROUPS AND
IN OTHER DEVELOPING COUNTRIES, 1986–2003

(Percentage of GDP)

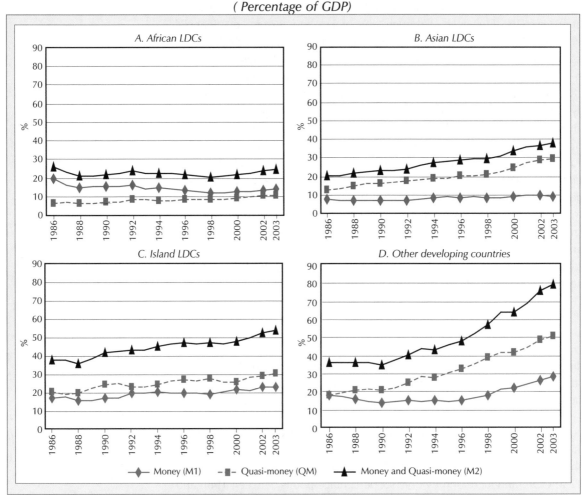

Source: UNCTAD secretariat estimates based on World Bank, *World Development Indicators 2005,* CD-ROM.

Note: Calculations are based on a group of 36 LDCs and 63 other developing countries.

As shown in box chart 6, in disaggregating the group of LDCs by region, it is seen that the average monetization level of Asian LDCs almost doubled from 20 per cent of GDP to 38 per cent of GDP between 1986 and 2003 as the main result of an increase in their ratio of quasi-money to GDP, which almost tripled between the same years. In contrast, in the group of African LDCs, the ratio of M2 to GDP was lower in 2003 (24 per cent of GDP) than in 1986 (26 per cent). This apparent demonetization process is attributed to a sluggish increase in the ratio of quasi-money to GDP (3.9 percentage points only between 1986 and 2003), which has not been sufficient to offset the concomitant decline in the ratio of M1 to GDP (-5.7 percentage points). In fact, the ratio of quasi-money was about twice as high in Asian LDCs (12.4 per cent of GDP) as in African LDCs (6.5 per cent of GDP) in 1986 and three times higher in 2003. According to Brownbridge

Box 18 (contd.)

and Gayi (1999), the better performance of Asian LDCs in enhancing financial depth relative to African LDCs may be attributable, at least in part, to the relatively greater macroeconomic stability prevailing in those countries, that is, lower inflation rates and higher real deposit rates. Data show that, on average, inflation rates were higher in African LDCs than in Asian LDCs in the late 1980s but not in the early 2000s.[2] With regard to island LDCs, data indicate that this group of countries showed an increase in their ratio of both quasi-money and money to GDP between 1986 and 2003. Their financial depth even appeared consistently higher than that of the group of Asian LDCs throughout the 1986–2003 period, although lower than that of the group of other developing countries.

These results tend to highlight the fact that despite an encouraging change in the LDCs' structure of monetization towards a relatively greater reliance on time and savings deposits, the financial depth of the group of LDCs compares particularly unfavourably with that of the group of other developing countries. The latter group of countries has showed substantial progress in their financial depth since the mid-1980s, while progress has been extremely sluggish in the group of LDCs and in African LDCs in particular. Such trends are significant as it has been estimated that a 10 per cent point increase in the M2/GDP ratio would increase GDP per capita growth by 0.2 per cent to 0.4 percentage points (World Bank, 1994: 22). The apparent demonetization of African LDCs in the aftermath of financial reforms is particularly preoccupying. In fact, with regard to the 22 African LDCs for which data are available, the level of monetization decreased in 10 and stagnated in 8 between 1986–1993 and 1996–2003. Weak monetization levels are a common feature of subsistence-oriented economies, where the main form of savings is often physical assets (commodity holdings) and where part of the agricultural sector is non-monetized. In those economies, monetization requires the economic development of rural areas (Akyüz, 1992).[3]

[1] For definition see footnote 5 in the text.
[2] In excluding Angola and the Democratic Republic of the Congo, two outliers, LDC data on inflation (based on the GDP deflator) are available for 39 LDCs in the periods 1986–1990 and 1999–2003, including 31 African LDCs and 5 Asian LDCs. Using simple averages, calculations show that inflation rates decreased from 22 per cent to 8 per cent in African LDCs and from 18 per cent to 14 per cent in Asian LDCs. In island LDCs, inflation rates decreased from 12 per cent to 5 per cent between the same periods. In comparison, inflation rates averaged 14 per cent in 1986–1990 in the group of other developing countries (in excluding four outliers, namely Argentina, Brazil, Nicaragua and Viet Nam) and decreased to 8 per cent in 1999–2003, which is the same level as the one displayed by African LDCs.
[3] The author also notes that interest policies such as increases in deposit rates cannot bring about monetization through the liquidation of commodity stocks.

in African, Asian and island LDCs, with a process of demonetization (reduction in the level of monetization) occurring in the African LDCs since 1986.

Interest rate spreads (the difference between deposit and lending interest rates) are used as a proxy for financial intermediation efficiency. Available data suggest that (i) the interest spread increased in the LDCs, while it decreased on average in the group of other developing countries, and that (ii) the interest spread remained consistently larger in LDCs than in other developing countries (see table 50). High interest spreads generally indicate the presence of high operating costs (including in particular high overhead costs commonly related to the low productivity and the overstaffing of banks), a poorly performing loan portfolio (reflecting a weak culture of repayment), a weakly competitive banking sector and a weak lending environment. According to McKinley (2005), large interest spreads may also imply that commercial banks charge large profit rates on disbursed loans so as to compensate for a low volume of loan disbursement. High profit margins on lending, which reflect high risk premiums charged, weak market infrastructure and weak enforcement of creditor rights, are also indicative of the weak intensity of competition (Èihák, M. and Podpiera, 2005).[6]

During the 1990s, interest rate spreads, commonly used as a proxy for financial intermediation efficiency, increased in the LDCs, while they decreased on average in the group of other developing countries.

Financial liberalization was accompanied by a lowering of domestic bank reserve requirements. Accordingly and as shown in chart 47a, the bank liquid reserves to bank assets ratio, which has constantly been higher in LDCs than in the group of low- and middle-income countries since the 1980s, experienced a declining trend during the 1990s in both groups of countries. This decline was accompanied by an increase in the GDP ratio of domestic credit provided by banks in the group of low- and middle-income economies, but by a decrease in the same ratio in the group of LDCs (chart 47b). As shown in table 51, between

TABLE 50. LENDING INTEREST RATES AND INTEREST RATE SPREAD IN LDCS AND IN OTHER DEVELOPING COUNTRIES, 1990–1993 AND 2000–2003

(Average in percentage)

	Lending interest rate			Interest rate spread		
	1990-1993 *(a)*	*2000-2003* *(b)*	*Change* *(b-a)*	*1990-1993* *(a)*	*2000-2003* *(b)*	*Change* *(b-a)*
Bangladesh	15.5	15.8	0.4	4.8	7.6	2.8
Cape Verde	10.0	12.7	2.7	6.0	8.2	2.2
Central African Republic	18.0	19.7	1.7	10.4	14.7	4.3
Chad	18.0	19.7	1.7	10.4	14.7	4.3
Equatorial Guinea	18.0	19.7	1.7	10.4	14.7	4.3
Ethiopia	8.5	9.6	1.1	4.7	4.8	0.1
Gambia	26.5	24.0	-2.5	13.7	11.4	-2.3
Guinea	24.3	19.4	-4.9	2.9	11.9	9.0
Lao PDR	25.8	29.5	3.7	8.5	21.7	13.2
Lesotho	18.6	16.7	-1.9	7.5	11.7	4.2
Madagascar	25.3	25.3	0.0	5.1	12.7	7.6
Malawi	23.1	52.2	29.1	7.4	21.8	14.4
Mauritania	10.0	21.0	11.0	3.8	13.0	9.3
Myanmar	8.0	15.1	7.1	-4.2	5.5	9.7
Nepal	14.4	8.6	-5.9	0.6	3.2	2.6
Samoa	13.2	10.1	-3.1	6.1	4.6	-1.6
Sao Tome and Principe	32.8	36.9	4.1	2.5	21.1	18.6
Sierra Leone	55.5	23.2	-32.3	13.0	14.8	1.8
Solomon Islands	18.8	16.0	-2.8	8.1	14.6	6.6
Uganda	36.5	20.9	-15.6	-10.4	12.5	22.8
United Rep. of Tanzania	31.0	18.2	-12.8	7.8	13.6	5.8
Vanuatu	16.9	8.0	-8.9	11.0	6.8	-4.2
Zambia	67.7	42.7	-25.0	32.2	20.5	-11.7
LDCs	23.3	21.1	-2.2	7.1	12.4	5.4
Other developing countries	42.8	16.2	-26.6	19.4	8.3	-11.1

Source: UNCTAD secretariat estimates based on World Bank, *World Development Indicators 2005,* CD-ROM.

Note: Averages are simple averages based on a group of 23 LDCs and 64 other developing countries.

Between 1980 and 2003, whereas the ratio of domestic credit to the private sector doubled from 30 per cent to almost 60 per cent in the group of low- and middle-income countries, it stagnated in the group of LDCs.

1990–1993 and 2000–2003, the bank liquid reserves to bank assets ratio declined in 29 out the 42 LDCs for which data are available, while the ratio of domestic credit provided by banks decreased in 60 per cent of them (as compared with 24 per cent of them in the group of other developing countries).

Another traditional indicator of financial intermediation is the GDP ratio of domestic credit to the private sector. This variable is supposed to capture the effective re-channelling of financial deposits/savings to the private sector through loan disbursements.[7] Chart 47c shows that between 1980 and 2003, whereas the ratio of domestic credit to the private sector doubled from 30 per cent to almost 60 per cent in the group of low- and middle-income countries, it stagnated at around 14–15 per cent in the group of LDCs. Data show that even the highest-ranked LDC, namely Cape Verde, in which domestic credit to the private sector averaged 37 per cent of GDP in 2003, did not reach the average level displayed by the group of low- and middle-income countries the same year. Those preliminary observations clearly indicate that on average and despite the implementation of financial reforms, domestic financial institutions failed to act as an engine for private sector development in the group of LDCs. As shown in table 52, the GDP ratio of domestic credit to the private sector increased from 12 to 15 per cent for the group of LDCs, but slightly declined in 19 out of the 33 LDCs for which pre-reform and post-reform data are available. With the exception of one country, namely the Solomon Islands, all of the 19 countries were African LDCs. In contrast, the same ratio increased in the five Asian LDCs for which data were available. According to Thisen, (2004), "[In

CHART 47. SELECTED INDICATORS OF FINANCIAL DEPTH IN LDCs AND LOW- AND MIDDLE-INCOME COUNTRIES, 1980–2003

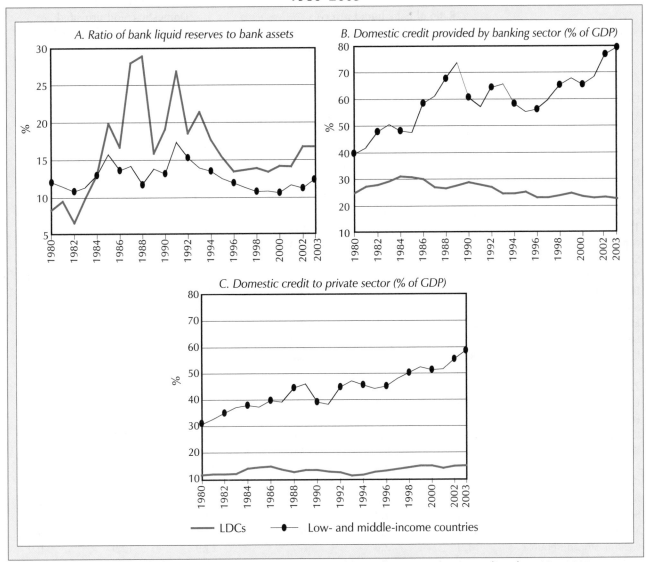

Source: UNCTAD secretariat estimates based on World Bank, *World Development Indicators*, online data, May 2005.

Africa] the one thing that industry and commerce lacked was a sufficient supply of money. Bankers, who were the only source of money, deliberately refused loans to industry, commerce and agriculture".

Although provision of domestic credit is very low in the LDCs, banks' portfolios are characterized by a high incidence of liquidity. In 2000–2003, the bank liquid reserves to bank assets ratio exceeded 11.4 per cent (the rate displayed by the group of low- and middle-income countries) in 32 out of the 45 LDCs for which data are available (see table 51).[8] Moreover, the coexistence of a situation of high liquidity and scarce bank domestic credit reveals that any intervention on bank reserve requirements to improve access to credit is expected to fail. Chart 48 shows that in 1999–2003 in the LDCs, the bank liquid reserves to bank assets ratio was invariably associated with a low level in the GDP ratio of domestic credit to the private sector. In contrast, in the group of other developing countries, relatively lower bank liquidity ratios were accompanied by relatively higher levels in the GDP ratio of domestic credit to the private sector.

It has often been argued that the weak level of domestic credit to the private sector is explained by the crowding-out effect of credit disbursed to the public

Domestic financial institutions failed to act as an engine for private sector development in the group of LDCs...

Yet banks' portfolios are characterized by a high incidence of liquidity.

TABLE 51. RATIO OF BANK LIQUID RESERVES TO BANK ASSETS AND DOMESTIC CREDIT PROVIDED BY BANKING SECTOR
IN LDCs AND IN LOW- AND MIDDLE-INCOME COUNTRIES, 1990–1993 AND 2000–2003

	Ratio of bank liquid reserves to bank assets (%)			Domestic credit provided by banking sector (% of GDP)		
	1990–1993 (a)	*2000–2003* (b)	*change* (b-a)	*1990–1993* (a)	*2000–2003* (b)	*change* (b-a)
Cape Verde	147.8	20.0	-127.8	44.8	67.6	22.8
Dem. Rep. of the Congo	109.5	7.5	-102.0	18.5	1.1	-17.4
Yemen	113.3	18.8	-94.4	56.8	3.1	-53.7
Myanmar	88.2	20.9	-67.3	38.2	33.6	-4.6
Samoa	72.5	11.4	-61.1	0.3	24.6	24.3
Bhutan	107.0	58.6	-48.4	7.3	7.2	0.0
Mali	65.4	17.2	-48.1	12.9	16.0	3.2
Benin	60.7	16.8	-43.9	14.9	7.1	-7.8
Haiti	83.1	40.9	-42.2	33.7	35.0	1.2
Togo	51.7	11.4	-40.4	23.4	18.8	-4.6
Niger	42.4	16.4	-26.0	14.6	8.7	-5.9
Sudan	50.5	25.9	-24.6	18.7	9.8	-8.9
Sierra Leone	33.2	10.0	-23.2	19.2	50.5	31.4
Burkina Faso	26.3	8.2	-18.1	9.9	13.5	3.6
Mozambique	30.4	13.5	-17.0	10.9	12.7	1.8
Ethiopia	26.0	12.6	-13.3	52.9	61.0	8.1
Lesotho	22.9	10.7	-12.2	20.4	6.0	-14.4
Liberia	70.8	60.2	-10.6	587.5	177.2	-410.2
Mauritania	13.0	3.9	-9.1	50.6	-4.4	-55.0
Zambia	24.7	17.6	-7.1	62.3	51.9	-10.4
Uganda	15.9	11.1	-4.8	14.9	12.7	-2.2
Rwanda	14.8	10.3	-4.4	15.8	12.6	-3.2
Gambia	16.2	12.2	-4.0	4.8	20.8	16.0
Bangladesh	12.7	8.8	-3.9	22.9	38.1	15.2
Malawi	25.4	22.4	-3.0	24.2	18.3	-5.9
Guinea-Bissau	31.3	29.5	-1.8	27.9	15.2	-12.8
Burundi	5.8	4.0	-1.8	21.7	34.2	12.5
Senegal	13.3	12.3	-1.0	32.6	23.7	-8.9
Maldives	54.1	53.4	-0.6	33.4	38.3	4.9
Central African Republic	1.9	2.6	0.7	13.9	12.9	-0.9
Djibouti	1.1	2.3	1.2	46.9	31.2	-15.6
Vanuatu	3.9	6.3	2.4	29.0	43.3	14.3
United Rep. of Tanzania	6.8	13.7	6.9	31.6	9.9	-21.7
Madagascar	13.8	21.2	7.4	28.9	16.9	-12.0
Nepal	11.5	20.2	8.6	28.3	43.2	14.9
Guinea	8.6	22.0	13.4	6.2	11.3	5.2
Chad	2.9	16.4	13.5	13.1	11.6	-1.5
Lao PDR	12.7	27.4	14.7	6.4	12.1	5.7
Solomon Islands	4.7	20.9	16.1	36.0	36.8	0.8
Equatorial Guinea	14.9	43.6	28.7	41.8	1.4	-40.4
Cambodia	2.9	56.5	53.6	5.1	6.4	1.3
Comoros	18.2	73.1	54.9	20.1	12.3	-7.8
Angola	..	15.9	..	..	-0.9	..
Eritrea	..	27.7	..	..	153.7	..
Sao Tome and Principe	..	64.0	..	..	11.3	..
LDCs	21.5	15.4	-6.1	27.1	23.1	-4.0
Low- and middle-income countries	14.9	11.4	-3.5	62.0	72.5	10.5

Source: UNCTAD secretariat estimates based on World Bank, *World Development Indicators 2005,* CD-ROM.

TABLE 52. DOMESTIC CREDIT TO PRIVATE SECTOR IN LDCS AND IN LOW- AND MIDDLE-INCOME COUNTRIES, 1980–1984 AND 1999–2003[a]

(Average, percentage of GDP)

	1980–1984 (a)	1999–2003 (b)	Change (b-a)
Mozambique	59.8	8.6	-51.3
Senegal	41.7	19.3	-22.4
Benin	28.2	12.1	-16.1
Niger	17.2	4.7	-12.5
Zambia	19.6	7.2	-12.3
Solomon Islands	30.8	19.0	-11.7
Togo	25.0	14.7	-10.2
Gambia	23.8	13.8	-10.0
Madagascar	18.6	9.0	-9.6
Sudan	12.9	3.4	-9.5
Chad	12.6	3.8	-8.8
Central African Republic	12.5	5.1	-7.4
Liberia	8.6	3.8	-4.9
Sierra Leone	6.8	3.0	-3.8
Mauritania	31.9	28.3	-3.6
Comoros	13.5	10.7	-2.9
Mali	19.6	18.0	-1.6
Dem. Rep. of the Congo	2.2	0.8	-1.5
Burkina Faso	13.3	12.4	-0.9
Haiti	16.0	16.6	0.6
Lesotho	12.1	12.8	0.7
Maldives	20.8	22.4	1.6
Uganda	3.3	6.5	3.1
Rwanda	6.1	10.2	4.1
Myanmar	5.3	10.4	5.1
Malawi	2.3	8.3	6.0
Vanuatu	33.9	40.0	6.1
Bhutan	2.6	9.8	7.2
Ethiopia	13.8	27.8	13.9
Burundi	11.2	25.6	14.5
Bangladesh	8.3	26.5	18.2
Nepal	8.6	29.8	21.2
Samoa	7.8	32.3	24.5
Angola	..	3.7	..
Cambodia	..	6.7	..
Cape Verde	..	33.0	..
Djibouti	..	26.8	..
Equatorial Guinea	..	3.3	..
Eritrea	..	32.8	..
Guinea	..	3.9	..
Guinea-Bissau	..	4.6	..
Lao PDR	..	8.4	..
Sao Tome and Principe	..	9.6	..
United Rep. of Tanzania	..	5.6	..
Yemen	..	5.9	..
LDCs	12.3	14.7	2.5
Low- and middle-income countries	34.8	53.9	19.1

Source: UNCTAD secretariat estimates based on World Bank, *World Development Indicators 2005*, CD-ROM.

a   The 1980-1984 period is a pre-reform period for many LDCs; the 1999-2003 period is a post-reform period for many LDCs.

CHART 48. BANK LIQUIDITY AND DOMESTIC CREDIT TO THE PRIVATE SECTOR IN LDCs
AND OTHER DEVELOPING COUNTRIES, 1999–2003

(Average in percentage)

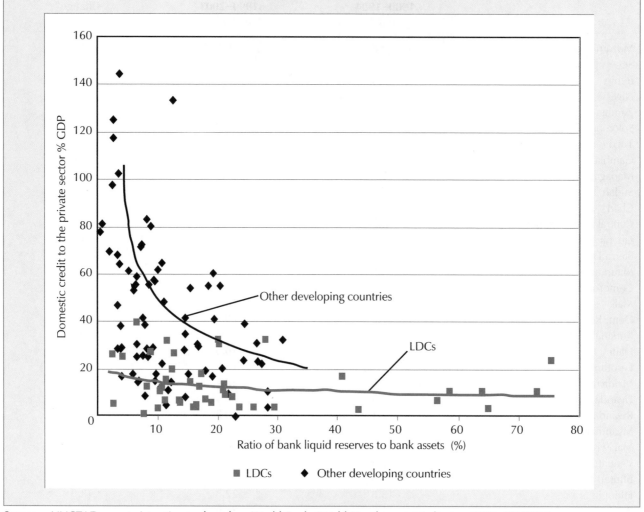

Source: UNCTAD secretariat estimates based on World Bank, *World Development Indicators 2005,* CD-ROM.

Note: Data are available for 119 developing countries, including 44 LDCs.

sector (which comprises credit to central government, local government and public enterprises) to finance the public deficit resulting from weak macroeconomic management (Nissanke, 2001). According to the IFS/IMF database (see table 53), claims on public entities absorb a significantly larger share of bank credit in the LDCs than in the group of other developing countries, a fact which may lead to the premature conclusion that the crowding-out effect of loans to the public sector is more pronounced in the LDCs than in other developing countries. Claims on public entities absorbed 39 per cent of total bank credit in the LDCs in 1990–1993 as compared with 24 per cent in the group of other developing countries in the same period. In 2000–2003 this ratio decreased to 34.5 per cent in the group of LDCs and to 18 per cent in the group of other developing countries. In both country groups the reduction in the contribution of credit to the public sector to total bank credit results from the reduction in the volume of such credit during the 1990s as part of stabilization reforms.

Although the contribution of bank credit to the public sector to total bank domestic credit was significantly higher in LDCs than in other developing countries, it is important to note that as a proportion of GDP, bank credit to the public sector was slightly lower in LDCs than in other developing countries (see table 53). Data also show that the GDP ratio of bank credit was consistently

TABLE 53. CLAIMS IN LDCS AND OTHER DEVELOPING COUNTRIES, BY BORROWER STATUS,1990–1993 AND 2000–2003
(Percentage)

	Period	% Bank credit		%GDP	
		LDCs	*Other developing countries*	*LDCs*	*Other developing countries*
Claims on public entities	1990–1993	38.7	24.3	10.0	11.6
Claims on private sector	1990–1993	59.9	72.2	15.5	34.6
Bank credit	1990–1993	100.0	100.0	25.9	47.9
Claims on public entities	2000–2003	34.5	18.0	8.3	9.6
Claims on private sector	2000–2003	64.9	78.0	15.6	41.4
Bank credit	2000–2003	100.0	100.0	24.0	53.0

Source: UNCTAD secretariat estimates based on IMF, *International Financial Statistics* March 2005, and World Bank, *World Development Indicators 2005,* CD-ROM.

Notes: The sum of claims on public and private sectors does not equal total bank credit. The residual may represent claims on financial institutions.
Averages are simple averages based on a group of 35 LDCs and 63 other developing countries.

smaller in LDCs than in other developing countries. This is largely due to the smaller level of domestic credit to the private sector prevailing in the LDCs than in the group of other developing countries. In comparing trends in bank credit provided to the public and the private sectors, it appears that as a proportion of GDP, claims on public entities decreased by the same level in the LDCs than in the group of other developing countries (around two percentage points) between 1990–1993 and 2000–2003. Interestingly, however, this decrease was accompanied by a strong surge in bank credit to the private sector in the group of other developing countries, in contrast with the group of LDCs, where this ratio remained flat between the two periods (see chart 49). These observations suggest that during the 1990s and contrary to expectation, credit to the public sector in the LDCs did not act as a major determinant of weak credit delivery to the private sector in those countries. The problem of credit rationing in a liberalized environment seems to be more related to the banking system itself. It arises more from the high perception of risk of bankers and their inability to address the principal–agent problem[9] than from the crowding-out effect of credit to the public sector per se.

Thus, in the group of other developing countries the increase in the GDP ratio of domestic bank credit since the mid-1980s has been driven by an increase in domestic bank credit to the private sector, which has been sufficient to offset the decrease in claims on the public sector. In the group of LDCs, however, the decrease in the GDP ratio of bank credit resulted from the decrease in credit to the public sector and the stagnation, if not decrease, in domestic bank credit to the private sector, particularly in African LDCs. In the group of LDCs, unlike in the group of other developing countries, neither the reduction in domestic credit to the public sector nor the reduction in bank reserve requirements proved sufficient to trigger bank credit to the private sector. Even after the implementation of financial reforms, banks in the majority of LDCs continued to bear the costs of weak loan repayments and were highly adverse to the risks of non-repayment. In poorly managed financial systems, commercial banks invest in weakly remunerative but risk-free government securities as a way of sterilizing excess liquidity, rather than lend to the domestic private sector.

To sum up, the implementation of market-oriented financial reforms has proved ineffective in supporting the domestic resource mobilization process in the LDCs. This is a basic reason for the persistently weak domestic savings and investment performance in most of these economies, and in African LDCs in

Neither the reduction in domestic credit to the public sector nor the reduction in bank reserve requirements proved sufficient to trigger bank credit to the private sector.

CHART 49. BANK CLAIMS ON PUBLIC ENTITIES AND ON PRIVATE SECTOR IN LDCs
AND OTHER DEVELOPING COUNTRIES, 1986–2003

(Percentage of GDP)

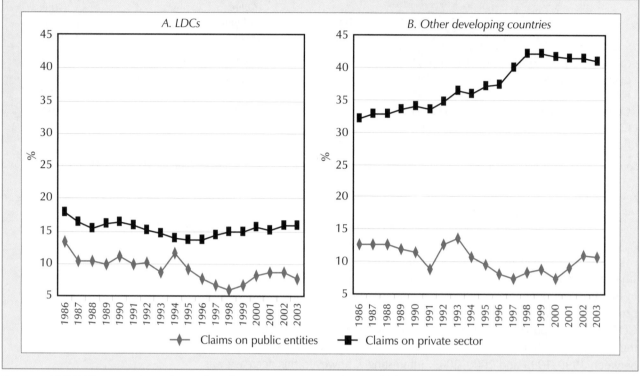

Source: UNCTAD secretariat estimates based on IMF, *International Financial Statistics,* March 2005; and World Bank, *World Development Indicators 2005,* CD-ROM.

Notes: Averages are simple averages based on a group of 35 LDCs and 63 other developing countries.

particular, which was shown in chapter 2. The high liquidity levels of the banking sector on the one hand and the weak level of domestic credit delivered to the private sector on the other hand are illustrative of the low intermediation trap[10] in which many LDCs are embedded. It is more likely that domestic financial resources are being underutilized in a number of LDCs and are inadequate to support the development of productive capacities.

3. INSTITUTIONAL WEAKNESSES OF LDC FINANCIAL SYSTEMS

The financial markets in LDCs are·dualistic. With formal and informal sectors often forming financial enclaves.

The financial markets in LDCs are dualistic. With formal and informal sectors often forming financial enclaves, the LDC financial market is characterized by a high degree of segmentation (few linkages between segments) and of fragmentation (high market power in each segment). Each segment serves a distinctive clientele on the basis of their respective capacity to manage risk (Nissanke, 2001). In the face of high information asymmetry, the dual feature of the LDC domestic financial sector is symptomatic of the existence of a shallow formal financial sector, which is often described as bank-dominated, highly concentrated, weakly competitive and highly vulnerable.

In 2002, banks held 78 per cent of total financial system assets in the United Republic of Tanzania, 82 per cent in Uganda, 88 per cent in Senegal and 95 per cent in Mozambique.[11] The vulnerability of the financial sector is notably characterized by the high degree of concentration of bank loan portfolios, which has been reported as being particularly acute in Mozambique, Rwanda, Senegal, the United Republic of Tanzania and Uganda, that is in all LDCs for which a Financial System Assessment Programme (FSAP) is available (IMF, 2003a, 2003b, 2004, 2005a and 2005b).[12] The large credit exposure to a small number of borrowers reflects the high perception of risk of commercial banks, which prefer to lend to a few corporations, namely to those located at the upper end of the market, than to expand their lending to clients that are new but less reputed, in other words, that are perceived as too risky. Trade and industry absorb the bulk of domestic credit. Comparatively, credit to the agricultural sector (i.e. to small farmers) is often limited. The closing down of rural banks during the financial restructuring process has generated an urban bias in the delivery and accessibility of financial services.

Owing to higher processing, administrative and monitoring costs and to the greater risk of default, small and medium-sized enterprises, which often lack the necessary collateral, are regarded as too costly and too risky and are simply marginalized from the banking system. The persistent credit gap facing the SMEs has important implications for private sector development and employment creation in LDCs. This is an important source of the "missing middle" and the stunted life cycle of business firms in LDCs. It is more likely that financial liberalization gave rise to another form of credit rationing, no longer based on the identification of priority sectors, as was the case during the period of financial repression, but rather based on the short-term profitability criteria imposed by a handful of credit suppliers. The problem of loan concentration or of loan exclusion is also sometimes exacerbated by the high degree of concentration in the banking system, which reveals the weak competition level prevailing in the sector. In Mozambique, while bank assets account for 95 per cent of total financial assets, the five largest banks account for 96 per cent of total deposits(IMF, 2004).

According to various FSAPs, gross non-performing loans (NPL) still represent a large share of total loans in a number of LDCs: the ratio of gross NPL to total gross loans averaged 33 per cent in Rwanda in 2004, 21 per cent in Mozambique in 2002 and 19 per cent in Senegal in 2000.[13] The weak quality of bank loan portfolios, the weak capacity of the oligopolistic banking sector (UNCTAD, 1996) to monitor/analyse risk and manage project proposals, and the high information asymmetry prevailing in those countries, in conjunction with weak contract enforcement and an inefficient judicial and legal framework, seriously act as a deterrent to loan access/delivery. Moreover, it should be noted that in countries with poor financial systems, domestic loans (and financial instruments in general) tend to be mostly short-term loans, reflecting the banks' preference for liquid assets or their high perception of risk. Consistent with the high liquidity ratio prevailing in the LDC banking sector, and with the high share of M1 in broad money supply (M2), particularly in African LDCs, the predominance of short-term financial instruments and the lack of long-term finance are common features of LDC banking systems. In Uganda and United Republic of Tanzania, most lending has a maturity of less than one year (Cihák and Podpiera, 2005). The weak delivery of long-term loans seriously impedes productive investment in LDCs. Overall, the agent problem is perpetuating the mismatch between borrowers' needs and lenders' supply, thus generating a high opportunity cost notably in terms of enterprise development and employment creation. The question of long-term finance in LDCs must be urgently addressed as part of a strategy to build productive capacities.

The poor delivery of private loans in LDC-type economies results from supply-side as well as demand-side constraints. On the demand side, it is usually argued that too few private investment projects are bankable. In other words, the rate of return of such projects is too low compared with the interest rate charged.[14] Moreover, the capacity of local entrepreneurs to formulate acceptable business plans is often too limited and their accounting records too

The persistent credit gap facing the SMEs has important implications for private sector development and employment creation in LDCs. This is an important source of the "missing middle" and the stunted life cycle of business firms in LDCs.

The question of long-term finance in LDCs must be urgently addressed as part of a strategy to build productive capacities.

poor (if they exist at all) to successfully go through the bank screening process, while the cost of creating and registering collaterals, when available, required by the banks also acts as a strong deterrent to loan access (see chart 50). In Senegal, where the cost of creating collateral averages 16.5 per cent of per capita income, it has been reported that 80 per cent of SME project applications are rejected owing to lack of collateral (IMF, 2005b). In the United Republic of Tanzania, because of low expectations, 84 per cent of micro-enterprises have never applied for bank loans, as compared with 41 per cent of large firms (Nissanke, 2001). It should be noted that the cost of creating collateral is, on average, much higher in African LDCs than in Asian ones.

In Senegal, 80 per cent of SME project applications are rejected owing to lack of collateral

On the supply side, it is argued that banks are simply not prepared to lend to the domestic private sector, and to SMEs in particular, as they are perceived as too risky. This is related to internal dysfunctions (lack of information capital, lack of skills) as well as regulatory ones (lack of contract enforcement and of regulation), both of which contribute to the increase in intermediation costs. Although Mozambique records the best credit information index amongst the LDCs according to the World Bank's doing business survey (see chart 51), three quarters of firms surveyed reported that the cost of financing and difficulty in accessing credit are the biggest obstacle to their business performance.[15] In eight out of the nine LDCs which are covered in the World Bank investment climate database, access to, or cost of, finance has been reported as acting as a severe obstacle to business performance by 38 per cent to 84 per cent of the firms surveyed. But, on the other hand, legal obstacles to credit recovery also represent a major hindrance to loan delivery: the average number of days to recover debt after insolvency is 540 in Mozambique. This is over twice as many as in Zimbabwe, and over five times as many as in South Africa (IMF, 2004). In the context of poor access to formal finance, small businesses have to rely on internal funds or on prohibitively expensive informal finance to finance their expansion or survival. Under these conditions, the shortage of working capital may explain the high exit rate of small enterprises.

In Mozambique, the average number of days to recover debt after insolvency is 540.

It is well recognized that the credit markets for small-scale farmers/enterprises suffer most from informational deficiencies as most banks avoid extending credit to them. These have found themselves excluded from liberalized financial markets. The closure of rural banks after the period of financial repression has further contributed to the exclusion of small farmers from the banking sector. In view of the structural and institutional constraints, the high information asymmetry and the weak legal and regulatory environment prevailing in LDC economies, it is less likely that private financial institutions alone will be able to take a lead role in supporting productive investment, notably through the financing of domestic enterprise development. Although a strengthened legal and regulatory system may contribute to increasing the confidence of the contractors, it will not be sufficient to respond to the financial needs of small and/or remote private operators.

In view of the structural and institutional constraints, the high information asymmetry and the weak legal and regulatory environment prevailing in LDC economies, it is less likely that private financial institutions alone will be able to take a lead role in supporting productive investment, notably through the financing of domestic enterprise development.

Microfinance is now perceived as the strategic tool for poverty reduction and SME development. According to the MIX Market database on microfinance, 130 microfinance institutions (MFIs) have been officially registered in 23 LDCs. They serve 8.5 million active borrowers for an average amount of $100 per loan. It is worth noting that on average these loans tend to be higher in African LDCs ($243 per borrower) than in Asian ones ($69 per borrower), which suggests that the outreach of Asian MFIs is larger than that of African ones. The literature on microfinance often argues that semi-formal and informal financial institutions interact increasingly with the formal financial sector, thus contributing to increased credit information and increased financial deepening. But according

CHART 50. COST TO CREATE COLLATERAL IN LDCS AND OTHER COUNTRY GROUPS, JANUARY 2004
(Percentage of per capita income)

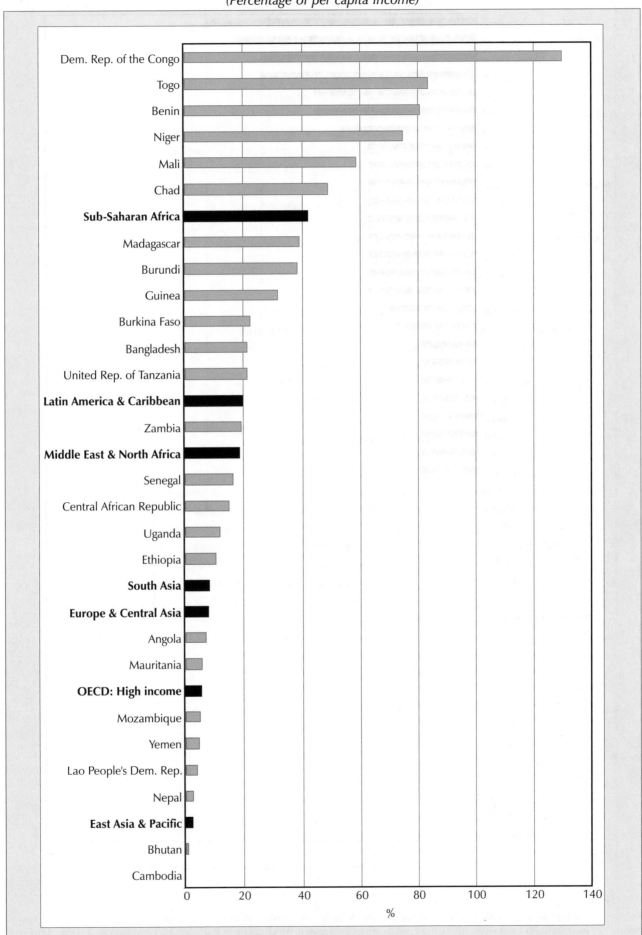

Source: UNCTAD secretariat estimates, based on World Bank, Doing Business 2005.

CHART 51. CREDIT INFORMATION INDEX AND LEGAL RIGHTS INDEX IN LDCS AND OTHER COUNTRY GROUPS, JANUARY 2005

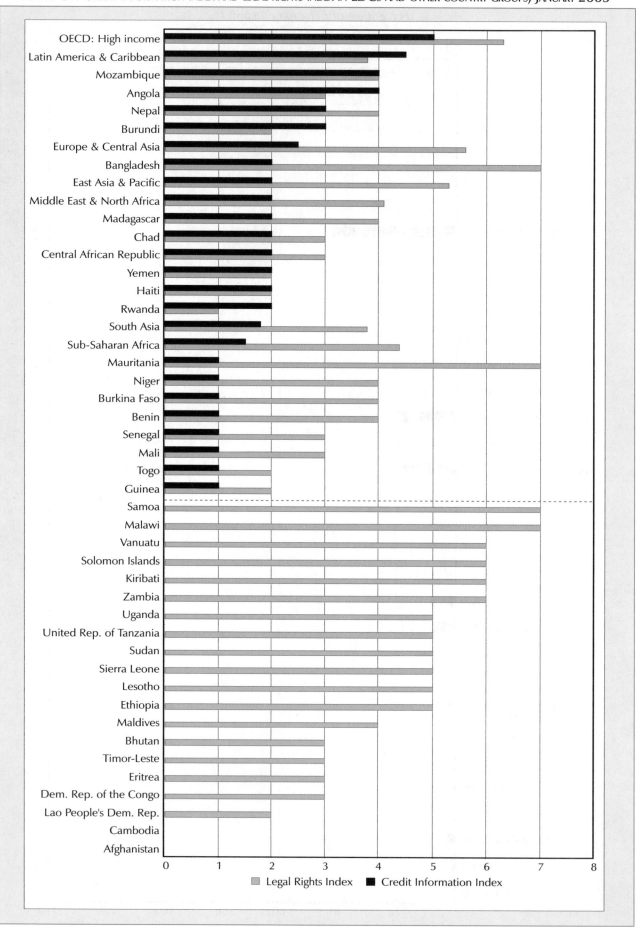

Source: UNCTAD secretariat estimates based on World Bank, Doing business survey online data May 2005.
Note: The Legal Rights Index ranges from 0 to 10 and measures the degree to which collateral and bankruptcy laws facilitate lending. The Credit Information Index ranges from 0 to 6 and measures rules affecting the scope, access and quality of credit information. The higher the index, the better the environment for credit delivery/access. Countries are ranked on the basis of credit information index. This index is zero for countries below the dotted lines. The legal rights index is zero for Afghanistan and Cambodia.

to Nissanke (2001), the scope for both information sharing and risk pooling has been limited in Africa owing to the small number of linkages and interactions between different segments of financial markets. Microfinance can play some role in supporting the start-up and limited growth of micro-enterprises. However, in view of the size of the LDCs financial needs for boosting the development of their domestic entrepreneurial sector, including that of formal sector SMEs, it is unlikely that this can be achieved without the support of a full spectrum of financial institutions.

One innovative approach to financing productive development, which could complement microfinance, is the practice of value-chain lending (i.e. lending that supports enterprises at different points along the supply chain). As discussed in box 19, GAPI in Mozambique provides an interesting illustration of this strategy. However, all such initiatives need to be part of an integrated and holistic strategy to finance, which promotes sound development of financial institutions supporting productive investment and long-term economic development, instead of favouring short-term profitability, in an environment of strengthened creditor rights.

One innovative approach to financing productive development, which could complement microfinance, is the practice of value-chain lending (i.e. lending that supports enterprises at different points along the supply chain).

Box 19. Value-chain lending: The example of GAPI, Mozambique

GAPI is a Mozambican non-bank financial institution that aims to bridge the gap between microfinance and formal finance. It operates mainly in rural areas by providing finance to firms in conjunction with business services. GAPI´s focus is on rural areas, because in Mozambique these are the areas from which most banks have withdrawn their activities, and 50 per cent of its portfolio is on activities related to agriculture, because this is the sector on which 80 per cent of Mozambique´s economically active population depends.

GAPI´s financial services arm provides concessional loans and in some cases, venture capital for SMEs in rural areas. The aim of the business services arm is to provide borrowers with business skills and form relationships with other institutions (i.e. suppliers, customers) in order to build a more sustainable productive system, by focusing on the entire supply chain and providing technical, business and training services to entrepreneurs. This approach may be called 'value-chain lending'.

GAPI's approach is novel since it focuses simultaneously on joint supply and demand action. On the supply side, GAPI focuses on reducing the asymmetry of information between borrowers and lenders by improving the lenders´ information about the nature of the borrower´s proposed investment project. The purpose is not only to focus on an assessment of creditworthiness but also to help actively improve the borrower's ability to repay in the future. On the demand side, this requires a focus on creating and improving productive and technological capabilities. The second key feature is the focus of the *whole system of production*. This includes careful assessment of economic incentives, market structure, ownership structure, and economies of scale and scope, and the promotion of quality and learning in the production system.

GAPI´s approach has the following characteristics:

- *Thinking beyond collateral:* The focus of improving "bankability" is on securing a stable future stream of profits, rather than focusing solely on collateral. This is made possible by GAPI´s relational rather than transactional approach to lending, in addition to the provision of business services.

- *Partnerships to overcome the potential constraints of this development approach to lending.* In order to address the extra risks that it may face in comparison with traditional banking institutions (i.e. lack of project finance, donor reliance, and breadth of areas in which productive expertise is available to assess projects proposed), GAPI works with external organizations (e.g. the NGO Technoserve), operating on the ground in specialist areas to improve production capabilities in rural regions. The purpose is not only to focus on an assessment of creditworthiness, but also to actively help improve the borrower's ability to repay in the future.

- *Value-chain lending*: This involves supporting the entire production system, including the supply chain and the economic and institutional environment in which it is embedded. It entails assistance to networks of producers structured around a particular value chain, rather than individuals or specific types of enterprises (i.e. micro-enterprises). This is facilitated by branch presence in rural areas, so as to facilitate a project´s prospects prior to

Box 19 (contd.)

the financing decision and monitor the implementation of projects after the loan is disbursed. This represents a break with traditional supply-driven development banking.

On the basis of GAPI´s experience in the creation of sustainable production systems, the following success factors have been identified as part of the value-chain lending approach:

(1) *Testing demand.* Market demand is required for any product, and for this reason, market access is essential. Production system creation therefore starts by testing the degree of market access and creates the distribution channels needed for a particular product.

(2) *The importance of scale.* Network formation, in GAPI´s experience, had been found to work best when linking medium-sized firms with associations of small producers and trading networks upstream and downstream by supply chain. This encourages more efficient division of labour, the internalization of externalities, and greater exploitation of economies of scale and of scope. This type of assistance is found to work in improving cluster-specific systemic capabilities as well as in improving systemic capabilities along the value chain to improve productivity and employment growth.

(3) *Building on existing capabilities.* GAPI ensures that its work corresponds to the whole value chain by forming partnerships with expert organizations which provide "islands of competencies".

(4) *Building new centres of competencies that will replace the initial expertise providers by providing them with an exit strategy.* In order to ensure the continuity of expertise provided in GAPI´s approach, which is reliant on time-limited donor funding (i.e. specific NGO expertise), centres of competencies are established to replace the role of NGOs in providing this expertise in the medium run.

(5) *Gradual increase in the internationalization of the value chain.* In order to increase value-added over time, successive layers of the value chain are gradually internalized.

(6) *Clustering.* Spatial concentration is necessary in countries such as Mozambique, in which economic infrastructure is widely dispersed, and in order to further internalize secondary multiplier effects from increased income generation from internalizing value added.

(7) *Attention to quality issues.* In order to help producers attain and maintain competitive edge, attention is paid to quality issues.

Two of GAPI´s key success stories include building the supply chain in Mozambique´s poultry sector by creating a successful import substitution system of production, and the recovery of the cashew-nut-processing sector in Mozambique´s Nampula region, which collapsed following the implementation of trade liberalization reforms.

Source: Fivawo, Simonetti and Wuyts (2005).

D. Domestic knowledge systems

The importance of domestic financial systems for economic growth and the development of productive capacities has long been recognized. However, the role of domestic knowledge systems in these processes has been largely neglected, at least until recently. As argued earlier in the Report, investment and innovation are interlinked and cumulative processes. Institutional weaknesses with regard to both domestic financial systems and domestic knowledge systems can thus act as key constraints on the development of productive capacities. This section defines how domestic knowledge systems will be conceptualized in this Report, describes the basic features of such systems within LDCs and includes some case studies to illustrate the major points.

The role of domestic knowledge systems for economic growth and the development of productive capacities has been largely neglected.

1. THE CONCEPT OF DOMESTIC KNOWLEDGE SYSTEMS

The concept of a domestic knowledge system is much less well defined than the concept of a domestic financial system. Malhotra (2003: 2) defines knowledge systems as "the national institutions, frameworks and infrastructures that can facilitate effective using, sharing, creation and renewal of knowledge for socio-economic growth", whereas Bell and Albu (1999: 1722) use the term to refer to "knowledge stocks within firms and knowledge flows to them, between them and within them which underlie change in the types of goods they produce and the methods they use to produce them", arguing that "it is the structure and functioning of that knowledge system which generates technological change at particular rates and with particular degrees of continuity and persistence".

In the present Report, domestic knowledge systems will be defined as *the set of institutions within a country, including regulatory frameworks, formal organizations, regular relationships amongst organizations and routine practices, which enable (or constrain) the creation, accumulation, use and sharing of knowledge*. This notion is broader than a national system of innovation. The latter term is associated with particular types of entrepreneurial capabilities, notably the necessary capabilities for transforming knowledge outputs from R&D into commercial innovations in the production of goods and services.[16] This is quite relevant within OECD countries, where the term has been elaborated most fully. But as argued earlier in the Report, the key entrepreneurial capabilities are much broader than R&D. The concept of the domestic knowledge system is preferred here for that reason, as well as because some question the appropriateness of the notion of a national innovation system as a standard for evaluating processes of knowledge accumulation in low-income countries (Bell, 2006).

Knowledge systems are the set of institutions within a country, including regulatory frameworks, formal organizations, regular relationships amongst organizations and routine practices, which enable (or constrain) the creation, accumulation, use and sharing of knowledge.

The major components of a domestic knowledge system are summarized in a schematic way in chart 52. The knowledge system is manifest in recurrent interactions, in the form of flows of people and information, amongst and between three basic types of agents.

CHART 52. DOMESTIC KNOWLEDGE SYSTEM

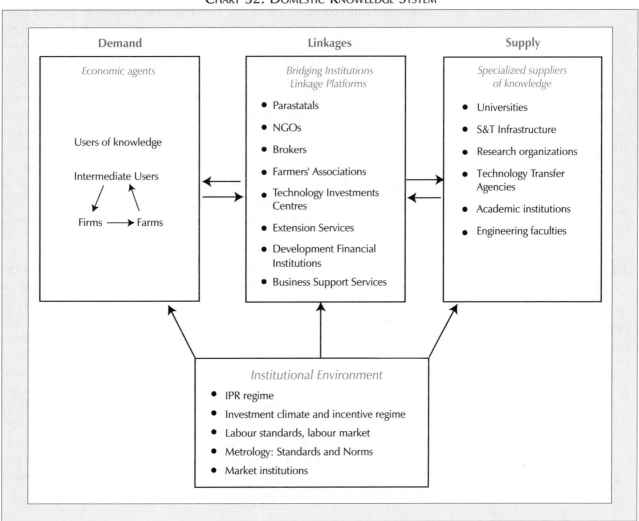

The first type, on the supply side (top right of the chart), is *specialized suppliers of knowledge*. These include universities, public research institutes, research laboratories, technology transfer agencies, education and training institutions which produce people who can create formal knowledge, (such as tertiary institutions providing education in science and engineering, vocational schools and formal skill formation entities), institutions that provide technology infrastructure, engineering research associations, and metrology, quality and standards institutions responsible for technical regulations, quality control and training.

The knowledge system is manifest in recurrent interactions, in the form of flows of people and information, amongst and between three basic types of agents: specialized suppliers of knowledge; economic agents that use knowledge; and various bridging institutions.

The second type, on the demand side (top left of the chart), is *economic agents* that use knowledge, but who also can produce formal and tacit knowledge (through internal R&D) and who, through linkages amongst themselves, also exchange and disseminate tacit knowledge. Linkages refer to different types of direct relationships that are established by firms engaged in complementary activities leading to external economies. They are external to anonymous pure market transactions and lead to "productivity spillovers" (Blomström and Kokko, 1998). Long-term relationships are important for close, inter-firm technology learning, where supply linkages are deepened over time as a result of recurrent experiences between firms and other actors. These interactions are deeper than arm's-length market transactions. It is these types of linkages that tend to facilitate technology transfer between TNCs and local suppliers (Ivarsson and Alvstam, 2005).

The third type of agent is various *bridging institutions* which act as specialized intermediary institutions to link these two — the specialized creators of knowledge and economic agents that use and apply knowledge — and build capabilities at the firm level by promoting linkages and knowledge flows amongst economic agents. They enable and facilitate knowledge flows throughout the system. They include technology support institutions, business associations, farmers' associations, public extension services (both in industry and in agriculture) and various types of business support services. They also include development financial institutions, specialized NGOs and parastatals, such as technology development centres (rather than formal R&D institutions), productivity centres, skill-building institutions, technology support institutions, specialized agencies that support entrepreneurship, and specialized institutions that provide public goods, technical assistance and skill formation as well as agencies responsible for information sharing and exchanges. In agriculture, they include, agricultural support institutions, extension services and technology training centres.

The linkages and knowledge flows amongst these basic components of the domestic knowledge system include various forms of interactions that are needed to build capabilities throughout the knowledge system. These interactions are shaped by the institutional environment.

The linkages and knowledge flows amongst these basic components of the domestic knowledge system include various forms of interactions – such as personnel mobility, licensing, importation of engineering services, flows of knowledge between components, inter-firm research collaboration, academic conferences and research networks — that are needed to build capabilities throughout the knowledge system. These interactions are also shaped by a fourth component of the knowledge system. This is the *institutional environment* for the creation, accumulation, use and sharing of knowledge. It is within the context of this overall enabling framework that the specific configuration of institutional arrangements between specialized creators of knowledge, economic agents who use knowledge and the bridging institutions and linkage platforms evolves. The institutional environment includes the intellectual property regime and various standards regimes, as well as the overall investment climate and economic incentive structure regimes.

Two final points are worth emphasizing with regard to this conceptualization of domestic knowledge systems. Firstly, although the term "domestic knowledge system" refers to institutions within a country, this does not mean that interactions with the rest of the world are irrelevant. Indeed, quite the contrary is the case in developing countries. An important feature of a domestic knowledge system is how open or closed it is with regard to the rest of the world, and the channels through which flows of information and personnel enter or leave the system.

Secondly, it is worth underlining that there are close interrelationships between the domestic financial system and the domestic knowledge system. This is evident in chart 52, in the sense that financial institutions are included as an important bridging institution. Domestic financial systems play a prominent role not only in providing investment for innovation and financial resources but also in supporting sector-specific technological learning.[17] The synthetic connections between finance and innovation have not been sufficiently explored in the context of low-income economies. But the weaknesses of the financial systems, which were discussed above, have important implications for the nature of domestic knowledge systems in LDCs and the generation and use of knowledge.

2. THE NATURE OF DOMESTIC KNOWLEDGE SYSTEMS IN LDCS

There has been limited research on domestic knowledge systems in low-income contexts. But work on technological capabilities has revealed a number of their features. The most basic one is that two knowledge systems coexist in the LDCs: a knowledge system based on modern science and technology, and a traditional knowledge system based on indigenous knowledge, which is often community-based (Sagasti, 2004; Bell, 2006). The latter is particularly important for lives and livelihoods. As Sagasti has put it, referring to developing countries in general, "more than three quarters of the world's population relies on indigenous knowledge to meet their medical needs, and at least half relies on traditional knowledge and techniques for crops and food supplies. As about one third does not have access to electricity, all modern technologies and production activities that depend on the source of energy are out of reach" (Sagasti, 2004: 54).

Production activities in LDC economies are largely based on traditional or indigenous knowledge and traditional knowledge systems. Although they are deeply rooted in the cultural heritage of local communities, traditional knowledge systems are severely constrained by their lack of ability to generate technical change and respond quickly to new opportunities and challenges. They are commonly disarticulated in the sense that component activities are weakly linked amongst the traditional stream of activities (World Bank, 2004a). Moreover, traditional knowledge systems tend to be small-scale relative to modern ones. They have also been described as "non-dynamic" (Oyeralan-Oyeyinka, 2005: 14), that is slow to learn.

The indigenous or traditional knowledge systems of the LDCs have great potential and represent a hidden reservoir of underutilized creativity and knowledge that could be harnessed, not only as a heritage from the past, but also as "a means and process for articulating what local people know, and involving them in the creation of new knowledge required for development" (World Bank, 2004b:42). Indigenous knowledge is a resource that can be harnessed to help solve local problems, to help grow more and better food, to

An important feature of a domestic knowledge system is how open or closed it is with regard to the rest of the world.

Owing to close interrelationships between the domestic financial and knowledge systems the weaknesses of the former have important implications for the nature of the latter and the generation and use of knowledge.

Two knowledge systems coexist in the LDCs: a knowledge system based on modern science and technology, and a traditional knowledge system based on indigenous knowledge, which is often community-based.

maintain healthy lives, to share wealth, and to contribute to global solutions. For example, the cotton farmers in Mali have their own vernacular and bilingual management systems for farmers' associations. Farmers in that country now manage the vertically integrated chain of production and process logistics, which is based on indigenous management techniques and has been used for many years. Releasing the potential of local knowledge in sub-Saharan Africa holds much promise in the areas of agriculture, health, capacity formation and conflict management. As recognized by UNESCO/ISCU (1999), traditional knowledge systems "represent an enormous wealth. Not only do they harbour information as yet unknown to modern science, but they are also expressions of other ways of living in the world, other relationships between society and nature, and other approaches to the acquisition and construction of knowledge". It has been also noted that "...local knowledge plays a very important role in traditional medicine, agriculture, the management of biological diversity, etc." (Touré, 2003:19).

The indigenous or traditional knowledge systems of the LDCs have great potential and represent a hidden reservoir of underutilized creativity and knowledge.

The role of local innovations and indigenous discoveries stemming from Africa's base of indigenous knowledge (IK) is being considered more seriously (see Nwokeabia, 2002; UN Millennium Project, 2005; World Bank, 2004b). The increased use of local innovations of economic significance in agricultural production, which include crop breeding, grafting against pests, water harvesting, soil management, conservation and processing, is currently being seriously re-evaluated. A case in point is the zaï technique for enhanced agricultural productivity used in northern Burkina Faso, although it originated in Mali. The zaï technique, which consists in building pits in the ground, to which organic matter is added, covered with a thin layer of soil into which seeds are placed, has important functions for soil and water conservation, and erosion control for encrusted soil. The upgrading of the traditional zaï technique has been very successful. The diffusion of improved traditional agricultural practices such as zaï has led to positive results. In the majority of the villages, the application of scaled-up zaï techniques has resulted in surplus production of over 50 per cent. This technique has been used to increase crop yields and reduce the risks for food insecurity in the rural areas. Linking traditional techniques such as zaï with modern scientific ones has produced superior knowledge and a more dynamic use of indigenous knowledge.

However, indigenous knowledge systems do not by and large enable the development of the necessary capabilities to attain international competitiveness. This requires synergies between modern and traditional knowledge systems.

Despite these potentials, indigenous knowledge systems — alone or taken from a static perspective — do not by and large enable the development of the necessary capabilities to attain international competitiveness, such as scientific, design and engineering and other types of productive capabilities (Bell, 2006; Mugabe, 2002a). This requires synergies between modern and traditional knowledge systems, which can lead to the emergence of a new hybrid knowledge system in the LDCs. In this context a major policy challenge is how to ensure the protection and promotion of traditional knowledge and to ensure effective ownership in the LDCs.

In practice, the modern knowledge systems within LDCs do not build on and utilize the potential of traditional knowledge systems and are characterized by various weaknesses. Firstly, there are weak linkages within the system between different actors, government agencies, national laboratories, universities, industries and grassroots innovators which are not functioning together in an integrated systemic framework (Oyelaran- Oyeyinka, 2006; Lall, 2004; Mugabe, 2002b; UNCTAD, 1999; Sagasti, 2004; Touré, 2003; Bell, 2006). The science and technology systems in LDCs, by and large, demonstrate an absence of a "system" of technical change and development, low spending rates on R&D,

and a dearth of linkages with the private sector to provide funding for R&D (Oyelaran-Oyelinka, 2006; Lall, 2005; Touré, 2003).

Secondly, in most LDCs, the modern knowledge system has been elaborated on the basis of a particular R&D-centred model of innovation which interprets innovation as a simple supply-push phenomenon, where the demand side exerts no influence on the innovation process. Even where the formal institutional technological regimes have been set up, these do not function as knowledge systems in a cohesive and integrated manner, but tend to be underperforming and are essentially delinked from the local productive apparatus. There are few institutional channels through which economic agents can articulate their needs to the specialized suppliers of knowledge. The dearth of linkages between the formal and informal institutions, private and public institutions, and indigenous and exogenous technological innovations dissipate the considerable inputs already invested over the years (UNCTAD, 2003; Mugabe, 2002b; Oyelaran-Oyeyinka, 2006). Knowledge-based research activities are not carried out by organizations that actually produce goods and services, — that is, research is not done at the farm or at enterprise level but in public laboratories and universities that are not oriented towards the production needs of domestic enterprises (UNCTAD, 1995). Sparse, often disconnected R&D activities have little, if any links with the needs of domestic enterprises or farmers' organizations. In other words, they are not carried out in response to articulated demand by productive sectors. In Africa, public research institutes, which undertake between 60 and 90 per cent of total national R&D (Bell, 2006), tend to have weak links with the rest of the system (Akin Adubifa, 2004; Oyelaran-Oyeyinka, 2006). Demand factors play little, if any, role in the content and design of research in sub-Saharan Africa (Touré, 2003; Bell, 2006). Articulated connectedness is an important component of capability formation in any system, but in traditional knowledge systems this is not generally the case, as linkages amongst the components are typically very weak. This is especially problematic as regards the weak role of demand from the productive enterprises to scientific activity, that is — articulation of demand by firms for technology development activities is either weak or non-existent (Bell, 2006).

Thirdly, the modern knowledge systems remain highly donor-driven and much of R&D requires large donor inputs. For instance, in Senegal, between 30 and 40 per cent of scientists are French nationals; and local researchers have a severe disadvantage with respect to funding. Both human and technological resources in Africa are considered to be well below the critical threshold necessary for providing effective and innovative leadership in R&D (Touré, 2003). As shown in chapter 2, basic education and training are very weak in the LDCs. Moreover a large proportion of the highly educated people who are vital for the creation and diffusion of knowledge leave to work in other countries (braindrain).

Fourthly, the modern knowledge systems in LDCs are not well integrated with international knowledge systems. One indication of this is the strikingly low number of international standards adopted in most LDCs (see table 54). The data indicate that as of 2002, Cambodia had adopted only 3 international standards, Zambia had adopted 12, Rwanda 6, Mozambique 5 and a number of LDCs none at all. This contrasts with Tunisia, which has adopted 4,320, and the Republic of Korea, which has adopted 7,054, whilst Ireland has adopted 12,619 and the Netherlands 10,092. Standards are important as they may enable LDCs to improve the technical quality of their products and processes. This is becoming critical for entry into high-income markets. The costs of complying with standards are sizeable; also standardization can be premature or there can

In most LDCs, the modern knowledge system has been elaborated on the basis of a particular R&D-centred model of innovation which interprets innovation as a simple supply-push phenomenon, where the demand side exerts no influence on the innovation process.

The dearth of linkages between the formal and informal institutions, private and public institutions, and indigenous and exogenous technological innovations dissipate the considerable inputs already invested over the years.

The modern knowledge systems remain highly donor-driven and are not well integrated with international knowledge systems. This is reflected in the low number of international standards adopted in most LDCs.

TABLE 54. NATIONAL AND INTERNATIONAL STANDARD DEVELOPMENT ACTIVITIES IN LDCs AS AT 2002

	ISO status	Staff directly employed by ISO[a] member	Annual budget 2002 (CHF '000)[b]	Number of organisa-tions to which standards development work is delegated	Government subsidy in % of total revenue	Total number of standards published at 31/12/2002	Voluntary standards in % of number of standards	Number of inter-national standards adopted as national standard 31/12/2002
African LDCs								
Angola	Correspondent	..	341	..	100	..	..	..
Benin	Subscriber	10	300	120	60	4	50	..
Burundi	Subscriber	..	44	..	100	..	..	..
Dem. Rep of the Congo	Correspondent	141	7375	..	..	2	100	..
Eritrea	Subscriber	34	495	17	..	334	0	..
Ethiopia	Member	328	..	..	..	389	0	..
Lesotho	Subscriber	11	100	100	..	..	..	..
Madagascar	Correspondent	..	175	..	53	67	90	..
Malawi	Correspondent	145	2100	..	52	450	70	155
Mali	Suscriber	45	250	..	100	..	75	..
Mozambique	Correspondent	15	97	..	82	16	94	5
Niger	Suscriber	7	48953	..	100	..	..	..
Rwanda	Correspondent	..	639	..	100	6	50	6
Sudan	Correspondent	720	3500	4	..	628	0	1100
Uganda	Correspondent	85	1696	..	75	467	70	121
United Rep. of Tanzania	Member	123	1884	..	39	738	68	328
Zambia	Correspondent	..	216	1	85	400	97	12
Asian LDCs								
Bangladesh	Member	478	2347	..	11	1729	92	115
Cambodia	Suscriber	..	..	25	100	10	80	3
Nepal	Correspondent	104	387	..	100	654	99	30
Yemen	Correspondent	134	965	..	85	..	..	..

Source: UNIDO (2005).

  a International Organization for Standardization.
  b Swiss franc.

be excessive standardization, both of which are inappropriate for countries' level of technological development (Blind, 2005). Governments have a key role to play in setting up the necessary standards infrastructure and helping firms to develop the capabilities to meet standards.

Governments have a key role to play in setting up the necessary standards infrastructure and helping firms to develop the capabilities to meet standards.

In terms of global links, joint R&D research activities with other countries are also rather weak, as reflected in low levels of R&D collaboration with other developing countries or developed countries (UNCTAD, 2005). Moreover, productive arrangements with LDCs mainly involve one-way knowledge flows such as technology licensing agreements (UNCTAD, 2005). The brain drain coexists with large amounts of aid for technical cooperation, much of which fails to build local capacities, supporting instead the salaries of foreign consultants.

Finally, the traditional and modern knowledge systems are weakly linked at best, and largely unsupported by formal education (see chapter 2). Traditional knowledge systems are largely disconnected from the formal sources of knowledge and learning. This dualism replicates the pattern with regard to enterprise structures and financial systems presented earlier in this chapter.

3. SOME CASE STUDIES

This section summarizes some of the diversity in domestic knowledge systems in LDCs. It includes discussion of (i) institutions supporting agricultural research in Bangladesh; (ii) institutions supporting industrialization in the United Republic of Tanzania; and (iii) institutions supporting integration of traditional and knowledge systems in Ethiopia. These cases illustrate some of the general points made above.

(a) Agricultural research in Bangladesh

Within Bangladesh, there is a well-developed set of institutions engaged in agricultural research. Most agricultural research is publicly funded and carried out by ten Agricultural Research Institutes (ARIs). These are governed by the apex body, the Bangladesh Agricultural Research Council (BARC), which coordinates research carried out by ARIs, and is in charge of coordination, human resource development and evaluation of research.

The institutional framework also includes a number of leading research institutions, such as the International Centre for Diarrhoeal Disease Research, the University of Dhaka, the Bangladesh Agricultural University, Rajshahi University, the Bangladesh Rice Research Institute, the Bangladesh Agricultural Research Institute, the Bangladesh Institute of Postgraduate Studies in Agriculture, the University of Chittagong, the Atomic Energy Research Establishment, Dhaka Shishu Hospital and Jahangirnagar University. Impressive research in biotechnology, carried out at the renowned Bangladesh Agricultural Research Institute, (BARI), and aided by the International Rice Research Institute (IRI) and the International Center for Wheat and Maize Improvement, has made a significant contribution to increasing cereal yields and total agricultural production in recent years.

The agricultural research system in Bangladesh is one of the most advanced knowledge systems in the LDCs. However, it is vastly underfunded, uncoordinated, fragmented and disarticulated.

Despite the existence of the formal science and technology institutional regime, recent evaluations suggest that the overall research capacity in Bangladesh is weak, with the exception of some types of agricultural research, namely in biotechnology (World Bank, 2005b). Biotech research is supported by the government and has recently been initiated in leading institutions. However, the availability of funding for research, while it has improved over the last decade, still remains very limited and inadequate to meet the growing demands of the rural sector. Relatively uncompetitive salaries for scientists lead to brain drain and exacerbate the already dire skill shortage to meet the growing demand. Major funding for research comes from the Ministry of Science and Information and Communication Technology, and a few foreign funding agencies that fund agricultural biotechnology research, together with the World Bank. Projects include genetic improvement of jute and lentils, and work is being carried out on developing new rice varieties. While funding of research by the ministry has increased substantially over the last five years, it is still considered inadequate to capitalize on the country's vast research potential, especially as regards the level of scientific human resources. But the considerable domestic scientific research capacity offers only limited opportunities for practical training and is largely limited by the lack of a supportive institutional environment that could translate local scientific creativity and ingenuity into commercial gains.

This system is one of the most advanced knowledge systems in the LDCs. However, the current agricultural research system is vastly underfunded, uncoordinated, fragmented and disarticulated. Agricultural Research Institutes, in partnership with private agricultural business enterprises and NGOs, could play a critical role in raising productivity levels in agriculture. However, the agricultural research system is largely delinked from local production: "Very weak linkage exists between the RDIs (research and development institutes) and the production sectors (downstream) or human resource development (upstream). Consequently, R&D efforts are unproductive and often inappropriate. Research and Development Institutes are run more as academic institutions rather than as industrial enterprises. Support to industry is weak and as the source of knowledge for new industry, RDIs are inadequate." (ISESCO, 2005: 10). It is difficult to generate new and profitable technologies to meet the changing needs of farmers and agribusiness enterprises. In order to improve the income of small and marginal farmers and facilitate the growth of high-value-added produce such as fruits, vegetables, shrimps, milk, meat and poultry, public research institutes need to become much more engaged with private sector initiatives. This engagement would require multiple partnerships, and not only in regard to increased allocation of resources. It would also require an increase in knowledge-based partnerships to facilitate information and knowledge flows throughout the incipient national innovation system. Better linkages between the ARIs and the domestic agribusiness enterprises would help to increase and improve the production of horticultural crops such as fruit and vegetables, as well increase the production of milk and poultry products. Increased production of these products would in turn increase rural employment as well as demand for labour and facilitate greater investment by the private sector in input supply distribution, reduce high risk management systems that would create more rural non-farm jobs (World Bank, 2004b).

In the United Republic of Tanzania, despite the formal existence of science and technology institutions, learning and innovation by the private sector basically take place through limited inter-firm linkages among the domestic firms only.

(b) Institutions supporting the development of technological capabilities in the United Republic of Tanzania

In the United Republic of Tanzania, domestic research capability was built in public research centres. Research priorities were determined by the Tanzanian Commission for Science and Technology. Several science and technology support institutions were set up in the 1970s, but they lack awareness of private sector needs as well as the sources of motivation to carry out their mandates successfully (Lall, 1999; Wangwe, 1995a, 1995b). The choice of sectors in research areas was supply-driven, rather than based on an analysis of technological needs and problems of domestic productive private enterprises. University-industry linkages remain weak.

In order to benefit from the TNC presence, local companies need to bridge the significant technology gap.

Despite the formal existence of these science and technology institutions, learning and innovation by the private sector basically take place through limited inter-firm linkages among the domestic firms only. Linkage with external sources of knowledge such as public research centres is weak and the technology gap with foreign firms is considered too large to facilitate close cooperation with TNCs to foster domestic innovation. Local companies are generally unable to benefit from TNC presence, as the domestic absorption capacity is too weak and the technology gap between them and the foreign enterprises is too great for any effective transfer of know-how or design, or for joint R&D. In order to benefit from the TNC presence, local companies need to bridge the significant technology gap (UNCTAD, 2003).

Financial systems can hinder as well as facilitate firms' learning performance (see Goedhuys, 2005). Recent work on firm-level learning processes suggests that dualistic financial markets exert a differential impact on the innovative performance of firms in the United Republic of Tanzania. Formal financial markets, which tend to favour larger enterprises or foreign-owned firms, exert an adverse impact on local firms' opportunities to learn and to build capabilities necessary for competing. In this context, product and process innovation in local firms is mainly taking place as a result of internal learning and inter-firm linkages among the domestic firms. The existing sources of knowledge are underutilized. This exemplifies the current situation in most LDCs.

(c) Linking traditional knowledge systems with modern knowledge systems in Ethiopia

Local traditional knowledge can become a dynamic basis for sustainable development through new initiatives, as is demonstrated by the case of PROFIEET (Promotion of Farmer Innovation and Experimentation). PROFIEET is an example of a recent initiative launched in Ethiopia to enhance rural development (Assefa, 2004). It has been designed as part of the new paradigm of agricultural research and development that is based on traditional knowledge embedded in farmers' and rural communities, and upgrading of local knowledge in support of increased agricultural productivity.

PROFIEET is a recent initiative aimed at promoting greater use of traditional knowledge and farmers' innovation by creating a new policy environment for farmer-led research and extension. Farmers from Amaro and Gojam are working with international experts to improve the use of traditional techniques to arrest the infestation of flea beetles in and bacterial wilt (an aggressive plant disease), for which modern techniques have proved ineffective. In these particular cases, traditional treatment is considered more effective and is being utilized in tandem with more modern techniques to improve farmers' productivity in the region.

Local traditional knowledge can become a dynamic basis for sustainable development such as PROFIEET, a recent initiative launched in Ethiopia, to enhance rural development and upgrading of traditional local knowledge.

As part of the new approach to agricultural research and extension services in Ethiopia PROFIEET is proving to be a successful model for modernizing the traditional knowledge base of local communities. Similar recent initiatives have been proposed in order to include the demand side of the innovation equation, by getting the users, namely, the farmers themselves, more involved in the design of science and technology aimed at enhancing direct stakeholder participation, based on increased use of local knowledge and participatory agricultural research. It is also envisaged that the PROFIEET Steering Committee will work closely with the national research and extension services, and organize workshops, seminars and training sessions for local farmers. These platforms are intended to benefit directly the users of knowledge, in order to share international experiences in stakeholder-based participatory research activities conducted in other countries and local communities.

E. Conclusions

Since the late 1980s, many LDCs have been implementing economic reforms designed to give a greater role to market forces and enable the private sector to lead the development process. The mixed results of the first generation of reforms have led to a greater focus on the importance of institutions for economic growth and poverty reduction, and in particular the role of good governance. But there is an equal need to focus on the nature of the private sector and the institutions within which entrepreneurship is embedded.

The development of productive capacities does not occur in an institutional vacuum. Such capacities are created through the interplay of institutions, incentives and entrepreneurship geared to investment and innovation. In that perspective, this chapter has examined three key institutions: the firms; domestic financial systems; and domestic knowledge systems. These institutions are interlinked and their nature can either enable or constrain the three core processes through which productive capacities develop – capital accumulation, technological progress and structural change.

The evidence of this chapter shows that most LDCs have serious institutional weaknesses with regard to their firms, financial systems and knowledge systems.

Firstly, the size distribution of enterprises within LDCs is generally characterized by a "missing middle" in which a multitude of informal micro-enterprises coexist with a few large firms, and there is weak development of formal sector SMEs, particularly medium-sized domestic firms. There are weak linkages between the large firms and other enterprises, and the life cycle of enterprises is stunted. Few informal micro-enterprises become formal sector enterprises. Moreover, small firms are often unable to grow even when they are efficient. There is also wide heterogeneity in firm performance, although it is often found that the large firms tend to be more productive than the small firms with regard to most productivity indicators.

The development of productive capacities does not occur in an institutional vacuum. Such capacities are created through the interplay of institutions, incentives and entrepreneurship geared to investment and innovation.

Secondly, and closely related to the phenomenon of the "missing middle", both the domestic financial systems and domestic knowledge systems are dualistic. The financial markets are characterized by an informal segment (including transactions between friends and relatives or small-scale group arrangements, as well as transactions conducted by moneylenders, traders and landlords), as well as by formal banks. The domestic knowledge system includes a modern knowledge system alongside a traditional knowledge system. Different types of enterprises are embedded within these different systems.

Thirdly, the domestic financial systems have large liquid reserves, but as a ratio of GDP, domestic credit loaned to the private sector is four times lower than in low- and middle-income countries (15 per cent as against 60 per cent). Moreover, it has declined in the aftermath of financial liberalization, particularly in African LDCs. During the same period, interest rate spreads have increased in LDCs, and the level of monetization has actually declined in African LDCs. Financial liberalization has simply failed to promote productive investment, as reflected in the poor delivery of credit to the private sector and to SMEs in particular. Banks are partly constrained because of the weak capacity of local entrepreneurs to formulate acceptable business plans and also because of weak contract enforcement. But at the same time, it is clear that the banks are very risk-averse and prefer to do business in the very safe areas of government bonds.

Closely related to the phenomenon of the "missing middle", both the domestic financial systems and domestic knowledge systems are dualistic.

Fourthly, modern knowledge systems are vital to international competitiveness, but they are fragmented. Specialized creators of knowledge, such as research institutions, are not responsive to the demands of users. A particularly striking feature of the case study evidence is that even LDCs which have done well in developing garment exports, mainly on the basis of different trade preference regimes, have very weak knowledge systems supporting these activities. Evidence on the use of international standards within LDCs also suggests that there is a particular problem in terms of the extent to which the domestic knowledge systems are outward-looking and able to keep up with ever-rising international standards.

These results have important policy implications. The weaknesses of the first-generation reforms have led to policy changes, and there is now a new emphasis on improving the overall investment climate. The thrust of this effort has been to improve the overall institutional environment in which market forces operate, rather than meso-level institutional arrangements. Moreover, it has particularly focused on reducing the costs of doing business which arise because of red tape and bureaucratic rules. These initiatives are certainly important. However, the weak development of firms in LDCs, their high degree of heterogeneity and the segmentation of financial and knowledge systems suggest that this will not be enough. Policy also needs to develop key meso-level institutional arrangements (such as firm linkages and networks) and firm-level capabilities. The evidence shows that markets are indeed very competitive at "pruning out" less efficient firms. However, the "churning" process may be so strong that it may not permit new entrants to survive, grow and prosper in an open global economy. The policy thrust should therefore shift from an exclusive focus on interventions that are intended to increase competition to a policy which develops both the framework conditions and the entrepreneurial capabilities which will enable firms to grow and prosper. This will be taken up in the last chapter of this Report.

In the previous chapter, it was shown that LDCs have a low level and poor-quality stock of physical infrastructure in transport, communications and energy. Increased infrastructure investment is certainly a necessary part of a strategy for development productive capacities in the LDCs. But from the analysis in this chapter, it is unlikely that infrastructure investment alone will work. What is needed is an infrastructure-plus policy which includes policies which address the institutional deficiencies with regard to the nature of domestic firms, financial systems and knowledge systems. Domestic financial systems and domestic knowledge systems also need to be addressed as complementary institutions supporting the twin processes of investment and innovation. Unless these institutions are created and strengthened, the LDCs are not likely to be able to compete effectively in the global economy and to reduce poverty. In the end, the development of productive capacities will depend on the actions of firms, linkages among them and the institutions which support them, together with public action that harnesses underutilized potentials, and catalyses and coordinates change. A private-sector-led approach which does not pay attention to the nature of the private sector will inevitably fail in very poor economies.

Domestic financial systems and domestic knowledge systems need to be addressed as complementary institutions supporting the twin processes of investment and innovation.

Notes

1. Baumol (1990), argued that different incentive structures in different environments can either result in entrepreneurship that contributes to economic growth (productive entrepreneurship) or in rent-seeking behaviour, speculation, tax evasion, limiting competition and corruption (unproductive entrepreneurship), or may even lead to entrepreneurial activities that are detrimental to economic growth (destructive entrepreneurship).

2. The website for these studies is http://www.worldbank.org/EnterpriseSurveys/ICAs.aspx

3. Unit labour costs estimated as the ratio of wages to value added in dollars at the firm level, averaged across the sample of firms using a deflator for physical value added (World Bank, 2004b).

4. For the cases of Nepal and Bhutan, median ratio of investment to capital: 0.05 (Bhutan), 0.01 (Nepal) vs. estimated depreciation capital rate of 0.1 (see World Bank, 2002).

5. The level of monetization refers to the ratio of money supply to GDP. As defined in the World Development Indicators database, money supply is defined as the sum of narrow money supply (M1) and quasi-money (QM). Money (M1) and quasi-money (QM) comprise the sum of currency outside banks, demand deposits other than those of the central Government (M1), and the time, savings and foreign currency deposits of resident sectors other than the central Government (QM) (World Bank, 2005a).

6. It has also been argued that financial liberalization tends to increase the rate of non-performing loans and to raise the interest rate spread thereafter as banks tend to pass the cost of bad loans onto other borrowers (Akyüz, 1993).

7. It is important to note that the private sector includes households. The domestic credit to the private sector to GDP ratio therefore captures credit disbursed for both private investment and household consumption. Data limitation makes it impossible to disentangle household credit from enterprise credit. International Financial Statistics, the IMF database which provides country monetary data, does not disaggregate the private sector into household and non-household. It is, however, largely recognized that in poor countries only high-income households have access to formal finance to finance consumption.

8. It would be interesting to measure the contribution of "structural liquidity" (resulting from aid-financed government domestic spending) to the excess liquidity prevailing in many African countries (IMF, 2003a) .

9. The principal–agent problem is concerned with difficulties that arise between the principal and the agent in situations where information is incomplete and asymmetric.

10. A situation in which "the formal financial system services only large firms leaving SMEs with little access to financial services" (World Bank, 2002, p. 75).

11. Financial institutions such as insurance, pension fund systems and leasing companies are weakly developed.

12. "The FSAP, a joint IMF and World Bank effort introduced in May 1999, aims to increase the effectiveness of efforts to promote the soundness of financial systems in member countries. Supported by experts from a range of national agencies and standard-setting bodies, work under the program seeks to identify the strengths and vulnerabilities of a country's financial system; to determine how key sources of risk are being managed; to ascertain the sector's developmental and technical assistance needs; and to help prioritize policy responses", available at http://www.imf.org/external/np/fsap/fsap.asp.

13. Foreign banks, which capture most creditworthy clients, tend to display better credit quality than domestic ones.

14. A high lending rate also implies that only highly risky projects can be considered bankable. On the one hand, this enhances the vulnerability of the banking system itself (a vicious circle of weak loan repayment), while on the other hand, considering the weak competitiveness of the financial sector, it may generate opportunities for rents for banks.

15. More precisely, 84 per cent of enterprises reported that the cost of finance was the greatest obstacle to their performance and 75 per cent and 74 per cent reported that access to domestic credit and to foreign credit respectively were major obstacles. In fact, financial problems were reported as more severe than corruption, electricity problems or even macroeconomic instability (IMF, 2004).

16. A national innovation system (NIS) has been defined as "a set of distinct institutions which jointly and individually contribute to the development and diffusion of new technologies and which provides the framework within which governments form and implement policies to influence the innovation process. As such, it is a system of interconnected institutions and formal institutions, to create, store and transfer the knowledge skills and artifacts which are defined as new technologies" (Metcalfe, 1995:38).

17. Recent research highlights the role of complementarities between innovation performance and countries' distinct financial infrastructure that can help to explain observable

differences in national industrial structures'. While market-dominated or "outsider" financial systems (equity-based) are more conducive to promoting new generic innovations (because of the capacity to underwrite higher degrees of risk and uncertainty), the "insider" or bank-based financial systems are more compatible with supporting the development of more established technologies (Block, 2002).

References

Acemoglu, D., Johnson, S. and Robinson, J. (2004). Institutions as the fundamental cause of long-run growth. Prepared for the *Handbook of Economic Growth* edited by Philippe Aghion and Steve Durlauf.

Akin Adubifa, O. (2004). An assessment of science and technology capacity building in sub-Saharan Africa. African Technology Policy Studies Network, Special Paper Series No. 19, Nairobi, Kenya.

Akyüz, Y. (1992). On financial deepening and efficiency. UNCTAD Discussion Paper No. 43, Geneva.

Akyüz, Y. (1993). Financial liberalization: The key issues. UNCTAD Discussion Paper No. 56, Geneva.

Albaladejo, M. and Schmitz, H. (2000). Helping African SMEs to compete in regional and global markets: A strategic framework. Institute for Development Studies, University of Sussex, UK.

Assefa, A. (2004). Promotion of former innovation and experimentation in Ethiopia (PROFIEET): A changing paradigm in agricultural research and extension approach, Addis Ababa, mimeo.

Bangladesh Enterprise Institute (2004). Taking stock and charting a path for SMEs in Bangladesh.

Bardhan, P. (2005). *Scarcity, Conflicts and Cooperation: Essays in the Political and Institutional Economics of Development*. Cambridge, Mass. MIT Press.

Baumol, W.J. (1990). Entrepreneurship: productive, unproductive and destructive. *Journal of Political Economy*, 98 (5): 893–921.

Bell, M. and Albu, M. (1999). Knowledge systems and technological dynamism in industrial clusters in developing countries. *World Development*, 27(9): 1715–1734.

Bell, M. (2006). Draft background discussion paper for the L20 workshop. L20 Communiqué: Science and Technology for Development Conference, Maastricht, March 7–8, MERIT/INTECH.

Biggs, T., and Shah, M. (2006). African SMEs, networks, and manufacturing performance. World Bank Policy Research Working Paper No. 4831.

Bigsten, A. et al. (2003). Credit constraints in manufacturing enterprises in Africa. *Journal of African Economies*, 12: 104-125.

Bigsten, A. and Soderbom, M. (2005). What have we learned from a decade of manufacturing enterprise surveys in Africa? World Bank Policy Research Working Paper No. 3798.

Blind, K. (2005). Standards, technical change and IPRs: Lessons from industrialized countries. Industrial Development Report 2005 Background Paper Series. UNIDO, Vienna.

Block, T. (2002). Financial systems, innovation and economic performance. MERIT-Infonomics Research Memorandum Series. Maastricht Economic Research Institute on Innovation and Technology, Maastricht, The Netherlands.

Blomström, M. and Kokko, A. (1998). Multinational corporations and spillovers. *Journal of Economic Surveys,* 12(3): 247–277.

Brilleau, A. et al. (2005). *Le secteur informel: Performances, insertion, perspectives*. Enquête 1-2-3, phase 2, STATECO No 99.

Brownbridge, M. and Gayi, S.K. (1999). Progress, constraints and limitations of financial sector reforms in the least developed countries. Finance and Development Research Programme, Working Paper Series, No. 7. Institute for Development Policy and Management, University of Manchester, UK.

Chandler, A.D. (1977). *The Visible Hand,* Cambridge, Harvard University Press, Mass., USA.

Èihák, M. and Podpiera, R. (2005). Bank behavior in developing countries: Evidence from East Africa. IMF Working Paper, 05/129, Washington, DC.

Coase, R. (1937). The nature of the firm. *Economica*, 4(16): 386–405.

Commission for Africa (2005). *Our Common Interest*. Report of the Commission for Africa, March 2005.

David, M. (2005). The LDC domestic financial sector. Background paper prepared for *The Least Developed Countries Report 2006*, UNCTAD, Geneva.

Dosi, G., Teece, D.J. and Winter, S.G. (1992). Toward a theory of corporate coherence: Preliminary remarks, in Dosi, G., Giannetti, R., and Toninelli, P.A. (eds.) *Technology and Enterprise in a Historical Perspective*.

Elhiraika, B. and Nkuunziza, J. (2005). Facilitating firm entry, growth and survival with special attention to SMEs. Economic Commission for Africa. Mimeo.

Fafchamps, M. (1999). Ethnicity and credit in African manufacturing. Stanford University, USA.

Fivawo, A., Simonetti, R. and Wuyts, M. (2005). Banking on rural productive capacities: the GAPI experience in Mozambique. Background paper prepared for the *The Least Developed Countries Report 2006*, UNCTAD, Geneva.

Gelbard, E.A. and Leite, S.P. (1999). Measuring financial development in sub-Saharan Africa. IMF Working Paper WP/99/105, Washington, DC.

Glick, R. and Hutchison, M. (2002). Capital controls and exchange rate instability in developing economies. Pacific Basin Working Paper Series, No. PB00-05, Federal Reserve Bank of San Francisco, USA.

Goedhuys, M. (2005). Learning, production innovation and firm heterogeneity in Tanzania. United Nations University, Institute for New Technologies, Discussion Paper Series No. 7, Maastricht, Netherlands.

Harding, A., Söderbom, M. and Teal, F. (2004). Survival and success among African manufacturing firms. Centre for Study of African Economies, Department of Economics, Working Paper No.5, University of Oxford, UK.

Ishikawa, S. (1998). Underdevelopment of the market economy and the limits of economic liberalization. In *Japanese Views on Economic Development: Diverse paths to the market*. (eds.) K. Ohno and I. Ohno, Routledge, London and New York.

ILO (2004). *World Employment Report 2004-05, Employment, Productivity and Poverty Reduction*, International Labour Office, Geneva.

IMF (2003a). Uganda: Financial system stability assessment, including reports on the observance of standards and codes on the following topics: monetary and financial policy transparency, banking supervision, securities regulation, insurance regulation, corporate governance, and payment systems. IMF Country Report No. 03/97. Washington, DC.

IMF (2003b). Tanzania: Financial system stability assessment, including reports on the observance of standards and codes on banking supervision. IMF Country Report No. 03/241, Washington, DC.

IMF (2004). Republic of Mozambique: Financial system stability assessment including report on the observance of standards and codes on the following topics: Banking supervision, payment systems, and anti-money laundering and combating the financing of terrorism. IMF Country Report No. 04/52. Washington, DC.

IMF (2005a). Rwanda: Financial system stability assessment, including reports on the observance of standards and codes on the following topics: Monetary and financial policy transparency, banking supervision, and the FATF recommendations for anti-money laundering and combating the financing of terrorism, Washington, DC.

IMF (2005b). Senegal: Financial system stability assessment update. IMF Country Report No. 05/126, Washington, DC.

ISESCO (2005). Transfer of scientific research results to the production sector. http://www.isesco.org.ma/pubEngTrSCResch/page 10.htm

Kaldor, N. (1967). *Strategic Factors in Economic Development*. New York State School of Industrial and Labor Relations, Cornell University, Ithaca, New York.

Kauffmann, C. (2005). Financing SMEs in Africa. Policy Insights No. 7, OECD Development Centre.

Kozul-Wright, Z. (2000). The firm in the innovation process. In: Singer, H., Hatti, M. and Tandon, R. (eds.) *Technological Diffusion in Third World*, Delhi.

Lall, S. (1999).(ed.) *The Technological Response to Import Liberalization in Sub-Saharan Africa 1999*. Macmillan: London.

Lall, S. (2004). Reinventing industrial strategy: The role of government policy in building industrial competitiveness. UNCTAD G-24 Discussion Paper Series, No. 28, United Nations, Geneva.

Lall, S. (2005). FDI, AGOA and manufactured exports by a landlocked, least developed African economy: Lesotho. *Journal of Development Studies*, 41 (6): 998–1022.

Liedholm, C. (2001). Small firm dynamics: evidence from Africa and Latin America. This paper was commissioned for the project on "The Role of Small & Medium Enterprises in East Asia" organized by the World Bank Institute.

Lundvall, B.A. (1988). Innovation as an interactive process: From user-producer to national system of innovation. In Dosi, G. et al. (1988). *Technology and Economic Theory*. Pinter Publishers, London.

Malhotra, Y. (2003). Measuring knowledge assets of a nation: Knowledge systems for development. Paper delivered at the Ad Hoc Group of Experts Meeting on Knowledge Systems for Development, United Nations, New York, 4–5 September 2003.

Mazumdar, D. and. Mazaheri, A. (2003), The African manufacturing firm: an analysis based on firm surveys in seven countries in sub-Saharan Africa, Routledge, London and New York.

McKinley, T. (2005). Economic alternatives for sub-Saharan Africa: "Poverty Traps", MDG-based strategies and accelerated capital accumulation. Draft paper for the G-24 Meeting, 15–16 September 2005. New York.

Mead, D.C. and Liedholm, C. (1998). The dynamics of micro and small enterprises in developing countries, *World Development*, 26: 61–74.

Mengistae, T. (2001). Indigenous ethnicity and entrepreneurial success in Africa: Some evidence from Ethiopia. Policy Research Working Paper No. 2543, World Bank, Washington, DC.

Metcalfe, J. (1995). The economic foundations of technology policy: equilibrium and evolutionary perspectives, in: Stoneman, P. (ed.), *Handbook of economics of innovation and technology change*, Oxford: Blackwell.

Mugabe, J. (2002a). Biotechnology in Sub-Saharan Africa: Towards a policy research agenda. African Technology Policy Studies Network, Special Series Paper No. 3. Nairobi, Kenya.

Mugabe, J. (2002b). Science and technology in the New Partnership for Africa's Development. Presentation at seminar in University Partnership Network for International Development (UniPID), 2 December 2002, University of Jyväskylä.

Nelson, R.R. and Winter, S. (1982). *An Evolutionary Theory of Economic Change*, Cambridge, Mass: Harvard University Press.

Nissanke, M.K. (2001). Financing enterprise development in sub-Saharan Africa. *Cambridge Journal of Economics*, (25): 343–367.

North, D.C. (1981). *Structure and Change in Economic History*. W.W. Norton and Company, New York and London.

Nwokeabia, H. (2002). Why the industrial revolution missed Africa: A "traditional knowledge" perspective, Economic Commission for Africa, ECA/ESPD/WPS/01/02.

Oyelaran-Oyeyinka, B. (2005). Systems of innovation and underdevelopment: An institutional perspective. Institute for New Technologies, Discussion Paper Series 2005-1, United Nations University, Maastricht, Netherlands.

Oyelaran-Oyeyinka, B. (2006). Learning hi-tech and knowledge in local systems: The Otigba computer hardware cluster in Nigeria. UNU-MERIT Working Paper Series, No. 007, United Nations University, Maastricht, Netherlands.

Penrose, E. (1959). *The Theory of Growth in the Firm*. Blackwells, Oxford.

Ramachandran, V. and Shah, M.K. (1999). Minority entrepreneurship and firm performance in sub-Saharan Africa. *Journal of Development Studies*, 36 (2): 71–87.

Ranis, G. and Stewart, F. (1999) V-Goods and the role of the urban informal sector in development. *Economic Development and Cultural Change*, 47 (2): 259–288.

Ranja, T. (2003). Success under duress: A comparison of indigenous Africans and East African Asian entrepreneurs. Globalisation and East Africa. Working Paper Series No. 7. Economic and Social Research Foundation.

Rodrik, D. (2004). Getting Institutions Right. Harvard University, Mass. Mimeo. http://ksghome.harvard.edu/~drodrik/ifo-institutions%20article%20_April%202004_.pdf

Sagasti, F.R. (2004). *Knowledge and Innovation for Development: The Sisyphus Challenge of the 21st Century*. Edward Elgar Publishing.

Schapiro, N. (1991). Firms, markets and innovation. Journal of Post Keynesian Economics, 14 (1): 49–60.

Schumpeter, J. (1947). *Capitalism, Socialism and Democracy*. London, Unwin, third edition, 1950, New York, Harper and Row.

Shiferaw, A. (2005). *Firm Heterogeneity and Market Selection in Sub-Saharan Africa: Does it Spur Industrial Progress?* Institute of Social Studies. Working paper No. 414, The Hague.

Thisen, J.K. (2004) Mobilization of savings through increased monetization of African economies. Powerpoint presentation at Economic Commission for Africa Workshop on "Financial Systems and Mobilization of Resources in Africa", Nairobi, 1–3 November 2004.

Touré, O. (2003). Research for development in West and Central Africa. Background paper prepared for the International Development Research Centre in preparation for the Corporate Strategy and Program Framework 2005-2010, IDRC, Canada.

Tybout, J.R. (2000). Manufacturing firms in developing countries: How well do they do, and why? *Journal of Economic Literature*, 38(1): 11–44.

UNCTAD (1995) Strengthening of linkages between the national research and development systems and industrial sectors. Report of the Panel of Experts to the Commission on Science and Technology for Development (E/CN.16/1995.8)

UNCTAD (1996). *The Least Developed Countries Report 1996*, United Nations publication, sales no. E.96.II.D.3.

UNCTAD (1999). Science, Technology and Innovation Policy Review, STIP, Jamaica. Geneva.

UNCTAD (2001). Growing micro and small enterprises in LDCs: The "missing middle" in LDCs: Why micro and small enterprises are not growing? Enterprise Development Series UNCTAD/ITE/TEB/5/, Geneva.

UNCTAD (2003). Africa's technology gap: Case studies on Kenya, Ghana, Tanzania and Uganda. UNCTAD/ITE/IPC/Misc. 13. United Nations publication.

UNCTAD (2005). *World Investment Report 2005: Transnational Corporations and the Internationalization of R&D.* United Nations publication, sales no. E.05.II.D.10.

UNESCO/ISCU (1999). Science Agenda: Framework for Action, agreed at the UNESCO/ ISCU World Conference on Science for the Twenty-first Century: A New Commitment, 1999.

UN Millennium Project (2005). Innovation: Applying Knowledge in Development. Task-force on Science, Technology and Innovation. Earthscan, London.

Van Biesebroeck, J. (2005). Firm size matters: Growth and productivity growth in African manufacturing. *Economic Development and Cultural Change*, 53(3): p. 545.

Wangwe, S. (ed.) (1995a). *Exporting Africa: Technology, Trade and Industrialization in sub-Saharan Africa.* Routledge, London and New York.

Wangwe, S. (1995b). Tanzania's growth potential: a background paper for the country's 1995 economic memorandum (CEM). Economic and Social Research Foundation (ESRF), Tanzania.

Williamson, O.E. (1983). Credible commitments: Using hostages to support exchange, *American Economic Review*, 73(4): 519–540.

Williamson, O. (1985). *Economic Institutions of Capitalism*, New York Free Press.

World Bank (1994). *Adjustment in Africa: Reforms, results and the road ahead.* World Bank Policy Research Report. Washington, DC.

World Bank (2004a). An assessment of the investment climate in Zambia. Investment Climate Assessment. Washington, DC.

World Bank, (2004b). Indigenous knowledge: Local pathways to development. Knowledge and Learning Group. Washington, DC.

World Bank (2005a). World Development Indicators Database 2005. Washington, DC.

World Bank (2005b). Revitalising the agricultural technology system in Bangladesh. Development Series, Agriculture and Rural Development. Washington, DC.

The Demand Constraint

A. Introduction

The development of productive capacities cannot be understood without addressing demand-side constraints as well as supply-side constraints. The previous two chapters have focused on the latter, examining the low stock and poor quality of physical infrastructure in the LDCs and also some key institutional weaknesses which constrain investment, technological learning and innovation. But even if these supply-side issues are successfully resolved, the development of productive capacities will still be constrained if there is no demand stimulus which provides an inducement to capital accumulation and technological progress. Decisions to spend on the expansion of physical production capacity are based on the expected growth of markets. Similarly, decisions of entrepreneurs to devote time and money to technological learning are based on the expected rents arising from innovations that increase their share of existing markets and also create new markets.

As noted earlier in this Report, the existence of productive capacities only creates a potentiality for production and growth. Whether or not that potential will be realized depends on whether productive capacities are also utilized. This depends on the stimulus of demand. In situations where there is a lack of effective demand, existing productive capacities will be underutilized. Moreover, where productive capacities are underutilized, there will be weak incentives for their further development. The sustained development of productive capacities occurs when there is a virtuous circle in which the development of productive capacities and the growth of demand mutually reinforce each other.

Starting and sustaining this interaction between growing demand and the development of productive capacities is particularly difficult in the LDCs. Generalized and persistent poverty means that national markets offer limited opportunities for efficient mass production. External markets are growing, but domestic entrepreneurs do not usually have the capabilities, the infrastructure or the institutions which can enable them to reach them, or in activities in which they do have such capabilities, they face fierce competition. As a result, productive resources and capabilities within LDCs are underutilized. This is yet another element of the poverty trap within which very poor countries are enmeshed.

Although the first generation of development economists were well aware of the influence of effective demand on the potential for development, the role of demand in processes of economic growth has been since neglected. As a result, there is a very limited literature on the role of demand in development in very poor countries. Against this background, this chapter addresses the subject in a preliminary and partial way. It seeks to provide a better understanding of the components of demand and also the constraints on demand in the LDCs.

The chapter is divided into three major sections. Section B identifies the relative importance of the five basic components of demand — private consumption, investment, government consumption expenditure, exports and imports — for a sample of the LDCs during the period 1993–2003. This shows that domestic demand makes the largest contribution to economic growth in almost all the LDCs. But there is also a strong association between export growth

The development of productive capacities cannot be understood without addressing demand-side constraints as well as supply-side constraints.

Generalized and persistent poverty means that national markets offer limited opportunities for efficient mass production. As a result, productive resources and capabilities within LDCs are underutilized.

and economic growth. Section C focuses more closely on domestic demand by considering intersectoral linkages. In particular, it examines how the growth of agricultural incomes can provide an important stimulus for investment in manufacturing industry and services within very poor countries. Such agricultural growth linkages are one of the most important mechanisms through which growing demand and the development of productive capacities can be linked in a virtuous circle in the LDCs. Section D extends the analysis by examining why exports also matter. It discusses this from a demand-side perspective by examining the extent to which the growth of a group of LDCs has been constrained by their balance of payments over the last 25 years. The analysis also identifies the contribution that capital inflows and transfers have made in financing current account deficits, and thus enabling the import content of domestic demand to be met. Section E summarizes the main points of the chapter.

B. The relative importance of different components of demand

This section identifies for a selected group of LDCs which components of demand have been driving their economic growth. It then highlights the complementarities between each of the components of demand and the crucial impact that exports have on current economic growth.

The traditional macroeconomic identity ($Y = C + I + G + X - M$, where Y is aggregate demand or GDP, C is private consumption, I is investment, G is government consumption expenditure, X is exports and M is imports) is used here to identify which components of demand have contributed most to the economic growth of a selected group of LDCs.[1] It is necessary to stress that all components of demand are highly interdependent, and particularly that all components of demand have an import content, so that how fast private consumption, investment and government consumption expenditure can grow partly depends on how fast exports grow.[2] Also, it is important to remember that in using accounting identities no unidirectional causation is implied between output and its components.

Table 55 ranks 15 LDCs in descending order according to their average annual growth rates of real GDP over the period 1993–2003. It also includes the accounting contributions of C, I, G, X and M to economic growth. The table gives the growth rates of each component of demand (section a); the weights, defined as the share of each component of demand in GDP (section b); and the contribution of each component of demand to GDP growth (section c), which is captured by the combined effect of the respective growth rates and weights.

Taking the countries as a whole, it can be seen that, on average, the weight of private consumption is the highest (79 per cent), followed by imports (34 per cent), exports (23 per cent), investment (17 per cent) and government consumption expenditure (12 per cent). The component of demand with the highest average annual growth rate for the group of LDCs is investment (7.9 per cent), followed by exports (6.8 per cent) and government consumption expenditure (5.3 per cent). Private consumption has grown the least. The fastest-growing countries are generally associated with the fast growth of investment and exports. The rate of growth of investment and exports is high in Mozambique, Rwanda, Cambodia, Bangladesh and Ethiopia. These countries are examples of the *virtuous* link that can exist between the two exogenous components of demand — investment and exports. By contrast, in other

---

All components of demand are highly interdependent, and they all have an import content, so that how fast private consumption, investment and government consumption expenditure can grow partly depends on how fast exports grow.

The fastest-growing countries are generally associated with the fast growth of investment and exports.

TABLE 55. CONTRIBUTION OF COMPONENTS OF DEMAND[a] TO REAL AVERAGE ANNUAL GDP GROWTH RATES IN SELECTED LDCs, 1993–2003

	Growth rates[b] (%) (1)						Weights[c] (2)					Contribution of components of demand[d] (3)							
	Y	C	I	G	X	M	C/Y	I/Y	G/Y	X/Y	M/Y	Y	C a	I b	G c	X d	M e	DD a+b+c	NE d-e
Mozambique	8.1	1.6	15.2	6.2	18.0	4.0	0.8	0.3	0.1	0.2	0.4	100	15.7	51.6	6.9	44.3	18.5	74.2	25.8
Rwanda	7.0	4.8	8.6	6.8	11.4	0.8	0.9	0.2	0.1	0.1	0.3	100	61.4	18.0	11.4	12.3	3.1	90.8	9.2
Cambodia	6.5	4.4	12.7	8.0	20.7	14.9	0.9	0.2	0.1	0.4	0.5	100	57.6	30.2	6.2	121.9	115.8	93.9	6.1
Benin	5.2	2.2	16.2	8.0	1.4	3.8	0.8	0.2	0.1	0.1	0.2	100	30.7	66.3	16.3	3.4	16.7	113.3	-13.3
Bangladesh	5.1	3.5	9.3	5.2	10.9	7.1	0.8	0.2	0.1	0.1	0.2	100	52.7	39.4	4.6	26.0	22.6	96.6	3.4
Senegal	4.9	1.2	10.0	7.3	7.2	1.8	0.7	0.2	0.1	0.3	0.3	100	15.8	32.5	20.3	40.8	9.4	68.5	31.5
Ethiopia	4.7	2.1	6.4	15.7	11.4	7.9	0.8	0.2	0.2	0.1	0.2	100	34.2	19.5	51.8	28.1	33.6	105.5	-5.5
UR of Tanzania	4.5	1.5	3.4	11.5	4.2	0.9	0.8	0.2	0.2	0.2	0.3	100	25.2	15.3	49.4	16.6	6.5	89.9	10.1
Burkina Faso	4.4	3.9	10.5	-1.4	2.7	4.3	0.8	0.2	0.1	0.1	0.2	100	68.9	47.5	-3.2	4.7	17.9	113.2	-13.2
Mauritania	4.2	4.5	11.5	5.0	-2.8	3.7	0.7	0.2	0.2	0.3	0.4	100	76.8	59.1	18.3	-19.1	35.1	154.2	-54.2
Togo	4.3	5.1	9.0	1.1	3.5	5.6	0.7	0.2	0.1	0.4	0.4	100	81.3	32.2	2.8	31.2	47.5	116.3	-16.3
Gambia	3.6	1.9	2.3	5.2	2.9	0.5	0.8	0.2	0.1	0.5	0.6	100	42.1	11.8	15.1	39.1	8.1	69.0	31.0
Malawi	3.0	4.2	-12.8	1.0	3.1	-0.1	0.9	0.2	0.2	0.3	0.5	100	132.1	-71.1	6.8	30.8	-1.4	67.9	32.1
Madagascar	2.6	2.9	7.1	2.7	3.4	7.6	0.8	0.1	0.1	0.2	0.2	100	93.0	34.8	8.3	22.8	58.9	136.1	-36.1
Zambia	2.0	-0.7	9.8	-2.0	5.1	2.1	0.7	0.2	0.1	0.4	0.4	100	-23.1	85.3	-12.1	88.2	38.3	50.1	49.9
Average	4.7	2.9	8.0	5.4	6.9	4.3	0.8	0.2	0.1	0.2	0.3	100	51.0	31.5	13.5	32.7	28.7	96.0	4.0

Source: UNCTAD secretariat estimates based on World Bank, *World Development Indicators 2005*, CD-ROM.

a   Y=GDP; the components of demand are: C=private consumption, I=investment, G=government expenditure, X=exports, and M=imports.
b   The countries have been ranked from the highest to the lowest real average annual GDP growth rate.
c   The weights have been calculated by dividing each component, measured in constant local currency, by GDP.
d   The figures were calculated by multiplying the growth rate of each GDP component by its weight and by normalizing their sum to 100.

countries where investment growth was strong, but exports grew slowly, growth performance was not so impressive, for example, Burkina Faso, Mauritania, Togo, Madagascar and Zambia. Private consumption has grown fastest in Togo (5.1 per cent), Rwanda (4.8 per cent), Mauritania (4.5 per cent) and Cambodia (4.4 per cent).

When the contribution of each component of demand to GDP growth is considered, the component with the highest contribution to GDP growth is private consumption (51 per cent), followed by exports (33 per cent) and investment (31 per cent), on average. These results reflect the weight of the different components of demand as well as their growth rates.

Table 56 orders countries according to the contribution of the two most important components to GDP growth for the whole period, 1993–2003, and for two sub-periods, 1993–1998 and 1998–2003. Private consumption and investment have been the most important in the majority of countries, which were not necessarily the fastest growers. Private consumption and investment have been the main driving forces through the two sub-periods in Bangladesh, Burkina Faso, Madagascar and Mauritania. In no other countries have the same two components of demand been the driving force in all three periods. But over the whole period, it can be seen that investment and exports have been the driving force in Mozambique, Zambia and Senegal; exports and private consumption in Cambodia, The Gambia and Malawi; and, private consumption and government consumption expenditure in Ethiopia and the United Republic of Tanzania.

There is no systematic pattern in the contribution of different demand components to GDP growth in the fastest-growing LDCs during this period. Regarding the six countries that have experienced the highest GDP growth over the full period, economic growth in Rwanda and Bangladesh has been driven by private consumption, the investment component played a leading role in Benin and Mozambique, and exports were the leading component in Cambodia and Senegal.

In the LDCs, where investment growth was strong, but exports grew slowly, growth performance was not so impressive.

The component with the highest contribution to GDP growth is private consumption, followed by exports and investment.

TABLE 56. LDCs CLASSIFIED ACCORDING TO THE CONTRIBUTION OF DEMAND COMPONENTS TO GDP GROWTH,
1993–2003, 1993–1998 AND 1998–2003

Contribution of demand to GDP growth, highest and second highest, respectively	1993–2003	1993–1998	1998–2003
C, I	Bangladesh Burkina Faso Madagascar Rwanda Mauritania Togo	Bangladesh Burkina Faso Madagascar Rwanda Mauritania	Bangladesh Benin Burkina Faso Madagascar Mauritania
I, C	Benin	Benin	Gambia
I, X	Mozambique Zambia	Mozambique	Zambia
X, I	Senegal	Zambia	Cambodia Mozambique Togo
X, C	Cambodia	Gambia Senegal	
C, X	Gambia Malawi	Cambodia Malawi Togo	
C, G	Ethiopia United Rep. of Tanzania	Ethiopia United Rep. of Tanzania	Rwanda
G, C			Malawi
G, I			Senegal
G, X			Ethiopia United Rep. of Tanzania

Source: UNCTAD secretariat estimates based on table 1.

Notes: Countries have been grouped according to their first and second highest GDP components.
C is private consumption, I is investment, G is government consumption expenditure and X is exports.

Domestic demand has contributed the most to GDP growth in the majority of the LDCs considered.

A further subdivision of GDP into domestic demand and net exports shows that the share of domestic demand in GDP is larger than the share of net exports in terms of its contribution to economic growth (see table 55).[3] Indeed, the share of domestic demand was greater than 50 per cent in all countries. For the countries (Mozambique, Rwanda, Cambodia and Benin) that experienced the highest GDP growth during the reference period, 1993–2003, most of the growth comes from the domestic demand. For nine out of fifteen LDCs, domestic demand grew at a faster rate than net exports. However, it would be fallacious to assume that this implies that exports do not matter as a component of demand. This is because the concept of net exports disguises the contribution that exports (and foreign exchange) make to economic growth. For instance, if exports and imports are equal, net exports are zero, which implies that there is no contribution to economic growth from exports, but exports are necessary in order to pay for the import content of domestic demand.

For nine out of fifteen LDCs, domestic demand grows at a faster rate than net exports.

Taking the countries as a whole, it can be seen, on average, that the share of private consumption in GDP is the highest (79 per cent). followed by imports (34 per cent), exports (23 per cent), investment (17 per cent) and government consumption expenditure (12 per cent). The component of demand with the highest growth rate, on average, is investment (7.9 per cent), followed by export growth (6.8 per cent) and government consumption expenditure (5.3 per cent). Private consumption has grown the least.

To summarize, domestic demand has contributed the most to GDP growth in the majority of the LDCs considered. This was expected since the share of domestic demand components in GDP is higher than that for exports.

But the evidence shows that high domestic demand growth is also associated with high export growth. This is particularly true of investment, which is not surprising since the import content of investment in most LDCs is high. Six of the seven fastest-growing countries have investment and exports growing faster than GDP — Mozambique, Rwanda, Cambodia, Bangladesh, Senegal and Ethiopia.

C. Agricultural growth linkages, employment and poverty reduction

In countries where the share of agriculture in GDP and employment is high, trends in domestic demand are closely related to what happens within the agricultural sector and also the nature of the linkages between agriculture and the rest of the economy. These linkages are critical for sustained economic growth (Fei and Ranis, 1997). On the supply side, agricultural productivity growth is particularly important for increasing domestic savings in very poor countries and also for ensuring an adequate supply of cheap foodstuffs. But demand-side linkages which result from agricultural growth are also an important mechanism which stimulates the development of local manufacturing industries and local services (Bhaduri and Skarstein, 2003). These intersectoral linkages can serve as a catalytic inducement mechanism which can set off a sequence of investment decisions and mobilize latent entrepreneurial capabilities within LDCs. They can also help to ensure that economic growth becomes more broad-based and inclusive.

In the initial literature on linkages, agriculture was identified as having very weak forward and backward intersectoral linkages. As Hirschman (1958: 109–110) put it, "Agriculture certainly stands convicted on the count of its lack of stimulus to the setting up of new activities through linkage effects; the superiority of manufacturing is crushing". But subsequent empirical research has nuanced this view.

Vogel (1994: 143–144) has shown that "(i) at low levels of development agriculture possess strong backward links to non-agricultural production activities; (ii) at low levels of development, the dominant linkage in the backward multiplier is rural household expenditures on non-agricultural commodities derived from increases in agricultural income; and (iii) the agricultural backward input–output linkage increases during the development process". This finding is based on the analysis of 27 social accounting matrices taken from countries at different levels of development. In low-income countries, every $1 of expenditure by agriculture generates $2.75 of induced demand for non-agricultural inputs and services, and 70 per cent of this backward linkage effect is attributable to rural household demand for consumer goods and services. Research in Africa has also found that growth in household incomes that comes from increases in agricultural production and incomes — due to technological changes, better prices or lower input costs — is largely spent on farm and non-farm items that are non-tradable, such as perishable foods, local services and locally produced non-farm goods. Adding $1 of new farm income potentially increases total income in the local economy — beyond the initial $1 — by an additional $1.88 in Burkina Faso, by $1.48 in Zambia, by $1.24 to $1.48 in two locations in Senegal, and by $0.96 in Niger (Delgado, Hopkins and Kelly, 1998: xii). Realizing this potential depends on the elasticity of the supply response of non-tradable activities.

Trends in domestic demand are closely related to what happens within the agricultural sector and also the nature of the linkages between agriculture and the rest of the economy.

Adding $1 of new farm income potentially increases total income in the local economy — beyond the initial $1 — by an additional $1.88 in Burkina Faso, by $1.48 in Zambia, by $1.24 to $1.48 in two locations in Senegal, and by $0.96 in Niger

Mellor (2000) has identified this demand linkage effect of agricultural growth as central to poverty reduction. As he puts it starkly, "(1) Poverty reduction takes place largely through increased employment in the production of non-tradables; (2) rising agricultural incomes are the dominant source of demand for non-tradeables; and (3) raising the aggregate of agricultural incomes requires substantial public sector expenditure to facilitate income increasing technological change, specialization and intensification" (p. 3). From this perspective, agricultural growth matters for poverty reduction directly because agriculture is the sector where most of the poor are located, and it is also generally a labour-intensive activity. But the most important reason why agriculture matters for poverty reduction is that rising income in agriculture leads to an increased demand for non-farm, non-tradable goods which are also very labour- intensive. This occurs primarily in the rural and small-town non-farm sector.

Rising income in agriculture leads to an increased demand for non-farm, non-tradable goods which are also very labour-intensive.

Poverty reduction, Mellor argues, requires employment growth outside agriculture because agriculture itself is likely to shed labour. But it is agricultural demand which stimulates the investment and entrepreneurship which generate such employment. However, the multiplier effects of agricultural growth on non-farm employment in non-tradables depend on the degree of income inequality in agriculture. The greater the income inequality, the more increased agricultural incomes are spent on imports and capital-intensive goods and less on non-farm, non-tradable, labour-intensive goods, and therefore there will be less employment growth and poverty reduction.

This model through which agricultural growth induces employment growth in local industry and services in rural areas and small towns is highly relevant to the LDCs.[4] Empirical research in Bangladesh suggests that this mechanism has been central to the process through which economic growth has translated into poverty reduction through expansion of more productive employment (Osmani et al,. 2003; Osmani, 2005). However, for most LDCs, inadequate levels of demand arising from agriculture have resulted in weak inter-sectoral linkages, thus contributing to labour market conditions such as those discussed in chapter 4.

The greater the income inequality, the more increased agricultural incomes are spent on imports and capital-intensive goods and less on non-farm, non-tradable, labour-intensive goods, and therefore there will be less employment growth and poverty reduction.

The research in Bangladesh begins by considering what are the sectors which have contributed most to the growth acceleration which occurred in Bangladesh in the 1990s. The two fastest-growing subsectors of the economy are fisheries and manufactures, both of which are export sectors. However, the sectors which contributed most to the improvement in the growth rate in Bangladesh between the 1980s and 1990s are non-tradables. As Osmani (2005: 59) puts it, "[o]n the whole, at least two-thirds to three-quarters of the incremental growth in the 1990s originated from the non-tradeable sectors — mainly services, construction and small scale industry". The analysis also shows that "the acceleration of the non-tradeable sector cannot be explained by autonomous productivity improvement within the sector. A more likely explanation lies in a more robust demand stimulus originating from outside the sector, especially in view of the existence of widespread underemployment in this sector, which ought to make it particularly responsive to demand stimulus" (p. 60).

The next question which arises is: what are the sources of demand stimulus for the growth of non-tradables in Bangladesh? Three are identified. The first is the phenomenal growth of the garments industry. The workers in this industry are the poorest among manufacturing workers and thus their spending patterns could provide a significant demand boost to the production of non-tradables. The second possible source is the accelerated increase in workers' remittances from emigrant Bangladeshis. The third is the growth in agricultural output and income associated with coordinated expansion of the use of agricultural inputs through the 1990s. When the sources of demand stimulus are disaggregated between increased crop production, garments output and foreign remittances from 1986/1987 and 1997/1998, Osmani (2005) finds that increased crop production provided the greatest stimulus to growth of non-tradables, followed by the growth of the garments industry and workers' remittances. Indeed, the demand stimulus from expanding crop production was equivalent to the combined stimulus from the other two sources.

There were also important differences in the structure of employment growth between the 1980s and 1990s in Bangladesh. In the 1980s the shift of labour was mainly into the rural non-farm sector, where people became self-employed with quite low productivity. The 1990s were characterized by faster growth of relatively larger-scale enterprises in the rural non-farm sector that are more productive and employ more wage labour. The poor rural workers found an increased opportunity to secure wage employment in the rural non-farm sector instead of overcrowding into petty self-employed activities. These developments have played a major role in reducing poverty in Bangladesh. Osmani et al (2003) summarize the growth–poverty nexus that took place in the 1990s as follows: "Faster growth enabled the non-farm enterprises to increase their scale of operation, thus tilting the structure of the rural-non-farm sector more towards the relatively larger enterprises. This structural change in turn brought about a change in the nature of labour absorption in this sector, as salaried wage employment became more plentiful with the emergence of large enterprises." (p. 26). However, lack of education, the shortage of physical assets and the lack of access to physical infrastructure act as impediments to moving up the hierarchy of salaried employment.

Bangladesh is not a unique case. Recent work on pro-poor growth which seeks to compare trends in growth and poverty in Viet Nam and Burkina Faso in the 1990s identifies mechanisms analogous to those operating in Bangladesh at work in Viet Nam (Bernabè and Krstic, 2005). In contrast, weak stimulus of demand is identified as a critical factor which is preventing the productive absorption of labour outside agriculture in Burkina Faso.

Focusing on the period 1993–1998, Bernabè and Krstic (2005) explain Viet Nam's success in terms of growth and poverty reduction as follows: "First, a broad-based increase in agricultural labour productivity combined with a strong domestic and foreign demand for crops produced, increased earning for the majority of the poor and stimulated domestic demand for non-agricultural goods produced by the poor. Second, an increase in (low-skilled) informal labour productivity combined with growing domestic and foreign demand for informal goods and services, created higher earning opportunities for agricultural workers. In turn, higher non-agricultural earnings further stimulated demand for agricultural goods and services, thereby creating a virtuous circle of growth and poverty reduction" (p. 37). In this process, although the high rates of economic growth were led by increasing exports of labour-intensive manufacturing goods, poverty reduction mainly occurred through rising agricultural incomes and the expansion of demand for non-tradables.

An important feature of the employment trends during this period was that there was "a massive informalization of non-agricultural employment" (p. 17). However, at the same time there has been "a decline in the rate of underemployment, particularly in the sectors where the poor were employed" (p. 18). Formal sector earnings grew faster than informal earnings, reflecting important productivity gains. But there was also a real increase in informal

The sectors which contributed most to the improvement in the growth rate in Bangladesh between the 1980s and 1990s are non-tradables.

In Bangladesh, the demand stimulus to non-tradables from expanding crop production was equivalent to the combined stimulus from the garments industry and workers' remittances.

earnings. This was partly as a result of productivity gains, but more importantly as a result of an increase in demand for informally produced goods. Within the agricultural sector, there was a shift to higher- value-added products and an increase in the intensity of agricultural employment. This was critically important for direct poverty reduction — two thirds of the workers who moved out of poverty remained or became employed in agriculture during the period 1993–1998. However, rising informal earnings were also related to the demand stimulus which came with the widespread increase in agricultural earnings. Moreover, some informally produced industrial goods were also exported and thus increased demand for Viet Nam's manufacturing exports supplemented the demand stimulus to informal sector activities.

In contrast to the pattern of growth and poverty reduction in Viet Nam, a shift to higher-value crops occurred in Burkina Faso but in a way which was limited to a small group of farmers, and the majority of food crop farmers faced weak domestic demand and essentially no foreign demand for their products. The strongest productivity gains were in the cotton sector. Output of food crops grew. But domestic demand was constrained by the small urban population and declining real urban incomes. There was also almost no foreign demand for food crops as they are effectively non-tradable. As agricultural earnings stagnated, there was little demand stimulus for non-farm goods and services, and there was also little demand for tradable non-agricultural goods. Thus "as informal labour supply expanded in the services sector, it was not matched by an increase in demand. As a result, although the expansion of employment generated growth in output, productivity and wages fell, leading to an increase in the poverty rate in the services sector" (p. 38).

From this analysis, it is now possible to get a clearer view of the problem of productive labour absorption within LDCs, which was discussed earlier in this Report. The analysis in chapter 3 identified declining non-agricultural labour productivity as a widespread tendency within the LDCs, and chapter 4 showed that in weak-growth economies this was associated with urban labour markets in which most people were employed in informal sector enterprises, and that there were high rates of underemployment. The cases of Bangladesh and Viet Nam show that in terms of their income-earning opportunities, informal sector activities do not necessarily have to be survivalist but may also be growth-oriented. However, the critical factor which enables increased informal sector earnings is the stimulus of demand. Moreover, the major source of demand stimulus comes from agricultural productivity growth. This pattern, in which there is a virtuous circle in which demand stimulus from agricultural growth induces investment, entrepreneurship and employment in non-agricultural activities, particularly non-tradables, is likely to be relevant in many LDCs and at the heart of efforts to create a more inclusive process of development which supports sustainable poverty reduction.

This growth and poverty reduction mechanism is influenced by the form of integration with the global economy. The opportunity of export markets can enable a faster rate of agricultural growth than would be possible if agricultural output was limited to domestic market. From this perspective, Mellor (2002) has argued that globalization could enable agricultural growth rates at 4 per cent to 6 per cent per annum rather than rates of 3 per cent, which were the maximum that they normally achieved in the past on the basis of domestic demand. However, at the same time, there is a possibility that agricultural imports could slow down agricultural growth. This could break down positive intersectoral linkages between agriculture and the rest of the economy, including the positive demand linkages discussed above. In this regard, a trend which is a matter of

Informal sector activities do not necessarily have to be survivalist but may also be growth-oriented. The critical factor which enables increased informal sector earnings is the stimulus of demand.

There is a possibility that agricultural imports could slow down agricultural growth. This could break down positive intersectoral linkages between agriculture and the rest of the economy, including the positive demand linkages.

Box 20. Food import surges into LDCs

The LDCs currently import more food than they export. This is particularly so in African LDCs. They were net food exporters in the 1980s, but in the early 1990s they changed to being net food importers. Their net imports increased at a steady rate during the 1990s, but since 2000 the growth of food imports has accelerated (box chart 7). This pattern has not occurred in either the Asian or island LDCs.

Box chart 7. Net food imports[a] in LDCs, 1980–2003
(Index, 1995 = 100)

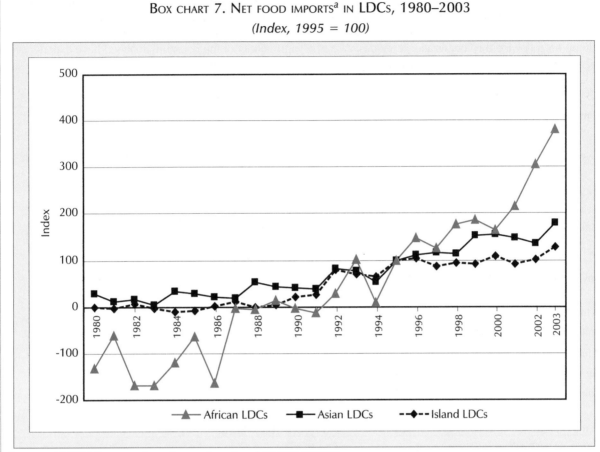

Source: UNCTAD secretariat estimates based on UN COMTRADE.
a   Food imports minus food exports.

Following the methodology used by FAO (2002), the number of import surges into LDCs that occurred in the 1970s, 1980s and 1990s and during 2000–2003 were calculated. An import surge is defined as a 20 per cent positive deviation from a five-year moving average for each commodity/country. The analysis was carried out for a selected number of commodities which were considered to be especially representative, namely wheat, maize, rice, bovine meat, pig meat, poultry meat, milk, tomatoes, tomato paste and sugar. The evidence shows that the number of import surges has been increasing over time and they became more frequent in the 1990s and, proportionally, more so in 2000–2003. In the case of pig meat, tomatoes and tomato paste, 60 per cent of the total import surges were experienced during 1990–2003 and 50 per cent of the total import surges of maize and poultry meat were experienced over the same period of 13 years. In the case of rice and sugar, slightly over 40 per cent of rice and sugar import surges were experienced over the past 13 years (box table 10).

Different countries have been affected differently by food import surges. Overall, African LDCs have been hit by import surges more than their Asian and island counterparts. African LDCs have been particularly hit in their domestic production of poultry meat over the last 13 years. The imports of processed agricultural goods also affect the domestic production of unprocessed agricultural goods. The case of tomato paste in African LDCs is a particularly good example. Imports of tomato paste by African LDCs have shown a rapid increase from the mid-1990s onward, while domestic production of tomatoes has remained stagnant. Imports of paddy rice show a different pattern. Rather than a steady increase in imports, there are spikes which probably reflect the effects of drought and other adverse weather conditions on domestic production.

According to recent research, food import bills in developing countries have increased recently because of (i) domestic exchange rate depreciation, and (ii) higher quantities of food imported on a commercial basis rather than through food

Box 20 (contd.)

aid (FAO, 2003). Many food prices also increased simultaneously in the period 2000–2003. Many of the products represented in box table 10 were also heavily subsidized by OECD countries. There is also likely to be a relationship between trade liberalization, which has proceeded far and fast in many LDCs, and increasing food imports in countries where local production is uncompetitive with imports. Using the liberalization episodes identified in *The Least Developed Countries Report 2004* (table 37, p. 186) for 26 LDCs, it was found that the majority of the countries that had liberalized by 2003 had increased their net food imports during and in the aftermath of their liberalization episodes (11 out of 15 countries), while the majority of those that are still liberalizing have experienced a fall in their net food imports during their ongoing liberalization policies (7 out of 11 countries). Only a minority of LDCs (4) have experienced a fall in food imports following the liberalization episodes. Also, the vast majority of the countries analysed have experienced a higher annual incidence of import surges in the post-liberalization period than in the pre-liberalization period.

Commodities	No. of import surges			Countries *particularly* hit by the import surges[a]
	1970–2003	*1990–2003*	*2000–2003*	
Rice	350	150	53	Bangladesh, Burkina Faso, Burundi, Central African Republic, Madagascar, Mali, Rwanda
Sugar	350	155	44	Benin, Burkina Faso, Central African Rep, Chad, Madagascar, Malawi, United Rep. of Tanzania
Maize	345	181	64	Benin, Burkina Faso, Guinea-Bissau, Malawi, Mali, Mauritania, Sierra Leone, Somalia, Togo, Uganda, Yemen
Bovine meat	344	160	54	Cape Verde, Guinea-Bissau, Madagascar, Malawi, Mali, Mozambique, Rwanda, Uganda
Wheat	301	143	34	Angola, Bangladesh, Liberia, Niger
Milk	290	136	34	Cambodia, Chad, Lao PDR, Uganda
Poultry meat	272	145	52	Central African Republic, Liberia, Mauritania
Pig meat	210	124	43	Democratic Republic of the Congo
Tomatoes	197	117	41	Cape Verde, Central African Republic, Liberia, Mauritania, Niger, Togo
Tomato paste	178	119	39	Burkina Faso

BOX TABLE 10. NUMBER OF IMPORT SURGES ON SELECTED COMMODITIES EXPERIENCED BY THE LDCs, 1970–2003

Source: UNCTAD secretariat estimates.

a Countries that have experienced a number of import surges greater than or equal to 10.

Most of the products in which the LDCs are experiencing food import surges are also produced by the LDCs. But even if they do not produce the very same products in respect of which they experience import surges, they typically do produce substitutes, which can also be negatively affected by these import surges (UNCTAD, 2004). However, the relationship between import surges and domestic production is complex. Domestic production of many of these goods either fell or slowed down during the period 1990–2003. But it is difficult to ascertain whether production is falling because of an inability to compete with cheaper imports, or whether imports are filling a demand gap left by falling domestic production. This is an important issue which requires further research, as it is potentially critical for the effectiveness of intersectoral linkages between agriculture and the rest of the economy in the LDCs.

concern is the rise in food import surges into LDCs, which was particularly apparent in the 1990s (see box 20).

D. Economic growth and the balance-of-payments constraint in LDCs

It is clear that domestic demand makes a critical contribution to economic growth. However, exports also matter because economic growth and the full utilization of productive capacities are constrained through the balance of payments. The empirical evidence clearly indicates that there is a conflict between sustaining an accelerated GDP growth rate and preserving an equilibrium in the balance of payments. The ultimate solution must lie in improving the balance of payments through trade, as will be discussed later.

Exports also matter because economic growth and the full utilization of productive capacities are constrained through the balance of payments.

As outlined in *The Least Developed Countries Report 2004*, exports can play a number of different roles in supporting economic growth. These are as follows: (a) static efficiency gains which arise through specialization according to current comparative advantage; (b) increased capacity utilization which arises if external demand enables the employment of previously idle factors of production; (c) increased physical and human capital investment owing to improved returns to investment; and (d) productivity growth through the transfer of technology or increased efficiency due to the exposure to international competition. This orthodox approach assumes that the balance of payments of a country looks after itself, so that the demand side of the economy is ignored. In practice, the exchange rate consequences of trade cannot be ignored and the balance of payments cannot be assumed to be self-correcting. Thus, the disequilibria within the balance of payments can become a constraint on economic growth from the demand side if deficits cannot be financed.

Theoretically, in the long run, no country can grow faster than the rate consistent with the balance-of-payments equilibrium on the current account unless it can finance ever-growing deficits through capital inflows. This is the idea behind the balance-of-payments-constrained growth model (Thirlwall, 1979). Empirical evidence suggests that most developing countries are demand-constrained by their balance of payments, although for short periods the constraint can be relaxed by capital inflows and transfers;[5] however, experience shows that the maximum current account deficit to GDP ratio sustainable by private financial flows is generally in the order of 2 to 3 per cent (Thirlwall, 2003).

The disequilibria within the balance of payments can become a constraint on economic growth from the demand side if deficits cannot be financed.

Each component of demand has an import content, which is essential for the continuation of the ongoing economic activities and development, and countries need foreign exchange to pay for those imports. In general, export earnings are the most important (and in many ways the most desirable) source of foreign exchange. However, if the rate of growth of exports is not enough to provide the foreign exchange needed, countries are obliged to attract capital flows to finance the difference between the value of imports and the foreign exchange provided by exports; if this does not happen, the components of demand have to be constrained in the long term in order for the balance of payments to be in equilibrium.

Chart 53 shows that the LDCs' trade deficit in goods and services worsened from 1985 to the late 1990s, as imports grew faster than exports. There was, however, a subsequent improvement, but this was mainly driven by oil-

CHART 53. EXPORTS, IMPORTS AND TRADE DEFICIT IN GOODS AND SERVICES IN LDCs, 1985–2003
(In current $ billions)

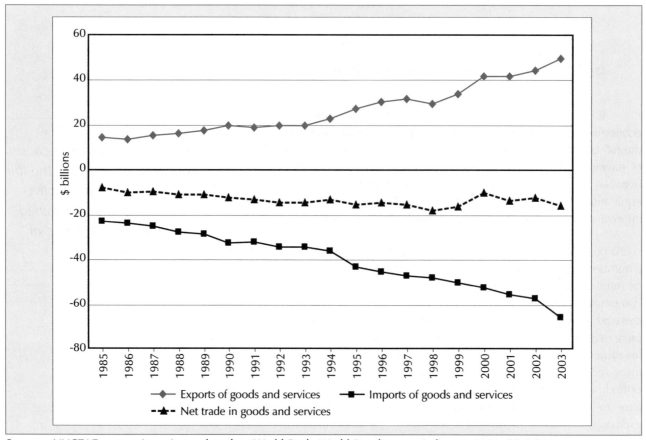

Source: UNCTAD secretariat estimates based on World Bank, *World Development Indicators 2005,* CD-ROM.

exporting LDCs. In the group of non-oil-exporting LDCs, the trade deficit in goods and services averaged 9 per cent of GDP in 2003. This suggests that the LDCs, and non-oil LDCs in particular, relied heavily on capital flows and transfers to finance their imports of goods and services.

Considering that export growth has not been enough to finance the import content requirement for the economic development of LDCs, Pacheco-López (2005b) used an extended version of the balance-of-payments-constrained growth model with capital flows and transfers for a sample of 18 LDCs (see box 21 for a technical review of the model).

Although the nominal terms of trade have been improving on average over the last three decades, the depreciation of LDCs' currencies has swamped any positive effects of the nominal terms of trade.

It was found that export growth has made a positive contribution to GDP growth in all countries except Mauritania, where the export growth rate was negative. The export growth rate exceeded the rate of GDP growth in 7 of the 18 countries. In the other 11 countries, the actual growth of GDP has been slowed down either by a negative pure terms of trade effect and/or slower growth of capital flows and transfers than exports. The pure terms of trade effect on growth can be estimated as the sum of the rate of change of the nominal terms of trade (measured as the ratio of domestic to foreign prices) and the rate of change of the nominal exchange rate (measured as the domestic price of foreign currency). Table 57 shows that although the nominal terms of trade have been improving on average over the last three decades, the depreciation of LDCs' currencies against the US dollar has swamped any positive effects of the nominal terms of trade. Eleven countries — Burundi, Ethiopia, Gambia, Haiti, Lesotho, Malawi, Mali, Senegal, Sierra Leone, Uganda and Zambia — have experienced adverse real terms of trade; and in eight of these countries this negative terms of trade effect can partly explain why the actual growth of GDP is

Box 21. Testing the balance-of-payments-constrained growth model for LDCs

Every country requires foreign exchange in order to pay for imports to support the growth and development process. How much imports grow with the growth of GDP is given by the income elasticity of demand for imports (holding relative prices constant). The magnitude of the income elasticity will depend on the structure of production, the import content of final demand and the trade regime in operation.

There can be no doubt from the evidence that virtually all of the LDCs are short of foreign exchange. Their current-account balance-of-payments deficits relative to GDP are huge, while their GDP growth rates are relatively modest, and there is also surplus labour. Often capital is also under-utilised because of a shortage of foreign exchange to buy spare parts. There are many ways of financing imports through: exports, ODA, FDI inflows, private lending, workers' remittances, and so forth. Use of the balance-of-payments framework, including both current and capital transactions, can give the relative importance of these components in financing imports and the growth process in LDCs.

The model, originally derived in Thirlwall (1979) and Thirlwall and Hussain (1982),[1] has the following form:

$$y_B^* = \frac{(p_{dt} - p_{ft} - e_t)(1 + w_1\eta + \psi) + w_1\varepsilon(z_t) + w_2(c_t - p_{dt})}{\pi}$$

where y_B^* is a country's growth rate consistent with the overall balance-of-payments equilibrium (including capital flows and transfers); p_{dt} is the rate of change of domestic prices; p_{ft} is the rate of change of foreign prices; e_t is the rate of change of the exchange rate (measured as the domestic price of foreign currency); z is world income growth; $(c_t - p_{dt})$ is the growth of real capital inflows that allow import growth to exceed export growth; h is the price elasticity of demand for exports which will be negative ($\eta < 0$) because a rise in the relative price of exports will reduce export demand; y is the price elasticity of demand for imports which will be negative ($\psi < 0$) because a rise in the price of imports will reduce import demand; ε is the income elasticity of demand for exports which will be positive (e > 0) because a rise in world income will lead to an increase in the demand for goods if they are "normal" goods; π is the income elasticity of demand for imports which will be positive ($\pi > 0$) because a rise in domestic income is partly spent on imports; and w_1 and w_2, respectively, are the shares of exports and capital flows and transfers in total receipts to pay for the import bill, and $w_1 + w_2 = 1$.

Since the overall balance of payments must balance, it can be seen from the equation that any country's growth rate can be disaggregated into four components:

1. The growth of exports determined by world demand conditions and the interaction of relative price changes and the price elasticity of demand for exports, i.e. $[w_1\eta(p_{dt} - p_{ft} - e_t) + w_1\varepsilon(z)]/\pi = w_1 x/\pi$, where x is the growth of exports;

2. The contribution of real capital flows and transfers, i.e. $w_2(c_t - p_{dt})/\pi$ (this can be disaggregated into component parts such as the growth of net ODA, net FDI inflows, net private lending, workers' remittances, etc. — each weighted by their share in total capital flows and transfers);

3. A pure terms of trade effect i.e. $(p_{dt} - p_{ft} - e_t)/\pi$;

4. A residual determined by the interaction of relative price changes and the price elasticity of demand for imports i.e. $[(p_{dt} - p_{ft} - e_t)\psi]/\pi$.

The full model has been applied to 18 LDCs over various periods between 1975 and 2003.[2] Box table 11 provides a summary of results for each of the countries in the sample. Column 1 gives the average growth of GDP. Column 2 gives the contribution of export growth to GDP growth. Column 3 gives the pure terms of trade effect and column 4 gives the contribution of real capital flows and transfers to GDP growth. The difference between the actual growth of GDP and the sum of the three components in the table is the fourth component, which is the residual mentioned above (including errors in the data).

276

Box 21 (contd.)

BOX TABLE 11. THE CONTRIBUTION OF EXPORT GROWTH, PURE TERMS OF TRADE MOVEMENTS, AND
REAL CAPITAL FLOWS AND TRANSFERS TO REAL GDP GROWTH OF SELECTED LDCs, 1975–2003[a]
(Percentage per annum)

	Average annual GDP growth rate	Average contribution[b] of:		
		Export growth $w_1 x / \pi$	Pure terms of trade movements $(p_{dt} - p_{ft} - e_t)/\pi$	Real capital flows and transfers $w_2(c_t - p_{dt})/\pi$
Bangladesh	4.3	+3.0	+1.2	+0.9
Benin	4.0	+0.8	+0.3	+0.4
Burkina Faso	3.8	+0.5	+1.4	-1.0
Burundi	1.7	+6.9	-6.0	+2.5
Ethiopia	3.1	+2.5	-7.0	+1.8
Gambia	3.6	+4.2	-3.4	+11.3
Haiti	0.5	+1.8	-3.7	+2.7
Lesotho	4.0	+3.4	-4.1	-3.9
Madagascar	0.9	+0.1	+0.2	+1.4
Malawi	3.3	+7.9	-7.4	+24.8
Mali	3.4	+1.9	-0.9	-0.9
Mauritania	3.7	-0.9	+0.8	+3.0
Rwanda	4.2	+6.7	10.8	+1.3
Senegal	3.0	+7.0	-5.4	+3.9
Sierra Leone	-0.4	+0.5	-4.1	+5.3
Togo	2.3	+1.4	+1.7	+4.6
Uganda	5.4	+2.6	-4.5	-2.4
Zambia	1.1	+0.4	-0.5	+2.2

a   Based on data availability; periods for variables and countries vary.
b   The sum of the contributions does not equal the average annual GDP growth rate due to the fact that not all capital flows were considered and also due to data errors.

Source: Pacheco-López (2005b).

1   For an up-to-date literature review on this topic, see McCombie and Thirlwall (2004).
2   The periods differ for countries according to the availability of data.

less than the combined contribution of export growth and real capital flows and transfers. The negative pure terms of trade effect is largely accounted for by nominal exchange rate depreciation — which coincides with the implementation of the Structural Adjustment Programmes implemented during the late 1980s and early 1990s.

Capital flows play an important part in the growth process of LDCs. Often capital flows and transfers pay for nearly 50 per cent of imports.

Capital flows play an important part in the growth process of LDCs. Often capital flows and transfers pay for nearly 50 per cent of imports. In general, the growth of real capital flows and transfers made a positive contribution to GDP growth in 14 of the 18 countries in the sample. In those countries, the growth of real capital flows and transfers made a more important contribution to GDP growth than the growth of exports. This is some measure of how many LDCs are reliant on capital flows and transfers to pay for their imports. When capital flows and transfers are disaggregated into net ODA, net FDI inflows (FDI), net private lending, workers' remittances and interest payments, it is possible to identify which type has the highest share in total capital flows and transfers (see box 22). However, a more revealing analysis is derived by considering the contribution of the real growth rate of each of these components to GDP growth.[6] Table 58 shows the actual GDP growth rate and the contribution of net ODA, net FDI inflows (FDI), net private lending, workers' remittances and interest payments on past net private lending to economic growth for the periods for which data are available. It is shown that:

TABLE 57. AVERAGE CHANGES OF THE NOMINAL TERMS OF TRADE, THE NOMINAL EXCHANGE RATE
AND THE REAL TERMS OF TRADE IN SELECTED LDCs, VARIOUS PERIODS[a]

(Annual average, percentage)

LDCs	Nominal terms of trade[b]	Nominal exchange rate[c]	Real terms of trade[b]
Bangladesh	+8.2	-6.2	+2.0
Benin	+6.8	-6.1	+0.7
Burkina Faso	+9.8	-7.1	+2.7
Burundi	+8.1	-12.8	-4.7
Ethiopia	+7.0	-15.5	-8.5
Gambia	+8.4	-10.6	-2.2
Haiti	+9.1	-17.0	-7.9
Lesotho	+10.7	-14.0	-3.3
Madagascar	+15.7	-15.0	+0.7
Malawi	+18.0	-21.0	-3.0
Mali	+3.1	-4.4	-1.3
Mauritania	+9.5	-8.1	+1.4
Rwanda	+15.7	-7.9	+7.8
Senegal	+3.7	-6.5	-2.8
Sierra Leone	+33.4	-41.8	-8.4
Togo	+8.4	-6.2	+2.2
Uganda	+48.4	-56.3	-7.9
Zambia	+53.0	-54.4	-1.4

Source: Based on Pacheco-López (2005b).

a   Data availability: Bangladesh (1976–2002), Benin (1976–2002), Burkina Faso (1980–2002), Burundi (1979–2002), Ethiopia (1982–2002), Gambia (1976–1994), Haiti (1976–2002), Lesotho (1981–2002), Madagascar (1976–2002), Malawi (1976–1984, 1986–2000), Mali (1986–1996), Mauritania (1986–2002), Rwanda (1976–1979, 1981–2002), Senegal (1976–2001), Sierra Leone (1976–1986, 1989–1993, 1995–2002), Togo (1976, 1978–2002), Uganda (1983–2002), and Zambia (1976–1978, 1980–1982, 1984–1986, 1990–1997).
b   + indicates improvement and – deterioration.
c   + indicates appreciation and – depreciation.

- The growth of net ODA in real terms has contributed positively to GDP growth in 8 of the 18 countries. In the other countries, real net ODA flows must have fallen on average resulting in a negative contribution of real net ODA growth to GDP growth.[7]

- From the limited data available on net FDI inflows, net private lending and workers' remittances to LDCs it appears that real FDI growth contributed positively to GDP growth in 11 of the 15 countries; the growth of real net private lending contributed positively to growth in 12 of the 18 countries; the growth of workers' remittances in real terms contributed positively to GDP growth in 8 of the 10 countries; and the payment of real interest on loans contributed negatively to growth in 6 of the 18 countries. Interestingly, in only 3 of the 18 countries has the growth of all capital inflows been positive simultaneously. In other countries, the impact of different flows has been offsetting.

Given the degree to which imports are financed by capital inflows and transfers, it is most likely that some of these LDCs would not be able to achieve their economic growth rates without these flows and transfers.

These results highlight the dependence on capital inflows in the form of net ODA, net FDI inflows, net private lending and workers' remittances in financing growth in the majority of LDCs.

The findings presented above lead to several policy implications for economic policymaking. First, it is clear from the size of their deficits that economic growth in LDCs has been constrained by their balance-of-payments position. Most LDCs have experienced current account deficits, which have been financed by capital flows and transfers. But when the latter are not sufficient to finance such deficits, or when they are volatile and with widespread fluctuations, the other components of demand may have to be limited owing to their import content. An alternative way of addressing this issue is to question

Box 22. Capital flows and transfers in LDCs

In the LDCs capital flows and transfers have been financing an excess of imports over exports. The main types of capital flows and transfers are the following: net ODA flows, net FDI inflows (FDI), net private lending, workers' remittances, interest payments (negatively) and other flows (not reported here). Box table 12, shows the average share of net ODA flows, net FDI inflows, net private lending, workers' remittances and interest payments to GDP for each country. For all countries, the share of net ODA flows is by far the highest. For many countries, the share of net ODA flows *alone* has exceeded total capital inflows so that net ODA flows are financing not only balance-of-payments deficits but also capital outflows presumably private capital flight.

Box table 12. Capital flows and transfers, as share of GDP, 1975–2003[a]
(Average, percentage)

	Net ODA flows	Net FDI inflows	Net private lending	Workers' remittances	Interest payments
Bangladesh	4.4	0.2	0.1	3.3	0.4
Benin	10.3	1.6	1.5	4.3	1.0
Burkina Faso	13.4	0.2	0.1	5.3	0.7
Burundi	16.7	0.2	-0.1	..	1.0
Ethiopia	11.6	n.a.	0.6	..	0.8
Gambia	27.8	2.6	0.3	..	2.0
Haiti	9.0	0.4	0.3	6.0	0.5
Lesotho	15.1	2.5	0.7	..	1.8
Madagascar	9.3	0.5	0.5	0.2	1.5
Malawi	21.2	0.4	0.1	..	2.2
Mali	19.4	0.7	-0.1	4.3	1.1
Mauritania	23.8	0.5	0.0	0.9	3.6
Rwanda	17.3	0.6	0.0	0.1	0.4
Senegal	12.0	0.7	0.1	2.3	2.2
Sierra Leone	13.7	-0.5	0.3	..	1.2
Togo	10.6	2.0	1.9	1.4	2.1
Uganda	11.4	2.3	0.1	..	0.6
Zambia	17.4	2.1	0.1	..	3.0

Source: Based on Pacheco-López (2005b).

a   Based on data availability; periods for variables and countries vary.

Supply-side reforms should lift the balance-of-payments constraint on demand by increasing the growth of exports and reducing the income elasticity of demand for imports.

the sustainability of the actual GDP growth rates in LDCs. Given the degree to which imports are financed by capital inflows and transfers, it is most likely that some of these countries would not be able to have their current economic growth rates without these flows and transfers.

Second, attempts by LDCs to grow faster by focusing on the supply-side of the economy will not succeed unless at the same time supply-side reforms should lift the balance-of-payments constraint on demand by increasing the growth of exports and reducing the income elasticity of demand for imports. Increasing the capacity to supply without a concomitant increase in demand would lead to further unemployed resources. Supply-side reforms should seek to improve the performance of the tradable sector, with particular emphasis on increasing export growth, by increasing the income elasticity of demand for exports, and on reducing the income demand elasticity of imports. As shown in chapter 3, the export composition of the LDCs is dominated by primary products, which in general lack market dynamism.

TABLE 58. CONTRIBUTION OF DIFFERENT CAPITAL FLOWS AND TRANSFERS TO REAL AVERAGE ANNUAL GDP GROWTH IN SELECTED LDCs, 1975–2003[a]

(Percentage)

	GDP growth rate	Contribution of:				Negative effect of interest payments on growth[c]
		Net ODA flows[b]	Net FDI inflows[b]	Net private lending[b]	Workers' remitt-ances to growth[b]	
Bangladesh	4.3	-0.5	0.7	-0.3	1.4	0.1
Benin	4.0	0.4	1.2	0.6	0.2	0.2
Burkina Faso	3.8	-0.1	-5.1	6.7	-0.4	0.1
Burundi	1.7	1.7	-43.2	1.6	..	-0.1
Ethiopia	3.1	3.7	..	-4.1	..	0.1
Gambia	3.6	4.5	..	2.2	..	2.4
Haiti	0.5	10.4	0.1	2.4	-0.1	1.4
Lesotho	4.0	-0.5	1.9	-1.4	..	0.0
Madagascar	0.9	-0.1	0.1	3.3	1.0	0.6
Malawi	3.3	-11.4	..	2.1	..	-1.2
Mali	3.4	-0.7	6.9	5.6	0.0	0.8
Mauritania	3.7	0.6	0.6	0.4	1.5	-0.1
Rwanda	4.2	-0.7	1.0	-9.0	0.4	0.3
Senegal	3.0	3.5	19.7	5.1	1.2	1.1
Sierra Leone	-0.4	-2.6	-13.0	-0.1	..	0.0
Togo	2.3	0.6	3.9	-0.2	4.2	0.5
Uganda	5.4	-9.1	9.7	0.8	..	-0.8
Zambia	1.1	-3.3	-0.7	11.7	..	-0.6

Source: UNCTAD secretariat estimates, based on Pacheco-López (2005b).

a Based on data availability; periods for variables and countries vary.
b A negative sign indicates that the particular capital flow has impacted negatively on real GDP growth.
c A negative sign indicates that interest payments have been declining.

E. Conclusions

The stimulus of demand is critically important for the development of productive capacities.[8] It animates the core processes through which productive capacities develop — capital accumulation, technological progress and structural change. Moreover, effective demand ensures that productive capacities are fully utilized. A proper understanding of the different components of demand, and of the constraints on their growth, is thus essential in any policy discussion of productive capacities. What are perceived as supply-side constraints cannot be divorced from demand-side constraints.

This chapter has shown that expansion of domestic demand has contributed to economic growth in most LDCs. This finding is based on a sample of 15 LDCs for the period 1993–2003. But it replicates a similar finding for a different sample of LDCs using a different methodology in an earlier LDC Report (UNCTAD, 2004: 143–148). Moreover, it confirms a tendency identified in earlier analysis of patterns of growth which shows that at the start of the development process, the expansion of domestic demand contributed just under 75 per cent of economic growth in both small primary-oriented and small manufactures-oriented countries (Chenery, Robinson and Syrquin, 1986).

Sluggish domestic demand is a central deficiency of the investment climate in LDCs.

Because domestic demand is such a large demand-side source of economic growth, its weak growth is a major constraint on the development of productive capacities in most LDCs. Sluggish domestic demand, which is associated with generalized and persistent poverty, is a central deficiency of the investment climate in those countries. Seeking to improve the investment climate is an important policy emphasis. But the current thrust of policy analysis in relation to the investment climate, which focuses on governmental constraints and bureaucratic red tape, addresses only a limited part of the problem. It ignores the stimulus to economic action which can be constrained through excessive regulation. Effective domestic demand must also be taken into account. To take it for granted is to leave out half the story. Supply creates demand; but demand induces supply.

Because the share of agriculture in GDP and total employment is high in most LDCs, trends in domestic demand are closely related to what happens in the agricultural sector and also the nature of the linkages between agriculture and the rest of the economy. In this regard, the chapter has shown that the demand linkage effects of agricultural growth constitute an important growth and poverty reduction mechanism. In Viet Nam and Bangladesh, it is possible to observe a virtuous circle in which demand stimulus from agricultural growth induces investment, entrepreneurship and employment in non-agricultural activities, particularly non-tradables. This virtuous circle is likely to be relevant in many LDCs and at the heart of efforts to create a more inclusive process of development which supports sustainable poverty reduction. Without the stimulus of domestic demand for non-tradables, it is difficult to envisage the productive absorption of labour outside agriculture, which, as shown earlier in this Report, is becoming a critical issue for poverty reduction in more and more LDCs.

Although domestic demand makes a critical contribution to economic growth in the LDCs, exports also matter.

Although domestic demand makes a critical contribution to economic growth in the LDCs, exports also matter. There are various supply-side reasons for this. But exports also matter because economic growth and the full utilization of productive capacities are constrained through the balance of payments. Each component of demand has an import content which is essential for the continuation of ongoing economic activities and their expansion, and countries need foreign exchange to pay for those imports. Analysis of the LDCs within this framework shows that export growth has made a positive contribution. But its contribution to relaxing the balance-of-payments constraint has been seriously reduced by declining terms of trade and currency depreciation. It is also clear that capital inflows and transfers have played an important role in the LDCs in alleviating the balance-of-payments constraint.

An exclusive emphasis on exports rather than domestic demand, or vice versa, or on developing productive capacities in tradables rather than non-tradables, or vice versa, is likely to be counter-productive. Both matter for growth and poverty reduction.

Overall, the analysis of this chapter suggests that an exclusive emphasis on exports rather than domestic demand, or vice versa, or on developing productive capacities in tradables rather than non-tradables, or vice versa, is likely to be counter-productive. Both matter for growth and poverty reduction. But what is more fundamentally important is to ensure that demand-side factors begin to be taken seriously in policy efforts to develop productive capacities. Policies which seek to engineer a supply-side fix in the LDCs, without due attention to the dynamics of demand, are likely to fail.

Notes

1. For which data are available and consistent.
2. Ideally, the import content of all items of C, I, G and X should be subtracted to find the *true* contribution of domestic demand.
3. Aggregate demand can be decomposed into the contribution of domestic demand (DD), which is the sum of C + I + G, and net exports (NE), which is the difference between exports and imports (X–M). For an example which applies this to five Asian countries, see Asian Development Bank (2005).
4. It is also relevant in other developing countries. Mellor (1999) applies the model to Egypt.
5. There is now an extensive literature that has tested empirically the balance-of-payments-constrained growth model, either for individual, or groups of, developing countries, for example Moreno-Brid and Perez (1999) for Central American countries; Hussain (1999, 2001) for East Asian and African countries; Perraton (2003) for several developing countries; and Moreno-Brid (1998) and Pacheco-López (2005a) for Mexico.
6. The contribution of each capital flow to growth is calculated by multiplying the average rate of growth of each flow by its share in financing imports.
7. This does not mean that net ODA flows do not contribute to welfare and living standards. However, in a growth model it is important to distinguish between the level of variables and their growth rates. Their level can be positive but their rate of growth negative. Another distinction that should be taken into account is that variables in nominal terms differ from variables in real terms.
8. The issue of demand stimulus also is central to the debate on market access; see Fugazza (2004).

References

Asian Development Bank (2005). *Asian Development Outlook 2005, Developing Asia and the World*, Hong Kong, China.

Bernabè, S. and Krstic, G. (2005). Labour productivity and access to markets matter for pro-poor growth. *World Bank*, within the context of the Operationalizing Pro-Poor Growth Work Program.

Bhaduri A. and Skarstein, R. (2003). Effective demand and the terms of trade in a dual economy: A Kaldorian perspective, *Cambridge Journal of Economics*, 27(4): 583–595.

Chenery, H., Robinson, S. and Syrquin, M. (1986). *Industrialization and Growth: A Comparative Study*. World Bank, Washington DC.

Delgado, C., Hopkins, J. and Kelly, V. (1998). *Agricultural Growth Linkages in Sub-Saharan Africa*. International Food Policy Research Institute, Research Report 107, Washington, DC.

FAO (2002). Some trade policy issues relating to trends in agricultural imports in the context of food security. CCP 03/10, Rome.

FAO (2003) Trade reforms and food security (http://www.fao.org/documents/show_cdr.asp?url_file=/DOCREP/005/Y4671E/Y4671E00.HTM).

Fei, J.C. and Ranis, G. (1997). *Growth and Development from an Evolutionary Perspective*, Blackwell, UK.

Fugazza, M. (2004). Export performance and its determinants: Supply and demand constraints. Policy Issues in International Trade and Commodities Study Series, No. 26. UNCTAD/ITCD/TAB/27, Geneva.

Hirschman, A. (1958). *The Strategy of Economic Development*. New Haven: Yale University Press.

Hussain, M.N. (1999). The balance of payments constraint growth and growth rate fifferences among African and East Asian economies, *African Development Review*, June, 103–137.

Hussain, M.N. (2001). "Exorcising the ghost": An alternate model for measuring the financing gap in developing countries, *Journal of Post Keynesian Economics*, 24(1): 89–124.

McCombie, J. and Thirlwall, A.P. (2004). *Essays on Balance of Payments Constrained Growth: Theory and Evidence*. London: Routledge.

Mellor, J. (1999). Faster, More Equitable Growth: The relationship between growth in agriculture and poverty reduction, *Agricultural Policy Development Project Research Report*, No.4, Abt Associates Inc., Cambridge, Mass.

Mellor, J. (2000). Agricultural growth, rural employment, and poverty reduction: Non-tradables, public expenditure and balanced growth. Paper prepared for the World Bank Rural Week 2000, "Poverty or Prosperity: Rural People in a Globalized Economy" 28–31 March.

Mellor, J. (2002). The impacts of globalization on the role of agriculture. Paper presented at the Expert Consultation on Trade and Food Security "Conceptualizing the Linkages", 11–12 July 2002, Rome.

Moreno-Brid J.C., (1998). 'Balance of payments constrained economic growth: The Case of Mexico', *Banca Nazionale del Lavoro Quarterly Review*, 207: 413–433.

Moreno-Brid J.C. and Perez, E. (1999). 'Balance of payments constrained growth in Central America, *Journal of Post Keynesian Economics*, 22(1): 131–147.

Osmani S.R. et al. (2003). The Macroeconomics of Poverty Reduction: The Case Study of Bangladesh. United Nations Development Programme, Asia-Pacific Regional Programme on Macroeconomics of Poverty Reduction: Kathmandu. Mimeo.

Osmani, S.R. (2005). *The Employment Nexus Between Growth and Poverty — An Asian Perspective*, Sida Studies No.15., Swedish International Development Cooperation Agency, Stockholm.

Pacheco-López, P. (2005a). The impact of trade liberalisation on exports, imports, the balance of payments and growth: The Case of Mexico, *Journal of Post Keynesian Economics*, 27(4): 595–619.

Pacheco-López, P. (2005b). Testing the balance of payments constrained growth model for the least developed countries. Background paper prepared for *The Least Developed Countries Report 2006*, UNCTAD, Geneva.

Perraton, J. (2003). Balance of payments constrained growth and developing countries: An examination of Thirlwall's hypothesis, *International Review of Applied Economics*, 17(1): 1–22.

Thirlwall, A.P. (1979). The balance of payments constraint as an explanation of international growth rate differences, *Banca Nazionale del Lavoro Quarterly Review*, 128: 45–53.

Thirlwall, A.P. (2003). *Trade, the Balance of Payments and Exchange Rate Policy in Developing Countries*. Cheltenham: Edward Elgar.

Thirlwall, A.P. and Hussain, M.N. (1982). The balance of payments constraint, capital flows and growth rate differences between developing countries, *Oxford Economic Papers*, 34: 498–509.

UNCTAD (2004). *The Least Developed Countries Report 2004, Linking International Trade with Poverty Reduction*. United Nations publication, sales no. E.00.II.D.21, Geneva and New York.

Vogel, S. (1994). Structural changes in agriculture: Production linkages and agricultural demand-led industrialization, *Oxford Economic Papers*, 46: 136–156.

Policy Implications

A. Introduction

The analysis and empirical evidence in the previous chapters have significant policy implications. The Report has sought to present the evidence in a comprehensive manner so that it can serve as a resource for policymakers and promote open policy dialogue both within the LDCs and between the LDCs and their development partners. Without seeking to pre-empt alternative locally-grounded interpretations, this final chapter draws some policy implications.

The basic message of this chapter is that there is a need for a paradigm shift in national and international policies to promote development and poverty reduction in the LDCs. The scaling-up of net ODA inflows into the LDCs since 2000, and promises of further increases in aid and enhanced complementary measures in the area of trade and debt relief, are potentially creating a major development opportunity. But the doubling and redoubling of external resources will not be effective if it is linked to the wrong development model. Unless external resources are geared to the development of the productive capacities of the LDCs, the recent growth spurts which many LDCs have experienced (see part I of this Report) will simply fizzle out and the past widespread pattern of growth collapses will reoccur. The paradigm shift which is required is one which places the development of productive capacities at the heart of national and international efforts to promote economic growth and reduce poverty in the LDCs.

This chapter is divided into three sections. Section B sets out why the development of productive capacities is so important for poverty reduction, why current policies are not adequately addressing the challenge of developing productive capacities and what is the nature of the paradigm shift which is required. Section C focuses on the three key constraints on the development of productive capacities in the LDCs which have been identified in the previous three chapters of the Report — the infrastructure divide, institutional weaknesses and the demand constraint. The section identifies policy priorities and policy measures in each of these areas. Finally, section D briefly discusses the implications of the focus on the development of productive capacities for national and global governance.

B. The paradigm shift: Its rationale and nature

1. THE RATIONALE FOR THE PARADIGM SHIFT

The need for the paradigm shift is based on the following two propositions:

- Substantial and sustained poverty reduction in the LDCs requires the development of their productive capacities so as to provide productive employment opportunities.

- National and international policies are not adequately addressing the challenge of developing productive capacities in the LDCs.

This section explains those propositions in turn.

There is a need for a paradigm shift in national and international policies to promote development and poverty reduction in the LDCs.

The development of productive capacities should be placed at the heart of national and international efforts to promote economic growth and reduce poverty in the LDCs.

(a) Productive capacities and poverty reduction in the LDCs

Substantial and sustained poverty reduction in the LDCs requires the development of their productive capacities because of the nature of poverty within the LDCs. It is not something which affects a minority of the population but rather is all-pervasive throughout society (see UNCTAD, 2002).

Generalized (or mass) poverty is rooted in low labour productivity and the underemployment of the labour force. Most persons have to earn a living using their raw labour, with rudimentary tools and equipment, little education and training, and poor physical infrastructure. They mainly work in household-based micro-enterprises rather than in firms, and the domestic financial systems and domestic knowledge systems which enable investment, technological learning and innovation are very weak. The economies of the LDCs are dominated by agriculture, which is subject to diminishing returns and the vagaries of the weather and climate; the extraction of mineral or oil resources which are non-renewable and will become exhausted; and petty services through which the poor compete with the poor to supply the basic needs of the poor. A few have also developed low-technology manufactures, mainly in clothing and garments, and also strong tourism sectors. Exports and imports constitute over half the GDP of the LDCs as a group. But there is a very limited range of products in which they are internationally competitive, and it is difficult for them to compete in their own markets even in simple products. Their export structure is dominated by primary commodities and, in spite of the recent boom in mineral and oil prices, most LDCs have experienced severe terms-of-trade losses since 1980. Food imports have been increasing significantly since the mid-1990s, particularly in African LDCs.

Mass poverty is rooted in low labour productivity and the underemployment of the labour force. Reducing poverty in this context requires the expansion of productive employment opportunities.

Reducing poverty in this context requires the expansion of productive employment opportunities. This in turn requires increased investment and technological learning to increase capital per worker, knowledge assets and productivity. It also requires structural change away from economic activities which are subject to diminishing returns, declining terms of trade and the vagaries of the natural environment towards economic activities which are likely to provide increasing returns and which offer increased opportunities for technological progress. One consequence of generalized poverty is that domestic markets are limited and stagnant, and thus incentives to invest and innovate are weak. But with the expansion of productive employment, the stimulus of domestic demand will strengthen. Investment and technological learning are also the basis of improved international competitiveness in tradable sectors, and the development of productive capacities is thus also essential for taking advantage of economic opportunities associated with demand in international markets. Poverty reduction can occur rapidly if policy can catalyse and sustain a virtuous circle in which the development of productive capacities and the growth of demand mutually reinforce each other.

The need to focus on the development of productive capacities is particularly important now because the LDCs are at a critical moment of transition.

The need to focus on the development of productive capacities is particularly important now because the LDCs are at a critical moment of transition in which they face a double challenge.

In the past, the major mechanism through which the growing labour force has found employment was through the expansion of agricultural land. But this is becoming more and more circumscribed as there is a general tendency for agricultural land per agricultural worker to decline and more and more farmers are working on fragile land. Even in land-abundant LDCs, inequalities in land access mean that the poorest smallholders have little access to land. In these circumstances it is becoming increasingly difficult to productively absorb labour within agriculture. More and more people are seeking work outside agriculture, and urbanization is accelerating. However, productive absorption of labour outside agriculture is simply not happening in many LDCs. For the LDC group as whole, non-agricultural labour productivity declined between 1980–1983 and 2000–2003. Moreover, this declining trend is evident in four fifths of the LDCs for which data are available.

For the LDCs as a group, the decade 2000–2010 is going to be the first decade in which the growth of the economically active population outside agriculture is predicted to be greater than the growth of the economically active population within agriculture. This transition will affect more than half the LDCs during the decade and even more in the decade 2010–2020. The past inability of most LDCs to generate productive non-farm jobs is thus a particularly serious problem. Real poverty reduction, which goes beyond palliative measures that alleviate the symptoms of suffering, will be impossible if this problem is not addressed now.

The challenge of generating productive employment to meet this urban transition is compounded by a second challenge – the challenge of globalization. As shown in earlier LDC Reports, very few LDCs have restrictive trade regimes at the present time and most have undertaken rapid and extensive trade liberalization. However, their existing production and trade structures offer very limited opportunities in a rapidly globalizing world driven by new knowledge-intensive products with demanding conditions of market entry. At the same time, the rapid opening up in more traditional sectors is exposing existing producers to an unprecedented degree of global competition. Benefiting from recent technological advances requires advancing towards and crossing various thresholds in human capital, R&D and management practice, which most LDC economies have lacked the resources to do. The relentless logic of cumulative causation threatens to push LDCs even further behind.

Against this background, it is essential that national and international action to reduce poverty in the LDCs focus on the development of their productive capacities and the concomitant expansion of productive employment opportunities. This is urgent in the current conjuncture in which on the one hand the LDCs are in an urban transition, with more and more people seeking work in non-agricultural activities, and on the other hand the LDCs must compete within the global economy.

b) The adequacy of current national and international policies

A paradigm shift is required because current national and international policies which seek to promote development and poverty reduction in the LDCs are not adequately addressing the challenge of developing their productive capacities.

Most of the LDCs have been engaged in economic reforms since the late 1980s. These were initially undertaken within the context of structural adjustment programmes and involved macroeconomic stabilization, liberalization and privatization in a package of measures widely referred to as the "Washington Consensus" (Williamson, 1990). Since 2000, they have been undertaken in the context of a second generation of economic reforms. These are generally being implemented through poverty reduction strategies which are undertaken within the context of the PRSP approach. As discussed in earlier Reports, the PRSP approach seeks to facilitate more context-specific and nationally-owned economic reforms, as well as to ensure greater donor coordination and alignment behind national strategies (see UNCTAD, 2002;

More people are seeking work outside agriculture, and urbanization is accelerating. However, productive absorption of labour outside agriculture is simply not happening in many LDCs.

Generating productive employment to meet the urban transition is compounded by the challenge of globalization and an unprecedented degree of global competition.

Current national and international policies are not adequately addressing the challenge of developing their productive capacities.

UNCTAD, 2004a). However, the poverty reduction strategies also implement the policy agenda of the second-generation reforms, which include a greater focus on poverty and human development outcomes and the social orientation of public expenditure, as well as an increased concern for institutions of governance and improving the administrative, legal and regulatory functions of the State. As part of this shift towards getting the institutions right, there is now increased emphasis on improving the investment climate. Recently too, there has been a much greater focus on infrastructure as part of the investment climate.

It is now widely agreed that the outcomes of the first-generation reforms were much less than expected. This, indeed, was the major rationale for the shift from first-generation to second-generation reforms. As the World Bank (2004a: 12) puts it, this shift "was not so much a planned strategy as a result of the disappointing supply response to first generation reforms". This disappointing response was found in LDCs as much as in other developing countries (UNCTAD, 2000).

The policy focus of reforms in the 1990s enabled better use of existing capacity but did not provide sufficient incentive for expanding that capacity.

There are disagreements over why the first-generation reforms failed. One view is that they were not properly implemented. But this view understates how much policy reform has actually taken place in developing countries. Within the LDCs, it has been considerable (UNCTAD, 2000). It is now becoming clear that the disappointing results of the first-generation reforms were rooted in design faults, rather than in weak implementation. Moreover, the fundamental weakness of these programmes was that they failed to develop productive capacities. They rarely led to increased capital accumulation and failed to address the complex issues in promoting technological learning and innovation. As the World Bank (2005a: 10) puts it, "The policy focus of reforms in the 1990s enabled better use of existing capacity but did not provide sufficient incentive for expanding that capacity". Griffin (2005: 9) has identified lack of investment as the "Achilles heel" of structural adjustment and globalization, whilst Lall (2004) argues that reforms were based on a faulty understanding of how technological learning and technology acquisition occur. Both of these authors show how the poor outcomes of the first-generation reforms were rooted in conceptual design faults with respect to how structural change, which ostensibly was the essence of structural adjustment programmes, could occur.

Second-generation reforms have recognized the problem of a weak investment response, and it is for this reason that much more emphasis is now being placed on improving the investment climate. This is certainly a move in the right direction from the perspective of the importance of developing productive capacities. However, what constitutes the investment climate can be understood in different ways. In broad terms, it is understood as "the set of location-specific factors shaping the opportunities and incentives for firms to invest productively, create jobs and expand" (World Bank, 2004b). But in practice, it is then defined in a narrower way in which "investment climate interventions" are firstly associated with institutions, governance and policies, and secondly, with deregulation, competition and the reduction of bureaucratic red tape. World Bank (2004b), for example, focuses on corruption, taxes, regulatory burdens and red tape, infrastructure and finance costs, labour market regulation, policy predictability and credibility, macroeconomic stability, rights to property, contract enforcement, expropriation, regulatory barriers to entry and exit, competition law and policy, functioning finance markets and infrastructure. World Bank (2004c: 4) uses the Heritage Foundation/Wall Street Journal Index of Economic Freedom to measure the quality of the investment climate, with higher scores on the index representing greater levels of government interference in the economy and a worse investment climate.

This approach to the investment climate has three weaknesses. Firstly, it focuses on *constraints* on investment but ignores the central role of effective demand as a *stimulus* for investment. Secondly, it prejudges the appropriate role of government in creating an appropriate investment climate. In the developing countries which have been most successful in promoting high rates of sustained economic growth, there has been a much more proactive approach to public action in which the animal spirits of investors have been animated through policies which create rents that are conditional on investment, technological progress or exporting (see UNCTAD, 1994, 1996; Amsden, 2004). Thirdly, the approach is concerned with establishing framework conditions for investment. But in an LDC context structural weaknesses mean that it is necessary also to address meso-level policy issues. These are related to the structure of production; persistent productivity gaps between agriculture and the rest of the economy, between formal sector and informal sector enterprises, between large and small firms, and between rich and poor farmers; and the nature of intersectoral linkages, inter-firm relationships and production complementarities. These weaknesses also mean that the development of enterprise capabilities at the micro-level is also essential. Indeed, a key finding of the Investment Climate Assessments undertaken within LDCs is that there is a high degree of firm heterogeneity in economic performance. Against this background, an approach which simply sets the overall incentives framework in place, although necessary, is insufficient.

A key finding of the Investment Climate Assessments undertaken within LDCs is that there is a high degree of firm heterogeneity in economic performance.

The recent adoption of poverty reduction as the central objective of national and international development policy has also served to complicate policymaking. As argued above, because of the essential links between production, employment and poverty, the divide between productive development and poverty reduction is certainly artificial. However, in practice the recent emphasis on poverty reduction has led to a strong focus on social sectors and related human development targets. These are certainly important, and they should constitute an essential element of a strategy to develop productive capacities. But whilst social sectors and human development targets have taken centre stage, production and employment issues have been neglected. Once this occurs, there is a danger that there will be a partial approach which addresses the symptoms of poverty rather than its causes. It has even been suggested that "Present policies run the risk of creating serious imbalances between efforts to create development and the palliative efforts of aid. What we may be creating is a system that could be described as 'welfare colonialism'" (Reinert, 2005: 15).

Because of the essential links between production, employment and poverty, the divide between productive development and poverty reduction is certainly artificial.

Analysis of trends in the composition of aid commitments shows that there has been a significant decline in the share of ODA to LDCs which is committed to economic infrastructure and production-oriented sectors. The recent interest in "aid for trade" is a welcome reversal of this tendency, provided that it focuses, inter alia, on support to enhance supply capacities in tradables. But there are ongoing discussions about how this notion can be defined. Moreover, regardless of however it is defined, an approach to developing productive capacities which is simply trade-centric will not be enough for sustained and inclusive economic growth in the LDCs. As shown in the last LDC Report, export expansion has frequently not been associated with poverty reduction in the LDCs, partly because export activities develop as enclaves which are weakly linked to the rest of the economy and partly because they do not, in themselves, generate sufficient employment opportunities for the expanding labour supply.

Substantial and sustained poverty reduction in the LDCs will require "aid for the development of productive capacities", a part of which is "aid for trade".

It is important, too, that international support for the LDCs builds on domestic potentials. One consequence of the combination of a deficiency of domestic demand on the one hand, and weak capabilities, infrastructure and institutions for being internationally competitive on the other hand, is that productive resources and entrepreneurial capabilities are underutilized within the LDCs owing to lack of demand. There is surplus labour, latent entrepreneurship, untapped traditional knowledge and unsurveyed natural resources. International support for the LDCs needs to be founded on Albert Hirschmann's insight that "Development depends not so much on finding optimal combination for given resources and factors of production as on calling forth and enlisting for development purposes resources and abilities that are hidden, scattered, or badly utilized" (Hirschman, 1958: 5). Too often now, when aid is provided to develop productive capacities, it is envisaged as a "supply-side fix" to rectify perceived deficiencies, gaps and lacks, rather than serving to mobilize the creative forces and latent potentials of LDCs. The way in which technical cooperation currently works is a good example of this phenomenon (Fukudu-Parr, Lopes and Malik, 2002).

2. THE NATURE OF THE PARADIGM SHIFT

The paradigm shift which is advocated here is one which places the development of productive capacities at the heart of national and international policies to promote economic growth and poverty reduction in the LDCs. In this approach, policies should focus on promoting capital accumulation, technological progress and structural change in the LDCs. They should seek to start and sustain a virtuous circle in which the development of productive capacities and the growth of demand mutually reinforce each other. This should be done in a way in which productive employment opportunities expand in order to ensure poverty reduction.

This paradigm shift is not something totally new. Such a policy orientation has been elaborated, for example, by ECLAC in a series of studies on productive development (box 23). Moreover, it is similar to the policy orientation of the Japanese approach to economic development (box 24), which has been so influential in spawning a variety of East Asian development models. But it would be a new policy orientation for the LDCs and their development partners, even though developing productive capacities is part and parcel of the Brussels Programme of Action for the LDCs.

This approach is different from current policies in three major ways: it involves a different approach to poverty reduction, to productive capacities and to international trade.

(a) The approach to poverty reduction

The paradigm shift advocated here places production and employment at the heart of efforts to reduce poverty. This does not mean that social sector spending and human development targets are unimportant. Indeed, health, education and social welfare should be seen as part of the process of developing productive capacities. However, it goes beyond this. It links sustained and substantial poverty reduction to the development of the productive base of a society. A society's capacity to consume is related to its capacity to produce. It also includes the essential role of employment expansion in poverty reduction.

Policies should focus on promoting capital accumulation, technological progress and structural change in the LDCs and seek to start and sustain a virtuous circle in which the development of productive capacities and the growth of demand mutually reinforce each other.

The paradigm shift advocated here places production and employment at the heart of efforts to reduce poverty.

Box 23. ECLAC´s approach to productive development

A *structuralist* strand of analysis has underpinned the approach of the Economic Commission for Latin America (ECLAC) since the 1950s, although a shift towards *neo-structuralism* has since around 1990 become the main thrust of the "ECLAC approach" to development. This is a holistic approach to productive development and is exemplified by its publication *Productive Development in Open Economies* (ECLAC, 2004).

The basic premise of the ECLAC approach is that the overall performance of the economy involves the interplay between macro-, meso- and microeconomic dynamics, the latter two referred to as *"structural" dynamics*. Because of the importance of these interactions, much emphasis in the ECLAC approach is put on understanding strategic complementarities between productive sectors. The existence of complementarities, according to ECLAC, is the basis for the system's competitiveness. The interaction between these levels also forms the basis for the delineation of a productive development strategy. It is additionally this interaction that is responsible for structural change which includes change in "productive and technological apparatuses, the configuration of factor and product markets, the availability of factors, the characteristics of entrepreneurial agents, and the way in which these markets and agents related to external circumstances" (ECLAC, 2000).

The recognition of *structural heterogeneity* is also critical to ECLAC´s approach. This heterogeneity derives from market failures, the underdevelopment of markets and asymmetries with regard to the varying ability of different economic agents to access information, factor markets and other assets. With increasing structural heterogeneity, the economy tends to exhibit deteriorating levels of aggregate productivity. If an economy is characterized by structural heterogeneity, there will be no spontaneous trend towards the full employment of productive resources (ECLAC, 2004). This is therefore the basis for concerted public action.

"Selective intervention" is needed owing to the recognition that although it is essential to have well-functioning markets, "getting the prices right" alone will not lead to economic growth that is socially equitable. "Selective intervention" is based on the justification of what is socially efficient for public policy to accomplish in areas in which it can have the greatest macroeconomic impact. A key feature of neo-structuralist thinking identifies the State as necessary for institutionalizing markets and encouraging *development from within;* this will not necessarily occur in a free-market environment.

In structurally heterogeneous economies, the application of apparently neutral policies has non-neutral outcomes. This is one of the main justifications for the reassessment of the role of public policy after the implementation of the neo-liberal policies. But the neo-structuralist approach represents a break with certain structuralist policies applied in the past, and therefore with the precepts underpinning these policies. This break represents an evolution in thinking towards recognizing the new dictates of the market economy, and that is evident in the incorporation of concepts of economic efficiency in current proposals, including an argumentation in favour of the "provision of incentives" but "on the basis of performance" (ECLAC, 2000: 233).

ECLAC´s 2004 Report entitled *Productive Development in Open Economies* provides an analysis of the main strategies available to the Latin American and Caribbean region to build, strengthen and modernize the region's productive apparatus. It includes the following three major strategies:

1) *An inclusion strategy*: intended to shift as many small productive units in the economy from the informal to the formal sector. Some mechanisms for this purpose include: the simplification of rules and administrative procedures, lower taxes with simplified declaration procedures, expanded access to credit for small investments, and basic training in management and technology skills.

2) *A modernization strategy*: based on selective measures directed at different production clusters or particular production chains. Criteria for selection could include the possibility of producing goods and services for exports, the possibility of introduction of higher levels of technology in the productive system, and so forth. It is suggested that support for modernizing production could include policies to improve access to information, credit, technology and marketing systems, and export activities enhanced by offering services for the provision of guidance on foreign markets by specialized public agencies, as well as by private sector business associations. Additionally, policies directed at training activities, the incorporation of improvements in production and technology, and procurement of new machinery and equipment should be adopted.

3) *A densification strategy,* which involves incorporating more knowledge into the national productive environment, to create a more interlinked web of productive, technological, entrepreneurial and labour relations. This simultaneously requires the necessary well-functioning institutions and public policy, and greater private sector involvement. This would include the implementation of programmes aimed at strengthening the links at the export base, public–private cooperation in particular areas of innovation, attracting higher-quality foreign investment for the creation of productive links and technological capacities, and strengthening services infrastructure to ease production bottlenecks.

Box 24. A Japanese approach to economic development

Like ECLAC (see box 23), various Japanese development economists have elaborated an approach to economic development which focuses on production development. Ohno (1998) summarizes the main features of the Japanese approach as follows:

- The highest priority should be given to the real economy, not financial targets.

- Real targets should be part of a long-term development strategy (not quarterly or monthly performance criteria) which would typically include "(i) setting long-term national goals (e.g. creating a certain number of jobs within five years, doubling income in ten years, building industries from scratch, achieving industrialization by 2020); and (ii) designing comprehensive and concrete annual steps towards these goals, identifying bottlenecks, appropriate budgetary resources and establishing implementing bodies' strategies. Working backwards from long-term goals thus determines action required today.

- Government plays an active role in promoting development.

- It is understood that fostering a market economy takes time.

- Strategies need to be country-specific.

Yanagihara (1998) distinguishes between the framework approach and the ingredients approach to development policy. As he puts it, "The 'framework' represents rules of the game according to which economic agents make decisions and take action in a given economy…In contrast, the 'ingredients' refer to tangible organizational units such as enterprises, official bureaus, and industrial projects and their aggregations such as industries, sectors and regions. They may, however, also relate to factors of production — land, labor, capital and technology — at different levels of aggregation and specificity. The ingredients approach conceives the economy as a collection of these components. It envisions economic development as the quantitative expansion and qualitative upgrading of the components, accompanied by shifts in composition" (pp. 70–71).

These approaches see development and structural adjustment policies in distinctly different ways. "In the 'framework approach' the central task of policy and institutional reforms is correcting distortions to the incentive scheme, defined by the policy environment and institutional arrangements. By contrast, in the 'ingredients approach' policies and institutions are viewed as tangible inputs, like conventional factors of production, that shape the process of economic change. They are the means to achieve a future vision of the economy, typically depicted in terms of a collection of industrial or regional economies". (p. 71)

In the "framework approach", "setting the framework right is considered a necessary, if not always sufficient, condition for successful development which will be manifested in improved macroeconomic indicators. By … [the] very essence of the approach, little consideration is given to what sort of real-sector economy will result once the framework is in place: that is left to the market to determine. Conversely in the ingredients approach the economic outcome in terms of sectoral composition or industrial organization occupies centre stage, while the mode of economic management remains flexible and uncommitted. Certain economic orientations, such as what sectors or activities ought to be given priority, come into play but they are derived from, and therefore subordinate to, the ultimate goal — or premeditated result — of economic development" (p. 71). This approach is "results-oriented, conceptualized in tangible rather than functional terms (building new factories versus enhancing the market mechanism in general). Development strategy aims to achieve economic expansion via accumulation of appropriate ingredients to increase productive capacity at the firm or project level" (p. 75).

In applying this approach in the context of very poor countries, a basic insight is that the market economy is underdeveloped and that markets have to be created (Ishikawa, 1998). Poverty reduction strategies should also focus on production and productivity rather than simply seeking to alleviate poverty directly (Ohno, 2002; Ishikawa, 2002).

Work within ILO on the employment nexus between growth and poverty has a similar emphasis (see box 13).

(b) The approach to productive capacities

From the foregoing discussion of the investment climate, it is clear that the development of productive capacities is not absent from the current policy approach. However, the paradigm shift advocated here involves a different approach to the development of productive capacities. This involves the following:

- Macroeconomic policies oriented to promoting growth, investment and employment;

- A multilevel approach which not only seeks to set the framework institutions and macroeconomic environment, but also includes policies to change meso-level production structures and institutions, as well as micro-level capabilities and incentives;

- An active approach to promoting entrepreneurship;

- A strategic approach to global integration.

Macroeconomic policies are an essential part of developing productive capacities. But if the development of productive capacities is adopted as the central policy goal, macroeconomic policies need to shift away from a focus on financial stabilization to promoting economic growth, investment and employment. Ffrench-Davies (2005) has called such an approach "a macroeconomics-for-development". This "requires a clear and systematic distinction between what is merely an economic recovery as opposed to generating additional productive capacity. Distinguishing between creating *new* capacity and using *existing* capacity should be a guiding principle for monetary, exchange rate and fiscal policy, as well as regulation of capital flows" (p. 7). He goes on to argue that "To ensure a policy environment that stimulates growth, countries must strive to get the *real* macroeconomic fundamentals right. This implies a sustainable external deficit, a moderate stock of external liabilities with a low liquid share, and a reasonable matching of terms and currencies. It also means a crowding in of domestic savings, limited exchange-rate appreciation and an effective demand consistent with the production frontier, together with responsible fiscal policies and a manageable inflation rate" (p. 7).

The *multilevel approach* is based on the insight that the dynamics of production structures matter for economic growth and that within any given macroeconomic framework, there are very heterogeneous outcomes amongst enterprises involved in the same economic activities. Meso-policies are thus required in addition to macro-economic policies in order to promote structural change and dynamic linkages, and these should be complemented with policies to build micro-level enterprise capabilities. This is not a matter of "picking winners", as it is often disparagingly described. Within the LDCs, increasing productivity and employment for long-run sustainable growth requires a twin strategy of investing in dynamically growing sectors while at the same time building capacity in sectors where the majority of labour is employed. A strategy of investing only in dynamic sectors in attempts to "leapfrog" may not be enough to reduce poverty, mainly because the fastest-growing sectors may often not be where the majority of the poor are employed and may require skills and training that the poor do not possess. The challenge then is to broaden the impact of the dynamically growing sectors of the economy, while deepening their linkages with other sectors in the economy — sectors where the majority of the poor are underemployed. At the same time, it is paramount to ensure that the poor can

Macroeconomic policies need to shift away from a focus on financial stabilization to promoting economic growth, investment and employment.

Increasing productivity and employment for long-run sustainable growth requires a twin strategy of investing in dynamically growing sectors while at the same time building capacity in sectors where the majority of labour is employed.

be provided with skills and training for labour absorption in these growing areas of the economy.

The most effective approach would support and stimulate simultaneous investments in agriculture, industry and services along the value chain of the promising sectors, as well as promotion of exports, which would stimulate upgrading and increased local value-added of abundant natural resources. The focus should be on integrated development that would set off an interactive growth process that recognizes the important role of intersectoral dynamics in rural and non-rural activities, particularly in those activities that can catalyse and sustain economic growth through a dynamic interrelationship between the primary, secondary and tertiary sectors. Agricultural growth linkages, in which there is a virtuous circle in which demand stimulus from agricultural growth generates investment, entrepreneurship and employment in non-agricultural activities, particularly non-tradables, are likely to be relevant in many LDCs and at the heart of efforts to create a more inclusive process of development which supports sustainable poverty reduction.

Entrepreneurship is a critical component within the process of developing productive capacities. It is essentially the deliberate act of creating economic value by seizing new opportunities through risk taking and the mobilization of human, social, financial and physical capital. There are two features of entrepreneurship which are important for channelling this animating force into the development of productive capacities. Firstly, rents (or the extra profits associated with innovative activity) play an important role in animating entrepreneurship (Kahn and Jomo, 2000). Secondly, entrepreneurship need not always be oriented to positive economic outcomes. If entrepreneurship is understood to involve rent seeking it is necessary to distinguish between productive and unproductive variants. Unproductive or destructive entrepreneurial activities involve individuals or firms that are engaging in profit-seeking activities based on asymmetric information, establishing illegal barriers to entry or reinforcing a monopoly position. Such activities require unproductive use of resources in securing rents and can become very destructive by encouraging predatory types of firm behaviour. On the other hand, productive entrepreneurship can help to direct resources towards productive uses. A major policy challenge in LDCs today is how to convert rent-seeking unproductive entrepreneurship into productive entrepreneurship and how to use public action to create entrepreneurial rents which act as incentives for productive entrepreneurship and thus to channel entrepreneurship into the development of productive capacities.

The development of productive capacities is a strategy of "development from within", as Sunkel (1993) has put it,[1] in the sense that it seeks to mobilize and develop domestic productive resources and capabilities and to increase production linkages within the national economy. However, it is important not to confuse this with an inward-looking strategy. There are major opportunities for the development of productive capacities through global integration. Thus *policies of global integration* are an essential part of the policy orientation being advocated here.

However, policies for global integration should not be equated with trade and capital account liberalization. There is a broader range of options for strategic integration with the rest of the world which include, but are not limited to, a permissive state of full openness. As Westphal (2004) has put it with regard to trade integration, "Openness in efficacious terms does not preclude a significant degree of import protection, but only so long as protectionist

> *The focus should be on integrated development that would set off an interactive growth process that recognizes the important role of intersectoral dynamics in rural and non-rural activities, particularly in those activities that can catalyse and sustain economic growth through a dynamic interrelationship between the primary, secondary and tertiary sectors.*

> *A major policy challenge in LDCs today is how to convert rent-seeking unproductive entrepreneurship into productive entrepreneurship and how to use public action to create entrepreneurial rents which act as incentives for productive entrepreneurship.*

measures do not unduly constrain a country's pursuit of its dynamic comparative advantage, as was true at least in the case of Taiwan [Province of China] and [the Republic of Korea]." Bradford (2005) notes that there is a role for targeted capital controls and intermediate exchange rate regimes in providing the macroeconomic policy space to prioritize economic growth.

What is best will vary between countries. But what is being advocated here is a strategic approach to global integration in which the speed and degree of liberalization in different types of economic interaction areas take account of the goal of developing productive capacities. In many LDCs, the regional dimension of global integration is likely to be important. Moreover, policies need to be adopted to maximize the opportunities and minimize the risks of global integration.

In this regard, three major opportunities can be underlined. Firstly, the external market, as a vent for surplus, can provide an outlet for domestic productive capacities that would otherwise remain underutilized, and can trigger a virtuous circle of higher demand, greater investment and increased productivity growth. Secondly, much of the effort in developing productive capacities should be concentrated on strengthening the role and size of domestic enterprises. However, foreign firms (through FDI and other channels) can be a beneficial factor in this process if domestic policy works to ensure that foreign enterprises crowd in rather than crowd out domestic enterprises, and if there are dynamic linkages between them promoting learning and investment. Thirdly, promoting the acquisition of imported technologies, technological learning and the diffusion of best practice amongst firms can provide important opportunities for accelerating economic growth through technological catch-up.

(c) The approach to international trade

The paradigm shift advocated here also involves a different approach to international trade. Since the early 1980s, there has been a strong tendency for ideas from international trade theory to dominate the understanding of development processes. This occurred initially through comparisons between the relative success of "outward-oriented" and "inward-oriented" development strategies, which were associated with particular trade policy regimes. But it was reinforced in the 1990s through arguments to the effect that fast and full integration with the world economy was the key to seizing the opportunities of globalization and minimizing the chance of being left behind. From this perspective, global integration began to replace national development as the major policy objective of Governments.

In the approach advocated here, international trade is seen as essential for the development of productive capacities, and the development of productive capacities is seen as essential for international trade. But the paradigm shift entails starting at the development end, rather than the trade end, of the relationship between trade and development.

As argued in the last LDC Report on trade and poverty, "International trade can play a powerful role in reducing poverty in the least developed countries as well as in other developing countries. But national and international policies which can facilitate this must be rooted in a development-driven approach to trade rather than a trade-driven approach to development" (UNCTAD, 2004a: 67). The policy approach advocated here thus first focuses on production, and then from this perspective identifies how international trade can support capital accumulation, technological change, structural change, employment creation

The paradigm shift entails starting at the development end, rather than the trade end, of the relationship between trade and development.

and poverty reduction. What matters is not to maximize trade, but to maximize the beneficial effects of trade.

C. Some policy options and policy measures

National and international policies to develop productive capacities in the LDCs should prioritize the relaxing of key constraints on capital accumulation, technological progress and structural change.

National and international policies to develop productive capacities in the LDCs should prioritize the relaxing of key constraints on capital accumulation, technological progress and structural change. The idea that public policy in developing countries should focus on relaxing key constraints on economic growth has been recently elaborated by Hausmann, Rodrik and Velasco (2005). They argue that economic reforms should be growth strategies and propose that the latter should be formulated "by identifying the most binding constraints on economic activity, and hence the set of policies that, once targeted on these constraints at any point in time, is likely to provide the biggest bang for the reform buck" (p. 2). The approach proposed here — to focus on relaxing key constraints on capital accumulation, technological progress and structural change — is analogous.

As Hausmann, Rodrik and Velasco argue, one of the advantages of such policy diagnostics is that it gets away from a one-size-fits-all approach to economic reform and identifies binding constraints in particular country contexts. It is important that in putting productive capacities at the heart of national and international policies to promote economic growth and poverty reduction in the LDCs, a context-specific approach be followed. However, in order to illustrate what the paradigm shift might mean in practice, this section focuses on the three key constraints which were identified in the previous three chapters of the Report and seeks to summarize briefly some of the key policy priorities and policy measures to relax these constraints. The three constraints are:

It is important that in putting productive capacities at the heart of national and international policies to promote economic growth and poverty reduction in the LDCs, a context-specific approach should be followed.

- The infrastructure divide;
- Institutional weaknesses — firms, financial systems and knowledge systems;
- The demand constraint.

The main message which follows from this discussion is that the paradigm shift does not entail wholesale changes in the subjects which policymakers are seeking to address. However, some policy issues which have been ignored or neglected assume more importance than previously, and some old policy issues are treated in a different way. Moreover, the focus on the development of productive capacities is likely to raise questions with regard to national and global governance, which is an issue which will be dealt with in the final section of this chapter.

1. Closing the infrastructure divide

Closing the physical infrastructure divide between LDCs and other developing countries is one of the quantitative targets of the Brussels Programme of Action for the LDCs. The evidence of this Report suggests that it is an important objective as the LDCs have the poorest transport, telecommunication and energy infrastructure in the world. Although possibilities for private financing of physical infrastructure should not be neglected, the past record shows that this source alone cannot meet infrastructure needs. There is thus a need for increased public investment and a reversal of the downward trend in aid for economic infrastructure which a number of LDCs, particularly in Africa, have experienced in the period 1990–2003. In the field of physical infrastructure there is a strong complementarity between private and public investment. This complementarity can serve as an important source of growth and an important influence on the composition and distribution of gains from growth. Public investment can be a key factor in raising the levels of productivity in order to generate a net surplus as a key source of accumulation in all sectors of the economy (UN Millennium Project, 2005).

Improved physical infrastructure can play an important role in reducing the costs and the amount of time with which exporters have to contend in international trade transactions. However, infrastructure investment should focus not only on investment in trade-related infrastructure. There is rather a need for a joined-up approach to infrastructure development which includes (i) rural infrastructure and district-level links between rural areas and small towns; (ii) large-scale national infrastructure (such as trunk roads, transmission lines and port facilities); and (iii) cross-border regional infrastructure. Increased public investment in the first is important for agricultural productivity growth and the development of a market economy in rural areas, as well as the creation of rural non-farm employment. Increased public investment in the second is important for diversification and structural change, as well as international trade integration. Increased public investment in the third is important for regional integration.

Particular efforts should be made to promote electrification and to close the electricity divide between LDCs and other developing countries. Most modern technologies require electricity, and the current low levels of access to electricity increase costs for firms, reducing their available funds for investment, and are a basic source of the technological incongruence between the LDCs and the rest of the world which is hampering the acquisition of technologies. This Report also shows that access to electricity affects the composition of exports in developing countries, and that differences in the degree of diversification into manufactures exports are partly related to the degree of electrification.

2. ADDRESSING INSTITUTIONAL WEAKNESSES: FIRMS, FINANCIAL SYSTEMS AND KNOWLEDGE SYSTEMS

The major thrust of current efforts to get institutions right is focused on good governance. With the paradigm shift advocated here, there needs to be a much greater focus on the nature of the domestic private sector and the financial systems and knowledge systems within which it is embedded. Productive capacities are developed and put to work at the level of the firm and the farm. But this does not happen in isolation from the wider institutional context and the systems of local production and consumption within which they are embedded.

A major problem in many LDCs is that there is a "missing middle" in the enterprise structure, with a multitude of informal sector micro-enterprises coexisting with a few large firms, and there are formal sector SMEs, particularly medium-sized firms, that are weakly developed. In addition, these SMEs face numerous obstacles to expansion. The current PRSP strategies recognize this and focus on providing support for SME development and small scale entrepreneurship. Also: "Most PSD [private sector development] work has focused on providing effective support to the development of small scale entrepreneurs, [and] micro-finance schemes" (World Bank, 2001: 12). SMEs are certainly important as they tend to use local inputs and thus are the agents that

Public investment can be a key factor in raising the levels of productivity in order to generate a net surplus as a key source of accumulation in all sectors of the economy.

Particular efforts should be made to promote electrification and to close the electricity divide between LDCs and other developing countries.

A major problem in many LDCs is that there is a "missing middle" in the enterprise structure, with a multitude of informal sector micro-enterprises coexisting with a few large firms.

link local primary and manufacturing activities. They also provide employment to the local population. But an exclusive focus on SMEs is based on a static view of the development process. From a dynamic efficiency perspective, large-size firms are in a better position to generate the resources to realize higher rates of capital formation, innovation, economies of scale and the accompanying learning effects. Such firms are also in a far better position to diversify into higher-value-added activities (Kozul-Wright, 1995). One major reason why SMEs do not grow is that there is an inadequate demand for their products. Fostering linkages between large firms and SMEs is an important demand-side measure to complement the supply-side measures for SME development. Moreover, such inter-firm linkages can also facilitate knowledge transfers, technology transfer and technological upgrading. This suggests the need for an alternative policy framework based on supporting firm growth and expansion, the promotion of linkages between SMEs and large firms, the development of subcontracting relations, and the promotion of clustering and spatial agglomeration.

The development of productive capacities depends on the ability of an economy to create enterprises with a high propensity to invest, learn and innovate. A major focus of investment climate reforms is on reducing obstacles to entry, lowering costs of credit, and encouraging competition and market efficiency. But the available evidence suggests that firm entry is not the major problem, and markets are very competitive and can prune out inefficient firms. However, that "churning" process may be so strong that it may not permit new entrants to acquire the required technological capabilities to grow. Greater attention thus needs to given to constraints on firm growth. Attention should also be given to dealing with the anti-competitive conduct of oligopolistic processors and exporters (some of which are vertically integrated with TNCs), which prevents diversification and the development of new processing industries.

The working of financial systems and knowledge systems is closely related to the issue of enterprise development. Financial markets are weak and subject to major market failures. Increasingly, in a more liberal policy environment, foreign financial institutions have come to dominate, but the narrow client base has not expanded and remains concentrated on either the Government or large domestic and foreign firms. Overcoming bottlenecks in financing for the private sector should be a critical priority for policymakers in the LDCs. Without access to capital by the private sector, the potential for development of productive capacities cannot be realized.

The importance of improving the financial systems in the LDCs is indeed widely recognized. However, new sources of financing urgently need to be identified and lessons may be drawn from the more successful cases in countries with deeper financial systems that are more responsive to the needs of the private sector. Experience suggests that a bank-based system is important at low levels of development. Possible financial instruments include, the following:

- Loan guarantee schemes between the public and the private sector to facilitate access to bank credit for SMEs and large enterprises investing in technical change;

- Public development banks, particularly to create long-term financing;

- Value-chain lending in which lending to enterprises along a value chain is coordinated;

- Innovative market-based financial instruments.

Knowledge systems are as important as financial systems in the development of productive capacities. Thus improving domestic knowledge systems should

Fostering linkages between large firms and SMEs is an important demand-side measure to complement the supply-side measures for SME development.

Without access to capital by the private sector, the potential for development of productive capacities cannot be realized.

Knowledge systems are as important as financial systems in the development of productive capacities.

complement efforts to improve domestic financial systems. This involves not only setting up special bodies oriented to creating knowledge which could be applied in production (such as research centres), but also creating bridging institutions with users and promoting linkages amongst users. For most LDCs the three most important sources for building their domestic knowledge base are education, foreign technology imports (through foreign licensing, FDI, turnkey plants and capital goods imports) and the mobility of experienced technical personnel. These are more important than seeking to increase levels of R&D. Investing in all levels of education is particularly important given the currently low levels of schooling which are found in most LDCs. This makes technology absorption difficult and slows down the technology catch-up process.

LDCs need to develop well-designed and coherent national technology learning strategies to increase access to technology and to improve the effectiveness of imported technology, as well as to benefit from linking to global knowledge. There are major opportunities for blending modern and traditional knowledge, particularly in areas of health and agriculture.

Investing in all levels of education is particularly important given the currently low levels of schooling which are found in most LDCs.

3. THE DEMAND CONSTRAINT

The greatest shifts in policy priorities arise when the demand constraint is brought into the analysis of the development of productive capacities. In the analysis in this Report, two mechanisms through which the development of productive capacities is either limited or stimulated by demand-side factors have been emphasized: the balance-of-payments constraint on the other components of domestic demand, — namely private consumption, investment and government consumption expenditure; and the linkages between agricultural growth and the expansion of non-tradables.

The greatest shifts in policy priorities arise when the demand constraint is brought into the analysis of the development of productive capacities.

With regard to the balance-of-payments constraint, it is clear that most LDCs have persistent trade deficits which have been financed by capital inflows and transfers. When these are insufficient to finance the deficits, or when they are volatile, the other components of demand have to be limited. Moreover, current growth rates are highly dependent on the level of capital inflows and transfers, which for most countries come in the form of ODA inflows. Policy needs to be explicitly geared to relax the balance-of-payments constraint on economic growth in order to decrease dependence on external sources of finance, particularly aid. This can be achieved by supply-side reforms which increase the income elasticity of demand for exports (by increasing the share of more dynamic products in the export structure) and reduce the income demand elasticity (through facilitating efficient import substitution and rationalizing import costs).

Upgrading of the export structure is particularly important in the LDCs because it is difficult to generate sufficiently fast export growth to finance the imports they need in order to develop their productive capacities, given the current pattern of trade integration with the global economy. The current LDC growth trajectories, based on export specialization of raw, unprocessed commodities, have evolved in line with the theoretical principles of static comparative advantage. The concentration on production and export of primary commodities and extractive industries largely oriented towards external markets has essentially failed in LDCs to contribute effectively to catching up, and has not provided the road out of persistent poverty. Instead, too often, such growth trajectories have led to enclave economies, dualistic economic structures, a poor poverty reduction record, and an increase in macroeconomic instability.

Upgrading of the export structure is particularly important in the LDCs... The policy measures to achieve export upgrading should not be limited to the trade regime but should also include a new kind of industrial policy.

BOX 25. INDUSTRIAL POLICY FOR THE 21ST CENTURY

Traditional activist industrial policy aimed at shifting the structure of production towards promising sectors was applied in most developing countries in the 1950s and 1960s through the strategy of import substitution, which called for (a) subsidies to targeted industries, and (b) the nurturing of infant industries through high tariffs on, and non-tariff barriers to, imported products in order to increase the domestic demand for locally produced products. With a view to expanding their industrial bases and developing strategic sectors, the strategy of "picking winners" was widely used. Interventions included targeting and subsidizing credit to selected industries, and protecting domestic import substitutes through trade and tariff policies. Public investment was directed towards the selected "winners", and public development banks supported the development of the selected firms or sectors through sectoral or vertical industrial policy. The State helped the "winners" to export by setting export targets, and getting "prices wrong" (Amsden, 2004) in order to promote the development of domestic enterprises.

These policies often gave rise to rent-seeking by special interest groups. State-owned enterprises were not subject to performance criteria or effective monitoring in line with development goals, and this often led to rampant rent-seeking and unproductive entrepreneurship (Baumol, 1990). The situation was made worse by the debt crisis, and, too often, industrial policy became the hostage of special interest groups and wasted scarce resources.

Beginning in the 1980s, these policies were dismantled in the context of structural adjustment programmes. However, with the disappointing results of these programmes there has recently been a revival of interest in industrial policies with a new approach (Oyelaran-Oyeyinka, 2005, Kuznetsov and Sabel, 2005; Cimoli, Dosi and Nelson, 2006).

The new model of industrial policy is based on a mixed, market-based model with private entrepreneurship and government working closely together in order to create strategic complementarities between public and private sector investment. The key role assigned to Governments relates to performing a strategic and coordinating role in the productive sphere that goes "beyond simply ensuring property rights, contract enforcement and macroeconomic stability" (Rodrik, 2004b: 2). The new industrial policy essentially perceives the State as a facilitator of learning and a provider of a regulatory framework that can accommodate a system of ensured private IPRs, attract FDI through fiscal incentives and indirect subsidies, and improve market governance by removing bottlenecks and correcting market failures. The role of the State is to provide a system of market-based political governance, based on the principles of a sound macroeconomic climate, in order to promote a pro-business investment climate. The new industrial policy focuses on innovation, and emphasizes the role of non-market institutions in the process of discovery. The private sector is perceived as the main agent of change (Kuznetsov and Sabel, 2005).

The new industrial policy is conceptualized as a discovery process, in which non-market institutions such as intellectual property rights, are critical in shaping industrial dynamics. The relevant institutions and cost structures are not given but need to be discovered. There are significant risks involved. This implies the need for a partnership and synergies with the public sector to socialize risks. The State generates and coordinates private investment through market-based incentives aimed at reducing risks and sharing benefits.

The policy needs to seek out new areas of comparative advantage, or to "acquire" comparative advantage, whereby goods with a high income elasticity of demand in the world markets are produced.

The policy measures to achieve export upgrading should not be limited to the trade regime but should also include a new kind of industrial policy. Such a policy is not like the old industrial policy but should draw lessons from policy innovations in developed countries which seek to develop new kinds of public–private partnerships (box 25). It may encompass proactive measures to promote agriculture and services as well as manufacturing industries.[2] The policy needs to seek out new areas of comparative advantage, or to "acquire" comparative advantage, whereby goods with a high income elasticity of demand in the world markets are produced. There is potentially a role for selective protection in LDCs based on arguments linked to addressing market failures, capturing externalities or welfare-enhancing policies, and in the case of international distortions. Given some unfortunate experiences in implementing trade reforms (see World Bank, 2006; Laird and Fernández de Cordoba, 2006, forthcoming), this implies that, in countries which have not yet undertaken extensive trade liberalization, there is a case for caution and a gradual approach. For those countries which have undertaken trade liberalization, this is not a call for a blanket reversal of this policy; rather, it is a call for a pragmatic analysis of policy options. This could include special safeguards against food import surges.

Policymakers should be cautious in relying on the effects of national currency devaluation as a policy for balance-of-payments adjustment. From a theoretical point of view, it is not clear that a one-off currency depreciation can put an economy on a higher growth path consistent with balance-of-payments equilibrium. Devaluation will not work from the demand side if the price elasticities of demand for imports and exports are low; and devaluation will not work from the supply side if devaluation is inflationary and raises costs in the traded goods sector, which reduce foreign exchange earnings per unit of domestic inputs. Currency devaluation can be highly inflationary and have effects that could erode an initial competitive advantage. The limited role for real exchange rate adjustment reinforces the need for a structural approach to balance-of-payments difficulties focusing on the income elasticities of demand for imports and exports, rather than on price elasticities working through relative price changes. However, equally, government needs to ensure that real exchange rates do not appreciate.

Policy analysis of the balance-of-payments constraint shows the importance of exports for growth processes within the LDCs. However, inclusive development and poverty reduction require a development strategy which also pays attention to the dynamics of domestic demand as well as external markets. This is particularly important since the domestic components of demand are the major demand-side source of economic growth in most LDCs. From this perspective, the most effective strategy is not simply to focus on the development of productive capacities within the tradable sectors, but also to develop productive capacities within non-tradable activities and to intensify the dynamic linkages between those activities. It is in the non-tradable sectors that labour can be more effectively absorbed.

The most effective strategy is not simply to focus on the development of productive capacities within the tradable sectors, but also to develop productive capacities within non-tradable activities and to intensify the dynamic linkages between those activities.

Because the majority of the population in most of the LDCs are employed in agriculture, the dynamics of domestic demand are strongly influenced by what happens in agriculture. In this regard, an important poverty reduction mechanism that has been identified is the backward linkage effects of agricultural growth on the development of non-tradable industries and services in rural areas and small towns. These linkage effects mainly work through consumer demand for these products. They can create a virtuous circle in which demand stimulus from agricultural growth generates investment, entrepreneurship and employment in non-agricultural activities, particularly non-tradables, and growth of these non-agricultural activities in turn enables and stimulates investment in agriculture. Policy needs to facilitate such dynamic inter-sectoral linkages. This is likely to be relevant in many LDCs and at the heart of efforts to create a more inclusive process of development which supports sustainable poverty reduction.

The formulation and the implementation of policies to promote capital accumulation, technological progress and structural change require government– business cooperation within the framework of a pragmatic developmental State.

D. Governance issues

Placing the development of productive capacities at the heart of national and international policies to promote economic growth and reduce poverty in the LDCs has implications for both national and global governance.

1. National governance

The formulation and the implementation of policies to promote capital accumulation, technological progress and structural change require government–business cooperation within the framework of a pragmatic developmental State. The policies should be implemented as far as possible through private initiative rather than public ownership and through the market mechanism rather than administrative controls. But the Government should play a key role in animating the animal spirits of the private sector and harnessing the aggressive pursuit of profits, which is the motor driving the system, to the realization of national development and poverty reduction goals. It should play a creative role in developing markets, and also in "allowing private agents to satisfy individually or collectively certain goals unattainable through market forces alone" (Moreau, 2004: 848). Often this can be achieved through improving coordination between economic agents to take account of production and investment complementarities.

Promoting the development of productive capacities will require the enhancement of State capacities rather than State minimalism. Honest, impartial and competent administrative, judicial and law enforcement systems are crucial not only for upholding the rule of law, protecting property rights and ensuring personal security but also for building an atmosphere of trust in public institutions. The developmental State also requires the creation of civil service capacities and of agencies capable of drawing up coherent development programmes and implementing specific policies so that they serve the broader national interest and are not captured by sectional or individual interests.

Honest, impartial and competent administrative, judicial and law enforcement systems are crucial not only for upholding the rule of law, protecting property rights and ensuring personal security but also for building an atmosphere of trust in public institutions.

It may be argued that in the LDCs the State capacities required in order to develop productive capacities simply do not exist.[3] There is an objective basis for this argument. In many LDCs, the cutbacks in State administrative services since the early 1980s have been particularly severe, as the data in chapter 3 indicate. In addition, government effectiveness has suffered from an internal brain drain from government offices to bilateral and multilateral aid agencies setting up parallel projects. There are also instances of inadequate governance which arise from rapacious leadership. In some countries, predatory behaviour associated with the exploitation of natural resources has interacted with civil conflict and instability to create growth collapses. Finally, it is clear that lack of financial resources is a key source of inadequate governance (UN Millennium Project, 2005). Good governance requires an adequately paid civil service, judiciary and police force; adequate communication and information technology; equipment and training for a reliable police force; and modern technological capabilities for customs authorities to secure borders. But in poor countries the magnitude of financial resources which can be mobilized domestically for good governance is severely constrained by the weak productive base of the economy and the consequent low revenue base.

Although State capacities are weak, this does not mean that the State is irrevocably incapable.

However, although State capacities are weak, this does not mean that the State is irrevocably incapable. The government capacities required in order to formulate and implement a strategy to develop productive capacities and expand productive employment opportunities are no more exacting than those required for formulating and implementing a poverty reduction strategy. Indeed, there are probably more working models to turn to with regard to the former than the latter.

It is important to see good governance not in static terms but rather in dynamic terms as a learning process.

With the publication of comprehensive sets of governance indicators which benchmark countries globally, it appears that there is now an objective basis for measuring governance. But the methodology which is used makes it difficult to see how an individual country is changing over time and governance is measured in relative terms (i.e. governance standards in relation to other countries) rather than absolute terms. There is a close relationship between higher governance scores and GDP per capita. As a result, most LDCs will always be towards the bottom 40 per cent of countries, those with bad governance.

In the end it is important to see good governance not in static terms but rather in dynamic terms as a learning process. For this to happen, Governments need the flexibility to experiment, to make mistakes and to make incremental improvements. It is through this process that learning will take place and good governance will develop. Such processes of trial and error and institutional and policy experimentation have characterized all previous examples of successful development. Through such processes Governments have discovered what actually works in their particular context.

2. GLOBAL GOVERNANCE

Developing productive capacities requires not only good national governance but also good global governance. With globalization, various international institutions matter for capital accumulation, technological progress and structural changes within countries. Critically important are the international regimes governing private capital flows and aid, technology transfer and intellectual property rights, and international migration, both globally and regionally. The nature of these international regimes has an important role to play in enhancing the opportunities for globalization and reducing its risks. They are generally characterized by asymmetries which constrain and enable different countries to a different extent. Improving these regimes is an important policy pressure point to promote the development of productive capacities within LDCs.

Developing productive capacities requires not only good national governance but also good global governance.

As shown in the first part of this Report, since 2000 there has been a major scaling up of international financial support for LDCs provided by their development partners, as well as increased debt relief and international initiatives to support trade expansion. But these positive developments need to be linked more closely to national policies to develop productive capacities if they are to be effective in creating a more self-sustaining growth process and reducing aid dependence. Moreover, any conditions attached to aid must not hamper a Government's efforts to discover the best ways to develop productive capacities and its ability to experiment to find the best approach in its local context.

Making productive capacities the focus of national and international policies to promote economic growth and poverty reduction in the LDCs also requires policy innovation with regard to international support measures for LDCs. Examples could be: a broad approach to "aid for trade" which links it not simply to physical infrastructure but also private sector development and the promotion of linkages, as well as the development of domestic financial systems and domestic knowledge systems; measures to deepen market access with supply-side support, for example through special incentives for encouraging FDI (Cline, 2004), particularly a type of FDI which has positive spillover effects for domestic enterprise; the activation of the provision in the TRIPS Agreement to support technology transfer to LDCs; a rethinking of the role of technical cooperation and the way in which ODA supports domestic knowledge systems; or new approaches to use aid for private sector development and to strengthen the domestic financial systems in LDCs. These are indicative suggestions. Devising new international support measures which can promote the development of productive capacities in the LDCs is an important frontier for development policy analysis which should be explored in the future.

Making productive capacities the focus of national and international policies to promote economic growth and poverty reduction in the LDCs requires policy innovation with regard to international support measures for LDCs.

Notes

1. Sunkel (1993) describes "development from within" as a "creative domestic effort to shape productive structure" (p. 46), writing that "The heart of development lies in the supply side: quality, flexibility, the efficient combination and utilization of productive resources, the adoption of technological developments, an innovative spirit, creativity, the capacity for organization and social discipline, private and public austerity, an emphasis on savings, and the development of skills to compete internationally. In short, independent efforts undertaken from within to achieve self-sustained growth" (pp. 8–9).

2. As part of the preparations for this Report, a small ad hoc expert meeting was held in Geneva on 3 and 4 October 2005 on the subject of "New productive development policies for LDCs". The experts participating were Anthony Bartzokas (UNU-INTECH), Mario Cimoli (ECLAC) and Andrew Dorward (Imperial College, London).

3. In Africa, for example, Mkandawire (2001) has identified a series of "impossibility theses" that are often put forward to argue that the State cannot play a developmental role.

References

Amsden, A.H. (2004). *The Rise of "The Rest": Challenges to the West from Late-industrializing Economies*. Oxford University Press, US.

Baumol, W. (1990). Entrepreneurship, productive, unproductive, and destructive. *Journal of Political Economy*, 98 (5): 893–921.

Bradford, C.J. (2005). Prioritizing economic growth: Enhancing macroeconomic policy choice. G-24 Discussion Paper, no. 27, UNCTAD, Geneva.

Cimoli, M., Dosi, G. and Nelson, R. (2006). Institutions and policies shaping industrial development: An introductory note. Prepared for the Task Force on Industrial Policies and Development within the Initiative for Policy Dialogue at Columbia University, New York.

Cline, W. (2004). Trade Policy and Global Poverty. Center for Global Development and Institute for International Economics, Washington, DC.

ECLAC (2000). *Equity, Development and Citizenship*. Santiago, Chile.

ECLAC (2004). *Productive Development in Open Economies*. LC/G.2234(SES.30/3), Thirtieth Session of ECLAC, San Juan, Puerto Rico.

Ffrench-Davies, R. (2005). The need for home-grown development strategies, International Poverty Centre, *In Focus*, April, pp. 6–7, UNDP, Brasilia, Brazil.

Fukuda-Parr, S., Lopes, C. and Malik, K. (2002). *Capacity for Development: New Solutions for Old Problems*. Earthscan and UNDP, New York.

Griffin, K. (2005). Relative prices and investment: An essay on resource allocation. International Poverty Centre, Working Paper No. 4, UNDP, Brasilia, Brazil.

Hausmann, R. and Rodrik, D. (2003). Economic development as self-discovery. *Journal of Development Economics*, 72 (2): 603–633.

Hausmann, R., Rodrik, D. and Velasco, A. (2004). Growth Diagnostics: Initiative for Policy Dialogue, Working Paper No. 11. Columbia University, New York.

Hirschman, A.O. (1958). *The Strategy of Economic Development*. Yale University Press, New Haven, Conn., USA.

Ishikawa, S. (1998). Underdevelopment of the market economy and the limits of economic liberalization. In: Ohno, K. and Ohno, I. (eds.), *Japanese Views on Economic Development: Diverse Paths to the Market*. Routledge, London and New York.

Ishikawa, S. (2002). Growth promotion versus poverty reduction: World Bank rethinking of aid policy and implications for developing countries. (Discussion paper is an English translation of the Japanese original) published in *Transactions of the Japan Academy (Nihon Gakushiin Kiyo)* 56: 2.

Kahn, M.H. and Jomo, K.S. (2000). *Rents, Rent-Seeking and Economic Development: Theory and Evidence in Asia*. Cambridge University Press, UK.

Kozul-Wright, Z. (1995). The role of the firm in the innovation process. UNCTAD Discussion Paper No. 98, Geneva.

Kuznetsov, Y. and Sabel, C. (2005). New industrial policy: Solving economic development problems without picking winners. World Bank Institute, Washington, DC.

Laird, S. and Fernández de Cordoba, S. (Forthcoming, 2006). *Coping with Trade Reforms: A Developing-Country Perspective on the WTO Industrial Tariff Negotiations*. Palgrave, London.

Lall, S. (2004). Reinventing industrial strategy: The role of government policy in building industrial competitiveness. UNCTAD G-24 Discussion Paper Series, No. 28, United Nations, Geneva.

Mkandawire, T. (2001). Thinking about developmental states in Africa. *Cambridge Journal of Economics*. 25, 289–313.

Moreau, F. (2004). The role of the state in evolutionary economics. *Cambridge Journal of Economics*, 28(6): 847–874.

Ohno, K. (1998). Overview: creating the market economy. In: Ohno, K. and Ohno, I. (eds.), *Japanese Views on Economic Development: Diverse Paths to the Market*. Routledge, London and New York.

Ohno, I. (2002). Diversifying PRSP: The Vietnamese model for growth-oriented poverty reduction. Updated version of background paper prepared for workshops at the World Summit on Sustainable Development, Johannesburg, 30 August – 1 September 2002.

Oyelaran-Oyeyinka, B. (2005). Partnerships for building science and technology capacity in Africa. Paper prepared for the Africa-Canada-UL Exploration: Building Science and Technology Capacity with African Partners, 30 January – 1 February 2005, Canada House, London.

Reinert, E. (2005). Development and social goals: Balancing aid and development to prevent "welfare colonialism". Paper prepared for the High-Level United Nations Development Conference on Millennium Development Goals, New York, 14–15 March 2005.

Rodrik, D. (2004a). Rethinking growth policies in the developing world. Draft of the Luca d'Agliano Lecture in Development Economics, Turin, Italy.

Rodrik, D. (2004b). Industrial policy for the twenty-first century. Paper prepared for UNIDO, Vienna.

Sunkel, O. (ed.) (1993) *Development from within: Toward a Neostructuralist Approach for Latin America*. Lynne Rienner Publishers, Boulder and London.

UNCTAD (1994). *Trade and Development Report 1994*. United Nations publication, sales no. E.94.II.D.26, Geneva.

UNCTAD (1996) *Trade and Development Report 1996*. United Nations publication, sales no. E.96.II.D.6, Geneva.

UNCTAD (2000). *The Least Developed Countries 2000 Report*. United Nations publication, sales no. E.00.II.D.21, Geneva.

UNCTAD (2002). *The Least Developed Countries Report 2002, Escaping the Poverty Trap*. United Nations publication, sales no. E.02.II.D.13, Geneva and New York.

UNCTAD (2003). *Trade and Development Report 2003: Capital Accumulation, Growth and Structural Change*. United Nations publication, sales no. E.03.II.D.7.

UNCTAD (2004a). *The Least Developed Countries Report 2004: Linking International Trade with Poverty Reduction*, United Nations publication, sales no. E.04.II.D.27, Geneva and New York.

UNCTAD (2004b). *Trade and Development Report, 2004*. United Nations publication, sales no. E.04.II.D.29, Geneva.

UN Millennium Project (2005). *Investing in Development: A Practical Plan to Achieve the Millennium Development Goals*. New York.

Westphal, L.E. (2000). Industrialization meets globalization: Uncertain reflections on East Asian experience. Paper derives from a Lecture and related Seminar on 18 April 2000 at Macalester College, St. Paul, Minn, USA.

Williamson, J. (ed.) (1990). What Washington means by policy reform? In: *Latin American Adjustment: How much has happened?* Washington Institute for International Economics, Washington, DC.

World Bank (2001). Private sector development strategy: issues and options. Discussion document. World Bank, Washington, DC.

World Bank (2004a). An evaluation of World Bank investment climate activities. Operations Evaluation Department. World Bank, Washington, DC.

World Bank (2004b). *World Development Report 2005: A Better Investment Climate for Everyone*. World Bank, Washington, DC.

World Bank (2004c). An evaluation of MIGA investment climate activities. MIGA, Operations Evaluation Unit. World Bank, Washington, DC.

World Bank (2005). An evaluation of IFC's investment climate activities: Operations evaluation group. Washington, DC.

World Bank (2005a). *Economic Growth in the 1990s: Learning from a Decade of Reform*. World Bank, Washington, DC.

World Bank (2005b). *World Development Report 2005: A Better Investment Climate for Everyone*. Washington, DC.

World Bank (2006). Assessing World Bank support for trade 1987–2004: An IEG evaluation. World Bank, Washington, DC.

Yanagihara, T. (1998). Development and dynamic efficiency: "framework approach" versus "ingredients approach". In: Ohno, K. and Ohno, I. (eds.), *Japanese Views on Economic Development: Diverse Paths to the Market*. Routledge, London and New York.

Statistical Annex

BASIC DATA ON THE
LEAST DEVELOPED COUNTRIES

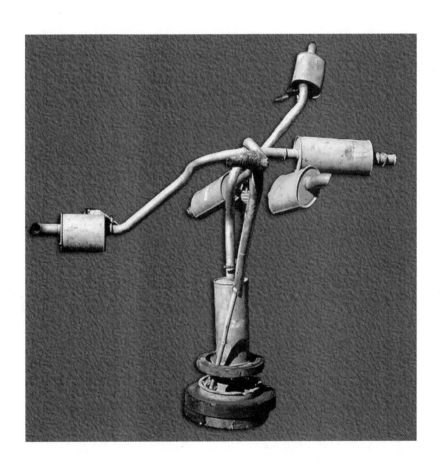

The Statistical Annex has been prepared using the same data sources as recent Least Developed Countries Reports. This is to ensure continuity.

Contents

Explanatory Notes

Definition of country groupings

Least developed countries

The United Nations has designated 50 countries as least developed: Afghanistan, Angola, Bangladesh, Benin, Bhutan, Burkina Faso, Burundi, Cambodia, Cape Verde, the Central African Republic, Chad, the Comoros, the Democratic Republic of the Congo, Djibouti, Equatorial Guinea, Eritrea, Ethiopia, Gambia, Guinea, Guinea-Bissau, Haiti, Kiribati, the Lao People's Democratic Republic, Lesotho, Liberia, Madagascar, Malawi, Maldives, Mali, Mauritania, Mozambique, Myanmar, Nepal, Niger, Rwanda, Samoa, Sao Tome and Principe, Senegal, Sierra Leone, Solomon Islands, Somalia, Sudan, Timor-Leste (as of December 2003), Togo, Tuvalu, Uganda, the United Republic of Tanzania, Vanuatu, Yemen and Zambia.

Major economic areas

The classification of countries and territories according to main economic areas used in this document has been adopted for purposes of statistical convenience only and follows that in the UNCTAD *Handbook of International Trade and Development Statistics 2005*.[1] Countries and territories are classified according to main economic areas as follows:

Developed market economy countries: Andorra, Australia, Canada, the European Union (Austria, Belgium, Czech Republic, Cyprus, Denmark, Estonia, Finland, France, Germany, Greece, Hungary, Ireland, Italy, Latvia, Lithuania, Luxembourg, Malta, the Netherlands, Poland, Portugal, Slovakia, Slovenia, Spain, Sweden and the United Kingdom), Faeroe Islands, Gibraltar, Iceland, Israel, Japan, Liechtenstein, Monaco, New Zealand, Norway, Switzerland and the United States.

South-East Europe and Commonwealth of Independent States (CIS):

South-East Europe: Albania, Bosnia and Herzegovina, Bulgaria, Croatia, Romania, Serbia and Montenegro, The former Yugoslav Republic of Macedonia.

Commonwealth of Independent States (CIS): Armenia, Azerbaijan, Belarus, Georgia, Kazakhstan, Kyrgyzstan, Republic of Moldova, Russian Federation, Tajikistan, Turkmenistan, Ukraine and Uzbekistan.

Developing countries and territories: All other countries, territories and areas in Africa, Asia, America, Europe and Oceania not specified above.

Other country groupings

DAC member countries: The countries members of the OECD Development Assistance Committee are Australia, Austria, Belgium, Canada, Denmark, Finland, France, Germany, Greece, Ireland, Italy, Japan, Luxembourg, the Netherlands, New Zealand, Norway, Portugal, Spain, Sweden, Switzerland, the United Kingdom and the United States.

OPEC member countries: The countries members of the Organization of the Petroleum Exporting Countries are Algeria, Indonesia, Iran (Islamic Republic of), Iraq, Kuwait, the Libyan Arab Jamahiriya, Nigeria, Qatar, Saudi Arabia, the United Arab Emirates and Venezuela.

Other notes

Calculation of annual average growth rates. In general, they are defined as the coefficient b in the exponential trend function $y^t = ae^{bt}$ where t stands for time. This method takes all observations in a period into account. Therefore, the resulting growth rates reflect trends that are not unduly influenced by exceptional values.

Population growth rates are calculated as exponential growth rates.

The term "dollars" ($) refers to United States dollars, unless otherwise stated.

Details and percentages in tables do not necessarily add to totals because of rounding.

The following symbols have been used:
A hyphen (-) indicates that the item is not applicable.
Two dots (..) indicate that the data are not available or are not separately reported.
A zero (0) means that the amount is nil or negligible.
Use of a dash (–) between dates representing years, e.g. 1980–1990, signifies the full period involved, including the initial and final years.

[1] United Nations Publication, Sales No. E/F.05.II.D.29.

Abbreviations

ACBF	African Capacity Building Foundation
ADF	African Development Fund
AfDB	African Development Bank
AFESD	Arab Fund for Economic and Social Development
AsDB	Asian Development Bank
BADEA	Arab Bank for Economic Development in Africa
BDEAC	Banque de Développement des Etats de l'Afrique Centrale
BITS	Swedish Agency for International Technical and Economic Cooperation
BOAD	West African Development Bank
CCCE	Caisse centrale de coopération économique
CEC	Commission of the European Communities
CIDA	Canadian International Development Agency
CIS	Commonwealth of Independent States
DAC	Development Assistance Committee
DANIDA	Danish International Development Agency
DCD	Development Cooperation Department
ECA	Economic Commission for Africa
EDF	European Development Fund
EEC	European Economic Community
ESAF	Enhanced Structural Adjustment Facility
ESCAP	Economic and Social Commission for Asia and the Pacific
EU	European Union
FAC	Fonds d'aide et de coopération
FAO	Food and Agriculture Organization of the United Nations
GDP	gross domestic product
GNI	gross national income
GTZ	German Technical Assistance Corporation
IBRD	International Bank for Reconstruction and Development
IDA	International Development Association
IDB	Inter-American Development Bank
IFAD	International Fund for Agricultural Development
ILO	International Labour Organization
IMF	International Monetary Fund
IRF	International Road Federation
IRU	International Road Transport Union
IsDB	Islamic Development Bank
ITU	International Telecommunication Union
KFAED	Kuwait Fund for Arab Economic Development
KfW	Kreditanstalt für Wiederaufbau
LDC	least developed country
ODA	official development assistance
OECD	Organisation for Economic Co-operation and Development
OECF	Overseas Economic Co-operation Fund
OPEC	Organization of the Petroleum Exporting Countries
PRGF	Poverty Reduction and Growth Facility
SAF	Structural Adjustment Facility
SDC	Swiss Development Corporation
SDR	special drawing rights
SFD	Saudi Fund for Development
SITC	Standard International Trade Classification (Revision I)
UNDP	United Nations Development Programme
UNESCO	United Nations Educational, Scientific and Cultural Organization
UNFPA	United Nations Population Fund

UNHCR	United Nations High Commissioner for Refugees
UNICEF	United Nations Children's Fund
UNTA	United Nations Technical Assistance
USAID	United States Agency for International Development
WFP	World Food Programme
WHO	World Health Organization

1. PER CAPITA GDP AND POPULATION: LEVELS AND GROWTH

Country	Per capita GDP (In 2004 dollars)			Annual average growth rates of per capita real GDP (%)			Population			
							Level (Millions)	Annual average growth rates (%)		
	1980	1990	2004	1980–1990	1990–2000	2000–2004	2004	1980–1990	1990–2000	2000–2004
Afghanistan	..	..	..	..	..	..	28.6	-0.8	5.0	4.8
Angola	1 398	1 304	1 298	0.4	-1.1	5.1	15.5	3.0	2.8	2.9
Bangladesh	246	280	408	1.3	2.6	3.1	139.2	2.4	2.2	1.9
Benin	445	415	498	-0.9	1.4	1.2	8.2	3.4	3.3	3.2
Bhutan	285	476	751	5.4	3.4	3.6	0.9	2.1	3.0	2.7
Burkina Faso	291	311	376	0.9	1.2	1.9	12.8	2.6	2.8	3.2
Burundi	109	123	90	1.1	-3.8	-0.2	7.3	3.3	1.2	2.9
Cambodia	..	..	333	..	4.2	3.5	13.8	4.1	2.7	2.0
Cape Verde	..	1 263	1 915	3.7	3.5	2.3	0.5	2.1	2.4	2.4
Central African Republic	456	392	334	-1.1	-0.3	-2.7	4.0	2.6	2.4	1.3
Chad	258	328	454	3.3	-1.1	10.3	9.4	2.7	3.1	3.6
Comoros	579	567	472	-0.3	-1.6	-0.5	0.8	3.1	2.9	2.7
Dem. Rep. of the Congo	337	272	118	-1.4	-7.5	0.7	55.9	3.0	2.8	2.8
Djibouti	..	1 178	851	-6.7	-3.7	0.6	0.8	5.2	2.4	2.2
Equatorial Guinea	..	1 127	6 572	-0.7	18.4	9.3	0.5	5.0	2.5	2.3
Eritrea	..	..	219	..	3.8ᵃ	-1.2	4.2	2.6	1.5	4.5
Ethiopia	..	97	107	-1.1ᵇ	1.1	1.2	75.6	3.3	3.0	2.5
Gambia	273	271	281	-0.1	-0.5	0.8	1.5	3.7	3.5	2.9
Guinea	..	341	381	1.6	1.2	0.7	9.2	2.6	3.1	2.2
Guinea-Bissau	192	244	182	1.5	-1.8	-4.1	1.5	2.4	3.0	3.0
Haiti	807	615	421	-2.5	-2.9	-2.4	8.4	2.4	1.4	1.4
Kiribati	550	482	636	-1.2	3.2	-0.3	0.1	2.8	2.2	2.1
Lao PDR	..	254	416	1.1	3.9	3.3	5.8	2.6	2.5	2.3
Lesotho	436	543	765	2.3	2.6	3.1	1.8	2.1	1.2	0.1
Liberia	814	222	138	-8.3	-0.2	-9.6	3.2	1.4	4.1	1.3
Madagascar	360	285	241	-1.7	-1.0	-1.9	18.1	2.9	3.0	2.8
Malawi	159	129	144	-1.9	1.8	-0.5	12.6	4.6	1.9	2.3
Maldives	..	..	2 345	..	5.6	4.1	0.3	3.2	3.0	2.6
Mali	345	287	371	-1.6	1.3	3.2	13.1	2.5	2.7	3.0
Mauritania	384	359	455	-0.5	1.7	2.2	3.0	2.3	2.7	3.0
Mozambique	188	172	286	-1.0	3.2	6.3	19.4	0.9	3.0	2.0
Myanmar	..	..	..	..	..	..	50.0	1.9	1.6	1.2
Nepal	152	191	252	2.2	2.4	0.4	26.6	2.3	2.5	2.1
Niger	359	260	228	-3.2	-1.0	0.6	13.5	3.2	3.4	3.5
Rwanda	234	209	208	-1.3	-1.4	2.6	8.9	3.5	1.2	2.5
Samoa	1 694	1 605	1 978	0.6	1.7	1.0	0.2	0.4	1.0	0.9
Sao Tome and Principe		375	407	-0.6	0.0	1.9	0.2	2.2	1.8	2.3
Senegal	564	572	673	0.1	0.9	2.1	11.4	3.0	2.6	2.4
Sierra Leone	278	241	202	-1.9	-5.9	11.0	5.3	2.4	0.8	4.4
Solomon Islands	493	677	519	3.2	-0.4	-2.8	0.5	3.3	2.8	2.7
Somalia	..	..	..	..	..	..	8.0	0.1	0.4	3.2
Sudan	348	341	551		3.0	4.0	35.5	2.7	2.4	1.9
Timor-Leste	..	..	382	..	-12.2	-5.7	0.9	2.6	-0.5	5.4
Togo	488	381	344	-1.9	0.4	-0.2	6.0	3.7	3.1	2.8
Tuvaluᵇ	..	..	..	..	..	..	0.0	1.6	0.8	0.5
Uganda	..	160	246	-0.7	3.8	2.3	27.8	3.5	3.2	3.4
United Rep. of Tanzania	..	239	288	1.9	0.1	4.7	37.6	3.3	2.9	2.0
Vanuatu	1 439	1 457	1 526	-0.3	1.1	-2.7	0.2	2.4	2.5	2.0
Yemen	..	538	631	..	1.9	0.4	20.3	3.9	4.0	3.2
Zambia	629	505	469	-2.2	-1.9	2.6	11.5	3.3	2.5	1.8
All LDCs	343	297	349	-0.1	0.9	2.5	740.4	2.6	2.6	2.4
All developing countries	964	1 079	1 604	1.1	3.1	2.0	5100.7	2.1	1.7	1.5
Developed market economy countries	21 543	25 621	32 732	2.6	1.9	1.3	956.6	0.6	0.6	0.5
South-East Europe and Commonwealth of Independent States	..	3 336	2 793	..	-4.0	6.6	331.9	0.8	-0.1	-0.3

Source: World Bank, *World Development Indicators 2005,* online data.

Note: GDP per capita data are based on World Bank data on GDP and population data are based on United Nations/DESA/Population Division. Data for Ethiopia prior to 1992 include Eritrea. Population data for Bhutan is from national sources.

a   1993–2000.

b   Population 10,466 and area 26 km².

2. Real GDP, total and per capita: Annual average growth rates
(Percentage)

Country	Real GDP							Real GDP per capita						
	1980–1990	1990–2000	2000–2004	2001	2002	2003	2004	1980–1990	1990–2000	2000–2004	2001	2002	2003	2004
Afghanistan	..	..	..	..	..	..	..	..	..	..	..	..	..	..
Angola	3.4	1.6	8.1	3.1	14.4	3.4	11.2	0.4	-1.1	5.1	0.4	11.2	0.5	8.0
Bangladesh	3.7	4.8	5.1	5.3	4.4	5.3	5.5	1.3	2.6	3.1	3.2	2.4	3.3	3.5
Benin	2.5	4.8	4.5	5.0	6.0	3.9	2.7	-0.9	1.4	1.2	1.8	2.7	0.6	-0.5
Bhutan	7.6	6.5	6.4	7.0	6.7	6.7	4.9	5.4	3.4	3.6	4.0	3.8	3.9	2.3
Burkina Faso	3.6	4.0	5.2	5.9	4.4	6.5	3.9	0.9	1.2	1.9	2.7	1.1	3.1	0.6
Burundi	4.4	-2.6	2.7	3.2	4.5	-1.2	5.5	1.1	-3.8	-0.2	0.9	1.7	-4.3	1.9
Cambodia	..	6.7	5.6	5.6	5.5	5.3	6.0	..	4.2	3.5	3.4	3.4	3.3	4.0
Cape Verde	5.9	6.0	4.7	3.8	4.6	5.0	5.5	3.7	3.5	2.3	1.4	2.2	2.5	3.1
Central African Republic	1.4	2.0	-1.4	1.5	-0.8	-5.4	0.9	-1.1	-0.3	-2.7	0.0	-2.1	-6.6	-0.4
Chad	6.1	1.9	14.3	9.9	9.9	11.3	31.0	3.3	-1.1	10.3	6.2	6.0	7.4	26.6
Comoros	2.8	1.3	2.2	2.3	2.3	2.1	1.9	-0.3	-1.6	-0.5	-0.4	-0.4	-0.6	-0.7
Dem. Rep. of the Congo	1.6	-4.9	3.5	-2.0	3.5	5.6	6.3	-1.4	-7.5	0.7	-4.4	0.8	2.6	3.2
Djibouti	-0.7	-1.4	2.8	1.9	2.6	3.5	3.0	-6.7	-3.7	0.6	-0.7	0.3	1.5	1.1
Equatorial Guinea	1.5	21.3	11.8	1.5	17.6	14.7	10.0	-0.7	18.4	9.3	-0.9	14.9	12.1	7.5
Eritrea	..	4.3[a]	3.3	9.2	0.7	3.0	1.8	..	3.8[a]	-1.2	4.8	-3.7	-1.5	-2.5
Ethiopia	2.2[b]	4.2	3.7	8.8	1.9	-3.7	13.4	-1.1[b]	1.1	1.2	6.1	-0.6	-6.0	10.7
Gambia	3.6	3.0	3.8	5.8	-3.2	6.7	8.3	-0.1	-0.5	0.8	2.6	-6.0	3.7	5.4
Guinea	4.6	4.4	2.9	3.8	4.2	1.2	2.6	1.6	1.2	0.7	1.6	2.0	-1.0	0.4
Guinea-Bissau	4.0	1.2	-1.2	0.2	-7.2	0.6	4.3	1.5	-1.8	-4.1	-2.7	-9.9	-2.4	1.2
Haiti	-0.2	-1.5	-1.0	-1.1	-0.5	0.4	-3.8	-2.5	-2.9	-2.4	-2.5	-1.9	-1.0	-5.2
Kiribati	1.5	5.5	1.8	1.8	1.0	2.5	1.8	-1.2	3.2	-0.3	-0.3	-1.1	0.4	-0.2
Lao People's Dem. Rep.	3.8	6.5	5.7	5.8	5.8	5.3	6.0	1.1	3.9	3.3	3.3	3.4	2.9	3.6
Lesotho	4.5	3.9	3.3	3.2	3.5	3.3	3.0	2.3	2.6	3.1	2.7	3.3	3.3	3.2
Liberia	-7.0	3.9	-8.4	4.9	3.3	-31.0	2.0	-8.3	-0.2	-9.6	1.7	1.8	-31.3	1.4
Madagascar	1.1	2.0	0.9	6.0	-12.7	9.8	5.3	-1.7	-1.0	-1.9	3.0	-15.1	6.8	2.4
Malawi	2.5	3.7	1.8	-5.0	2.7	4.4	3.8	-1.9	1.8	-0.5	-7.3	0.3	2.1	1.6
Maldives	..	..	6.7	3.3	6.1	8.4	8.8	..	5.6	4.1	0.6	3.4	5.7	6.1
Mali	0.8	4.1	6.3	12.1	4.2	7.4	2.2	-1.6	1.3	3.2	8.9	1.1	4.3	-0.8
Mauritania	1.8	4.4	5.3	2.8	3.2	8.3	6.6	-0.5	1.7	2.2	-0.2	0.1	5.1	3.5
Mozambique	-0.1	6.4	8.5	13.0	7.4	7.1	7.8	-1.0	3.2	6.3	10.6	5.2	5.0	5.7
Myanmar	..	..	..	..	..	..	..	..	..	..	..	..	..	..
Nepal	4.6	4.9	2.6	5.5	-0.6	3.1	3.7	2.2	2.4	0.4	3.2	-2.7	1.0	1.6
Niger	-0.1	2.4	4.1	7.1	3.0	5.3	0.9	-3.2	-1.0	0.6	3.5	-0.5	1.8	-2.4
Rwanda	2.2	-0.3	5.1	6.7	9.4	1.0	3.7	-1.3	-1.4	2.6	2.2	6.5	-0.7	2.2
Samoa	1.0	2.7	1.9	6.2	1.2	-1.0	3.2	0.6	1.7	1.0	5.2	0.3	-1.8	2.4
Sao Tome and Principe	1.8	1.8	4.3	4.0	4.1	4.5	4.5	-0.6	0.0	1.9	1.8	1.8	2.1	2.1
Senegal	3.1	3.6	4.6	5.6	1.1	6.5	6.0	0.1	0.9	2.1	3.0	-1.3	3.9	3.5
Sierra Leone	0.5	-5.1	15.8	18.2	27.4	9.2	7.4	-1.9	-5.9	11.0	13.8	21.9	4.4	3.0
Solomon Islands	6.6	2.4	-0.1	-9.0	-1.6	5.1	3.8	3.2	-0.4	-2.8	-11.5	-4.2	2.4	1.1
Somalia	..	..	..	..	..	..	..	..	..	..	..	..	..	..
Sudan	2.3	5.4	6.0	6.1	6.0	6.0	6.0		3.0	4.0	4.0	4.0	4.0	4.0
Timor-Leste	..	..	-0.6	16.5	-6.7	-6.2	1.8	..	-12.2	-5.7	14.0	-11.1	-12.1	-5.0
Togo	1.7	3.5	2.6	-0.2	4.1	2.7	3.0	-1.9	0.4	-0.2	-3.1	1.3	0.0	0.4
Tuvalu	..	..	..	..	..	..	..	..	..	..	..	..	..	..
Uganda	2.9	7.1	5.8	6.1	6.8	4.7	5.7	-0.7	3.8	2.3	2.7	3.3	1.2	2.1
United Rep. of Tanzania	5.4	2.9	6.8	6.2	7.2	7.1	6.3	1.9	0.1	4.7	4.1	5.1	5.0	4.3
Vanuatu	2.1	3.7	-0.7	-2.7	-4.9	2.4	3.0	-0.3	1.1	-2.7	-4.6	-6.8	0.4	1.0
Yemen	..	6.0	3.6	4.6	3.9	3.1	2.7	..	1.9	0.4	1.3	0.7	0.0	-0.5
Zambia	1.0	0.5	4.4	4.9	3.3	5.1	4.6	-2.2	-1.9	2.6	2.9	1.5	3.3	2.9
All LDCs	2.6	3.6	5.0	5.2	4.6	4.6	5.9	-0.1	0.9	2.5	2.7	2.1	2.1	3.4
All developing countries	3.5	4.9	3.4	2.5	2.3	3.7	5.5	1.1	3.1	2.0	1.1	1.0	2.2	4.1
Developed market economy countries	3.3	2.6	1.9	1	1.3	2.2	3.3	2.6	1.9	1.3	0.4	0.7	1.6	2.7
South-East Europe and Commonwealth of Independent States	..	-3.9	6.4	5.8	5.1	7.1	7.8	..	-4.0	6.6	6.1	5.4	7.4	8.1

Source: World Bank, *World Development Indicators 2005*, online data; United Nations/DESA/Population Division.

a   1993–2000.   b   Data for Ethiopia prior to 1992 include Eritrea.

3. Agricultural production, total and per capita: Annual average growth rates

Country	Percentage share of agriculture in:				Annual average growth rates (%) Total agricultural production*					Annual average growth rates (%) Per capita agricultural production*				
	Total labour force		GDP											
	1990	2002	1990	2004	1990–1994	2000–2004	2002	2003	2004	1990–1994	2000–2004	2002	2003	2004
Afghanistan	70	66	..	52ᵃ	..	..	..	..	..	..	..	..	..	..
Angola	75	71	18	9ᵇ	4.9	2.5	0.2	2.0	-1.1	1.8	-0.7	-3.0	-1.3	-4.3
Bangladesh	65	54	30	21	0.1	0.9	2.2	3.0	-1.3	-2.3	-1.2	0.2	0.9	-3.3
Benin	64	52	36	36	6.3	7.5	9.3	15.2	2.9	2.8	4.7	6.3	12.2	0.2
Bhutan	94	94	43	33ᵇ	1.8	0.8	-6.6	5.1	-1.7	0.5	-2.2	-9.5	2.1	-4.4
Burkina Faso	92	92	28	31	5.8	8.6	3.7	6.3	0.7	2.8	5.5	0.6	3.2	-2.1
Burundi	92	90	56	51	-2.2	2.1	4.7	-1.7	-2.7	-3.8	-1.0	1.6	-4.9	-6.0
Cambodia	74	69	47ᶜ	36	0.7	2.2	-4.3	15.6	-7.5	-2.7	-0.2	-6.6	12.9	-9.7
Cape Verde	31	22	14	7	0.4	-1.4	-5.8	3.0	-2.3	-1.9	-3.3	-7.7	0.9	-4.3
Central African Rep.	80	71	48	61ᵇ	2.5	0.3	0.0	-2.1	1.8	-0.2	-1.0	-1.3	-3.2	0.5
Chad	83	73	29	61	1.5	3.9	-1.1	-0.3	5.7	-1.3	0.9	-4.1	-3.1	2.6
Comoros	78	73	39	41ᵇ	2.7	1.1	-0.5	2.9	0.2	-0.3	-1.7	-3.3	0.1	-2.6
Dem. Rep. of the Congo	68	62	30	58ᵃ	1.3	-0.6	-0.9	0.6	-0.7	-2.3	-3.4	-3.6	-2.4	-3.8
Djibouti	82	78	3	4ᵈ	-4.9	2.9	3.3	6.4	0.0	-6.2	1.2	1.4	4.9	-1.3
Equatorial Guinea	75	69	62	7ᵇ	-2.4	-1.7	-5.3	1.2	0.0	-4.8	-4.3	-7.8	-1.5	-2.5
Eritrea	80	77	22ᶜ	15	35.8	-2.5	-22.1	13.7	-0.8	35.3	-6.0	-24.9	9.6	-4.4
Ethiopia	86	82	49	46	1.1	2.6	2.6	-2.8	4.3	-1.9	0.1	0.1	-5.2	1.8
Gambia	82	78	29	32	0.9	-11.0	-40.1	9.8	-3.8	-2.6	-13.4	-41.7	6.8	-6.1
Guinea	87	83	24	25	5.0	2.9	1.4	3.3	2.4	1.2	1.3	-0.1	1.9	0.8
Guinea-Bissau	85	82	61	71	1.4	1.9	-1.8	2.5	5.2	-1.8	-1.1	-4.7	-0.6	2.2
Haiti	68	61	33ᵉ	28ᵃ	-2.0	-0.1	2.4	1.7	-2.7	-3.6	-1.4	1.1	0.3	-3.9
Kiribati	30	26	19	14ᵃ	4.8	2.2	1.6	0.5	6.2	3.1	0.6	-0.7	-0.7	5.1
Lao Peoples. Dem. Rep.	78	76	61	49ᵇ	2.0	2.3	8.4	-3.9	4.1	-0.6	0.0	6.0	-6.1	1.7
Lesotho	41	39	24	16	3.4	0.4	-5.7	-1.2	9.0	2.0	0.2	-6.1	-1.3	9.0
Liberia	72	67	..	..	-5.3	-0.6	-2.5	0.1	2.4	-4.4	-4.7	-6.7	-3.7	-1.1
Madagascar	78	73	29	29	1.1	1.5	-2.0	1.9	8.0	-1.7	-1.3	-4.8	-0.9	4.9
Malawi	87	82	45	39	-0.8	-3.9	-25.6	9.9	8.5	-1.9	-5.8	-27.1	7.8	6.4
Maldives	33	21	..	..	3.7	3.1	9.4	0.2	1.0	0.7	0.1	6.2	-2.6	-2.1
Mali	86	80	46	38ᵇ	2.6	6.1	-6.6	15.6	-1.1	-0.2	3.0	-9.2	12.1	-4.2
Mauritania	55	52	30	19	-1.1	2.1	5.6	2.4	0.5	-3.5	-0.9	2.5	-0.7	-2.5
Mozambique	83	81	37	26ᵇ	-3.4	2.7	1.8	3.1	0.0	-6.7	0.9	0.0	1.2	-1.6
Myanmar	73	70	57	57ᵈ	6.7	3.9	2.9	6.6	-2.7	4.9	2.5	1.5	5.3	-4.0
Nepal	94	93	52	40	1.0	2.7	2.8	4.9	-0.7	-1.4	0.5	0.5	2.7	-3.0
Niger	90	87	35	40ᵇ	3.0	5.9	2.5	7.8	-1.4	-0.3	2.2	-1.2	4.0	-4.9
Rwanda	92	90	33	42ᵇ	-12.9	3.0	24.7	-9.1	0.0	-6.8	0.7	21.6	-10.4	-1.2
Samoa	42	33	..		-3.5	0.6	-0.4	1.7	0.0	-4.1	-0.3	-1.0	0.5	-1.1
Sao Tome and Principe	71	63	28	16	9.8	2.2	1.2	4.5	0.9	7.1	-0.4	-1.4	2.0	-1.6
Senegal	77	73	20	17	1.5	-5.0	-35.7	36.2	-0.8	-1.0	-7.3	-37.1	32.9	-3.2
Sierra Leone	67	61	32	53	-1.1	4.8	4.8	5.4	-0.9	-1.2	0.7	0.5	1.0	-4.6
Solomon Islands	77	72	..	..	3.0	8.5	2.1	4.6	42.3	-0.2	5.4	-0.8	1.5	38.3
Somalia	75	70	65	..	..	..	..	..	..	..	..	..	..	..
Sudan	69	59	43ᵉ	39ᵃ	8.2	2.8	-3.2	9.6	-3.6	5.7	0.6	-5.4	7.3	-5.7
Timor-Leste	..	..	41ᶠ	26ᵈ	5.4	3.1	7.4	-0.6	3.6	2.1	-1.0	3.5	-5.6	-1.8
Togo	66	59	34	41	4.0	3.6	10.8	-0.5	1.4	1.8	1.2	8.1	-2.6	-0.8
Tuvalu	33	25	..	..	..	..	..	..	..	..	..	..	..	..
Uganda	85	79	57	32	2.1	2.2	4.1	-2.9	3.7	-1.0	-1.0	0.9	-6.0	0.3
Utd. Rep. of Tanzania	84	80	46	45ᵇ	-1.0	1.6	1.6	-0.8	3.8	-4.3	-0.4	-0.4	-2.7	1.8
Vanuatu	43	35	21	15ᵈ	-2.7	-0.6	-9.3	4.7	3.5	-5.4	-3.0	-11.5	2.2	1.0
Yemen	60	48	24	15	4.3	2.1	-0.7	-0.7	4.6	-0.7	-1.5	-4.2	-4.1	0.9
Zambia	74	68	21	21	3.6	2.5	0.3	11.0	0.0	0.8	1.2	-0.9	9.8	-1.1
LDCs	76	69	36	28ᵇ	1.6	2.3	1.2	4.0	-0.2	..	..	..	..	..
Developing countries	61	51	15	11	3.7	3.2	2.7	4.1	3.1	1.8	1.6	1.2	2.5	1.6

Source: UNCTAD secretariat calculations based on data from FAO online data; World Bank, *World Development Indicators 2005*, CD-ROM, UNDP, *Human Development Report 2005*.

Note: * base year 1999–2001.
a 2002. b 2003. c 1993. d 2000. e 1996. f 1998.

4. FOOD PRODUCTION, TOTAL AND PER CAPITA: ANNUAL AVERAGE GROWTH RATES
(Percentage)

Country	Total food production[a]					Net per capita food production[a]				
	1990–1994	2000–2004	2002	2003	2004	1990–1994	2000–2004	2002	2003	2004
Afghanistan	..	..	..	..	..	..	..	..	..	..
Angola	5.2	2.7	0.4	2.0	-1.1	2.0	-0.6	-2.8	-1.3	-4.3
Bangladesh	0.0	0.9	2.5	3.0	-1.4	-2.4	-1.2	0.4	1.0	-3.4
Benin	4.2	9.1	6.1	23.0	3.2	0.8	6.2	3.3	19.7	0.5
Bhutan	1.8	0.8	-6.6	5.1	-1.7	0.5	-2.2	-9.5	2.1	-4.6
Burkina Faso	7.2	6.8	-1.5	7.2	-4.6	4.2	3.7	-4.3	4.0	-7.3
Burundi	-2.4	2.1	2.5	0.2	-2.8	-4.0	-1.0	-0.4	-3.1	-6.2
Cambodia	0.5	2.2	-4.2	15.0	-7.7	-2.9	-0.2	-6.4	12.3	-9.9
Cape Verde	0.4	-1.4	-5.8	3.0	-2.3	-1.9	-3.3	-7.7	0.9	-4.3
Central African Republic	3.2	1.3	1.3	-0.2	1.9	0.4	0.0	0.0	-1.4	0.6
Chad	2.6	3.9	-1.4	3.3	1.1	-0.4	0.9	-4.3	0.3	-2.0
Comoros	2.7	1.1	-0.5	2.9	0.2	-0.3	-1.7	-3.3	0.1	-2.6
Dem. Rep. of the Congo	1.5	-0.6	-1.5	1.0	-0.5	-2.2	-3.4	-4.3	-2.0	-3.5
Djibouti	-4.9	2.9	3.3	6.4	0.0	-6.2	1.2	1.4	4.9	-1.3
Equatorial Guinea	-1.8	-1.9	-5.9	1.3	0.0	-4.2	-4.5	-8.5	-1.4	-2.6
Eritrea	36.4	-2.5	-22.2	13.9	-0.8	35.7	-6.0	-25.1	9.7	-4.4
Ethiopia	0.3	2.6	3.0	-2.9	3.6	-2.9	0.1	0.4	-5.2	1.1
Gambia	0.5	-11.1	-40.2	9.8	-3.8	-2.9	-13.5	-41.8	6.8	-6.1
Guinea	5.0	3.8	3.9	3.5	2.5	1.2	2.2	2.5	2.0	0.9
Guinea-Bissau	1.6	1.8	-1.9	2.5	5.4	-1.6	-1.1	-4.8	-0.5	2.2
Haiti	-1.9	-0.1	2.4	1.7	-2.7	-3.5	-1.4	1.0	0.4	-3.9
Kiribati	4.8	2.2	1.6	0.5	6.2	3.1	0.6	-0.7	-0.7	5.1
Laos	3.4	3.2	9.2	-2.7	2.6	0.8	0.9	6.7	-4.9	0.4
Lesotho	2.5	0.4	-6.0	-1.2	9.3	1.1	0.2	-6.2	-1.4	9.4
Liberia	-4.9	-1.5	-4.0	-0.2	1.8	-4.1	-5.6	-8.2	-4.0	-1.7
Madagascar	1.3	1.5	-1.4	1.5	8.0	-1.5	-1.3	-4.1	-1.4	5.1
Malawi	-1.1	-3.5	-28.1	12.0	9.3	-2.2	-5.4	-29.6	10.0	7.2
Maldives	3.7	3.1	9.4	0.2	1.0	0.7	0.1	6.2	-2.6	-2.1
Mali	2.8	3.8	-1.4	9.4	0.9	0.1	0.7	-4.3	6.2	-2.2
Mauritania	-1.1	2.1	5.6	2.4	0.5	-3.5	-0.9	2.5	-0.7	-2.5
Mozambique	-3.8	2.3	1.7	2.9	0.0	-7.1	0.5	-0.1	1.1	-1.6
Myanmar	6.8	4.0	3.0	6.6	-2.9	5.0	2.6	1.5	5.4	-4.0
Nepal	1.0	2.7	2.9	4.9	-0.9	-1.3	0.5	0.6	2.6	-3.0
Niger	2.9	6.3	2.4	8.7	-1.3	-0.4	2.5	-1.2	4.8	-4.8
Rwanda	-12.5	3.1	25.9	-9.1	-0.3	-6.3	0.8	22.8	-10.4	-1.4
Samoa	-3.5	0.6	-0.4	1.7	0.0	-4.1	-0.3	-1.0	0.5	-1.1
Sao Tome and Principe	9.8	2.2	1.3	4.5	0.9	7.2	-0.4	-1.4	1.9	-1.5
Senegal	1.7	-5.6	-36.3	35.4	-0.9	-0.9	-7.9	-37.7	32.3	-3.3
Sierra Leone	-1.3	4.9	5.0	5.4	-1.0	-1.4	0.8	0.9	1.0	-4.7
Solomon Islands	3.0	8.5	2.1	4.6	42.5	-0.2	5.4	-0.8	1.5	38.4
Somalia	..	..	..	..	..	..	..	..	..	..
Sudan	9.4	2.7	-2.9	9.4	-4.1	6.9	0.4	-5.1	7.1	-6.1
Timor-Leste	5.8	3.4	9.3	-0.6	4.2	2.4	-0.6	5.1	-5.6	-1.1
Togo	3.8	2.1	7.3	0.1	-0.1	1.6	-0.3	4.7	-2.1	-2.3
Tuvalu	..	..	..	..	..	..	..	..	..	..
Uganda	1.7	2.0	3.6	-2.4	3.3	-1.4	-1.2	0.4	-5.5	-0.1
United Rep of Tanzania	-0.9	1.2	2.9	-0.5	1.1	-4.2	-0.7	0.9	-2.4	-0.7
Vanuatu	-2.7	-0.6	-9.3	4.7	3.6	-5.4	-3.0	-11.5	2.2	1.1
Yemen	4.2	2.0	-0.7	-0.8	4.8	-0.7	-1.5	-4.2	-4.3	1.3
Zambia	3.5	2.7	0.2	12.3	0.0	0.8	1.4	-1.0	11.0	-1.1
LDCs	1.7	2.3	1.4	4.1	-0.6	..	..	..	..	..
Developing countries	4.0	3.1	2.8	4.3	2.4	2.1	1.6	1.3	2.7	0.9

Source: UNCTAD secretariat calculations, based on data from FAO online data.

a   base year 1999-2001.

5. THE MANUFACTURING SECTOR: ANNUAL AVERAGE GROWTH RATES AND SHARES IN GDP
(Percentage)

Country	Share in GDP			Annual average growth rates						
	1980	*1990*	*2004*	*1980–1990*	*1990–2000*	*2000–2004*	*2001*	*2002*	*2003*	*2004*
Afghanistan	..	..	18[a]	..	..	..	..	..	..	..
Angola	10[b]	5	4[c]	-11.1[d]	-0.3	11.3	9.8	10.2	12.1	13.5
Bangladesh	14	13	16	5.2	7.2	6.5	6.7	5.5	6.7	7.4
Benin	8	8	9	5.1	5.8	5.9	9.0	5.5	4.6	5.4
Bhutan	3	8	8[c]	13.0	6.5	5.8[h]	9.3	0.3	10.1	..
Burkina Faso	15	15	14	2.0	1.6	2.2[h]	8.1	-0.3	0.0	..
Burundi	7	13	9[e]	..	..	..	..	..	..	..
Cambodia	..	9[f]	22[c]	..	17.9[g]	13.9[h]	14.2	15.1	12.0	..
Cape Verde	7[i]	8	1	8.6[j]	4.8	4.7	4.7	4.7	4.7	4.7
Central African Republic	7	11	9[k]	5.0	-0.2	4.0[h]	4.0	4.0	4.0	..
Chad	11[l]	14	7	..	..	..	..	..	..	..
Comoros	4	4	4[c]	4.9	1.7	1.3	4.1	-0.6	1.4	1.0
Dem. Republic of the Congo	14	11	4[a]	..	..	..	..	..	..	..
Djibouti	..	5	3[k]	..	-7.3	..	..	..	..	..
Equatorial Guinea	..	2[f]	..	..	..	..	..	..	..	..
Eritrea	..	9[f]	11	..	8.2[g]	6.6	8.0	10.0	5.5	2.0
Ethiopia	8	8	..	..	..	..	..	..	..	..
Gambia	6	7	5	7.8	0.9	4.2	2.7	4.5	4.7	4.7
Guinea	..	5	4	..	4.0	2.0	5.5	6.0	-4.0	2.0
Guinea-Bissau	14[i]	8	9	9.2	-2.0	14.6	5.9	14.4	27.5	6.0
Haiti	..	..	..	-1.7	-8.4	-3.3	-9.6	1.6	0.5	-9.3
Kiribati	2	1	1[a]	-10.7	8.9	7.3	18.6	-3.0	..	..
Lao People's Dem. Republic	..	10	19[a]	8.7[d]	11.7	10.7[h]	12.1	13.0	6.3	..
Lesotho	8	14	20[a]	9.8	6.6	5.8	7.9	6.9	5.2	3.0
Liberia	..	..	..	..	..	..	..	..	..	..
Madagascar	11[b]	11	15	2.4[m]	2.0	1.4	10,7	-18.3	15.3	6.1
Malawi	14	19	10	3.6	0.5	-2.1	-14.2	-0.2	0.8	4.0
Maldives	..	..	..	..	..	..	..	..	..	..
Mali	7	9	3[c]	6.8	-1.4	5.3	-14.0	22.7	-5.5	20.9
Mauritania	13[b]	10	9	-2.1[d]	-1.3	5.9[n]	5.9	..	..	..
Mozambique	..	10	15[a]	..	19.1[o]	12.2	27.2	4.0	12.8	10.0
Myanmar	10	8	7[k]	..	..	..	..	..	..	..
Nepal	4	6	9	9.3	8.9	-2.5[h]	3.8	-10.0	2.0	..
Niger	4	7	7[c]	-2.7[d]	2.6	3.9[h]	3.4	3.3	5.0	..
Rwanda	15	18	11	2.6	-6.0	5.8	7.8	5.0	5.2	5.8
Samoa	..	..	..	..	-2.6[o]	5.8[h]	12.2	-0.9	8.8	..
Sao Tome and Principe	9[i]	5	4	0.5[j]	1.4	2.9[h]	2.7	3.0	3.0	..
Senegal	11	13	13	4.6	4.0	5.3	5.1	10.1	0.3	5.9
Sierra Leone	5	5	5	..	..	..	..	..	..	..
Solomon Islands	..	..	..	..	..	..	..	..	..	..
Somalia	5	5	..	..	..	..	..	..	..	..
Sudan	7	..	9[a]	4.8	4.4	-7.5[q]	-16.2	2.1	..	..
Timor-Leste	..	..	3[p]	..	-26.0	6.9[n]	6.9	..	..	..
Togo	8	10	9	1.7	1.8	7.6	6.5	10.6	6.3	6.6
Tuvalu	..	..	..	..	..	..	..	..	..	..
Uganda	4	6	9	3.9[m]	14.1	5.0	7.0	5.3	4.0	4.0
United Republic of Tanzania	..	9	7[c]	..	2.7	7.6	5.0	8.0	8.6	8.0
Vanuatu	4	5	4[p]	12.2[m]	2.3	-8.5[n]	-8.5	..	..	..
Yemen	..	9	5	..	3.7	2.5	3.3	4.8	-2.0	5.3
Zambia	18	36	12[c]	4.1	0.8	5.8	4.2	5.7	7.6	5.1
All LDCs	11	11	12[c]	2.9	4.8	5.4[h]	5.2	4.8	6.3	..

Source: UNCTAD secretariat calculations, based on data from the World Bank , *World Development Indicators 2005*, online data.

a 2002. b 1985. c 2003. d 1985-1990. e 1999. f 1993. g 1993-2000. h 2000-2003. i 1986. j 1986-1990. k 2000. l 1983. m 1983-1990. n 2000-2001. o 1994-2000. p 2001. q 2000-2002.

6. GROSS CAPITAL FORMATION: ANNUAL AVERAGE GROWTH RATES AND SHARES IN GDP
(Percentage)

Country	Share in GDP			Annual average growth rates						
	1980	1990	2004	1980-1990	1990-2000	2000-2004	2001	2002	2003	2004
Afghanistan	..	..	..	..	..	..	..	..	..	..
Angola	18[a]	12	12	..	..	..	..	..	..	..
Bangladesh	14	17	23	7.2	9.2	7.5	5.8	8.2	7.9	7.7
Benin	15	14	20	-5.3	12.2	6.4	6.4	-1.5	12.2	10.3
Bhutan	31	32	53[b]	..	..	..	..	..	..	..
Burkina Faso	15	18	19	8.6	7.0	7.7	10.5	10.6	1.1	10.8
Burundi	14	15	11	6.9	0.4	4.8[c]	2.8	6.9	..	..
Cambodia	9[d]	8	23	..	11.2[e]	13.2	19.4	10.5	19.5	2.8
Cape Verde	33[f]	23	22	-4.7[g]	0.2	7.7	-3.6	19.5	1.5	12.8
Central African Republic	7	12	7		..	..	..	..	..	..
Chad	3	7	25	19.0[h]	4.4	12.8	102.0	56.7	-16.6	-39.5
Comoros	33	19	11	-4.2	-4.1	-2.4	4.4	6.3	-2.0	-9.4
Dem. Rep. of the Congo	10	9	18	-5.1	2.6	-4.1[c]	-12.1	4.7	..	..
Djibouti	..	8[i]	13[j]	..	..	..	..	..	..	..
Equatorial Guinea	..	17	..	..	..	..	..	..	..	..
Eritrea	..	8[k]	22	..	19.1	-13.5	-2.5	-12.4	-26.7	-3.4
Ethiopia	13[l]	12	20	4.7[m]	6.4	10.8	15.8	13.3	2.4	15.4
Gambia	27	22	24	0.0	1.9	2.3	3.2	1.0	0.0	6.9
Guinea	15[f]	18	11	3.3[g]	2.8	-7.7	5.6	-2.2	-21.9	-5.1
Guinea-Bissau	28	30	12	12.9	-6.5	-8.6	-1.6	-43.3	2.7	21.8
Haiti	17	13	23	-0.6	7.7	-0.5	-2.1	-3.9	24.9	-21.4
Kiribati	33	93	..	..	..	..	..	..	..	..
Lao PDR	7[a]	26[i]	19	..	..	..	..	..	..	..
Lesotho	29	53	41	5.0	1.5	-7.1	-4.0	-11.6	-6.0	-4.7
Liberia	..	..	14	..	..	..	..	..	..	..
Madagascar	15	17	24	4.9	3.4	12.0	22.6	-31.4	33.8	63.8
Malawi	25	23	11	-2.8	-8.0	-6.0	-87.4	-15.9	-1.7	-0.6
Maldives	..	31[i]	26[b]	..	9.2[n]	1.9[c]	8.6	-4.4	..	..
Mali	16	23	20	3.6	0.4	4.7	55.4	-28.2	35.2	-15.2
Mauritania	26	20	17[b]	6.9	8.6	..	13.8	..	..	..
Mozambique	8	22	22	3.8	11.4	12.7	0.9	12.2	19.1	-5.9
Myanmar	22	13	12[j]	..	..	..	..	..	..	..
Nepal	18	18	24[b]	..	..	..	..	..	..	..
Niger	28	8	16	..	..	..	..	..	..	..
Rwanda	16	15	21	4.3	1.4	0.4	1.6	-11.3	2.8	14.0
Samoa	..	..	..	..	..	..	..	..	..	..
Sao Tome and Principe	17	16	33	-0.8[g]	0.7	..	-28.5	..	..	..
Senegal	12	14	21	5.2	7.6	10.0	5.2	5.4	16.4	12.4
Sierra Leone	16	10	20	..	..	..	..	..	..	..
Solomon islands	36	29	..	..	..	..	..	..	..	..
Somalia	42	16	..	..	..	..	..	..	..	..
Sudan	15	..	20	-1.8	0.2[o]	19.5	6.9	25.6	21.7	20.5
Timor-Leste	..	..	27	..	..	..	..	..	..	..
Togo	28	27	18	2.7	-0.1	5.8	2.8	7.7	5.0	7.6
Tuvalu	..	..	..	..	..	..	..	..	..	..
Uganda	6	13	22	8.0[p]	8.9	6.2	-6.0	9.9	10.0	8.1
United Rep.Tanzania	..	26	19	..	-1.6	9.6	5.8	17.8	4.6	9.1
Vanuatu	26[a]	35	..	..	..	..	..	..	..	..
Yemen	..	15	17	..	10.9	6.6	4.2	0.0	11.2	13.0
Zambia	23	17	25	-4.3	5.4	7.4	15.9	10.7	12.8	-11.8
All LDCs	16	16	21	3.0[g]	6.1	8.1	8.4	7.3	9.5	6.8

Source: UNCTAD secretariat calculations based on data from World Bank, *World Development Indicators 2005*, online.

a 1985. b 2002. c 2000-2002. d 1988. e 1993-2000. f 1986. g 1986-1990. h 1983-1990. i 1995. j 2000. k 1992. l 1981. m 1981-1990. n 1995-2000. o 1996-2000. p 1982-1990.

7. INDICATORS ON AREA AND POPULATION

Country	Area				Population				
	Total	% of arable land and land under permanent crops	% of land area covered by forests	Density	Total	Urban	Activity rate[a] %		
	(000 km²) 2004	2002	2002	Pop./km² 2004	(millions) 2004	% 2004	M	F	T
								2002	
Afghanistan	652.1	12.4	2.1	44	28.6	24	88	50	69
Angola	1 246.7	2.6	56.0	12	15.5	36	90	75	83
Bangladesh	144.0	58.5	10.2	967	139.2	25	87	56	78
Benin	112.6	25.0	24.0	73	8.2	45	83	76	79
Bhutan	47.0	3.5	64.2	19	0.9	9	91	60	76
Burkina Faso	274.0	16.1	25.9	47	12.8	18	90	78	84
Burundi	27.8	48.5	3.7	262	7.3	10	94	86	90
Cambodia	181.0	21	52.9	76	13.8	19	86	85	86
Cape Verde	4.0	11.2	21.1	123	0.5	57	90	50	68
Central African Republic	623.0	3.2	36.8	6	4.0	43	87	68	77
Chad	1 284.0	2.8	10.1	7	9.4	25	90	70	80
Comoros	2.2	59.2	4.3	348	0.8	36	86	64	75
Dem. Rep. of the Congo	2 344.9	3.3	59.6	24	55.9	32	85	63	74
Djibouti	23.2	0.1	0.3	34	0.8	84	..	..	..
Equatorial Guinea	28.1	8.2	62.5	18	0.5	49	91	48	69
Eritrea	117.6	4.3	13.5	36	4.2	20	87	77	82
Ethiopia	1 104.3	9.7	4.2	68	75.6	16	86	59	73
Gambia	11.3	22.6	48.1	131	1.5	26	90	70	80
Guinea	245.9	6.3	28.2	37	9.2	35	87	80	84
Guinea-Bissau	36.1	15.2	60.5	43	1.5	35	91	60	75
Haiti	27.8	39.6	3.2	303	8.4	38	82	58	70
Kiribati	0.7	53.4	38.4	134	0.1	47	..	..	..
Lao People's Dem. Republic	236.8	4.2	54.4	24	5.8	21	90	78	84
Lesotho	30.4	11.0	0.5	59	1.8	18	85	50	67
Liberia	111.4	5.4	31.3	29	3.2	47	83	56	70
Madagascar	587.0	6.0	20.2	31	18.1	27	89	71	80
Malawi	118.5	20.6	27.2	106	12.6	17	87	79	83
Maldives	0.3	40.0	3.3	1078	0.3	29	86	68	77
Mali	1 240.2	3.8	10.8	11	13.1	33	90	74	82
Mauritania	1 025.5	0.5	0.3	3	3.0	63	87	65	76
Mozambique	801.6	5.5	39.0	24	19.4	37	91	83	87
Myanmar	676.6	15.7	52.3	74	50.0	30	90	68	79
Nepal	147.2	22.4	27.3	181	26.6	15	86	58	72
Niger	1 267.0	3.6	1.0	11	13.5	23	93	71	82
Rwanda	26.3	52.6	12.4	337	8.9	20	94	86	90
Samoa	2.8	45.4	37.2	65	0.2	22	..	..	..
Sao Tome and Principe	1.0	56.3	28.3	159	0.2	38	..	..	..
Senegal	196.7	12.7	32.2	58	11.4	50	87	63	75
Sierra Leone	71.7	8.4	14.7	74	5.3	40	85	46	65
Solomon Islands	28.9	2.6	88.8	16	0.5	17	89	82	86
Somalia	637.7	1.7	12.0	12	8.0	35	87	65	76
Sudan	2 505.8	6.6	25.9	14	35.5	40	86	35	61
Timor-Leste	14.9	9.2	34.3	60	0.9	8	..	..	..
Togo	56.8	46.3	9.4	105	6.0	36	87	55	71
Tuvalu[b]	0.0	..	..	400	0.0	55	..	..	..
Uganda	241.0	29.9	21	115	27.8	12	91	81	86
United Republic of Tanzania	883.7	5.4	43.9	43	37.6	36	88	83	86
Vanuatu	12.2	9.8	36.7	17	0.2	23	..	..	..
Yemen	528.0	3.2	0.9	39	20.3	26	84	32	58
Zambia	752.6	7.0	42.0	15	11.5	36	87	67	77
All LDCs	20 740.9	6.8	27.6	36	740.4	27	88	66	77
All developing countries	80 828.5	11.5	20.3	63	5 100.7	42	87	60	73

Sources: UNCTAD; *Handbook of Statistics 2005*; FAO, online data and *State of the World's Forest 2003*; ILO, *World Labour Report 2000*; and UNDP *Human Development Report 2005*.

a Economically active population, labour force participation rates calculated as a percentage of those in the labour force at age 15–64 to total population at age 15–64.   b Population 10,466 and area 26 km².

8. INDICATORS ON DEMOGRAPHY

Country	Infant mortality rate (Per 1,000 live births)		Under-5 mortality rate		Average life expectancy at birth (Years)						Crude birth rate		Crude death rate (Per 1,000 population)	
	1990	2004	1990	2004	1990 M	1990 F	1990 T	2004 M	2004 F	2004 T	1990	2004	1990	2004
Afghanistan	153	147	260	248	45	45	45	46	47	46	51	49	21	19
Angola	158	136	275	241	38	42	40	40	42	41	53	48	25	22
Bangladesh	96	56	138	74	54	55	55	62	64	63	35	27	12	8
Benin	119	103	190	157	52	54	53	54	55	54	47	42	15	13
Bhutan	91	53	145	79	53	55	54	62	65	63	39	30	14	8
Burkina Faso	129	120	214	194	46	50	48	47	49	48	50	47	18	17
Burundi	121	104	210	183	43	47	45	43	45	44	47	45	20	19
Cambodia	113	93	176	136	53	56	54	53	60	56	44	30	13	11
Cape Verde	49	28	63	34	62	68	65	67	73	71	39	30	8	5
Central African Republic	104	97	179	174	46	52	49	38	40	39	42	37	17	22
Chad	121	115	213	202	44	48	46	43	45	44	48	48	19	20
Comoros	88	55	125	73	55	58	56	62	66	64	41	36	11	7
Dem. Rep. of the Congo	117	117	205	208	44	48	46	43	45	44	48	50	19	20
Djibouti	116	90	175	136	49	52	51	52	54	53	43	35	14	13
Equatorial Guinea	123	100	215	178	44	48	46	42	43	43	44	43	20	20
Eritrea	98	62	147	90	46	50	48	52	56	54	42	39	16	11
Ethiopia	118	97	206	168	45	49	47	47	49	48	47	40	18	16
Gambia	106	74	185	123	48	51	50	55	58	56	43	35	16	12
Guinea	142	103	240	159	47	48	47	54	54	54	45	42	18	13
Guinea-Bissau	145	117	255	206	41	44	42	43	46	45	50	50	23	20
Haiti	88	60	145	107	47	51	49	51	53	52	38	30	16	13
Kiribati	..	..	..	..	..	..	..	..	..	..	..	..	..	..
Lao People's Dem. Republic	110	86	181	136	48	51	50	54	56	55	43	35	17	12
Lesotho	80	65	116	122	56	60	58	34	36	35	35	28	11	25
Liberia	159	139	244	219	42	45	43	42	43	42	50	50	21	21
Madagascar	103	76	176	127	49	52	51	54	57	56	44	39	15	12
Malawi	141	108	237	179	44	48	46	40	40	40	51	44	19	21
Maldives	74	40	101	51	62	59	60	67	67	67	41	31	9	6
Mali	146	131	251	216	45	47	46	47	49	48	50	49	20	17
Mauritania	112	94	186	152	47	51	49	51	55	53	42	41	16	14
Mozambique	140	98	242	176	42	45	43	41	42	42	44	40	21	20
Myanmar	94	72	147	108	54	58	56	58	63	61	31	20	12	10
Nepal	98	61	142	83	54	54	54	62	62	62	39	30	13	8
Niger	178	150	315	259	40	40	40	45	45	45	57	54	26	21
Rwanda	123	115	205	190	30	34	32	43	46	44	48	41	33	18
Samoa	40	25	50	30	62	68	65	68	74	70	34	28	7	6
Sao Tome and Principe	83	81	113	110	61	62	62	62	64	63	37	34	10	9
Senegal	94	82	152	129	52	54	53	55	57	56	44	37	14	11
Sierra Leone	183	163	326	286	38	40	39	40	42	41	48	47	26	23
Solomon Islands	38	33	63	56	60	62	61	62	63	63	38	33	9	7
Somalia	150	122	250	203	40	44	42	46	48	47	46	45	22	18
Sudan	95	70	159	116	51	54	52	55	58	57	39	33	14	11
Timor-Leste	150	90	224	128	45	47	45	55	57	56	40	50	18	12
Togo	101	91	152	135	56	60	58	53	56	54	44	39	12	12
Tuvalu	..	..	..	..	..	..	..	..	..	..	..	..	..	..
Uganda	94	80	167	136	44	48	46	48	49	48	50	51	18	15
United Republic of Tanzania	108	105	166	164	52	56	54	46	46	46	44	37	13	17
Vanuatu	46	33	58	40	62	65	64	67	71	69	37	31	7	5
Yemen	97	66	140	90	54	55	54	60	62	61	51	40	13	8
Zambia	101	93	175	170	45	48	47	38	37	38	46	41	17	23
ALL LDCs	114	96	187	157	48	59	49	50	52	51	43	38	16	14
All developing countries	75	61	111	92	60	62	61	62	66	64	29	23	9	9

Source: United Nations Population Division, *World Population Prospects: 2004 Revision.*

9. INDICATORS ON HEALTH

Country	Low birth-weight[a] infants (%) 1998–2003[c]	Percentage of women attended childbirth by trained personnel 1995–2003[c]	Percentage of 1-year-old children immunized against: Tuber-culosis 2003	DPT3[b] 2003	Measles 2003	Estimated number of people living with HIV/AIDS children (0–14 years) End 2003	adults and children (0–49 years) End 2003	Adult prevalence rate (15–49) years End 2003
Afghanistan	..	14	59	54	50	…	…	…
Angola	12	45	62	46	62	23 000	240 000	3.9
Bangladesh	30	14	95	85	77	…	…	…
Benin	16	66	99	88	83	5 700	68 000	1.9
Bhutan	15	24	93	95	88	…	…	…
Burkina Faso	19	31	83	84	76	31 000	300 000	4.2
Burundi	16	25	84	74	75	27 000	250 000	6.0
Cambodia	11	32	76	69	65	7 300	170 000	2.6
Cape Verde	13	89	78	78	68	..	..	..
Central African Republic	14	44	70	40	35	21 000	260 000	13.5
Chad	17[d]	16	72	47	61	18 000	200 000	4.8
Comoros	25	62	75	75	63	…	…	…
Dem. Republic of the Congo	12	61	68	49	54	110 000	1100 000	4.2
Djibouti	..	61	63	68	66	680	9 100	2.9
Equatorial Guinea	13	65	73	33	51	…	…	…
Eritrea	21[d]	28	91	83	84	5 600	60 000	2.7
Ethiopia	15	6	76	56	52	120 000	1 500 000	4.4
Gambia	17	55	99	90	90	500	6 800	1.2
Guinea	12	35	78	45	52	9 200	140 000	3.2
Guinea-Bissau	22	35	84	77	61	…	…	…
Haiti	21	24	71	43	53	19 000	280 000	5.6
Kiribati	5	85	99	99	88	..	..	..
Lao People's Dem. Republic	14	19	65	50	42	…	1 700	0.1
Lesotho	14	60	83	79	70	22 000	320 000	28.9
Liberia	..	51	43	38	53	8 000	100 000	5.9
Madagascar	14	46	72	55	55	8 600	140 000	1.7
Malawi	16	61	91	84	77	83 000	900 000	14.2
Maldives	22	70	98	98	96	…	…	…
Mali	23	41	63	69	68	13 000	140 000	1.9
Mauritania	..	57	84	76	71	…	9 500	0.6
Mozambique	14[d]	48	87	72	77	99 000	1 300 000	12.2
Myanmar	15	56	79	77	75	7 600	330 000	1.2
Nepal	21	11	91	78	75	…	61 000	0.5
Niger	17	16	64	52	64	5 900	70 000	1.2
Rwanda	9	31	88	96	90	22 000	250 000	5.1
Samoa	4[d]	100	73	94	99	…	…	…
Sao Tome and Principe	..	79	99	94	87	…	…	…
Senegal	18	58	97	73	60	3 100	44 000	0.8
Sierra Leone	..	42	80	70	73	…	…	…
Solomon Islands	13[d]	85	76	71	78	…	…	…
Somalia	..	34	65	40	40	…	…	…
Sudan	31	86	53	50	57	21 000	400 000	2.3
Timor-Leste	24	24	80	70	60	…	…	…
Togo	15	49	84	64	58	9 300	110 000	4.1
Tuvalu	5	99	99	93	95	…	…	…
Uganda	12	39	96	81	82	84 000	530 000	4.1
United Republic of Tanzania	13	36	91	95	97	140 000	1 600 000	8.8
Vanuatu	6	89	63	49	48	…	…	…
Yemen	32[d]	22	67	66	66	…	12 000	0.1
Zambia	12	43	94	80	84	85 000	920 000	16.5
All LDCs	18	32	79	68	67	1 009 480	11 822 100	3.2
All developing countries	17	59	85	76	75	2 100 000	34 900 000	1.2

Source: UNICEF, *The State of the World's Children 2005*; UNAIDS, *2004 Report on the global AIDS epidemic.*

a Less than 2,500 grams.
b Diphtheria, pertussis and tetanus.
c Data refer to the most recent year available during the period specified in the column heading.
d Indicates data that refers to years or periods other than those specified in the column heading, differ from the standard definition, or refer to only part of the country.

10. INDICATORS ON NUTRITION AND SANITATION

Country	Total food supply (dairy calories intake per capita)		Population using improved drinking water sources (%)			Population using adequate sanitation facilities (%)		
	1990	2003	2002 Total	Urban	Rural	2002 Total	Urban	Rural
Afghanistan			13	19	11	8	16	5
Angola	1 791	2 089	50	70	40	30	56	16
Bangladesh	2 071	2 187	75	82	72	48	75	39
Benin	2 305	2 455	68	79	60	32	58	12
Bhutan	..	..	62	86	60	70	65	70
Burkina Faso	2 297	2 485	51	82	44	12	45	5
Burundi	1 888	1 612	79	90	78	36	47	35
Cambodia	1 809	1 967	34	58	29	16	53	8
Cape Verde	2 940	3 308	80	86	73	42	61	19
Central African Republic	1 863	1 949	75	93	61	27	47	12
Chad	1 697	2 245	34	40	32	8	30	0
Comoros	1 898	1 735	94	90	96	23	38	15
Dem. Rep. of the Congo	2 204	1 535	46	83	29	29	43	23
Djibouti	1 779	2 218	80	82	67	50	55	27
Equatorial Guinea	..	..	44	45	42	53	60	46
Eritrea	1 483	1 690	57	72	54	9	34	3
Ethiopia	1 510	2 037	22	81	11	6	19	4
Gambia	2 412	2 300	82	95	77	53	72	46
Guinea	2 013	2 362	51	78	38	13	25	6
Guinea-Bissau	2 252	2 481	59	79	49	34	57	23
Haiti	1 783	2 045	71	91	59	34	52	23
Kiribati	2 592	2 922	64	77	53	39	59	22
Lao People's Dem. Rep.	2 158	2 309	43	66	38	24	61	14
Lesotho	2 400	2 320	76	88	74	37	61	32
Liberia	2 102	1 946	62	72	52	26	49	7
Madagascar	2 138	2 072	84	75	34	33	49	27
Malawi	1 927	2 168	48	96	62	46	66	42
Maldives	2 324	2 587	56	99	78	58	100	42
Mali	2 235	2 376	42	76	35	45	59	38
Mauritania	2 517	2 764	80	63	45	42	64	9
Mozambique	1 849	1 980	84	76	24	27	51	14
Myanmar	2 620	2 822	46	95	74	73	96	63
Nepal	2 426	2 459	73	93	82	27	68	20
Niger	2 165	2 118	88	80	36	12	43	4
Rwanda	1 827	2 086	79	92	69	41	56	38
Samoa	..	..	72	91	88	100	100	100
Sao Tome and Principe	2 299	2 567	57	89	73	24	32	20
Senegal	2 306	2 277	70	90	54	52	70	34
Sierra Leone	1 991	1 913	57	75	46	39	53	30
Solomon Islands	1 953	2 272	70	94	65	31	98	18
Somalia	..	..	29	32	27	25	47	14
Sudan	2 136	2 288	69	78	64	34	50	24
Timor-Leste	2 510	2 819	52	73	51	33	65	30
Togo	2 279	2 358	51	80	36	34	71	15
Tuvalu	..	..	93	94	92	88	92	83
Uganda	2 321	2 360	56	87	52	41	53	39
United Rep. of Tanzania	2 065	1 959	73	92	62	46	54	41
Vanuatu	2 498	2 604	60	85	52	50	78	42
Yemen	2 022	2 019	69	74	68	30	76	14
Zambia	1 961	1 975	55	90	36	45	68	32
All LDCs	2 082	2 148	58	80	50	35	58	27
All developing countries	2 517[a]	2 669	79	92	70	49	73	31

Source: FAO, Food Balance sheets online data; and UNICEF, The State of the World's Children 2005.
a 1993.

11. INDICATORS ON EDUCATION AND LITERACY

Country	Adult literacy rate (%) 2000–2004			Youth literacy rate (%) 2000–2004			School enrolment ratio (%) Primary[a] 1999–2005[d]			Secondary[b] 1999–2005[d]			Tertiary[c] 1999–2005[d]		
	M	F	T	M	F	T	M	F	T	M	F	T	M	F	T
Afghanistan	51	21	36	..	..	..	...	...	...	...	...	...	...	...	...
Angola	82	54	67	83	63	71	66	57	61	...	...	...	...	...	...
Bangladesh	49	30	40	..	..	..	82	86	84	42	47	44	8	4	6
Benin	46	23	34	58	33	44	69	47	58	26	12	...	6	1	4
Bhutan	61	34	47	..	..	..	...	...	...	...	...	...	...	...	...
Burkina Faso	19	8	13	25	14	19	42	31	36	11	7	9	2	1	1
Burundi	67	52	59	76	69	72	62	52	57	10	8	9	3	1	2
Cambodia	85	64	74	88	79	83	96	91	93	30	19	24	5	2	3
Cape Verde	85	66	74	..	..	..	100	98	99	55	61	58	4	5	5
Central African Republic	65	33	49	70	47	58	...	...	...	...	...	...	3	1	2
Chad	41	13	26	55	23	37	72	49	61	17	6	12	2	...	1
Comoros	63	49	56	..	..	..	59	50	55	...	...	...	3	2	2
Dem. Rep. of the Congo	80	52	65	77	61	69	...	...	...	...	...	...	...	...	...
Djibouti	76	54	65	..	..	..	40	32	36	25	17	21	2	2	2
Equatorial Guinea	92	76	84	94	94	94	91	78	85	...	...	24	4	2	3
Eritrea	67	45	56	..	..	..	49	42	45	25	18	22	3	...	3
Ethiopia	47	31	39	..	..	..	55	47	51	23	13	18	4	1	3
Gambia	44	30	37	..	..	..	79	78	79	39	27	33	...	...	1
Guinea	55	27	41	..	..	..	73	58	65	28	13	21	...	...	...
Guinea-Bissau	54	24	38	..	..	..	53	37	45	11	6	9	1	...	...
Haiti	52	48	50	..	..	..	...	...	...	...	...	...	...	...	...
Kiribati	..	..	..	..	..	..	...	...	...	...	...	...	...	...	...
Lao People's Dem. Rep.	77	61	69	83	75	79	88	82	85	38	32	35	7	4	5
Lesotho	74	90	81	..	..	..	83	89	86	18	27	22	2	4	3
Liberia	70	37	54	..	..	..	79	61	70	23	13	18	...	15	...
Madagascar	76	65	71	72	68	70	78	79	79	11	12	11	2	2	2
Malawi	75	54	64	82	71	76	...	...	100	32	26	29	1	...	...
Maldives	96	96	96	98	98	98	92	93	92	48	55	51	...	...	...
Mali	27	12	19	32	17	24	50	39	44	...	...	...	...	...	2
Mauritania	60	43	51	68	55	61	68	67	68	...	...	...	6	2	4
Mozambique	60	29	44	..	..	..	58	53	55	14	10	12	1	1	1
Myanmar	94	86	90	96	93	94	84	85	84	36	34	35	8	15	12
Nepal	63	35	49	81	60	70	75	66	70	...	...	...	8	3	5
Niger	20	9	14	26	14	20	45	31	38	7	5	6	2	1	1
Rwanda	70	59	64	77	76	76	85	88	87	...	...	...	4	2	3
Samoa	99	98	99	..	..	..	99	96	98	59	65	62	7	6	7
Sao Tome and Principe	..	..	..	..	..	..	100	94	97	32	26	29	1	1	1
Senegal	51	29	39	58	41	49	71	66	69	...	...	...	...	...	...
Sierra Leone	40	21	30	47	30	38	...	...	...	...	...	...	3	1	2
Solomon Islands	..	..	..	..	..	..	...	...	72	...	...	...	...	...	...
Somalia	..	..	..	..	..	..	...	...	...	...	...	...	...	...	...
Sudan	69	50	59	82	69	75	50	42	46	...	...	...	7	6	7
Timor-Leste	..	..	..	..	..	..	...	...	...	...	...	20	10	15	12
Togo	68	38	53	83	63	74	99	83	91	36	17	27	6	1	4
Tuvalu	..	..	..	..	..	..	...	...	...	...	...	...	...	...	...
Uganda	78	57	67	..	..	..	...	...	...	17	16	16	4	2	3
United Rep. of Tanzania	78	62	69	81	76	78	83	81	82	5	4	5	2	1	1
Vanuatu	..	..	74	..	..	..	93	95	94	27	28	28	...	...	4
Yemen	68	25	46	72	33	53	84	59	72	47	21	35	17	5	11
Zambia	76	60	68	73	66	69	69	68	68	25	21	23	3	2	2
All LDCs	63	43	53	70	57	64	..	..	..	..	..	..	..	..	..
All developing countries	83	69	76	89	81	85	..	..	..	..	..	..	..	..	..

Source: UNESCO Institute for Statistics (UIS) estimates and projections, online data (September 2005), UIS May 2005 Assessment 2005 and *World Culture Report 2000*; UNDP, *Human Development Report 2005*; UNICEF, *The State of the World's Children 2005*.

a   Net primary school enrolment.
b   Net secondary school enrolment.
c   Gross tertiary school enrolment.
d   Or latest year available.

12. INDICATORS ON COMMUNICATIONS AND MEDIA

Country	Post offices open to the public[a] (Per 100,000 inhabitants)	Circulation of daily newspapers[a]	Radio receivers[a]	Television sets[a]	Telephone main-lines[a]	Cellular sub-scribers[a]	Personal computers[a]	Internet users[a]
				(Per 1,000 inhabitants)				
	2004	2001	2001	2003	2003	2003	2003	2003
Afghanistan	2	5	132	14	2	10	..	1
Angola	0	11	54	20	7	10	2	3
Bangladesh	7	53	50	61	5	10	8	2
Benin	2	5	110	33	9	30	4	10
Bhutan	5	..	19	27	34	10	14	20
Burkina Faso	1	1	33	12	5	20	2	4
Burundi	0	2	152	35	3	10	2	2
Cambodia	1	2	128	7	3	40	2	2
Cape Verde	11	..	183	100	156	120	76	44
Central African Republic	1	2	83	5	2	10	2	1
Chad	0	0	242	5	2	10	2	2
Comoros	4	..	141	23	17	..	6	6
Democratic Rep. of the Congo	1	3	376	2	..	20	..	1
Djibouti	1	..	84	76	15	30	22	10
Equatorial Guinea	4	5	428	..	18	80	6	4
Eritrea	2	..	484	53	9	10	3	2
Ethiopia	1	0	196	6	6	..	2	1
Gambia	1	2	394	15	29	80	14	19
Guinea	1	..	49	17	3	10	6	5
Guinea-Bissau	1	5	44	40	8	..	..	15
Haiti	1	3	55	60	17	40	..	18
Kiribati	26	..	212	44	51	10	11	23
Lao People's Democratic Rep.	4	4	143	53	12	20	4	3
Lesotho	9	8	49	37	16	50	..	14
Liberia	0	13	329	..	2	..	..	..
Madagascar	3	5	198	17	4	20	5	4
Malawi	3	3	250	6	8	10	2	3
Maldives	67	20	129	128	105	230	70	53
Mali	1	1	54	27	6	20	2	3
Mauritania	1	1	151	44	14	130	11	4
Mozambique	2	3	40	163	4	20	4	33
Myanmar	3	9	70	16	7	..	6	3
Nepal	16	12	39	..	16	..	4	..
Niger	0	0	66	119	2	10	1	17
Rwanda	0	0	102	8	3	20	..	3
Samoa	20	..	1 035	148	73	60	7	22
Sao Tome and Principe	6	..	272	92	46	30	..	99
Senegal	1	5	142	39	22	60	21	22
Sierra Leone	-	4	274	13	5	10	..	2
Solomon Islands	6	..	141	10	13	..	38	5
Somalia	..	1	53	17	8	20	2	7
Sudan	1	26	271	378	27	20	6	9
Timor-Leste	..	..	..	..	..	..	..	..
Togo	1	4	227	120	12	40	32	42
Tuvalu	..	..	384	..	68	..	..	188
Uganda	1	2	127	15	2	30	4	5
United Republic of Tanzania	1	4	279	42	4	30	6	7
Vanuatu	16	..	350	13	31	40	14	36
Yemen	1	15	64	298	28	30	7	5
Zambia	2	12	160	59	8	20	8	6
All LDCs	3	7	170[b]	50[c]	8	16	..	4
All developing countries	8	40	321[b]	183[c]	113	134	..	53

Source: UNDP, *Human Development Report 2005*; UNCTAD, *Handbook of Statistics 2005*; UNESCO, *Statistical Yearbook 1999* and *World Culture Report 2000*; Universal Postal Union, *Postal Statistics* online data.

a   Or latest year available.   b Data refer to 1997.   c Data refer to 2002.

13. INDICATORS ON TRANSPORT AND TRANSPORT NETWORKS

Country	Road networks[a]			Railways[b]				Civil aviation[c]	
	Total km	Paved %	Density km/ 1,000 km²	Network km	Density km/ 1,000 km²	Freight mill. ton per km	Passenger mill. pass. per km	Freight mill. tons. per km.	Passenger thousands
Afghanistan	21 000	13.3	32.2	..	..	..	..	7.8[d]	150[d]
Angola	51 429	10.4	41.3	2 523	2.0	1 890	360	56.5	198
Bangladesh	207 486	9.5	1 440.9	2 746	19.1	718	5 348	179.0	1 579
Benin	6 787	20.0	60.3	579	5.1	220	230	7.4[e]	46[e]
Bhutan	4 007	60.7	78.5	..	..	..	..	0.2	36
Burkina Faso	12 506	16.0	45.6	607	2.2	72	152	7.4[e]	55
Burundi	14 480[f]	..	520.2	..	..	..	..	..	12[g]
Cambodia	12 323[d]	16.2[d]	68.1[d]	601	3.3	34	80	2.6	116
Cape Verde	1 100	78.0	272.7	..	..	..	..	0.4	253
Central African Republic	23 810	2.7[e]	38.2	..	..	..	..	7.4[e]	46[e]
Chad	33 400	0.8	26.0	..	..	..	..	7.4	46e
Comoros	880	76.5	393.7	..	..	..	..	..	27f
Dem. Rep. of the Congo	157 000[h]	..	67.0	5 088	2.2	1 836	580	7.4	9.5[e]
Djibouti	2 890	12.6	124.6	100	4.3	..	..	..	..
Equatorial Guinea	2 880	..	102.7	..	..	..	..	..	21[g]
Eritrea	4 010	21.8	34.1	..	..	..	..	..	..
Ethiopia	31 571	12.0	28.6	781	0.7	103	185	93.5	1147
Gambia	2 700	35.4	239.0	..	..	..	..	..	..
Guinea	30 500	16.5	124.1	940	3.8	660	116	1.4[g]	59[g]
Guinea-Bissau	4 400	10.3	121.8	..	..	..	..	0.1[h]	20[e]
Haiti	4 160	24.3	149.9	100	3.6	..	..	..	..
Kiribati	670	..	922.9	..	..	..	..	0.8[g]	28[g]
Lao People's Dem. Rep.	21 716	44.5	91.7	..	..	..	..	1.9	219
Lesotho	5 940	18.3	195.7	16	0.5	..	..	..	1[g]
Liberia	10 600	6.2	95.2	493	4.4	..	..	..	..
Madagascar	49 827	11.6	84.9	1 030	1.8	93	46	9.6	404
Malawi	28 400	18.5	239.7	789	6.7	48	40	1.2	109
Maldives	..	..	..	..	..	..	..	13.2[d]	60
Mali	15 100	12.1	12.2	642	0.5	4	9	7.4[e]	46[e]
Mauritania	7 660	11.3	7.5	650	0.6	16 623	7	7.4[e]	116
Mozambique	30 400	18.7	37.9	3 150	3.9	1 420	500	6.6	281
Myanmar	28 200	12.2	41.7	2 775	4.1	648	4 675	2.1	1117
Nepal	15 308	30.8	89.8	52	0.4	..	..	18.9	625
Niger	10 100	7.9	8.0	..	..	..	..	7.4	46[e]
Rwanda	12 000	8.3	455.6	2 652	100.7	2 140	2 700	..	..
Samoa	790	42.0	279.1	..	..	..	..	1.5	198
Sao Tome and Principe	320	68.1	332.0	..	..	..	..	0.1	36
Senegal	14 576[d]	29.3[d]	74.1[d]	906	4.6	386	179	7.4[e]	130
Sierra Leone	11 300	8.0	157.9	84	1.2	..	..	6.7	14
Solomon Islands	1 360	2.5	47.1	..	..	..	..	0.7	68
Somalia	22 100	11.8	34.7	..	..	..	..	..	..
Sudan	11 900	36.3	4.7	4 756	1.9	1 970	985	36.3	421
Timor-Leste	..	..	..	..	..	..	..	..	..
Togo	7 520	31.6	132.4	514	9.1	17	132	7.4[e]	46[e]
Tuvalu	8	..	307.7	..	..	..	..	..	..
Uganda	27 000	6.7	112.0	1 100	4.6	82	315	23.4	40
United Rep. of Tanzania	88 200	4.2	99.8	3 575	4.0	523	935	1.8	150
Vanuatu	1 070	23.9	87.8	..	..	..	..	1.5	83
Yemen	67 000	11.5	126.9	..	..	..	..	48.7	844
Zambia	91 440	22.0	88.7	1 924	2.6	1 625	547	0.5[d]	51

Source: World Bank, *World Development Indicators 2005*, online data; IRU, *World Transport Statistics 1996.*

　　a　Data refer to 2002 or latest year available.
　　b　Data refer to 1996 or latest year available.
　　c　Data refer to 2003.
　　d　2000. e 2001. f 1996. g 1999. h 1997.

14. INDICATORS ON ENERGY AND THE ENVIRONMENT

Country	Coal, oil, gas and electricity		Fuelwood, charcoal and bagasse		Net installed electricity capacity		Electricity consumption per capita		Carbon dioxide emissions per capita	
	Consumption per capita in kg. of coal equivalent				Kilowatt/ 1,000 inhabitants		Kilowatt-hours		Metric tons	
	1980	2000	1980	1996	1980	2002	1980	2002	1980	2002
Afghanistan	48	23	99	99	25	26	..	..	0.1	0
Angola	135	174	362	183	85	31	214	135	0.7	0.5
Bangladesh	45	114	23	24	11	26	30	119	0.1	0.3
Benin	51	116	347	344	4	7	37	92	0.1	0.3
Bhutan	9	172	777	262	8	404	17	236	0	0.2
Burkina Faso	33	43	277	312	6	6	16	32	0.1	0.1
Burundi	14	20	252	255	2	6	12	25	0	0
Cambodia	22	20	213	218	6	3	15	10	0	0.1
Cape Verde	194	155	..	..	21	15	55	99	0.4	0.3
Central African Rep.	26	38	358	335	13	11	29	28	0	0.1
Chad	22	8	206	208	8	3	10	12	0	0
Comoros	48	54	..	..	10	8	26	25	0.1	0.1
Dem. Rep. of the Congo	75	37	298	335	64	61	161	91	0.1	0
Djibouti	326	290	..	..	124	117	416	296	0.9	0.5
Equatorial Guinea	124	170	645	383	32	38	83	54	0.3	0.4
Eritrea	..	76	..	..	..	44	..	66	..	0.2
Ethiopia	21[a]	40	296	285	9	8	..	32	0	0.1
Gambia	128	93	452	338	17	21	70	96	0.2	0.2
Guinea	85	69	246	221	39	22	85	95	0.2	0.1
Guinea-Bissau	81	104	177	134	9	14	18	41	0.2	0.2
Haiti	56	89	322	288	22	32	58	73	0.1	0.2
Kiribati	220	141	..	..	33	32	..	..	0.5	0.3
Lao People's Dem. Rep.	30	62	354	308	78	51	68	133	0.1	0.2
Lesotho	..	..	..	..	..	..	..	..	..	..
Liberia	480	72	709	589	163	104	..	..	1.1	0.1
Madagascar	86	57	194	242	11	13	49	42	0.2	0.1
Malawi	58	38	288	314	24	16	66	80	0.1	0.1
Maldives	129	875	..	..	13	144	25	448	0.3	3.4
Mali	27	23	196	191	6	9	15	33	0.1	0
Mauritania	178	530	1	1	35	41	60	58	0.4	1.1
Mozambique	151	76	351	323	156	127	364	378	0.3	0.1
Myanmar	65	99	143	149	19	32	44	135	0.1	0.2
Nepal	18	70	305	282	5	18	17	62	0	0.2
Niger	50	46	191	200	6	8	39	40	0.1	0.1
Rwanda	28	36	292	232	8	5	32	23	0.1	0.1
Samoa	310	405	145	149	84	133	252	597	0.6	0.8
Sao Tome and Principe	213	317	..	..	43	41	96	115	0.4	0.6
Senegal	214	191	..	..	30	22	115	141	0.6	0.4
Sierra Leone	79	48	709	237	29	27	62	54	0.2	0.1
Solomon Islands	212	177	..	126	53	27	93	69	0.4	0.4
Somalia	108	48[b]	192	315	5	11	..	..	0.1	..
Sudan	81	93	282	289	16	22	47	89	0.2	0.3
Timor-Leste	..	..	..	..	..	..	..	..	..	..
Togo	72	152	66	94	13	7	74	120	0.2	0.3
Tuvalu	..	..	..	..	..	..	..	..	..	..
Uganda	29	38	235	236	12	10	28	61	0.1	0.1
United Rep. of Tanzania	44	58	331	392	14	15	41	83	0.1	0.1
Vanuatu	248	193	68	48	85	60	171	208	0.5	0.4
Yemen	187	211	45	8	20	42	..	159	..	0.7
Zambia	403	159	496	502	301	204	1125	603	0.6	0.2
All LDCs	66	82	212	210	28	30	83	106	0.1	0.2
All developing countries	521	886	125	135	88	232	388	1155	1.3	2

Source: United Nations, *Energy Statistics Yearbook 1983* and *2002,* and *Statistical Yearbook 1985/86.* UNDP, *Human Development Report 2005,* and World Bank, *World Development Indicators 2005,* online data.

a Includes Eritrea.   b 1989.

15. INDICATORS ON THE STATUS OF WOMEN IN LDCs

Country	Education, training and literacy: Female–male gaps[a]				Health, fertility and mortality			Economic activity, employment					Political participation	
	Adult literacy rate	School enrolment ratio[b]			Average age at first marriage (years)	Total fertility rate (births per woman)	Maternal mortality (per 100,000 live births)	Women as a percentage of total:				Female labour force: Agriculture/total	Women in government at ministerial level	Seats in parliaments held by women
		Primary	Secondary	Tertiary				Labour force	Employees	Self-employed	Unpaid family	(%)	(% of total)	
	2003	2002–2003			1997[c]	2002-2005	2005[d]	2004	1998[c]	1998[c]	1998[c]	2002	2005[g]	2005[h]
Afghanistan	..	..	..	..	18	7	1900	36	..	..	..	83	..	..
Angola	66	0.86	..	0.65[f]	18	7	1700	46	..	..	..	83	6	15
Bangladesh	62	1.04	1.11	0.50	17	3	380	43	14	8	74	64	8	2
Benin	49	0.69	0.48	0.24	18	6	850	40	..	64	40	52	19	7
Bhutan	..	..	..	..	..	4	420	40	..	..	..	98	0	9
Burkina Faso	44	0.73	0.67	0.34[i]	17	7	1000	48	13	16	66	93	15	12
Burundi	78	0.84	0.78[i]	0.45[i]	22	7	1000	48	13	53	60	97	11	18
Cambodia	76	0.95[i]	0.64[i]	0.40	21	4	450	52	..	..	..	73	7	10
Cape Verde	80	0.98	1.11	1.09	25	4	150	39	32	30	54	21	19	11
Central African Republic	52	..	..	0.19[f]	19	5	1100	46	10	52	55	78	10	..
Chad	31	0.68i	0.31[i]	0.17[f]	17	7	1100	45	..	..	..	84	12	7
Comoros	77	0.84	..	0.77	22	5	480	43	24	25	..	86	..	3
Dem. Rep. of the Congo	65	..	..	..	20	7	990	43	..	..	..	76	13	12
Djibouti	..	0.90	0.69	0.81	19	5	730	40	33	28	22	83	5	11
Equatorial Guinea	83	0.85	0.58	0.43[f]	..	6	880	36	..	..	74	89	5	18
Eritrea	67	0.86	0.48	0.24[i]	..	6	630	47	..	..	..	81	18	22
Ethiopia	69	0.65	0.57	0.33	18	6	850	41	26	28	67	79	6	8
Gambia	..	0.99[i]	0.68[i]	0.29[i]	..	5	540	45	..	..	64	89	20	13
Guinea	..	0.8	0.48[i]	..	16	6	740	47	..	..	60	88	15	19
Guinea-Bissau	..	0.71[f]	0.55	0.18[f]	18	7	1100	41	..	..	4	95	38	14
Haiti	93	..	..	..	24	4	680	43	44	57	37	49	25	4
Kiribati	..	..	..	..	..	..	..	..	..	..	..	14	..	5
Lao People's Dem. Rep.	79	0.93	0.83	0.57	..	5	650	47	..	..	..	79	0	23
Lesotho	123	1.07	1.53[i]	1.48	21	4	550	38	38	24	39	54	28	12
Liberia	..	..	..	..	19	7	760	40	..	..	..	75	..	8
Madagascar	85	1.00	1.03[i]	0.83[i]	20	5	550	44	..	..	..	82	6	7
Malawi	72	..	0.81[i]	0.41	18	6	1800	49	13	57	58	95	14	14
Maldives	100	1.01	1.15[f]	..	19	4	110	44	17	44	29	18	12	12
Mali	44	0.77	..	..	16	7	1200	46	17	15	53	81	19	10
Mauritania	73	0.97	0.77[i]	0.27[i]	19	6	1000	44	15	23	38	63	9	4
Mozambique	50	0.91	0.70	0.73	18	6	1000	49	..	..	82	95	13	35
Myanmar	92	1.01	0.94	1.75[e]	22	3	360	44	..	..	..	73	..	..
Nepal	56	0.88[i]	..	0.34	18	4	740	40	15	36	61	98	7	6
Niger	48	0.69	0.67	0.34[i]	16	8	1600	43	8	17	24	97	23	12
Rwanda	84	1.04	..	0.46	21	6	1400	49	15	33	53	97	36	49
Samoa	99	0.98	1.11	0.90	25	4	130	37	37	9	8	33	8	6
Sao Tome and Principe	..	0.94[f]	0.83[f]	0.56	18	4	..	..	32	26	54	74	14	9
Senegal	57	0.89	..	..	18	5	690	43				81	21	19
Sierra Leone	52	..	..	0.4[i]	18	7	2000	37	20	24	72	76	13	15
Solomon Islands	..	..	..	..	21	4	130	48	20	39	..	83	0	0
Somalia	..	..	..	..	20	7	1100	43	..	..	..	82	..	..
Sudan	72	0.83[i]	..	0.92[i]	19	4	590	31	..	..	..	74	3	10
Timor-Leste	..	..	..	1.58[f]	..	8	660	45					22	25
Togo	56	0.84	0.48[i]	0.20[i]	19	5	570	40	15	48	54	61	20	6
Tuvalu	..	..	..	..	..	..	..	..	..	..	..	..	..	0
Uganda	75	..	0.90i	0.52[i]	18	7	880	47	..	39	74	83	23	24
United Rep. of Tanzania	80	0.98	..	0.44	19	5	1500	49	..	..	88	87	15	21
Vanuatu	..	1.02[i]	1.01[f]	..	23	4	130	..	..	..	..	37	8	4
Yemen	41	0.71	0.46[i]	0.28[i]	18	6	570	29	8	13	69	75	3	0
Zambia	78	0.98	0.83[i]	0.46[i]	19	6	750	43	16	55	54	75	25	13
All LDCs	70	..	..	..	19	5	..	43	..	..	..	78	..	..

Source: UNDP, *Human Development Report 2005;* United Nations, *The World's Women 1970–1990* and *2000: Trends and Statistics; Women's Indicators and Statistics* (Wistat); UNESCO, *2005 Statistical data online, Statistical Yearbook 1999, World Culture Report 2000;* UNICEF, *The State of the World's Children 2005;* and FAO, online data.

a Females as percentage of males. b Net primary school enrolment, Net secondary school enrolment, and Tertiary school enrolment is generally calculated as a gross ratio. c Or latest year available. d UNICEF, WHO and UNFPA adjusted from the reported data and estimates for the year 2005. e Data refer to the 2000/2001 school year. f Data refer to the 2001/2002 school year. g Data are as of 1 January 2005. h Data are as of 1 March 2005 and refer to the lower or single house. i Estimates subject to revision.

TABLE 16. LDCs REFUGEES POPULATION BY COUNTRY OR TERRITORY OF ASYLUM OR RESIDENCE, END-2004

Country[a]	Refugees population[b]		Asylum-seekers[c]	Returned refugees[d]	Internally displaced[e]	Returned IDPs[f]	Others	Total
	begin year	end year						
Afghanistan[g]	22	30	29	940469	159549	27391	-	1127468
Angola	13381	13970	929	90246	-	-	-	105145
Bangladesh	19792	20449	10	-	-	-	250000	270459
Benin	5034	4802	1053	-	-	-	-	5855
Bhutan	-	-	-	-	-	-	-	-
Burkina Faso	466	492	518	-	-	-	-	1010
Burundi	40971	48808	11893	90321	-	1970	-	152992
Cambodia	76	382	316	-	-	-	-	698
Cape Verde	-	-	-	-	-	-	-	-
Central African Rep.	44753	25020	2748	368	-	-	-	28136
Chad	146400	259880	-	184	-	-	-	260064
Comoros	-	-	-	-	-	-	-	-
Dem. Rep. of the Congo	234033	199323	354	13843	-	-	-	213520
Djibouti	27034	18035	-	-	-	-	-	18035
Equatorial Guinea	-	-	-	-	-	-	-	-
Eritrea	3889	4240	449	9893	-	-	7	14589
Ethiopia	130276	115980	40	7	-	-	-	116027
Gambia	7465	7343	602	-	-	-	-	7945
Guinea	184341	139252	6317	2	-	-	-	145571
Guinea-Bissau	7551	7536	141	-	-	-	-	7677
Haiti	-	-	-	-	-	-	-	-
Kiribati	-	-	-	-	-	-	-	-
Lao People's Dem. Rep.	-	-	-	-	-	-	-	-
Lesotho	-	-	-	-	-	-	-	-
Liberia	33998	15172	5	56872	498566	33050	35	603700
Madagascar	-	-	-	-	-	-	-	-
Malawi	3202	3682	3335	-	-	-	-	7017
Maldives	-	-	-	-	-	-	-	-
Mali	10009	11256	1085	-	-	-	-	12341
Mauritania	475	473	117	-	-	-	29500	30090
Mozambique	311	623	4892	-	-	-	-	5515
Myanmar	-	-	-	210	-	-	-	210
Nepal	123667	124928	654	-	-	-	10737	136319
Niger	328	344	41	-	-	-	-	385
Rwanda	36608	50221	3248	14136	-	-	-	67605
Samoa	-	-	-	-	-	-	-	-
Sao Tome and Principe	-	-	-	-	-	-	-	-
Senegal	20726	20804	2412	-	-	-	-	23216
Sierra Leone	61194	65437	138	26271	-	-	-	91846
Solomon Islands	-	-	-	-	-	-	-	-
Somalia	368	357	334	18069	-	-	-	18760
Sudan	138163	141588	4271	290	662302	-	37416	845867
Timor-Leste	3	3	10	-	-	-	-	13
Togo	12396	11285	390	120	-	-	-	11795
Tuvalu	-	-	-	-	-	-	-	-
Uganda	230903	250482	1809	91	-	-	-	252382
United Rep. of Tanzania	649770	602088	166	2	-	-	-	602256
Vanuatu	-	-	-	-	-	-	-	-
Yemen	61881	66384	1270	39	-	-	-	67693
Zambia	226697	173907	84	-	-	-	-	173991
Total LDCs	2476183	2404576	49660	1261433	1320417	62411	327695	5426192

Source: UNHCR: 2004 Global Refugee Trends

Notes: The data are generally provided by Governments, based on their own definitions and methods of data collection.
   a   Country or territory of asylum or residence.
   b   Persons recognized as refugees under the 1951 UN Convention/1967 Protocol, the 1969 OAU Convention, in accordance with the UNHCR Statute, persons granted a humanitarian status and those granted temporary protection.
   c   Persons whose application for asylum or refugee status is pending at any stage in the procedure or who are otherwise registed as a asylum-seekers.
   d   Refugees who have returned to their place of origin during the year.
   e   Persons who are displaced within their country and to whom UNHCR extends protection and/or assistance,
   f   Persons who have returned to their place of origin during the year.
   g   According to the Government, the number of Afghans in the Islamic Rep. of Iran and Pakistan are estimated to be   some 2.0 million and 1.8 millions, respectively.

17. LEADING EXPORTS OF ALL LDCs IN 2002–2003

SITC	Item	Value[a] ($ millions)	As percentage of:		
			LDCs	Developing countries	World
	All commodities	37'159.5	100.00	1.69	0.54
333	Petroleum oils, crude and crude oils obtained from bituminous minerals	12'041.8	32.41	4.66	3.33
845	Outergarments and other articles, knitted	2'394.3	6.44	6.32	4.29
334	Petroleum products, refined	1'982.6	5.34	2.76	1.23
842	Outer garments, men's, of textile fabrics	1'465.7	3.94	6.59	4.00
846	Undergarments knitted or crocheted	1'322.6	3.56	5.77	3.60
843	Outergarments, women's, of textile fabrics	1'059.5	2.85	3.20	1.96
263	Cotton	1'049.4	2.82	37.67	12.86
844	Undergarments of textile fabrics	1'021.5	2.75	11.58	8.78
036	Crustaceans and molluscs, fresh, chilled, frozen, salted, in brine or dried	902.2	2.43	8.11	5.20
667	Pearls, precious and semi-precious stones unworked or worked	888.4	2.39	4.61	1.51
341	Gas, natural and manufactured	737.5	1.98	2.21	0.80
971	Gold, non-monetary	677.2	1.82	5.14	2.54
034	Fish, fresh, chilled, frozen	563.6	1.52	5.82	2.30
682	Copper	559.2	1.50	4.33	1.82
247	Other wood rough, squared	501.4	1.35	29.89	6.77
054	Vegetables, fresh,chilled,frozen or simply preserved	483.9	1.30	5.99	1.76
071	Coffee and coffee substitutes	427.4	1.15	7.59	4.71
684	Aluminium	424.9	1.14	3.72	0.82
892	Printed matter	422.7	1.14	7.51	1.21
121	Tobacco, unmanufactured	337.2	0.91	12.07	6.24

Source: UNCTAD secretariat calculations, based on data from the United Nations Statistics Division.

a   Annual average 2002–2003.

18. Main markets for exports of LDCs: Percentage shares in 2004 (or latest year available)

Country	Developed economies					South-East Europe and CIS	Developing economies			Un-allocated
	Total	EU 25	Japan	USA and Canada	Others		Total	OPEC	Others	
Afghanistan	34.4	20.3	0.6	12.9	0.6	5.0	60.7	3.9	56.8	0.0
Angola	50.7	10.4	0.1	40.2	0.0	0.0	49.3	1.1	48.2	0.0
Bangladesh	78.3	50.0	1.0	26.5	0.9	0.1	8.7	1.2	7.5	12.9
Benin	11.3	11.0	0.0	0.3	..	0.1	88.4	8.5	79.9	0.2
Bhutan	..	..	..	..	..		..	..	..	..
Burkina Faso	16.3	13.4	2.6	0.1	0.2	..	81.0	1.9	79.2	..
Burundi	59.0	27.3	0.6	5.6	..	0.8	14.7	0.0	14.7	25.6
Cambodia	90.9	25.6	3.5	60.8	0.9	0.1	9.1	0.1	9.0	0.0
Cape Verde	96.1	78.3	0.5	17.7	..	..	3.4	2.0	1.5	..
Central African Republic	77.3	69.2	1.6	6.4	0.1	0.1	22.7	8.7	14.0	-0.1
Chad	83.9	7.9	0.0	76.0	0.0	0.0	16.1	0.1	16.0	0.0
Comoros	72.9	28.8	1.4	42.5	0.3	0.0	26.0	0.0	26.0	1.1
Dem. Rep. of the Congo	76.1	65.6	0.7	9.5	0.2	0.0	23.5	0.0	23.5	0.3
Djibouti	3.8	3.3	0.0	0.4	0.0	0.0	96.2	0.1	96.1	0.0
Equatorial Guinea	74.7	28.6	1.4	44.3	0.5	0.0	25.3	0.0	25.3	0.0
Eritrea	..	..	..	..	..	..	..	..	..	..
Ethiopia	47.5	28.9	8.7	6.0	3.8	0.6	35.7	8.1	27.6	16.2
Gambia	57.0	53.2	2.2	1.3	0.0	0.8	42.2	0.0	42.2	0.0
Guinea	50.1	40.4	0.1	9.5	0.1	23.3	26.6	3.2	23.4	0.0
Guinea-Bissau	28.6	4.9	0.4	23.3	..	..	71.4	13.9	57.5	..
Haiti	90.3	3.4	0.2	85.9	0.8	0.0	9.5	0.7	8.8	0.2
Kiribati	87.9	48.3	28.7	9.2	2.3	..	12.1	..	..	..
Lao People's Dem. Rep.	31.8	27.7	1.3	1.8	1.0	0.1	39.1	0.8	38.3	29.0
Lesotho	..	..	..	..	..	..	..	..	..	..
Liberia	88.8	72.7	0.0	12.7	3.4	0.2	11.0	0.2	10.8	0.0
Madagascar	87.5	47.5	2.3	37.2	0.6	0.1	10.8	0.2	10.6	1.7
Malawi	52.8	35.7	2.5	12.5	2.1	6.4	39.7	0.9	38.8	1.0
Maldives	63.4	14.8	8.6	39.9	0.1	0.0	36.6	6.8	29.8	0.0
Mali	23.7	21.9	0.1	1.2	0.5	0.1	72.9	1.9	71.0	3.3
Mauritania	67.5	52.8	12.9	0.9	0.9	5.4	25.5	2.8	22.7	1.6
Mozambique	75.6	73.4	1.2	0.8	0.1	0.6	17.7	0.5	17.1	6.1
Myanmar	21.9	15.6	5.1	0.6	0.6	0.1	76.4	0.7	75.7	1.7
Nepal	43.0	17.5	1.1	23.4	1.1	0.0	54.0	0.0	54.0	3.0
Niger	66.4	48.8	8.0	9.7	0.0	..	33.5	24.4	9.1	..
Rwanda	13.3	10.7	0.0	2.5	0.1	0.9	53.6	37.6	16.0	32.2
Samoa	70.3	3.8	1.0	5.1	60.5	0.0	24.8	19.0	5.8	4.9
Sao Tome and Principe	64.4	62.4	..	1.0	1.0	..	35.6	2.0	33.7	..
Senegal	28.1	26.0	1.2	0.3	0.7	0.0	57.0	0.5	56.5	14.8
Sierra Leone	88.9	81.5	0.1	7.2	0.1	0.2	10.5	0.5	10.0	0.4
Solomon Islands	20.8	6.9	9.5	1.8	2.5	..	76.8	0.5	76.3	..
Somalia	2.0	1.0	0.6	0.4	0.1	0.0	97.9	29.9	68.0	0.1
Sudan	19.0	5.0	13.7	0.4	0.0	0.1	80.1	7.6	72.4	0.8
Timor-Leste	..	..	..	..	..	..	..	..	..	..
Togo	19.2	13.9	0.1	0.4	4.9	0.3	79.8	3.4	76.4	0.7
Tuvalu	68.4	68.4	..	..	0.0	0.0	26.3	..	..	5.3
Uganda	54.3	37.0	1.1	4.1	12.1	0.7	38.8	2.3	36.5	6.2
United Republic of Tanzania	44.6	33.3	5.5	2.7	3.1	1.4	47.1	4.9	42.2	7.0
Vanuatu	22.0	12.1	7.3	1.1	1.5	0.0	77.7	6.0	71.7	0.2
Yemen	6.3	1.6	1.4	1.3	2.0	0.0	93.5	9.8	83.7	0.1
Zambia	35.4	17.4	7.7	2.5	7.8	0.1	64.5	0.9	63.6	0.0
LDCs	50.2	26.0	2.7	20.3	1.2	0.7	42.8	2.6	40.2	6.3
Total Developing	53.1	18.0	8.7	24.0	2.4	1.2	43.4	3.8	39.7	2.2

Source: UNCTAD, *Handbook of Statistics 2005,* based on data from IMF, *Direction of Trade Statistics,* CD-ROM.

19. Main sources of imports of LDCs: Percentage shares in 2004 (or latest year available)

Country	Developed economies					South-East Europe and CIS	Developing economies			Un-allocated
	Total	EU 25	Japan	USA and Canada	Others		Total	OPEC	Other	
Afghanistan	27.2	14.9	3.4	8.4	0.6	14.9	57.9	1.5	56.4	0.0
Angola	64.7	43.8	6.7	13.2	1.0	0.9	34.3	0.4	33.9	0.0
Bangladesh	20.8	8.7	5.6	3.2	3.3	2.0	66.3	10.3	56.0	10.9
Benin	33.6	29.0	0.7	2.7	1.3	0.1	65.8	3.2	62.6	0.5
Bhutan	..	..	..	..	..	..	..	..	..	..
Burkina Faso	48.3	44.3	0.4	3.1	0.5	3.9	44.1	3.0	41.2	3.7
Burundi	46.8	32.7	4.4	8.7	1.1	0.3	49.2	0.8	48.3	3.8
Cambodia	9.3	4.1	2.5	1.9	0.8	0.2	90.5	3.3	87.2	0.0
Cape Verde	80.7	68.3	0.2	12.1	0.2	0.4	15.0	3.1	11.9	3.8
Central African Republic	46.3	29.1	1.0	15.9	0.1	0.2	26.9	0.9	26.0	26.6
Chad	66.7	54.2	0.1	11.6	0.7	2.6	30.7	6.3	24.5	0.0
Comoros	41.4	40.1	0.4	0.8	0.1	1.2	56.1	9.3	46.8	1.4
Dem. Republic of the Congo	48.4	40.3	0.8	6.2	1.1	0.2	49.0	0.4	48.5	2.4
Djibouti	27.1	18.4	3.5	5.0	0.3	0.2	68.5	24.1	44.4	4.2
Equatorial Guinea	71.3	41.3	1.0	27.3	1.8	0.1	28.5	0.1	28.4	0.0
Eritrea	..	..	..	..	..	..	..	..	..	..
Ethiopia	38.0	18.3	3.1	15.7	0.9	4.9	48.7	26.6	22.1	8.4
Gambia	29.4	24.0	0.6	4.4	0.4	0.5	70.1	3.3	66.8	0.0
Guinea	54.1	42.8	1.4	6.3	3.6	1.9	43.7	3.4	40.3	0.3
Guinea-Bissau	40.7	39.4	0.1	1.0	0.1	0.3	46.7	0.0	46.7	12.2
Haiti	62.2	7.5	2.8	51.2	0.7	0.1	37.5	2.4	35.1	0.1
Kiribati	61.5	7.7	10.3	2.6	40.9	0.0	38.5	0.3	38.1	0.0
Lao People's Dem. Republic	12.3	8.4	1.4	0.7	1.8	0.6	85.2	0.1	85.1	2.0
Lesotho	..	..	..	..	..	..	..	..	..	..
Liberia	33.0	10.8	19.9	1.3	0.9	5.5	61.6	0.1	61.5	0.0
Madagascar	33.3	28.9	1.6	2.3	0.5	0.3	57.6	10.5	47.1	8.8
Malawi	23.8	18.0	1.5	3.9	0.3	0.1	73.8	0.2	73.5	2.4
Maldives	20.2	12.3	1.2	2.2	4.5	0.0	79.6	9.6	70.0	0.2
Mali	31.1	27.3	0.3	2.9	0.6	1.6	57.3	0.7	56.5	10.0
Mauritania	57.3	44.9	2.7	7.6	2.1	2.9	30.2	3.2	26.9	9.6
Mozambique	25.1	9.9	1.2	3.8	10.2	0.0	48.2	1.9	46.3	26.6
Myanmar	7.3	3.0	3.1	0.4	0.9	1.9	90.6	1.9	88.7	0.1
Nepal	9.8	5.0	1.4	2.1	1.2	0.5	86.8	16.9	69.9	2.9
Niger	47.1	40.4	0.5	5.6	0.6	0.7	50.1	8.8	41.2	2.1
Rwanda	29.9	25.1	0.8	2.9	1.1	1.2	45.3	2.5	42.8	23.7
Samoa	46.5	2.3	7.2	4.6	32.4	0.0	52.7	3.3	49.4	0.8
Sao Tome and Principe	85.3	75.3	3.3	5.7	0.0	0.3	14.6	1.1	13.4	-0.1
Senegal	54.9	49.5	0.8	3.8	0.8	2.7	42.3	13.8	28.5	0.1
Sierra Leone	56.0	47.1	0.7	7.8	0.5	6.4	34.0	1.4	32.6	3.6
Solomon Islands	39.4	3.0	3.6	1.8	30.9	0.0	47.2	1.6	45.6	13.4
Somalia	6.8	4.8	0.0	1.8	0.2	0.0	80.4	6.0	74.4	12.7
Sudan	32.5	20.7	3.8	3.1	4.9	2.2	55.1	19.6	35.5	10.3
Timor-Leste	..	..	..	..	..	..	..	..	..	..
Togo	44.1	39.9	1.5	2.4	0.3	2.8	51.8	2.9	48.9	1.3
Tuvalu	46.2	13.8	17.1	1.2	14.4	0.0	53.8	0.0	53.8	0.0
Uganda	30.5	20.0	4.6	4.9	1.0	0.3	68.5	8.9	59.6	0.7
United Republic of Tanzania	30.9	19.9	2.8	5.4	2.8	0.2	64.8	11.4	53.4	4.1
Vanuatu	36.2	3.2	9.5	3.7	19.8	0.0	62.2	0.3	61.9	1.6
Yemen	31.3	21.3	2.7	4.9	2.4	3.5	64.4	27.8	36.7	0.8
Zambia	15.5	10.6	1.0	2.5	1.3	0.1	84.4	5.5	79.0	0.0
All LDCs	32.9	20.8	4.1	5.8	2.3	2.2	60.1	8.7	51.3	4.8
All developing countries	50.8	23.6	10.8	13.2	3.3	2.4	43.6	6.5	37.1	3.3

Source: UNCTAD, *Handbook of Statistics 2005,* based on data from IMF, *Direction of Trade Statistics,* CD-ROM.

20. Composition of total financial flows to all LDCs
IN CURRENT AND IN CONSTANT DOLLARS
(Net disbursements)

	Millions of current dollars						Millions of 2000 dollars[f]					
	1985	1990	2001	2002	2003	2004	1985	1990	2001	2002	2003	2004
Concessional loans & grants	**9 503**	**16 752**	**13 838**	**18 094**	**23 791**	**24 908**	**10 677**	**14 567**	**14 120**	**18 094**	**22 235**	..
Of which:												
DAC	8 835	16 175	13 594	17 358	23 678	24 703	9 927	14 065	13 871	17 358	22 129	..
Bilateral	5 484	9 888	7 766	10 365	16 513	15 852	6 162	8 598	7 924	10 365	15 433	..
Multilateral[a]	3 351	6 287	5 828	6 993	7 165	8 852	3 765	5 467	5 947	6 993	6 696	..
Grants	6 413	11 842	10 822	14 135	20 271	21 626	7 206	10 297	11 042	14 135	18 944	..
Loans	2 422	4 333	2 772	3 223	3 407	3 078	2 721	3 768	2 829	3 223	3 184	..
Technical assistance	2 221	3 375	2 848	3 391	4 085	4 080	2 496	2 935	2 907	3 391	3 818	..
Other[b]	6 614	12 800	10 745	13 967	19 592	20 623	7 431	11 130	10 965	13 967	18 311	..
OPEC	729	581	290	751	50	303	819	505	296	751	47	..
Bilateral	648	571	187	653	11	59	728	497	191	653	10	..
Multilateral[c]	81	9	102	98	40	244	91	8	104	98	37	..
Grants	434	520	55	156	20	48	488	452	56	156	18	..
Loans	295	60	235	595	31	255	331	52	239	595	29	..
Non-concessional flows	**430**	**737**	**1 355**	**-2 481**	**4 205**	**1 742**	**483**	**641**	**1 383**	**-2 481**	**3 930**	..
Of which:												
DAC	402	743	1 356	-2 485	4 205	1 746	451	646	1 383	-2 485	3 930	..
Bilateral official	497	692	- 119	- 403	1 037	- 607	559	601	- 122	- 403	969	..
Multilateral[a]	248	35	- 57	- 178	48	156	279	30	- 59	- 178	45	..
Export credits[d]	- 330	- 528	67	- 658	-2 022	- 483	- 371	- 459	69	- 658	-1 890	..
Direct investment	- 64	250	135	- 985	1 611	1 665	- 72	217	138	- 985	1 506	..
Other[e]	50	295	1 329	- 261	3 530	1 015	56	257	1 356	- 261	3 299	..
Total financial flows	**9 933**	**17 489**	**15 193**	**15 613**	**27 996**	**26 650**	**11 160**	**15 208**	**15 503**	**15 613**	**26 165**	..

Source: UNCTAD secretariat calculations, based on OECD/DAC: *International Development Statistics,* online data.

a From multilateral agencies mainly financed by DAC member countries.
b Grants (excluding technical assistance grants) and loans.
c From multilateral agencies mainly financed by OPEC member countries.
d Guaranteed private.
e Bilateral financial flows originating in DAC countries and their capital markets in the form of bond lending and bank lending (either directly or through syndicated "Eurocurrency credits"). Excludes flows that could not be allocated by recipient country.
f The deflator used is the unit value index of LDCs imports 2000 = 100. Data are not available for 2004.

21. Distribution of financial flows to LDCs and to all developing countries, by type of flow
(Percentage)

	To least developed countries						To all developing countries					
	1985	1990	2001	2002	2003	2004	1985	1990	2001	2002	2003	2004
Concessional loans & grants	**95.7**	**95.8**	**91.1**	**115.9**	**85.0**	**93.5**	**68.0**	**70.9**	**28.4**	**68.0**	**39.8**	**40.3**
Of which:												
DAC	88.9	92.5	89.5	111.2	84.6	92.7	61.5	62.9	27.6	63.8	39.3	39.7
Bilateral	55.2	56.5	51.1	66.4	59.0	59.5	42.8	45.4	18.2	42.2	28.1	27.4
Multilateral[a]	33.7	35.9	38.4	44.8	25.6	33.2	18.7	17.4	9.4	21.6	11.2	12.3
Grants	64.6	67.7	71.2	90.5	72.4	81.1	40.6	43.9	21.7	52.5	36.0	37.6
Loans	24.4	24.8	18.2	20.6	12.2	11.5	20.9	19.0	5.9	11.4	3.4	2.1
Technical assistance	22.4	19.3	18.7	21.7	14.6	15.3	16.1	15.4	8.3	19.3	11.8	10.4
Other[b]	66.6	73.2	70.7	89.5	70.0	77.4	45.4	47.5	19.3	44.5	27.6	29.3
OPEC	7.3	3.3	1.9	4.8	0.2	1.1	6.6	8.1	0.7	3.9	0.2	0.5
Bilateral	6.5	3.3	1.2	4.2	0.0	0.2	6.3	8.0	0.6	3.7	0.2	0.3
Multilateral[c]	0.8	0.1	0.7	0.6	0.1	0.9	0.3	0.1	0.1	0.2	0.0	0.2
Grants	4.4	3.0	0.4	1.0	0.1	0.2	5.4	7.9	0.3	1.7	0.1	0.2
Loans	3.0	0.3	1.5	3.8	0.1	1.0	1.3	0.1	0.4	2.2	0.1	0.3
Non-concessional flows	**4.3**	**4.2**	**8.9**	**-15.9**	**15.0**	**6.5**	**32.0**	**29.1**	**71.6**	**32.0**	**60.2**	**59.7**
Of which:												
DAC	4.0	4.2	8.9	-15.9	15.0	6.6	32.6	28.8	71.6	30.1	58.3	57.2
Bilateral official	5.0	4.0	-0.8	-2.6	3.7	-2.3	8.3	11.6	-1.4	-0.5	-3.6	-5.1
Multilateral[a]	2.5	0.2	-0.4	-1.1	0.2	0.6	20.1	15.0	5.8	-8.6	-5.4	-3.7
Export credits[d]	-3.3	-3.0	0.4	-4.2	-7.2	-1.8	3.7	-0.7	2.9	1.7	4.0	6.2
Direct investment	-0.6	1.4	0.9	-6.3	5.8	6.2	10.5	28.5	62.8	90.2	45.9	56.5
Other[e]	0.5	1.7	8.7	-1.7	12.6	3.8	-9.9	-25.5	1.6	-52.6	17.4	3.4
Total financial flows	**100.0**	**100.0**	**100.0**	**100.0**	**100.0**	**100.0**	**100.0**	**100.0**	**100.0**	**100.0**	**100.0**	**100.0**

For source and note, see table 20.

22. SHARE OF LDCS IN FINANCIAL FLOWS TO ALL DEVELOPING COUNTRIES, BY TYPE OF FLOW
(Percentage)

	1985	1990	2001	2002	2003	2004
Concessional loans & grants	**38.0**	**35.5**	**37.2**	**41.7**	**48.0**	**45.5**
Of which:						
DAC	39.1	38.6	37.5	42.6	48.4	45.8
Bilateral	34.9	32.7	32.5	38.5	47.1	42.6
Multilateral[a]	48.9	54.2	47.1	50.6	51.4	52.9
Grants	43.1	40.5	38.0	42.2	45.3	42.4
Loans	31.5	34.3	35.9	44.4	81.2	106.7
Technical assistance	37.6	32.9	26.1	27.5	27.8	28.9
Other[b]	39.7	40.5	42.5	49.1	57.1	51.8
OPEC	29.9	10.8	31.5	30.2	17.3	44.3
Bilateral	27.9	10.8	23.4	27.6	4.3	17.1
Multilateral[c]	70.2	14.6	87.1	81.9	94.0	72.1
Grants	22.1	9.8	13.9	14.1	14.0	18.5
Loans	62.6	70.2	44.9	43.1	20.4	60.1
Non-concessional flows	**3.7**	**3.8**	**1.4**	**..**	**5.6**	**2.1**
Of which:						
DAC	3.4	3.9	1.4	..	5.8	2.2
Bilateral official	16.2	9.0	6.3	136.4	..	8.7
Multilateral[a]	3.4	0.3	..	3.2	..	..
Export credits[d]	.	110.1	1.8	..	..	..
Direct investment	..	1.3	0.2	..	2.8	2.2
Other[e]	..	..	64.9	0.8	16.3	22.1
Total financial flows	**27.1**	**26.3**	**11.6**	**24.4**	**22.5**	**19.6**

Note: No percentage is shown when either the net flow to all LDCs or the net flow to all developing
countries in a particular year is negative.
For other notes and sources, see table 20.

23. NET ODA*a* FROM INDIVIDUAL DAC MEMBER COUNTRIES TO LDCs AS A GROUP

Donor country*b*	% of GNI					Millions of dollars					% change
	1990	*2000*	*2002*	*2003*	*2004*	*1990*	*2000*	*2002*	*2003*	*2004*	*2004/1990*
Norway	0.52	0.26	0.27	0.27	0.33	532	455	424	449	625	17.6
Portugal	0.17	0.11	0.10	0.14	0.53	100	118	120	205	878	777.2
Norway	0.52	0.27	0.33	0.36	0.33	532	424	625	801	837	57.4
Denmark	0.37	0.34	0.32	0.32	0.31	462	537	547	673	735	58.9
Luxembourg	0.08	0.26	0.30	0.27	0.31	10	46	58	65	87	770.9
Netherlands	0.30	0.21	0.29	0.20	0.25	834	793	1180	981	1453	74.2
Sweden	0.35	0.24	0.26	0.27	0.22	775	528	629	822	762	-1.7
Ireland	0.06	0.14	0.21	0.21	0.21	21	113	210	266	322	1430.4
Belgium	0.19	0.09	0.14	0.35	0.18	367	213	353	1088	645	75.6
France	0.19	0.09	0.16	0.11	0.15	2286	1141	1626	2965	3169	38.6
United Kingdom	0.09	0.10	0.07	0.12	0.14	834	1406	1153	2273	2988	258.2
Switzerland	0.14	0.10	0.08	0.12	0.11	325	269	250	405	399	22.7
Finland	0.24	0.09	0.12	0.11	0.08	317	109	154	183	153	-51.8
Germany	0.12	0.06	0.07	0.10	0.08	1769	1207	1332	2508	2312	30.7
Total DAC	**0.09**	**0.05**	**0.06**	**0.08**	**0.08**	**15153**	**12169**	**15137**	**22237**	**23490**	**55.0**
New Zealand	0.04	0.06	0.06	0.06	0.07	18	27	30	45	65	257.1
Canada	0.13	0.04	0.05	0.07	0.07	740	307	349	634	702	-5.1
Austria	0.07	0.05	0.08	0.07	0.06	61	59	170	169	168	175.7
Australia	0.06	0.06	0.05	0.05	0.06	171	211	192	259	350	104.4
Italy	0.13	0.04	0.09	0.08	0.05	1382	388	1045	1104	788	-43.0
Japan	0.06	0.04	0.04	0.04	0.04	1753	2127	1813	1922	1684	-3.9
Spain	0.00	0.03	0.04	0.04	0.04	194	142	252	342	424	118.0
United States	0.04	0.02	0.03	0.04	0.04	2199	1986	3012	4474	4504	104.8
Greece	-	0.02	0.03	0.03	0.03	-	18	37	55	65	-

Source: UNCTAD secretariat calculations, based on OECD, *Development Co-operation Report*, various issues, and OECD/DAC, *International Development Statistics,* online database.

a Including imputed flows through multilateral channels.
b Ranked in descending order of the ODA/GNI ratio in 2004.

24. BILATERAL ODA FROM DAC MEMBER COUNTRIES AND TOTAL FINANCIAL FLOWS FROM MULTILATERAL AGENCIES[a] TO ALL LDCs

(Millions of dollars)

	Net disbursements						Commitments					
	1985	*1990*	*2001*	*2002*	*2003*	*2004*	*1985*	*1990*	*2001*	*2002*	*2003*	*2004*
A. Bilateral donors												
Australia	58.2	104.5	151.7	172.8	204.4	296.5	59.1	97.0	179.6	138.0	236.6	249.7
Austria	12.1	60.9	71.7	125.6	64.3	54.8	11.9	132.4	66.3	137.2	75.4	46.2
Belgium	179.2	273.5	190.8	252.7	959.9	458.9	83.5	273.5	209.5	260.7	959.9	488.6
Canada	329.6	391.6	198.6	224.8	487.7	548.6	352.0	354.0	208.5	316.4	466.7	655.7
Denmark	126.0	295.1	396.6	371.1	448.0	493.5	148.6	269.2	177.1	371.0	254.8	663.2
Finland	60.6	194.6	70.6	78.3	99.3	109.9	127.7	129.8	101.9	97.9	97.5	109.9
France	723.9	1857.1	645.4	1108.7	2247.6	2269.3	901.7	1480.3	765.5	1279.9	2755.8	2503.6
Germany	584.9	1160.6	601.6	819.6	1551.4	963.2	843.8	1323.2	576.6	952.1	1709.3	1009.5
Greece	-	-	2.3	9.7	10.8	14.4	-	-	2.3	9.7	10.8	14.4
Ireland	10.4	13.9	123.6	181.1	226.1	270.7	10.4	13.9	123.6	181.1	226.1	270.7
Italy	420.1	968.8	187.2	772.6	722.1	287.6	530.7	846.0	211.4	782.4	723.2	302.2
Japan	562.9	1067.2	1188.8	1036.5	1078.0	914.9	633.2	1144.7	1709.7	1207.9	1127.3	1848.8
Luxembourg	-	7.9	40.5	50.6	55.9	70.8	-	-	40.5	50.6	55.9	70.8
Netherlands	256.2	592.8	761.9	920.2	980.7	957.5	251.9	681.7	753.7	857.7	733.9	802.1
New Zealand	7.0	13.3	25.4	25.5	37.0	56.3	12.2	9.7	25.4	27.9	35.4	57.6
Norway	156.8	356.7	314.9	452.0	577.6	617.4	151.1	187.0	428.2	478.0	649.2	634.2
Portugal	-	99.6	155.0	155.9	150.8	824.5	-	-	155.0	155.9	152.6	829.1
Spain	-	96.7	78.5	130.4	160.4	169.2	-	-	87.0	138.9	170.4	195.6
Sweden	200.8	530.2	325.7	344.7	608.8	586.9	210.5	332.4	355.1	367.9	739.7	527.7
Switzerland	87.2	232.1	163.3	190.0	255.2	257.7	137.4	214.9	174.2	165.7	269.0	278.8
United Kingdom	281.6	473.0	1079.2	855.7	1348.6	2195.7	232.3	480.0	1119.3	885.0	1402.3	2204.1
United States	1427.0	1098.0	992.4	2086.3	4238.6	3433.5	1362.4	1152.2	1227.3	2321.3	4774.0	4421.2
Total bilateral concessional	5484.4	9888.0	7765.6	10364.8	16513.0	15851.5	6060.4	9121.7	8697.6	11183.3	17625.8	18183.5
B. Multilateral donors												
1. Concessional												
AfDF	173.4	561.3	307.2	437.0	374.1	675.6	344.4	864.4	973.3	661.1	971.4	967.0
AsDF	229.6	448.2	271.9	330.6	293.5	161.8	383.7	536.4	422.1	708.5	721.4	638.8
EC	554.8	1168.4	1499.8	1686.8	2309.7	2642.6	579.0	790.8	1316.6	1947.8	3380.5	2585.8
IBRD	0.6	-	-	-	-	-	-	-	-	-	-	
IDA	1178.9	2138.0	2394.5	2897.2	3186.5	3925.7	1584.4	2986.0	3532.4	3253.6	3764.9	4614.7
IDB Sp.Fund	10.7	11.7	0.3	3.8	25.8	18.7	24.7	56.0	2.0	1.9	203.7	2.3
IFAD	108.0	120.6	88.8	76.7	85.1	109.4	83.2	72.1	158.7	130.0	187.3	185.6
SAF+ESAF+PRGF(IMF)	-108.8[b]	297.9	86.0	305.6	-272.3	-3.7	-	-	-	-	-	-
Other:	1204.1	1541.1	1163.4	1239.3	1148.9	1305.5	1314.9	1748.3	269.2	263.1	117.5	91.1
Of which:												
UNDP	276.2	366.6	157.2	154.7	171.8	220.0	-	-	-	-	-	-
UNFPA	26.4	46.3	89.3	106.1	110.9	114.1	-	-	-	-	-	-
UNHCR	201.8	197.6	201.4	254.9	203.5	164.1	-	-	-	-	-	-
UNICEF	126.6	232.7	184.2	168.9	194.5	202.8	-	-	-	-	-	-
UNTA	62.0	59.0	81.9	113.2	123.7	114.9	-	-	-	-	-	-
WFP	346.3	501.3	234.8	241.9	229.0	186.0	-	-	-	-	-	-
Total	3351.4	6287.1	5828.3	6993.4	7164.6	8851.6	4314.3	7053.9	6724.2	7008.5	9406.1	9144.8
2. Non-concessional												
AfDB	142.9	106.9	-66.1	-77.3	-51.7	-87.9						
AsDB	-0.9	-0.5	20.6	24.3	19.1	95.9						
EC	20.0	-14.0	8.3	30.6	61.1	165.3						
IBRD	55.0	-82.0	-17.7	-118.6	-14.9	-10.4						
IFC	20.5	18.5	-2.5	-36.5	34.8	-7.0						
Total	237.6	28.9	-57.5	-177.6	48.4	155.8						
Total concessional(A+B1)	8835.7	16175.1	13593.9	17358.2	23677.6	24703.1						
Grand total	9073.3	16203.9	13536.4	17180.6	23725.9	24859.0	10374.7	16175.7	15421.7	18191.8	27031.9	27328.3

Source: UNCTAD secretariat calculations, based on OECD/DAC, *International Development Statistics*, online data.

   a Multilateral agencies mainly financed by DAC countries.
   b IMF Trust Fund.

25. ODA TO LDCs FROM DAC MEMBER COUNTRIES AND MULTILATERAL AGENCIES MAINLY FINANCED BY THEM: DISTRIBUTION BY DONOR AND SHARES ALLOCATED TO LDCs IN TOTAL ODA FLOWS TO ALL DEVELOPING COUNTRIES

(Percentage)

	Distribution by donor						Share of LDCs in ODA flows to all developing countries					
	1985	*1990*	*2001*	*2002*	*2003*	*2004*	*1985*	*1990*	*2001*	*2002*	*2003*	*2004*
Bilateral donors												
Australia	0.7	0.6	1.1	1.0	0.9	1.2	11.9	15.4	27.7	29.1	27.6	32.0
Austria	0.1	0.4	0.5	0.7	0.3	0.2	7.5	153.1	19.9	59.1	48.1	23.9
Belgium	2.0	1.7	1.4	1.5	4.1	1.9	75.6	72.2	60.7	59.8	85.6	71.4
Canada	3.7	2.4	1.5	1.3	2.1	2.2	44.6	39.5	44.0	32.8	77.2	49.3
Denmark	1.4	1.8	2.9	2.1	1.9	2.0	60.6	61.3	55.5	54.4	67.1	57.4
Finland	0.7	1.2	0.5	0.5	0.4	0.4	54.9	53.1	54.4	54.1	54.5	52.8
France	8.2	11.5	4.7	6.4	9.5	9.2	39.2	38.7	25.5	31.2	45.6	43.1
Germany	6.6	7.2	4.4	4.7	6.6	3.9	35.6	29.9	30.0	41.8	50.5	35.9
Greece	-	-	0.0	0.1	0.0	0.1	-	-	25.6	53.9	26.4	32.0
Ireland	0.1	0.1	0.9	1.0	1.0	1.1	92.2	87.3	85.2	81.9	78.5	81.1
Italy	4.8	6.0	1.4	4.5	3.0	1.2	65.0	54.4	99.4	91.6	86.7	64.3
Japan	6.4	6.6	8.7	6.0	4.6	3.7	23.3	17.2	20.0	19.8	25.1	21.6
Luxembourg	-	0.0	0.3	0.3	0.2	0.3	-	60.4	52.4	55.2	49.2	55.0
Netherlands	2.9	3.7	5.6	5.3	4.1	3.9	40.0	37.4	45.6	52.4	56.2	60.9
New Zealand	0.1	0.1	0.2	0.1	0.2	0.2	22.1	22.6	40.9	37.1	37.4	46.1
Norway	1.8	2.2	2.3	2.6	2.4	2.5	58.1	62.2	56.3	63.8	63.2	66.7
Portugal	-	0.6	1.1	0.9	0.6	3.3	-	100.0	97.1	95.3	94.2	97.8
Spain	-	0.6	0.6	0.8	0.7	0.7	-	19.5	8.6	18.7	19.8	15.8
Sweden	2.3	3.3	2.4	2.0	2.6	2.4	50.1	57.8	52.2	55.6	64.1	57.5
Switzerland	1.0	1.4	1.2	1.1	1.1	1.0	51.6	60.1	53.4	50.9	53.5	52.8
United Kingdom	3.2	2.9	7.9	4.9	5.7	8.9	43.4	44.1	57.4	41.8	49.6	55.2
United States	16.2	6.8	7.3	12.0	17.9	13.9	28.3	20.2	23.2	35.7	42.0	34.1
Total	62.1	61.1	57.1	59.7	69.7	64.2	34.9	32.7	32.5	38.5	47.1	42.6
Multilateral donors												
AfDF	2.0	3.5	2.3	2.5	1.6	2.7	83.8	94.4	76.1	73.8	80.9	82.8
AsDF	2.6	2.8	2.0	1.9	1.2	0.7	59.3	41.3	36.6	38.6	37.6	26.2
EC	6.3	7.2	11.0	9.7	9.8	10.7	59.6	53.0	42.7	50.1	53.3	48.3
IBRD	0.0	-	-	-	-	-	1.9	-	-	-	-	-
IDA	13.3	13.2	17.6	16.7	13.5	15.9	45.4	54.7	51.7	54.6	61.2	59.8
IDB Sp.Fund	0.1	0.1	0.0	0.0	0.1	0.1	3.3	10.4	0.1	2.7	10.0	7.9
IFAD	1.2	0.7	0.7	0.4	0.4	0.4	41.8	49.2	56.9	57.3	63.1	76.1
SAF+ESAF+PRGF(IMF)	n.a	1.8	0.6	1.8	n.a	0.0	36.5	92.7	856.8	56.5	n.a	2.5
UN	11.8	8.7	7.0	6.0	4.4	4.1	45.4	46.3	40.5	41.2	41.4	41.5
Other	0.6	0.9	1.7	1.2	0.5	1.3	42.8	136.0	70.1	60.0	49.7	52.4
Total	37.9	38.9	42.9	40.3	30.3	35.8	48.9	54.2	47.1	50.6	51.4	52.9
Grand Total	100.0	100.0	100.0	100.0	100.0	100.0	39.1	38.6	37.5	42.6	48.4	45.8

Source: UNCTAD secretariat calculations, based on OECD/DAC, *International Development Statistics*, online data.

n.a Percentage share can not be expressed because of the numerator is negative.

26. TOTAL FINANCIAL FLOWS AND ODA FROM ALL SOURCES TO INDIVIDUAL LDCs

(Net disbursements in millions of dollars)

Country	Total financial flows						Of which: ODA					
	1985	1990	2001	2002	2003	2004	1985	1990	2001	2002	2003	2004
Afghanistan	- 6	129	390	1 305	1 611	2 225	17	131	408	1 305	1 595	2 190
Angola	258	91	854	- 337	446	1 084	92	268	289	421	497	1 144
Bangladesh	1 105	2 167	985	895	1 273	1 515	1 129	2 095	1 030	913	1 396	1 404
Benin	97	243	291	235	286	373	95	268	274	216	293	378
Bhutan	24	50	60	96	57	78	24	47	61	73	77	78
Burkina Faso	190	347	391	490	524	643	195	331	392	473	507	610
Burundi	154	255	149	186	224	342	139	264	137	172	225	351
Cambodia	15	42	443	207	383	316	15	42	420	487	509	478
Cape Verde	71	107	130	161	186	206	70	108	77	92	143	140
Central African Rep.	112	254	66	54	50	106	104	250	67	60	50	105
Chad	179	315	201	247	299	325	181	314	187	229	247	319
Comoros	51	45	16	- 105	26	24	48	45	27	32	24	25
Congo Dem.Rep.	462	1 410	288	1 025	4 707	1 782	306	897	263	1 188	5 421	1 815
Djibouti	103	192	71	94	99	74	81	194	58	78	79	64
Equatorial Guinea	28	62	24	- 415	845	848	17	61	13	20	21	30
Eritrea	-	-	281	216	302	252	-	-	281	230	316	260
Ethiopia	790	988	1 061	1 093	1 594	1 673	720	1 016	1 116	1 307	1 553	1 823
Gambia	48	108	46	47	68	67	50	99	54	61	63	63
Guinea	108	284	230	232	230	230	115	293	282	250	240	279
Guinea-Bissau	63	135	59	60	93	75	58	129	59	59	145	76
Haiti	142	154	166	170	202	243	150	168	171	156	200	243
Kiribati	12	20	13	21	18	17	12	20	12	21	18	17
Laos	67	151	242	265	152	260	40	151	245	278	299	270
Lesotho	118	148	- 41	- 44	- 50	96	93	142	56	76	78	102
Liberia	- 294	519	1 033	- 259	4 522	1 225	91	114	39	52	107	210
Madagascar	210	430	374	369	550	1 217	186	398	374	373	539	1 236
Malawi	118	518	457	392	517	471	113	503	404	377	518	476
Maldives	11	38	38	52	55	76	9	21	25	27	21	28
Mali	377	474	333	330	559	533	376	482	354	467	543	567
Mauritania	224	219	260	306	228	211	207	237	268	345	239	180
Mozambique	330	1 051	1 057	2 091	864	1 368	300	1 003	933	2 203	1 039	1 228
Myanmar	311	117	107	78	61	84	346	163	127	121	126	121
Nepal	244	429	475	280	464	416	234	426	394	365	465	427
Niger	285	382	229	194	486	453	303	396	257	298	457	536
Rwanda	184	286	296	360	341	471	180	291	299	355	333	468
Samoa	20	54	43	38	40	21	19	48	43	37	33	31
Sao Tome & Principe	12	54	41	28	45	32	13	55	38	26	38	33
Senegal	306	759	456	541	524	996	289	818	413	445	446	1 052
Sierra Leone	56	64	343	353	296	361	65	61	345	353	303	360
Solomon Islands	22	58	54	25	62	124	21	46	59	26	60	122
Somalia	380	488	153	197	179	191	353	494	150	194	175	191
Sudan	1 117	740	173	423	610	902	1 129	822	185	351	617	882
Tanzania	556	1 128	1 296	1 019	1 623	1 750	484	1 173	1 271	1 233	1 704	1 746
Timor-Leste	- 5	- 5	249	397	346	527	-	0	195	220	155	153
Togo	91	257	43	60	65	94	111	260	44	51	47	61
Tuvalu	3	5	10	37	6	8	3	5	10	12	6	8
Uganda	220	665	757	702	991	1 143	180	668	793	712	977	1 159
Vanuatu	39	149	- 374	24	32	21	22	50	32	28	32	38
Yemen	402	331	496	759	389	193	397	405	461	584	234	252
Zambia	523	583	382	618	517	909	322	480	349	641	581	1 081
LDCs,Total	9 933	17 489	15 193	15 613	27 996	26 650	9 503	16 752	13 838	18 094	23 791	24 908
Developing countries	36 708	66 608	131 161	63 861	124 454	135 853	24 975	47 216	37 237	43 404	49 578	54 759
memo items:												
In current dollars per capita:												
All LDCs	25	34	22	22	39	36	24	32	20	26	33	34
All Developing countries	10	16	27	13	25	27	7	12	8	9	10	11
In constant 2000 dollars (millions)[a]												
All LDCs	11 160	15 208	15 503	15 613	26 165	..	10 677	14 567	14 120	18 094	22 235	..
All Developing countries	40 787	64 668	135 218	67 222	125 711	..	27 750	45 841	38 389	45 688	50 079	..
In constant 2000 dollars per capita												
All LDCs	28	29	23	22	36	..	27	28	21	26	31	..
All Developing countries	11	16	28	14	25	..	8	11	8	9	10	..

Source: UNCTAD secretariat calculations, based on OECD/DAC, *International Development Statistics*, online data.

a The deflator used is the unit value indices of LDCs imports 2000 = 100.

27. ODA FROM DAC MEMBER COUNTRIES AND MULTILATERAL AGENCIES MAINLY FINANCED BY THEM, TO INDIVIDUAL LDCs

Country[a]	Average: 1990–1994						Average: 2000–2004					
	Per capita ODA $	Total ODA $ mill.	Of which: Technical assistance	Bilateral ODA	Of which: Grants	Multilateral ODA	Of which: Grants	Per capita ODA $	Total ODA $ mill.	Of which: Technical assistance	Bilateral ODA	Of which: Grants	Multilateral ODA	Of which: Grants

(Bilateral/Multilateral columns expressed "As percentage of total ODA")

Country[a]	Per capita ODA $	Total ODA $ mill.	Tech. assist.	Bilateral ODA	Grants	Multilateral ODA	Grants	Per capita ODA $	Total ODA $ mill.	Tech. assist.	Bilateral ODA	Grants	Multilateral ODA	Grants
Mozambique	85.0	1 177.3	11.9	71.5	61.4	28.5	16.8	70.7	1 286.9	14.0	77.8	84.0	22.2	9.4
Dem. Rep. of the Congo	9.8	397.5	15.7	67.1	62.2	32.9	18.9	33.6	1 773.8	4.5	76.3	73.7	23.7	12.0
United Rep. of Tanzania	39.1	1 100.6	15.9	66.2	69.9	33.8	12.3	38.6	1 396.8	10.6	66.2	65.8	33.8	16.9
Ethiopia	19.7	1 075.6	8.2	44.9	44.0	55.1	36.5	17.6	1 269.0	10.2	51.9	52.0	48.1	22.5
Mozambique	82.6	1 181.0	10.1	69.0	58.6	31.0	17.6	67.1	1 253.3	14.2	70.7	74.5	29.3	15.2
Bangladesh	16.1	1 756.5	11.4	49.0	49.5	51.0	11.5	8.7	1 163.0	16.0	52.3	59.8	47.7	11.1
Afghanistan	10.7	182.0	28.2	62.7	64.7	37.3	37.3	42.3	1 102.4	18.8	77.9	78.5	22.1	18.6
Uganda	34.7	659.5	10.9	44.8	40.7	55.2	18.1	34.2	889.0	16.9	60.8	62.5	39.2	21.5
Zambia	90.1	797.6	15.0	66.1	70.2	33.9	11.7	61.9	687.1	16.0	71.5	72.7	28.5	17.5
Madagascar	29.3	374.1	18.3	62.9	72.5	37.1	14.9	33.2	569.6	14.1	46.4	50.3	53.6	21.7
Senegal	76.1	641.4	23.4	71.8	77.5	28.2	11.8	51.1	555.2	29.3	65.7	72.5	34.3	13.5
Angola	28.9	324.6	10.8	54.7	43.0	45.3	40.6	36.3	531.5	10.6	76.8	49.6	23.2	20.6
Burkina Faso	45.5	411.9	24.5	62.9	60.5	37.1	17.7	37.4	450.4	17.3	56.6	57.6	43.4	30.8
Cambodia	18.6	193.7	21.3	56.9	59.3	43.1	35.3	33.7	446.6	27.7	62.8	62.1	37.2	10.0
Mali	46.1	432.1	21.8	59.9	55.1	40.1	17.8	36.0	445.3	24.5	61.3	68.1	38.7	28.1
Malawi	52.4	511.9	10.9	40.7	36.2	59.3	32.7	36.3	438.2	22.3	59.9	62.7	40.1	25.2
Sudan	22.3	610.8	9.8	43.1	44.9	56.9	39.6	12.1	414.4	8.1	72.7	73.2	27.3	28.4
Nepal	21.2	426.0	21.6	62.0	53.9	38.0	11.4	15.7	401.6	26.8	70.7	69.1	29.3	12.4
Rwanda	64.8	411.4	17.2	62.8	61.6	37.2	25.2	41.6	355.2	19.7	53.7	54.2	46.3	29.4
Niger	40.8	368.2	24.3	70.4	71.4	29.6	20.6	27.8	351.1	12.4	50.4	55.3	49.6	24.9
Sierra Leone	38.0	156.2	9.0	43.7	37.2	56.3	21.3	62.5	306.9	11.2	57.3	57.0	42.7	24.0
Benin	48.3	269.4	15.2	55.4	51.6	44.6	16.8	36.4	279.5	24.5	63.1	68.7	36.9	24.3
Lao PDR	40.1	174.5	17.0	47.1	48.3	52.9	14.6	49.3	272.8	26.5	65.3	63.8	34.7	6.8
Yemen	19.1	254.5	25.7	65.2	53.0	34.8	15.2	13.8	264.2	15.8	49.8	52.4	50.2	16.9
Mauritania	116.8	249.1	15.0	52.8	44.3	47.2	22.8	88.9	249.7	12.6	42.4	49.5	57.6	37.7
Eritrea	13.8	42.2	26.7	170.4	170.4	79.6	79.6	64.0	248.6	10.4	60.2	57.4	39.8	16.7
Guinea	56.1	378.3	11.8	48.5	41.2	51.5	19.7	27.1	239.0	23.1	54.7	63.0	45.3	32.7
Chad	38.7	249.3	18.3	57.6	53.8	42.4	18.4	25.1	221.3	11.8	40.8	43.5	59.2	27.0
Burundi	46.5	274.2	17.4	48.4	46.7	51.6	31.5	28.5	195.5	7.2	49.7	49.6	50.3	37.4
Haiti	33.1	234.7	19.1	87.5	95.7	12.5	11.0	23.9	195.3	40.9	79.6	80.4	20.4	18.5
Timor-Leste	-	-	-	-	-	-	-	241.3	190.6	41.3	85.4	86.8	14.6	14.6
Somalia	81.6	531.4	4.7	75.6	75.6	24.4	21.9	20.2	150.9	7.3	66.3	67.4	33.7	33.7
Myanmar	3.4	144.1	5.9	68.3	44.8	31.7	18.3	2.4	116.6	29.8	68.8	70.3	31.2	31.0
Cape Verde	305.3	113.9	25.2	69.9	69.3	30.1	19.6	232.2	109.8	28.4	62.5	60.0	37.5	13.9
Liberia	55.0	114.6	5.0	32.3	33.4	67.7	62.1	30.0	95.3	15.1	62.6	71.1	37.4	38.2
Guinea-Bissau	111.9	121.2	21.6	61.8	48.3	38.2	17.8	58.0	84.1	14.5	53.2	52.7	46.8	36.9
Central African Rep.	59.0	186.5	21.6	55.3	55.4	44.7	19.2	18.3	71.2	26.9	63.9	74.4	36.1	36.2
Lesotho	81.7	133.3	24.4	52.1	48.8	47.9	25.8	39.5	71.0	15.4	42.0	44.4	58.0	34.2
Bhutan	95.5	60.8	20.7	63.3	63.3	36.7	28.4	81.3	69.1	24.3	64.9	63.2	35.1	14.8
Djibouti	194.1	112.8	33.9	80.0	72.1	20.0	11.6	90.5	67.7	35.1	54.2	56.0	45.8	19.7
Solomon Islands	136.9	45.9	41.3	75.2	63.9	24.8	17.8	151.3	66.9	62.3	71.7	80.9	28.3	28.7
Gambia	93.2	93.8	18.4	53.4	52.0	46.6	20.5	39.8	55.6	13.4	27.7	29.7	72.3	29.2
Togo	43.5	181.4	20.2	61.2	56.8	38.8	16.1	9.3	52.6	44.4	83.0	101.3	17.0	22.4
Vanuatu	276.5	43.8	51.6	80.8	78.6	19.2	11.0	175.6	35.0	62.5	78.6	79.4	21.4	13.1
Samoa	310.4	50.9	25.1	59.4	59.3	40.6	14.7	189.3	34.2	54.2	74.7	74.8	25.3	17.0
Sao Tome & Principe	427.8	51.8	17.1	52.4	48.1	47.6	17.9	233.0	34.1	31.3	62.3	59.4	37.7	24.3
Comoros	87.6	48.8	23.8	53.5	54.6	46.5	31.4	32.8	24.2	31.7	46.6	53.4	53.4	28.9
Maldives	129.6	29.8	14.7	53.1	53.1	46.9	17.9	74.7	22.8	16.8	51.6	53.8	48.4	14.5
Equatorial Guinea	141.3	52.3	30.6	60.8	58.0	39.2	20.5	45.3	21.3	33.5	80.4	103.7	19.6	30.3
Kiribati	259.9	19.6	38.8	81.0	81.0	19.0	17.4	184.1	17.2	52.5	77.5	77.5	22.5	12.1
Tuvalu	616.7	5.9	47.2	85.5	85.5	14.5	13.8	759.2	7.8	36.6	83.6	83.6	16.4	13.0
LDCs, Total	29.5	16 281.8	15.3	58.4	56.5	41.6	20.4	26.0	18 364.2	16.4	63.6	64.7	36.4	19.6
All developing countries	10.6	44 469.0	25.9	69.0	54.8	31.0	14.7	8.6	42 710.0	29.1	68.7	69.4	31.3	16.7

Source: UNCTAD secretariat calculations, based on OECD/DAC, International Development Statistics, online data.

a Ranked in descending order of total ODA received in 2000–2004.

28. FOREIGN DIRECT INVESTMENT: INFLOW TO AND OUTFLOW FROM LDCs

(Millions of dollars)

Country	FDI inflow						FDI outflow					
	1985	1990	2000	2003	2003	2004	1985	1990	2000	2002	2003	2004
Afghanistan	..	..	0.2	0.5	2.0	1.0	..	..	..	..	..	..
Angola	278.0	-334.5	878.5	1672.1	3504.7	2047.5	..	0.9	20.0	28.7	23.6	30
Bangladesh	- 6.7	3.2	280.4	52.3	268.3	460.4	- 0.3	0.5	2.0	2.7	2.8	4.4
Benin	- 0.1	62.4	59.7	13.5	44.7	60.0	..	0.3	3.6	1.4	0.3	..
Bhutan	..	1.6	-0.1	0.3	1.1	1.0	..	..	..	..	..	..
Burkina Faso	- 1.4	0.5	23.1	15.0	29.1	35.0	0.0	-0.6	0.2	1.7	1.9	1.0
Burundi	1.6	1.3	11.7	0.0	0.0	3.0	..	0.0	0.0	0.0	0.0	..
Cambodia	..	..	148.5	145.1	84.0	131.4	..	..	6.6	6.0	9.7	10.2
Cape Verde	..	0.3	32.5	12.1	13.8	20.5	..	0.3	1.4	0.0	..	..
Central African Republic	3.0	0.7	0.9	5.6	3.3	-12.7	0.6	3.8	0.0	1.3	0.0	..
Chad	53.7	9.4	114.8	924.1	712.7	478.2	0.3	0.1	0.0	0.0	0.0	..
Comoros	..	0.4	0.1	0.4	1.0	2.0	..	1.1	..	..	..	..
Dem. Rep. of the Congo	69.2	-14.5	23.1	117	158	900	..	..	-1.8	-1.9	..	..
Djibouti	0.2	0.1	3.3	3.5	11.4	33	..	..	..	..	..	..
Equatorial Guinea	2.4	11.1	107.8	323.4	1430.7	1664.1	..	0.1	-3.6	0.0	0.0	..
Eritrea	..	..	27.9	20	22.0	30.0	..	..	..	..	..	..
Ethiopia	0.2	12	134.6	255	465.0	545.1	..	..	-1.0	..	..	..
Gambia	- 0.5	14.1	43.5	42.8	25.0	60.0	..	2.8	4.7	4.8	6.7	1.0
Guinea	1.1	17.9	9.9	30	79.0	100.0	..	0.1	0.0	7.0	..	..
Guinea-Bissau	1.4	2	0.7	3.5	4.0	5.0	..	..	..	1.0	0.5	0.5
Haiti	4.9	8	13.3	5.7	7.8	6.5	..	-8.0	..	1.0	..	..
Kiribati	0.2	0.3	..	..	..	..	..	..	..	..	..	..
Lao People's Dem. Rep.	- 1.6	6	34	25	19.5	17	..	0.2	9.8	..	0.1	..
Lesotho	4.5	16.1	31.5	27.2	41.9	51.8	..	..	..	0.1	0.0	0.1
Liberia	- 16.2	225.2	20.8	2.8	1.0	20.0	245.0	-3.1	780.3	385.6	80.0	60.0
Madagascar	- 0.2	22.4	83.0	8.3	12.7	45.0	..	1.3	..	..	..	..
Malawi	0.5	23.3	26.0	5.9	10.0	16.0	..	..	..	..	..	..
Maldives	1.2	5.6	13.0	12.4	13.5	13.0	..	..	..	..	..	..
Mali	2.9	5.7	82.4	243.8	132.3	180.0	..	0.2	4.0	1.6	1.4	1.0
Mauritania	7.0	6.7	40.1	117.6	214.1	300.0	..	..	0.5	..	-1.0	..
Mozambique	0.3	9.2	139.2	347.6	336.7	131.9	..	0.2	-0.2	0.0	0.0	0.0
Myanmar	..	225.1	208	191.4	291.2	556.4	..	..	..	..	..	..
Nepal	0.7	5.9	-0.5	-6.0	14.8	10.0	..	..	..	..	..	..
Niger	- 9.4	40.8	8.4	2.4	11.5	20.0	1.9	0.0	-0.6	-1.7	0.0	..
Rwanda	14.6	7.7	8.1	7.4	4.7	10.9	0.0	0.0	..	..	..	..
Samoa	0.4	6.6	-1.5	-0.1	0.5	0.5	..	..	..	..	..	..
São Tomé and Principe	..	..	3.8	3.0	7.0	54.0	..	..	..	..	..	..
Senegal	- 18.9	56.9	62.9	78.1	52.5	70	3.1	-9.5	0.6	34	2.7	4.0
Sierra Leone	- 31.0	32.4	38.9	1.6	3.1	4.9	0.0	0.1	..	..	..	..
Solomon Islands	0.7	10.4	1.4	-1.4	-2.0	-5.0	..	..	..	..	..	..
Somalia	- 0.7	5.6	0.3	0.1	0.3	9.0	..	..	..	..	..	..
Sudan	- 3.0	-31.1	392.2	713.2	1349.2	1511.1	..	..	..	..	..	..
Togo	16.3	22.7	41.5	53.4	33.7	60.0	0.3	4.6	0.4	2.4	-6.3	-3.0
Tuvalu	..	..	-0.9	2.1	0.0	8.5	..	..	..	..	..	..
Uganda	- 4.0	-5.9	180.8	202.9	210.5	237.2	- 34.0	..	-27.6	..	..	..
United Rep. of Tanzania	14.5	0	282	429.8	526.8	469.9	..	..	..	..	..	..
Vanuatu	4.6	13.1	20.3	8.8	15.5	21.9	..	..	..	0.6	0.7	0.8
Yemen	3.2	-130.9	6.4	101.7	5.5	-20.9	0.5	..	-9.8	11.3	..	..
Zambia	51.5	202.8	121.7	82.0	172.0	334.0	..	..	..	..	..	..
All LDCs	445.2	578.7	3758.1	6327.2	10350.6	10702.1	217.6	-4.5	789.6	487.6	123.1	110.0
Developing countries	14 908.8	35 736.3	253 178.8	155 528.4	166 336.6	233 227.3	4 262.9	225 965	1 092 747	599895	577323	637360

Source: UNCTAD, FDI/TNC database and Handbook of Statistics 2005.

29. EXTERNAL DEBT (AT YEAR END) AND DEBT SERVICE, BY SOURCE OF LENDING
($ millions)

	External debt (at year end)[a]						% of total		Debt service						% of total	
	1985	1990	2000	2002	2003	2004	1985	2004	1985	1990	2000	2002	2003	2004	1985	2004
I. Long-term	**59 024**	**106 240**	**119 963**	**126 118**	**136 956**	**140 360**	**80.2**	**86.1**	**2202**	**3060**	**4509**	**4255**	**4483**	**5533**	**100.0**	**100.0**
Public and publicly guaranteed	58 539	105 387	117 546	123 870	134 746	138 320	79.5	84.8	2145	2979	4441	4187	4381	5417	97.4	97.9
Official creditors	50 739	90 630	107 691	113 708	124 345	127 482	68.9	78.2	1510	2227	2872	2686	2822	3915	68.6	70.7
A. Concessional	38 328	69 406	91 022	100 243	110 090	114 525	52.1	70.2	682	1244	2240	2089	2108	2891	31.0	52.2
Of which:																
Bilateral	25 447	39 481	36 965	37 768	39 222	37 148	34.6	22.8	457	756	1155	850	922	1262	20.7	22.8
Multilateral	12 881	29 925	54 057	62 475	70 868	77 377	17.5	47.4	226	487	1085	1239	1186	1629	10.3	29.4
B. Non-concessional	12 411	21 224	16 669	13 466	14 255	12 958	16.9	7.9	827	984	632	596	714	1024	37.6	18.5
Private creditors	7 800	14 757	9 855	10 161	10 401	10 838	10.6	6.6	635	753	1568	1502	1559	1503	28.9	27.2
Bonds	7	10	7	12	7	5	0.0	0.0	1	1	0	0	2	1	0.1	0.0
Commercial banks	2 512	3 174	5 038	4 755	5 423	6 533	3.4	4.0	227	174	1273	1315	1012	1084	10.3	19.6
Other private	5 281	11 573	4 810	5 394	4 971	4 301	7.2	2.6	407	578	295	187	545	418	18.5	7.6
Private nonguaranteed	486	852	2 418	2 249	2 211	2 039	0.7	1.3	57	81	68	68	102	116	2.6	2.1
II. Short-term	**9 400**	**13 072**	**16 767**	**14 880**	**15 119**	**16 314**	**12.8**	**10.0**	..	..	..	..	..	..	..	..
III. Use of IMF credit	**5 181**	**5 397**	**5 839**	**6 030**	**6 191**	**6 397**	**7.0**	**3.9**	..	..	..	..	..	..	.	..
Total external debt	**73 605**	**124 708**	**142 569**	**147 029**	**158 266**	**163 070**	**100.0**	**100.0**	..	..	..	..	..	..	..	..

Source: UNCTAD secretariat calculations, based on World Bank, *Global Development Finance*, online data.

a Refers to debt stocks.

30. TOTAL EXTERNAL DEBT AND DEBT SERVICE PAYMENTS OF INDIVIDUAL LDCs
($ millions)

Country	External debt[a] (at year end)						Debt service[b]					
	1985	1990	2000	2002	2003	2004	1985	1990	2000	2002	2003	2004
Afghanistan	..	..	..	..	..	..	..	..	..	..	..	..
Angola	..	8 592	9 408	9 189	9 316	9 521	..	283	1 680	1 425	1 352	2 044
Bangladesh	6 658	12 439	15 717	17 046	18 759	20 344	195	495	684	624	584	646
Benin	854	1 292	1 591	1 836	1 828	1 916	41	33	60	45	48	60
Bhutan	9	84	204	378	419	593	0	5	7	6	7	12
Burkina Faso	513	834	1 426	1 548	1 736	1 967	25	28	38	34	43	62
Burundi	455	907	1 108	1 214	1 328	1 385	21	40	14	19	28	59
Cambodia	7	1 845	2 628	2 900	3 139	3 377	0	29	19	7	11	16
Cape Verde	95	134	327	414	486	517	5	6	16	21	19	24
Central African Rep.	344	699	858	1 065	1 038	1 078	12	17	12	0	0	15
Chad	217	529	1 138	1 323	1 590	1 701	12	7	24	20	33	35
Comoros	134	189	238	276	293	306	2	1	2	5	3	3
Dem. Rep. of the Congo	6 183	10 259	11 693	10 060	11 254	11 841	300	137	0	412	141	126
Djibouti	144	205	262	335	396	429	4	11	11	9	14	18
Equatorial Guinea	132	241	248	260	319	291	2	1	2	2	5	5
Eritrea	..	..	311	520	635	681	..	..	3	9	11	19
Ethiopia	5 206	8 630	5 483	6 526	7 187	6 574	111	201	123	73	82	117
Gambia	245	369	483	576	635	674	1	30	19	14	20	22
Guinea	1 465	2 476	3 388	3 401	3 457	3 539	61	149	132	111	114	149
Guinea-Bissau	318	692	804	699	745	765	5	6	19	9	10	43
Haiti	749	911	1 169	1 248	1 309	1 225	21	14	33	15	35	125
Kiribati	..	..	..	..	..	..	0	0	0	0	0	0
Lao PDR	619	1 768	2 502	2 665	2 846	2 961	5	8	32	35	40	45
Lesotho	175	396	672	658	707	764	18	23	56	64	64	52
Liberia	1 243	1 849	2 032	2 324	2 568	2 706	19	2	0	0	0	0
Madagascar	2 520	3 689	4 691	4 511	4 952	3 462	94	155	102	58	64	73
Malawi	1 021	1 558	2 706	2 888	3 099	3 418	76	103	51	28	33	56
Maldives	83	78	206	272	281	345	9	7	19	21	21	31
Mali	1 456	2 468	2 980	2 827	3 114	3 316	34	43	68	61	56	91
Mauritania	1 454	2 113	2 378	2 240	2 328	2 297	76	118	66	44	44	53
Mozambique	2 871	4 650	7 000	4 592	4 543	4 651	57	64	84	64	73	74
Myanmar	3 098	4 695	5 928	6 583	7 319	7 239	185	57	75	102	107	105
Nepal	590	1 640	2 846	2 972	3 200	3 354	13	54	95	97	109	113
Niger	1 195	1 726	1 673	1 791	2 084	1 950	95	71	22	23	28	46
Rwanda	366	712	1 273	1 437	1 540	1 656	14	15	21	14	19	29
Samoa	76	92	197	234	365	562	5	4	6	5	6	6
Sao Tome and Principe	63	150	322	343	349	362	3	2	3	5	7	11
Senegal	2 566	3 739	3 607	4 121	4 447	3 938	103	226	185	189	206	311
Sierra Leone	711	1 197	1 229	1 443	1 607	1 723	15	17	19	20	23	27
Solomon Islands	66	121	155	180	178	176	3	10	9	6	9	17
Somalia	1 639	2 370	2 562	2 689	2 838	2 849	5	7	0	0	0	0
Sudan	8 955	14 762	16 394	17 297	18 389	19 332	89	23	185	118	246	281
Timor Leste	..	..	..	..	..	..	0	0	0	0	0	0
Togo	935	1 281	1 432	1 587	1 715	1 812	90	60	15	1	1	4
Tuvalu	..	..	..	..	..	..	0	0	0	0	0	0
Uganda	1 231	2 583	3 497	3 992	4 555	4 822	56	84	47	49	57	77
United Rep. of Tanzania	9 105	6 454	6 931	6 800	6 990	7 800	140	137	150	96	77	95
Vanuatu	16	38	75	91	95	118	1	2	2	2	2	2
Yemen	3 339	6 352	5 075	5 225	5 375	5 488	95	108	127	139	150	175
Zambia	4 487	6 905	5 723	6 452	6 914	7 246	87	171	177	157	485	164
Total LDCs	73 605	124 708	142 569	147 029	158 266	163 070	2 202	3 060	4 509	4 255	4 483	5 533

Source: UNCTAD secretariat calculations, based on information from the World Bank, *Global Development Finance 2005.*

a Figures for total debt cover both long-term and short-term debt as well as the use of IMF credit.
b Figures on debt service cover long-term debt only.

31. Debt and debt service ratios
(Percentage)

Country	Debt/GDP						Debt service/exports[a]					
	1985	*1990*	*2000*	*2002*	*2003*	*2004*	*1985*	*1990*	*2000*	*2002*	*2003*	*2004*
Afghanistan	..	..	..	..	..	..	..	..	..	..	..	..
Angola	..	84	103	85	67	47	..	8	21	17	15	..
Bangladesh	31	41	35	36	36	36	19	26	9	7	6	..
Benin	82	70	71	68	51	47	13	8	12	..	..	..
Bhutan	5	29	42	63	70	88	0	5	5	5	..	..
Burkina Faso	32	27	55	48	42	41	10	7	15	14	10	..
Burundi	40	80	163	193	223	211	20	43	40	61	66	..
Cambodia	..	166	73	72	76	73	..	..	2	1	1	..
Cape Verde	..	40	62	67	61	55	10	5	7	8	5	..
Central African Republic	40	47	90	102	86	81	14	13	..	..	..	..
Chad	21	30	82	66	61	40	17	4	..	..	..	..
Comoros	117	72	117	112	92	83	9	2	..	..	..	..
Dem. Rep. of the Congo	86	110	272	181	198	180	..	..	..	..	..	..
Djibouti	42	49	47	57	63	65	..	..	..	..	..	..
Equatorial Guinea	166	182	18	12	11	9	..	12	..	..	..	..
Eritrea	..	..	49	82	85	74	..	..	3	7	14	..
Ethiopia	78	100	84	108	108	81	25	39	13	8	7	..
Gambia	109	116	115	156	173	162	10	22	..	..	..	..
Guinea	..	88	109	106	95	101	..	20	20	15	15	..
Guinea-Bissau	221	284	373	344	312	273	52	31	..	14	16	..
Haiti	37	32	30	36	45	35	11	11	4	3	4	..
Kiribati	..	..	..	..	..	..	..	..	..	..	..	..
Lao PDR	26	204	145	147	136	123	9	9	8	10	10	..
Lesotho	60	64	78	94	66	56	7	4	11	12	9	..
Liberia	133	481	375	414	581	604	9	..	0	0	0	..
Madagascar	88	120	121	103	90	79	42	45	10	9	6	..
Malawi	90	83	155	155	182	189	40	29	13	8	9	..
Maldives	65	36	33	42	41	46	11	5	4	4	4	..
Mali	111	102	123	85	72	68	17	12	13	7	..	..
Mauritania	213	207	253	226	197	169	25	30	..	..	..	..
Mozambique	64	189	190	128	105	84	34	26	12	7	7	..
Myanmar	..	..	..	..	..	..	58	18	4	4	4	..
Nepal	23	45	52	53	55	50	7	16	7	6	6	..
Niger	83	70	93	83	76	63	34	17	..	..	..	..
Rwanda	21	28	70	83	91	90	10	14	24	11	14	..
Samoa	63	46	85	89	115	155	15	6	..	..	..	..
Sao Tome and Principe	121	261	692	682	586	582	29	34	26	26	31	..
Senegal	100	66	82	82	69	51	21	20	14	12	10	..
Sierra Leone	83	184	194	154	162	160	15	10	67	18	12	..
Solomon Islands	41	57	52	76	75	73	5	12	..	..	..	..
Somalia	187	258	..	..	..	..	16	..	..	..	..	..
Sudan	72	112	134	112	103	99	14	9	10	5	7	..
Timor-Leste	..	..	..	..	..	..	..	..	..	..	..	..
Togo	123	79	108	107	98	88	27	12	6	2	2	..
Tuvalu	..	..	..	..	..	..	..	..	..	..	..	..
Uganda	35	60	59	68	72	71	42	81	8	6	7	..
United Rep. of Tanzania	..	152	76	70	68	72	40	33	13	7	5	..
Vanuatu	13	25	30	38	34	37	1	2	1	2	1	..
Yemen	..	132	54	53	49	43	..	6	4	3	3	..
Zambia	199	210	177	175	159	134	16	15	20	20	40	..
All LDCs	64	87	85	80	76	68	21	16	..	..	..	..

Source: UNCTAD secretariat calculations, based on World Bank, *World Development Indicators 2005,* online data, and *Global Development Finance 2005,* online data.

Note: Figures for total debt cover both long-term and short-term debt as well as use of IMF credit.

a Exports of goods and services (including non-factor services).

32. LDCs' DEBT RESCHEDULINGS WITH OFFICIAL CREDITORS, 1990–2005

Country	Number of debt[a]	Date of meeting	Cut-off date	Consolidation period (months)	Terms	Arrears	Rescheduling of previously rescheduled debt	Goodwill clause	Amounts rescheduled/consolidated ($ million)
Benin	II	December 1991	31 March 1989	15	London terms	Yes	Yes	Yes	152
	III	June 1993	31 March 1989	29	London terms	Yes	No	Yes	25
	IV[b]	October 1996	31 March 1989	-	Naples terms (67%)[c]	Yes	Yes	No	209
	V	October 2000	31 March 1989	12	Cologne terms	No	Yes	Yes	5
	VI	April 2003	31 March 1989	-	Cologne terms	Yes	Yes	No	65
Burkina Faso	I	March 1991	1 January 1991	15	Toronto terms	Yes	No	Yes	63
	II	May 1993	1 January 1991	32	London terms	Yes	No	Yes	36
	III[b]	June 1996	1 January 1991	-	Naples terms (67%)[c]	No	Yes	No	64
	IV	October 2000	1 January 1991	12	Cologne terms	No	Yes	Yes	1
	V	June 2002	1 January 1991	-	Cologne terms	Yes	-	-	33
Cambodia	III[b]	January 1995[d]	31 December 1985	30	Naples terms (67%)	No	Yes	No	249
Central African Republic	V	June 1990	1 January 1983	12	Toronto terms	No	Yes	No	4
	VI	April 1994	1 January 1983	12	London terms	Yes	Yes	Yes	33
	VII[b]	September 1998	1 January 1983	34	Naples terms (67%)	Yes	Yes	Yes	26
Chad	II[b]	February 1995[d]	30 June 1989	-	Naples terms (67%)	..	-	-	24
	III[b]	June 1996[d]	30 June 1989	32	Naples terms (67%)	Yes	Yes	No	..
	IV	June 2001	30 June 1989	23	Cologne terms	No	Yes	Yes	15
Dem. Rep. of the Congo	X	September 2002	30 June 1983	36	Naples terms	Yes	Yes	Yes	8 980
	XI	November 2993	30 June 1983	-	Cologne terms	No	No	Yes	not stated
Djibouti	I	May 2000	31 March 1998	32	Non-concessional	Yes	-	Yes	16
Equatorial Guinea	III	April 1992[d]	..	-	London terms	Yes	Yes	Yes	32
	IV	Febuary 1994[d]	..	-	London terms	Yes	-	Yes	51
Ethiopia	I	December 1992	31 December 1989	37	London terms	Yes	Yes	Yes	441
	II[b]	January 1997	31 December 1989	34	Naples terms (67%)	Yes	No	Yes	184
	III[b]	April 2001	31 December 1989	37	Naple terms (67%)	Yes	Yes	Yes	430
	IV	April 2002	31 December 1989	29	Cologne terms	No	Yes	Yes	7
	V	May 2004	31 December 1989	-	Cologne terms	Yes	-	-	1 487
Gambia	II	January 2003	1 July 1986	36	Cologne terms	No	Yes	Yes	203
Guinea	IV[b]	November 1992	1 January 1986	-	London terms	Yes	Yes	Yes	156
	V[b]	January 1995	1 January 1986	12	Naples terms (50%)	Yes	Yes	Yes	..
	VI	February 1997	1 January 1986	36	Naples terms (50%)	Yes	Yes	Yes	151
	VII	May 2001	1 January 1986	40	Cologne terms	Yes	-	Yes	195
Guinea-Bissau	III[b]	February 1995	31 December 1986	36	Naples terms (67%)	No	Yes	Yes	141
	IV	January 2001	31 December 1986	37	Cologne terms	Yes	Yes	Yes	117
Haiti	I[b]	May 1995	1 October 1993	13	Naples terms (67%)	No	No	No	139
Madagascar	VII	July 1990	1 July 1983	13	Toronto terms	Yes	Yes	Yes	1 247
	VIII[b]	March 1997	1 July 1983	35	Naples terms (67%)	Yes	Yes	Yes	254
	IX	March 2001	1 July 1983	39	Cologne terms	Yes	Yes	Yes	1 057
	X	November 2004	1 July 1983	-	Cologne terms	Yes	-	-	..
Malawi	IV	January 2001	1 January 1997	37	Cologne terms	Yes	Yes	Yes	20
Mali	III	October 1992	1 January 1988	35	London terms	No	No	No	33
	IV[b]	May 1996	1 January 1988	-	Naples terms (67%)[c]	Yes	Yes	Yes	4
	V	October 2000	1 January 1988	10	Cologne terms	Yes	Yes	Yes	155
	VI	March 2003	1 January 1988	-	Cologne terms	Yes	Yes	No	
Mauritania	V	January 1993	31 December 1984	24	London terms	Yes	Yes	Yes	218
	VI[b]	June 1995	31 December 1984	36	Naples terms (67%)	No	Yes	Yes	66
	VII	March 2000	31 December 1984	36	Cologne terms	Yes	Yes	Yes	80
	VIII	July 2002	31 December 1984	30	Cologne terms	Yes	Yes	No	384
Mozambique	III	June 1990	1 February 1984	24	Toronto terms	Yes	Yes	Yes	719
	IV	March 1993	1 February 1984	32	London terms	Yes	Yes	Yes	440
	V[b]	November 1996	1 February 1984	32	Naples terms (67%)	Yes	Yes	Yes	664
	VI[e]	May 1998	1 February 1984	-	Lyon terms	Yes	Yes	Yes	..
	VII	July 1999	1 February 1984	-	90% NPV reduction	yes	yes	yes	1 860
	VIII	November 2001	1 February 1984	-	Cologne terms	No	Yes	No	2 800

Table 32 (cont.)

Country	Number of debt[a]	Date of meeting	Cut-off date	Consolidation period (months)	Terms	Arrears	Rescheduling of previously rescheduled debt	Goodwill clause	Estimated amounts rescheduled ($ million)
Niger	VII	September 1990	1 July 1983	28	Toronto terms	Yes	Yes	Yes	116
	VIII	March 1994	1 July 1983	15	London terms	Yes	Yes	Yes	160
	IX[b]	December 1996	1 July 1983	31	Naples terms (67%)	Yes	Yes	Yes	128
	X	January 2001	1 July 1983	37	Cologne terms	Yes	Yes	Yes	115
	XI	May 2004	1 July 1983	-	Cologne terms	Yes	-	-	250
Rwanda	I[b]	July 1998	31 December 1994	35	Naples terms (67%)	Yes	-	Yes	64
	II	March 2002	31 December 1994	17	Cologne terms	No	Yes	Yes	..
	III	May 2005	31 December 1994	-	Cologne terms	Yes	-	-	90
Sao Tome and Principe	I[b]	May 2000	1 April 1999	37	Naples terms (67%)	Yes	-	Yes	27
Senegal	VIII	February 1990	1 January 1983	12	Toronto terms	Yes	Yes	Yes	107
	IX	June 1991	1 January 1983	12	Toronto terms	Yes	Yes	No	114
	X	March 1994	1 January 1983	15	London terms	Yes	Yes	Yes	237
	XI[b]	April 1995	1 January 1983	29	Naples terms (67%)	Yes	Yes	No	169
	XII[b]	June 1998	..	-	Naples terms (67%)[c]	Yes	Yes	Yes	428
	XIII	October 2000	1 January 1983	18	Cologne terms	No	Yes	No	21
	XIV	June 2004	1 January 1983	-	Cologne terms	Yes	-	-	463
Sierra Leone	V	November 1992	1 July 1983	16	London terms	Yes	Yes	Yes	164
	VI	July 1994	1 July 1983	17	London terms	Yes	Yes	Yes	42
	VII[b]	March 1996	1 July 1983	24	Naples terms (67%)	No	Yes	No	39
	VIII[b]	October 2001	1 July 1983	36	Naples terms (67%)	Yes	Yes	Yes	180
	IX	July 2002	1 July 1983	31	Cologne terms	No	Yes	No	3
Togo	VIII	July 1990	1 January 1983	24	Toronto terms	No	Yes	No	88
	IX	June 1992	1 January 1983	24	London terms	No	Yes	Yes	52
	X[b]	February 1995	1 January 1983	33	Naples terms (67%)	No	Yes	Yes	239
Uganda	V	June 1992	1 July 1981	18	London terms	Yes	Yes	Yes	39
	VI[b]	February 1995[d]	1 July 1981	-	Naples terms (67%)[c]	No	Yes	No	110
	VII	April 1998	1 July 1981	-	Lyon terms (80%)[f]	No	Yes	No	110
	VIII	September 2000	1 July 1981	-	Cologne terms[c]	-	-	-	145
United Rep. of Tanzania	III	March 1990	30 June 1986	12	Toronto terms	Yes	Yes	Yes	200
	IV	January 1992	30 June 1986	30	London terms	Yes	Yes	Yes	691
	V[b]	January 1997	30 June 1986	36	Naples terms (67%)	Yes	Yes	Yes	608
	VI	April 2000	30 June 1986	36	Cologne terms	Yes	Yes	Yes	390
	VII	January 2002	30 June 1986	-	Cologne terms	-	Yes	No	1 245
Yemen	I[b]	September 1996	1 January 1993	10	Naples terms (67%)	Yes	-	Yes	113
	II[b]	November 1997	1 January 1993	36	Naples terms (67%)	Yes	No	No	..
	III[b]	June 2001	1 January 1993	-	Naples terms (67%)[c]	-	No	No	420
Zambia	IV	July 1990	1 January 1983	18	Toronto terms	Yes	Yes	Yes	963
	V	July 1992	1 January 1983	33	London terms	Yes	Yes	Yes	917
	VI[b]	February 1996	1 January 1983	36	Naples terms (67%)	Yes	Yes	Yes	566
	VII[b]	April 1999	1 January 1983	36	Naples terms (67%)	No	Yes	Yes	1 063
	VIII	September 2002	1 January 1983	27	Cologne terms	Yes	-	-	..
	IX	May 2005	1 January 1983	-	Cologne terms	Yes	-	-	1 763

Source: Paris Club Agreed Minutes.

a   Roman numerals indicate the number of debt reschedulings for the country since 1976.
b   Naples terms; number in brackets indicates the percentage of reduction applied.
c   Stock reduction.
d   Dates of informal meeting of creditors on the terms to be applied in the bilateral agreements, as creditors did not call for a full Paris Club meeting.
e   Amendment to the November 1996 agreement.
f   Additional stock reduction ("Topping up") on previously rescheduled debt.

33. ARRANGEMENTS IN SUPPORT OF STRUCTURAL ADJUSTMENT IN LDCs (As OF DECEMBER 2004)
Millions of SDRs (except where otherwise indicated)

Country	IMF arrangements — Stand-by/Extended Facility Period	Amount	SAF/ESAF/PRGF Period	Amount	World Bank — Structural adjustment Date of approval	IDA	African Facility[1]	Co-financing[2]	Sector and other adjustment Date of approval	IDA	African Facility[1]	Co-financing[2]	Purpose
Afghanistan									Jul. 2005	18.8			Emergency reconstruction
									May 2005	40.0 ($)			Education
									May 2005	29.9			Transport
									Jan. 2005	27.0 ($)			Public administration capacity
									Jul. 2004	17.1			Urban reconstruction
									Jul. 2004	54.7			Institution building
									Jul. 2004	35.0 ($)			Education
									Jul. 2004	3.5			Investment guarantees
Angola									Feb. 2005	16.9			Multi-sector recovery
									Dec. 2004	14.1			Health
Bangladesh	July 1979 - July 1980	85.0							June 1987	147.8			Industrial policy reform
	Dec. 1980 - Dec. 1983[3]	800.0[4]	Feb. 1987 - Feb. 1990	201.3					Apr. 1989	137.0		Germany (DM 26m)	Energy sector
	March 1983 - Aug. 1983	68.4							Oct. 1989	1.8[6]			"
	Dec. 1985 - June[1] 1987	180.0	Aug. 1990 - Sep. 1993	345[5]					June 1990	132.7		USAID (18.2)	Financial sector
									Nov. 1990	2.5[6]			"
									Nov. 1991	2.2[6]			"
									May 1992	109.3			Public resource management
									Oct. 1992	72.2			Industry
									Dec. 1992	2.5[6]			"
									Feb. 1994	175.0			Jute sector
									May 1994	2.4[6]			"
									Dec. 1994	2.3[6]			"
			June 2003 - June 2006	400.3					Dec. 1995	2.3[7]0			"
									Nov. 1996	2.0			"
									Jul. 2004	136.8			Development support
									Aug. 2004	68.4			Education
									Apr. 2005	196.1			Health
Benin			June 1989 - June 1992	21.9[7]	May 1989	33.5			Nov. 1993	3.7		DANIDA (4); ACBF (2)	Public expenditure
			Jan. 1993 - May 1996	51.9[5]	June 1991	41.3							Economic management
			Aug. 1996 - Jan. 2000	27.2[7]1	March 2001	7.8			July 2004	31.1			Energy
			July 2000 - July 2003	27.0[7]1	May 1995	25.8			Oct. 2004	34.1			Community-driven development
					June 2005	19.9							
Bhutan									Mar. 2005	4.6			Rural development
Burkina Faso			Mar. 1991 - Mar. 1993	22.1[8]	June 1991	60.0		EC (30); AfDB (20); France (17); Canada (13); Germany (12)	Feb. 1985	13.8			Fertilizers
			Mar. 1993 - May 1996	53.0[5]					Feb. 1992	49.6		France/CCCE (3.2); Netherlands (2.1); Germany/GTZ (2); France/FAC (1.7); EDF (99); AfDB (60.6); CIDA (29.8); Germany (28.6); West African Development Fund (10.2); BADEA (8.5); CCCE & FAC (7.8); BOAD (3.1); IsDB (5.5); UNDP (0.6); France (21); EC (20); AfDB (13)	Transport sector
			June 1996 - Sep. 1999	39.8[5]	Nov. 1998	11.0			June 1992	20.6			Agriculture
			Sep. 1999 - Sep. 2002	39.1[7]1	Dec. 1999	18.0			Mar. 1994	18.0			Economic recovery
			June 2003-June 2006	24.1	May 2005	39.9			Nov. 2004	43.4			Economic management
									Mar. 2005	4.6			Structural adjustment credit III
									May 2005	3.4			Energy / Administration capacity building / HIV/AIDS

Table 33 (cont.)

Country	IMF Stand-by/Extended Facility — Period	Amount	IMF SAF/ESAF/PRGF — Period	Amount	WB Structural adjustment — Date of approval	IDA	African Facility[1]	Co-financing[2]	WB Sector and other adjustment — Date of approval	IDA	African Facility[1]	Co-financing[2]	Purpose
Burundi	Aug. 1986 - March 1988	21.0	Aug. 1986 - Aug. 1989	29.9	May 1986	13.2	14.3	Japan (11); Switzerland (7.7); Japan (18.1); Germany (6); Saudi Arabia (2.9)	July 2004	24.0			Agriculture
			Nov. 1991 - Nov. 1994	42.7[5]	June 1988	64.9							
			Jan. 2004 - Jan. 2007	69.3									
Cambodia			Oct. 1999 - Feb. 2003	84.0[5]	June 1992	22.0			July 1988	11.9	(16.2)		Economic rehabilitation
			Oct. 1999 - Oct. 2002	58.5[7]	Feb. 2000	21.9			Sep. 1995	25.4			Structural adjustment credit
									May 2005	18.4			Education
									June 2005	6.6			Trade facilitation
Cape Verde	Feb. 1998 - May 1999	2.1	Apr. 2002 - Apr. 2005	9.0[71]	Dec. 2001	11.6			Dec. 1997	21.8			Economic reforms support
	Feb. 1998 - Mar. 2000	2.1			Feb. 2005	9.7			May 2005	17.1			Structural adjustment credit; Road sector
Central African Republic	Feb. 1980 - Feb. 1981	4.0	June 1987 - May 1990	21.3	Sep. 1986	12.3	14	ADF (25)	July 1987	11.5		Saudi Arabia (2); Japan (6)	Cotton sector
	April 1981 - Dec. 1981	10.4[9]			June 1988	28.9			Dec. 1999	14.4			Fiscal consolidation credit
	April 1983 - April 1984	18.0[10]			June 1990	34.5							
	July 1984 - July 1985	15.0											
	Sep. 1985 - March 1987	15.0[11]											
	June 1987 - May 1988	8.0											
Chad	Mar. 1994 - Mar. 1995	16.5	July 1998 - Jan. 2002	49.4[71]	Feb. 1996	20.2			July 1988	11.9	(16.2)	USAID (23); Germany (22.7); CCCE (13.1); ADF (11.3); BDEAC (10.6); EDF (4.8); OPEC Fund for Int.Dev.(4.5); FAC (3.3); UNDP (0.5)	Public finance and cotton sector
			Oct. 1987 - Oct. 1990	21.4	June 1997	18.0			April 1989	45.4			Transport sector
			Sep. 1995 - Apr. 1999	49.6[5]	May 1999	22.2			Mar. 1994	14.4			Economic recovery
			Jan. 2000 - Jan. 2003	48.0[71]	Dec. 2001	31.4							Public sector; structural adjustment credit III
			Feb. 2005 - Feb. 2008	25.2					Sep. 2004	16.4			Structural adjustment credit; Decentralised development
									Nov. 2004	17.1			Institutional reform
Comoros			June 1991 - June 1994	3.2					June 1991	6.0	ADF (17); UNDP (1)		Macroeconomic reform and capacity-building
Dem. Republic of the Congo	Aug. 1979 - Feb. 1981	118.0[59]	May 1987 - May 1990	203.7[63]	June 2002	360.4			June 1986	17.6	(60)	Japan (15.7)	Industrial sector
	June 1981 - June 1984[21]	912.0[60]	June 1996 - June 1999	69.5[5]					June 1987	42.2	(94.3)		Agricultural and rural dev.
	Dec. 1983 - March 1985	228.0[61]	June 2002 - June 2005	580.0					Aug. 2004	41.1			Economic recovery; Emergency social action
	April 1985 - April 1986	162.0							May 2005	53.9			Restore basic services
	May 1986 - Mar. 1988	214.2[62]											
	May 1987 - May 1988	100.0[64]											
	June 1989 - June 1990	116.4[65]											
Djibouti	April 1996 - June 1997	4.6	Oct. 1999 - Oct. 2002	19.1[71]					Sep. 2004	4.4			Emergency assistance
Equatorial Guinea	July 1980 - June 1981	5.5	Dec. 1988 - Dec. 1992	12.9[13]									
	June 1985 - June 1986	9.2[12]	Feb. 1993 - Feb. 1996	12.9[5]									

Table 33 (cont.)

	IMF arrangements				World Bank loans and credits								
	Stand-by/Extended Facility		SAF/ESAF/PRGF		Structural adjustment				Sector and other adjustment				
						Amount				Amount			
Country	Period	Amount	Period	Amount	Date of approval	IDA	African Facility[1]	Co-financing[2]	Date of approval	IDA	African Facility[1]	Co-financing[2]	Purpose
Eritrea									July 2004	34.5			Energy
									June 2005	15.9			Health
Ethiopia	May 1981 - June 1982	67.5	Oct. 1992 - Nov. 1995	49.4	June 1993	176.5			Sep. 2004	110.0			Economic rehab. support
			Oct. 1996 - Oct. 1999	88.5[5]	Jan. 1994	0.3[6]			Sep. 2004	17.1			Structural adjustment credit
			Mar. 2001 - Mar. 2004	100.0[71]	Dec. 1994	0.1[6]			Sep. 2004	27.4			Roads
					June 2001	150.0			Sep. 2004	47.8			ICT
					June 2002	96.2			Nov. 2004	16.1			Education
					Nov. 2004	88.6			Dec. 2004				Food security
													Private sector development
Gambia	Nov. 1979 - Nov. 1980	1.6	Sep.1986 - Nov. 1988	12.0[16]	Aug. 1986	4.3	9.9	United Kingdom (4.5); ADF (9)	June 2005	2.7			Local govt. capacity-building
	Feb. 1982 - Feb. 1983	16.9	Nov. 1988 - Nov. 1991	20.5[5]	June 1989	17.9		ADF (6); Netherlands (2.5)					
	April 1984 - July 1985 15	12.8[14]	June 1998 - Dec. 2001	20.6[71]									
	Sep.1986 - Oct. 1987	5.1	July 2002 - July 2005	20.2									
Guinea	Dec. 1982 - Nov. 1983	25.0[17]	July 1987 - July 1990	40.5[19]	Feb. 1986	22.9	15.6	France (26.7); Germany (9.4); Japan (27.8); Switzerland (4.8); ADF (12); Japan (11.2)	June 1990	15.4			Education sector
	Feb. 1986 - March 1987	33.0[18]	Nov. 1991 - Dec. 1996	57.9[5]	June 1988	47.0							Public sector
	July 1987 - Aug. 1988	11.6	Jan. 1997 - Jan. 2001	70.8[71]	Dec. 1992	0.1[6]							Structural adjustment credit IV
			May 2001 - May 2004	64.0[71]	Dec. 1997	50.8							Rural infrastructure
					July 2001	39.3							Health
Guinea-Bissau			Oct. 1987 - Oct. 1990	5.3[20]	May 1987	8.0	4	Switzerland (5.2); Saudi Arabia (3.2); ADF (11.3); IFAD (5.3); Netherlands (4.8); USAID (4.5); ADF (12.0)[22]	Dec.1984	10.1		Switzerland (SwF 4.5 m)	Economic recovery programme[21]
Haiti	Oct. 1978 - Oct. 1981[24]	32.2[23]	Dec. 1986 - Dec. 1989	30.9[26]	May 1989	18.0			Nov. 2004	2.1			Environment
	Aug. 1982 - Sep. 1983	34.5	Oct.1996 - Oct. 1999	91.1[5]	May 2000	18.0			Dec. 2004	2.8			Health
	Nov. 1983 - Sep. 1985	60.0[25]			Jan. 2005	40.7			Mar.1987	32.8			Economic recovery
	Sep.1989 - Dec.1990	21.0[18]							Dec. 1994	26.8			
	Mar. 1995 - Mar.1996	20.0							Jan. 2005	1.4			Economic governance
									Jan. 2005	8.0			Emergency recovery
Lao People's Dem. Republic	Aug. 1980 - Aug. 1981	14.0	Sep.1989 - Sep. 1992	20.5	June 1989	30.8							
			June 1993 - May 1997	35.2[5]	Oct. 1991	30.0							
			Apr. 2001 - Apr. 2004	32.0[71]	Feb. 1996	26.9			Mar. 2005	40.5			Financial management adj.
					June 2002	13.5			June 2005	2.7			Social and environment
					Mar. 2005	6.6							Environment
Lesotho	Sep.1994 - Sep. 1995	8.4	June 1988 - June 1991	10.6					July 2004	3.5			HIV/AIDS
	July 1995 - July 1996	7.2	May 1991 - Aug. 1994	18.1					Oct. 2004	9.6			Water
			Sep.1996 - Sep. 1997	7.2[5]									
			Mar. 2001 - Mar. 2004	25.0[71]									

Table 33 (cont.)

	IMF arrangements				World Bank loans and credits								
	Stand-by/Extended Facility		SAF/ESAF/PRGF		Structural adjustment				Sector and other adjustment				
Country	Period	Amount	Period	Amount	Date of approval	IDA	African Facility[1]	Co-financing[2]	Date of approval	IDA	African Facility[1]	Co-financing[2]	Purpose
Madagascar	June 1980 - June 1982[31]	64.5[27]											
	April 1981 - June 1982	76.7[28]											
	July 1982 - July 1983	51.0[14]											
	April 1984 - Mar. 1985	33.0											
	April 1985 - April 1986	29.5							May 1986	19	(33)		Agricultural sector
	Sep.1986 - Feb. 1988	30.0	Aug. 1987 - May 1989	46.5[29]					June 1988	90.5		KfW (4); Japan (3); ADF (40); Switzerland (8)	Public sector
	Sep.1988 - July 1989	13.3[30]	May 1989 - May 1992	76.9[5]					Mar.1989	1.1[6]			Public sector
									Oct.1989	0.9[6]			"
									Nov.1990	1.2[6]			"
									Nov.1991	1[6]			"
			Nov. 1996 - Nov. 1999	81.4[5]	Mar. 1997	48.6			Dec.1992	1[6]			Multisector rehabilitation
					Mar. 1997	0.4							Structural adjustment credit II
			Nov. 1996 - Nov. 2000	24.0[71]	May 1999	73.5							Structural adjustment credit
			Mar. 2001 - Feb. 2004	79.0[71]	July 2000	15.2							"
					Dec. 2000	23.5			July 2004	34.2			Community development
					July 2004	85.7			June 2005	12.3			Health
Malawi	Oct. 1979 - Dec. 1981[31]	26.3[32]			June 1981	36.7[33]							
	May 1980 - March 1982	49.9[32]							April 1983	4.6		IFAD (10.3)	Smallholder fertilizers
	Aug. 1982 - Aug. 1983	22.0			Dec. 1983	51.9	37.3	Germany/KfW (6.4); Japan/OECF (22.6); USAID (15)					
	Sep.1983 - Sep. 1986	81.0[34]			Dec. 1985	28.0							
	March 1988 - May 1989	13.0	July 1988 - Mar. 1994	67.0[5]	Jan. 1987		8.4	Japan (17.7); United Kingdom (7.5); Germany (5)	June 1988	50.6		OECF (30); USAID (25); ADF (19.5); EEC (16)	Industrial and trade policy adjustment
									Mar. 1989	4.0[6]			"
			Oct.1995 - Dec. 1999	51.0[5]					Oct. 1989	3.8[6]		USAID (25); United Kingdom (16.5); Netherlands (5); Germany, EEC and Japan (6.1)	Agriculture
									April 1990	52.6			"
Malawi (cont.)									Nov. 1990	5.1[6]			Industry and trade
									Nov. 1991	4.0[6]			Agriculture
	Nov. 1994 - June 1995	15.0							June 1992	85.4		AfDB (13.4)	Entrepreneurship dev.
									Dec. 1992	4.3[6]			& drought recovery
									Nov. 1994	27.6[6]			"
									Dec. 1994	3.2[6]			"
									April 1996	70.3			Fiscal restructuring & deregulation programme
			Dec. 2000 - Dec. 2003	45.0[71]	Nov. 1996	2,4[70]			April 1996	2.9[70]			"
					Dec. 1998	67.2							Fiscal restructuring and and de-regulation program. II
					Dec. 2000	0.4							Program Credit III-IDA reflow
					Dec. 2000	43.1							Program Credit III
									Dec. 2004	10.1			Health
									May 2005	22.0			Education
Mali	May 1982 - May 1993	30.4							June 1988	29.4		Japan (38.7); Saudi Arabia (5.9); ADF (45)	Public enterprise sector
	Dec. 1983 - May 1985	40.5											
	Nov. 1985 - March 1987	22.9[36]											
	Aug. 1988 - June 1990	12.7	Aug. 1988 - Aug. 1991	35.6[14]	Dec. 1990	50.3		EC (20); AfDB (18)	June 1990	40.7		FAC/CCCE (50.8); SDC (6.9); Netherlands (5.2); Germany (2.9)	Agricultural sector/ investment
			Aug. 1992 - April 1996	79.2[5]					Mar. 1994	18.2			Economic recovery
			April 1996 - Aug. 1999	62.0[5]	Dec. 2000	19.6			Jan. 1995	34.3			Education
			Aug. 1999 - Aug. 2003	52.0	Dec. 2001	55.0			June 1996	41.6			Economic management
			June 2004 - June 2007	9.3	Mar. 2005	16.6			Feb. 2005	35.6			Economic management / Structural adjustment credit / Growth support

Table 33 (cont.)

Country	IMF arrangements — Stand-by/Extended Facility — Period	Amount	SAF/ESAF/PRGF — Period	Amount	World Bank loans and credits — Structural adjustment — Date of approval	IDA	African Facility[1]	Co-financing[2]	Sector and other adjustment — Date of approval	IDA	African Facility[1]	Co-financing[2]	Purpose
Mauritania	July 1980 - March 1982[38]	29.7[37]											
	June 1981 - March 1982	25.8											
	April 1985 - April 1986	12.0	Sep.1986 - May 1989	23.7[39]	June 1987	11.7	21.4	Saudi Arabia (4.8); Germany (2.8)	Feb. 1990	19.4		CCCE (8); Germany (2); WFP (1);	Agricultural sector/investment
	April 1986 - April 1987	12.0	May 1989 - Jan. 1995	50.9[5]					June 1990	30.7		Japan (50); SFD (19.8); KFAED (13.7); AFESD (10.3); Abu Dhabi Fund (6.1); Spain (5); Germany (4)	Public enterprises
	May 1987 - May 1988	10.0							Nov. 1990	2.9[6]			Public enterprises
			Jan. 1995 - July 1998	42.8[5]					Nov. 1991	1.9[6]			"
									Dec. 1992	1.6[6]			"
			July 1999 - July 2002	42.5[71]	Feb. 1999	0.1			Jan. 1994	1.0[6]			"
					Nov. 1999	0.1			Nov. 1996	0.4[6]			Public resource management
					May 2000	22.4			Dec. 1997	0.3			Public resource management
			July 2003 - July 2006	6.4	Dec. 2000	14.1			Aug. 2004	10.2			Fiscal reform
													Fiscal reform
													Education
									Mar. 2005	25.7			Agriculture
Mozambique			June 1987 - June 1990	42.7					May 1985	45.5			Economic rehabilitation programme I
									Aug. 1987	54.5	(18.6)	Switzerland (11.2)	Economic rehabilitation programme II
			June 1990 - Dec. 1995	130.1[5]					May 1989	68.2		United Kingdom (17.5); Switzerland (12.8); Germany (10.9); Sweden (9.4); Finland (8.9)	Economic rehabilitation programme III
			June 1996 - Aug. 1999	75.6[5]					June 1992	132		Switzerland (6)	Economic recovery
			June 1999 - June 2002	87.2[71]					June 1994	141.7			Economic recovery II
			July 2004 - July 2007	11.4					Oct. 2004	75.6			Railways
Myanmar	June 1981 - June 1982	27.0											
Nepal	Dec. 1985 - April 1987	18.7	Oct. 1987 - Oct. 1990	26.1	Mar. 1987	40.9		KfW (5)	July 2004	34.5			Education
			Oct. 1992 - Oct. 1995	33.6[5]	June 1989	46.2			Sep. 2004	34.2			Health
			Nov. 2003 - Nov. 2007	49.9	July 2004	40.9			June 2005	2.0			Economic reform
									June 2005	21.2			Rural development
Niger	Oct. 1983 - Dec. 1984	18.0	Nov. 1986 - Nov. 1988	23.6[40]	Feb. 1986	18.3	36.6		June 1987	46.0	15.4		Public enterprises
	Dec. 1984 - Dec. 1985	16.0	Dec. 1988 - Dec. 1991	47.2[5]					Mar. 1994	18.2			Economic recovery
	Dec. 1985 - Dec. 1986	13.5	June 1996 - Aug. 1999	58.0[5]	Mar. 1997	21.6							
	Dec. 1986 - Dec. 1987	10.1			Oct. 1998	48.0							Public sector
	Mar. 1994 - Mar. 1995	18.6	Dec. 2000 - Dec. 2003	59.0[71]	Sep. 2000	26.5							Public finance reform
					Dec. 2000	9.4			May 2005	26.6			Finance recov. adjustment
			Jan. 2005 - Jan. 2008	26.3	Nov. 2001	54.5							Public expenditure
													Public expenditure reform

Table 33 (cont.)

| | IMF arrangements | | | | World Bank loans and credits | | | | | | | | |
| Country | Stand-by/Extended Facility | | SAF/ESAF/PRGF | | Structural adjustment | | | | Sector and other adjustment | | | | Purpose |
	Period	Amount	Period	Amount	Date of approval	IDA	African Facility [1]	Co-financing [2]	Date of approval	IDA	African Facility [1]	Co-financing [2]	
Rwanda	Oct. 1979 - Oct. 1980	5.0[42]	April 1991 - April 1994	30.7[26]	June 1991	67.5		Switzerland (SwF 10m); Belgium (BF 400m)					
			June 1998 - Jan. 2002	71.4[71]					Jan. 1995	34.3			Emergency recovery
			Aug. 2002 - Aug. 2005	4.0					July 2004	13.7			Economic recovery; Public sector capacity building
									Jan. 2005	16.7			Electricity
Samoa	Aug. 1979 - Aug. 1980	0.7[42]											
	June 1983 - June 1984	3.4											
	July 1984 - July 1985	3.4											
Sao Tome and Principe			June 1989 - June 1992	2.8[43]	June 1987	3.1							Management credit
			Apr. 2000 - Apr. 2003	6.7[71]	June 1990	7.5	2.3	ADF (8.5); ADF(12); IMF (2.6)					
					Nov. 2000	5.8			Oct. 2004	3.5			Governance capacity building
Senegal	Oct. 1987 - Oct. 1988	21.3	Nov. 1986	43.0	Feb. 1986	18.3							
			Nov. 1986 - Nov. 1988	59.6	May 1987	35.0	31.4	7.1					
				144.7	Mar. 1989	4.2			Dec. 1989	35.3			Str.adjustment credit III (supplement); Structural credit IV
	Mar. 1994 - Aug. 1994	48.0	Nov. 1988 - June 1992	131.0	Feb. 1990	62.4							
			Aug. 1994 - Jan. 1998	107.0[71]	May 1990	3.5			Dec. 1995	1.8			Agricultural sector
			Apr. 1998 - Apr. 2002		Nov. 1990	5.1			Nov. 1996	1.3			
			Apr. 2003 - Apr. 2006	24.3	Apr. 1992	3.5							Energy sector
					May 1998	74.0			Sep. 2004	20.6			Trade reform
					Sep. 2000	75.7			Sep. 2004	13.8			Electricity
					Dec. 2004	20.5			Nov. 2004	6.9			Emergency recovery; Marine resources
									May 2005	10.5			Electricity
Sierra Leone	Nov. 1979 - Nov. 1980	17.0	Nov. 1986 - Nov. 1989	40.5[47]					June 1984	20.3		IFAD (5.4)	Agriculture
	March 1981 - Feb. 1984[45]	186.0[44]							April 1992	31.4			Reconstruction
	Feb. 1984 - Feb. 1985	50.2[46]							April 1992	0.2[6]			Imports
	Nov. 1986 - Nov. 1987	23.2							Dec. 1992	0.2[6]			"
			Mar. 1994 - Mar. 1995	27.0	Oct. 1993	35.9							
			Mar. 1994 - May 1998	101.9[5]	Jan. 1994	0.1[6]							
					Dec. 1994	0.2[70]							
			Sep. 2001 - Sep. 2004	131.0[71]	Dec. 1995	0.2[70]							
					Nov. 1996	0.1			July 2004	24.2			Economic recovery
					Feb. 2000	21.9			June 2005	2.2			Economic recovery II
					Dec. 2000	7.9			June 2005	10.0			Electrocity and water; Water
					Dec. 2001	39.4			June 2005	50.2 ($)			Economic recovery; Electricity
Solomon Islands					June 1999	8.9							Structural adjustment credit
Somalia	Feb. 1980 - Feb. 1981	11.5[48]	June 1987 - June 1990	30.9[26]					June 1989	54.2		ADF (25); BITS (0.5)	Agriculture
	July 1981 - July 1982	43.1											
	July 1982 - Jan. 1984	60.0											
	Feb. 1985 - Sep. 1986	22.1											
	June 1987 - Feb. 1989	33.2											
Sudan	May 1979 - May 1982[49]	427.0							June 1983	46.4			Agricultural rehabilitation
	Feb. 1982 - Feb. 1983	198.0[50]											
	Feb. 1983 - March 1984	170.0											
	June 1984 - June 1985	90.0[51]											

Table 33 (cont.)

	IMF arrangements				World Bank loans and credits								
	Stand-by/Extended Facility		SAF/ESAF/PRGF		Structural adjustment				Sector and other adjustment				
						Amount				Amount			
Country	Period	Amount	Period	Amount	Date of approval	IDA	African Facility[1]	Co-financing[2]	Date of approval	IDA	African Facility[1]	Co-financing[2]	Purpose
Timor-Leste					Oct. 2004	3.4			July 2004	1.4 (5)			Power sector
Togo	June 1979 - Dec. 1980	15.0[52]			May 1983	36.9							
	Feb. 1981 - Feb. 1983	47.5[53]			May 1985	28.1							
	March 1983 - April 1984	21.4			Aug. 1985								
	May 1984 - May 1985	19.0											
	May 1985 - May 1986	15.4											
	June 1986 - April 1988	23.0	Mar. 1988 - May 1989	26.9[54]	Mar. 1988	33.0		ADF (17.3); Japan (20.8)					
	Mar. 1988 - April 1989	13.0	May 1989 - May 1993	46.1[5]	Mar. 1989	0.1[6]							
					Oct. 1989	0.2[6]							
					Dec. 1990	39.6							
			Sep.1994 - June 1998	65.2[5]					Feb. 1991	10.2			Population and health
									April 1996	32.2			Economic recovery and adjustment
Uganda	Jan. 1980 - Dec. 1980	12.5							Feb. 1983	63.5		Italy/DCD (10)	Agricultural rehabilitation
	June 1981 - June 1982	112.5							May 1984	47.2	18.8	United Kingdom/ODA (16)	Reconstruction
	Aug. 1982 - Aug. 1983	112.5							Sep.1987	50.9			Economic recovery
	Sep.1983 - Sep. 1984	95.0[55]	June 1987 - April 1989	69.7[56]					Mar. 1989	1.3[6]			"
			April 1989 - June 1994	219.2[57]					April 1989	19[6]	(12.8)		"
									Oct. 1989	1.2[6]			"
									Feb. 1990	98.1			"
					Dec. 1991	91.9			Nov. 1990	1.5[6]			Agriculture
					Dec. 1992	1.0[6]			Dec. 1990	69.5			Economic recovery
			Sep. 1994 - Nov. 1997	120.5[5]	May 1994	57.8			Nov. 1991	1.2[6]			Finance
					Dec. 1994	0.4[6]			May 1993	72.8			"
					June 1997	90.4			Jan. 1994	0.8[6]			
			Nov. 1997 - Mar. 2001	100.4[71]					Mar. 1998	59.2			Education sector
			Sep. 2002 - Sep. 2005	13.5	Dec. 2000	19.6			Sep. 2004	47.9			Structural adjustment III
					Sep. 2004	102.6			Sep. 2004	73.2			Private sector; Roads
United Republic of Tanzania	Sep.1980 - June 1982	179.6[58]							Nov. 1986	41.3	38.2	Germany (17.3); Switzerland (9.2);	Multisector rehabilitation
	Aug. 1986 - Feb. 1988	64.2	Oct. 1987 - Oct. 1990	74.9					Jan. 1988	22.5	(26.0)	United Kingdom (7.3); Saudi Arabia (4);	Multisector rehabilitation
									Dec. 1988	97.6		ADF (24); United Kingdom (15); Switzerland (14);	Industrial rehabilitation and trade adjustment
									Mar. 1989	9.7[6]		Netherlands (10)	"
									Oct. 1989	8.3[6]			Industrial rehabilitation
			July 1991 - July 1994	181.9[5]					Mar. 1990	150.4			Industry and trade adjustment
									Dec. 1990	11.5[6]		Netherlands (40)	Agriculture
									Nov. 1991	8.6[6]		United Kingdom (20)	Agriculture
									Nov. 1991	150.2			"
			Nov. 1996 - Feb. 2000	181.6[5]	June 1997	93.2[70]			Dec. 1992	8.2[6]		United Kingdom (16.8); Switzerland (6.6)	Finance
					Dec. 1997	1.8							"
					Dec. 1999	0.8							
			Apr. 2000 - Apr. 2003	135.0[71]	June 2000	141.8							
					Jan. 2001	0.6			Oct. 2001	119.1			Stru.adjustment credit
			Aug. 2003 - Aug. 2006	19.6	Feb. 2002	0.5			Oct. 2004	2.4			Stru.adjustment I-IDA
					July 2004	102.6			Nov. 2004	102.3			Education development
									Nov. 2004	35.6			Stru.adjustment I-IDA; Environment; Social sector; Local government

Table 33 (cont.)

| Country | IMF arrangements — Stand-by/Extended Facility | | IMF arrangements — SAF/ESAF/PRGF | | World Bank loans and credits — Structural adjustment | | | | World Bank loans and credits — Sector and other adjustment | | | | |
	Period	Amount	Period	Amount	Date of approval	IDA	African Facility[1]	Co-financing[2]	Date of approval	IDA	African Facility[1]	Co-financing[2]	Purpose
Yemen	Mar. 1996 - June 1997	132.4			Nov. 1997	58.9			April 1996	53.7			Economic recovery
	Oct. 1997 - Oct. 2001	105.9	Oct. 1997 - Oct. 2001	264.8[71]	Mar. 1999	35.8							Financial sector
													Public sec. mgmt. adj. credit
									Sep. 2004	44.3			Education
Zambia	April 1978 - April 1980	250.0							Jan. 1985	24.7	(10)	AfDB (23.4); CIDA (6.8); USAID (5); Switzerland (4.8); Germany (18.8)	Agricultural rehabilitation
	May 1981 - May 1984[24]	800.0[66]							Mar. 1991	149.6			Economic recovery
	April 1983 - April 1984	211.5[67]							Mar. 1991	19.4[6]			"
	July 1984 - April 1986	225[68]							May 1992	7.6[6]			Privatization and industry
	Feb. 1986 - Feb. 1988	229.8[69]							June 1992	146.0			"
			Dec. 1995-Dec. 1998	701.7[5]	Aug. 1996	62.4			Dec. 1992	15.1[6]			"
					Nov. 1996	5.4			June 1993	72.1			"
					Jan. 1999	122.7			Aug. 1993	7.0[6]			Economic and social adjustment
			Mar. 1999 - Mar. 2003	254.5[71]	June 2000	2.0			Jan. 1994	12.1[6]			"
					Nov. 2000	105.5			Mar. 1994	108.9			"
					Dec. 2000	1.6			Dec. 1994	9.7[6]			Economic recovery and investment promotion
			June 2004 - June 2007	220.1	May 2002	23.5			June 1995	19.1			"
					Dec. 2004	27.4			July 1995	90.0			Economic and social adjustment
									Dec. 1995	8[70]			Public sector reform and export promotion
									June 1996	16.0			Fiscal sustainability credit.
									July 2004	19.2			Fiscal sustainability
													Fiscal sustainability
													Fiscal sustainability 5th dim.
													Economic expansion

Sources: IMF, *Annual Report, 2002* and various issues; *IMF Survey* (various issues); World Bank, *Annual Report, 2002* and various issues; *World Bank News* (various issues).

m = million

1. Special Facility for Sub-Saharan Africa; amounts in parentheses are expressed in millions of dollars.
2. Including special joint financing and bilateral support; amounts are in millions of dollars unless stated otherwise.
3. Extended Facility arrangement, cancelled as of June 1982.
4. SDR 580 m not purchased.
5. ESAF.
6. Supplemental credit.
7. SDR 6.3 m not purchased.
8. SDR 15.8 m not purchased.
9. SDR 2.4 m not purchased.
10. SDR 13.5 m not purchased.
11. SDR 7.5 m not purchased.
12. SDR 3.8 m not purchased.
13. SDR 3.7 m not purchased.
14. SDR 10.2 m not purchased.
15. Cancelled as of April 1985.
16. SDR 3.4 m not purchased.
17. SDR 13.5 m not purchased.
18. SDR 6.0 m not purchased.
19. SDR 11.6 m not purchased.
20. SDR 1.5 m not purchased.
21. Supported by IMF; (SDR 1.88 m purchased in first credit tranche).
22. Additional financing.
23. SDR 21.4 m not purchased.
24. Extended Facility arrangement.
25. SDR 39 m not purchased.
26. SDR 22.1 m not purchased.
27. Cancelled as of April 1981; SDR 54.5 m not purchased.
28. Augmented in June 1981 with SDR 32.3 m; SDR 70 m not purchased at expiration of arrangement.
29. SDR 33.2 m not purchased.
30. Cancelled as of May 1989; SDR 10.5 m not purchased.
31. Cancelled as of May 1980; SDR 20.9 m not purchased.
32. SDR 9.9 m not purchased.
33. IBRD loan.
34. Original amount decreased from SDR 100 m; SDR 24 m not purchased.
35. Extended Facility arrangement; cancelled as of August 1986.
36. SDR 6.6 m not purchased.
37. SDR 20.8 m not purchased.
38. Cancelled as of May 1981.
39. SDR 6.8 m not purchased.
40. SDR 6.7 m not purchased.
41. ESAF; original amount decreased from SDR 50.6 m.
42. Not purchased.
43. SDR 2 m not purchased.
44. Including an increase of SDR 22.3 m in June 1981. SDR 152 m not purchased.
45. Extended Facility arrangement; cancelled as of April 1982.
46. SDR 31.2 m not purchased.
47. SDR 29 m not purchased.
48. SDR 5.5 m not purchased.
49. Extended Facility arrangement; cancelled as of February 1982; SDR 176 m not purchased.
50. SDR 128 m not purchased.
51. SDR 70 m not purchased.
52. SDR 1.75 m not purchased.
53. SDR 40.3 m not purchased.
54. SDR 19.2 m not purchased.
55. SDR 30.0 m not purchased.
56. SDR 19.9 m not purchased.
57. ESAF; original amount increased from SDR 179.3 m.
58. SDR 154.6 m not purchased.
59. SDR 9.0 m not purchased.
60. Cancelled as of June 1982; SDR 737 m not purchased.
61. SDR 30 m not purchased.
62. Cancelled as of April 1987; SDR 166.6 m not purchased.
63. SDR 58.2 m not purchased.
64. SDR 75.5 m not purchased.
65. SDR 41.4 m not purchased.
66. Cancelled as of July 1982; SDR 500 m not purchased.
67. SDR 67.5 m not purchased.
68. Cancelled as of February 1986; SDR 145 m not purchased.
69. Cancelled as of May 1987; SDR 194.8 m not purchased.
70. From IDA reflows.
71. PRGF, Poverty Reduction and Growth Facility Trust, formerly Enhanced Structural Adjustment Facility.